New York Criminal Procedure

New York Criminal Procedure

An Analytical Approach to Statutory, Constitutional and Case Law for Criminal Justice Professionals

THIRD EDITION

Christopher J. Morse

Brian J. Gorman

Jared J. Hatcliffe

CAROLINA ACADEMIC PRESS

Durham, North Carolina

Library of Congress Cataloging-in-Publication Data

ISBN: 978-1-5310-1673-9
eISBN: 978-1-5310-1674-6
LCCN: 2022029364

See catalog.loc.gov for complete Library of Congress
Cataloging-in-Publication Data

Carolina Academic Press
700 Kent Street
Durham, North Carolina 27701
Telephone (919) 489-7486
www.cap-press.com

Printed in the United States of America

Contents

Preface   xiii
Acknowledgments   xvii

PART ONE
GENERAL PROVISIONS

Chapter 1 • Introduction, Definitions and Basic Constitutional Law Summary   3
1.1 Historical Background and Sources of the Law   3
1.2 Overview of the Process   6
1.3 Basic Constitutional Law Summary   12
1.4 Key Definitions (Article 1)   33
1.5 Peace Officers (Article 2)   37

Chapter 2 • The Criminal Courts   39
2.1 Article 10; Organization and Subject Matter Jurisdiction   39

Chapter 3 • Requirements for and Exemption from Criminal Prosecution   41
3.1 Geographical Jurisdiction of Offenses (Article 20)   41
3.2 Timeliness of Prosecution and Speedy Trial (Article 30)   46
3.3 Exemption from Prosecution by Reason of Previous Prosecution (Article 40)   51
3.4 Compulsion of Evidence by Offer of Immunity (Article 50)   55

Chapter 4 • Rules of Evidence, Standards of Proof and Related Matters   59
4.1 Rules of Evidence (Article 60)   59
4.2 Use of Closed Circuit Television for Certain Child Witnesses (Article 65)   65
4.3 Standards of Proof (Article 70)   67

PART TWO
THE PRINCIPAL PROCEEDINGS

Chapter 5 • Preliminary Proceedings in Local Criminal Court; Commencement of the Action, Arrest, Summons, Fingerprinting, Photographing and Criminal Identification   73

5.1 Commencement of the Action in, and Local Criminal Court
      or Youth Part of a Superior Court — Accusatory
      Instruments (Article 100)   73
5.2 Requiring Defendant's Appearance for Arraignment (Article 110)   74
5.3 Warrant of Arrest (Article 120)   75
5.4 The Summons (Article 130)   79
5.5 Arrest without a Warrant (Article 140)   79
5.6 The Appearance Ticket (Article 150)   89
5.7 Fingerprinting and Photographing of Defendant after Arrest—
      Criminal Identification Records and Statistics (Article 160)   91

**Chapter 6 • Preliminary Proceedings in Local Criminal Court; upon
             Local Criminal Court Accusatory Instruments;
             Arraignment, Hearings and Dispositions**   95
6.1 Proceedings in Local Criminal Court upon Accusatory
      Instruments (Article 170)   95
6.2 Proceedings in Local Criminal Court upon Felony
      Complaint (Article 180)   102

Chapter 7 • Preliminary Proceedings in Superior Court   109
7.1 The Grand Jury and Its Proceedings (Article 190)   109
7.2 Waiver of the Grand Jury Indictment (Article 195)   127
7.3 The Indictment and Related Instruments (Article 200)   128
7.4 Proceedings from Filing of Indictment to Plea (Article 210)   136
7.5 Adjournment in Contemplation of Dismissal for the Purpose
      of Referral to Dispute Resolution (Article 215)   144

**Chapter 8 • Prosecution of Indictments in Superior Court; from
             Plea to Pre-Trial Motions**   147
8.1 The Plea (Article 220)   147
8.2 Removal of the Action (Article 230)   153
8.3 Discovery (Article 245)   154
8.4 Pre-Trial Notices of Defenses (Article 250)   161
8.5 Pre-Trial Motions (Article 255)   164

**Chapter 9 • Prosecution of Indictments in Superior Court: From
             Trial to Sentence**   167
9.1 The Jury Trial — Generally (Article 260)   167
9.2 The Formation and Conduct of the Jury (Article 270)   170
9.3 The Jury Trial — Motion for a Mistrial (Article 280.10)   175
9.4 Trial Order of Dismissal (Article 290.10)   176
9.5 The Court's Charge and Instructions to the Jury (Article 300)   177
9.6 Deliberation and Verdict of the Jury (Article 310)   178
9.7 Waiver of Jury Trial and Conduct of Non-Jury Trial (Article 320)   180
9.8 Proceedings from Verdict to Sentence (Article 330)   181

Chapter 10 • Prosecution of Informations in Local Criminal Court: From Plea to Sentence   185
10.1 Pre-Trial Proceedings (Article 340)   185
10.2 Non-Jury Trials (Article 350)   186
10.3 The Jury Trial (Article 360)   187
10.4 Proceedings from Verdict to Sentence (Article 370)   187

Chapter 11 • The Sentence   189
11.1 Sentencing in General (Article 380)   189
11.2 Pre-Sentence Reports (Article 390)   191
11.3 Pre-Sentence Proceedings (Article 400)   193
11.4 Sentences of Probation and Conditional Discharge (Article 410)   196
11.5 Fines, Restitution and Reparation (Article 420)   199
11.6 Sentences of Imprisonment (Article 430)   201

Chapter 12 • Proceedings after Judgment   203
12.1 Post-Judgment Motions (Article 440)   203
12.2 Appeals — In What Cases Authorized and to What Courts Taken (Article 450)   206
12.3 Appeals — Taking and Perfecting, and Stays during Pendency (Article 460)   209
12.4 Appeals — Determination Thereof (Article 470)   211

PART THREE
SPECIAL PROCEEDINGS AND MISCELLANEOUS PROCEDURES

Chapter 13 • Securing Attendance at Court of Defendants and Witnesses under Control of the Court — Recognizance, Bail and Commitment   219
13.1 Recognizance, Bail and Commitment — Definitions (Article 500.10)   219
13.2 Recognizance, Bail and Commitment — Application for; Securing Orders and Related Matters (Article 510)   221
13.3 Bail and Bail Bonds (Article 520)   223
13.4 Recognizance or Bail Re: Defendants; When and by What Courts Authorized; Orders of Protection (Article 530)   225
13.5 Forfeiture of Bail and Remission Thereof (Article 540)   234

Chapter 14 • Securing Attendance at Court of Defendants Not Securable by Conventional Means and Related Matters   237
14.1 In General (Article 550)   238
14.2 Defendants Confined in Institutions within the State (Article 560)   238
14.3 Defendants Outside the State but within the U.S., Rendition to Other Jurisdictions of Defendants within the State; the Uniform Criminal Extradition Act (Article 570)   239

14.4 Securing Attendance of Prisoners from Other U.S. Jurisdictions
and Rendition to Other Jurisdictions of Prisoners in N.Y.S.
Prisons; Agreement on Detainers (Article 580)   244
14.5 Securing Attendance of Defendants Who Are outside the
United States (Article 590)   246
14.6 Securing Attendance of Corporate Defendants (Article 600)   246

Chapter 15 • Securing Attendance of Witnesses   247
15.1 Securing Attendance of Witnesses by Subpoena (Article 610) 247
15.2 Securing Attendance of Witnesses by Material Witness
Order (Article 620)   248
15.3 Securing Attendance of Witnesses Confined in Institutions
within the State (Article 630)   250
15.4 The Uniform Witness Act; Securing as Witnesses Persons at
Liberty outside the State and Rendition to Other States of
Witnesses at Liberty within New York State (Article 640)   250
15.5 Securing Attendance as Witnesses, and Rendition as Witnesses,
of Prisoners (Article 650)   252

**Chapter 16 • Securing Testimony for Future Use and Using
Testimony from a Prior Proceeding**   255
16.1 Securing Testimony for Future Use — Examination of Witnesses
Conditionally (Article 660)   255
16.2 Use of Testimony Previously Given (Article 670)   256
16.3 Securing Testimony outside the State; Examination of Witnesses
on Commission (Article 680)   257

**Chapter 17 • Securing Evidence by Court Order and Suppressing
Evidence Unlawfully or Improperly Obtained**   259
17.1 Search Warrants (Article 690)   259
17.2 Eavesdropping and Video Surveillance Warrants (Article 700) 264
17.3 Pen Registers and Trap and Trace Devices (Article 705)   272
17.4 Motion to Suppress Evidence (Article 710)   273
17.5 Destruction of Dangerous Drugs (Article 715)   276

**Chapter 18 • Special Proceedings Which Replace, Suspend or
Abate Criminal Actions**   279
18.1 Youthful Offender Procedure (Article 720)   279
18.2 Establishment of Youth Part (Article 722)   282
18.3 Removal of Adolescent Offender to Family Court (Article 722.23) 282
18.4 Removal of Proceeding against a Juvenile Offender to Family
Court (Article 725)   282
18.5 Mental Disease or Defect Excluding Fitness to
Proceed (Article 730)   284

PART FOUR
ILLUSTRATIVE CASES FOR ANALYSIS

Chapter 1; Introduction 291
Sec. 1.3; Basic Constitutional Law Summary 291

Chapter 3; Exemption from Prosecution 298
Sec. 3.1; Article 20; Geographical Jurisdiction 298
Sec. 3.2; Article 30; Speedy Trial 306
Sec. 3.3; Article 40; Double Jeopardy 311
Sec. 3.4; Article 50; Immunity 316

Chapter 4; Rules of Evidence, Standards of Proof and Related Matters 320
Sec. 4.1; Article 60; Rules of Evidence 320
Sec. 4.3; Article 70; Standards of Proof 327

Chapter 5; Preliminary Proceedings in Local Criminal Court 331
Sec. 5.5; Article 140; Arrest without a Warrant 331

Chapter 6; Preliminary Proceedings in Local Criminal Court 345
Sec. 6.1; Article 170; Proceedings on Complaints Other Than
Felony Complaints 345
Sec. 6.2; Article 180; Proceedings on Felony Complaints 351

Chapter 7; Preliminary Proceedings in Superior Court 353
Sec. 7.1; Article 190; The Grand Jury and Its Proceedings 353

**Chapter 8; Prosecution of Indictments in Superior Court; from
Plea to Pre-Trial Motions** 359
Sec. 8.1; Article 220; The Plea 359
Sec. 8.3; Article 245; Discovery 364
Sec. 8.5; Article 255; Pre-Trial Motions 370

**Chapter 9; Prosecution of Indictments in Superior Court; from
Trial to Sentence** 373
Sec. 9.1; Article 260; Jury Trial — Generally 373
Sec. 9.2; Article 270; Jury Trial — Formation and Conduct of Jury 377
Sec. 9.3; Article 280; Jury Trial — Motion for a Mistrial 382
Sec. 9.4; Article 290; Jury Trial — Trial Order of Dismissal 384
Sec. 9.6; Article 310; Jury Trial — Deliberation and Verdict of Jury 386
Sec. 9.8; Article 330; Proceedings from Verdict to Sentence 390

**Chapter 10; Prosecution of Informations in Local Criminal Courts;
Plea to Sentence** 393
Sec. 10.1; Article 340; Pre-Trial Proceedings 393

Sec. 10.2; Article 350; Non-Jury Trial   395
Sec. 10.3; Article 360; Jury Trial   397

Chapter 11; The Sentence   397
Sec. 11.1; Article 380; Sentencing in General   397
Sec. 11.2; Article 390; Pre-Sentence Reports   398
Sec. 11.3; Article 400; Pre-Sentence Proceedings   402

Chapter 12; Proceedings after Judgment   405
Sec. 12.1; Article 440: Post-Judgment Motions   405
Sec. 12.2; Article 450; Appeals — In What Cases Authorized and
        to What Courts Taken   412
Sec. 12.4; Article 470; Appeals — Determination Thereof   413

**Chapter 13; Securing Attendance at Court of Defendants;
        Recognizance, Bail and Commitment**   419
Sec. 13.2; Article 510; Rules of Law and Criteria Controlling
        Determinations   419
Sec. 13.4; Article 530; Recognizance or Bail; When and by What
        Courts Authorized   421

**Chapter 14; Securing Attendance at Court of Defendants Not Securable
        by Conventional Means and Related Matters**   424
Sec. 14.3; Article 570; Securing Attendance of Defendants from
        outside the State but within the U.S.; Rendition to
        Other States; Uniform Criminal Extradition Act   424
Sec. 14.4; Article 580; Securing Attendance of Prisoners from
        Other United States Jurisdictions; Agreement
        on Detainers   429

Chapter 15; Securing Attendance of Witnesses   433
Sec. 15.1; Article 610; by Subpoena   433
Sec. 15.4; Article 640: Persons at Liberty outside N.Y.S. and
        Rendition to Other Jurisdictions of Persons at Liberty
        within the State; the Uniform Witness Act   438

**Chapter 16; Securing Testimony for Future Use and Use of
        Testimony Previously Given**   441
Sec. 16.1; Article 660; Securing Testimony for Future Use —
        Examination of Witness Conditionally   441
Sec. 16.2; Article 670; Use of Testimony Previously Given   442

Chapter 17; Securing Evidence by Court Order and Suppressing
      Evidence Unlawfully or Improperly Obtained   446
   Sec. 17.1; Article 690; Search Warrants   446
   Sec. 17.2; Article 700; Eavesdropping and Video Surveillance Warrants   454
   Sec. 17.4; Article 710; Motion to Suppress Evidence   457

Chapter 18; Special Proceedings That Replace, Suspend or Abate
      Criminal Actions   464
   Sec. 18.1; Article 720; Youthful Offender Procedure   464

Index   469

Preface

The third edition of this book brings to bear one of a very few periods of major reform within New York's Criminal Procedure Law. These reforms are not mere updates of the CPL Article. Rather, they represent substantive changes in law reflecting changes in attitudes and values consistent with certain criminal justice reform movements. For instance, one of the more significant reforms flows from the "Raise the Age" campaign, with its mission to raise the age of criminal responsibility generally from 16 to 18. This is a departure from sentiments holding sway in the late 1990s, which led to changes holding offenders of more serious violent crimes responsible at lower ages. The age of criminal responsibility remains staggered, and dependent upon the nature of the crime. Campaigns like "Raise the Age," however, resulted in adjustments and new presumptions pertaining to the age of criminal responsibility for various crimes, and the creation of an entirely new "Youth Part," staffed with specially trained judges. Other major reforms include liberalized bail requirements, rules of discovery and speedy trial requirements. Bail reform was the most notorious of these reforms due to the confusion and controversy they caused in the courts and community upon implantation. Thus, initial bail reforms made effective January 1, 2020, needed to be reassessed and adjusted in the months that followed. More adjustments may yet arrive down the road; however, the dust has settled on these most recent reforms, and are contained within for study by students and criminal justice professional alike.

The literature review leading to the first edition of this book found that there were many books on constitutional criminal procedure but virtually no comprehensive works on statutory criminal procedure. Therefore, this book was designed to stimulate and enable students and criminal justice professionals to critically analyze and understand statutory criminal procedure law. This body of law contains precise procedural rules that must be followed in order to ensure the constitutional rights of defendants and other players in the criminal process are not violated.

The provisions of the United States Constitution relating to criminal procedure are embodied in its Fourth, Fifth, Sixth and Eighth Amendments. These amendments contain such well-known rights as those against unreasonable search and seizure, the right not to be compelled to be a witness against oneself, the right to the assistance of counsel, the right to a speedy, public, jury trial and the due process clause; however, these are rights not procedure. These provisions, as written, at one and the same time, are ambiguous and the supreme law of the land. Their meaning is set forth in the decisions of the United States Supreme Court and lower courts of the federal and state governments. The due process clause requires criminal procedure to be fair, in order to enable a defendant to be able to defend against criminal charges. However, these court decisions do not translate directly to a comprehensive set of criminal procedure rules designed to insure fairness in the criminal procedure process as required by the due process clause.

The legislative bodies of the United States and each individual state have enacted statutes that constitute the criminal procedure law of that jurisdiction. These statutory schemes are similar since they are based upon the same constitutional principles as set forth above. Statutes are by their very nature ambiguous or if precisely drawn, create difficulties in application to the varying factual situations to which they must be applied. When the meaning or intent of a criminal procedure statutory provision is brought into question, the courts must decide its meaning or how it should be appropriately applied. There is a myriad of such decisions.

In order to stimulate students and criminal justice professionals into thinking critically about the criminal procedure process, we must look first to the criminal procedure statute, then to the court decisions interpreting them and then to the applicable constitutional provisions. It is difficult, if not impossible, for students and criminal justice professionals, who have little or no formal education in constitutional law or methods of constitutional interpretation, to acquire a reasonable understanding of the criminal procedure process. This book is designed to enable these constituencies to overcome these problems. The analysis is of the Criminal Procedure Law of New York State; however, since the criminal procedure law is similar in each jurisdiction due to its constitutional underpinnings, this book may be used in any jurisdiction in order to provoke readers into thinking critically and understanding criminal procedure law.

Absent this book, teachers in an academic environment or training facility for criminal justice professionals would be required to use the statute as a primary text which, from a pedagogical view is wholly inadequate. The statute itself is not comprehensive and is at times misleading when viewed alone. This book takes one through the criminal procedure statute in its entirety, from arrest, arraignment, hearings, motions, discovery, evidence, trial and appeal to special procedures such as immunity, jurisdiction, wiretapping, death penalty and extradition. This work analyzes and integrates the statute with court decisions and constitutional considerations, presenting the reader with a comprehensible, thought provoking, understandable knowledge of the criminal procedure process. In addition, it contains over eighty edited, illustrative cases for analysis on various aspects of the criminal procedure process such as stop and frisk, search warrants, no knock entry, grand jury proceedings, plea bargaining, bail, admission at trial of previous statements of witnesses, bodily intrusions, DNA testing, suppression of evidence, jury trial, sentencing and sex offender registration.

The exposure of students, criminal justice professionals and the public at large to the criminal procedure process has increased significantly due to the plethora of criminal procedure news, television dramas, and the live televising of criminal actions and trials. This book will assist members of these constituencies to more fully analyze and understand the criminal procedure process they are experiencing.

The overarching goal of this book is to encourage students and criminal justice professionals to think critically about criminal procedure law. Those armed with the tools and insights learned, will then be equipped for further study and best uses of criminal procedure law.

Acknowledgments

The authors would like to thank their families, colleagues, and students for support and encouragement in furtherance of this work.

This book is dedicated to Marilyn and Henry R. Morse, J.D., for their unending support and encouragement.

Every author knows that his or her completed project is actually the result of a larger team effort, and this work was no exception. The authors would like to take this opportunity to thank the many players on the different teams who helped develop this project from concept to completion. To our families and close friends who endured endless hours away from them: Antonietta Morse, Brianna, Alanna, Danny and Anastasia Morse, Michael Morse, J.D., Adam Algaze, Esq., Susan Koscis, Jenifer Chin, J.D., Cynthia Beamish, J.D., James, Kerri, Patti and Jaime Hatcliffe.

To all of our friends and colleagues at Towson University, those in the Department of Law, Police Science and Criminal Justice Administration at John Jay College of Criminal Justice and at the Elisabeth Haub School of Law at Pace University who provided critical analysis and commentary: Maria (Maki) Haberfeld, Chair, Serguei Cheloukhine, T. Kenneth Moran (Chair Emeritus), Robert McCrie, Anthony Carpi, Todd Clear, Heath Grant, William Heffernan, Zelma Henriques, Delores Jones-Brown, Irving Klein, Gloria Browne-Marshall, Norman Olch, Robert Panzarella, Alison Pease, Dorothy Schulz, Eli Silverman, and Louis V. Fasulo.

We must also acknowledge friends and colleagues at John Jay College of Criminal Justice outside of the department, who supported this work in numerous ways: Karol Mason, (President), Gerald Lynch, Yi Li (Provost), Basil Wilson, Ellen Hartigan, (VP), Magarita Argumedo, Selman Berger, Michael Blitz, Joseph Buttagheri, Jannette Domingo, Karen Kaplowitz, Lawrence Kobilinsky, James Malone, Rubie Malone, Richard Mills, Jose Luis Morin, John Pittman, Ralph Rosado, Patrick Ryder, Prem Sukhan, Sean Williams, Roger Witherspoon, Kathryn Wylie-Marques, and Jack Zlotnick.

To those in the larger sphere of academia who contributed as well: Paul Bompas (Bramshill, U.K.), Ned Benton, Michael Buerger, Gary Cordner, James Fyfe, Rodney Harrison, Marta Arias-Klein, Mary and Michael Loughrey, M.L. Moran, Jeffrey Roth, Joseph Bizzarro, Ed Lehman, Eric Sandseth, Sonia Thomas, Amanda Nazar, Victoria Seeger, Mike LoForte, James Li, Santiago Correa, Kamela Gjoka, Howard Cheng, and Natale Corsi.

Of course, to the team at Carolina Academic Press, for their editorial and technical expertise: Ryland Bowman, Beth Hall, Kasia Krzysztoforska, and Susan Trimble.

Perhaps most importantly, to our students at Towson, John Jay College of Criminal Justice and the Elisabeth Haub School of Law at Pace University, for their advice, encouragement, and friendship along the way, and for teaching us about facing incredible challenges with maturity and aplomb beyond their years, especially, Robert Bolstadt, Anthony Cangelosi, Marius Sniarowski, Richard Mills, Ron Rafailov, Tim Bremer, Mike Conroy, Sal Russo, Alex Sinclair, Jillian Snyder, Kris Allen, Rosty Kostiv, Fillip Shinelev, Nate Ullman, Hannah Stone, Nisha Desai, Mattison Stewart and Michaela Petersen.

Finally, we wish to thank the many International Orphan Hosting and Adoption agencies we work with in the fight for Justice for Orphan Children. Please visit the following websites to learn more about how you yourself can help in the struggle for Justice for Orphan Children:

New Horizons for Children Orphan Hosting Program: NHFC.org

Project 143 Orphan Hosting Program: P143.org

Non scholae, sed vitae.

Part One

General Provisions

Chapter 1

Introduction, Definitions and Basic Constitutional Law Summary

Sec. 1.1 Historical Background and Sources of the Law
Sec. 1.2 Overview of the Process
Sec. 1.3 Basic Constitutional Law Summary
Sec. 1.4 Article 1; Definitions
Sec. 1.5 Article 2; Peace Officers

1.1 Historical Background and Sources of the Law

The Criminal Procedure Law of New York State is an extremely important statute for all criminal justice professionals, aspiring professionals and citizens throughout the state. It contains the procedural requirements and processes by which criminal actions and special proceedings must be conducted within the state, and the rights and obligations of citizens, defendants, suspects and criminal justice professionals alike.

The statute itself is however only one element of the state's criminal procedure law. Criminal procedure also consists of provisions of the Constitution of the United States of America and the Constitution of the State of New York, in addition to decisions of the federal and New York State judiciary which interprets statutory and constitutional language. Taken together these elements comprise the procedural law (the rules so to speak), that must be followed in order to enforce the substantive law of the state.

Criminal law consists of two kinds of law: substantive and procedural. The substantive law sets forth the definition of criminal and lesser prohibited offenses, such as what constitutes larceny, robbery, assault or disorderly conduct; the defenses an accused has available if charged with violating a substantive provision; and the punishments a convicted defendant would incur for violating the provision. Procedural law sets forth the rules which must be followed in enforcing the prohibitions of the substantive law. These rules are critical since the stakes are with punishment that can result in the loss of life, liberty and property. A cardinal principle in our system of criminal procedure is fairness, as represented by the due process clauses of our federal and state constitutions. The procedural law strives to balance the power between the government and the accused by recognizing the presumption of innocence of the accused and the state's burden of proof throughout the judicial process.

Civilized societies establish rules governing the bounds of relations amongst its people. The role of government, however, is likewise limited when enforcing these rules. Our representative democratic form of government is the result of a social contract entered into by the people of the original thirteen states in 1789 in the form of an agreement set forth in the document known as the Constitution of the United States of America. The agreement was amended in 1791 by the addition of its first ten amendments, commonly called the Bill of Rights. The original document of 1789 established the organization of the federal government into three branches — the executive, legislative and judicial — and the powers and duties of each branch and the relationship of the new federal government and the states who joined together with the people of the states to establish the new government. The Bill of Rights set forth prohibitions against the new federal government taking away without due process of law (fairness) certain fundamental rights and freedoms of the people of the states, e.g., freedom of speech, press, religion, freedom from unreasonable search and seizure or from being compelled to be a witness against one's self.

History and human experience have shown the wisdom and necessity for people to join together in the formation of "governments" in order to assure peace, stability, security and civil order in life. The accomplishment of these objectives, however, is attained at the cost of surrendering to the government the freedom to decide how to achieve them. The Constitution, the charter of government, the supreme law of the land, is designed to control the decisions and actions of the government's agents so that the delicate balance is maintained between government's legitimate interest in securing and maintaining civil order (the reason for establishing a government) and the freedom, liberty and privacy interests of individual persons. The criminal procedure law of New York is designed to accomplish these aims.

New York State has its own constitution, as do the other states. It sets forth structural arrangements for the government of the state and relations between the state and the people, similar to, and in conformity with the United States Constitution. It also contains a "Bill of Rights" in its Article One. The relationship between the federal government and the states constitutes a federal republic. It establishes a federal government of limited powers (only those granted by the U.S. Constitution) and state governments of limited powers (those not given to the federal government by the U.S. Constitution nor prohibited by it to the states). The United States Constitution is the supreme law of the land. The federal and state governments must conduct the business of governing in such a way as to not violate any of its provisions. For example, one of the enumerated powers of the federal government is to coin money; therefore, states may not develop their own monetary systems. On the other hand, a state may conduct its own business of governing without the interference of the federal government as long as in doing so the state does not violate any of the provisions of the U.S. Constitution or transgress the enumerated powers of the federal government set forth in the U.S. Constitution.

The provisions of the Bill of Rights, added to the United States Constitution in 1791, originally prohibited the federal government only from unnecessarily interfering with a person's fundamental freedoms. These provisions did not control actions of state governments in the same areas of concern. For example, due to the Fourth Amendment, federal government agents are prohibited from interfering with a person's right to be free of unreasonable searches and seizures; but, the Fourth Amendment could not be used to prevent an agent of state government from conducting an unreasonable search and seizure. The state's own constitution or statutes had to be used to control the actions of state officers. When the United States Constitution was developed the people feared their freedoms might be infringed by the new powerful central government they were creating, in the same way strong central governments had done throughout history. There was, however, more trust in local state governments where people felt greater comfort with more direct control over government.

As the nation grew and prospered, societal values changed. Slavery became the great divisive issue in a nation founded upon principles of equality and liberty. The Fourteenth Amendment was added to the United States Constitution in 1868. This amendment contains a number of extremely important provisions which have been utilized in the development of state criminal procedure law through application of the criminal procedure provisions of the Bill of Rights to the states. The amendment provides in part, "… nor shall any state deprive a person of life, liberty or property without due process of law." The amendment was intended to prevent the states, particularly the former Confederate states, from taking away a person's constitutional rights after the Civil War. Utilizing the due process clause of the Fourteenth Amendment and the theory that due process includes the various criminal procedure rights found in the Bill of Rights, the United States Supreme Court has held all of these rights to be applicable to the states except for the right to trial for a serious crime by grand jury indictment and the right not to be held in excessive bail. This process was accomplished through the use of the Incorporation Doctrine. What it accomplished was the nationalization of the basic criminal procedure rights set forth originally as checks upon the power of the federal government. When a right is incorporated into the Fourteenth Amendment's due process clause, it establishes the minimum protections citizens are entitled to under the United States Constitution. A state is still free to interpret the same or similar provisions of its own constitution to provide greater protection within the state than the minimum protection offered by the Bill of Rights provision of the United States Constitution. It may not, however, interpret its own constitution so as to provide lesser protection for such rights than that provided in the United States Constitution. New York State's criminal procedure law constitutes an intricate, complex set of rules governing criminal actions and proceedings in the state, derived from the state criminal procedure statute, the federal and state constitutions and the decisions of federal and state courts interpreting the statutory and constitutional provisions and the actions of state officers in application of these provisions.

The United States' and New York State's system of law is based upon Anglo-American traditions of justice and fair play and the common law system of England. It must be remembered that for some 150 years prior to the Revolutionary War, the thirteen colonies were possessions of England and governed by the English Common Law. The common law was derived from the decisions of English judges. They were not codified into written statutes. With the adoption of the Constitution, the federal government and many of the states supplanted the common law rules with codified or statutory law. New York was one of these states. Until today, when interpreting law or in the absence of statutory law, common law provisions, ideas or concepts are looked to for understanding and guidance as to the appropriateness of a governmental action or procedure.

There are different systems of justice found in the free world. The Anglo-American adversarial system of justice is followed in our nation and state as opposed to the inquisitorial system found in other nations. There are significant differences between the two which lead to fundamental differences in the protection afforded individual rights. Basically, under our adversarial system, the accused is presumed innocent until proven guilty beyond a reasonable doubt. The burden of proof of guilt always resides with the government. The accused may not be compelled to be a witness against himself and no inference of guilt may be made from the fact the accused did not take the witness stand in his own defense. In the inquisitorial system there is no presumption of innocence, the accused bears the burden of proving his innocence and he may be compelled to give testimony. The protection afforded individual rights under the two systems is clearly different, to say the least. The adversarial system pits the state against the accused in a contest to see which of them can convince a neutral fact finder that their version of events is the truth; it gives each adversary a strong incentive to expose the other's shortcomings.

In order to convict a defendant of a criminal offense at trial, the government prosecutor must prove two facts beyond a reasonable doubt:

1. A violation of the criminal (substantive) law of the state occurred; and,

2. The defendant (accused) is the one who committed the violation.

Evidence of these facts constitutes the prosecutor's case in chief. These are the two ultimate facts that the trier of fact (the jury in a jury trial) must determine. The criminal trial, the most visible part of the criminal justice process, is just that: only a part of the process involved in criminal actions and proceedings. Before going into specific procedures governing the process it will be beneficial to take an overview of the parts of the process since the rules govern the permissible actions of either party in each of these parts.

1.2 Overview of the Process

The criminal justice process in New York as in other jurisdictions is a complex process and this overview is necessarily an oversimplification. It is beneficial however to begin with an overview since it will assist in understanding the specific parts and how each fits into the overall context of the process.

Commission of the Crime

The process begins with the police becoming aware of the commission of a criminal offense. This may occur in a number of different ways. The police may discover a crime in progress, they may happen upon a past crime, a victim or witness may call to report the commission of a crime or police may receive information of suspicious activity which may upon investigation be determined to amount to criminal activity. The fact of the crime is recorded in official documents and becomes part of the criminal records of the locality and the state.

Preliminary Investigation

When police become aware of the commission of a criminal offense a preliminary investigation is conducted in order to discover evidence needed to legally prove:

1. The elements of the criminal offense committed; and,

2. Who committed it.

The investigation usually entails observations by the police, the questioning of the victim, witnesses and suspects, visits to the crime scene and searches for and seizures of evidence. The law requires enough evidence to establish reasonable cause to believe (probable cause) that it is more likely than not that the criminal offense was committed and that the suspect did it. The investigative process is circumscribed by the criminal procedure law. Failure to abide by the rules set forth in the law governing the investigative stage might result in a violation of a suspect's legal rights and could lead to prosecutorial difficulties.

Arrest of the Subject

Once probable cause exists, police activity centers upon finding the suspect and arresting him. An **arrest** is the taking of a person into custody to be held to answer for a criminal offense. The procedures to be followed in making an arrest are set forth in the criminal procedure statute and since an arrest constitutes the seizure of a person, these procedures must comport with the requirements of both the federal and state constitutions. Arrests may be made without a warrant of arrest (the vast majority are) or with a warrant of arrest. Under certain circumstances a warrant of arrest is required in order to accomplish a lawful arrest. There are also occasions when police may stop a person on less than probable cause, without a warrant, and make a superficial search of the person for weapons (stop and frisk procedures) which may result in an arrest. Contemporaneous with the arrest a search of the arrestee and the surrounding area will be undertaken by the police. The person in custody may be advised of his constitutional rights and interrogated. The arrestee will then be taken to the police station for required administrative purposes permitted by the law and in some instances continuing investigative activities.

The Booking Process

At the police station a record of the arrest will be made. The charge, evidence and circumstances of the arrest will be reviewed by a booking officer to assure probable cause for the arrest exists. The prisoner will be fully searched and will be afforded an opportunity to telephone a friend, relative or attorney for assistance. In an appropriate case he will be fingerprinted and photographed and further investigative activities may take place such as requiring the prisoner to stand in a line-up for identification purposes by the victim of the crime or witnesses to it. He may also be further interrogated.

The Charging Process

Depending upon the seriousness of the charge, a member of the prosecutor's office (the district attorney of the county) may be present at the police station and take part in the investigatory process by reviewing evidence, questioning victims, witnesses and the police, interrogating prisoners and taking statements. At any rate the law requires the prisoner to be brought before a court without unnecessary delay for the opportunity of a probable cause hearing before a judge. This limits the time available for the "booking process."

So far, the principle criminal justice actors in the procedure involving receipt of the report of crime, the preliminary investigation, and the arrest and booking process have been the police. From this point on the principle figure will be the prosecutor, the district attorney of the county in which the criminal offense occurred and the judge. The prisoner will be transported to the courthouse and detained there by custodial personnel. The victim (the complaining witness or complainant in the case) and/or the arresting or investigating officer in the case will appear in the complaint room of the court. They will be interviewed by a complaint clerk, usually an assistant district attorney, who will assure himself the facts and circumstances of the case, supported by the available evidence, amount to probable cause a criminal offense was committed by the person arrested. The complaint clerk will then prepare an appropriate accusatory instrument which when filed in the court at the initial appearance of the defendant (the prisoner is now referred to as the defendant) will commence the criminal action and may form the basis of prosecution. The defendant will be brought before the judge of the court and arraigned on this accusatory instrument. The judge will advise the defendant of his constitutional rights and inform him of the charge against him.

At this point the issue of representation by an attorney will be initially resolved, release of the defendant on bail or recognizance will be determined and an adjourned date set for the next appearance which may be a preliminary hearing to decide if probable cause exists for the charge in the accusatory instrument. From this point the process diverges dependent upon the seriousness of the charge against the defendant. If the charge constitutes a felony (a crime punishable by more than a year in prison) the matter will be referred to the Grand Jury to ascertain if probable cause exists to try the defendant. The New York State Constitution requires trial by indictment for felony charges. If the accusatory instrument sets forth a lesser charge the grand jury process will not occur and generally speaking the case could be disposed of at this point by the judge or resolved at the adjourned date. From this point on this overview will focus upon felony proceedings.

Grand Jury Function and Process

The Grand Jury constitutes another of the legal safeguards built into the system to help assure a defendant's liberty is not being deprived without due process of law. The police, prosecutor and judge at the initial appearance and the preliminary hearing, if any, have reviewed primarily whether or not there was probable cause to deprive the defendant of his liberty. These are all government officials however. The Grand Jury constitutes a body of private citizens who will determine whether or not probable cause exists in the case.

The Grand Jury serves as a buffer between official government and the liberty of the defendant. The district attorney will present the evidence in the case to the grand jurors. If they determine probable cause exists they will find an indictment, which is the form of accusatory instrument required as the basis of prosecution for a felony. If they determine probable cause does not exist then the original complaint must be dismissed and the defendant released. In the alternative they might find grounds for a lesser charge and direct the prosecutor to cause the filing of an appropriate accusatory instrument in the lower criminal courts. All the court proceedings set forth above take place in the lower criminal courts of the county. The Grand Jury is an arm of the superior criminal courts of the county, however, and its proceedings are considered part of that division of the court structure.

Filing of and Procedures on the Indictment

The indictment of the Grand Jury must be filed in a superior court of the county since felonies must be tried in a superior court. The defendant will be required to appear in the superior court to be arraigned on this new accusatory instrument, the indictment. At the arraignment on the indictment, the judge takes control of the case and determines the course of future events such as the next appearance, representation of counsel and bail (procedures similar to those discussed at the arraignment on the original accusatory instrument in the lower criminal court).

Pre-Trial Procedures

The defendant will be required to enter a plea to the indictment of guilty or not guilty in whole or in part. If the defendant pleads guilty the judge will adjourn the case for sentencing. If the defendant pleads not guilty then various pre-trial procedures will occur in preparation of the case for trial.

A. Discovery

Discovery is a procedure which allows each party to inspect property in possession of the adverse party and which may be used as evidence in the case. The people's or prosecutor's discovery rights are limited by constitutional protections afforded the defendant. The process serves to eliminate surprise evidence and particularly affords the defendant an opportunity to prepare a defense to the charges. It also requires disclosure by the defendant of evidence relating to certain defenses available to him in order to give the people an opportunity to rebut such claim. Property that may be subject to discovery consists of any existing tangible property such as (but not exclusively) records, reports, books, memos, photos, fingerprints and weapons. Rules relate to the process that must be followed in order to utilize discovery. Discovery gives the defendant, who usually has far fewer resources than the state, an enhanced opportunity for a fair trial through awareness of evidentiary material in possession of the prosecutor and increases his ability to defend against it if the prosecutor chooses to use it at trial.

In some instances it also supplies a defendant with evidence favorable to his case that he might never have become aware of. Discovery may also be had on pre-trial hearings and upon trial. In these instances, it is limited, however, to criminal history information relative to either party's witnesses.

B. Pre-Trial Motions

A motion consists of a request to the judge to make a favorable ruling on a legal issue in the case. Pre-trial motion procedure may be used by the defendant to request the judge to dismiss the charge on various legal grounds, to suppress evidence believed to have been illegally seized, to change the trial venue or to request a separate trial. The motion must be made in writing within specified time limits and must be decided by the court on the basis of information in the request and the prosecutor's response to the request. If the judge cannot decide on the basis of this information he will order a hearing held on the motion. The hearing will usually be held by a hearing officer. The rules of evidence must be followed and a record made of witnesses and testimony offered at the hearing. This information and the hearing officer's recommendation are placed in a report to the judge. The judge must then decide the motion. Decisions on the motion resolve questions of law and serve to structure the trial. In criminal actions there are two types of questions that must be resolved: questions of law and questions of fact. Legal questions are answered by the judge and fact questions by the trier of fact, the jury in a jury trial. The ultimate fact question to be decided is the guilt or innocence of the defendant.

The Trial

Once the legal issues in the case have been decided by the judge, the search for an answer to the fact question takes place in the form of the trial. The defendant has a right under the federal and state constitutions to a trial by jury but the defendant may waive such right. If he does the trial judge will also be the trier of fact in what is termed a bench trial, as opposed to a jury trial.

The jury trial commences with the selection and swearing in of the jurors. After instructions to the jury by the judge, opening statements are made and the prosecutor presents his case. Each witness presented is subject to cross examination by defense counsel. The defendant may then put on his case. His witnesses are subject to cross examination by the prosecutor. Each party may then give a summation to the jury. The judge will then instruct the jurors as to their deliberations. The jury will then retire to the jury room to consider the evidence presented at trial in order to attempt to reach a verdict.

The verdict is presented in open court and will consist of some finding of guilt or innocence on the various charges against the defendant. If the jurors cannot agree upon a verdict (a unanimous verdict is required by law) they will so inform the judge who will declare a mistrial. The defendant possesses the constitutional right to remain silent and is under no obligation to do anything or present any evidence at trial. The defendant may choose not to give an opening statement, present evidence or make a summation. The burden of proof of guilt always remains with the prosecutor although the burden of coming forth with evidence shifts during the course of the trial. If the defendant is found not guilty of the charges, they are dismissed and the defendant is free to go. If the jurors cannot agree on a verdict the jurors will be thanked for their effort and discharged from duty. The defendant may be remanded to custody or released on bail or recognizance to await a new trial. If the verdict is guilty the judge will set an adjourned date for sentencing.

Sentencing

During the time between trial and sentencing the probation department will conduct a pre-sentencing investigation and make recommendations to the judge as to the sentence. The prosecutor and defense counsel will also submit recommendations to the judge. The trial judge will determine the sentence within the requirements of the law and taking into consideration the pre-sentence report and recommendations of the prosecutor and defense counsel. Punishments may range from a fine, probation or community service to a prison term of up to life imprisonment or for Murder first degree, the death penalty. The permissible punishment under the law is part of the substantive law of the state.

Appeals

After imposition of sentence the defendant has the right to appeal his conviction to the Appellate Division of the New York Supreme Court. Appeals are generally made on the basis of the legal rulings of the judges made pre-trial or during the trial. If the appellate court finds a legal error in the proceedings that it considers substantial (could affect the outcome), it will reverse the conviction and remand the case to the trial court for further necessary action. This may result in a new trial to be conducted without the legal error giving rise to the reversal or, if not possible, a dismissal of the charge against the defendant.

The highest court in New York State, the New York State Court of Appeals, may be requested by the losing party on the first appeal as a matter of right, to review the findings of the lower appellate court. The Court of Appeals has discretion under the law as to whether or not to review the case. This is the court of last appeal in New York State. Depending upon the sentence the defendant may be subject to the supervision of other government officials such as probation officers, prison officials or parole officers until such time as the sentence is completed.

Collateral Challenges

If the defendant's appeal is unsuccessful there may be other avenues available for him to attack the conviction such as habeas corpus proceedings in the state or federal courts or a writ of certiorari to the United States Supreme Court. These are beyond the scope of this consideration and will not be addressed here.

Succeeding chapters will delve into the intricacies of the processes and procedures inherent in statute and case law governing the above steps in the criminal justice process. Certain special proceedings will also be reviewed.

1.3 Basic Constitutional Law Summary

In 1791 the first ten amendments to the United States Constitution (the Bill of Rights) became effective. These provisions, designed to prevent the new federal government from taking away the people's hard-fought civil and human rights, as originally passed, were not intended to be used to control the actions of the various state governments. In addition to the federal Bill of Rights, each state, including New York, has its own constitution and "Bill of Rights" provisions which act as a deterrent to the state government from taking away these same rights. After the Civil War, in 1868, the Fourteenth Amendment to the United States Constitution was enacted into law. It contains the due process clause, "... no state shall deprive a person of life, liberty or property without due process of law." By its very language this clause is designed to control state actions rather than federal government action. Crime is considered essentially a local matter and constitutionally states are to handle it except for those matters declared federal crimes, which would be handled by the federal government. The social, economic, legal and political climate in each state is generally different. Different social problems appear and different approaches and procedures are found in the various states designed to take care of them. Consequently the criminal law and procedures in each state are somewhat different.

As communications and transportation modernized, the differences became more readily apparent. Many felt injustices occurred in the criminal law due purely to the incidence of geography and rather than have some innocuous happenstance such as this control the fate of defendants, it would be better to have one national set of criminal rules, particularly in those areas set forth in the national Bill of Rights. The Incorporation Doctrine was developed to try to accomplish this goal. Theoretically it may be argued the phrase "due process of law" includes those rights set forth in the Bill of Rights, such the right to be free of unreasonable search and seizure, the right not to be compelled to be a witness against oneself, and so on. The debate over this issue in a criminal context raged for some thirty odd years, from the early 1930s until the 1960s when the United States Supreme Court, beginning with the famous case of *Mapp v. Ohio*, found all of the criminal provisions of the Bill of Rights to be of the essence of due process, therefore included in the language of the Fourteenth Amendment and, as a consequence, applicable to the states. All the criminal provisions of the Bill of Rights except for two, the right to trial by grand jury indictment and not to be held in excessive bail, have been made applicable to the states. Since the United States Supreme Court is the final interpreter of the language of the United States Constitution and since that is the supreme law of the land, the interpretation of the Court as to the meaning, procedures and scope of a Bill of Rights provision establishes the minimum rights of persons under the law throughout the nation in every court of the nation. A state court is free to interpret its own state constitutional provision that reads the same or similar to that of the federal constitution in such a way as to afford greater rights to persons under the state's own constitution but never in such a way as to diminish the rights persons have under the federal constitution. In effect the federal constitution establishes the floor under which these rights may not go in the state courts or, in another sense, they establish the minimum protections guaranteed under the laws of the land.

Constitutional criminal procedure in New York State is therefore different in certain aspects than federal law due to decisions of the New York State Court of Appeals interpreting constitutional provisions of the state constitution so as to provide greater protection in the area of concern than that provided by the United States Constitution.

This material will set forth basic federal constitutional criminal procedure rules as well as those provisions in the New York State Constitution which differ from the federal rule, if any.

I. Search and Seizure

General Principles

The Fourth Amendment to the United States Constitution and Article I, Section 12 of the New York State Constitution contain identical language. They have two clauses:

> **The Reasonableness Clause.** No person shall be subject to an unreasonable search or seizure of his person, houses, papers or effects; and,

The Warrant Clause. No warrants shall issue but upon probable cause, particularly describing the place to be searched and the person or things to be seized.

Probable cause constitutes that amount of evidence which would cause a reasonable person to conclude it is more likely than not that crime has been committed or the property is in the place to be searched.

- Probable cause is also required in order to make warrantless searches and seizures.
- Not all searches violate the constitution, only unreasonable ones.
- A search is not unreasonable if made under the authority of a valid search warrant, or, in the absence of a valid warrant, if the search falls within one of the "… narrow, well delineated exceptions …" to the warrant requirement.

The search and seizure provisions are applicable to both arrests (seizures of persons) and searches and seizures of property. An arrest in violation of the constitution raises no valid defense to the charge. The defendant can still be convicted. However, any evidence gotten by the government as the result of an invalid search or seizure of such person or his property is prohibited from being used to convict him at trial. (The exclusionary rule of *Mapp v. Ohio,* 367 U.S. 643 (1961)).

The constitution prefers searches to be made under the authority of a valid search warrant because a neutral, detached magistrate determines if probable cause exists prior to the search as opposed to warrantless searches where the original probable cause decision is made by the police whose duty it is to ferret out crime, even though their probable cause decision is subject to a post-search determination by a judge (after the fact of the search) in a suppression hearing.

The right against unreasonable search and seizure is a personal right of each person, as are all other constitutional rights. It may only be invoked to protect one's own personal right to privacy, not someone else's. A defendant can't get evidence excluded on the basis of an illegal search of someone else's. The constitution constrains government agents only—not private citizens. The search and seizure provisions are not intended to hamper police but to protect persons' privacy rights.

The Exclusionary Rule

The **exclusionary rule** may be stated as: any evidence seized in violation of a defendant's constitutional rights may not be used by the prosecutor as part of her case in chief to prove defendant's guilt. In the search and seizure context the rule arose out of the case *Weeks v. U.S.* 232 U.S. 383 (1914). It was and is extremely controversial. Its many pros and cons can be gleaned by a reading of the opinions in *Mapp* (1961) which held that the Fourth Amendment provision regarding search and seizure is applicable to the states and by that same amendment any evidence in violation of that amendment is inadmissible at trial in a state court. The main purpose of the rule is to deter police misconduct. (If police know illegally seized evidence will not be admissible in court they will not engage in illegal searches and seizures.) New

York was a state whose constitution had not been interpreted by its state courts as containing an exclusionary rule at that time; therefore, as a result of *Mapp*, New York was required to follow the same search and seizure rules of the federal government (at the minimum) and it was thus bound to the exclusionary rule.

The rule is controversial due to the fact that real evidence of criminality is sometimes kept out of the trial process and as a result criminals go free when otherwise they would in all probability be convicted. Over the years the Supreme Court has cut back on the rule, particularly so in the last two decades. In *U.S. v. Leon*, 468 U.S. 897 (1984), the court developed the **"good faith exception"** to the exclusionary rule to this effect: If police act in reasonable reliance on a search warrant, ultimately found to be invalid due to lack of probable cause, the evidence seized would not be excluded. The rationale for this decision is that the sole deterrent of the rule is to deter misconduct by police, not judges. The court also stated in its opinion that the rule is not of constitutional origin but merely a judge-made remedy. The exception was expanded to allow the good faith exception to be operative in situations where the police make good faith errors in executing valid search warrants. Once again the deterrent effect is not operative if police make a good faith error (*Maryland v. Garrison*, 480 U.S. 79 (1987)). In *People v. Bigelow*, 66 NY.2d 417 (1985), the New York Court of Appeals refused to adopt the good faith exception, on state constitutional grounds. It reasoned that it would frustrate the exclusionary rule in the state constitution; it would place a premium on illegal police activity and would act as a positive incentive for others to follow.

Probable Cause

Probable cause is a nebulous, ambiguous phrase that has no one clear cut definition; but, it is one of the most important concepts in constitutional law. It has to do with fairness and the elimination or prevention of arbitrary action by government officials in reference to their dealings with the people. For search and seizure it has to do not only with fair procedures being utilized in connection with the taking away by government of persons' life, liberty and property but also with the amount of facts and circumstances (the quantum of evidence) necessary to establish the probability of crime or the presence of evidence or contraband.

Probable cause is based upon probabilities. Its determination is non-technical. It is based upon the factual and practical considerations of everyday life on which reasonable persons act, not legal technicians (*Brinegar v. U.S.*, 338 U.S.160 (1949)). It is less than needed to convict but more than mere or reasonable suspicion. A good working definition of **probable cause** is:

> **Probable cause** consists of ARTICULABLE FACTS AND CIRCUM-STANCES, which would cause a REASONABLE PERSON to conclude, it is MORE LIKELY THAN NOT, that crime IS BEING, HAS BEEN, or IS ABOUT TO BE, committed;
>
> or, in a search context,
>
> that the property IS IN THE PLACE to be searched.

By definition probable cause determinations involve an analysis of the articulable facts and circumstances inherent in a given situation in order to determine if enough are present to warrant the arrest or search (more likely than not). The police officer's experience and expertise, the basis of his knowledge (personal observation or what someone else has told him), the nature of the facts and circumstances (criminal in nature or mere innocent activity), the environment surrounding the situation (high crime area, drug area, known criminals, time of day, modus operandi of the suspects), the actions of the suspects — are all kinds of **ARTICULABLE FACTS AND CIR-CUMSTANCES** analyzed to determine if probable cause is present. Information that police officers possess as a result of their own personal knowledge (through the use of their own senses) and their training, experience and expertise utilized to analyze all the factors present is given a great deal of credibility as well as information offered by private citizens and other police, particularly if known as a result of their own personal knowledge. What is at stake here is the credibility of the information. If probable cause is present a person's life, liberty or property may be taken from her under the law as the result of a reasonable search and seizure. The legal presumption regarding the credibility of police and average private citizens is they have no reason to lie, and absent a showing to the contrary, such information is very worthy of belief. Courts apply the totality of circumstances test to determine if probable cause exists from information as indicated above. However, information from criminal informants or anonymous informants does not possess the same worthiness of belief. Criminal informants may have motivation to lie to protect themselves from jail or to protect criminal activity, and the basis of anonymous informants' knowledge is not known. Therefore the Supreme Court fashioned the two-pronged *Aguilar-Spinelli* test for determining probable cause when criminal or anonymous informants are involved. It is more technical and difficult of proof than totality of circumstances and consequently gives greater protection to individuals. Under this test the prosecutor must independently prove two things:

1.   The informant was reliable (*Aguilar v. Texas*, 378 U.S. 108 (1964)), and,

2.   The basis or reliability of the information (*Spinelli v. U.S.*, 393 U.S. 410 (1969)).

To satisfy the first prong of the test the prosecutor must show the informant previously gave valid information of crime. The second prong is satisfied by demonstrating that the informant possesses this information due to his own personal knowledge and it is not the product of mere rumor, gossip or what someone else may have told her. Unless each prong is independently satisfied a finding of probable cause may not be made, despite how reliable the informant or the information may be. In many instances police utilize criminal informants as part of their investigative strategy. Due to the difficulties of proving probable cause in such instances many complaints were raised relative to the *Aguilar-Spinelli* requirement since in many cases the overwhelming quantum of evidence present in one prong of the two prong test would certainly amount to enough evidence to warrant a probable cause finding under the traditional totality of circumstances test.

The Supreme Court decided to review the constitutional necessity of Aguilar/ Spinelli in *Illinois v. Gates*, 482 U.S. 213 (1983). It decided the *Aguilar-Spinelli* rule was not required by the Fourth Amendment and that the required constitutional test was the totality of circumstances test. It revoked the requirement of the two-pronged test. The New York State Court of Appeals refused to abandon the use of *Aguilar-Spinelli* in favor of totality of circumstances however. In two subsequent cases involving probable cause determination issues, *People v. Johnson,* 66 N.Y.2d 398 (1985) (warrantless arrest), and *People v. Griminger,* 71 N.Y.2d 635 (1988) (search warrant), the court looked to the New York State Constitution and interpreted its search and seizure provision as requiring the *Aguilar-Spinelli*, two-pronged test for probable cause to be used in assessing probable cause involving criminal or anonymous informants' information.

What the Search and Seizure Provisions of the Constitutions Protect

Until the decision of the Supreme Court in *Katz v. U.S.*, 389 U.S. 347 (1967), the Fourth Amendment was thought to protect places. In deciding cases courts looked to the nature of the place or property invaded by the government, if it the kind of place that was to receive constitutional protection and whether or not there was a trespass into said property. Under this traditional mode of analysis the home received the greatest protection under the Fourth Amendment as well as buildings within its curtilage (that area in close proximity to the home and used in daily family activities, e.g., barns, tool sheds). In *Katz* the court shifted the jurisprudence from the concept of a trespass into property to that of an invasion of one's **REASONABLE EXPECTATION OF PRIVACY**. The court found the Fourth Amendment protects people, not places and that the trespass doctrine was no longer controlling. What one knowingly exposes to the public, even in his own home, is **not** protected; but what one seeks to preserve as private, even in an area accessible to the public, **may** be protected (emphasis added). Justice Harlan in his concurring opinion, as a matter of clarification, set forth what has become as famous as the new rule itself, a two-pronged test for use in determining if a person was entitled to Fourth Amendment protection under the new rule:

1. Did the person exhibit an actual (subjective) expectation of privacy? If so,

2. Is that expectation one that society is prepared to recognize as reasonable?

If the answer to these two queries is yes, then the person is entitled to the protections of the Fourth Amendment in the situation at issue.

The nature of the property searched has not been totally divorced from the analytical picture; however, the primary analysis method is the two-pronged test of Justice Harlan. If a search or seizure is found to violate a person's reasonable expectation of privacy it is unreasonable and therefore violates that person's Fourth Amendment rights.

Searches and seizures may be lawfully made with a warrant or without a warrant. Most arrests (seizures of persons) are made without a warrant. It is only when the arrest is to be made in a residence that a warrant of arrest may be required. Generally speaking, if an officer has probable cause a person has committed a crime the officer may make a warrantless arrest. The main reason for this is that the delay inherent in applying for and issuance of the arrest warrant may result in the suspect's flight and escape from any arrest. On the other hand it is said that the constitution prefers searches to be made under the authority of a warrant, so as to have a judge make the necessary probable cause decision as opposed to the police officer whose duty it is to ferret out crime. However, the constitution recognizes a number of narrow, well delineated circumstances under which the search may be made without the issuance of a search warrant. These are known as the exceptions to the search warrant requirement:

1. Search Incident to Arrest

2. Plain View Seizure

3. The Automobile Exception

4. Consent Searches

5. Exigent Circumstances

6. Hot Pursuit

7. Inventory Procedures

8. Stop and Frisk

9. Open Fields

Exceptions to the Search Warrant Requirement (Warrantless Searches)

1. Search Incident to Arrest

The basic search incident to arrest rule was set forth by the Supreme Court in *Chimel v. California*, 395 U.S. 752 (1969). When a person is arrested the police may search the person arrested and that area within her immediate control:

1. the arrest must be lawful (based upon probable cause) and

2. the search must be contemporaneous with the arrest (within a reasonable time before or after the arrest).

The area within her immediate control is that area from which the arrestee might grab a weapon or destructible evidence. It is known as the grabbable area. As such the rule is designed to protect the safety of the officer and to preserve evidence. The rule applies to all custodial arrests, i.e., arrests for charges that the officer may not issue a summons for.

There has been much litigation over the rule. The main issues are the "grabbable area" under factual circumstances, searches of containers carried or possessed by the arrestee and the search of residences. Without a special rule, the grabbable area depends upon the facts in the case — the size and reach of the arrestee, for example, and the place where the arrest was made. For arrests made outside the home, the home may not be searched incident to the arrest.

The grabbable area for search incident to arrest of the occupant of a vehicle is the passenger compartment of that vehicle and, under federal law, any compartment or container found therein (*New York v. Belton,* 453 U.S. 454 (1981)). Container search rules under the predicate of search incident to arrest are different under New York law. In New York containers found on the person of the arrestee, such as in her pocket, may be searched. However, portable containers carried by the person or in her possession (such as handbags, attaché cases, shopping bags, gym bags or luggage) require additional factors that must be satisfied before being searched incident to arrest. If such container is in the grabbable area of the arrestee the police may seize it. The container may not be searched incident to arrest unless there also exists a reasonable, articulable belief it contains a weapon or destructible evidence. Reasonable belief is less than probable cause or reasonable suspicion. It consists of some evidence which would justify a reasonable conclusion the container contains a weapon or destructible evidence. Factors that might be considered are the violent nature of the crime, wearing a bullet proof vest, known violent offender or something found on the person of the arrestee such as a holster, bullets, etc., (*People v. Gokey, People v. Smith, People v. Belton*). If factors add to reasonable belief and, if the contents of the container are accessible, the container may be searched. It is accessible if it is open, or unlocked, or if locked the key is present or, if no key, it can be opened without damaging the lock. Under New York law a container carried or possessed by the arrestee may not be searched unless the foregoing factors are present using search incident to arrest as the predicate or justification for the search. In order to search it the predicate of some other permissible search rule would have to be sought or in its absence, if probable cause was present, a search warrant sought.

In addition to the basic rule of *Chimel* the Supreme Court addressed the issue of protective sweeps in conjunction with arrests made in houses. Under *Chimel*, the grabbable area for the arrest of a person in a house is the room in which the arrest is made. The basic search incident to arrest rule does not allow a search of other rooms or areas of the house. However in order to preclude unnecessary danger to police making an arrest in a strange environment usually without full knowledge of possible danger in the house the Supreme Court has found no unreasonableness in protective sweeps made in conjunction with arrests in houses. In *Maryland v. Buie,* 494 U.S. 325 (1990), the court decided that as an incident to the arrest in a house, the officers could, as a precautionary matter and without probable cause or reasonable suspicion, look in closets and other spaces immediately adjoining the place of arrest from which an attack could be immediately launched and, based upon articulable facts and circumstances providing reasonable suspicion of other persons posing a danger in the home, may make a protective sweep of the entire home.

A protective sweep consists of a cursory look into those places in which or where a person might hide. It does not give police the authority to look into other places such as night table drawers where a person could not hide. If police find any evidence in plain view in a place they have the authority to sweep they may seize it under the Plain View Exception.

2. Plain View Seizures

The general rule is: objects falling within the plain view of a police officer who has a right to be in the place the officer is in, which are immediately apparent as evidence, and are inadvertently discovered may be seized by the officer in accord with any applicable warrant or warrantless search rules.

A person has no reasonable expectation of privacy in what she exposes to others. Immediately apparent means there must be at least probable cause the item is evidence. Inadvertence means the officer should not be consciously searching for the item. This is a requirement of New York Law; however, the Supreme Court in 1990 eliminated this requirement from Fourth Amendment law (*Horton v. California*, 496 U.S. 128 (1990)).

In addition to the elements of the general definition, the seizure must comport with other search and seizure rules in this sense. Assume an officer is walking along the street and looks into an apartment through an open window and observes contraband (e.g., marijuana plants) on the kitchen table. He may not enter that apartment to seize the evidence based upon the plain view doctrine. In order to enter a house a search warrant or other appropriate warrantless predicate must be present before the home may be entered to make the seizure. On the other hand should he observe the plants in a car on the street he may enter the car to seize the evidence not on the sole ground of plain view but also on the warrantless predicate of the automobile exception. Should the officer see them growing in an unfenced vacant lot he may immediately enter the lot to seize the plants. Thus we see the plain view seizure rule allows the officer to seize evidence in plain view; in addition, whether the place where the object lies may be entered without some other authority must be ascertained.

The use of mechanical devices to enhance the officer's view is permissible, such as flashlights or binoculars and flyovers in planes or helicopters.

3. The Automobile Exception

The existing auto exception rule emanates from three federal cases; *Carroll v. U.S.*, 267 U.S. 132 (1925); *Chambers v. Maroney*, 399 U.S. 42 (1970); and *U.S. v. Ross*, 456 U.S. 798 (1982).

If the police have probable cause a car contains contraband, they may search it without a warrant (*Carroll*). The search may be made at the scene of the stop or later at the police station (*Chambers*). They may search the whole car, including any compartments and containers found therein. The search may be as thorough as if a search warrant was had, the only limitation being the nature of the object being sought (*Ross*).

The reason for the exception is the mobility of the vehicle. If the search was delayed for the time necessary to obtain a warrant the car, due to its mobility, might be gone upon return with the warrant. The courts have also found a lesser expectation of privacy in a vehicle than a home. The search may be delayed in order not to unnecessarily endanger police by requiring the search to be made at the scene (traffic, nighttime, darkness, number of suspects). Under the automobile exception the whole car may be searched. Compare the rule under search incident to arrest of the occupant of an auto, which only permits a search of the passenger compartment (*N.Y. v. Belton*). There is no probable cause needed to search the passenger compartment of a vehicle as per the search incident to arrest rule of *Belton*. Such search must be confined to the passenger compartment of the vehicle; however, if something is found in the passenger compartment during its search which would lead to the conclusion of probable cause that evidence may be elsewhere in the vehicle, the automobile exception comes into play and the entire vehicle may be searched. This is a good example of a narrow predicate that during the course of its execution gives rise to one which allows a much more thorough search.

The phrase in the *Ross* portion of the rule," ... the only limitation being the nature of the object being sought," limits the scope or extent of the search related to the size of the object being sought. You could not look for a suitcase in the glove compartment since it would not be able to fit in it. The scope of all searches is limited by this principle.

The automobile exception may be applied to all types of vehicles, as long as they are mobile, including vessels and aircraft. A motor home or recreational vehicle as long as it is mobile and not permanently parked is a vehicle and subject to the auto exception. If it is not capable of being readily moved it might be considered a home. The use to which it is put is the determining factor (*California v. Carney*, 471 U.S. 386 (1985)). New York follows the auto exception as developed in the federal rules (*People v. Belton*, 1982).

4. Consent Searches

The constitutional rights possessed by each person, such as the right to be free of unreasonable search and seizure, may be waived (given up) by a person. The waiver to be valid must be freely and voluntarily given. When one consents to a search, she has in effect waived her Fourth Amendment rights. The burden of proving voluntariness rests upon the prosecutor and it is a heavy one because the presumption is people don't willingly give up their constitutional rights. Any coercion, physical, psychological or legal tricks to get people to give consent will void a waiver. The police do not have to advise a person that she does not have to consent to a search (*Schneckloth v. Bustamonte*, 412 U.S. 218 (1973)). The test the courts use to determine voluntariness is the totality of circumstances test. All the facts surrounding the purported consent are examined to ascertain if coercion has brought it about.

Third Party Consent. A person who has an ownership or a possessory interest in property may give consent to the search of it even though another has such an interest in it as well. The **assumption of risk theory** states that one who shares property with another assumes the risk the other may consent to its search (*U.S. v. Matlock*, 415 U.S. 164 (1974); *People v. Cosme*, 48 N.Y.2d 286 (1979)). In a typical case, domestic partners are living together, have a fight, one leaves and calls police to retrieve belongings or to report the other has drugs or weapons in the apartment. The police ask questions to establish the interest in the apartment and for permission to enter to help. Permission is granted and evidence is found leading to the arrest of the other. Only shared property is subject to third party consent. If one party in the typical incident had exclusive access to a closet or storage bin or room, the other would not be able to give valid consent to its search. In a recent case the Court of Appeals allowed school authorities permission to search a student's locker and to give police consent to search a student's locker (*People v. Overton*, 24 N.Y.2d 522 (1969)).

5. Exigent Circumstances

General Rule: If police have probable cause there is

a. danger to life,

b. a suspect may escape, or

c. evidence may be destroyed

they may enter a premises without a warrant since speed is essential to deal with the exigency. The need for immediate fast action must be present. The rule allows police to enter into premises for exigent circumstances purposes; however, once in, their actions must be related to the reason for entry. Rummaging through drawers is not permitted. Plain view seizures are permitted, since they are in a place they have a right to be. The weakest of the exigencies is the destruction of evidence justification. In many instances evidence may be subject to destruction; but if the police were allowed to enter to cover any possibility, the exception would swallow up the warrant requirement. Courts construe the destruction of evidence exigency very strictly. The facts must indicate more than the possibility of destruction. The facts must indicate the evidence is in the process of destruction or in imminent danger of destruction before the exigency will be accepted (*Cupp v. Murphy*, 412 U.S. 291 (1973)).

The Court of Appeals has developed the Emergency Circumstances Doctrine for guidance in exigent circumstances situations involving danger to life. It is also called the Public Safety Exception to the warrant requirement. It arose out of *People v. Mitchell*, 39 N.Y.2d 173 (1976) (overruled in part by *Brigham City v. Stuart*, 547 U.S. 398 (2006)). The exception comes into play when the police have reasonable grounds to believe (probable cause) there is an emergency and an immediate need for their action to protect life or property. The police may enter premises to search for people whose lives may be at risk, explosives or some other source of danger. Totality of circumstances is the test used to determine if the entry and exigency under the circumstances were reasonable and thus not in violation of the constitutional provisions.

6. Hot Pursuit

Hot pursuit is that form of exigent circumstances involving escape of a suspect. There are special pursuit requirements connected to it, however. Courts have decided for hot pursuit to be present there must be "… some kind of chase …" (*Johnson v. U.S.*, 333 U.S. 10 (1948)). The chase does not have to be a hue and cry chase on the street. It can be short and in a public place (*U.S. v. Santana,* 427 U.S. 38 (1976)). If a fleeing suspect enters a premises the police may within a reasonable time enter the place in hot pursuit to prevent her escape and to prevent danger to the public (suspect has gun). Once inside police must confine their actions to the reason for entry and may seize evidence in plain view (*Warden v. Hayden,* 387 U.S. 294 (1967)).

7. Inventory Procedures

The police may inventory the contents of vehicles they impound (*South Dakota v. Opperman,* 428 U.S. 364 (1976)); *People v. Galak,* 80 N.Y.2d 715 (1993)) and containers possessed by a prisoner as part of the booking process (*Illinois v. Lafayette,* 462 U.S. 640 (1983)) without any search warrant as an exception to the warrant requirement. No probable cause is required for these procedures. The courts have found them not to be in the nature of a traditional search of the type the Fourth Amendment was designed to control since the purpose of the inventory is not to seek evidence. The purpose of the inventory procedure (notice it is not called a search) is to:

- protect the property of the owner against loss or theft,
- protect the police against false claims of lost or stolen property, and,
- protect the police against the danger of explosives secreted in the cars or containers carried by the prisoners.

To utilize this procedure the police department in question must have a regularized procedure controlling the inventory policy so as not to leave the inventory procedure to the discretion of the individual officer. If the procedure is found to be merely a procedure to accomplish an otherwise unreasonable search the courts will find a violation of the Fourth Amendment and any evidence seized will be subject to the exclusionary rule.

In the process of carrying out an inventory procedure the police may force open any closed or locked container if the key is not available. They may do more than minimum damage in the process if they reasonably suspect it contains explosives, guns, hazardous or perishable materials or such contents are in plain view or ascertainable from the packaging. They may also do so if they have consent of the owner (*Colorado v. Bertine,* 479 U.S. 367 (1987)).

8. Stop and Frisk

In 1968 the Supreme Court, in deciding *Terry v. Ohio,* 392 U.S. 1 (1968), established a new form of warrantless search commonly referred to as stop and frisk. The court for the first time permitted the police to interfere with a person's liberty without probable cause. In *Terry* the Court sanctioned the stop (a temporary interference with liberty) of persons who acted in a reasonably suspicious manner (acted in such a way that a reasonable person would believe crime **may be afoot**). The court rationalized that since the stop is a temporary interference with liberty, it would not be unreasonable to permit it upon facts and circumstances amounting to less than probable cause. The purpose of the stop is to allow the police to ask questions to ascertain if the suspicious circumstances relate to crime or not. If it is ascertained there is no probable cause for an arrest, the subject of the stop is to be released. If in conjunction with the encounter, the officer has reasonable suspicion the subject may be armed and pose a danger the officer may frisk (pat down the outer clothing) for a weapon. If something that might be a weapon is felt the officer may remove it from the clothing of the person. The same rationale exists for the frisk (a limited search) as for the stop. Since the frisk is a limited search, it is not unreasonable to permit it on reasonable suspicion.

New York has codified the stop and frisk procedure in the arrest article of its Criminal Procedure Law (Section 140.50). The *Terry* decision was quite revolutionary and it spawned many legal issues which are explored in the chapter on Article 140, Arrests.

9. Open Fields

Open fields under federal law have never enjoyed the protection of the Fourth Amendment, even if they were fenced or posted. Under the trespass doctrine open fields were not the kind of property protected and under the reasonable expectation of privacy doctrine society was not ready to accept as reasonable a person's subjective expectations of privacy such as fencing or posting since traditionally no one pays much attention to these measures when taken (*Oliver v. U.S.*, 466 U.S. 170 (1984)). The rule was followed in New York (*People v. Reynolds*, 71 N.Y.2d. 552 (1988)) but in *People v. Scott*, 79 N.Y.2d 474 (1992), the Court of Appeals ruled that when persons post, fence or take some other action to indicate unmistakably that entry is not permitted their reasonable expectation of privacy will be protected.

Standards, or, Quantums of Proof

The law requires differing amounts of evidence in order establish the basis for different legal conclusions. Evidence of, or proof of, the existence of probable cause (reasonable grounds to believe), mere suspicion or beyond a reasonable doubt depends upon the amount of articulable facts and circumstances offered to convince a reasonable person that such conclusion is warranted. The amount of evidence needed to establish various legal conclusions is set forth below, beginning at the bottom with "mere suspicion," which consists of an absence of articulable facts and circumstances, and going to the top, "absolute certitude," which is never required by the law:

Absolute certitude (without a doubt): never required by the law.

Beyond a reasonable doubt: that amount of articulable facts and circumstances that would establish beyond a doubt a reasonable person could give for having, as to the guilt of a person charged with crime.

Clear and convincing evidence: that amount of articulable facts and circumstances which constitutes more than that amount required to establish a preponderance of evidence but less than that needed to establish guilt beyond a reasonable doubt.

Preponderance of evidence: that amount of articulable facts and circumstances that establishes the greater weight of evidence as to the existence of a contested issue. The standard of proof required to prevail in civil actions and in certain criminally related issues such as the existence of mental disease or defect of a defendant.

Reasonable cause to believe (probable cause): that amount of articulable facts and circumstances that would cause a reasonable person to conclude it is more likely than not that crime is being, has been or is about to be committed; or, the property is in the place to be searched. This is the standard required by the search and seizure provisions of the Fourth Amendment to the U.S. Constitution and Article 1, Section 12 of the N.Y.S. Constitution.

Reasonable suspicion: that amount of articulable facts and circumstances that would lead a reasonable person to conclude crime may be afoot. This is the standard required for stops and frisks to be constitutional.

Mere suspicion: the absence of articulable facts and circumstances necessary to conclude reasonable suspicion or probable cause is present.

II. Confessions, Admissions and Interrogation

The Fifth Amendment to the United States Constitution and Article 1, Section 6 of the New York State Constitution provide protection against self-incrimination; to wit, no person shall be compelled in any criminal case to be a witness against himself. The provision traces its origins to fifteenth-century England as a reaction to the infamous Star Chamber proceedings, in which the Crown engaged in the torture of defendants until they either confessed to treasonous acts against the king (usually political activities) for which they would be put to death, or they died from the torture. With the demise of Henry VII, the practice was eventually abolished but the experience led to the inclusion of self-incrimination provisions in England and later in the colonies as well. It has long been the law that in order to be admissible, the defendant's confession must be found to be voluntary. The admissibility of coerced confessions is addressed in Section 60.45 CPL. Involuntary confessions were always inadmissible in the federal system due to the interpretations of the provisions of the Fifth Amendment right not to be compelled to be a witness against oneself. Since this amendment was not originally applicable to the states, the issue of their admissibility was decided differently in some states. In 1964, the Fifth Amendment was made applicable to the states in *Malloy v. Hogan,* 378 U.S. 1 (1964). Also in 1964, the Supreme Court for the first time declared a "voluntary" confession to be inadmissible due to the fact the police refused to allow a defendant to speak to his attorney (*Escobedo v. Illinois,* 378 U.S. 478 (1964)). This case began the process of intertwining the provisions of the Fifth Amendment provision against self-incrimination and the Sixth Amendment right to the assistance of counsel for one's defense in a criminal prosecution.

Miranda v. Arizona, 1966

The decision of the Supreme Court in *Miranda* is arguably the most important case in criminal procedure history as well as its most controversial. The decision was very broad. For the first time the police were required to advise persons of their constitutional rights in custodial interrogation situations, and otherwise admissible evidence was to be excluded from trial if the police were found to be deficient in accomplishing their affirmative duty to provide notice. The decision addresses four issues: custody, interrogation, constitutional notice and waiver.

The court held the prosecutor may not use confessions or admissions of the defendant stemming from custodial interrogation unless the police use procedural safeguards which effectively secure the defendant's right against self-incrimination:

CUSTODY — means deprived of one's freedom in any significant way.

INTERROGATION — means police initiated questioning designed to get the person to incriminate herself (confess or make an admission, exculpatory or inculpatory).

WARNINGS — means prior to any questioning, the person must be warned that

- you have the right to remain silent;
- anything you say may be used as evidence against you;
- you have the right to the presence of an attorney during any questioning;
- if you can't afford one, one will be provided for you.

WAIVER — means the defendant may waive these rights provided the waiver is made voluntarily, knowingly and intelligently.

If the person indicates in any manner at any stage of the process that he wishes to consult with an attorney or he does not wish to speak there can be no questioning. The mere fact that he may have answered some questions or volunteered some information does not preclude him from exercising his rights at anytime thereafter.

The court discussed the "coercive" atmosphere of station house interrogation and the psychological pressures inherent in interrogation at great length to justify its decision. The decision was and is quite controversial since it prevents otherwise voluntary confessions and admissions from being utilized as evidence to the consternation of prosecutors, police and many citizens. On the other hand, it was applauded by civil libertarians and others in favor of curbing police abuses and protecting individual rights.

The decision spawned much litigation involving interpretation of the key issues in the decision (custody, interrogation, the warnings and waiver). Remember, the two elements of custody and interrogation must both be present in a given situation for the Miranda rule to apply.

1. Custody explicitly occurs when the police pronounce a person to be under arrest. During the investigative process this may not occur and it is not specific as to whether the suspect was under arrest. In *U.S. v. Mendenhall*, 446 U.S. 544 (1980), the Supreme Court established an objective test for determining if custody exists in ambiguous situations. Custody is present when a reasonable person in the situation of the suspect would believe she was not free to leave. In order to make a determination the setting of the incident must be analyzed to determine if custody was present. Did it take place in the suspect's home, the police station, in a police car? How many officers were present? Were they in uniform, have their guns drawn, use bullying tactics? How long did the encounter take? These and similar factors are considered. Brief encounters such as traffic stops and other non-custodial arrest situations, common law inquiries and stop and frisk situations where police have not drawn their guns do not amount to custody. Voluntary visits to the police station at the request of the police are not custodial, as long as the facts indicate the person is free to leave. If a person is not deemed to be in custody, no *Miranda* warnings need be given prior to questioning by police.

2. Interrogation is present in two circumstances. The most common consists of police initiated questioning designed to elicit a confession or admission — to get her to incriminate herself The other occurs when police engage in what the courts have labeled indirect questioning, the functional equivalent of interrogation (*Brewer v. Williams*, 430 U.S. 387 (1977)). In this situation the police ask no questions but make statements which they should believe are likely to elicit an incriminating response from the suspect, e.g., knowing a suspect to be a religious fanatic, playing upon this weakness in order to get him to make a confession or admission, talking to him while not asking any questions. If the facts indicate a conversation between two officers in the presence of the suspect led to his incriminating statement but the officers were not aware of any weaknesses and had no intent to elicit the response the situation would not be considered indirect questioning (*Rhode Island v. Innis*, 446 U.S. 291 (1980)). Volunteered statements do not constitute interrogation, nor do on-scene clarifying questions or questions designed to uncover facts to enable police to determine what is occurring or pedigree questions at the time of booking.

3. Warnings given by police need not consist of the exact language in the holding of *Miranda*. As long as they convey the same meaning they are sufficient, although the closer the language the better. Many police departments provide written materials to officers which they are required to read to the suspect. The specific warnings given are then easier to prove at a hearing on the adequacy of the warnings. If the warnings were not proper in form or content any waiver of the defendant subsequent to them would be invalid and any confessions or admissions gotten as a result would be excluded as evidence against the suspect defendant.

4. Waiver of the right to remain silent and to the assistance of counsel, similar to any other waiver of constitutional rights, must be voluntary, intelligent and knowing, i.e., the expression of one's free will after a thoughtful determination to waive these rights. After the questions embodying the warnings are asked, the suspect will be asked to the effect, do you understand? Upon an affirmative response, the question will be asked, Are you now willing to answer questions? or, Are you now willing to make a statement? If the person answers in the affirmative he is deemed to have waived his rights to remain silent and to an attorney. The burden of proof as to waiver rests upon the prosecutor, by a preponderance of evidence, which must demonstrate the suspect understood his rights and intended to relinquish them (*Nix v. Williams*, 467 U.S. 431 (1984)). There have been many cases over the issue of the validity of the waiver such as the adequacy of the warnings, the setting in which they were given, the behavior of the police and the suspect, trickery or deception, attenuation and right to counsel. The law coming from decisions in cases established many rules of procedure. Silence does not constitute a waiver. Nods or shrugs may. A waiver does not have to be in writing. A suspect does not have to be informed of the subject of the interrogation before he executes a Miranda waiver (*Colorado v. Spring*, 479 U.S. 564 (1987)), but the police must not mislead the suspect as to the subject. In New York, any trickery or deception used to get the waiver will invalidate it, although some forms of trickery or deception are allowed during the interrogation process (it is adversarial in nature). Lying about the existence of evidence, the condition of a victim or witness or the results of a line-up are permissible. Lying about the prosecution, a lesser charge or lighter sentence are not. Threats relative to jobs, condition of loved ones or posing falsely as a religious person are not.

5. Right to Counsel. If the suspect in answer to the question as to waiver (are you now willing to answer questions or make a statement) answers in the negative or at that time or any time during the proceedings states he does not wish to speak or answer questions or he wants an attorney, no questions may be asked and questioning must be discontinued immediately. At this point in the proceedings the suspect's right to counsel attaches. New York believes the greatest protection for a suspect's constitutional rights is the assistance of counsel and as a consequence New York's right to counsel rules are greater than those in the federal system. In addition to the above, a defendant's right to counsel attaches upon the commencement of a criminal action against the defendant (the filing of the first accusatory instrument) or when an attorney enters the picture (makes aware his representation of the suspect to the police). In New York, once a suspect's right to counsel attaches, it may not be waived except in the presence of an attorney since to do so would not amount to a knowing and intelligent waiver. The right to counsel rules in New York are quite complicated; however, they may be summarized as follows:

a. If the defendant is in custody and the right to counsel has attached there may be no interrogation of the subject without the presence of an attorney for any crime except if the right to counsel was triggered by the filing of an accusatory instrument. In this latter instance, the interrogation may not be conducted regarding the crimes in the accusatory instrument but may be conducted for other crimes. Obviously, Miranda rules govern such questioning.

b. If the defendant is not in custody she may be questioned regarding crimes not contained in the accusatory instrument after waiving her rights under the Miranda rule.

In order to obtain an arrest warrant an accusatory instrument must be filed for the crime the arrest warrant relates to. Therefore the arrestee's right to counsel has attached and she may not waive her Miranda rights without the presence of an attorney.

There is an exception to the Miranda rule, the Public Safety Exception to the Miranda Rule (*New York v. Quarles*, 467 U.S. 649 (1984)). Under this rule the police may question a person in custody before administering the Miranda warnings in order to resolve an imminent danger to the public, such as the presence or whereabouts of a gun, explosives, a missing or kidnapped person or similar problem. Once the problem is resolved, no further questions may be asked without first administering the Miranda warnings. The public safety exception exists in the face of the suspect's request for counsel as well (*People v. Krom*, 61 N.Y.2d 187 (1984)).

III. Right to Counsel

Aspects of the right to counsel have been discussed above in connection with *Miranda* and earlier in conjunction with Section 60.45 CPL. A remaining issue to be discussed of relevance to criminal justice is that of the right of indigent defendants to be represented by free counsel provided by the government. The notion that one's ability to pay to hire counsel might determine whether a defendant is found guilty or not can be disturbing. A literal reading of the Sixth Amendment constitutional right forbids the government from preventing a defendant from having the assistance of counsel for her defense and at the time of the adoption of the constitution there was no procedure whereby a defendant was entitled to free counsel as a matter of right.

The societal conscience was aroused over the infamous case of *Powell v. Alabama*, 287 U.S. 45 (1932) (the Scottsboro Boys case), in which the Alabama court sentenced to death a number of young, illiterate black youths without their having been represented by counsel at trial. Their plight was highly publicized and was brought to the Supreme Court by a number of civil rights interest groups that interceded on the boys' behalf. The court found the due process clause of the Fourteenth Amendment required a state to provide free counsel to indigent defendants in capital cases.

The Sixth Amendment was interpreted to require free counsel for indigent defendants in *Johnson v. Zerbst*, 304 U.S. 458 (1938); however, the Sixth Amendment had not been made applicable to the states. Indigent defendants in federal court could look to the Sixth Amendment for protection of their right to counsel, but in state courts defendants had to seek relief on a case by case basis under the due process clause as applied in *Powell, supra.* A huge difference existed between the protections offered. The Sixth Amendment provision applied to defendants charged with a felony while the due process protection of the Fourteenth Amendment applied only to capital cases. This anomalous situation was finally resolved in the famous case of *Gideon v. Wainwright,* 372 U.S. 335 (1963).

Gideon was convicted of a burglary related offense of the grade of felony. He was without funds and asked the state court for free counsel. The Court ruled the U.S. Constitution only required states to provide free counsel in capital cases, denied his request and proceeded. Upon review the U.S. Supreme Court found the Sixth Amendment to be applicable to the states and reversed the conviction of *Gideon.* The constitutional right to free counsel for indigent defendants in federal courts under the Sixth Amendment was recognized and made applicable to indigents facing similar charges in state courts.

The issue continued to bubble, since most cases involved offenses below the grade of felony, misdemeanors or other petty offenses. The Court finally resolved this issue in *Argersinger v. Hamlin,* 407 U.S. 25 (1972), in which it decided there could be no jail sentence applied to an indigent defendant convicted without benefit of counsel.

The Court was also asked to resolve the issue of the indigent's right to counsel for appeals. In *Douglas v. California,* 372 U.S. 353 (1963), the Court interpreted the Sixth Amendment to require free counsel for indigents for first appeals as a matter of right. It refused to extend this right any further in *Ross v. Moffitt,* 417 U.S. 600 (1974).

In *Faretta v. California,* 422 U.S. 806 (1975), the Court upheld the right of a defendant to waive the assistance of counsel guaranteed by the Sixth Amendment. It found it to be as any other right. As long as the waiver was found to be valid (voluntary, intelligent and knowing) such right could be waived. New York requires the assignment of counsel to assist the defendant to defend herself but such counsel may not act in such a manner as to appear to take over the defense.

IV. Identification Procedures

Lineups, Showups and Photo Arrays

The prosecutor's case in chief consists of proving each element of the offense charged was committed and that the defendant did it. Proving the defendant is the one who committed the offense can be accomplished in different ways. One of these ways is by eyewitness identification. In this method one who witnessed the commission of the crime, either the victim or another eyewitness, would be called as a witness at trial in order to make an in court identification of the defendant as the one she saw commit the crime. CPL Sections 60.25 and 60.30 specify how this may be accomplished. As part of the investigation the police will seek to gain an identification of a suspect as the one who committed the offense as part of the evidence in the case. The police may use one or more of three procedures to accomplish this purpose: a lineup, showup or photo array. The constitutional due process clause requires the police to conduct these procedures fairly and in certain instances a suspect's attorney may be required to be present. Generally speaking, prior to the commencement of the criminal action the suspect has no right to counsel at a lineup (*Kirby v. Illinois*, 406 U.S. 682 (1972)); however, if the suspect asks for one the police should attempt to accommodate the request and delay the lineup for a reasonable time in order to allow the attorney an opportunity to be present. If the attorney does not arrive in a reasonable time, the lineup may be held without his presence. Once the criminal action has commenced the defendant's right to counsel attaches and the lineup may not be conducted without the attorney's presence, unless waived (*U.S. v. Wade*, 388 U.S. 218 (1967), and *Gilbert v. California*, 388 U.S. 263 (1967)). The suspect may not interpose the Fifth Amendment right against self incrimination in order to attack the constitutionality of the lineup since that right is testimonial in nature. The lineup procedure does not compel the witness to say anything.

Lineups. The lineup procedure must be devoid of suggestiveness as to who the suspect may be. It should consist of approximately six similar looking persons. Nothing in the make-up of the lineup should direct attention to the suspect. The officers conducting the lineup can make no suggestions as to whom the suspect might be. The persons in the lineup can be required to speak for identification purposes as to sound of voice, or to wear a wig or glasses or other such action for identification purposes. If the suspect's attorney is present at the lineup he is to take no role in its conduct. He is merely there as an observer to make note of its conduct, to protect his client's due process rights and later to be able to protect her legal interests at the criminal action.

Showups. The showup procedure is highly suggestive and except for two circumstances will not withstand constitutional attack upon due process grounds. It consists of a one on one confrontation between the eyewitness and the suspect. There is no opportunity for comparison and the mere fact the police have the suspect in custody might readily suggest she must be the one whom the witness saw commit the offense. Showups are permitted in only two situations;

1. **Prompt on-scene showups** made within a reasonable time after the offense was committed. The suggestiveness is less in this circumstance since the identity of the offender is fresh in the mind of the eyewitness and there is minimum chance of an erroneous identification. There is also less of an infringement on the personal liberty of the subject, since if the eyewitness does not make a positive identification of the suspect he will be released at that point. If a lineup was to be held it would usually take some hours before the failure to identify would occur and the suspect's liberty would be infringed upon far more significantly (*People v. Johnson*, 66 N.Y.2d 398 (1985) and *People v. Duuvon*, 77 N.Y.2d 541 (1991)).

2. **Exigent circumstances showups**. If an eyewitness may die or otherwise become unable to attend a lineup to make an identification, a showup may be permissible. Hospital showups are most common.

Photo Arrays. This procedure is utilized when a suspect is not in custody. Usually reasonable cause to believe a suspect committed the offense has not developed. If, in accordance with descriptive information, modus operandi utilized in the offense or other investigative lead, a possible suspect is under suspicion, if police have a photo of her they may ask the eyewitness to view a number of similar pictures, including that of the suspect, in order to make a positive identification. The same rules of fairness discussed in reference to the lineup are applicable here. No suggestiveness may be permitted as to which of the photos might be the one of the suspect. Since no suspect is present there is no right to counsel involved. If a positive identification is made from a photo array the suspect will usually be arrested and then a lineup held to establish the identification with more certainty.

In a modern twist to the photo array, in *People v. Edmonson*, 75 N.Y.2d. 672 (1990), the Court of Appeals upheld a videotape canvass and identification procedure. The police videotaped passers-by fitting the description of an offender in the vicinity of the offense. Later, following procedures similar to those entailed in photo array identifications, they had the eyewitness view the videotape to see if she could identify the offender. She did and the police returned to the scene at a later time, observed the offender and arrested him.

See Illustrative Cases

People v. Gokey, 60 N.Y.2d 309 (1983), p. 289
People v. Settles, 46 N.Y.2d 154 (1978), p. 291
People v. Griminger, 71 N.Y.2d 635 (1988) p. 294

Table of Cases (for Sec. 1.3)

Aguilar v. Texas, 378 U.S. 108 (1964)
Argersinger v. Hamlin, 407 U.S. 25 (1972)
Brewer v. Williams, 430 U.S. 387 (1977)
Brinegar v. U.S., 338 U.S. 160 (1949)
California v. Carney, 471 U.S. 386 (1985)
Carroll v. U.S., 267 U.S. 132 (1925)
Chambers v. Maroney, 399 U.S. 42 (1970)
Chimel v. California, 395 U.S. 752 (1969)
Colorado v. Bertine, 479 U.S. 367 (1987)
Colorado v. Spring, 479 U.S. 564 (1987)
Cupp v. Murphy, 412 U.S. 291 (1973)

Douglas v. California, 372 U.S. 353 (1963)
Escobedo v. Illinois, 378 U.S. 478 (1964)
Faretta v. California, 422 U.S. 806 (1975)
Gideon v. Wainwright, 372 U.S. 335 (1963)
Gilbert v. California, 388 U.S. 263 (1967)
Horton v. California, 496 U.S. 128 (1990)
Illinois v. Lafayette, 462 U.S. 640 (1983)
Illinois v. Gates, 462 U.S. 213 (1983)
Johnson v. U.S., 333 U.S. 10 (1948)
Johnson v. Zerbst, 304 U.S. 458 (1938)

Katz v. U.S., 389 U.S. 347 (1967)
Kirby v. Illinois, 406 U.S. 682 (1972)
Malloy v. Hogan, 378 U.S. 1 (1964)
Mapp v. Ohio, 367 U.S. 643 (1961)
Maryland v. Buie, 494 U.S. 325 (1990)
Maryland v. Garrison, 480 U.S. 79 (1987)
Miranda v. Arizona, 384 U.S. 436 (1966)
New York v. Belton, 453 U.S. 454 (1981)
New York v. Quarles, 467 U.S. 649 (1984)
Nix v. Williams, 467 U.S. 431 (1984)
Oliver v. U.S., 466 U.S. 170 (1984)
People v. Belton, 55 N.Y.2d 49 (1982)
People v. Bigelow, 66 N.Y.2d 417 (1985)
People v. Cosme, 48 N.Y.2d 286 (1979)
People v. Duuvon, 77 N.Y.2d 541 (1991)
People v. Edmonson, 75 N.Y.2d 672 (1990)
People v. Galak, 80 N.Y.2d 715 (1993)
People v. Gokey, 60 N.Y.2d 309 (1983)
People v. Griminger, 71 N.Y.2d 635 (1985)
People v. Johnson, 66 N.Y.2d 398 (1985)
People v. Johnson, 81 N.Y.2d 828 (1993)

People v. Krom, 61 N.Y.2d 187 (1984)
People v. Mitchell, 39 N.Y.2d 173 (1976)
People v. Overton, 24 N.Y.2d 522 (1969)
People v. Reynolds, 71 N.Y.2d 552 (1988)
People v. Scott, 79 N.Y.2d 474 (1992)
People v. Smith, 59 N.Y.2d 454 (1983)
Powell v. Alabama, 287 U.S. 45 (1932)
Rhode Island v. Innis, 446 U.S. 291 (1980)
Ross v. Moffitt, 417 U.S. 600 (1974)
Schneckloth v. Bustamonte, 412 U.S. 218 (1973)
South Dakota v. Opperman, 428 U.S. 364 (1976)
Spinelli v. U.S., 393 U.S. 410 (1969)
Terry v. Ohio, 392 U.S. 1 (1968)
U.S. v. Leon, 468 U.S. 897 (1984)
U.S. v. Matlock, 415 U.S. 164 (1974)
U.S. v. Mendenhall, 446 U.S. 544 (1980)
U.S. v. Ross, 456 U.S. 798 (1982)
U.S. v. Santana, 427 U.S. 38 (1976)
U.S. v. Wade, 388 U.S. 218 (1967)
Warden v. Hayden, 387 U.S. 294 (1967)
Weeks v. U.S., 232 U.S. 383 (1914)

1.4 Key Definitions (Article 1)

The current statute, the Criminal Procedure Law of New York State, was enacted by the New York State legislature and became law in 1971. It may be cited as "CPL." It replaced the state's previous statute, the Code of Criminal Procedure. The CPL applies to all criminal actions and proceedings within the state.

Article One contains numerous definitions of terms utilized in the statute and must be understood in order to grasp the meaning and intent of its provisions. Many of the sections of the CPL also have definitions at the beginning of the section which are applicable to that section. This chapter will set forth and discuss the definitions found in Article One.

A **criminal action** may be defined as a proceeding by which a person charged with a criminal offense is brought to trial and found guilty or not guilty (*Black's Law Dictionary*). A **criminal proceeding** is any proceeding in court which is part of a criminal action or if not part of a criminal action is related to crime (e.g., application for a search warrant) (1.20/18). A **criminal action** commences with the filing in an appropriate court of an accusatory instrument. It includes all subsequent proceedings and ends with the imposition of sentence or other final disposition (e.g., not guilty verdict, constitutional bar to conviction such as double jeopardy) (1.20/16).

An **accusatory instrument** constitutes an accusation of a violation of a criminal statute on behalf of the people of the state (in whose name the case is prosecuted) against a designated named person as defendant. The title of a criminal action is People v. (Name of designated person) (1.20/1). Several different accusatory instruments are set forth in the CPL: Indictment, Information (a number of different kinds), Misdemeanor Complaint and Felony Complaint. They may commence a criminal action and/or, except for the felony complaint, form the basis for prosecution. These considerations as well as the seriousness of the criminal offense and the court having jurisdiction of the matter determine which form of accusatory instrument is to be used. The details of each of the accusatory instruments are set forth in subsequent portions of the statute. It will serve the purposes of this writing to review some of the details of those most commonly encountered.

An **indictment** is a written accusation, by a grand jury, filed with a superior court, which charges a defendant with a crime and which serves as the basis of prosecution and may commence the criminal action. The New York State Constitution (article 1, section 6) requires that felonies be tried by grand jury indictment. A defendant may waive such right and be prosecuted by a Superior Court Information. The Penal Law of the State sets forth the classification of offenses within the state as: felony, misdemeanor, criminal violation and traffic violation.

Felonies are the most serious classification and are punishable in terms of imprisonment in a state prison for more than one year. Misdemeanors are punishable by more than 15 days but not more than one year. A criminal violation is punishable by up to 15 days in jail, and a traffic violation is classified as set forth in the Vehicle and Traffic Law of the State (NYPL sec. 10) (1.20/3). Felonies and misdemeanors are also classified as crimes.

An **information** is a verified written accusation, by a person, filed in a local criminal court, which charges defendant with a criminal offense below the grade of felony, which may serve both to commence a criminal action and as the basis of prosecution (1.20/4).

The **misdemeanor complaint** is a verified written accusation, by a person, filed with a local criminal court, which charges defendant with a misdemeanor and commences the criminal action and may in certain circumstances serve as the basis of prosecution (1.20/7).

The **felony complaint** is a verified written accusation, by a person, filed with a local criminal court, which charges a defendant with a felony (1.20/8). It serves to commence a criminal action but may not serve as the basis for prosecution due to the New York State constitutional requirement of grand jury indictment in such cases.

There are five elements in each of the definitions of accusatory instruments and one way of determining differences among them is through comparison of the elements:

Comparison of Accusatory Instrument Elements

Instrument	Form	By	Court	Charge	Use
Indictment	Written Accusation	Grand Jury	Superior	Crime	Commence Pros. & Basis of Pros.
Information	Verified Written Accusation	Person	Local	Below Felony	Same
Misdemeanor Complaint	Same	Same	Same	Misdemeanor	Same
Felony Complaint	Same	Same	Same	Felony	Commence Pros.; But Not Basis of Pros.

The first appearance of the defendant in court constitutes the **arraignment**. On this occasion the court acquires control over the defendant and determines the course of future events such as counsel for the defendant, the next appearance and whether defendant should be released on some form of recognizance or held in custody (1.20/9).

Most commonly the defendant will be taken before the court to answer to the charge by an arrest without a warrant, an arrest under the authority of a warrant, a court summons or an appearance ticket. If the defendant is not at liberty within the state, special procedures are provided for in order for the court to gain control over the defendant, such as securing attendance of those outside the state or in institutions inside the state (*see* Articles 550 to 600).

An **arrest** is the taking of a person into custody to be held to answer for a criminal offense. A **warrant of arrest** is an order of a local criminal court, while a **superior court warrant of arrest** is an order of a superior court. They both direct a police officer to arrest the person named in the warrant and to bring him to the appropriate court. In order to secure arrest warrants there must first be an accusatory instrument filed with the court which commences the criminal action against the person (1.20/28,29). The warrants of arrest are utilized to secure the initial appearance of the defendant before the court. If she does not appear for a subsequent appearance in the criminal action, the court may issue a **bench warrant**, directed to a police officer to accomplish this purpose (1.20/30).

A defendant may be gotten into court initially through the use of procedures less drastic upon one's liberty than an arrest. Where less serious crimes and criminal offenses are the gravamen of the accusatory instrument the court may issue a **summons** or a police officer may issue an **appearance ticket**. Each of these processes directs the defendant to appear in court at a future date to answer the charge and the defendant remains at liberty during the proceedings (1.20/26,27).

A defendant may enter a **plea** to the charge, usually guilty or not guilty or some other as prescribed in Article 220 of the CPL. A guilty plea will eliminate the need for a trial to determine the defendant's guilt and constitutes a conviction. In the absence of a guilty plea, a trial will be had in order to determine the guilt or innocence of the defendant. In New York State the pleadings are separate and distinct from the process of arraignment although they may or may not take place at the same court appearance (1.20/10, 13).

There are two kinds of trials provided for, a **jury trial** and a **non-jury trial**. A defendant has the right under the New York State Constitution to a jury trial for felony charges and serious misdemeanors. The constitution also contains specific requirements for waiver of the right to trial by jury and gives the legislature the right to establish detailed procedures governing the waiver of this right. A jury trial may not be waived for a crime the punishment for which may be death (NYS Const. art. 1., sec. 2). The jury trial commences with the selection and swearing in of the jury. For felony trials there must be twelve jurors and for lesser trials, six jurors. A non-jury trial commences with the first opening address, or if none the swearing in of the first witness. The trial ends with the **verdict**, which constitutes the decision of the jury or judge as to the guilt or innocence of the defendant. A verdict of guilty will be followed with the announcement and imposition of **sentence** (the punishment to be allotted to the defendant) such as execution, imprisonment, fine or other such penal discipline (1.20/11,14).

The prosecutor has the burden of proof of two essential facts at trial in order to secure a conviction: proof of the commission of each element of the crime charged and that the defendant committed it. Evidence constituting such proof is called **evidence in chief** (1.20/40).

If one crime is necessarily included within the definition of another it is defined as a **lesser included offense**. For example, the crimes of assault and larceny are lesser included offenses within the crime of robbery. A lesser included offense also includes a less serious, in the eyes of the law, form of the same class of crime which has as an element a lesser form of mens rea or mental culpability. For example the crimes of negligent or reckless homicide are lesser included offenses of the crime of intentional murder. The concept is used broadly in the plea bargaining process or in determining whether a guilty plea is acceptable under the law (1.20/37 and PL Articles 15,120,125, 155 and 160).

In order to insure truthfulness of witnesses they may be required to testify under **oath**, which includes any form authorized by law of attesting to the truth, including affirmation (a promise of truth binding upon one's conscience for those who do not believe in a Supreme Being) (1.20/38).

The peoples' attorney is called the **prosecutor**. The prosecutor in New York State is usually the district attorney of the county in which the court is located. The term includes assistant district attorneys and the attorney general of the state and assistant attorneys general in cases appropriate to the functions of that office (1.20/31,32).

New York State is comprised of sixty-two counties. When the term **county** is used in the CPL it refers to counties outside New York City or New York City as a whole even though the City is comprised of five separate counties (1.20/36).

Geographical area of employment refers generally to the geographical jurisdiction of a peace or police officer's employing agency. For example, the geographical area of employment of a police officer employed by the state is the State of New York; of a New York City police officer, the City of New York. This term is used primarily in reference to the authority to arrest (1.20/34a).

The CPL provides for two different types of law enforcement officers — **police officers** and **peace officers**. At this point, police officers may be thought of as having general police powers, while peace officers may be thought of as those with more narrow or specialized functions or powers. Compare New York State or New York City Police Officers and Triboro Bridge and Tunnel Authority Officers or Dog Control Officers of the Town of Brookhaven. The distinctions are most sharply drawn regarding the powers of arrest, the use of force, the carrying of firearms and the authority to obtain and execute warrants. Peace officers have less authority in these areas of concern (1.20/33,34; 2.10/ 20,40).

Armed felony relates to crimes committed with the use of deadly weapons. Plea bargaining opportunities of defendants are restricted in such cases (1.20/41).

The effect of the term **juvenile offender** is to lower the age of criminal responsibility below sixteen years for crimes of serious personal violence committed by adolescents. Thirteen-year-olds who commit murder and fourteen- and fifteen-year-olds who commit murder, manslaughter, forcible sex crimes, dangerous robberies and other like acts of serious personal violence may be charged, tried and punished as adults upon conviction. Absent these provisions such young persons would only be chargeable as juvenile delinquents, not deemed criminally responsible for their acts and subject to limited punishment for them. There are many factors that must be considered by the judge in determining whether to treat such persons as adult criminals or to cause the action to be transferred to the Family Court for treatment as a juvenile delinquent (1.20/42).

Judicial hearing officers constitute retired judges appointed to conduct preliminary hearings in pending criminal actions (1.20/43).

In addition to the definitions contained in this article, at the beginning of some other articles, definitions specific to that article are set forth. Those set forth in Article One are applicable to the CPL wherever appropriate.

1.5 Peace Officers (Article 2)

Article Two speaks to the issue of peace officer status. It sets forth some sixty positions, the holders of which become peace officers. It sets forth the powers of peace officers and training requirements required for employment as such. It also identifies twenty different federal law enforcement officers and clothes them with the power of peace officers in New York State, which allows them to make arrests for violations of New York law upon reasonable cause to believe such violation occurred in their presence, to make permissible warrantless searches and use reasonable and necessary force as though they were state peace officers.

Peter Priesser's *Practice Commentaries to McKinney's Criminal Procedure Law* notes that comprehensive legislation in 1980 delineated police officers from peace officers and identifies distinctions between them. Police officers are employed by agencies whose mission is law enforcement, while peace officers perform law enforcement functions for agencies whose mission is other than law enforcement (Vol. 11A, p. 55).

Police officers possess greater authority than peace officers and are required to undergo more extensive training. Where a statute grants powers to peace officers, police officers absorb that power also; but where the statute confers powers upon police officers it does not extend to peace officers as well. The sections that delineate who are peace officers many times limit the authority to carry or possess firearms (2.10).

Section 2.20 sets forth peace officers' powers to arrest, use force, search and seize and issue appearance tickets in conjunction with their special duties. It also sets forth indemnification against lawsuits arising out of the exercise of powers vested in peace officers while engaged in their official duty or otherwise enforcing state law.

Training is required for full- and part-time peace officers and no firearms may be utilized without initial training in the use of the firearm and in the lawful use of force. Refresher training may also be required. The training is overseen by the Municipal Police Training Council of the State Division of Criminal Justice Services. Certificates of successful completion of training are issued by the Council and are required for employment as a peace officer. The mandated training program for full-time employment encompasses 35 hours and 10 hours for part-time employment. In addition employers may provide additional training specific to the agency's concerns (2.30).

Chapter 2

The Criminal Courts

2.1 Article 10; Organization and Subject Matter Jurisdiction

The criminal trial courts of the state are divided into two general categories: superior courts and local criminal courts. In this article and Article 20, the term **jurisdiction** is frequently used. It means the right of a court to try and convict a defendant. There are two aspects to jurisdiction. One has to do with the authority of a court to exercise jurisdiction based upon the criminal offense charged. This is termed subject matter jurisdiction. The other aspect has to do with what the CPL terms geographical jurisdiction in Article 20. Under the common law and in other jurisdictions this is also called personal jurisdiction. It is based upon contacts with the place where the crime was committed. Usually the case will be tried in the state, county or city where the crime was committed. This establishes a nexus between the crime, the people of the community affected and the defendant. New York's CPL statute replaces the common law but continues to embrace a number of principles within it.

The Superior Courts and Their Subject Matter Jurisdiction (10.20)

The Superior Courts are the:

a. supreme court; and,

b. county court.

There is a supreme court in each county of the state and a county court in each county of the state outside of New York City (10.10).

The superior courts have trial jurisdiction of all criminal offenses in the state. They are principally concerned with serious criminality, felonies, and generally only try lesser criminal offenses if contained in an indictment. The subject matter provisions reflect this intent. The superior courts have:

a. exclusive trial jurisdiction of felonies;

b. concurrent trial jurisdiction with local criminal courts of misdemeanors;

   c. trial jurisdiction of petty offenses, but only when contained in an indictment which also charges a crime; and,

   d. preliminary jurisdiction of all offenses through the agency of their grand juries (the investigative arm of the courts) (10.20).

The Local Criminal Courts and Their Subject Matter Jurisdiction (10.30)

The local criminal courts are (10.30):

   a. the district courts;

   b. the New York City criminal court;

   c. the city town or village courts; and,

   d. a supreme court justice or county court judge sitting as a local criminal court. Local criminal courts have trial jurisdiction of all offenses except felonies. They also have preliminary jurisdiction of all offenses. Their jurisdiction in all areas is subject to divestiture by the superior courts. For the superior court to take jurisdiction of misdemeanors, there must be an indictment for the misdemeanor in question and for petty offenses, only in an indictment charging a crime in addition to the petty offense. A superior court judge sitting as a local criminal court may only exercise preliminary jurisdiction (conduct arraignments and issue arrest warrants and search warrants) (10.30).

Criminal cases are handled in several types of courts in New York. Criminal cases can be heard in local city courts, town courts, village courts, district courts (in Nassau and Suffolk Counties only), the Supreme Court in New York City, county courts and New York City Criminal Court. The nature of the crime and stage of the process, i.e., pre- or post-indictment, will determine the court venue in each locality. For instance, post-indictment felonies are only heard in the Supreme Courts of the City of New York and county courts of all other counties in New York. Otherwise local courts may handle preliminary proceedings for felony charges in addition to misdemeanors and petty offenses including violations of local city, town or village statutes.

Chapter 3

Requirements for and Exemption from Criminal Prosecution

Sec. 3.1 Article 20; Geographical Jurisdiction of Offenses
Sec. 3.2 Article 30; Timeliness of Prosecution and Speedy Trial
Sec. 3.3 Article 40; Exemption of Prosecution by Reason of Previous Prosecution
Sec. 3.4 Article 50; Compulsion of Evidence by Offer of Immunity

3.1 Geographical Jurisdiction of Offenses (Article 20)

Article 20 addresses the broad question of under what circumstances the State of New York or one of its political subdivisions may exercise criminal jurisdiction over a person. There generally must be some nexus between the criminal offense committed and the political entity seeking to exercise jurisdiction. The statute addresses the questions, When does the state have geographical jurisdiction? (20.20). The individual counties within the state? (20.40). And within the counties, the cities, towns and villages? (20.50). The statute replaces the common law rule that jurisdiction lies in the place where the offense was committed but absent a statutory rule the common law would be followed.

Definitions (20.10)

20.10 defines the state and its 62 counties in terms of their legal territorial boundaries and the space over each. Two technical terms are also defined. "**Result of an offense**" exists when a specific consequence of an offense is also an element of the offense. For example, the death of the victim is an element of the crime of murder. Consequently, the dead body is both a consequence and an element of the crime. "**Particular effect of an offense**" exists when the results of criminal conduct do not constitute an element of an offense but rather the consequences have a materially harmful impact upon the governmental processes or community welfare of the state or one of its political subdivisions, or result in the defrauding of persons in such jurisdiction (*People v. Fea*, 47 N.Y.2d 70 (1979)). For example, a defendant's threats against an eyewitness to the crime was deemed likely to have a materially harmful effect upon government processes and community welfare of the county in which the defendant was to be prosecuted for murder (*People v. Griffen*, 469 N.Y.S.2d 881 (1983)).

State Jurisdiction (20.20)

State jurisdiction relates to three possible situations:

1. Conduct occurs within the state; or,
2. No conduct occurs within the state; or,
3. Acts of omission constitute the criminal offense.

1. Conduct within the State

A person may be convicted in the criminal courts of the state of a criminal offense when his own conduct, or the conduct of one for whom he is legally responsible under Section 20.00 of the Penal Law of the state, constitutes:

a. an element of the criminal offense,
b. an attempt to commit such offense, or,
c. a conspiracy or criminal solicitation.

PL Section 20.00 makes a person criminally liable for the acts of others when such person, with the intent to commit a crime, gets another to actually commit it or any of its elements.

2. No Conduct within the State

If none of the acts occurred within the state, jurisdiction would still lie if the conduct amounted to;

a. a result offense,
b. a particular effect offense,
c. an attempt to commit a crime within the state, or,
d. a conspiracy to commit a crime within the state; and an overt act in furtherance of the agreement occurred within the state.

3. Acts of Omission

The offense committed was one of omission to perform a duty imposed by the laws of the state, such as non-support of a child (PL 260.05) or official misconduct by a public official refraining to perform a duty imposed by law (PL 195.00).

Effects of Laws of Other Jurisdictions (20.30)

Section 20.30 deals with the effects of laws of other jurisdictions upon New York's jurisdiction when crimes and their consequences span more than one state. Two possibilities are addressed:

1. A person commits elements of a crime within New York which results in a crime being committed in another state. For New York to have jurisdiction, the crime committed in the other state must also satisfy all elements of a crime in New York State.

2. If a person commits an act in another state which results in a crime being committed in New York State, New York has jurisdiction whether or not the crime committed in New York is a crime in the other state. Each state has the right to protect itself from such conduct committed outside its boundaries if an element of the crime occurred within its jurisdiction, and the state's rule on territorial jurisdiction allows the prosecution.

County Jurisdiction (20.40)

Section 20.40 sets forth the rules for determining geographical jurisdiction of counties within the state. Many criminal offenses occur across county lines, thus bringing into play Section 20.40. Like 20.20 it sets forth rules for conduct which occurs within the county (20.40/1), when no conduct actually occurs within the county (20.40/2), and for acts of omission (20.40/3). In addition, 20.40/4 establishes special rules for certain crimes and for crimes committed on conveyances traveling over county lines or on roads, bridges or tunnels spanning more than one county, when it may not be certain within which county the crime was committed.

1. Conduct within the County

A county has jurisdiction when a defendant commits conduct within the county which constitutes an element of a criminal offense or an attempt or conspiracy to commit such offense.

2. No Conduct in the County

If no conduct was committed in the county, jurisdiction would still lie if the offense was a result or particular effect offense. (If the offense was a homicide, jurisdiction would lie if the body or a part was found in the county.) The same holds if the offense committed constituted an attempt, conspiracy, or solicitation to commit a crime in the county, or criminal facilitation of a felony in the county (20.40/2).

3. Acts of Omission

If the offense was omission of an act required by law, jurisdiction would rest upon whether the defendant was in or out of the county at the time of the omission (20.40/3).

4. Special Rules

Section 20.40/4 establishes special rules for unique jurisdictional problems arising in conjunction with certain specific criminal offenses or for crimes occurring on transportation conveyances or routes, waterways, bridges and tunnels:

a. Criminal Offenses

1) Jurisdiction for **abandonment** or **non-support** lies in any county in which the child or defendant resided during such period, or any county defendant was present in during said period, if he was arrested therein, or the criminal action occurred therein during such period.

2) Jurisdiction for **bigamy** lies in the county in which the offense was committed, or in which subsequent cohabitation occurred, or in which defendant was present and arrested in, or the criminal action was commenced.

3) Jurisdiction for **forgery** lies in any county in which the forged instrument was possessed by the defendant or one for whom he is legally liable under PL 20.00.

4) Jurisdiction for **filing false instruments** or **larceny by false pretenses** is in any county in which such instrument was executed or in which goods and services were provided.

In the above criminal offenses the general provisions of 20.40 would not permit jurisdiction in certain affected counties thereby making prosecution difficult under certain circumstances (e.g., availability of witnesses or evidence).

b. Transitory Offenses

It may be difficult to determine the county of commission (where jurisdiction lies) when crimes are committed during the course of transportation across county lines. There are six specific special provisions in 20.40/4 which address this kind of problem:

1) For any offense committed on the Hudson River, south of the northern boundary of New York City or on New York Bay between Staten Island and Long Island, jurisdiction lies in any of the five counties of New York City.

2) For crimes committed on vessels on any river, canal or lake, jurisdiction lies in any county bordering such waters or through which it passes.

3) For offenses committed on the Atlantic Ocean within two miles of the high water mark, jurisdiction lies in the county closest to the point of occurrence and for crimes committed over two miles, in the supreme court of such county.

4) For offenses on bridges or tunnels with terminals in different counties, jurisdiction lies in any terminal county.

5) Offenses on board common carrier planes, trains or buses may be prosecuted in any county through which the trip passes or county in which the trip was scheduled to terminate.

6) Offenses in private vehicles may be prosecuted in any county through which the vehicle passed during the trip.

The New York Court of Appeals has held that these transitory provisions are to be used where it is not possible to determine the exact location of the commission of the offense (*People v. Moore*, 46 N.Y.2d 1 (1978)).

7) For offenses occurring within 500 yards of the boundary between two counties, jurisdiction lies in either county.

City, Town and Village Jurisdiction (20.50)

The jurisdiction of cities, towns and villages is to be governed by the provisions of 20.40 (county jurisdiction) as logically would be applied to these entities and in addition one special provision applies. Offenses committed and prosecutable in a city (other than New York City), town or village within 100 yards of the boundary line of another such political subdivision may be prosecuted in either subdivision.

Transportation, Communication and Computer Use (20.60)

Certain criminal offenses may be committed without the defendant ever personally entering the state or a county, but rather by the use of telephone, mail, common carrier or computer. In order to apply certainty to the rules in such instances, 20.60 sets forth the following special rules:

1. Oral or written statements by a person from one jurisdiction to another are deemed to have been personally made in each jurisdiction.

2. A person who causes property to be transported from one jurisdiction to another by any method is deemed to have personally transported it and if delivery has been made, to have personally delivered it.

3. Use of computers or computer services from one jurisdiction to another is deemed to be personal use in each jurisdiction.

Article 20 in its entirety sets forth New York's statutory rules for determining jurisdiction. Although not an element of an offense, the people bear the burden of proof of geographical jurisdiction by a preponderance of evidence (*People v. Ribowsky*, 77 N.Y.2d 284 (1991)).

See Illustrative Cases

People v. Fea, 47 N.Y.2d 70 (1979), p. 296
People v. Carvajal, 6 N.Y. 3d 305 (2005), p. 300
People v. Moore, 46 N.Y.2d 1 (1978), p. 302

3.2 Timeliness of Prosecution and Speedy Trial (Article 30)

This article deals with statutory time limitations placed upon the government by the legislature in both commencing criminal actions (timeliness), and once the criminal action has been commenced, in bringing the defendant to trial (speedy trial).

Time within Which the Criminal

Criminal Offense	Action Must Be Commenced
Class A Felony	May be commenced at anytime
Other Felony	5 years
Misdemeanor	2 years
Petty Offense	1 year

I. Timeliness

Timeliness statutes are also called statutes of limitations. Absent a statute of limitations government has substantial leeway in determining when to commence a criminal action (*People v. Bryant*, 398 N.Y.S.2d 21 (1977)). 30.10 sets forth the timeliness or statute of limitations restrictions. Deliberate delay in commencing an action might violate the due process clause of the state constitution which requires governmental action and procedures to be fair (*People v. Singer*, 44 N.Y.S.2d 241 (1978)). Statutorial time limits are placed upon the commencement of the criminal action, since undue delay would not be fair concerning the defendant's ability to gather evidence with which to defend herself, and to require a presumptively innocent person to live with the fear of punishment or the aura of criminality above her head (*Toussie v. U.S.*, 397 U.S. 112 (1970)).

Timeliness or **statute of limitations** then address the time within which a criminal action must be commenced. It is measured from the date the criminal offense is committed to the date the accusatory instrument is filed in court. The statute sets forth a general statutory rule based upon the seriousness of the criminal offense, some special rules deemed necessary due the nature of the criminal offenses addressed and rules for calculating time (30.10).

The general statutory rule of 30.10/2 provides, except for the existence of a special rule, the following periods of limitations:

The special rules set forth in 30.10/3 provide for the following periods of limitation:

In calculating the time to be counted the following periods shall not be included (30.10/4):

1. Any time following commission of the offense during which the defendant is continuously out of the state; or, the whereabouts of the defendant were continuously unknown and unascertainable by the exercise of reasonable diligence.

Time within Which the Criminal

Criminal Offense	Action Must Be Commenced
Larceny by a Fiduciary	Within 1 year of the discovery of the crime or from the date it should have been discovered by reasonable diligence.
Any offense involving misconduct in public office by a public servant.	Anytime during the defendant's service in office or within 5 years after leaving office, but in no case more than 5 years over the period in subd. 2 for the criminal offense charged.
Any crime in Articles 27 or 71 of the Environmental Conservation Law	Within 4 years after discovery or the date it should have been discovered by reasonable diligence.
A misdemeanor in the tax law or Ch. 46, Administrative Code of New York City	3 years.
Sexual Conduct 1st or 2d degree (PL 130.75 & 130.80)	5 years from the commission of the most recent sexual act.
Sexual offense against a Child (PL art.130; Incest Against a child under 18 (PL 255); or, use of child in a sexual performance (PL 263)	Time does not run until child reaches 18 or offense is reported to police or state central register of child abuse. Whichever occurs first.

2. The time between the commencement of the first criminal action and its defeat and circumstances allow another charge to be lodged.

In interpreting the provisions of 30.10 the courts have decided the statute cannot be tolled by the filing of an insufficient accusatory instrument or the filing of a valid one in a court without jurisdiction (*People v. Kase*, 53 N.Y.2d 989 (1981)). The date of commission of the offense for a usual criminal offense such as a robbery or assault is readily determinable; but for continuing offenses such as conspiracy, which is not complete until the commission of the last provable overt act, problems arise (*People v. Leisner*, 73 N.Y.2d 140 (1989)). Failure to comply with the statute is a bar to prosecution but the statute must be raised in timely fashion by a pre-trial motion to dismiss by the defendant or he is deemed to have waived the statutory provision (210.20).

II. Speedy Trial (30.20)

30.20 is the only true speedy trial provision in the CPL (*McKinney's CPL*, vol. 11, *Preiser's Practice Commentaries*, p. 151). It states unequivocally in subdivision 1 that, after a criminal action is commenced, the defendant is entitled to a speedy trial. The New York State Constitution has no speedy trial provision but the Sixth Amendment speedy trial provision of the federal constitution is applicable to the states (*Klopfer v. North Carolina*, 386 U.S. 213 (1967)).

In New York, speedy trial rights are protected under the due process clause of its constitution and the entire period of statute of limitations and speedy trial may be viewed as one time period for these purposes (*People v. Singer, supra*). Although the provisions of 30.30 might cause one to believe there are specific time limitations governing speedy trial rights, this is not so. 30.30 is a "ready rule" but does not require the start of a trial. Speedy trial is an amorphous, vague concept and a violation of it has to be determined on a case by case basis, based upon the facts in each case. The main speedy trial case decided by the United States Supreme Court, *Barker v. Wingo* (407 U.S. 514 (1972)), states it is impossible to determine with precision when the right has been denied. The court chose four factors within that case to determine if the Sixth Amendment speedy trial right had been violated. New York followed this lead in *People v. Taranovich* (37 N.Y.2d 442 (1975)), in which it determined 5 factors in the case to be critical to the analysis. Both courts indicated the factors it used were not exclusive of others that might also be pertinent in other cases. The courts considered factors such as length of the delay, reason for the delay, did defendant assert his right and any deprivation of due process.

Time for speedy trial purposes commences with the filing of the accusatory instrument and ends with the date the trial begins. Speedy trial claims must be raised by pre-trial motion (170.30, 210.20) and if not raised may not be the basis of an appeal (*People v. Jordan*, 62 N.Y.2d 825 (1984)). While a guilty plea waives any statutory speedy trial claims, it does not waive any such constitutional claims (*People v. Blakely*, 34 N.Y.2d 311 (1974)). 30.20 gives criminal trials preference over civil trials and any case in which the defendant is incarcerated is to be given preference over those in which the defendants are not.

Speedy Trial: Time Limitations, "The Ready Rule" (30.30)

Despite its heading, this section is not a speedy trial provision. It sets forth rules expressing time within which the people must be ready for trial. It does not mean that if the people are ready the trial must begin for there are other pre-trial matters that may lead to further delay. It does mean, however, that if the people are not ready in accordance with the provisions of 30.30 the charges will be dismissed and act as a bar to further prosecution if the charge was contained in an indictment but not if it was one in an information (170.30, 210.20).

30.30 is a complex, much litigated section. It has eight subdivisions which shall be reviewed more or less in depth. In summary, the subdivisions contain the following provisions:

Subdivision Provisions

1   States a general time rule based upon specific criminal offenses.

2   Requires, based on time frames, the release of incarcerated defendants on conditions of bail or personal recognizance.

3   Sets forth exceptions to the application of subdivisions 1 and 2.

4   Sets forth don't count time for subdivisions 1 and 2.

5   Deals with procedures when accusatory instruments are dismissed, replaced or changed for various types of criminal offenses following the court's inquiry on readiness.

Criminal Offense	(Sub. 1) Time for Dismissal	(Sub. 2) Time for Release
Felony	6 months	90 days
Misdemeanor, punishable by more than 3 months in prison	90 days	30 days
Misdemeanor, punishable by 3 months or less in prison	60 days	15 days
Criminal violation	30 days	5 days

6   Applies the motion to dismiss rules of 210.45 to this section.

7   Designates a new commencement date for the criminal action and period held in custody following a change in circumstances such as withdrawal of a plea or retrial.

8   Permits a request for a prompt hearing upon oral argument over excludable time periods with respect to a motion to dismiss.

Subdivision 1, the general rule, provides for dismissal of the charges on pre-trial motion of the defendant if the people are not ready for trial within the time indicated, measured from the commencement of the criminal action;

Subdivision 2 requires the release from custody of a defendant on bail or personal recognizance on just and reasonable conditions upon pre-trial motion of a defendant if the people are not ready for trial in the time frames indicated, measured from the commencement of defendant's commitment;

Subdivision 3 provides that subdivisions 1 and 2 do not apply under the following circumstances:

a.   Defendant is charged with Murder 1st or 2nd degree, Manslaughter 1st or 2nd degree or Criminally Negligent Homicide (PL 125.10,15,20,25,27).

b.   The people are not ready, after they were, due to some exceptional fact or circumstance including but not limited to unavailability of material evidence when the district attorney has exercised due to diligence and there is reason to believe the evidence will become available in a reasonable time (*see People v. Staley*, 41 N.Y.2d 789 (1977), for discussion of factors).

c.   It also provides that subdivision 2 only will not;

1.   apply to a defendant serving time for another offense;

2.   require release of a defendant being held on another criminal charge for which the applicable time has not elapsed; nor,

3.   apply to a defendant who on release does not show up in court on an adjourned date.

Subdivision 4 sets forth provisions regarding don't count time for subdivisions 1 and 2:

a. **Preliminary Proceedings** — reasonable periods of pre-trial delay due to pre-liminary proceedings such as discovery, motions, incompetency and other hearings and trials of other charges.

b. **Continuances** — periods of delay resulting from continuances requested by or with the consent of the defendant. Defendants without counsel must be specifi-cally advised as to this provision. Failure to object to a continuance by a de-fendant will not be considered consent. It must be clearly expressed.

c. **Defendant's Absence or Unavailability** — if due to escape or bail jumping, don't count the period from the issuance of a bench warrant to the day the defendant appears. Absence means the defendant's location is unknown, he is avoiding apprehension or prosecution and his whereabouts cannot be de-termined by due diligence. Unavailable means his location is known but his presence for trial cannot be obtained due to diligence.

If the defendant's behavior did not cause the delay the time may or may not be counted. If the delay is caused by the inefficiency of the prosecutor's office the time will be counted. If the prosecutor, on the other hand, has a consistently administered policy of not presenting a case to the grand jury due to defendant's absence the time will not be counted (*People v. Bratton*, 65 N.Y.2d 675 (1985)).

d. **Co-defendant's Joinder** — co-defendant's joinder and the co-defendant time has not run.

e. **Detained Elsewhere** — periods during which defendant is detained in another jurisdiction and prosecutor has made a reasonable effort to secure his presence for trial (*see*, e.g., *People v. Santana*, 568 N.Y.S.2d 650 (1991) (psychiatric fa-cility); *People v. Wallace*, 26 N.Y.2d 371 (1970) (federal prison); *People v. Mis-sirian*, 546 N.Y.S.2d 455 (1989) (other state prison)).

f. **No Counsel** — periods during which defendant is, without fault of the court except when defendant waives counsel and is defending self.

g. **Exceptional Circumstances** — other periods of delay caused by exceptional circumstances and requested by the prosecutor, such as, evidence is unavailable but prosecutor is using due diligence to find it or case is complicated and district attorney is granted more time to prepare.

h. **ACDs** — periods of adjournment in contemplation of dismissal for misde-meanors or non-serious felonies (170.55,56; 215.10).

Subdivision 5 deals with counting time in cases in which a defendant withdraws a guilty plea; is to be retried for various reasons; in appearance ticket cases; and when the charge and/or accusatory instrument is changed.

There are a large number of cases relative to the ready rule of 30.30. Two gener-alities appear. They generally reflect the notion that if the prosecutor does not exercise reasonable effort, due diligence or other such effort the delay will be charged to the people; but if the prosecutor makes the good effort the time will not be counted. If delay is caused by the defendant the time is not charged against the people. If caused by the people or the system it is; however, for some of the rules causation is not a factor.

The procedural rules of timeliness and speedy trial are regulated by statutes. The statutes and procedures must comport with the requirements of constitutional due process and the Sixth Amendment of the United States Constitution guaranteeing speedy trial.

See Illustrative Cases

People v. Taranovich, 37 N.Y.2d. 442 (1975), p. 304
People v. Romeo, 47 N.Y.S.2d 666 (2008), p. 307

3.3 Exemption from Prosecution by Reason of Previous Prosecution (Article 40)

The Fifth Amendment of the U.S. Constitution and Article 1, Section 6 of the New York State Constitution provide protections against multiple prosecutions or punishments for the same offense. The Fifth Amendment provision, "... nor shall any person be subject for the same offense to be twice put in jeopardy of life or limb," has been made applicable to the states (*Benton v. Maryland*, 395 U.S. 784 (1969)) and the provision of Article 1, Section 6 has not been interpreted by the New York Court of Appeals to offer any additional protections than those provided by the Fifth Amendment provision. Statutory protection against double jeopardy from multiple punishments is found in Penal Law Sections 70.25, 70.30 and 80.15. These two forms of statutory protection provide greater protection than that afforded by the constitutional provisions for the same offense or for different offenses arising from the same act or criminal transaction (40.20) and entire separate procedures for enterprise corruption (40.50), which by definition includes previously committed crimes or offenses for which previous jeopardy may have occurred.

At its outset, Article 40 sets forth two important definitions: offense and criminal transaction (40.10) An **offense** is defined as occurring whenever:

1. any conduct violates a statute, or

2. the same conduct or criminal transaction violates two or more statutes in which each case is a separate and distinct offense (e.g., the offenses of unlawful imprisonment and endangering the welfare of a child out of the same transaction are separate and distinct offenses), or

3. the same conduct or criminal transaction violates only one statute but results in multiple deaths, losses to victims and such result is an element of the offense (e.g., defendant sprayed a room with gunfire killing three people (*People v. D'Arcy* 359 N.Y.S.2d 453 (1974)).

Criminal transaction means conduct which violates at least one statute and is comprised of two or more acts so closely related in time, circumstance, purpose or objective as to constitute the elements or parts of a single criminal incident or venture. For example, defendant in a one hour period, while illegally possessing a handgun, constantly changed his intent and after killing his wife, he left the building to shoot his son and then threatened to shoot others with the same gun (*People v. Okafore*, 72 N.Y.2d 81 (1988)).

The substantive protections of the statute are contained in 40.20. Section 40.20/1 provides that a person may not be twice prosecuted for the same offense. This provision offers the same kind of protection as offered in Article 1, Section 6 of the state constitution but is broader in its protections due to provisions governing what constitutes a previous prosecution in 40.30. This section provides protection from a second prosecution after conviction or acquittal and in some circumstances after a trial has been terminated without a verdict being reached. 40.20/2 is a complex statute consisting of a general rule with multiple exceptions that has led to much litigation. While subdivision 1 is concerned with multiple prosecutions for the same offense, subdivision 2 is concerned with multiple prosecutions for different offenses arising out of the same act or criminal transaction: for example, driving a vehicle in an intoxicated condition, jumping the divider, striking another vehicle and killing its passengers. The same act resulted in two offenses. 40.20/2 specifically provides that a person may not be separately prosecuted for two offenses based upon the same act or criminal transaction, *UNLESS*:

a. the offenses have different elements and are clearly distinguishable from the others (e.g., forging of a hunting permit and illegally taking deer have different elements and are clearly distinguishable from each other (*Fuller v. Plumadore*, 450 N.Y.S.2d 918 (1982)), or

b. the offenses have different elements and are designed to prevent different kinds of harm or evil (growing marijuana without a license and criminal possession of marijuana have different elements and the statutes are designed to prevent different kinds of unlawful activity (*Parmeter v. Feinberg*, 482 N.Y.S.2d 78 (1984)), or

c. one offense is criminal possession of contraband and the other involves its use, other than its sale (e.g., prosecution for possession of a controlled substance after conviction of sale of other controlled substances from the same possession violated the statute (*People v. Flower*, 545 N.Y.S.2d 384 (1989)), or

d. one offense is assault of a person and the other is homicide based upon the death of such person from the injury inflicted during the assault (e.g., *People v. Rivera*, 60 N.Y.2d 110 (1983)), or

e. each offense involves harm to a different victim (e.g., defendant under same plan commits larceny by false pretense of a number of persons, *People v. Luongo*, 47 N.Y.S.2d 418 (1979)), or

f. one offense is a violation of and prosecuted in another jurisdiction but is dismissed for insufficient evidence of an element of the offense; but that element is not an element of the offense charged in this state (e.g. reversal of a federal conviction under the Travel Act for insufficient evidence of use of interstate facilities did not bar state prosecution for conspiracy and bribery since the federal and state prosecutions were for different offenses (*Klein v. Murtagh*, 355 N.Y.S.2d 622 (1974)), or

g. present prosecution is for a consummated result offense in this state due to a conspiracy, facilitation or solicitation prosecuted in another state (e.g., a prosecution for murder in this state is not barred by a previous prosecution in another state for conspiracy to commit murder, *McKinney's CLS, CPL* 11A *Practice Commentaries*, p. 1311), or

h. one offense is enterprise corruption under 460.20 of the penal law or a similar racketeering offense under federal or other state's law and a separate or subsequent prosecution is not barred by CPL 40.50, since the intent of the statute is to place all the rules regarding enterprise corruption into this section.

i. one offense is the object of conspiracy to evade federal or state income taxes.

40.30/1 provides a person is prosecuted for an offense within the meaning of 40.20 when he is charged in an accusatory instrument filed in a court of this state or any other jurisdiction of the United States and the defendant pleads guilty or a trial commences. This statutory provision provides greater protection to defendant than that offered by constitutional double jeopardy in that it eliminates the traditional dual sovereignty doctrine whereby a prosecution in one jurisdiction does not bar a prosecution in another. Many states have similar provisions and in the federal government the Justice Department has a policy which bars federal prosecution after a state prosecution, unless an assistant attorney general approves re-prosecution (LaFave & Isreal, *Criminal Procedure*, West, 1984, pp. 98–102).

Despite the above provision, a person will not be deemed to have been prosecuted when:

1. the court lacked jurisdiction, or

2. the prosecution was improperly procured by the defendant for a lesser offense than possible without the knowledge of the prosecutor in order to avoid a greater charge (e.g., a district attorney told the defendant the matter would be submitted to the grand jury but another district attorney agreed to a plea for a misdemeanor when the defendant told him the plea was authorized by the other district attorney. The court declared the misdemeanor conviction a nullity and no bar to subsequent prosecution on the indictment (*People v. Dishaw*, 388 N.Y.S.2d 795 (1976)), or

3. the previous proceedings have been nullified by court order which directs a new trial and such trial is not otherwise barred (40.30/3,4).

Generally this procedure refers to mistrials. If caused by or consented to by the defendant (*People v. Key*, 45 N.Y.2d 111 (1978)), or if the doctrine of manifest necessity applies (*People v. James*, 489 N.Y.S.2d 527 (1985)), re-prosecution is permitted by this section. Manifest necessity applies to mistrials caused by hung juries (*Plumer v. Rothwax*, 63 N.Y.2d 243 (1984)), illness of the judge or jurors, defective indictments or to appellate reversals due to errors of law. It is not applicable to trials terminated due to a finding of insufficient evidence (*People v. Gentile*, 466 N.Y.S.2d 405 (1983)). This acts as an acquittal and an acquittal may never be reversed. Reversals on findings of against the weight of evidence do not bar future prosecution.

40.40 bars separate prosecution of joinable offenses arising out of the same criminal transaction although not barred by any other of the provisions of Article 40. Two situations are addressed:

1. If one joinable offense for which jeopardy has attached is charged in an accusatory instrument and another is not, in that or any other accusatory instrument, and the people have evidence to support a conviction of the uncharged offense, subsequent prosecution for the uncharged offense is barred if either a trial is commenced or a guilty plea is entered on the existing accusatory instrument (e.g., where reckless assault was not charged in the first indictment for reckless endangerment, defendant could not subsequently be prosecuted for the assault, *People v. Rivera*, 445 N.Y.S.2d 678 (1981)).

2. If the court improperly denies a pre-trial motion for consolidation of two such charges contained in separate accusatory instruments, and the defendant fails to move for consolidation, there can be no denial and thus no satisfaction of the required elements of this provision. Commencement of the action on one, bars subsequent commencement of the action on the other (e.g., *People v. Green*, 392 N.Y.S.2d 804 (1977)).

In 1986 the crime of enterprise corruption was added to the Penal Law as part of an effort to deal with the activities of organized crime (P.L. Article 460). Section 40.50 was also added to the CPL to separately deal with the double jeopardy implications of the statute. Since the crime may involve as an element the commission of other crimes, the possibility of multiple prosecutions for the same criminal conduct arises. Other states and the federal government have similar statutes. Thus, three distinct double jeopardy situations are possible:

1. Separate prosecutions for enterprise corruption and separate and distinct crimes which are part of the elements of the enterprise corruption charge. A crime previously prosecuted may be included as an element of enterprise corruption as long as another not prosecuted crime which occurred after the previous prosecution is also a part of the enterprise corruption charge (40.50/2).

2. A subsequent prosecution may not be had for a crime included as an element of the enterprise corruption unless it is a class A felony that was not prosecutable in the enterprise corruption action (40.50/3.ld).

3. Multiple prosecutions for enterprise corruption within the state or for enterprise corruption and similar statutes without the state. Use of the same crime as an element of more than one such offense is prohibited but the state is not prohibited from separately prosecuting a specific crime over which it has jurisdiction due to the fact it was an element of a racketeering prosecution in another jurisdiction (40.50/6,7,9).

To seek the protections of the claim of previous prosecution the defendant must make it part of a motion to dismiss. If the motion is denied an Article 78 proceeding may be commenced to attack the power of the court to proceed (*Wiley v. Altman*, 52 N.Y.2d 410 (1981)). A guilty claim waives a statutory claim of double jeopardy but not a constitutional one (*People v. Dodson*, 48 N.Y.2d 36 (1979)).

See Illustrative Cases

People v. Rivera, 60 N.Y.2d 110 (1983), p. 309
People v. Kurtz, 51 N.Y.2d 380 (1980), p. 311

3.4 Compulsion of Evidence by Offer of Immunity (Article 50)

The United States and New York State constitutions contain the provision no person shall be compelled to be a witness against himself (U.S. Const. amend. 5; N.Y.S. Const. art.1, sec. 6). The purpose of the provision is to preclude the government from engaging in the abhorrent practice of forcing witnesses to convict themselves by words forced out of their own mouths. The provision is called the right against self-incrimination. When a witness is called upon to give testimony, he must answer the questions put to him unless he believes the answer would tend to incriminate him. In that case the witness may refuse to answer on that ground. However, if offered immunity, the witness must answer but will not be held liable on the basis of the answer.

The federal constitutional provision was originally construed to provide transactional immunity (*Counselman v. Hitchcock*, 142 U.S. 547 (1892)) which gives immunity for any crime arising out of the transaction testified to under the immunity grant. The concept was narrowed, however, to mere use immunity in certain situations. Use immunity protects from the government's use of the witnesses words or any evidence derived from them (*Kastigar v. U.S.*, 406 U.S. 441 (1972)). The scope of use immunity is narrower than transactional immunity but was held to be coextensive with the testimonial nature of the self-incrimination provision. The state constitutional provision has never been construed differently than the federal provision.

Article 50 contains the statutory provisions against self-incrimination and the procedures to be followed for grants of transactional immunity to witnesses. In any situation other than in conformance with the provisions of Article 50, where evidence is compelled over a claim of privilege, only the constitutional protection of use immunity may be claimed (*Matter of Matt v. LaRocca*, 71 N.Y.2d 154 (1987)). Transactional immunity is statutory and is only available under the provisions of Article 50 (*People v. Laino*, 10 N.Y.2d 161 (1961)). Thus, Article 50 offers greater protection than the constitution in the scope of the immunity provided and, in addition, protects against compulsion to produce physical evidence as well as testimony (CPL 50.10/ 3; *People v. Perri*, 53 N.Y.2d 957 (1981); *People v. Middleton*, 54 N.Y.2d 42 (1981)). **Immunity** is defined as a witness in a legal proceeding who cannot be convicted of any offense or subjected to any penalty or forfeiture on account of anything concerning which he gave evidence. Such witness however may be convicted of perjury for giving false testimony in such legal proceeding and may be held in contempt for contumaciously refusing to give evidence when so ordered (50.10/1). **Legal proceeding** means a proceeding before any court and grand jury or before any body, agency or person authorized by law to conduct the proceeding and to administer or cause to be administered the oath (50.10/2). Amongst the other authorities authorized to grant immunity in criminal proceedings are joint legislative committees (Leg. Law 62b), the State Board of Elections (Elec. Law 17-146), the Public Service Commission (Pub. Ser. Law 520/2), the Secretary of State in matters involving real estate brokers licenses (Real Prop. Law 442.e/7), and the State Rent Control Commission (Uncon. Laws Ch. 153.13/2). In addition to authorities such as these who have been authorized by legislation to grant immunity, the courts have also found the authority in family court fact finding hearings (*In Re M.* 403 N.Y.S.2d 979 (1978)), juvenile proceedings (*People v. Elliot,* 403 N.Y.S.2d 901 (1978)) and probation proceedings (*People v. Moschelle,* 410 N.Y.S.2d 764 (1978)). Therefore a witness in a legal proceeding, other than a grand jury proceeding (50.20/5), may refuse to give evidence on the ground it may tend to incriminate him and he may not be compelled to do so unless the legal proceeding is one by which a statute declares the person conducting it as a competent authority to grant immunity, such competent authority orders the witness to give the evidence requested and advises the witness that upon doing so he will receive immunity (50.20/2). To receive immunity the witness must refuse to give evidence on the ground of self-incrimination. The ground of fear for self or family (*Piemonte v. U.S.,* 367 U.S. 556 (1961)) or personal disgrace for self or someone else (*Brown v. Walker,* 161 U.S. 591 (1896)) are not grounds for such refusal.

Any evidence freely given by a witness without first asserting the privilege against self-incrimination will not be given immunity. It acts as a waiver of the right and may be used against him. The immunity procedure is given on a question by question basis unless the prosecutor, defense counsel and court agree on a different mode of procedure. Although cumbersome, the question by question procedure is designed to prevent conferring overly broad and unnecessary grants of immunity (*Brockway v. Monroe,* 59 N.Y.2d 179 (1983)). In a criminal proceeding the court is the competent authority to grant immunity but only upon the express request of the district attorney (50.30). The prosecutor has discretion as to whether or not immunity should be granted (*People v. Gonzalez,* 465 N.Y.S.2d 471 (1983)) and is not obligated to give immunity to defense witnesses (*People v. Osorio,* 449 N.Y.S.2d 968 (1982)); however, prosecutorial discretion is not unlimited and is reviewable for abuse when acting in bad faith or otherwise violating a defendant's due process right to a fair trial (*People v. Sapia,* 41 N.Y.2d 160 (1976)). The provisions of Article 50 do not apply to grand jury proceedings. A witness who gives evidence before such a body does so with transactional immunity, unless he waives it (190.40).

Although the grant of immunity protects against the use of immunized evidence in subsequent criminal actions, it does not protect against its use in civil actions such as loss of license (*Greco v. Board of Examiners*, 458 N.Y.S.2d 343 (1983)), disbarment (*Matter of Anonymous Attorneys v. Bar Association*, 41 N.Y.2d 506 (1977)) or revocation of probation or parole (*Matter of Dellacroce*, 398 N.Y.S.2d 811 (1977)). A defendant may invoke the protection of immunity by pre-trial motion to dismiss (210.20/1d) and, if denied, through collateral attack under Article 78, CPLR (CPLR 506.b/1). A plea of guilty acts as a waiver of a claim of statutory transactional immunity under Article 50 (*People v. Filhan*, 73 N.Y.2d 729 (1988)).

The U.S. Constitution, Fifth Amendment, and its protection against self-incrimination are applicable to the states (*Malloy v. Hogan*, 378 U.S. 1 (1964)). This provision protects a state witness against use of his immunized testimony in other state or federal criminal proceedings or a federal witness from its use in state proceedings (*Murphy v. Waterfront Commission*, 378 U.S. 52 (1964)).

The transactional immunity afforded by Article 50 gives the witness in New York State the ultimate in protection against being compelled to be a witness against oneself.

See Illustrative Cases

Brockway v. Monroe, 59 N.Y.2d 179 (1983), p. 314

Chapter 4

Rules of Evidence, Standards of Proof and Related Matters

Sec. 4.1 Article 60; Rules of Evidence
Sec. 4.2 Article 65; Use of Closed Circuit Television for Certain Child Witnesses
Sec. 4.3 Article 70; Standards of Proof

4.1 Rules of Evidence (Article 60)

Article 60 sets forth the rules of evidence to be followed in criminal cases. Evidence may be defined as all the means used to prove or disprove a fact in issue. Not all evidence offered by a party may be acceptable to a court. The admissibility of evidence constitutes a legal question which requires the decision of the court. In accord with the rules of evidence, which constitute a separate body of law, that which is offered may be found to be admissible or inadmissible. If what is offered as evidence is found to be relevant (related to a fact in issue), material (has proof value relating to a fact in issue), and competent (not otherwise inadmissible according to the rules of evidence), the evidence will be admitted and permitted to be used in the case.

The rules of evidence applicable to civil cases are applicable to criminal cases unless otherwise provided by statute or court decision (60.10).

What Witnesses May Be Called (60.15)

In any criminal proceeding, as a matter of right, each party may call and examine witnesses and cross examine the other party's witnesses. A defendant may testify in his own behalf, but failure to do so is not a factor from which any unfavorable inference may be drawn against him. The judge or prosecutor may not comment on the defendant's failure to do so. To make such comment would violate defendant's constitutional right not to be compelled to be a witness against oneself. An exception to this rule is that a judge may instruct jurors as to this provision in his discretion if he believes it necessary to preclude the inference from being drawn or upon request of the defendant (*People v. Grice*, 474 N.Y.S.2d 152 (1984)).

Witness	Must Testify	Unless
Under 9	Without an oath (unsworn)	Understands oath (sworn)
9 or over	Under oath (sworn)	Does not understand oath (unsworn)

Testimonial Capacity; Evidence Given by Children (60.20)

Any person may be a witness unless he does not have sufficient intelligence or capacity to justify reception of his evidence due to mental disease, mental defect or infancy. A witness under nine years of age is considered an infant and as such may not testify under oath unless the court is satisfied he understands the nature of an oath. A witness nine years of age or older, considered to be an adult, must testify under oath unless due to mental disease or defect he does not understand the nature of an oath. Such a witness, if the court is satisfied he possesses enough intelligence and capacity to justify it, may be permitted to give unsworn testimony. Graphically illustrated these rules are:

The significance of these rules is that no conviction may be had based solely on unsworn testimony. It must be corroborated by truly independent evidence as to each material fact testified to. Sworn testimony has a greater assurance of truth due to the promises inherent in the oath (*People v. Parks*, 41 N.Y.2d 36 (1976)).

Corroboration of Accomplice Testimony (60.22)

There can be no conviction of a defendant based upon the testimony of an accomplice without corroborative evidence tending to connect the defendant with the commission of the offense. An **accomplice** is defined as a witness in a criminal action who according to evidence in the case may reasonably be considered to have participated in the offense charged or an offense arising out of the same transaction. A witness is considered an accomplice even though he cannot be prosecuted or convicted due to some defense or exemption such as age or immunity. Whether corroboration is sufficient depends on the facts in each case. Corroborative evidence must be truly independent. The reason corroboration is required is the accomplice cannot be trusted to tell the truth (*People v. Hudson*, 51 N.Y.2d 233 (1980)). A confession of an accomplice may not be admissible if the defendant has no opportunity to cross examine the maker at trial. This would be deemed to violate the defendant's confrontation right under the constitution.

Identification of the Defendant (60.25, 30)

The prosecutor's case in chief at trial consists of proving beyond a reasonable doubt the elements of the criminal offense charged and the defendant is the one who committed it. Without such proof there can be no conviction. Sections 60.25 and 60.30, address the identification of the defendant issue. They set forth the matters an eyewitness may testify to at trial. The procedures governing eyewitness identification are carefully structured because eyewitness testimony is powerful evidence and if not controlled could lead to undue prejudice against the defendant in the minds of the jurors. Research has shown it to be frequently faulty. 60.30 is utilized when the witness is able to identify the defendant in court after having viewed him at the scene and then, usually, at a police line-up. It allows the witness to testify to this effect;

1. I saw the defendant (do what he did) at the crime scene.

2. I again saw that person on a second occasion (usually the police line-up).

3. The defendant is the person I saw on the previous two occasions.

No bolstering of this eyewitness testimony is permitted.

Section 60.25 allows the following testimony by the eyewitness and testimony of a third party to establish the identity of the defendant as the perpetrator of the criminal offense, when the eyewitness is unable to identify the defendant in court:

1. I saw a person (do what he did) at the crime scene.

2. I again saw that person on a second occasion (usually the police line-up).

3. I cannot recollect if the defendant is the one I previously saw.

If this eyewitness testimony was not allowed to be bolstered, the identification attempt would fail. Trials may occur months after the event. Memories fade. Appearances change. In this situation:

4. Another witness may testify (usually a police officer present at the line-up) that at the line-up the previous witness picked the defendant in this case as the person he saw at the crime scene.

Impeachment of Own Witness by Proof of Prior Contradictory Statement (60.35)

When a party calls a witness to testify on a material issue of the case and the testimony of the witness tends to disprove the position of the party calling the witness, such party may introduce a prior signed statement or oral statement made under oath by such witness that contradicts the witness's testimony. The prior contradictory statement of the witness may only be introduced for impeachment purposes and the court must so instruct the jurors. If the prior contradictory statement does not tend to disprove the position of the party who called the witness, it may not be introduced in evidence and it may not be used to refresh the recollection of the witness in such a way that discloses its content to the trier of facts.

Proof of Previous Conviction; When Allowed (60.40)

Any witness including a defendant may be properly asked if he was previously convicted of a specific offense or any offense. If he denies or equivocates, the party may independently prove such conviction. If a witness testifies as to the good character of the defendant, the people may introduce evidence of a conviction that tends to negate the trait testified to. The issue of whether or not a previous conviction of a defendant may be brought out will be decided by the judge. The judge must balance the probative value of such evidence against the danger of creating unfair prejudice against the defendant. If the previous conviction would tend to indicate a propensity to commit the type of crime defendant is charged with, it may not be admitted unless the intent of its use is to prove motive, intent, absence of mistake, accident or common scheme or plan. The people may prove a previous conviction if it is an essential element of the present charge unless the defendant admits to it in a special proceeding. In that event no mention of it may be made at the trial (200.60).

Admissibility of Evidence of Victim's Sexual Conduct in Sex Offense Cases (60.42)

Evidence of the victim's sexual conduct in Penal Law Article 130 cases (Rape, Sodomy and Sexual Abuse) or 230 (Sex trafficking of a child) shall not be admissible unless such evidence:

1. Proves or tends to prove specific instances of the victim's prior sexual conduct with the accused; or

2. Proves or tends to prove that the victim has been convicted of an offense under Section 230.00 of the penal law within three years prior to the sex offense which is the subject of the prosecution; or

3. Rebuts evidence introduced by the people of the victim's failure to engage in sexual intercourse, oral sexual conduct, anal sexual conduct or sexual contact during a given period of time; or

4. Rebuts evidence introduced by the people which proves or tends to prove that the accused is the cause of pregnancy or disease of the victim, or the source of semen found in the victim; or

5. Is determined by the court after an offer of proof by the accused outside the hearing of the jury, or such hearing as the court may require, and a statement by the court of its findings of fact essential to its determination, to be relevant and admissible in the interests of justice.

This section is designed to preclude the defense from cross-examining the victim in such matters so as to delve into sexual aspects of the victim's life not believed to be relevant to the charge at hand. A defense to forcible sex crimes may be consent of the victim or creation of a reasonable doubt the defendant was the perpetrator. These rules are designed to limit invasions of the victim's privacy but at the same time permit the introduction of evidence by the defendant in his attempt to defend himself against the charge. In addition, 60.48 precludes admissibility of the victim's manner of dress in a sex offense case and, in 60.43, evidence of the victim's past sexual conduct in a non-sex offense case is also precluded. In these latter two instances the court may allow such evidence if after a hearing it finds it in the interest of justice to do so.

Use of Anatomically Correct Dolls (60.44)

Any person under sixteen years of age may, in the discretion of the court, use an anatomically correct doll in testifying in a criminal proceeding for a violation of Penal Law Article 130, 260 or Section 255.25 (Rape, Sodomy, Sexual Abuse, Offenses Against Children or Incest). Children of tender years may not be able to testify specifically as to the facts of an offense due to lack of knowledge of the names of the various parts of the sexual anatomy or embarrassment. The doll may be used by the child to point to that part of the body that was involved in the sexual act.

Admissibility of Statements of Defendants (60.45)

Written or oral confessions, admissions or exculpatory statements made by a defendant are inadmissible as evidence against him if involuntarily made. **Involuntarily made** means gotten from defendant;

1. By any person, by use of physical force or threat of use of physical force against the defendant or any person; or,

2. Through the use of undue conduct or pressure which impaired defendant's ability to decide to make a statement or not; or,

3. By a public servant or one acting at his direction, by means of a promise that creates a substantial risk that defendant may falsely incriminate himself in violation of his constitutional right.

Involuntariness is a legal question to be answered by the judge, but on motion of the defendant the jury may decide the issue. The constitutional rights to due process and not to be compelled to be a witness against oneself are protected by this rule.

Statements of Defendants; Corroboration (60.50)

A defendant may not be convicted solely on his confession or admissions. Corroboration in the form of additional proof that the criminal offense has been committed must be shown.

Psychiatric Testimony in Certain Cases (60.55)

When the defendant claims the affirmative defense of lack of criminal responsibility due to mental disease or defect, the burden of proof of such defense lies with the defendant by a preponderance of evidence. The defendant's proof will consist of expert witness testimony from a psychiatrist or licensed psychologist, concerning the defendant's mental state at the time of the commission of the offense. The expert witness must be allowed to testify as to:

1. the nature of his examination;

2. his diagnosis;

3. his opinion as to defendant's ability to know or appreciate the nature and consequences of his act or its wrongfulness, due to mental condition (this constitutes the legally recognized mental state that is assessed in reference to culpability for one's acts).

The defendant's statements to the psychiatrist or psychologist during the course of the examination are inadmissible as proof except as to the issue of mental disease or defect. The privileged communication regarding statements of a patient to a doctor or psychologist is not a bar to the doctor's testimony as to the affirmative defense. The court must instruct the jurors as to these provisions and of the fact they may not consider such statements in determining whether or not the defendant committed the act constituting the criminal offense charged.

Certificates Concerning Judgments of Conviction and Fingerprints (60.60)

Criminal court certificates stating a person has been convicted of a criminal offense and reports of government custodians of fingerprint records, certifying the fingerprints of a defendant are the same as those of a person previously convicted of a criminal offense, may be entered into evidence and are presumptive evidence of previous convictions of crime. There are occasions when a previous conviction must be proven in a trial. Without the above provision the clerk of the court or a representative of the identification section would be required to appear in court to testify as to the above fact. Certified copies of the records may be used instead.

Dangerous Drugs Destroyed Pursuant to Court Order (60.70)

Article 715 provides for destruction of dangerous drugs. The destruction of the drugs in question at a trial shall not preclude testimony or evidence relating to the drugs if such testimony or evidence would have been admissible if such drugs had not been destroyed; e.g., if such drugs had been found to have been seized by the government in violation of the defendant's constitutional rights at a suppression hearing such drugs would not be admissible notwithstanding this section.

Chemical Test Evidence (60.75)

If defendant is charged with more than one count of driving while intoxicated in the same indictment, chemical test evidence of intoxication admitted into evidence regarding one count may be received in evidence with regard to the remaining counts. This eliminates the necessity of relitigating the admissibility of such evidence on the subsequent counts.

The provisions of Article 60 set forth special rules relating to the application of the criminal procedure law. It must be remembered there is a separate body of law; the law of evidence is also applicable. All the rules have been developed in order to try to assure truth in the fact finding process and to ensure a fair trial so that justice may be done.

See Illustrative Cases

People v. Felder, 485 N.Y.S.2d 576 (1985), p. 318
People v. Sandoval, 34 N.Y.2d 371 (1974), p. 319
People v. Jovanovic, 700 N.Y.S.2d 156 (1999), p. 322

4.2 Use of Closed Circuit Television for Certain Child Witnesses (Article 65)

In 1985 the legislature enacted Article 65 as a three-year experiment permitting a vulnerable child witness, 12 years of age or less, to give testimony relating to its victimization of a sex offense under Article 130 (N.Y. Penal Law, Article 130, defines the crimes of sexual misconduct, rape, sodomy and sexual abuse) or Section 255.25 of the penal law (N.Y. Penal Law, Section 255.25, defines the crime of incest), in any criminal proceeding, other than a grand jury proceeding, by use of a two way closed circuit television system, from a testimonial room separate from the courtroom and in some instances out of the physical presence of the defendant. Whether the procedure was constitutional under the U.S. Constitution, amend. 6, and the N.Y. Constitution art.1, sect. 6, both of which contain the "confrontation clause" (right of the defendant to be confronted with the witnesses against him), was settled by the U.S. Supreme Court in *Maryland v. Craig* (110 S. Ct. 3157 (1990)) and the N.Y. Court of Appeals in *People v. Cintron* (75 N.Y.2d 249 (1990)). The *Craig* court found no constitutional impediment in the use of one way closed circuit television systems and the court in *Cintron* found no facial constitutional violations in the procedures set forth in Article 65. Both decisions however stressed the need to demonstrate the specific necessity requiring the use of such procedures.

In order for the procedure to be utilized the child witness must be declared "vulnerable" by the court, upon clear and convincing evidence, and that as the result of extraordinary circumstances the child witness will suffer severe mental or emotional harm (65.10/1) if required to testify without the use of the two way television procedure. One way television is not permitted (65.10/2) nor is the court's power to close the court room curtailed (65.10/3).

Application Procedures (65.20)

Either party upon pre-trial, written motion, may apply to the court for an order declaring the child witness is vulnerable, with reasonable notice to the other party and an opportunity to be heard. At any time, if the court believes the child witness is vulnerable the judge may invoke the procedure as if it was requested by either party upon pre-trial motion. The papers must state the basis for the motion and sworn allegations of fact based upon personal knowledge or information and belief. The answer may admit or deny and in addition may contain sworn allegations of fact including the rights of the defendant, the need to protect the child witness and the integrity of the finder of fact.

Unless the facts in the motion are conceded, the court must hold a hearing to determine the motion. It may subpoena and examine witnesses. The child witness may not be compelled to testify at the hearing on the motion and such action shall not be a ground for denying the motion. Prior statements of the child regarding the crimes and attempts to deter it from testifying are admissible but alone they may not form the basis of a vulnerability finding. A doctor, psychologist, nurse or social worker who has treated the child may testify as to the treatment rendered the child without violating any privileged communication and the court shall examine, in camera, any reports relative thereto; and, if it deems any information material and relevant, it shall disclose such information to both parties.

At any time after the motion is made, upon demand, discovery is allowed by either party of records, reports or documents. Prior to the hearing, the district attorney and defense counsel, subject to protective orders, will make known to the other party prior statements of witnesses they intend to call at the hearing and any known records of prior convictions of crime or pending criminal actions.

The court may consider, in determining whether extraordinary circumstances exist (*People v. Costa*, 554 N.Y.S.2d 930 (1990)) that would cause the child witness severe mental or emotional harm, a finding that any one or more of the following factors (relating to the offense, the child or defendant) have been established by clear and convincing evidence:

a. the offense; the offense was particularly heinous or aggravating circumstances were present; or, was part of an ongoing course of conduct over an extended period of time;

b. the child; the child is particularly young or subject to psychological harm due to a condition pre-dating the offense; or, has previously been the victim of Article 130 or Section 255.25 penal law offenses; or, an expert witness testifies the child would be particularly susceptible to psychological harm if required to testify in open court or in the physical presence of the defendant;

c. the defendant; the defendant at the time of the offense occupied a position of authority over the child; or, used a deadly weapon or instrument in the offense; or, inflicted serious injury upon the child; or, threatened physical violence to the child if the child reported the incident or the break-up of the family relationship of the child and its family if reported; or, is living in the same house as the child or has access to or is providing financial support for the child; or, a threat has been made to a third party witness on behalf of the defendant.

The court must consider these and other relevant factors and the relationship between them and the child's vulnerability. If the court is satisfied the child witness is vulnerable and the defendant's constitutional rights to an impartial jury and confrontation will not be impaired, it may enter an order granting the use of live, two way, closed circuit television. If the court finds the child will likely suffer severe mental or emotional harm if the defendant was in the same room during the testimony of the child witness it shall direct the defendant to remain in the court room.

Taking Testimony of the Vulnerable Child Witness (65.30)

When the order is granted the testimony of the vulnerable child witness will be taken in a separate testimonial room equipped with closed circuit television equipment which will transmit the testimony and image of the child witness and the image of all others in the testimonial room (except that of the equipment technician) to the courtroom which will be equipped with sufficient television monitors to permit viewing by the judge, jury, defendant and attorneys. The public will also be permitted to view the monitors. The image of the jury shall be transmitted to the testimonial room for view of the child witness and, where the court order specifies the testimony to be out of the physical presence of the defendant, the image of the defendant shall also be visible to the child witness. The attorney must also remain in the courtroom unless the court determines presence in the testimonial room will not impede full communication between the defendant and his attorney and will not create an inference adverse to defendant's interest. If the court determines no equipment is available, the procedure may not be used. The testimony of the child witness in the testimonial room will be given as by any other witness and recorded by the court stenographer.

The courts have decided the state interest in protecting the well-being of child sex victims more than outweighs the minimal infringement upon the defendant's constitutional rights of the two way, closed circuit procedure set forth in Article 65 (*People v. Algarin*, 498 N.Y.S.2d 977 (1986)), but only upon an individualized determination that the child is a vulnerable child witness caused by extraordinary circumstances which are factually proven by clear and convincing evidence (*People v. Logan*, 535 N.Y.S.2d 322 (1988)).

4.3 Standards of Proof (Article 70)

There are a number of standards of proof in law utilized to describe the amount and kind of evidence required to establish the basis for different legal conclusions (*see* chart, Standards of or Quantums of Proof, in Chapter 1). Article 70 speaks to three important concepts within the parameters of standard of proof. It defines the terms "**legally sufficient evidence**" and "**reasonable cause to believe a person has committed an offense**"; and, it sets forth the standard of proof required for a trial verdict of conviction, or "**guilt beyond a reasonable doubt.**" Standards of proof relate to the kind of and/or the quantity or quality of facts, circumstances or information (evidence) which may be relied upon to form the basis for decisions such as arrest, search, charging or conviction and they differ in this regard, depending upon the impact upon the liberty of a person. For example, it takes less to arrest than to indict and more to convict than to indict.

Legally sufficient evidence is defined as:

a. competent evidence,

b. which if accepted as true,

c. would establish every element of an offense charged,

d. and the defendant's commission thereof,

e. except that such evidence is not legally sufficient when corroboration required by law is absent (70.10).

The term is synonymous with the term "prima facie case" (*People v. Anderson*, 344 N.Y.S.2d 15 (1973)). Thus, legally sufficient evidence may be explained as relevant and material evidence which if uncontradicted or explained (accepted as true) would be sufficient to sustain a decision to arrest or a conviction; however, if other evidence to the contrary was introduced (no longer accepted as necessarily true) or if required corroboration was absent, the relevant and material evidence would not be considered legally sufficient. In addition, the term competent evidence rules out the use of inadmissible evidence, such as hearsay, in determining if a given set of facts and circumstances constitutes legally sufficient evidence.

Reasonable cause to believe a person has committed an offense is defined as existing when:

a. evidence or information which appears reliable,

b. discloses facts or circumstances,

c. which are collectively of such weight and persuasiveness,

d. as to convince a person of ordinary intelligence, judgment and experience,

e. that it is reasonably likely that such offense was committed, and

f. that such person committed it (70.10(2)).

Except as otherwise provided in the CPL, such apparently reliable evidence may include or consist of hearsay evidence. For example, an officer may take into account hearsay evidence in order to determine if reasonable cause exists to arrest a person; but a grand jury may not include hearsay evidence to determine whether reasonable cause to believe a person committed an offense exists in order to find an indictment, since the statute (190.65/1) does not permit its use for such purpose.

A fundamental difference between legally sufficient evidence and reasonable cause to believe is the former does not take into account the quality or quantity of evidence present or its persuasiveness, whereas the latter deals with these factors.

Reasonable cause is also synonymous with the federal constitutional standard of probable cause (*People v. Johnson*, 66 N.Y.2d 398 (1985)).

Guilt beyond a reasonable doubt, the standard of proof set forth in 70.20, is not defined in the statute. It merely states that no conviction by verdict (after trial) is valid unless:

a. based upon trial evidence,

b. which is legally sufficient, and

c. it establishes beyond a reasonable doubt,

d. every element of the offense, and

e. the defendant's commission thereof.

The guilt beyond a reasonable doubt standard of proof is extremely important. It has been declared to be a fundamental right under the due process clause of the Fourteenth Amendment to the U.S. Constitution (*In re Winship*, 397 U.S. 358 (1970)) and recognized as such by New York State (*People v. Di Manno*, 182 N.Y.S.2d 937 (1959)). It is also a very complex and at times ambiguous concept. One of the problems is that the standard must be applied in the context of the various factual situations present in differing crimes. Despite this fact it is important to have a general understanding of the meaning of the standard. Judges must address this problem as part of their charge to juries prior to their deliberations on the evidence in an attempt to reach a verdict. Some general understandings may be found in case law. Each of us must be able to understand and define the concept of guilt beyond a reasonable doubt. It has been defined in different ways, by different jurists and scholars, in an effort to achieve understanding. It may be defined as:

a. that amount of articulable facts and circumstances,

b. that would establish beyond a doubt a reasonable person could give for having,

c. the guilt of a person charged with crime.

Such a definition arises from a review of cases dealing with the issue. For example, it is an actual doubt you are conscious of after going over in your mind the entire case, giving consideration to all the testimony and every part of it. If you then feel uncertain and not fully convinced that the defendant is guilty and believe you are acting in a reasonable manner, and you believe that a reasonable man in any matter of like importance would hesitate to act because of such doubt as you are conscious of having, that is a reasonable doubt that the defendant is entitled to have the benefit of (*People v. Insogna*, 281 N.Y.S.2d 124 (1967)).

The foundation for the finding of guilt may not be based on conjecture or suspicion but on facts and inferences which common human experience would lead a reasonable man, putting his mind to it, to accept (*People v. Pena*, 50 N.Y.2d 400 (1980)). A reasonable doubt is one which arises from the evidence and its character, or from the absence of satisfactory evidence, and is such a doubt as a reasonable man has a right to entertain after a fair review and consideration of all the evidence (*People v. Fried-*

land, 37 N.Y.S. 974 (1896)). At a criminal trial, the burden is on the people to prove every material element of the crime charged, beyond a reasonable doubt (*People v. Guarino*, 391 N.Y.S.2d 699 (1977)). The prosecution's burden to establish guilt beyond a reasonable doubt extends to every issue raised at trial, including rebuttal of defendant's defense (*People v. Butts*, 201 N.Y.S.2d 926 (1960)). The reasonable doubt rule is a rule of evidence which deals with the quantum of proof necessary to convict (*People v. De Cillis*, 14 N.Y.2d 203 (1964)). And finally, the identification of the defendant must be proved beyond a reasonable doubt (*People v. Coleman*, 471 N.Y.S.2d 380 (1983)).

These are the elements that must be understood in order to grasp the meaning of the all-important standard, guilt beyond a reasonable doubt.

See Illustrative Cases

People v. Graham, 626 N.Y.S.2d 95 (1995), p. 325
People v. Guarino, 391 N.Y.S.2d 699 (1977), p. 328

Part Two

The Principal Proceedings

Chapter 5

Preliminary Proceedings in Local Criminal Court; Commencement of the Action, Arrest, Summons, Fingerprinting, Photographing and Criminal Identification

Sec. 5.1 Article 100; Commencement of the Action in, and Local Criminal Court Accusatory Instruments

Sec. 5.2 Article 110; Requiring Defendant's Appearance for Arraignment

Sec. 5.3 Article 120; Warrant of Arrest

Sec. 5.4 Article 130; The Summons

Sec. 5.5 Article 140; Arrest without a Warrant

Sec. 5.6 Article 150; The Appearance Ticket

Sec. 5.7 Article 160; Fingerprinting, Photographing and Criminal Identification Records and Statistics

5.1 Commencement of the Action in, and Local Criminal Court or Youth Part of a Superior Court — Accusatory Instruments (Article 100)

A **criminal action is commenced** by the filing of an accusatory instrument against a defendant in a criminal court or youth part of the superior court of the state. The various kinds of accusatory instruments, namely: an information, simplified information, a prosecutor's information, a misdemeanor complaint, or a felony complaint. The criminal action usually commences in a local criminal court by the filing of an information or misdemeanor or felony complaint unless the first accusatory instrument filed is an indictment, which must be filed in a superior court. If more than one accusatory instrument is filed, the criminal action commences with the filing of the first. This is significant since the commencement of the criminal action triggers a number of important rights of the defendant such as the right to counsel, and calculations of time for statute of limitations purposes begin from the date of such filing (100.05).

The form and content of the various local criminal court accusatory instruments is comprised of the name of the court, the title of the action, the verification part and most importantly the accusatory and factual parts. The title of the action will be People v. (a designated named defendant). It must be signed by the complainant, either a police or peace officer or citizen who has knowledge of the offense. In order to assure truthful information in the instrument, the complainant is required to sign the verification part which indicates it is a criminal offense to give false information in the factual part of the instrument. The verification may also be accomplished by means of a swearing under oath by an officer authorized to administer same.

The government may not take a person's liberty away unless probable cause (reasonable cause to believe) exists that such person violated a statute. The accusatory part contains the specific section of law the defendant is charged with violating and the factual part must contain facts of an evidentiary character, based upon the personal knowledge of the complainant or upon her information and belief, tending to support the charge in the accusatory part of the instrument. If the defendant consents, the misdemeanor complaint prepared in this manner may form the basis of prosecution. If the defendant does not consent to its use, then the basis for the prosecution must be an information. The factual part of the information must contain non-hearsay allegations which, if true, establish every element of the offense charged and the defendant's commission thereof.

The felony complaint may never serve as the basis for prosecution since the New York State Constitution requires trial by indictment for felony charges (art. 1; sec. 6). If the felony complaint charges a violent felony offense as set forth in Section 70.02 of the Penal Law (sets forth crimes of personal violence for which additional penalties may be imposed), the accusatory part of the complaint must designate it as such and the factual part must contain facts of an evidentiary character tending to support such designation.

The accusatory instrument must be filed in the appropriate court having jurisdiction of the offense. If the form and content of the accusatory instrument are not in conformance with the provisions of the statute there could be a failure of the court to obtain jurisdiction, leading to invalidity of the courts process (e.g., invalid arrest warrants) and a dismissal of the charges (100.05 to 100.55).

5.2 Requiring Defendant's Appearance for Arraignment (Article 110)

A defendant is brought before the court by various means, usually by an arrest either under the authority of an arrest warrant or without a warrant. Most arrests are made without warrants. In order to obtain a warrant of arrest a police officer must demonstrate to the court reasonable cause to believe an offense was committed by the person sought to be arrested. The officer may make a warrantless arrest on the same grounds. In cases of lesser criminal offenses, the court in its discretion may issue a summons rather than a warrant of arrest if it believes the defendant would appear as required in response to same, and an appearance ticket may be issued by the police in conjunction with a warrantless arrest. These procedures are set forth in sections below. If the defendant is not at liberty within New York State, e.g., is in jail or confined to a mental institution in the state or is not physically in the state, procedures are set forth in Chapter 14 for securing their attendance. When the offense charged is a crime, other than in New York City, a copy of the accusatory instrument must be given to the prosecutor, before arraignment, by the officer if she is the complainant or is assisting an arresting citizen, or by the court clerk in other cases.

5.3 Warrant of Arrest (Article 120)

A **warrant of arrest** is a process of a local criminal court, directing a police officer to arrest a defendant designated in an accusatory instrument filed with such court and to bring the defendant before the court for arraignment (120.10).

Form and Content

The warrant must contain the name of the issuing court, date issued, the offense charged, the name of or a description of the defendant, the officer, officers or class of officers issued to and a direction that the defendant is to be brought before the issuing court. The warrant must be signed by the issuing judge (120.10).

When Issuable

The warrant is issuable after the filing of an accusatory instrument sufficient on its face and before arraignment. Such an instrument establishes the constitutional requirement of probable cause the offense was committed by the defendant. The court in its discretion may satisfy itself as to the sufficiency of the instrument by a hearing under oath. A simplified traffic information may not form the basis for the issuance of a warrant of arrest. The court in its discretion may issue a summons if satisfied the defendant would respond thereto and in such a case it may not issue a warrant of arrest (120.20). This provision that the court "may not issue a warrant of arrest" is not a mandatory direction but is merely permissive (*People v. McNeil*, 393 N.Y.S.2d 662 (1977)). The court in its discretion may also authorize the district attorney to direct the defendant to appear on a designated date, if satisfied the defendant will so appear. The warrant is issuable and returnable in a court having geographical jurisdiction (120.30). A copy of the underlying accusatory instrument may be attached to warrants issued by city, town or village courts since in certain instances the defendant will have the opportunity to appear before a court in the county in which the arrest was made for bail or recognizance purposes (120.40; 120.90).

Execution of the Warrant

The warrant may be executed by the officer designated in the warrant or by an officer delegated for such purpose. The delegation may be made by the designated officer in the warrant when she has reasonable cause to believe the defendant is in a county other than the one in which the warrant is returnable, is executable in such county without a place endorsement by a judge in such county and said county is within the geographical area of employment of the delegated officer. The delegation may be made by any means and it is not necessary that a copy of the warrant be transmitted, although if possible this would amount to good police practice (120.60). If the defendant is a parolee or probationer, the warrant may also be executed by a probation or parole officer (120.55). A warrant issued by a district court or the New York City Criminal Court or a superior court judge sitting as a local criminal court may be executed in any county of the state. A warrant issued by any other local criminal court may ordinarily only be executed in the county of issuance or an adjoining county. If to be executed in another county it must be first endorsed by a local criminal court judge in such county for execution in said county (120.70).

When and How Executed

The warrant may be executed on any day of the week and at any hour of the day or night. The arresting officer must inform the defendant he is being arrested under the authority of a warrant unless the defendant resists, attempts to flee or some other factors arise making it impractical to carry out the requirement. The officer must show the warrant upon the request of the defendant — if not in possession of it at the time of the arrest, then as soon as practicable thereafter (120.80).

Use of Force to Effect the Arrest or Prevent Escape

The arresting officer may use justifiable physical force to effect the arrest or prevent an escape as authorized by Penal Law Section 35.30 (the officer may use reasonable and necessary force to effect the arrest or prevent escape or defend against the use of physical force, but may not use deadly physical force unless she reasonably believes the offense to be a felony involving the use of physical force against a person; or, the crimes of kidnapping, arson, escape 1st degree, or burglary 1st degree; or, a felony and in the course of resisting arrest or attempting escape the person is armed with a firearm or deadly weapon; or, the use of deadly force is necessary for defense of self from the use of deadly physical force) (120.80).

Entering Premises

The officer may enter any premises to execute the arrest warrant in which she reasonably believes the defendant to be present (before such entry the officer must give or make reasonable effort to give notice of her authority and purpose, unless exigent circumstances exist) except the residence of a third party (i.e., the residence of someone other than the defendant). In order to enter the third-party residence, non-consensually, the officer must also be in possession of a search warrant for such residence (690.05) or exigent circumstances must be present, i.e., to delay entry for purposes of obtaining consent to enter or to obtain a search warrant would result in the escape of the defendant, danger to life or the loss of evidence. If after giving notice of her authority and purpose the officer is refused admittance or no response is forthcoming, or due to exigent circumstances such notice is not required, the officer may break in if necessary (120.80). This section pertaining to execution of arrest warrants is designed as much to protect the officer's safety as the individual's privacy (*People v. Reiff*, 407 N.Y.S.2d 534 (1978)). Defendants have no right to be speedily arrested (*People v. Bryant*, 398 N.Y.S.2d 216 (1977)). Officers' forced entry into apartment after recognizing voices of two defendants from outside apartment was justifiable to prevent destruction, damaging or secretion of material evidence they had reason to believe was in the apartment (*People v. Cage*, 339 N.Y.S.2d 6 (1972)). The fact the defendant is not advised of the offense designated in the arrest warrant does not vitiate the arrest. A defendant is in custody for Miranda purposes at the moment the officer informs the defendant he has a warrant for the defendant's arrest (*People v. Duncan*, 660 N.Y.S.2d 81 (1997)).

Procedure after Arrest

The procedure after arrest will differ depending upon the offense for which the warrant was issued, the county of execution and the officer involved.

1. If the warrant charged a felony; or, if the warrant charged a lessor offense but was executed in the county of issuance or an adjoining county:

   a. If the arrest was made by the officer to whom the warrant was addressed, the officer shall bring the defendant directly to the court that issued the warrant without unnecessary delay.

   b. If the arrest was made by a delegated officer, she shall deliver the defendant to the officer to whom the warrant was issued without unnecessary delay and such officer shall deliver the defendant to the issuing court without unnecessary delay.

2. For other than a felony warrant, executed in a county other than the one in which the warrant was issued or in an adjoining county:

   a. If the arrest was made by the officer to whom the warrant was addressed, the officer shall inform the defendant of his right to appear before a local court in the county of arrest for bail or personal recognizance purposes. If the defendant does not wish to appear before this court, the officer will require the defendant to endorse the warrant to that effect and the officer shall then deliver him to the court that issued the warrant without unnecessary delay. If the defendant wishes to avail himself of the opportunity to appear before the former court or refuses to endorse the warrant indicating he wants to go to the court that issued the warrant, the officer shall bring the defendant to the court in the county in which the arrest was made for bail or recognizance purposes without unnecessary delay.

b. If the arrest was made by the delegated officer, she shall turn the defendant over to the officer to whom the warrant is addressed within two hours of the arrest. Otherwise, the delegated officer must inform the defendant that he has a right to appear before a local criminal court for the purpose of being released on his own recognizance or having bail fixed. If the defendant does not desire to avail himself of such right, the officer must request him to make, sign and deliver to him a written statement of such fact, and if the defendant does so, the officer must retain custody of him but must without unnecessary delay deliver him or cause him to be delivered to the custody of the delegating police officer. If the defendant does desire to avail himself of such right, or if he refuses to make and deliver the aforementioned statement, the delegated or arresting officer must without unnecessary delay bring him before a local criminal court of the county of arrest and must submit to such court a written statement reciting the material facts concerning the issuance of the warrant, the offense involved and all other essential matters relating thereto. Upon the submission of such statement, such court must release the defendant on his own recognizance or fix bail for his appearance on a specified date in the court in which the warrant is returnable (120.90).

An arrested defendant must be arraigned without unnecessary delay and such obligation arises immediately upon arrest and continues until arraignment (*People v. McCray*, 313 N.Y.S.2d 772 (1970)). Undue delay in arraignment is to be avoided to protect a defendant's constitutional rights and to prevent inherent abuses and evils that attend delay such as secret interrogation, improper obtaining of admissions or confessions and coercion of the accused (*People v. Johnson*, 313 N.Y.S.2d 768 (1969)).

Processing of the Arrest

Before bringing a defendant before a local criminal court after arrest upon a warrant, the officer shall record the arrest and perform all necessary fingerprinting and other preliminary police duties required by the particular case. If the arrest is not so processed before the appearance in court, before any release of the defendant on bail or recognizance, the court shall direct such processing to take place. Upon arresting a juvenile offender, the officer shall immediately notify the parent, guardian or person with whom he is domiciled of the fact of the arrest and the location of the facility where he is being detained (120.90). The Family Court Act and this section reflect the legislature's concern that when very young people are arrested they may be in need of parental guidance and support during police interrogation (*People v. Susan H.*, 477 N.Y.S.2d 550 (1984)).

5.4 The Summons (Article 130)

A **summons** is a process of a local criminal court directing a defendant named in an information, prosecutor's information, felony complaint or a misdemeanor complaint, to appear before the court at a specified time for arraignment upon the charge in the accusatory instrument. It may also be issued by a superior court to direct the defendant to appear before it in connection with an accusatory instrument filed in such court. It must be signed by the issuing judge and is returnable only in the issuing court. It may be served by a police officer or by a complainant or other person over the age of 18 designated by the court. The summons may be served in the county of issuance or an adjoining county. If the defendant does not appear on the returnable date, the court may issue a warrant of arrest for his appearance. Upon arraignment the court shall direct the defendant to be fingerprinted when such action is required by the charge against the defendant. It should be remembered that the judge, in his discretion, may not issue a warrant of arrest if he is satisfied the defendant would appear in response to the direction in the summons. The summons should be thought of as a less drastic alternative to the liberty interests of a defendant in a less serious criminal case.

5.5 Arrest without a Warrant (Article 140)

A warrantless arrest may be made of a person at liberty within the state when such person has in fact committed any offense or there is reasonable cause to believe such person has committed an offense (140.05). Article 140 sets forth different authority for warrantless arrests for police officers, peace officers and private citizens. Police officers are given the greatest authority in that they may make warrantless arrests upon reasonable cause to believe an offense has been committed. While performing their duties, peace officers are given similar authority; but when not performing their duties, they may make arrests for serious offenses on reasonable cause to believe but may only make arrests for lesser criminal offenses which have in fact been committed. Private citizens may only make arrests for offenses in fact committed. Reasonable cause to believe is synonymous with probable cause. Reasonable cause to believe allows the arresting officer a reasonable margin for error in making arrests and shields her somewhat from civil liability for false arrest suits. It also permits evidence to be admitted at trial compared to the in fact standard, required particularly of private citizens. Criminal offenses are classified as felonies, misdemeanors, criminal violations and traffic violations. Felonies and misdemeanors constitute crimes, while criminal and traffic violations are classified as petty offenses or non-criminal offenses (10.00 Penal Law).

When the intrusion involved is of sufficient magnitude, an arrest will be said to occur, whether or not the person is eventually transported to the police station and charged with crime, but not every seizure constitutes an arrest (*People v. Chestnut*, 51 N.Y.2d 14 (1980)). A defendant was subjected to full scale arrest when he was handcuffed at gunpoint so that he could be transported to the scene of a murder (*People v. Crosby*, 457 N.Y.S.2d 831 (1983)). Briefly handcuffing defendant while awaiting victim's arrival did not elevate detention to an arrest (*People v. Tucker*, 636 N.Y.S.2d 759 (1996)). The police officers' approach of the defendant outside a bus station and the initial questioning of him, limited to a request for information regarding his identity, citizenship and destination was reasonable and permissible and did not constitute an arrest (*People v. Mejia-Guzman*, 590 N.Y.S.2d 623 (1992)). A defendant was under arrest at the time of a show-up identification, where he was left in the rear of a police car for a period of at least 20 minutes with no way of opening the door from the inside (*People v. Cooper*, 616 N.Y.S.2d 442 (1994)).

Warrantless Arrests by Police Officers (140.10)

A police officer may make a warrantless arrest upon:

1. reasonable cause to believe a person has committed a crime (felony or misdemeanor); or,

2. reasonable cause to believe a person has committed a petty offense (criminal or traffic violation);

    a. in his presence,

    b. within his geographical area of employment or one hundred yards of such area, and

    c. the arrest is made in the county of commission of the offense or an adjacent county, unless made in hot pursuit from such county, in which case it may be made in any county of the state. The police officer may pursue a person in hot pursuit into another state and make the arrest in such state if it has a reciprocal hot pursuit statute (*See* 140.55).

Special procedures exist for family offense cases and arrests under orders of protection, which restrict an officer's discretion whether or not to arrest.

When and How Made (140.15)

The arrest may be made on any day of the week and at any time of the day or night. The arresting officer:

1. must inform the person arrested of his authority and purpose and the reason for the arrest unless due to flight, resistance to the arrest or some other factor to do so would be impracticable;

2. may use justifiable physical force to effect the arrest as per P.L. 35.30. (These provisions are set forth in reference to arrests under the authority of a warrant of arrest 120.80 above.) (*People v. Hill*, 17 N.Y.2d 185 (1966));

3. may enter a premises to make the arrest when he reasonably believes the person to be arrested is present therein unless the premises is a residence;

a. In order to enter the residence of the person to be arrested, non-consensually, to make a routine arrest (no exigent circumstances are present) the officer must have an arrest warrant. (*Payton v. New York*, 445 U.S. 573 (1980));

b. In order to enter the residence of a third party, non-consensually, to make a routine arrest, the officer must have an arrest warrant and a search warrant. (*Steagald v. U.S.*, 451 U.S. 204 (1981); 690.05);

4. must announce his authority and purpose before forcing entry into any premises unless he reasonably believes to do so would result in the escape of the suspect, endanger the life or safety of the officer or someone else or result in destruction, damage to or the hiding of evidence. (*See* 120.80/4,5; *People v. Floyd*, 26 N.Y.2d 558 (1970); *People v. Hyter*, 402 N.Y.S.2d 602 (1978).)

In the Payton and Steagald cases, the U.S. Supreme Court declared entry into residences without the authorization specified to constitute a violation of the U.S. Constitution, Fourth Amendment (*Matter of Lynell H.*, 469 N.Y.S.2d 883 (1983)).

Procedure after Arrest (140.20)

Upon arresting a person without a warrant, the police officer will usually take the prisoner to the local police station and without unnecessary delay, record the arrest and perform other necessary police preliminary procedures such as fingerprinting, photographing and conducting a lineup. The officer must then, without unnecessary delay, bring the prisoner to the appropriate local criminal court for the filing of an appropriate accusatory instrument charging him with the offense or offenses related to the arrest, unless an appearance ticket is in order. In such a case the appearance ticket will be issued and the prisoner will be released from custody and appear in the court specified in the ticket at the time and date indicated.

The ambiguous phrase "… without unnecessary delay …" is an important one. The U.S. Constitution gives a defendant the right to a prompt judicial determination of probable cause for the arrest (*Gerstein v. Pugh*, 420 U.S.103 (1975)). In *County of Riverside v. McLaughlin*, 500 U.S. 44 (1991), the U.S. Supreme Court decided that a probable cause hearing within 48 hours was prompt and that systems should be designed to accomplish the hearings within that period of time. The decision takes into account the competing needs of society to record and preliminarily prepare the case for court and the defendant's right to a prompt hearing. The case does not mean that a defendant held for longer than 48 hours without the opportunity for the hearing has had his rights violated, for there may have been extraordinary circumstances involved that made the longer period of time reasonable. The N.Y.S. Court of Appeals has not interpreted the state constitution in this matter; however, it let stand an affirmation of the Appellate Division of a lower court ruling that 24 hours was a reasonable period of time for preliminary matters to be taken care of and that in New York County delays beyond this time frame would be presumed to be unnecessary (*People ex rel. Maxian v. Brown*, 77 N.Y.2d 422 (1991)). Delays due to continuing the investigation are not appropriate for extending the time frame nor are those motivated by malice or ill will.

It is imperative the defendant be brought to the appropriate court for the filing of the accusatory instrument otherwise the defendant's jurisdictional rights will be violated. The reasonable cause decision is made by the court on the basis of the factual part of the accusatory instrument. If it is not filed in the appropriate court as set forth in Sec. 100.55, the court in which it is misfiled does not acquire geographical jurisdiction, the criminal action has not commenced and any orders, warrants or other process issued by the court are a nullity. The provisions regarding the appropriate court in Sec. 100.55 are quite liberal. The general rule that geographical jurisdiction lies in the county in which the offense occurred is followed; however, more than one local criminal court may cover the same geographical area due to the political entities of counties, cities, towns and villages. In addition there are a number of local criminal court accusatory instruments (see the organization of the criminal courts in Article 10 and the definitions of the various accusatory instruments, above). Any local criminal court accusatory instrument may be filed in a district court, the New York City Criminal Court, or a city court of a particular city when the offense charged was committed in the county where the district court is located; or in the New York City Criminal Court if the offense was committed in New York City; or in the city court of a particular city if the offense was committed in that city. In addition to these provisions the statute addresses specific kinds of local criminal court accusatory instruments and the jurisdiction of town and village courts and that of the superior court judge sitting as a local criminal court judge:

1. A felony complaint may be filed in any town or village court of a particular county when the felony charged was alleged to have been committed in any town of that county;

2. An information or misdemeanor complaint may be filed in the village court of the village in which the offense has been allegedly committed;

3. An information or misdemeanor complaint may be filed in a town court of a particular town in which the offense has allegedly been committed, unless it was allegedly committed in a village within such town that has a village court;

4. An information, simplified information, misdemeanor or felony complaint may be filed with a superior court judge sitting as a local criminal court when the offense charged was allegedly committed in a county in which such judge is present and he also resides in or is holding or assigned to hold a term of a superior court in said county.

In the event more than one court is authorized as a proper court, the accusatory instrument may be filed in any such court, but not more than one. If a law expressly provides for a different method of filing, that law may be followed rather than the above provisions (100.55).

140.20 allows for the issuance of an appearance ticket and release from custody for arrests for E felonies (excepting rape or sodomy 3d degree, escape 2d degree, absconding 1st degree and bail jumping 2d degree) and for lesser criminal offenses. For these offenses an appearance ticket or the fixing of bail must be done when the defendant cannot be promptly arraigned due to the unavailability of a local criminal court. Such procedures are not required if the defendant appears to be under the influence of alcohol or drugs to the extent of possibly endangering himself or others if released. The specific provisions relating to appearance tickets are set forth in Article 150 below. If, after the arrest is made, further investigation reveals there is no longer reasonable cause to believe the person committed any offense such person must be immediately released from custody. Also, upon arresting a juvenile offender, an immediate notification of such arrest and the location of the detention facility must be made to the parent or guardian or other person legally responsible for his care.

Warrantless Arrests by Peace Officers (140.25)

As indicated above, a peace officer has less authority to make warrantless arrests than a police officer but greater authority to make such an arrest than a private person. In general, the peace officer has the same authority to make warrantless arrests as a police officer when acting "pursuant to his special duties." When not so acting and he is outside his "geographical area of employment," he has less authority and, other than arrests for alleged felonies, has no more authority than the private, ordinary citizen.

1. A peace officer, acting pursuant to his special duties, may arrest a person for:

    a. A crime (felony or misdemeanor) upon reasonable cause to believe the person to be arrested has committed such crime; or,

    b. A lessor offense (traffic or criminal violation) upon reasonable cause to believe the person to be arrested has committed such offense, in his presence.

A peace officer acts "pursuant to his special duties" when the arrest is for a statutory offense he is required or authorized to enforce or the circumstances are such that the arrest of the offender constitutes an integral part of his specialized duties. Sec. 2.10 describes who are peace officers and specific duties and purposes, as well as specific statutes which must be consulted in specific cases in order to determine if the arrest was made "pursuant to his special duties."

2. A peace officer, not acting pursuant to his special duties, may arrest a person:

    a. Within his geographical area of employment, for;

        1) a felony, upon reasonable cause to believe the person to be arrested committed such felony; or,

        2) a lesser offense (misdemeanor, criminal or traffic violation) when such person has in fact committed such offense, in his presence.

    b. Outside his geographical area of employment, for;

        1) a felony, upon reasonable cause to believe the person to be arrested committed the felony in his presence and the arrest is made during its commission or immediately thereafter or during the immediate flight therefrom.

The "geographical area of employment" of a peace officer is coextensive with the political jurisdiction of his employer if employed by a government agency (state, county, city, etc.) or, if employed by a private employer, any place in the state where he is at a particular time acting in the course of his duties. Note how the authority of the peace officer narrows as the seriousness of the offense diminishes and as he becomes further removed from his employment. He ultimately has no more authority to make warrantless arrests than private citizens for lesser offenses. For an analysis of the elements involved in peace officer arrests for lesser offenses, see *People v. Hartman*, 451 N.Y.S.2d 347 (1982).

Procedures to Be Followed in Making Arrests and after by Peace Officers (140.27)

The rules governing the manner of arrest by peace officers are the same as prescribed for police officers in Section 140.15. Upon arrest the peace officer may take the prisoner directly to an appropriate local criminal court for the filing of the accusatory instrument. If the charge is one requiring fingerprinting of the defendant, the peace officer may enlist the aid of an appropriate police officer. If the arrest is one for which an appearance ticket may be issued or must be issued, the defendant shall be taken to a police facility for processing and issuance of same. If the defendant is a juvenile offender, the peace officer must make the required notification of the arrest and place of detention to the parent or guardian.

Warrantless Arrests by Private Persons (140.30)

The private person's authority to arrest is severely limited since in every instance the law allows no margin for error on the basis of reasonable cause or good faith. If the person arrested did not in fact commit the crime, civil liability lies for false arrest.

A private person may arrest:

1. for a felony, anywhere in the state, when the person to be arrested has in fact committed such felony; and,

2. for a lesser offense, only in the county of commission, when the person to be arrested has in fact committed it in his presence.

The statutory provision recognizes the fact that private citizens generally do not possess knowledge or experience in the law and the fact that it is more likely "citizen arrests" will result in resistance by the person to be arrested, leading to further breaches of the peace. To be arrested constitutes a seizure of the person and is a major intrusion on the liberty of persons presumed innocent until proven guilty. Therefore the authority of private citizens to arrest is severely limited. The private person who chooses to make an arrest does so at his own legal peril.

The process of the arrest by the private person is similar in some respects but different in others from arrests by police and peace officers. The arrest may be made at any time of the day or night and the person to be arrested must be informed of the reason for the arrest unless physical resistance, flight or other factors make such procedure impracticable. The private person may use justifiable force to effect the arrest, but such authority is much more limited than that allowed police and peace officers (140.35). Subdivision four of Section 35.30, Penal Law, allows the use of force by private citizens making arrests under the following circumstances:

1. Use of force, other than deadly physical force;

   a. upon reasonable belief such to be necessary to effect the arrest or prevent the escape of a person he reasonably believes committed the offense; AND, who has in fact committed such offense.

2. Use of deadly physical force;

   a. in defense of self or another from what he reasonably believes to be the use or imminent use of deadly physical force; or,

   b. to effect the arrest of a person who has committed murder, manslaughter in the first degree, robbery, forcible rape or sodomy; and, who is in immediate flight therefrom.

There is no authority in the statute for private citizens to enter premises to affect the arrest.

Procedure after an Arrest by a Private Person (140.40)

The private person making an arrest must without unnecessary delay deliver or attempt to deliver the person arrested to a police officer. From there on the police officer must process the arrest as if he himself made the arrest (fingerprinting, photographing, follow-up investigation, recording the arrest, appearance ticket issuance where appropriate and any other similar procedures set forth in 140.20 that may be appropriate in the case). The officer must then, without unnecessary delay, bring the person to the appropriate court for arraignment and the private person must file an appropriate accusatory instrument with such court without delay. A police officer is not required to take such an arrested person into custody or perform any of the above actions if he reasonably believes the person arrested did not commit the offense or that the arrest was otherwise unauthorized. If the accusatory instrument filed is not sufficient on its face and the court is satisfied, based upon the available facts, that it would be impossible to draw and file an accusatory instrument valid on its face, it must dismiss such accusatory instrument and discharge the defendant (140.45).

Temporary Questioning of Persons in Public Places; Search for Weapons (Stop & Frisk Law, 140.50)

As mentioned in Chapter 1, Basic Constitutional Law Summary, New York has codified the constitutional right to stop a person (interfere with a person's right to be free of interference with liberty by government agents or the right to be left alone, under the Fourth Amendment to the U.S. Constitution). The timeless activity of police of stopping and investigating suspicious persons and circumstances was given constitutional favor in the landmark decision of the United States Supreme Court in *Terry v. Ohio*, 392 U.S. 1 (1968). New York's Statute 140.50 codifies the constitutional provisions set forth in *Terry*. Case law therefore is based not only on the statute but most importantly upon the constitutional provisions enunciated in *Terry*. 140.50 provides:

1. A police officer,

2. may **stop** a person,

3. in a public place,

4. within his geographical area of employment,

5. when he **reasonably suspects**, such person,

6. is committing, has committed, or is about to commit,

7. a felony or misdemeanor under the penal law, and

8. may demand of him his name, address and an explanation of his conduct.

    (A peace officer providing court security duty may do the same in or about the courthouse to which assigned.)

9. Upon stopping a person under the circumstances described above,

    a. if the officer **reasonably suspects**,

    b. danger of physical injury,

    c. he may search such person for a weapon.

    d. If he finds such a weapon, or other property he reasonably believes may constitute the commission of a crime,

    e. he may seize it and keep it until the completion of questioning and then,

    f. return it, if lawfully possessed, or arrest such person.

In *Terry v. Ohio* and a myriad of subsequent cases interpreting the language of the search and seizure provisions of the United States and New York State constitutions, the U.S. Supreme Court and the New York Court of Appeals have attempted to define and explain the meaning of the terms stop and search, under the concepts of the stop and frisk situation and the all-important term — reasonable suspicion.

The Stop

When a police officer restrains a person from walking away either through the authority of the badge or physical restraint, he has constitutionally seized that person. All seizures of persons, to pass constitutional muster, must meet the constitutional test of reasonableness. In order to determine if the seizure was reasonable, the articulable facts surrounding the seizure must be examined. In determining reasonableness, the law weighs the right of the person to be free of arbitrary interference with her liberty and society's right to take action in order to protect itself from crime. Historically, an arrest, the taking of a person into custody to be held to answer for a criminal offense, constitutes a seizure of a person. The arrest constitutes a major or significant interference with one's liberty and the constitution requires a seizure to be based upon probable cause the person to be arrested has committed a criminal offense (in New York State the term reasonable cause is the term used which is synonymous with probable cause). These terms relate to the amount of evidence of crime required to cause a reasonable person to conclude it is more likely than not that crime has been, is being or is about to be committed. In *Terry*, the Court was asked to determine if an investigative stop, a temporary interference with one's liberty, constituted a seizure, and if so, does the requirement of probable cause have to be satisfied in such situations.

The court determined that when police interfere with a person's freedom of movement, temporarily, to determine if crime is occurring, a seizure of the person has occurred.

Reasonable Suspicion

After defining a stop and determining it to be a constitutionally protected seizure of the person, the court determined that since it was a lesser interference with a person's liberty than an arrest it could be conducted upon a lesser standard of articulable facts and circumstances than that which would amount to probable cause, reasonable suspicion. The court defined **reasonable suspicion** as that amount of articulable facts and circumstances that would cause a reasonable person to believe crime may be afoot, as opposed to the conclusion required in probable cause determinations, that crime has been, is being or is about to be committed.

The Frisk

Section 140.50, set forth above, states that upon reasonable suspicion of danger an officer may search a person for a weapon. The term search is unqualified and as such can denote a full search. The constitutions, however, require full searches to be made upon probable cause as opposed to the lesser standard of reasonable suspicion. In *Terry*, based upon reasonable suspicion of danger, the officer patted down the outer clothing of Terry in order to determine if he was armed and upon feeling what he believed to be a gun, the officer reached into that portion of Terry's clothing in order to retrieve it. This action is a limited intrusion upon the person's right to be free of unreasonable search under the constitution, and is commonly called a frisk. The court determined that the frisk is a search in constitutional terms but since it is a limited intrusion upon one's freedom it may constitutionally be performed upon a lesser showing of articulable facts and circumstances (reasonable suspicion of danger) than that required for a full search (probable cause). The search provision of 140.50 then must be read as a limited one or a frisk.

There are a substantial number of cases at the state and federal levels, involving various sets of facts and circumstances, in which the courts have been required to apply the above terms in order to determine if the action of the officers involved was constitutionally and statutorily appropriate. These cases further defined and clarified the definitions and issues of stop, frisk and reasonable suspicion and involve comparisons with the terms arrest, search and probable cause. Issues include how to determine if a stop has occurred; how a stop can develop into an arrest; if facts and circumstances amount to an arrest or a stop, reasonable suspicion or probable cause; and whether the search was a frisk or a full-blown search. In-depth analysis of the issues raised by stop and frisk is beyond the scope of this work; however, a reading of *Terry v. Ohio* and *People v. De Bour*, 40 N.Y.2d 210 (1976), will lead to the ability to better understand stop and frisk law.

Warrantless Arrests by Peace Officers of Other States for Offenses Committed Outside New York State (Provisions of the Uniform Close Pursuit Act, Sec. 140.55)

A peace officer of another state, who enters New York in close pursuit of and arrests a person for a crime committed in another state, which would also be a crime in New York State, and such other state has a reciprocal act, has the same arrest powers in New York as a police officer under New York law, and may arrest and hold in custody such person.

The peace officer of the other state shall deliver the person arrested, without unnecessary delay, to a local criminal court, where a hearing will be held in order to determine if the arrest was made in conformance with the above provisions. The local criminal court shall not determine the guilt or innocence of the person arrested. If the court determines the arrest was made in conformance with the above provisions, it shall commit the person arrested to the custody of the officer making the arrest for return, without unnecessary delay, to the state from which he fled. If not, it shall discharge the person arrested. This section represents New York's adoption of the Uniform Close Pursuit Act. It has been adopted by most other states as have other uniform laws which make it possible for one state jurisdiction to cooperate with another without involved legal impediments.

See Illustrative Cases

People v. De Bour, 40 N.Y.2d 210 (1976), p. 329
People v. Carroll, 868 N.Y.S.2d 866 (2008), p. 334
People v. Floyd, 26 N.Y.2d 558 (1970), p. 337
People ex rel. Maxian v. Brown, 561 N.Y.S.2d 418 (1990), p. 338
People v. Carney, 58 N.Y.2d 51 (1982), p. 341

5.6 The Appearance Ticket (Article 150)

Just as the summons (Article 130) may be thought of as a less drastic alternative to the liberty interests of a defendant than an arrest under the authority of an arrest warrant, the appearance ticket may be thought of as a less drastic alternative to the liberty interests of a defendant subject to a warrantless arrest. The **appearance ticket** is a device used primarily as an alternative to a warrantless custodial arrest for less serious criminal offenses. It is a written notice issued and signed by a police officer or other authorized public servant (authorized by state or local law) directing the person to appear before a local criminal court at a certain time to answer a charge of a designated offense. As long as the notice contains these elements, it satisfies the requirements of an appearance ticket despite its being labeled a traffic ticket, summons or any other name or title (150.10). The procedure may be used as an alternative to a warrantless arrest or after a warrantless arrest has been made for a:

1. class E felony, except;

Rape 3d Degree (PL 130.25)	Absconding 1st Degree (PL 205.17)6
Sodomy 3d Degree (PL 130.40)	Absconding (PL 205.19)A
Escape 2d Degree (PL 205.10)	Bail Jumping 2d Degree (PL 215.56); or,

2. lesser criminal offense (misdemeanor, criminal violation or traffic offense).

The appearance ticket may be issued by non-police personnel public servants, designated by state or local law (150.20). The procedure is far less restrictive upon the liberty of the defendant than the normal requirements of custody inherent upon a warrantless arrest. The decision to utilize the appearance ticket procedure is within the discretion of the police officer unless the defendant cannot be promptly arraigned due to the unavailability of a local criminal court. In this situation however, as in any other appearance ticket situation, release may be conditioned upon the posting of station house bail (140.20 subd. 2,3). The issuance of an appearance ticket is mandatory if the sole charge for which the person has been arrested is the non-criminal violation of possession of marijuana (Sec. 221.05 P.L.).

Pre-Arraignment Bail (150.30)

The issuance of the appearance ticket may be made conditional upon the posting of pre-arraignment station house bail after an arrest for an offense for which the appearance ticket procedure may be utilized. If the arrested person fails to comply with the directions of the appearance ticket, the bail will be forfeited. The person posting the bail must complete and sign a form which serves to place him on notice as to the terms of release under the appearance ticket and that failure to comply with these terms by the principal will result in the forfeiture of the amount posted as bail. The desk officer in charge of the police station or jail where the principal is held, or his superior officer will fix the amount of bail to be posted, issue the appearance ticket and a receipt for the bail posted and release the principal from custody. The amount of bail will be fixed as follows:

Arrest for	Bail = Any Amount Not Exceeding
Class E felony	$750.00
Class A misdemeanor	$500.00
Other misdemeanor	$250.00
Petty offense	$100.00

The police officer has discretion to take road bail for traffic infractions where she reasonably believes the violator to be not licensed by New York or any state covered by a reciprocal compact guaranteeing appearance as provided in Sec. 517, VTL. The road bail shall be fixed at $50.00 and must be posted by credit card. The posting of station house bail by credit card for traffic infractions is also permitted.

Service and Related Procedures

An appearance ticket is made returnable to the local criminal court in which the accusatory instrument must be filed prior to the appearance of the person. It may be served in the county in which the offense was committed, an adjoining county or, in the case of close pursuit, any county of the state. It must be served personally unless issued for a parking violation (150.40,50). If the defendant fails to appear after the filing of the accusatory instrument, the court may issue a summons or warrant of arrest, depending upon the charge, or the officer may rearrest without a warrant (150.60). If the offense involved is one for which fingerprints are to be taken in accordance with 160.10, the officer shall take them before release of the principal from custody if the appearance ticket is issued after arrest; or, if issued in lieu of arrest, the court shall direct they be taken after arraignment on the accusatory instrument in court (150.70).

Mandatory Requirement (150.75)

If the sole offense the person is arrested for is Sec. 221.05 P.L., the non-criminal offense of possession of marijuana (punishable by fine only), an appearance ticket must be issued. It may not be made contingent upon station house bail unless there is reasonable suspicion the defendant does not reside in the state or the residence given is not accurate.

The appearance ticket procedure benefits both the individual citizen and the people as well. The citizen's liberty interests are enhanced and there is assurance the defendant will respond to answer the charge but pressure is taken off the correction and court facilities.

5.7 Fingerprinting and Photographing of Defendant after Arrest — Criminal Identification Records and Statistics (Article 160)

No two persons have ever been found to possess the same fingerprints. A classification system for identifying fingerprint patterns has been developed which makes it possible for individuals to be uniquely identified on the basis of their fingerprint patterns. This systematization makes it possible for each state to maintain accurate criminal identification records and for the various states and the federal government to participate in one national criminal identification system.

When Fingerprints Taken (160.10)

Whether or not fingerprints are to be taken depends upon the criminal offense the defendant is charged with. The taking of prints is mandatory in certain cases, discretionary with the police in others and absent either of these categories, fingerprints are not to be taken.

When the arrested person is charged with the following criminal offenses the police must take the fingerprints of such person:

a. a felony,

b. a misdemeanor defined in the penal law,

c. any other misdemeanor which would constitute a felony based upon a prior conviction,

d. loitering as defined in 240.35 or 240.37 of the Penal Law. (240.35 sets forth various behaviors the legislature has determined to be annoyingly unacceptable in public places. The courts have struck down some of these as unconstitutional but others remain viable. 240.37 prohibits loitering for prostitution purposes.)

In addition, fingerprints may be taken upon an arrest for any offense if the police officer:

a. is unable to ascertain the arrested person's identity, or,

b. reasonably suspects the arrested person,

   - has given false identification, or,

   - is wanted for the commission of some other offense.

In any of the above cases in which fingerprints are required or permitted, the police may also take palmprints and photographs of the arrested person.

The File Search and Distribution Processes (160.20, 30, 40)

Two copies of the fingerprints must be forwarded without unnecessary delay to the state Division of Criminal Justice Services in Albany. This is accomplished by transmitting the contents of the fingerprint card by fax. The state DCJS is connected by computer with the national criminal identification system located in Washington, D.C., which enables nationwide record searches to be conducted of persons arrested.

Upon receipt of the copies of the fingerprints, the Division of Criminal Justice Services must:

a. classify them,

b. search its records for any previous record of the defendant, and,

c. transmit a report of the record search to the submitting police officer or agency.

The report shall contain all information on file with respect to the defendant's previous criminal record, if any, or, if no information is found in the files, the statement of no previous record. Such a report, if certified, constitutes presumptive evidence of the facts so certified. If the prints received by DCJS are not sufficiently legible they must be returned to the submitting agency with an explanation of the legibility problem and a request to retake and submit them if possible. Defendants are entitled to arraignment without unnecessary delay; therefore police agencies have procedures in place requiring prompt taking and forwarding of fingerprints to enable the report to be available in timely fashion for arraignment. Upon receipt of the report, the police must give a copy to the district attorney of the county and two copies to the court. The court must give one of its copies to the defendant.

Sealing of Records and Return of Fingerprints and Photos upon Termination of the Criminal Action in Favor of the Accused or upon Conviction for a Non-Criminal Offense (160.50, 55)

In order to protect a defendant against acquiring the stigma of criminality due to an arrest without a conviction for a criminal offense that might impede his opportunities for employment, education, professional licensing and the like, the statutes provide for the sealing of court records and the destruction or return of fingerprints and photographs taken of the defendant in connection with the arrest. The statute also contains a few exceptions to this general rule.

When the entire criminal action is finally terminated in the defendant's favor, the clerk of the court initiates the sealing and return process. The court records are sealed except for published decisions, opinions or records or briefs on appeal, unless the court on motion of the district attorney or upon its own initiative determines the interests of justice require otherwise. The reasons therefore must be entered on the record. If the records are sealed, then they may not be accessed other than for a few exceptions set forth in the statute. For example, the defendant may have access as well as the prosecutor in connection with ACD proceedings, probation and parole officials when the defendant was arrested while on probation or parole, the police upon ex parte motion convincing a superior court that justice requires such action, a gun licensing agency when the defendant has made application for a gun license and a police agency when the defendant has made application for employment as a police or peace officer. In addition to these statutory provisions the courts have decided access may be had in other circumstances, such as upon a compelling demonstration that it is required for a public purpose (*Hynes v. Karassik*, 47 N.Y.2d 659 (1979)) or the defendant is deemed to have waived the provisions of the statute upon initiating a civil action connected to the arrest, such as a false arrest suit (*Maxie v. Gimbel Bros., Inc.*, 423 N.Y.S.2d 802 (1979)).

In addition to the sealing of the records, the court clerk shall notify the Division of Criminal Justice Services and the appropriate police and law enforcement agencies that the action has been terminated in favor of the accused. Upon receipt of the notification of termination, all fingerprints, palmprints and photographs of the accused shall be immediately destroyed or returned to the accused or his attorney, unless the court has directed otherwise or the dismissal is an ACD dismissal in a marijuana case (170.56 or 210.46). If such agency has forwarded prints or photos of the accused to any other law enforcement agency, it shall formally request in writing that such items be returned to the department or destroyed forthwith.

Despite these return procedures, there have been occasions where police have failed to return all prints or photos and utilized them in subsequent investigations leading to arrest of the person whose prints or photos were not destroyed or returned. In these cases, the accused may bring a civil action for failure to comply with the statute but may not have such evidence suppressed as a result of the use of the photos or prints (*People v. Anderson*, 411 N.Y.S.2d 830 (1978); *Anderson v. City of New York*, 611 F.Supp. 481 (1985)).

Persons whose cases were terminated prior to the effective date of this section (9/1/76) may obtain the same relief but must petition the appropriate court for an order directing same. Similar relief may be gotten by an accused whose case has been terminated by a conviction for a non-criminal offense other than that of loitering (P.L. 240.35/3 or 240.37/2) or that of operating a motor vehicle while ability is impaired (V.T.L. 1192.1). The only difference is that the sealing of records is only required at the State Division of Criminal Justice Services and the court, but not at other police or law enforcement agencies. The provisions relating to the destruction or return of prints and photos is the same.

Upon the termination of a criminal action in favor of the defendant, the arrest and prosecution of the accused shall be a nullity and he shall be restored to the status he enjoyed prior thereto. The arrest and prosecution shall not operate as a disqualification for any lawful occupation or calling and no such person shall be required to divulge information relating to the arrest or prosecution. In addition, Executive Law 296.16 declares it to be an unlawful discriminatory practice for anyone to make inquiry about or to discriminate against such person. There are exceptions to these provisions as set forth above. For example, the application for employment in governmental agencies such as the Department of Correctional Services allows such agencies to inquire into the arrest and prosecution in order to evaluate the candidate's fitness for employment.

Finally, 160.45 prohibits any district attorney or law enforcement officer from requiring, as a prerequisite to initiating a criminal investigation, a victim of a sex crime, as specified in P.L. Article 130 or in Section 255.25, to submit to a polygraph or psychological stress evaluator test to determine the truth or falsity of their statements. Article 130 contains the sex offenses of sexual misconduct, rape, sodomy and sexual abuse. Section 255.25 defines the crime of incest.

Chapter 6

Preliminary Proceedings in Local Criminal Court; upon Local Criminal Court Accusatory Instruments; Arraignment, Hearings and Dispositions

---

Sec. 6.1 Article 170; Proceedings upon Accusatory Instruments Other Than Felony Complaints from Arraignment to Plea

Sec. 6.2 Article 180; Proceedings upon Felony Complaints from Arraignment to Its Disposition

6.1 Proceedings in Local Criminal Court upon Accusatory Instruments Other Than Indictments and Felony Complaints from Arraignment to Plea (Article 170)

The preliminary proceedings in local criminal court conclude with the arraignment of the defendant upon whom an accusatory instrument has been filed in the local criminal court. The proceedings are covered in Article 170 regarding accusatory instruments other than felony complaints. Article 180, next, deals with the proceedings concerning felony complaints. Arraignment on the charges in the accusatory instrument is addressed here. It should be remembered that the plea is not part of the arraignment process in New York. The plea is addressed separately in Article 340. On the occasion of the arraignment a plea may be taken; however, it is governed by a separate proceeding and is not part of the arraignment process.

Arraignment (170.10)

After the filing of the accusatory instrument the defendant must be arraigned. The defendant must appear personally at the arraignment unless:

    a.   it is a corporation; or,

    b.   the accusatory instrument is in the form of a simplified information for which the proceedings may be conducted by mail. The substantive statute, such as the Vehicle and Traffic Law, will permit the proceedings to be entirely conducted in this manner; or,

    c.   the defendant is appearing in response to a summons or appearance ticket, in which case for good cause shown, the defendant may be permitted by the court to appear by counsel instead of in person.

If the defendant personally appears at the arraignment the court must inform the defendant:

    a.   of the charge and give her a copy of the accusatory instrument;

    b.   of the right to an adjournment in order to secure counsel;

    c.   that she may communicate free of charge in order to secure counsel or to notify a friend or relative of her situation;

    d.   of the right to free counsel if defendant cannot afford to hire one (except in traffic infraction cases).

The court must take affirmative action to effectuate the above rights. In New York it is felt the best way to ensure the accused of the protection of her rights and a fair trial is through the representation of counsel.

    e.   If the charge is a traffic infraction or misdemeanor, a plea of guilty constitutes a conviction and a conviction may cause her license to drive and vehicle registration to be suspended or revoked, in addition to the sentence which may be imposed for the offense charged;

    f.   If the accusatory instrument is a simplified traffic information, the defendant has a right to a supporting deposition;

    g.   If the accusatory instrument is a misdemeanor complaint, the defendant must consent to be prosecuted thereunder, otherwise an information must be drawn to form the basis of the charge.

Waiver of Counsel

The right to have the assistance of counsel for one's defense is a constitutional guarantee and like all constitutional guarantees it may be waived and the defendant permitted to represent herself. A waiver of a constitutional right, however, must be voluntary, intelligent and knowing and therefore the court must assure itself that such waiver meets these criteria in order for it to be valid. If defendant wishes to defend herself for a traffic infraction charge she will be permitted to do so. In all other cases the court may only permit waiver of the right to counsel if it is satisfied that the waiver is knowingly made and the defendant is aware of all the ramifications of the waiver decision. The court must also inform defendant that she may invoke the right to counsel, if permitted to waive, at any stage of the proceedings. There are many cases regarding waiver. See, for example, *People v. Kaltenbach*, 60 N.Y.2d 797 (1983).

If no final disposition is reached at arraignment, then the court must issue a securing order which sets forth the terms of release on bail or recognizance; however, if the defendant appeared by counsel rather than personally, the order may only specify release upon personal recognizance. If the defendant is charged in a simplified traffic information with a violation of driving while impaired or intoxicated or any traffic offense arising therefrom and the court is aware that an accident was involved in the case in which a person was killed or suffered serious physical injury, the court may not accept a guilty plea without consent of the district attorney in order to preclude such final disposition from becoming a bar to a more serious charge due to the protections of double jeopardy.

Divestiture of Jurisdiction over Misdemeanor Charge by Indictment (170.20, 25)

The prosecutor (170.20) and the defendant (170.25) may petition a court for presentation of a misdemeanor charge in an accusatory instrument filed in a local court to a grand jury for consideration. Generally, the prosecutor would be seeking an indictment for a felony in connection with the transaction whereas the defendant would be seeking a dismissal, notwithstanding the fact that the prosecutor could refile an appropriate accusatory instrument in the lower court to reinstitute the original charge or another growing out of the same transaction.

At any time prior to a plea of guilty or the commencement of trial on a misdemeanor charge the prosecutor may apply for an adjournment on grounds he intends to present the facts to a grand jury in order to try to prosecute it in a superior court by indictment. The court must grant an adjournment for a reasonable period of time for the prosecutor to do so and the court may grant subsequent adjournments for that purpose as are reasonable under the circumstances. If the grand jury finds an indictment or directs dismissal of the charge the local court is divested of jurisdiction over such charge and all proceedings in the local court are terminated. If the prosecutor does not present the charge to the grand jury within the allotted time, the proceedings in the local criminal court must continue.

Before entry of a guilty plea or the commencement of trial or within 30 days of arraignment, the defendant may apply to the local criminal court for an adjournment on grounds he intends to make a motion before a superior court for an order that the charge must be prosecuted by indictment. The court must grant a reasonable period of time and may, as circumstances reasonably require, grant further adjournments. The defendant may then make a motion to that effect before a superior court having jurisdiction to try an indictment for the charge in question. Notice of such motion must be given to the prosecutor. The motion must show good cause to believe that the interests of justice require prosecution by indictment in the superior court. There have been many cases involving the factors which would demonstrate good cause such as bias, fair trial, complexity and lay judges. See, for example, *People v. Charles F.*, 60 N.Y.2d 474 (1983). If the defendant does not make the motion in the superior court or if such court denies the motion if made, the proceedings in the local court must continue. The proceedings in the local court are stayed if the motion is made to the superior court and if such court grants the motion the proceedings in the local court are stayed until the grand jury acts. If the grand jury finds an indictment or a dismissal of the charge, the action in the lower court is terminated. If the defendant is committed for more than 45 days awaiting the action of the grand jury he may make application for and the superior court must release him on his own recognizance unless the delay was caused by the defendant or the prosecutor shows good cause why the defendant should not be so released (some compelling fact or circumstance which precluded the grand jury action within the specified time).

Motion to Dismiss (170.30, 35, 40, 45, 50)

The procedures set forth for a motion to dismiss local criminal court accusatory instruments generally mirror the procedures set forth for a motion to dismiss an indictment in superior courts (Article 210). The motion to dismiss is an effective defense tool in that, if granted, it ends the prosecution early on, thus saving much time, money, effort and anguish for the defense. It must be remembered, however, that the prosecutor may obtain a subsequent accusatory instrument in an appropriate case to reinstitute a criminal action for the same charge against the defendant as long as the basis for the dismissal may be cured. The motion to dismiss must be made within 45 days of arraignment or securance of counsel, in writing, with a copy given to the prosecutor. The grounds upon which the motion may be based are:

a. the accusatory instrument is defective;

b. the defendant has immunity;

c. double jeopardy;

d. statute of limitations would be violated;

e. speedy trial violation;

f. some other jurisdictional or legal impediment exists; or

g. the interests of justice.

All grounds must be put in the same motion unless good cause exists for not doing so. It is within the court's discretion to either summarily deny a subsequent motion or to entertain and dispose of such motion on its merits in the interests of justice for good cause shown. The motion to dismiss based upon speedy trial grounds may be made prior to the commencement of trial or entry of a guilty plea. The procedure for written pre-trial motions of 255.20 are to be followed and the procedural rules for making, considering and disposing of a motion to dismiss an indictment of 210.45 are also to be followed.

The Ground of Defective Accusatory Instrument (170.35)

The motion to dismiss on the ground of a defective accusatory instrument may be based upon defects such as:

a. the instrument is defective upon its face (no reasonable cause to believe an offense was committed or that defendant did it);

b. the court does not have jurisdiction;

c. the statute charged is unconstitutional or otherwise defective;

d. the information used to replace the misdemeanor complaint does not contain at least one of the counts contained in the complaint; or,

e. a prosecutor's information does not contain one of the offenses authorized by the grand jury.

The Grounds of Interests of Justice (170.40)

The motion to dismiss on grounds of the interests of justice is utilized when no other legal basis for dismissal set forth in 170.30 exists; but, such dismissal is required as a matter of judicial discretion based upon the existence of some compelling factor clearly demonstrating that prosecution or conviction of the defendant would be an injustice. In order to make such determination the court must consider the following factors; and the judge who dismisses the accusatory instrument on this ground must put the factors considered and his reasoning in deciding them on the record to enable appellate review:

a. seriousness of the offense;

b. harm caused by the offense;

c. evidence of guilt;

d. background of the defendant;

e. any serious law enforcement misconduct;

f. effect of sentence on defendant;

g. impact on safety of community;

h. impact on criminal justice system;

i. attitude of complainant;

j. any other relevant fact.

This motion may be made by the court and district attorney as well as the defendant. A motion to dismiss a prosecutor's information on grounds of insufficient evidence or defective grand jury may also be made to and decided by the local criminal court in accordance with procedures set forth regarding the motion to dismiss indictments on the same grounds set forth in 210.30,35,45 (170.50).

Adjournment in Contemplation of Dismissal (ACD) (170.55, 56)

Adjournment in contemplation of dismissal is a procedure that stays proceedings after arraignment for a specified period of time. If the conditions for adjournment as specified in the statute or as directed by the court are not violated within that period, the charge will be dismissed in the interest of justice, the records sealed and the arrest and prosecution deemed a nullity. If the charge is a misdemeanor or less, the general provisions of 170.55 apply except that if the charge is possession of marijuana, misdemeanor or less, then 170.56 is applicable.

On arraignment on a charge other than marijuana possession (misdemeanor or less) the court upon motion and consent of either party, or the court on its own motion with the consent of both parties, may order the action be adjourned in contemplation of dismissal with a view towards ultimately dismissing the action in furtherance of justice. Upon issuing the order the court must release the defendant in his own recognizance. The court may require certain conditions of the defendant in conjunction with the issuance of the order such as an order of protection or participation in an educational or dispute resolution program. Notice the absence of any criteria requirements for the issuance of the order. All that is required is the consent of all parties. Within six months of the order the prosecutor may apply to the court for restoration of the action to the calendar for prosecutorial purposes. The grounds may be a violation of one of the conditions set forth for the issuance of the order or some other factor indicating dismissal would not be in the interests of justice. It is within the court's discretion to restore the case to the calendar or not.

If the case has not been restored to the calendar within this six month period the accusatory instrument is deemed to have been dismissed in furtherance of justice. The ACD is not deemed a conviction or admission of guilt, the arrest and prosecution shall be deemed a nullity, the record shall be sealed and the defendant restored in contemplation of law to the status she enjoyed prior to the arrest and prosecution.

In Preiser's *Practice Commentaries*, he points out that this procedure replaced the pre CPL practice of "D.O.R." (discharge on own recognizance) which was similar to a nolle prosequi, and used mainly in cases where the prosecutor believed the case was not appropriate for criminal prosecution. Typically such cases involved minor technical charges such as disorderly conduct or simple assault between family members, neighbors or businessmen; or, in some instances, cases arose out of a confrontation between a police officer and an indignant citizen. In this regard these procedures are less technical and more easily accomplished than the other provisions for dismissal in furtherance of justice in 170.40 (*McKinney's, CPL*, vol.11A, p. 93) (170.55).

The procedures for an ACD in misdemeanor or less marijuana cases differ from the above procedures in these respects:

a. The court as an alternative may order an immediate dismissal in furtherance of justice. To do so the court must find an ACD is not necessary and put the reasons therefore on the record;

b. The court may not order this ACD or a dismissal in furtherance of justice if the defendant has previously been;

- granted such ACD or dismissal in furtherance of justice; or,

- convicted of any controlled substance offense, or, a crime and the district attorney does not consent; or,

- adjudged a youthful offender involving controlled substances and the district attorney does not consent;

c. The court may require and modify conditions for the ACD and set and adjust the time but the time shall not exceed 12 months. Upon violation of the conditions the court may revoke the order, restore the case to the calendar and proceed with the prosecution. If the case is not so restored the case will be deemed dismissed in the furtherance of justice;

d. Upon dismissal, the court shall order the record sealed. In addition to the exceptions to access to the records specified in 160.50.1/d, the court subsequently may order access to determine if the person qualifies for ACD under this section. Upon issuance of the order to seal, the arrest and prosecution shall be deemed a nullity and the defendant restored to the legal status he enjoyed prior to the arrest (170.56).

Requirement of a Plea (170.60)

If the accusatory instrument is not dismissed the defendant will be required to enter a plea. The procedures are set forth in 340.20; e.g., it must be made in person unless the court approves entry by counsel or by mail; if by a corporation, by counsel; and, if a plea bargain is involved, the agreements must be put on the record. Recall that a plea is a separate and distinct proceeding even though it may take place on the occasion of the arraignment.

Proceedings upon Misdemeanor Complaint (170.65, 70)

The misdemeanor complaint may not be used as the basis for prosecution unless the defendant waives his right to trial by information or the complaint is supported by a deposition setting forth reasonable cause to believe the offense was committed and the defendant committed it, by factual and non-hearsay evidence. Waiver of the information must be by some affirmative act, not mere silence. The entry of a plea to the misdemeanor complaint in and of itself does not constitute a waiver of the right to the information. An information replacing a misdemeanor complaint need not contain the same offense charged in the misdemeanor complaint but at least one count in the information must be based upon conduct giving rise to the misdemeanor complaint. The defendant may not be held in custody more than five days on a misdemeanor complaint unless the defendant has waived prosecution by information or the court is satisfied as to good cause why an order of release should not be issued.

See Illustrative Cases

People v. Ross, 67 N.Y.2d 321 (1986), p. 343
People v. O'Grady, 667 N.Y.S.2d 895 (1997), p. 345
Hollender v. Trump Village Cooperative, Inc., 58 N.Y.2d 420 (1983), p. 347

6.2 Proceedings in Local Criminal Court upon Felony Complaint (Article 180)

The prosecution of a felony charge is begun in either of two ways:

1. The filing of a felony complaint in a local criminal court; or,

2. The filing of a grand jury indictment in a superior court.

In the vast majority of cases the charge is commenced by the filing of the felony complaint. Recall the state constitution requires felonies to be prosecuted by indictment and hence we shall see the passage from felony complaint to indictment. Also, no plea may be accepted on the basis of a felony complaint.

Arraignment (180.10)

The procedures upon arraignment on a felony complaint in local criminal court are virtually the same as those for arraignment therein upon a misdemeanor complaint or information as set forth in Article 170. Upon arraignment, the court must:

1. Immediately inform the defendant

    a. of the charge against her and give her a copy of the felony complaint;

    b. that the purpose of the proceeding is to determine if the defendant is to be held for the action of the grand jury;

    c. of the right to a prompt hearing on the issue of whether or not there is sufficient evidence to hold her for the action of the grand jury and that she may waive such right;

    d. of the right to counsel at the arraignment and all subsequent stages of the proceeding and if she appears at arraignment without counsel, she has the right

        - to an adjournment for the purpose of obtaining counsel;

        - to communicate free of charge by letter or phone for the purpose of obtaining counsel or to notify a relative or friend she has been charged with an offense and to have free counsel assigned if she is financially unable to obtain one; and

        - to waive counsel and of the right to defend herself.

The court must afford the defendant the opportunity to exercise such rights and must itself take such affirmative action as is necessary to effectuate them.

If the defendant desires to proceed without counsel the court must permit her to do so if satisfied the waiver was made knowingly, voluntarily and intelligently. If the court does not so find, then the proceedings must be stayed until the defendant secures counsel or one is assigned. The court must inform the defendant, if she chooses to proceed without counsel, the right to counsel may be exercised at any future stage of the proceedings.

The right to a hearing to determine if the defendant should be held for the action of the grand jury may be illusory in that the prosecutor may go directly to the grand jury to seek an indictment. An indictment terminates the proceedings in local criminal court on the felony complaint including the right to a hearing.

Unless the court intends to immediately dismiss the felony complaint and thereby terminate the action it must enter a securing order which either releases the defendant in her own recognizance, fixes bail or commits her to custody to await future appearances in the matter.

Removal from One Local Criminal Court to Another (180.20)

When an arrest is made in a town and the case is not brought for arraignment to the local town or village court but to another local court in the county, such court may, after arraignment, retain jurisdiction of the case or remit the action to the town or village court. When an arrest is made in a city and the case is not brought for arraignment to the local city court but to another local criminal court in the county, such court may after arraignment retain jurisdiction of the case or remit the action to the city court. Similarly, if the defendant is brought before a superior court judge sitting as a local criminal court such judge may dispose of the felony complaint in one of two ways:

1. If the disposition is a reduction to a misdemeanor or less, remit the case to a local criminal court having jurisdiction and such court must finally dispose of the case; or,

2. Remit the felony complaint to a local criminal court having jurisdiction over the charge and such court must dispose of it as set forth above.

A superior court judge may conduct preliminary proceedings, sitting as a local criminal court but may not conduct trials while so sitting.

Waiver of Hearing (180.30)

If the defendant waives a hearing, after entering a securing order, the papers and case will be referred to the superior court having jurisdiction for the action of the grand jury. Until such papers are received by the superior court the action is still deemed to be pending in the local court. While awaiting such action, the local court may still entertain negotiations for a reduction in the charge to a misdemeanor before termination of its jurisdiction. Before the matter is submitted to the grand jury the district attorney may apply to the superior court for an order to return the matter to the local criminal court for reconsideration. The superior court may issue such order if it is satisfied the felony complaint is defective or such action is required in the interest of justice. This procedure is only available to the people and is designed to prevent questionable felony charges from going to the grand jury. For example, there may be a weakness in evidence to prove a felony or it may be more appropriate to plea bargain the charge (180.40).

Reduction of Charge (180.50)

With the district attorney's consent, the court may conduct an inquiry to determine if a charge less than a felony would be appropriate and if so should the felony charge be reduced. The court may question any person in such inquiry whom it believes possesses information relative to the matter including the defendant if he wishes to be questioned. If the court finds reasonable cause to believe the defendant committed a lesser offense it may reduce the charge to such lesser offense if it finds that there is not reasonable cause to believe a felony was also committed. If it believes a felony was also committed it may only reduce the charge if the district attorney consents and if the judge is satisfied it is in the interest of justice to do so; however, the court may not order a reduction where there is reasonable cause to believe the defendant committed a class A felony other than a drug felony or any armed felony as defined in 1.20/41.

The charge is reduced by replacing the felony complaint with another local criminal court accusatory instrument such as a misdemeanor complaint or information, either by having the district attorney or complainant file the new accusatory instrument or by the judge noting the new charge on the felony complaint as long as the factual allegations and any supporting depositions are sufficient to support the non-felony charge.

If the court reduces the charge to a non-felony and a final disposition on that charge is reached it constitutes a bar to a subsequent prosecution for the felony that was originally charged on the grounds of double jeopardy. The district attorney can avoid this situation however by immediately applying for an adjournment to present the case to the grand jury. The judge must grant such request and it immediately stays the proceedings in the local court (170.20).

The Hearing (180.60, 70)

The purpose of the preliminary hearing is to determine if reasonable cause exists to believe the defendant committed a felony and, if so, to hold her for the action of the grand jury. It is a first screening of the charge and does not decide the merits of the case. It does not require the same degree of proof or quality of evidence as that required to support an indictment or a conviction; but, on the other hand, it protects a person from being held over for the action of the grand jury merely on the basis of a complaint. It should be remembered though that the right to a hearing may be illusory due to the fact the district attorney may stay the proceedings and go directly to the grand jury for an indictment. A hearing upon a felony complaint must be conducted as follows:

1. The district attorney must be present and conduct the hearing on behalf of the people.

2. The defendant as a matter of right may be present.

3. The court must read the felony complaint and any supporting depositions to the defendant unless he waives the reading.

4. The people must call and examine witnesses and offer evidence in support of the charge. The defendant may testify and in the discretion of the court offer other witnesses and evidence in his behalf. Each witness must testify under oath, unless he would be authorized to give unsworn testimony at trial and be subject to cross examination. The burden of proof is on the people in the hearing.

5. Only non-hearsay evidence is admissible to show reasonable cause to believe the defendant committed a felony, except reports of expert witnesses as allowed in grand jury hearings (190.2,3). The court may require such expert to testify if upon application of the defendant good cause is shown that a report is unreliable.

6. Upon application of the defendant the court may exclude the public and direct that no disclosure of the proceedings be made. This includes the press; however, the First Amendment right of freedom of the press and this provision collide. The court must have good reason to override the First Amendment provision such as prejudice to the defendant.

7. The hearing should be completed in one session; however, it may be adjourned in the interest of justice but not for more than one day in the absence of good cause shown.

The defendant may waive any of the rights set forth for the hearing as well as the right to the hearing as well. After the hearing the court must dispose of the felony complaint.

1. If the court finds reasonable cause to believe the defendant committed a felony and no non-felony offense, the defendant shall be held for the action of the grand jury. All papers shall be promptly transmitted to the superior court for this purpose. Until such papers are received by the superior court the action is deemed to be pending in the local court.

    a. If the court finds reasonable cause to believe a non-felony was committed in addition to the felony offense the court may reduce the charge to a non-felony offense if satisfied it is in the interest of justice to do so and the district attorney consents. This is not permitted if the felony offense believed to be committed is a class A felony, other than a narcotic felony, or an armed felony as per 1.20/41.

2. If there is reasonable cause only that the defendant committed a non-felony offense the court may reduce the charge as per 180.50/3.

3. If there is not reasonable cause to believe the defendant committed any offense the court must dismiss the felony complaint, discharge the defendant from custody if being held and if she is at liberty on bail, exonerate the bail.

Juvenile Offenders (180.75)

A juvenile offender as defined in 1.20/42 is generally a person of the ages 13,14 or 15 who has committed a felony involving serious personal violence against another such as murder, robbery, felonious assault or forcible rape. Absent the juvenile offender classification, such a person (under the age of 16) would not be triable as an adult but would be treated in the family court as a juvenile delinquent. A rash of crimes of serious personal violence by young people led the legislature to establish the juvenile offender category and related special procedures such as these from arraignment through verdict. The juvenile offender therefore is a young person who may be treated as a juvenile delinquent and receive more lenient treatment or as an adult depending upon the presence or absence of mitigating circumstances in the case. When a juvenile offender is arraigned before a local criminal court this section sets provisions for waiver of the hearing, disposition of the felony complaint and removal of the case to family court, which replace the provisions of 180.30, 50 and 70.

If the defendant waives the hearing on the felony complaint, she must be held for the action of the grand jury. All related papers will be promptly forwarded to the superior court for presentation of the case before a grand jury. The action remains pending in the local court until such papers are received by the superior court.

If there is a hearing on the case, at the conclusion of the hearing, the court must dispose of the felony complaint in one of three ways:

1. If the court finds reasonable cause to believe the defendant committed a crime for which she could be tried as an adult under the juvenile offender category, she shall be held for the action of the grand jury.

2. If the court finds the defendant did not commit a crime which would require submission of the matter to the grand jury but finds reasonable cause to believe the defendant has committed another offense which would classify the defendant as a juvenile delinquent the court must direct the action be removed to the family court for such proceedings.

3. If the court finds no reasonable cause to believe the defendant committed any criminal offense, the felony complaint must be dismissed, the defendant released from custody and any bail exonerated if she is at liberty on bail.

The case may also be removed to family court upon motion of the district attorney or the defendant:

1. At the request of the district attorney the court shall order the case removed to the family court if upon consideration of criteria such as the seriousness of the crime, its harm, or the past record of the defendant (*see* 210.43/2) it finds it would be in the interest of justice to do so. If the charge is murder, rape or sodomy first degree or an armed felony (1.20/41) removal to family court must also be based upon a finding of one or more of the following factors:

   a. mitigating circumstances that bear directly upon the manner in which the crime was committed; or,

   b. where defendant was not the sole participant in the crime, her role was relatively minor but not so minor as to constitute a defense to the prosecution; or,

   c. possible deficiencies in the proof of the crime.

2. The defendant may make a motion in the superior court for removal of the case to family court if she has not waived the hearing and the hearing has not yet commenced. Upon receipt of the motion the judge shall sit as a local criminal court and determine the disposition to be made of the case, i.e., hold for action of the grand jury, dismissal of the felony complaint or removal to family court. The judge is required to follow the procedures set forth in 210.45/1,2, for a motion to dismiss an indictment (defendant and district attorney may offer evidence on the motion) in determining this motion and the procedures in 210.43 for removal of a charge in an indictment to the family court. Consent of the district attorney is not required unless the charge is murder, rape, or sodomy first degree or an armed felony. If this motion is denied it may not be made again at any time.

In either of the above circumstances if the court orders removal of the action to the family court it must state its reasons therefore and the factors upon which the decision is based. The prosecutor must also state the same for his consent wherever it is required. For the purpose of making its decision the court may make any such inquiry as it deems necessary. Any evidence which is not legally privileged may be introduced. If the defendant testifies, such testimony may not be used against him in any future proceedings except for impeachment purposes on the basis of prior inconsistent statements.

Release from Custody (180.80)

In order to assure a defendant is not held in custody for an unreasonable period of time solely on the basis of the felony complaint while awaiting a determination of the court or the grand jury, the defendant may apply for release from custody to the local criminal court. If since the time of her arrest the defendant has been in custody for more than 120 hours or 144 hours if a weekend or holiday is involved, the court must release the defendant on her own recognizance unless:

1. the delay is due to the defendant's action, request or consent; or,

2. prior to the application the grand jury finds an indictment against the defendant; or,

3. for good cause showing it would not be in the interest of justice to release her.

See Illustrative Cases

People v. Hodge, 53 N.Y.2d 313 (1981), p. 349

Chapter 7

Preliminary Proceedings in Superior Court

Sec. 7.1 Article 190; The Grand Jury and Its Proceedings
Sec. 7.2 Article 195; Waiver of Indictment
Sec. 7.3 Article 200; The Indictment and Related Instruments
Sec. 7.4 Article 210; Proceedings from Filing of Indictment to Plea
Sec. 7.5 Article 215; Adjournment in Contemplation of Dismissal for Purpose of Referral to Dispute Resolution

7.1 The Grand Jury and Its Proceedings (Article 190)

Under the constitution of New York State (art. 1, sec. 6), a felony may only be prosecuted by grand jury indictment. The institution of the grand jury had its origins in 12th-century England. It was established as a buffer between the all-powerful monarch and the people, in the bringing of criminal charges against them. It was brought to these shores by the English colonists and imbedded into the Fifth Amendment of the United States Constitution, to wit: "No person shall be held to answer for a capital, or otherwise infamous crime, unless on a presentment or indictment of a grand jury, except...." Due to the relative independence of the judiciary and prosecutors in our system of government the importance of the institution of the grand jury has diminished. The constitutional provision has not been interpreted by the U.S. Supreme Court as being applicable to the states and all but 19 states have abandoned its use. They have found it to be expensive and time consuming and adding nothing to the protection of the individual rights of citizens. In place of the grand jury indictment, these states have adopted some form of verified prosecutor's information in order to cut costs, save time and protect individual rights.

Definition, Functions and Organization (190.05, 10, 15, 20)

The grand jury consists of not less than 16 nor more than 23 persons. These persons are selected randomly from the lists of registered voters in the county and must meet the qualifications of jurors as set forth in the Judiciary Law. The grand jury's functions are to hear and examine evidence concerning criminal offenses and concerning mis-conduct in public office, criminal or otherwise, occurring in the county and to take appropriate action thereon (190.05; 190.55). In order to find an indictment against a defendant, 12 of the grand jurors must vote to indict (190.05). A grand jury is em-paneled for each superior court and becomes the investigatory part of the court. The grand jury is under control of the court, statutes and the Rules of the Chief Admin-istrator of the Courts. The grand jury need not simply await charges against suspects to be brought before it by the prosecutor. It may initiate investigations upon its own knowledge (190.10). Performing the dual role of a sword and a shield the grand jury's responsibilities include not only determining if the evidence warrants charges being brought against a suspect but also to protect the citizenry against unfounded, arbitrary and unjust prosecution (*People v. Monroe*, 480 N.Y.S.2d 259 (1984)).

A grand jury, once impaneled, remains in existence until the opening date of the next term of the court. The life of the grand jury may be extended past its usual ex-piration date by the court, upon application and declaration of the grand jury and the district attorney that it has not finished certain business and will not be able to do so before the end of its term. During its extension this grand jury may only finish work upon matters that were previously before it and may not undertake any new business (190.15). As mentioned above, the selection and drawing of the grand jury is governed by the Judiciary Law and the qualifications for grand jurors are the same as those for trial jurors. The grand jury panel or individual grand jurors are not subject to challenge; but, the court has the authority to discharge a grand jury panel if it finds it does not substantially meet the requirements of the Judiciary Law. An indicted de-fendant, however, may attack the legality of the grand jury that found the indictment against her through a motion to dismiss as part of the pre-trial motion procedure (art. 210, 255). The court may also refuse to swear a grand juror in or discharge her after being sworn for not meeting the requirements of the Judiciary Law, or bias, prejudice or misconduct in performance of her duties which would impair the proper functioning of the grand jury. After impaneling, the court must appoint one of its members as foreman and another as assistant foreman. The grand jurors must appoint one of themselves as secretary (190.20). The foreman has no greater power or authority than any other member but in the absence of the court she is the presiding officer of the inquiry and reports on the actions and proceedings of the grand jury (*People v. Whalen*, 208 N.Y.S.2d 130 (1960)). The grand jurors must be sworn in by the court and be given instructions as to their duties and each member must be given a copy of this Article, 190, of the CPL. If more than one grand jury is seated for the court the court may assign members for good cause from one panel to another (190.20).

Proceedings and Operations Generally; Secrecy Provisions; Instructions (190.25)

Sixteen members of the grand jury must be present for the grand jury to conduct business. In order to take any affirmative action or make any decision such as finding an indictment, filing a prosecutor's information or issuing a report, at least twelve members must vote for such action to be taken. Witnesses appearing before the grand jury may be given an oath by the foreman or any other grand juror.

Secrecy

Secrecy measures are provided for grand jury proceedings for a variety of reasons. They are mainly for the protection of witnesses against improper influence or reprisal which might cause them or future witnesses to withhold the truth or even make them unwilling to appear, and also to similarly protect the grand jurors (*People v. Di Napoli*, 27 N.Y.2d 229 (1970)). Secrecy is accomplished in two ways: by limiting the persons permitted to be present during the proceedings and by not permitting disclosure of what transpired at the grand jury. During deliberations and voting of the grand jury, only the grand jurors may be present in the grand jury room. During other proceedings, in addition to witnesses, various functionaries may be present such as the district attorney, a clerk, stenographer and interpreter, prisoner guards, a video operator, an attorney for a witness who has waived immunity and a child witness's counselor. These are persons whose presence is necessary in order for the proceedings to take place and in some instances to protect the due process rights of witnesses (*People v. Leite*, 355 N.Y.S.2d 930 (1974)). No one is permitted to disclose the nature or substance of any testimony, evidence, decision, result or any other matter that took place before the grand jury except upon written order of the court; however, a witness before the grand jury may disclose her own testimony. On application of the district attorney the judge must permit previously unknown evidence of child abuse or molestation to be reported to the state central register of child abuse and maltreatment, unless the court finds such disclosure would jeopardize the life or safety of any person or would interfere with a continuing grand jury investigation. The courts have said that for disclosure of grand jury minutes to be made a compelling and particularized need for disclosure must be made in order to overcome the presumption in favor of secrecy and that secrecy is an integral feature of grand jury proceedings but it is not absolute (*In Re FOJP Service Corp.*, 463 N.Y.S.2d 681 (1983)).

Instructions

The grand jury is the exclusive judge of the facts before it. The court and district attorney are the exclusive legal advisors to the grand jury. The grand jury may not seek or receive advice from any other source. Where necessary or appropriate, the court or the district attorney, or both, must instruct the grand jury concerning the law with respect to its duties or any matter before it, and such instructions must be recorded in the minutes (190.25/5,6). Even though the purposes of the grand jury can only be fulfilled if it is independent of external influence, it must operate within the statutes establishing it and exercise its discretion in light of the law relating to each matter before it. Therefore, the grand jury should properly be instructed in the law by the court and/or district attorney in each case so as to guide the members in their deliberations (*People v. Randolph*, 387 N.Y.S.2d 389 (1976)). Where a witness renders legal advice to a grand jury, the indictment should be dismissed (*People v. Richard*, 561 N.Y.S.2d 351 (1990)). Although it is the duty of the court to charge the grand jury with respect to its duties and advise it when requested, in the absence of any further requests, it is neither necessary nor appropriate for the court to give further instructions concerning the law with respect to the grand jury's duties or the matter before it. In performing his function of guiding the grand jury as to the law and weight of evidence, the district attorney may place evidence before it, sum it up, charge the jury as to the law and even ask for an indictment, but he may not dominate the jury nor control its findings. Any violation of this rule accompanied by prejudice to the defendant should give rise to ground for a motion to dismiss a resulting indictment (*Application of Kelley*, 372 N.Y.S.2d 538 (1975)). As grand jurors may well need guidance as to the law and the weight of the evidence, the district attorney may place the evidence before them, sum it up, and charge them as to the law, but he cannot dominate the grand jury or control its findings (*U.S. v. Rintelen*, 235 F. 787 (1916)). In presenting a case before the grand jury, the district attorney need not instruct the grand jury with the same degree of precision required when a petit jury is instructed on the law; however, he must provide the grand jury with enough information to enable it to intelligently decide whether a crime has been committed and whether there exists legally sufficient evidence to establish the material elements of the crime (*People v. Nelson*, 486 N.Y.S.2d 979 (1985)).

Rules of Evidence (190.30)

The provisions of Article 60 regarding the admissibility of evidence in criminal proceedings are, in general, applicable to grand jury proceedings, unless otherwise provided in this section. In addition to those provisions, 190.65 (discussed below) requires, for an indictment to be found, legally sufficient, competent and admissible evidence, providing **reasonable cause to believe** the person committed the offense. Evidence which would be incompetent and inadmissible for trial purposes is not totally barred before the grand jury. Such evidence would be ruled inadmissible at grand jury proceedings if subsequent, extrinsic proof nullifies its admissibility or if a specific statute forbids its admission (*People v. Oakley*, 28 N.Y.2d 309 (1971); *People v. De Martino*, 422 N.Y.S.2d 949 (1979); *People v. Cunningham*, 390 N.Y.S.2d 547 (1976)).

1. Reports or copies of reports of the results of technical examinations of evidence by public servants or experts hired by the people, related to the case, may be admitted at grand jury proceedings when certified as authentic by the maker. Fax copies of such reports may also be received as evidence if:

   a. a transmittal memo by the sender certifies the copy and the number of pages, and

   b. the receiver certifies the document and transmittal memo were so received, and

   c. the certified report or copy are received by the court within 20 days of indictment.

These provisions are designed to save valuable time of the government's experts and, more importantly, permitted since the reports are straight forward and the setting at the grand jury is non-adversarial in nature.

2. Written or oral statements, under oath, by a person attesting to the following matters may be received by the grand jury as evidence of the facts stated therein:

    a. a person's lawful ownership of property and defendant's lack of license or privilege to enter or remain on it (*see* 140.00 PL);

    b. a person's ownership of property and the nature and monetary amount of damage to it, and defendant's lack of right to damage it;

    c. a person's ownership of property including a vehicle and its value, and defendant's lack of right to possession of it (*see* 155.00 PL);

    d. a person's ownership of a vehicle and the absence of her consent to the defendant's use of it.

    e. a person's qualifications as an expert in the appraisal of a particular type of property, her opinion as to the value of a piece of that type of property and the basis for such opinion;

    f. a person's identity as ostensible maker or signator of a written instrument and its falsity (*see* 170.00 PL).

None of the above statements shall be admitted when the maker has been required to appear personally to testify to the same at a preliminary hearing on the sufficiency of a felony complaint in the local criminal court (*see* 180.60). Opinions of owners of property as to its value or damage may not be merely conclusory but the basis for the evaluation must be stated when such evaluation is an element of the offense charged (*People v. Lopez*, 79 N.Y.2d 402 (1992)).

3. An examination of a child witness or special witness by the district attorney, videotaped as per 190.32 (discussed below) may be admitted as the testimony of such witness. In any of the above situations (1–3) the grand jury has the right to call such person as a witness (190.50/3, discussed below).

Whenever Article 60 provides the court must rule on the competency of a witness, the admissibility of evidence or instruct the jury concerning the evidence in a criminal proceeding, in a grand jury proceeding, the district attorney may make such ruling or give such instruction. The courts have decided numerous cases relative to the admissibility, or lack thereof, of certain kinds of evidence before the grand jury, such as:

1. Prior convictions. Use of prior convictions for impeachment purposes is limited to cases in which convictions are related to the issue of credibility and use of prior drug convictions in a drug case is highly prejudicial to the defendant (*People v. Hargrove*, 363 N.Y.S.2d 241 (1975)).

2. Prior bad acts. Use of prior bad acts for impeachment purposes only is permitted when accompanied by instructions regarding such use and that it is

not to be used to consider defendant's propensity to commit crimes (*People v. Rosa*, 546 N.Y.S.2d 803 (1989)).

3. Expert testimony. Some testimony of respective complainants required medical conclusions and could not be rendered by lay witnesses, such as receipt on assault of a "fractured jaw"; however, their other evidence as to assault could be admitted (*People v. Brandon*, 476 N.Y.S.2d 370 (1984)).

4. Hearsay. Assault victims could testify as to readily apparent external physical injuries of which they obviously had personal knowledge (ibid).

5. Identification testimony. Identification testimony which did not inform grand jury that identification had been made from photographs was not hearsay where grand jury heard no evidence concerning when or how identification was made (*People v. Brewster*, 63 N.Y.2d 419 (1984)).

6. Privileged communications. Once there exists relevant evidence indicating a patient has been subject of possible criminal activities by a hospital, that hospital may not use the medical privilege to block the grand jury from investigating the records of any patient connected with the act (*People v. Doe*, 455 N.Y.S.2d 945 (1982)).

7. Searches and seizures. Exclusionary rule regarding search and seizure under U.S. Const. amend. 4 is not applicable to grand jury proceedings (*In re Grand Jury Proceedings*, 452 N.Y.S.2d 643 (1982)).

8. Competency of witnesses. The grand jury must be allowed to make its own determination as to the competency and credibility of witnesses before it; and, an indicted person is not permitted to have a hearing to determine the mental capacity of a witness who testified before the grand jury (*People v. Gelia*, 192 N.Y.S.2d 43 (1959)).

9. Oaths. Although there are differences between grand jury proceedings and petit jury proceedings, the requirement that a person testifying do so under oath is equally as necessary (*People v. Vasquez*, 464 N.Y.S.2d 685 (1983)).

10. Presumptions. Since purpose of indictment is to bring defendant to trial on prima facie case which, if unexplained, would warrant conviction, the people are justified in relying on the presumption of sanity in presentation to the grand jury (*People v. Lancaster*, 69 N.Y.2d 20 (1986)).

Videotaped Examination of Child Witnesses and Special Witnesses (190.32)

Instead of requiring persons classified as Child Witnesses and Special Witnesses to appear in person to give evidence before the grand jury, their testimony may be videotaped and played before the grand jury as evidence.

A **child witness** is a person twelve years of age or younger, whom the people intend to call as a witness before the grand jury, to give evidence concerning any crime in PL Articles 130 (Sex Offenses), 260 (Offenses Involving Children & Incompetents) and Section 255.25 (Incest), of which the person was a victim. The district attorney, without leave of the court, may cause the examination of the child witness to be videotaped in accordance with the procedures set forth below.

A **special witness** is a person the people intend to call as a witness and who is either:

1. unable to attend and testify personally due to physical illness or incapacitation; or,

2. over twelve years of age and likely to suffer very severe emotional or mental stress if required to testify in person before the grand jury, concerning the crimes listed above, of which the person was a victim or witness.

Whenever the district attorney believes a witness is a special witness, she may make a written, ex parte application to the court requesting an order authorizing the videotaping and subsequent use of it before the grand jury, in lieu of requiring the person to testify personally. If the court is satisfied the person is a special witness, the court shall issue the order in accord with the procedure that follows. The court order, application and all supporting papers shall not be disclosed to anyone without further court order. A videotaped examination of a child witness or special witness pursuant to these procedures may be:

a. conducted anywhere and at any time, provided at the beginning of the tape the operator records the district attorney's statement as to the date, time, and place of videotaping and identifying himself as the district attorney, the videotape operator and any other persons present. The videotape operator must be employed by the district attorney.

b. an accurate clock with a sweep second hand, must be positioned so it is videotaped along with the witness; or, a date and time generator shall be used to superimpose the day, hour, minute and second over the videotape.

c. Only those functionaries listed in Section 190.25/3 may be present during the videotaping, as necessary, and any required doctor, nurse or medical assistant as dictated by the circumstances. Each person present must take the grand jury secrecy oath and an oath to keep secret the fact of the videotaping.

d. The district attorney shall state for the record the name of the witness and the caption and grand jury number, if any. If the witness is a child witness, the child's date of birth must be recorded. If the witness is a special witness, the date of the authorizing order and name of the justice who issued the order must be recorded.

e. If the witness is to give sworn testimony the administration of the oath must be recorded; or, if unsworn testimony is to be given, a statement to that fact must be recorded.

f. If more than one tape must be utilized, the operator shall record at the end of each a statement by the district attorney that the tape is concluded and refer to the continuation on the succeeding tape. At the beginning of each succeeding tape the operator shall videotape a statement of the district attorney identifying himself, the witness being examined and the number of tapes that have been used. At the conclusion of the examination the operator shall record the statement of the district attorney certifying the recording has been completed, the number of tapes used and that such tapes constitute a complete and accurate record of the examination of the witness.

g. The videotape shall not be edited except upon further order of the court.

When the videotape is played at the grand jury, the stenographer shall record the examination in the same manner as if the witness had testified in person. Custody of the videotape shall be maintained in the same manner as the grand jury minutes.

Failure of the prosecutor to turn over to the defendant the videotaped examination of the child witness constitutes reversible error. The transcribed minutes are not deemed to be the duplicative equivalent of the videotape (*People v. Gaskins*, 575 N.Y.S.2d 564 (1991)). Neither the statute nor case law required the dismissal of the indictment where the videotaped examination of a special witness was utilized before the grand jury as opposed to the witness personal appearance upon release from the hospital prior to the utilization of the videotape (*People v. Lenahan*, 533 N.Y.S.2d 664 (1988)).

These procedures were added to the statutes with others in 1984 to enable more effective prosecution of difficult child and sex abuse cases and to provide protection for the health and emotional well-being of victims and witnesses, and the constitutional due process and confrontation rights of suspects or defendants. As such, they should be strictly adhered to.

Compulsion of Evidence; Immunity; Waiver of Immunity; Witnesses (190.40, 45, 50)

The basic statute setting forth the general immunity provisions of New York State law is contained in Article 50. The definitions contained in 50.10 are applicable to Sections 190.40, 45 and 50 relating to witnesses before the grand jury (190.35). It should be remembered that statutory immunity in New York State clothes a witness with transactional immunity which is broader in the protection granted than that provided by constitutionally required use immunity; and, the statute also protects against requiring the production of physical evidence in addition to testimony which is the only protection provided by the constitutional right not to be compelled to be a witness against oneself.

Every witness in a grand jury proceeding must give evidence legally requested of him, even though the witness believes it may incriminate him; however, a witness who gives evidence in the grand jury proceeding automatically receives transactional immunity unless:

1. he has waived such immunity, or

2. such evidence is not responsive to the question, or

3. it is voluntarily given with knowledge it is not responsive, or

4. it is gratuitously given, or

5. it consists of physical evidence in the form of books, papers or records of a business enterprise (defined in PL175.00).

All other physical evidence which may be required of a witness by the grand jury is, like testimony, also clothed with transactional immunity, unless waived. For example, a corporate officer or employee is required to produce corporate books or records even if the documents would tend to incriminate him personally (*People v. MacLachlan*, 395 N.Y.S.2d 106 (1977)), whereas the forced production of a handwriting exemplar was sufficient to confer immunity upon such person (*People v. Perri*, 423 N.Y.S.2d 674 (1980)).

The grant of immunity for all witnesses before the grand jury is automatic and the witness does not have to, nor may he, assert his privilege against self incrimination (190.40). A person has no right to remain silent after a grant of immunity even if he is a target of the grand jury investigation (*Gold v. Menna*, 25 N.Y.2d 475 (1969)). Nor may a witness refuse to testify before the grand jury on ground that the questions put to him are based upon evidence obtained by an unlawful search and seizure (*In re Kronberg*, 464 N.Y.S.2d 466 (1983)). A person must testify before the grand jury even though she may be subject to prosecution in another state (*People v. Woodruff*, 270 N.Y.S.2d 838 (1966)) even though constitutional immunity grants only use immunity for prosecutions in other jurisdictions (*People v. Lev*, 398 N.Y.S.2d 593 (1977)).

Since the grand jury proceeding is an ex parte proceeding, no person has a right to call a witness or to appear before the grand jury, except a person who is subject to a criminal charge before the grand jury and who signs and submits a written waiver of immunity. The district attorney has the duty to inform a defendant held in a local criminal court on an undisposed-of felony complaint of his right to appear before the grand jury. A motion to dismiss the indictment on ground of failure of the district attorney to so notify such a defendant must be filed within five days of arraignment on the indictment. Failure to do so constitutes a waiver of the provision (190.50). There is no obligation on the part of the prosecutor in a grand jury investigation to supply evidence which is being sought for the purpose of rebutting the prosecutor's presentation before the grand jury (*People v. Russo*, 491 N.Y.S.2d 951 (1985)), nor does the defendant have any right of cross examination or introduction of evidence thereat (*People v. Perez*, 433 N.Y.S.2d 541 (1980)).

Any person asked to sign a waiver of immunity by the district attorney must be advised of his right to, and be given the opportunity to, confer with an attorney. To be effective the waiver must be sworn to before the grand jury. The waiver may be a limited waiver in which there is set forth an agreement between the person and the district attorney as to the specific subject matters or areas of conduct for which immunity will be waived. If the person is questioned and testifies regarding any other subject matter or conduct, such testimony is clothed with immunity (190.45). A waiver of immunity signed by a police officer under compulsion of losing his job is ineffective and when he appears before the grand jury he retains all the protection available to a nonwaiving witness; however, he could be indicted for perjury for willfully testifying falsely before the grand jury, even though the waiver was ineffective

(*People v. Straehle*, 294 N.Y.S.2d 42 (1968)). The witness who has signed a waiver of immunity has the right to the assistance of an attorney when appearing before the grand jury. The attorney may be present in the grand jury room and may advise the witness but not otherwise take any part in the proceeding (190.52). No other witness has the right to the presence of an attorney in the grand jury room (*People v. Ellwanger*, 417 N.Y.S.2d 402 (1979)). The distinction between the rights of the two categories of witnesses is due to the fact the witness testifying under the waiver of immunity is most likely a target of an investigation or a defendant already charged in the local court and anything disclosed by such witness would be able to be used by the prosecutor in the case against the witness.

The grand jury, in addition to the district attorney, may also call witnesses by requesting the district attorney to issue a subpoena to such person. However, the district attorney may require such witness, called at the instance of the grand jury, to sign a waiver of immunity before being called to testify. A defendant or person against whom a criminal charge may be drawn may also request the grand jury to call a person designated by him as a witness before the grand jury. The grand jury, in its discretion, may do so but the appearance of such a witness is also subject to the requirement of testifying under a waiver of immunity if required by the district attorney (190.50). The authority of the district attorney to require the defendant, a person who may be charged with an offense or one requested to be heard by the grand jurors, to sign a waiver of immunity before being permitted to testify is warranted in order to prevent such a person to be automatically given a grant of immunity when the district attorney knows the person may be subject to prosecution for an offense. No person who has been asked to testify under a waiver of immunity by the district attorney may do so without first signing and submitting the requisite waiver of immunity before the grand jury. A defendant who appears before the grand jury must be given a reasonably fair and uninterrupted opportunity to present his narrative testimony and cannot merely be required to answer the prosecutor's questions nor have his narrative continuously interrupted (*People v. Lerman*, 497 N.Y.S.2d 733 (1986)). A defendant who pleads guilty waives any claims of improperly being prevented from appearing before the grand jury (*People v. Grey*, 522 N.Y.S.2d 965 (1987)). The court has the duty to dismiss an indictment obtained in violation of the defendant's right to appear before the grand jury (*People v. Massard*, 528 N.Y.S.2d 954 (1988)). Papers relating to subpoenas and motions in connection therewith in the courts are subject to the grand jury secrecy rules and may not be disclosed without the person subpoenaed and the prosecutor waiving the secrecy provision (190.50).

Duties and Authority of the District Attorney (190.55)

District Attorneys are required or authorized to submit evidence to grand juries under the following circumstances:

1. A district attorney must submit to a grand jury evidence concerning:

    a. a felony by a defendant held on a felony complaint in the local criminal court of the county for the action of the grand jury (unless defendant has waived indictment); and,

    b. a misdemeanor by a defendant charged in an accusatory instrument in the local criminal court of the county where upon petition of the defendant (in accord with 170.25), a superior court has ordered that such misdemeanor be prosecuted by indictment in a superior court.

2. A district attorney submit to a grand jury any available evidence concerning:

    a. any offense prosecutable in the courts of the county; or,

    b. misconduct, nonfeasance or neglect in public office by a public servant, criminal or otherwise.

The grand jury's jurisdiction to indict is not dependent upon the receipt of a felony complaint or other pertinent papers (*People v. Talham*, 342 N.Y.S.2d 921 (1973)). The grand jury, in investigating whether a crime has been committed, may proceed on its own knowledge or upon information brought to its attention from any reliable source (*People ex rel. Van Der Beek v. McKloskey*, 238 N.Y.S.2d 676 (1963)).

The prosecutor performs a dual role as an advocate and public officer; he is charged with the duty not only to seek convictions, but also to see that justice is done. In his position as a public officer he owes a duty of fair dealing to the accused and candor to the courts (*People v. Monroe*, 480 N.Y.S.2d 259 (1984)). The decision whether to prosecute or submit matter to the grand jury is entrusted to the discretion of the prosecutor (*Johnson v. Town of Colonie*, 477 N.Y.S.2d 513 (1984)). In a grand jury proceeding, since there is no judge present to safeguard the defendant's rights, the prosecutor stands in a position of vouching for the truth of the evidence he presents (*Monroe*, ibid). Although the district attorney has sole authority in determining who is, or is not, to be prosecuted, his primary duty is to see that justice is done (*People v. Davis*, 465 N.Y.S.2d 404 (1983)). It is within the power of the district attorney to directly submit a case pending in a lower court to the grand jury even though an indictment returned after such submission would divest the lower court of all jurisdiction over the matter and remove any procedural rights the defendant may have had therein (*People v. McDonnell*, 373 N.Y.S.2d 971 (1975)).

The people do not have an obligation to present to the grand jury every piece of evidence they possess, nor must every matter which may have a tendency to reflect upon the credibility of a witness be revealed (*People v. Suarez*, 505 N.Y.S.2d 728 (1986)). The duty of the district attorney before the grand jury is to present enough evidence to support an indictment, not to supply all evidence at his disposal for consideration by that body (*People v. Campisi*, 369 N.Y.S.2d 322 (1975)). The people enjoy wide discretion in presenting a case to the grand jury and are not obligated to search for evidence favorable to the defense or present all evidence in their possession that is favorable to the accused (*People v. Lancaster*, 69 N.Y.2d 20 (1986)). The prosecution does not always have to bring before the grand jury all statements given by the defendant, even if the statement contains exculpatory material, as long as the

presentation is fair (*People v. Smalls*, 488 N.Y.S.2d 712 (1985)). In making a presentment to the grand jury, the prosecution has wide discretion, but this discretion is
not unbounded; for instance, the prosecutor has a duty not to let a case go to trial
when he knows the indictment is founded on perjury. If he is in possession of evidence
which clearly negates the defendant's guilt, he must submit such evidence to the
grand jury (*People v. Perez*, 433 N.Y.S.2d 541 (1980)).

Actions the Grand Jury May Take (190.60, 65, 70, 71, 75, 80, 85, 90)

After hearing and examining evidence as prescribed in 190.55, a grand jury may:

1.   indict a person for an offense;
2.   direct the district attorney to file a prosecutor's information with a local crim-
     inal court;
3.   direct the district attorney to file a request for removal to the family court;
4.   dismiss the charge; or,
5.   submit a grand jury report (190.60).

When the Grand Jury May Indict (190.65)

A grand jury may indict a person when:

1.   the evidence before it is legally sufficient to establish such person committed
     an offense, and if the corroboration required by law for conviction, if any, is
     present; and if,
2.   competent and admissible evidence before it provides reasonable cause to be-
     lieve such person committed the offense (190.65).

The terms legally sufficient evidence and reasonable cause to believe have been
defined and discussed in Chapter 4, Section 4.3, *supra*. Legally sufficient, by way of
review, means the presence of some evidence which tends to prove each element of
the offense charged and that the defendant committed it, whereas reasonable cause
to believe relates to the amount and quality of evidence that is present. To find an
indictment the evidence must establish a **prima facie case**; that is, evidence which if
uncontradicted or unexplained would warrant a conviction after trial (*People v.
Williams*, 487 N.Y.S.2d 862 (1985)). The test for legally sufficient evidence is the
prima facie test, to wit, whether the evidence before the grand jury, if unexplained
and uncontradicted, would warrant conviction by a trial jury (*People v. Danzy*, 480
N.Y.S.2d 567 (1984); *see also People v. Cox*, 486 N.Y.S.2d 143 (1985)). **Reasonable
cause to believe**, on the other hand, is present if the legally sufficient evidence is of
such weight and quality that it would appear to a reasonable person more likely than
not that the offense was committed and that the defendant committed it. For the
grand jury to find an indictment what is required is a prima facie case together with
probable cause (*People v. Karl*, 344 N.Y.S.2d 118 (1973)).

Under certain circumstances no conviction may be had on uncorroborated evidence, meaning the presence of other evidence on the same point. If such is the case, the grand jury may not find an indictment. Corroboration is a requirement of "legally sufficient evidence" to support an indictment and the district attorney must inform the grand jury of the nature, degree and extent of the particular corroboration statute involved in the criminal proceeding (*People v. Sanchez*, 479 N.Y.S.2d 602 (1984)). For example, evidence before the grand jury, consisting of defendant's confession, was not legally sufficient to indict, in absence of corroboration of the confession by additional proof that the offense charged had been committed (*People v. Esposito*, 503 N.Y.S.2d 611 (1986)); *see also* 60.50, *supra*, and 60.22 (no conviction on testimony of an accomplice without corroborative evidence tending to connect the defendant with the crime).

Direction to File Prosecutor's Information (190.70)

The grand jury may direct the district attorney to file a prosecutor's information charging a person with an offense below the grade of felony, in a local criminal court when:

1. there is legally sufficient evidence the person committed the offense; and,

2. there is competent and admissible evidence that provides reasonable cause to believe such person committed the offense (190.70).

The one exception to this authority of the grand jury is when the case has been directed to be tried by indictment by a superior court upon application of a defendant being proceeded against in the lower criminal court (170.25).

The direction of the grand jury to file a prosecutor's information must be signed by the foreman or assistant foreman and filed with the court by which the grand jury was impaneled. It must contain a plain and concise statement of the conduct constituting the offense to be charged, similar to the factual statement required in an indictment (*see* 200.50/7). Where appropriate it may contain multiple offenses below the grade of felony and multiple defendants (*see* 200.20, 40). Unless such direction is insufficient on its face, the court must issue an order approving such direction and ordering the district attorney to file such a prosecutor's information in the appropriate court having trial jurisdiction (190.70).

Direction to File Request for Removal to Family Court (190.71)

A person under the age of 16, who commits an act which, if committed by a person sixteen years of age or older, would constitute a criminal offense, is classified under the law as a juvenile delinquent or a juvenile offender. The juvenile delinquent cannot be held criminally responsible for his unlawful acts but the effect of the juvenile offender status is to lower the age of criminal responsibility below sixteen years of age for crimes of serious personal violence committed by adolescents. Juvenile offenders constitute thirteen-year-olds who commit the crime of murder and fourteen- and fifteen-year-olds who commit the crimes of murder, manslaughter, kidnapping, arson, forcible sex crimes, the most dangerous robberies and other like crimes of serious personal violence (*see* 1.20/42). The grand jury may not indict a person under sixteen years of age who commits a criminal offense except if the circumstances are such as to trigger the juvenile offender classification. If this is the case the grand jury can indict the person and based upon mitigating circumstances the trial court will determine if such person will be tried as an adult or as a juvenile delinquent. The grand jury under these circumstances does not have the discretion to remove a juvenile offender charge to the family court; if it finds such a charge it must indict (*People v. Rios*, 432 N.Y.S.2d 120 (1980)).

A grand jury may vote to file a request to remove a charge to the family court if it finds that a person 13, 14 or 15 years of age committed an act which if done by a person over the age of 16 would constitute a crime provided:

1. such act is one for which it may not indict (i.e., not a crime which would invoke juvenile offender status);

2. it does not indict such person for a crime; and,

3. the evidence is legally sufficient to establish such person did the act and competent and admissible evidence provides reasonable cause to believe such person did the act.

Upon voting to remove a charge to the family court, the foreman will file the request for transfer of the charge with the court for which it was impaneled. The request must:

1. allege that the person did an act which if committed by one over the age of 16 would constitute a crime;

2. specify the act and its time and place of commission; and,

3. be signed by the foreman.

The court must, unless the request is improper or insufficient on its face, issue an order approving such request and direct the charge to be removed to the family court (*see* art.725).

Dismissal of a Charge (190.75)

Upon a charge a designated person committed a crime, the charge must be dismissed if either:

1. the evidence before the grand jury is not legally sufficient; or,

2. the grand jury does not find reasonable cause to believe the person charged committed any offense.

The foreman of the grand jury must file its finding of dismissal with the court by which it was impaneled. If the defendant was previously held for the action of the grand jury by a local criminal court, the superior court in which the finding of dismissal was filed must order the sheriff to release the defendant from custody or, if he was released on bail, to exonerate the bail. When all charges against a person have been dismissed by the grand jury, the district attorney must notify the person of such dismissal within 90 days of the filing of the dismissal, unless permission to resubmit the matter to another grand jury or an order of postponement of such notification has been granted by the court.

When a charge has been so dismissed, it may not be resubmitted to the same or another grand jury unless the court in its discretion authorizes or directs the people to resubmit the charge. If in such a case the charge is once again dismissed it may not again be resubmitted to a grand jury. The spirit of the grand jury procedure would be violated and nullified if the district attorney, because he disagreed with the findings of one grand jury resubmitted the same charge until he could find a grand jury that agreed with his opinion that a prosecution was warranted (*People v. Westbrook*, 361 N.Y.S.2d 584 (1974)). The purpose of this provision is to prevent abuse by prosecutors; and, when faced with an application for resubmission, the court's role is not purely ministerial and the court's power should be exercised sparingly and discriminately (*People v. Dykes*, 449 N.Y.S.2d 284 (1982)). Only when additional facts are offered may a judge exercise the judicial power to order resubmission to a second grand jury after the first has refused to indict (*People ex rel. Besser v. Ruthazer*, 158 N.Y.S.2d 803 (1957)). A determination by a grand jury that evidence before it does not warrant resubmission should end the matter and there should not be a resubmission unless it appears, for example, that new evidence has been discovered, that the grand jury failed to give the case a complete and impartial investigation or there is a basis for believing the grand jury otherwise acted in an irregular manner (*People v. Dykes*, ibid). Each situation in which a district attorney withdraws a matter from one grand jury and submits it to another must be examined individually to determine whether the district attorney's conduct was proper or merely a pretext to circumvent the function of a grand jury; where, as far as the prosecutor was concerned, all witnesses had testified and all that was left was to instruct the grand jury on the law and the grand jurors then asked for additional witnesses whom the prosecutor could not present, his withdrawal of the case from the grand jury was the equivalent of a dismissal requiring the consent of the court for resubmission to a second grand jury (*People v. Wilkins*, 68 N.Y.2d 269 (1986)). However, where an indictment is dismissed by a court because of the insufficiency or illegality of the evidence before the grand jury, no permission of the court is necessary for resubmission of the charges to another grand jury (*People v. Bedjanzaden*, 306 N.Y.S.2d 498 (1969)).

Release of a Defendant upon Failure of Timely Grand Jury Action (190.80)

In order to prevent unreasonably long detention of a defendant awaiting grand jury action, upon application of a defendant who has been held for the action of the grand jury on a felony complaint who has been in custody for more than 45 days (if a juvenile offender, 30 days) without any action or disposition of the grand jury (indictment or direction to file a prosecutor's information or referral to family court), the superior court which impaneled him must release him on his own recognizance, unless

1. the lack of action was due to the defendant's request, action or condition, or occurred with his consent; or,

2. the people have shown good cause why the order of release should not be issued. Such good cause must consist of some compelling fact or circumstance which precluded grand jury action within the 45-day period or would render the release against the interest of justice.

Delays in grand jury action due to scheduling problems (*People v. Hosler*, 543 N.Y.S.2d 631 (1989)) or proceedings inquiring into defendant's *sanity* (*People ex rel. Robinson v. Denno*, 227 N.Y.S.2d 276 (1962)) were determined to be for good cause, thereby barring defendant's release.

Grand Jury Reports (190.85)

Article 1, Section 6 of the N.Y.S. Constitution gives grand juries the power to investigate willful misconduct of public officials in public office. It is silent as to the issuance of reports on the results of these investigations. Obviously if the conduct of the public official violated a statute an indictment or prosecutor's information could be utilized to commence a criminal action. If the results of the investigation fell short of the ability to bring criminal charges, the grand jury issued a report of its findings. The problem with such reports was they named the names of public officials, charged no crimes, but set forth basically a moral condemnation of the public official's performance. Great weight was given to these official reports and great publicity; however, since no crime was charged, the named public officials had no forum or opportunity to defend themselves against these allegations of misconduct. Many felt this system violated the due process rights of the persons and called for reform. In 1961, the Court of Appeals, in *Wood v. Hughes* (9 N.Y.2d 144), found that grand juries had no authority to issue reports and the constitution only gave them the authority to inquire into the conduct of public officials and issue criminal charges. The court went on to explain the due process implications of such reports similar to as indicated above. In 1964, the legislature added this provision to the then Code of Criminal Procedure authorizing the issuance of reports short of criminal findings and also setting forth safeguards for the due process rights of named public officials.

1. The grand jury may submit to the court which impaneled it, a report:

   a. Concerning misconduct, non-feasance or neglect in public office, by a public servant, as the basis for a recommendation of removal or disciplinary action; or,

   b. Stating that after the investigation of a public official it finds no misconduct, non-feasance or neglect in office by him provided that such public servant has requested the submission of such report,

    c. Proposing recommendations for legislative, executive or administrative action in the public interest based upon stated findings.

2. The court to which such report is submitted shall examine it and the grand jury minutes and make an order accepting and filing such report as a public record, if the court is satisfied it complies with the provisions of subdivision 1. (above) and that:

    a. the report is based on facts uncovered in an authorized investigation and is supported by the preponderance of credible and legally sufficient evidence; and,

    b. when the report is submitted pursuant to subdivision;

        - 1.a., that each person named in the report had an opportunity to testify before the grand jury prior to the filing of the report, and if,

        - 1.b. or c., that it is not critical of an identified or identifiable person.

If, however, the court finds the filing of the report as a public record may prejudice a pending criminal matter, it must order such report sealed and not disclosed except upon an order of the court.

3. The order accepting a report concerning subdivision 1.a. (wrongdoing and recommendation of dismissal or discipline) and the report itself;

    a. must be sealed by the court and not filed as a public record nor disclosed until at least 31 days after a copy of the order and report are served upon each public servant named in it, or,

    b. if an appeal is taken, until the appeal is disposed of.

4. The public servant may file an answer to the report within 20 days after its receipt and except for scandalous, prejudicial or unnecessary matter (so determined by the court) his answer shall become an appendix to the report. The district attorney shall deliver a copy of the report, and appendix, if any, to each public servant or body having removal or disciplinary authority over each public servant named in the report.

5. Whenever the court is satisfied that the report submitted complies with the provisions of subdivision 2. (above), it may;

    a. direct additional testimony be taken by the same grand jury, or,

    b. it must make an order sealing such report and it may not be filed as a public record or otherwise disclosed (190.85).

Before any report is prepared pursuant to a vote of the grand jury it must vote upon whether or not a report should be issued at all, and if so, what type of report should be prepared (*Matter of Report of Special Grand Jury of Nassau County, Panel 3, Second Term*, 477 N.Y.S.2d 34 (1984)). The district attorney must instruct the grand jurors regarding the issuance of a report. A grand jury report recommending removal from office of a public servant would be ordered sealed where the district attorney failed to advise the grand jury as to what duties and responsibilities were attributable to the public servant or the law bearing upon the burden of proof and no detailed record existed as to how the report was actually prepared and it was not clear the grand jury ever approved the actual content of the report (*Matter of June, 1982 Grand Jury of Supreme Court of Renssalaer*, 471 N.Y.S.2d 378 (1983)). The grand jury record must indicate, inter alia, that at least 16 grand jurors were present and that 12 voted in favor of the report (*Matter of Nassau County Grand Jury*, 382 N.Y.S.2d 1013 (1976)). Matter concerning misconduct by a public servant should not be combined in one report with matter proposing recommendations for legislative, executive or administrative action (*Report of August "A" 1977 Grand Jury of Westchester County*, 406 N.Y.S.2d 107 (1978)). The grand jury report alleging misconduct in office without making a recommendation for disciplinary action was required to be sealed since there was no authority for making such report unless a recommendation for removal or disciplinary action was made (*In re Talerico*, 309 N.Y.S.2d 511 (1970)). A specific recommendation as to a minimum disciplinary penalty on a public servant was not authorized by subdivision 1(a) and exceeded the grand jury's authority (*In re Richard Roe investigation of August 1973 Monroe County Grand Jury*, 360 N.Y.S.2d 123 (1974)). A grand jury report recommending removal from office or disciplinary action against a public servant who has since resigned or against whom no recommendations were made requires the redacting of the names of such employees (*Matter of Report of 1985–1986 Special Grand Jury, Nassau County*, 541 N.Y.S.2d 842 (1989)) or the sealing of the report (*Matter of Report of April, 1979 Grand Jury of Montgomery County*, 436 N.Y.S.2d 414 (1981)). The purpose of the answer is to assist the court in deciding whether a grand jury report should be accepted for filing (*Matter of Report of Special Grand Jury of Monroe County*, 433 N.Y.S.2d 300 (1980)).

Appeals from Orders Concerning Grand Jury Reports (190.90)

Court orders regarding the acceptance or sealing of grand jury reports may be appealed in accordance with the provisions of 190.90. A court order accepting a report of a grand jury regarding misconduct, non-feasance or neglect (190.85/1a) may be appealed by any public servant named in such report. A court order sealing a report of a grand jury (190.85/5) may be appealed by the grand jury that issued the report by the district attorney. If the report relates to the district attorney or his office, the appeal may be made by any attorney designated by the grand jury.

Such appeals are to be made exclusively to the appropriate appellate division of the supreme court and the order of the appellate division determining such appeal shall not be subject to any further review or appeal (190.90/5) unless the review is sought upon grounds of the constitutionality of the procedure itself (*In re Second Report of November, 1968 Grand Jury of Erie County*, 26 N.Y.2d 200 (1970)).

The record on appeal shall remain sealed except that upon:

1. the reversal of the order sealing the report, or,
2. dismissal of the appeal by the public servant,

the report of the grand jury shall be filed as a public record in accord with the provisions of 190.85/3.

See Illustrative Cases

People v. Di Napoli, 27 N.Y.2d 229 (1970), p. 351
People v. Straehle, 294 N.Y.S.2d 42 (1968), p. 352
People v. Feerick, 93 N.Y.2d 433 (1999), p. 353
People v. Williams, 56 N.Y.2d 916 (1982), p. 354
People v. Evans, 29 N.Y.2d 407 (1992), p. 355

7.2 Waiver of the Grand Jury Indictment (Article 195)

As noted at the beginning of Section 7.1 above, the New York State Constitution (art.1, sec. 6) requires a felony to be prosecuted by grand jury indictment unless the indictment is waived. The waiver provision is quite specific and forms the basis of the statutory procedures set forth in Article 195. The constitutional exception provides that a person held for the action of a grand jury upon a charge other than one punishable by death or life imprisonment, with the consent of the district attorney, may waive indictment by a grand jury and consent to be prosecuted on an information filed by the district attorney. Such waiver shall be evidenced by a written instrument signed by the defendant in open court in the presence of his counsel.

A defendant may waive indictment and consent to be prosecuted by a superior court information when:

1. a local criminal court has held the defendant for the action of the grand jury; and,

2. the defendant is not charged with a class A felony; and,

3. the district attorney consents to the waiver.

The defendant may waive the indictment in either:

1. the local criminal court in which the order holding the defendant for the action of the grand jury was issued, at the time such order is issued; or,

2. the appropriate superior court at any time prior to the filing of an indictment by the grand jury (195.10).

The Written Waiver (195.20, 30, 40)

The waiver must be in writing. It must contain the name, date and approximate time and place of each offense to be charged in the superior court information to be filed by the district attorney. The offenses named may include any for which the defendant was held for the action of the grand jury and any properly joinable offenses (e.g., lesser included offenses). A higher degree of the offense charged may not be included in the waiver or the superior court information as this is deemed by the courts to exceed the provision of the statute confining the waiver procedure to those offenses for which the defendant was held for the action of the grand jury (*People v. Zanghi*, 79 N.Y. 2d 815 (1991)). The written waiver must also contain a statement of the defendant that he is aware that:

1. under the New York State Constitution he has the right to be tried by grand jury indictment;

2. he waives such right and consents to be prosecuted by a superior court information to be filed by the district attorney;

3. the superior court information will charge the offenses named in the waiver; and,

4. the superior court information will have the same force and effect as an indictment filed by a grand jury.

This written waiver must be signed by the defendant in open court in the presence of his attorney, and the consent of the district attorney must be endorsed thereon (195.20).

The court before whom the waiver is executed shall determine if it complies with the above provisions and if so satisfied shall approve it and execute a written order to that effect. If the approval is by the local criminal court, it shall transmit the waiver and approval order to the appropriate superior court along with any other pertinent documents to the action (195.30).

When the indictment is waived in a superior court the district attorney shall file the superior court information in such court at the time the waiver is executed. If it is waived in the local criminal court the superior court information shall be filed within ten days of the execution of the order approving the waiver. If the superior court information is not filed within this ten-day period, the court must, on application of an incarcerated defendant, release him on his own recognizance unless:

1. the failure to timely file was caused by or consented to by the defendant; or,

2. the people show good cause, consisting of some compelling fact or circumstance which precluded timely filing, why such order of release should not be issued (195.40).

7.3 The Indictment and Related Instruments (Article 200)

General Provisions (200.10, 15)

An indictment serves the purpose of providing a defendant with fair notice of the accusations against him so that he will be able to prepare a defense, of preventing the prosecutor from usurping the powers of the grand jury by insuring that the crime for which the defendant is tried is the same crime for which she was indicted, and by pre-

venting later retrial for the same offense in contravention of the constitutional prohibitions against double jeopardy (*People v. Grega*, 72 N.Y.2d 489 (1988)). In order
for a superior court to exercise trial jurisdiction over a case the charges must be contained in an indictment or its functional equivalent, a superior court information.

An **indictment** is a written accusation by a grand jury, filed with a superior court,
charging a person(s) with the commission of a crime, or the commission of two or
more offenses at least one of which is a crime (200.10). Note that by definition an
indictment may not be used solely to charge a criminal offense below the grade of a
crime. An indictment should be liberally construed in determining its sufficiency
and any technical or impracticable objection to it should be rejected (*People v. Fox*,
128 N.Y.S.2d 9 (1954)). It is important to remember that an indictment is merely a
finding by a grand jury that reasonable cause to believe exists that the defendant has
committed a crime and is not a determination of guilt or a conviction (*People v.
Block*, 74 N.Y.S.2d 430 (1947)).

A **superior court information** is a written accusation by a district attorney, filed
in a superior court after the defendant has waived his right to trial by indictment
(art. 195), charging a person(s) with a crime or two or more offenses, at least one of
which is a crime. It may include any offense for which the defendant was held for
the action of the grand jury in a local criminal court or offenses properly joinable
with it, but shall not include any offense not named in the defendant's written waiver
of grand jury indictment. The superior court information has the same force and
effect as an indictment and all procedures applicable to indictments are likewise applicable to it, except if otherwise provided (200.15).

What Offenses May Be Charged; Joinder; Consolidation of Indictments (200.20)

Charges

An indictment must charge at least one crime and, in separate counts, one or more
other offenses including petty offenses, provided all such offenses are joinable.

Joinder

Two offenses are joinable when:

a. they are based upon the same act or criminal transaction (e.g., a defendant
   who shoots another with an unlawfully possessed gun can be charged in two
   counts of an indictment with felonious assault and unlawful possession of a
   gun); or,

b. if based upon different criminal transactions, the proof of one would be material
   and admissible as evidence in chief for the other (e.g., count of indictment
   charging defendant with sex abuse of one victim was joinable with counts involving attempted rape, robbery and sexual abuse of another victim, where
   the proof of the first count would be material and admissible as evidence in

chief upon trial of the latter counts) (*People v. Griffin*, 517 N.Y.S.2d 296 (1987)), usually to show motive, intent, identity, common scheme or plan, etc.; or,

c. if such proofs are not present, they are defined by the same or similar statutes or are similar in law (e.g., possession of stolen property counts of indictment were properly joined with other possession of stolen property counts arising from stolen credit cards, inasmuch as both sets of charges were defined by the same or similar statutes) (*People v. Blackwell*, 548 N.Y.S.2d 197 (1989)); or,

d. if not directly joinable with each other but they are so joinable with a third offense contained in the indictment, then the three may be properly joined, not only with each other, and the chain of joinder may be further extended in accord with these joinder rules (e.g., count of indictment charging criminal possession of a weapon was properly joined with kidnapping and sodomy counts even though it was not shown to be part of these latter transactions, since it was not totally unrelated to such charges and all the witnesses who would testify as to the weapons count would necessarily be witnesses on the kidnapping and sodomy counts also) (*People v. De Vyver*, 453 N.Y.S.2d 915 (1982)).

Severance

Where joinability rests solely on the fact of the same or similar law (see above) the court, in the interest of justice and for good cause shown, on application of the defendant or the people, in its discretion, may order such offenses to be tried separately. Good cause includes situations such as:

a. Substantially more proof exists on one count than the other and it is such that the jury would be unable to separate the proof as it relates to each count; or,

b. The defendant has both important testimony to give on one count but a genuine need to refrain from testifying on the other, and the court is satisfied that the risk of prejudice to the defendant is substantial.

Consolidation

Whereas severance is the procedure either party may use in an attempt to obtain separate trials of two or more counts contained in a single indictment, consolidation is the procedure utilized to attempt to have two or more separate indictments combined for a single trial (*People v. Lane*, 56 N.Y.2d 1 (1982)). When two or more indictments against the defendant charge joinable offenses as discussed above, it is in the court's discretion, upon application of either party to order the indictments to be consolidated and treated as a single indictment for trial purposes. In exercising such discretion, the judge weighs the public interest in avoiding duplicative, lengthy and expensive trials, against the defendant's interest in being protected from unfair disadvantage. While the court must be afforded reasonable latitude in exercising discretion with respect to consolidation, the compromise of a defendant's right to a fair trial, free of undue prejudice as the quid pro quo for the mere expeditious disposition of criminal cases will not be tolerated (*People v. Lane, supra*).

a. If the application by the defendant seeks consolidation with respect to offenses arising from the same act or transaction (2a above) the court must order such consolidation unless good cause to the contrary is shown. This is to prevent prosecutorial attempts to obtain two trials for crimes arising from the same act or transaction and thereby increase chances of conviction of a defendant.

Mixed Juvenile Offender/Delinquency Charges

If a person under the age of sixteen commits, as the result of the same act or criminal transaction, two or more joinable offenses, one of which subjects him to criminal trial as a juvenile offender and the other(s) do not, but are charges for which treatment as a juvenile delinquent in family court would ordinarily be required, the indictment may contain all the charges in separate counts in order avoid bifurcation of the charges and separate proceedings in the criminal and family courts. If the defendant is found guilty of the juvenile offender charge, and the juvenile delinquency charge, the juvenile delinquency charge will be declared a nullity and not be referred to the family court for disposition. If, however, the defendant is found not guilty on the juvenile offender charge but guilty on the juvenile delinquency charge, the matter will be referred to the family court for disposition (310.85).

An indictment may accuse a defendant of as many criminal offenses as may be properly joined but each offense must be placed in a separate count. A count that accuses a defendant of more than one offense is called a duplicitous count and duplicitous counts are prohibited (200.30). An indictment containing duplicitous counts may be remedied by an election of counts by the prosecutor or by correct instructions given to the jury by the court (*People v. Horne*, 468 N.Y.S.2d 433 (1983)).

Joinder of Defendants and Consolidation of Indictments vs. Different Defendants (200.40)

Two or more defendants may be jointly charged in a single indictment provided that:

1. all such defendants are jointly charged with every offense in the indictment; or,
2. all the offenses are based upon a common scheme or plan or the same criminal transaction; or,
3. if the indictment includes a count of enterprise corruption:
    a. all the defendants are jointly charged with every count of enterprise corruption; and,
    b. every offense other than enterprise corruption is included in the pattern of activity upon which enterprise corruption is based; and,
    c. each defendant could have properly been jointly charged with one of the other defendants absent the enterprise corruption counts.

When filing an indictment charging enterprise corruption, the district attorney must submit a statement to the court attesting he has reviewed the legislative findings on enterprise corruption in art. 460 PL, and the substantive evidence in this case, and concurs in the judgment of the grand jury that the charge is consistent with these legislative findings (200.65). In any of the above cases the court upon good cause shown, such as the finding that prejudice to the defendant or people will arise by the joint trial, may order a severance of the defendants.

When two or more defendants are charged in separate indictments with charges that could have been charged in a single indictment, the court upon application of the people may order them consolidated in a single indictment and any charges in these indictments that are not proper for consolidation shall remain in existence and be separately prosecuted. In determining consolidation and severance issues the court must weigh the factors of economy and prejudice to the defendant or people (*People v. Rowley*, 462 N.Y.S.2d 366 (1983)).

Form and Content of Indictments (200.50)

An indictment must contain the name of the court in which filed, the title of the action, a separate count for each offense charged, the county of commission of the offense, the date of commission, the signatures of the foreman of the grand jury and district attorney and a plain and concise factual statement in each count, without allegations of an evidentiary nature, which:

1. asserts facts supporting every element of the offense charged and the defendant's commission thereof with sufficient precision to apprise the defendant of the conduct which is the subject of the accusation; and,

2. if an armed felony, a statement to that effect including the weapon involved.

The primary function of an indictment is to inform a defendant of the crimes with which he is charged and to do so with sufficient fullness and clarity to allow him to prepare for trial (*People v. Branch*, 426 N.Y.S.2d 291 (1980)). An indictment should contain specifications of the acts and a description of the criminal offense to enable the defendant to adequately defend himself and bar further prosecution arising out of the same facts (*People v. Cirillo*, 419 N.Y.S.2d 820 (1979)). Further particulars concerning the alleged crime are a matter of evidence and need not be set forth in the indictment, and the defendant who desires additional information may seek it through a bill of particulars (*People v. Shapiro*, 279 N.Y.S.2d 220 (1967); *rev'd on other grounds*, 20 N.Y.2d 694 (1967)).

Previous Convictions May Not Be Included in an Indictment (200.60)

When a defendant is charged with a crime which has as one of its elements the previous conviction of another crime, the fact of the previous conviction may not be set forth in the indictment and if the title of the crime includes reference to a previous conviction, the title may not be used. In such a case the grand jury shall provide a special information to accompany the indictment charging the defendant was previously convicted of a specified offense and the title of the crime must be improvised such as by use of the words "as a felony," without mentioning the previous conviction. After the commencement of the trial and before the close of the people's case, the defendant shall be arraigned on the special information, out of the presence of the jury. If the defendant admits to the previous conviction, no mention will be made of it at trial as if such previous conviction was not an element of the offense charged. If the defendant denies the previous conviction or remains mute, the people may prove it before the jury as a part of their case.

The purpose of this provision is to protect the defendant against the district attorney's providing at trial the very damaging fact of the defendant's previous conviction, if he does not dispute the fact of such conviction (*People v. Giuliano*, 383 N.Y.S.2d 878 (1976)). A certificate of conviction from the appropriate court may be used to prove the previous conviction but it must state facts demonstrating the defendant is the person named in the certificate (*People v. Vollick*, 539 N.Y.S.2d 187 (1989)). If the defendant contests the validity of the evidence of previous conviction, the appropriate remedy is for the court to hold a hearing. The defendant has the initial burden of introducing sufficient evidence to overcome the presumption of regularity in the proof of the people. If the defendant does so, the prosecutor has the burden of proving the previous conviction beyond a reasonable doubt (*People v. Ryan*, 485 N.Y.S.2d 933 (1985)).

Amendments and Superseding Indictments (200.70, 80)

Amendments

At any time before or during trial, the court may, upon application of the people and with notice to the defendant and opportunity to be heard, amend an indictment to correct:

1. errors, defects or variances from proof relating to form, time, place, names, etc., when such amendment does not change;

    a. the theory of the prosecution as reflected in the evidence before the grand jury; or,

    b. otherwise tend to prejudice the defendant on the merits of the case.

When such an amendment is permitted, upon application of the defendant, an adjournment must be granted which may be necessary to give the defendant adequate opportunity to prepare his defense.

No amendment is permitted which would change the theory of the prosecution as reflected in the evidence before the grand jury that filed the indictment nor for the purpose of curing:

1. a failure to charge or state an offense; or,

2. legal insufficiency of the factual allegations; or,

3. a misjoinder of offenses or defendants (200.70).

The reason no amendment may be made that changes the theory of the prosecution as reflected in the evidence before the grand jury is due to the state constitutional requirement that all indictments for felonies emanate from grand juries (*People v. Carmona*, 478 N.Y.S.2d 759 (1984)). Except for unessential details set forth in this section a court cannot usurp the authority of a grand jury by a unilateral amendment of an indictment (*People v. Kramer*, 175 N.Y.S.2d 508 (1958)). For example, it was error to permit an amendment to an indictment that the defendant caused physical injury to the victim by striking him with a baseball bat rather than a lamp, where there was evidence at trial that the victim had been struck by the defendant with both a bat and a lamp and it was the bat which caused the injury, as the amendment made a substantive change in the theory of the prosecution (*People v. Powell*, 549 N.Y.S.2d 276 (1989)). The purpose of this section is to promote the ends of justice by rendering of no avail a purely technical objection to an indictment without depriving a defendant of any substantial right (*People v. Fiske*, 85 N.Y.S.2d 240 (1949)).

Superseding Indictments

If at any time before the defendant pleads guilty or the trial commences, another indictment is filed in the same court, charging the defendant with an offense charged in the first indictment, the first indictment with respect to such offense is superseded by the second and upon defendant's arraignment on the second indictment the superseded count in the first must be dismissed by the court. Other counts in the first indictment are not superseded nor dismissed (200.80). This section was intended to clarify procedure rather than to make any substantive change in the law (*People v. Benson*, 143 N.Y.S.2d 563 (1955)).

Bill of Particulars (200.95)

The purpose of a bill of particulars is to clarify the matter contained in an indictment and thus to allow the defendant an opportunity to prepare his defense (*In re L*, 320 N.Y.S.2d 570 (1971)). It is not a discovery device (*People v. Davis*, 41 N.Y.S.2d 678 (1977)). It is not intended to furnish a defendant with a preview of the prosecutor's proof but has as its sole function a more specific definition of the crime charged in the indictment. The motion for a bill of particulars may not be used as a "fishing expedition," i.e., it is not meant to furnish the defendant with a preview of some or all of the prosecutor's proof (*People v. Raymond G.*, 387 N.Y.S.2d 174 (1976)). Sec. 200.50/7 requires merely that the indictment contain sufficient precision of facts to clearly apprise the defendant of the conduct which is the subject of the accusation. This provision is satisfied when such facts support each element of the offense charged without offering much detail. Hence, the importance of a bill of particulars to a defendant.

A **bill of particulars** is a written statement by the prosecutor specifying items of factual information not in the indictment, which pertain to the offense charged, including:

   a. the substance of the defendant's conduct encompassed in the charge, and,

   b. whether the people intend to prove the defendant acted as principal or accomplice or both; however,

the prosecutor is not required to include in it matters of evidence relating to how the people intend to prove the elements of the offense, or items of factual information not in the special forfeiture information which pertains to:

   a. the substance of each defendant's conduct re the forfeiture claim,

   b. the approximate value of the forfeiture property,

   c. the nature and extent of the defendant's interest in such property, and,

   d. the extent of his gain if any from the offense charged.

Special forfeiture and prosecutor's forfeiture informations are utilized in conjunction with prosecution of felony drug offenses under art. 480 P.L. and the bill of particulars in reference to them gives the defendant necessary information to defend against seizure of property authorized under that article.

Request for a Bill of Particulars

A request for a bill of particulars is:

   a. a written request served by a defendant upon the people,

   b. without leave of the court,

   c. requesting a bill of particulars,

   d. specifying the items of factual information desired and alleging the defendant cannot adequately prepare or conduct his defense without such information.

The bill of particulars may be gotten by a demand to the prosecutor, or if such demand is refused by the prosecutor, by court order upon a pre-trial motion. If the prosecutor refuses the demand, the refusal shall contain the reasons therefore, either:

   a. a reasonable belief the information requested is not authorized to be included; or,

   b. such information is not necessary for the defendant to adequately prepare or conduct his defense; or,

   c. a protective order would be warranted; or,

   d. the request is untimely made.

Upon the defendant's motion, the court will order the bill of particulars to be delivered upon the motion, if it is satisfied the information requested is authorized and is necessary for the defendant to adequately prepare or defend against the charges:

   a. If the request to the prosecutor was not timely made the court will order the request complied with upon finding good cause for the delay.

   b. If the prosecutor has not made a timely refusal, the court must order compliance with the request, unless the people show good cause why the order should not be given (See 255.20).

A protective order may be issued by the court upon written motion of the prosecutor or another affected person, or by the court upon its own initiative. The protective order will limit the substance or utilization of the material set forth in the bill of particulars for good cause shown, including intimidation, economic reprisal, danger to the integrity of physical evidence, etc., or any other factors which outweigh the need for the bill of particulars.

Much of the litigation concerning the appropriateness of material requested in a bill of particulars revolves about whether the material requested is evidence or information regarding the theory of the prosecutor to be used at trial. The purpose of the bill of particulars is not to enable the defendant to examine the people's evidence but merely to give the defendant and the court reasonable information as to the nature and character of the crime charged (*People v. Golly*, 250 N.Y.S.2d 210 (1964)). Access to evidence may be had through the discovery procedures of Article 245.

7.4 Proceedings from Filing of Indictment to Plea (Article 210)

The only methods of prosecuting an offense in the superior courts are by grand jury indictment or, in the event the defendant waives the right to be tried by that form of accusatory instrument, by superior court information (210.05).

Securing the Defendant's Appearance for Arraignment (210.10)

After the indictment has been filed the defendant must be gotten into court to personally appear at the arraignment on the charge in the indictment. The method of securing this appearance depends upon the circumstances of the defendants whereabouts.

If the defendant was previously held for the action of the grand jury in the local criminal court and is confined in the custody of the sheriff:

   a. the superior court must order the sheriff to produce the defendant for arraignment at a specified time and date; and,

   b. give at least two days' notice of such arraignment to defendant's counsel, if any has filed a notice of appearance with the local criminal court.

If the defendant is at liberty on bail or recognizance as a result of a pending action in the local criminal court, the superior court must, upon two days' notice, direct the defendant, his surety and attorney, if any, to appear for arraignment on the specified date and time.

   a. If the defendant fails to appear on such date the court may issue a bench warrant and forfeit any bail that has been posted. The police officer executing the bench warrant must bring the defendant before such superior court without unnecessary delay. If the court is not in session at the time, the officer may deliver the defendant to the local correctional facility of the county for detention until the opening of the court on the next business day.

If the defendant has not previously been held by a local criminal court for the action of the grand jury, is at liberty, and the filing of the indictment constitutes the commencement of the criminal action, the court must order the indictment sealed and:

    a. issue a superior court warrant of arrest; or,

    b. at the request of the district attorney and if the court is satisfied the defendant would appear for arraignment:

        (i) issue a summons; or,

        (ii) authorize the district attorney to direct the defendant to appear (210.10).

Superior Court Warrants of Arrest

A superior court warrant of arrest is executable anywhere in the state and may be addressed to any police officer whose geographical area of employment embraces the place where the crime was committed or where the court is located. It must be executed in the same manner as an ordinary warrant of arrest (120.80) and following the arrest the executing officer must perform all the required preliminary police duties such as recording, fingerprinting and photographing, and deliver the defendant to the superior court without unnecessary delay. If the court is not in session the officer may deliver the defendant to the local correctional facility for detention until the commencement of business of the superior court on the next business day.

The superior court warrant of arrest may be executed by any police officer to whom addressed or who has been delegated to execute it under the following circumstances.

    1. When the issuing court has so authorized, the officer to whom the warrant is addressed may delegate another police officer to execute it when:

        a. he has reasonable cause to believe the defendant is in a county other than the one to which the warrant is returnable; and,

        b. the geographical area of employment of the delegated officer embraces the county where the arrest is to be made; and,

        c. the delegated police officer, upon the arrest, must deliver the defendant to the officer holding the warrant for delivery to the court and performance of preliminary duties as indicated above (210.10).

Arraignment upon Indictment; Defendant's Rights, Court's Instructions and Bail (210.15)

At arraignment the court must inform the defendant of the charges against him and the district attorney must give him a copy of the indictment (210.15/1). The defendant has the right to the aid of counsel at arraignment and every subsequent stage of the action. If the defendant appears at arraignment without counsel, the court must inform him of the following rights, accord the defendant the opportunity to exercise such rights and must itself take such affirmative action as is necessary to effectuate them:

1. to an adjournment for the purpose of obtaining counsel; and,

2. to communicate free of charge, by letter or telephone, for the purpose of obtaining counsel and informing a relative or friend that he has been charged with an offense; and,

3. to have counsel assigned if he is financially unable to obtain one (210.15/2,3).

If the defendant desires to defend himself without the aid of counsel the court must permit him to do so if it is satisfied he made such decision with knowledge of its significance; but, if the court is not so satisfied, it may not proceed until the defendant is provided with counsel, either of his own choosing or by assignment. A defendant who proceeds without counsel does not waive his right to counsel and the court must inform him he may invoke his right to counsel, or any of the above mentioned rights, at any subsequent stage of the action (210.15/5).

The right to counsel is fundamental (*People v. Friedlander*, 16 N.Y.2d 248 (1965)). An accused, once indicted, has an absolute right to counsel (*People v. Jamison*, 423 N.Y.S.2d 184 (1980)). The purpose of the right to counsel requirement is to assure protection of all the defendant's constitutional guaranties (*People v. McKie*, 25 N.Y.2d 19 (1969)). Although a criminal defendant has the right to represent himself if he so chooses, it is incumbent upon the court to determine if his decision to forego counsel is knowing and intelligent (*People v. Williams*, 465 N.Y.S.2d 332 (1983)). Although the constitutional right to counsel does not justify forcing counsel upon an accused who does not want one, where the defendant has not intelligently and understandably waived counsel and where circumstances show that his rights could not be fairly protected without an attorney, the right to counsel becomes of such critical concern as to be an element of due process and the finding of a waiver under such circumstances is not to be lightly made (*People v. Amos*, 249 N.Y.S.2d 740 (1964)). The question of whether a person knowingly and intelligently waives his right to counsel is one of fact to be determined by the court on all the evidence and the circumstances; the question to be determined is one of the accused's being in touch with the realities of the situation, his volitional competency, his degree of specific awareness of particular facts or general understanding and, basically, whether the accused was of such mental state as to be able to understand the meaning of his statements (*People v. Bunk*, 312 N.Y.S.2d 889 (1970)).

Unless the court disposes of the action by final disposition immediately, it must enter a securing order either releasing him in his own recognizance, or fixing bail or committing him to the custody of the sheriff for his future appearance in such action (210.15/6).

Motion to Dismiss or Reduce an Indictment (210.20)

After arraignment on an indictment, the superior court may, upon motion of the defendant, dismiss such indictment or any count within it, upon any of the following grounds:

a. The indictment or count is defective; or,

b. The evidence before the grand jury was not legally sufficient to establish the offense charged or any lesser included offense; or,

c. The grand jury proceeding was defective; or,

d. The defendant has immunity; or,

e. The prosecution is barred due to a previous prosecution (double jeopardy); or,

f. The prosecution is untimely (statute of limitations); or,

g. A speedy trial violation; or,

h. Some other jurisdictional or legal impediment to conviction; or,

i. Dismissal is required in the interest of justice.

The Procedure

1. The motion must be in writing, within the time period specified in 255.20 (within 45 days of arraignment or securance of counsel (210.20/2)), with reasonable notice to the people, and contain sworn allegations of fact and any documentary evidence tending to support the motion.

2. The people may file an answer with the court, with a copy to the defendant, denying or admitting the allegations in the defendant's motion, supported by any documentary evidence refuting such allegations.

3. After receipt of all the papers the court may determine the motion with or without a hearing.

    a. The court must grant the motion without a hearing if the grounds are either conceded by the people or are conclusively substantiated by unquestionable documentary proof.

    b. The court may deny the motion without a hearing if the defendant's papers do not state one of the legal grounds for the motion, do not contain sworn allegations of fact, or if an allegation of fact in the defendant's motion is refuted by unquestionable documentary proof.

4. If the court does not make one of the above determinations it must hold a hearing to gather additional facts it feels necessary to make the determination. The defendant has the right to be present at the hearing and has the burden of proof by a preponderance of the evidence of every essential fact to support the motion.

5. If the court denies the defendant's motion, the indictment remains valid and the criminal action continues. If the court dismisses the entire indictment it may do so:

   a. without authorizing the prosecutor to resubmit the charges to a grand jury, in which case the court must order the defendant discharged from custody or if released on bail, the exoneration of the bail; or,

   b. if it authorizes the prosecutor to resubmit the charges to a grand jury, such action is deemed to constitute an order holding the defendant for the action of the grand jury. The securing order issued by the court remains in effect until the first of any of the following events occur:

      (i) the people state they do not intend to resubmit the case; or,

      (ii) as a result of resubmission of the case the defendant is arraigned upon a new indictment or prosecutor's information; or,

      (iii) after resubmission of the case the grand jury files a dismissal of the case; or,

      (iv) after 45 days, during which time none of the above actions were taken. Such time may be extended for good cause upon application of the people.

If the case is terminated as indicated above the securing order is terminated and the defendant must be ordered released from custody or the bail be exonerated (210.45). If the defendant has more than one ground to support the motion he must raise them all in his motion. If he fails to do so the court will not permit it to be raised at a later time unless in the interest of justice, for good cause shown by the defendant (210.20/2).

The Ground of Lack of Legal Sufficiency of the Evidence (210.30)

If the court finds, after motion of the defendant to dismiss on grounds of lack of legal sufficiency of evidence before the grand jury, that no offense charged in the indictment was supported by legally sufficient evidence but the evidence does support a lesser included offense, it shall order the count or counts reduced to the highest lesser included offense so supported; however, if the only lesser included offense would be a petty offense, the indictment shall be dismissed and the prosecutor ordered to file a prosecutor's information in the appropriate local criminal court. The court shall order an appropriate securing order in conjunction with the action taken (210.20/1b). The motion to dismiss or reduce an indictment on grounds of lack of legally sufficient evidence must be preceded or accompanied by a motion to inspect the grand jury minutes. The purpose of this motion to inspect is to enable the court and defendant to examine the stenographic notes of the grand jury proceeding to determine the sufficiency of the evidence that was presented before it. Unless good cause exists for denying the motion to inspect, the court must grant such motion.

If the court determines there is not reasonable cause to believe the evidence was insufficient, it may deny the defendant's motions or proceed, despite such finding. The court must then examine the minutes and make a determination. If it deems it necessary, the court shall release the relevant portions of the minutes to the parties to see if they can assist in the determination. Prior to such release the district attorney shall be given an opportunity to present argument that the release of the minutes would not be in the public interest. The court must place its ruling on the motion on the record (210.30).

The Ground of Defective Indictment (210.25)

The motion to dismiss on the ground the indictment is defective on its face may be made when:

a. It does not substantially conform to the provisions in Article 200. The indictment may not be dismissed due to this form of defect if it is one that can be cured by an amendment and the people move for such an amendment as per 200.70;

b. The defect is that the court does not have jurisdiction of the offense charged;

c. The statute defining the offense is unconstitutional or otherwise invalid (210.25).

Dismissal of indictments for technical defects is not favored in absence of a showing of fraud or prejudice to the defendant (*People v. Heller*, 472 N.Y.S.2d 824 (1984)). Trial, judgment or proceedings on an indictment are not affected by reason of an imperfection as to form which in no way prejudices the defendant (*People v. Hardy*, 310 N.Y.S.2d 357 (1970)). An indictment is jurisdictionally defective only if it does not effectively charge the defendant with the commission of a particular crime (*People v. Branch*, 426 N.Y.S.2d 291 (1980)). Indictments that fail to state each element of the offense charged do not result in the charging of the defendant with the commission of a criminal offense by the grand jury. Since the constitutional and statutory requirements require prosecution upon grand jury indictment for felonies, such defects may not be merely corrected by the court, and result in the dismissal of the indictment. Defects as to form and other imprecision may generally be corrected by amendment and generally will not result in dismissal.

The Ground of a Defective Grand Jury Proceeding (210.35)

The motion to dismiss upon the ground that the grand jury proceeding was defective requires a showing that:

1. The grand jury was illegally constituted; or,

2. The grand jury lacked a quorum (less than sixteen members present), or fewer than twelve members voted the indictment; or,

3. The defendant was not given an opportunity to appear and testify before the grand jury as per 190.05; or,

4. The grand jury proceeding in some other way failed to conform with the requirements of Article 190, and due to such failure, the integrity of the process was impaired and prejudice to the defendant may result (210.35).

Violations of the first three categories listed above are fatally defective and result in the dismissal of the indictment. The fourth category requires a showing of possible prejudice against the defendant as a result before dismissal may be granted. A defendant need not show actual prejudice (*People v. De Ruggiero*, 409 N.Y.S.2d 88 (1978)). The issue of possible prejudice has arisen, for example, in cases in which unauthorized persons have appeared before the grand jury, the use of confessions as evidence before the grand jury, prosecutorial misconduct and improper instructions to the grand jurors.

The Ground of Dismissal in Furtherance of Justice (210.40)

An indictment or any count in it may be dismissed on the ground the prosecution would not be in the furtherance of justice, even though there is no basis for dismissal as a matter of law upon any other ground; but, such dismissal is required as a matter of judicial discretion due to some compelling factor clearly demonstrating conviction of the defendant would result in an injustice. In making such determination, the court must consider:

1. the seriousness and circumstances of the offense;

2. the extent of harm caused by the offense;

3. the evidence of guilt, whether admissible or not at trial;

4. the history, character and condition of the defendant;

5. any exceptionally serious misconduct of law enforcement personnel;

6. the impact upon the public confidence in the criminal justice system or upon the safety and welfare of the community if dismissed;

7. the attitude of the victim with respect to the motion;

8. any other relevant factor indicating a conviction would serve no useful purpose.

The motion on this ground may be made by the prosecutor or the court itself in addition to the defendant (210.40). The dismissal of an indictment when "required in the interest of justice" only applies when there is no basis for dismissal as a matter of law, that is, when the defendant, despite his apparent guilt, shows that for some reason of compassion he should not be prosecuted (*People v. Coppa*, 394 N.Y.S.2d 219 (1977); *rev'd on other grounds*, 45 N.Y.2d 244 (1978)). The purpose of the discretionary authority of a court to dismiss an indictment in the furtherance of justice is to allow the letter of the law to succumb to the spirit of justice, in rare circumstances, but the court must be cognizant of the fact that the honest labors of the grand jury and district attorney should not be lightly set aside (*People v. O'Neill*, 379 N.Y.S.2d 244 (1975)). The court's power to dismiss a criminal prosecution without the consent of the public officer elected by the people to enforce the criminal law should be exercised most sparingly and only in those cases where some "compelling factor" warrants the conclusion the court should substitute its discretion for that of the district attorney (*People v. Field*, 555 N.Y.S.2d 437 (1990)). The court's discretion to dismiss is to be exercised sparingly and dismissal granted in absence of a "crying need" will likely be overturned as an abuse of discretion (*People v. Walsh*, 394 N.Y.S.2d 374 (1977)).

The Motion to Remove a Juvenile Offender to Family Court (210.43)

The motion to remove a juvenile offender to family court may be made by any of the parties or the court on its own motion. The court may order such removal if, after consideration of the factors set forth in Section 210.40 above (except for the subdivision dealing with the misconduct of the police), it determines that to do so would be in the interests of justice; unless the indictment charges the juvenile offender with murder 2d, rape or sodomy 1st or an armed felony, the district attorney must consent to such removal and the court may only so order if it finds one or more of the following factors present:

1. mitigating circumstances that bear directly on the manner in which the crime was committed;

2. where the defendant was not the sole participant, the defendant's role was relatively minor, although not so minor as to constitute a defense to the charge; or,

3. possible deficiencies in the proof of the crime exist and, after consideration of the above-mentioned factors, the court determined that removal of the action to the family court would be in the interests of justice.

If the court orders removal of the action to the family court and if the district attorney consents, they must put on the record their reasons therefore in detail and not in conclusory terms (210.43). If an indictment also charges a juvenile offender with offenses for which he ordinarily would be proceeded against as a juvenile delinquent and the charge for which he is held as a juvenile offender is dismissed, the court must direct that the action be removed to the family court for proceedings of juvenile delinquency against the defendant (210.20).

Adjournment in Contemplation of Dismissal in Marijuana Cases below the Grade of Felony (210.46)

Where the sole remaining counts in an indictment charge a violation of the marijuana laws, below the grade of felony, before the entry of a plea of guilty thereon or the commencement of trial, the court upon motion of the defendant may order the suspension of the case and the action adjourned in contemplation of dismissal; or, it may dismiss the charge in accordance with the provisions of 170.56 (210.46).

The effective date of an order to dismiss or reduce a charge shall be stayed for thirty days unless the stay is waived by the people. On or before the conclusion of the thirty-day period, the people shall exercise one of the following options:

1. accept the court's order by filing a reduced indictment or a prosecutor's information, as appropriate; or,

2. resubmit the case to a grand jury as the court may permit upon a showing of good cause. This option may only be utilized once by the prosecutor; or,

3. appeal the order (210.20/6).

Unless an indictment is dismissed or otherwise terminated in accordance with some other provision of law, the defendant must be required to enter a plea thereto (210.50). The pleadings constitute a separate and distinct procedure and are not part of the arraignment process.

7.5 Adjournment in Contemplation of Dismissal for the Purpose of Referral to Dispute Resolution (Article 215)

As provided for misdemeanors in Section 170.55/4, this article provides for the referral of certain felonies for the purpose of dispute resolution procedures. The local criminal court or a superior court may, with the consent of the people and defendant, and notice to the victim (one who has sustained physical or financial injury due to the crime), with an opportunity to be heard, may order certain felonies be adjourned in contemplation of dismissal, for the purpose of referring the case to a community dispute center established pursuant to Article 21A of the Judiciary Law. These centers, privately run, operate under contract with the court administration and conduct mediation and conciliation programs to deal with selected cases which are deemed amenable to such procedures. The courts may not utilize these procedures for:

1. class A felonies; or,

2. violent felony offenses (70.02 PL); or,

3. any drug offense in 220 PL; or,

4. second felony or persistent felony cases (70.04,06,08,10 PL) (215.10,15).

Upon issuance of the order, the court must release the defendant on his own recognizance and refer the action to the appropriate dispute resolution center. No later than 45 days after such referral, the center must advise the district attorney as to whether the charges against the defendant have been resolved. If the defendant has agreed to pay a fine, restitution or reparation the district attorney must be advised every 30 days as to the status of such payments. The center is authorized to make monetary awards of up to $5,000 (849b.4e Judiciary Law). The court may restore the action to the calendar under the following circumstances:

1. upon application of the people;
    a. within 6 months of the order upon a finding the dismissal of the accusatory instrument would not be in the furtherance of justice; or,
    b. within 1 year of the order, where the defendant has agreed to pay a fine, etc., upon a determination the defendant has failed to pay the fine, etc. (215.30).

The accusatory instrument will be deemed to have been dismissed by the court in furtherance of justice where the order has not been restored to the calendar within the six month or one year periods specified in the procedures listed above. Upon dismissal of the action the arrest and prosecution shall be deemed a nullity and the record subject to sealing in accord with 160.50 (215.40).

Chapter 8

Prosecution of Indictments in Superior Court; from Plea to Pre-Trial Motions

Sec. **8.1** Article 220; The Plea
Sec. **8.2** Article 230; Removal of the Action
Sec. **8.3** Article 245; Discovery
Sec. **8.4** Article 250; Pre-Trial Notices of Defenses
Sec. **8.5** Article 255; Pre-Trial Motions

8.1 The Plea (Article 220)

The **plea** constitutes the defendant's response to the criminal offense or offenses contained in the accusatory instrument filed against the defendant, which in the case of a felony charge is the indictment or superior court information. An indictment or pleading is essential to the prosecution of a crime and to the acceptance of a plea in regard thereto (*McDonald v. Sobel*, 72 N.Y.S.2d 4 (1947)). Recall that each offense charged must be contained in a separate count of the indictment and the corollary, counts may not be duplicitous. One of the reasons for this provision is to assure the defendant understands what criminal offenses are being plead to. The defendant must enter a plea to each count of the indictment.

Entry of Plea (220.50)

The plea to an indictment must be made orally and in person by the defendant, unless the defendant is a corporation, in which case the plea must be entered by counsel, or the charge in the indictment is a misdemeanor, in which case the plea may be made by the individual defendant's counsel. Despite this statutory provision requiring the defendant to personally enter the felony plea, courts have held that the acceptance of a defendant's plea of guilty through his counsel in open court did not amount to such statutory non-compliance as to constitute grounds for reversal of the judgment of conviction had thereunder (*People v. Sadness*, 300 N.Y. 69 (1949)). If the defendant refuses to enter a plea or remains mute, the court must enter a plea of not guilty on his behalf. The conditions of plea bargaining agreements and the required permission of the court and consent of the prosecutor must be entered in the record either orally or in a writing filed with the court, stating the reasons for such approval or consent. If the plea bargain involves forfeiture of property under the drug felony forfeiture law (480 PL), the value and description of the property involved must be included in the record as well. If the court decides not to implement the conditions agreed upon, either party must be given an opportunity to withdraw from the bargain.

Kinds of Pleas (220.10)

There are different pleas available to the defendant:

a. Not guilty to the entire indictment;

b. Guilty to the entire indictment;

c. If the indictment charges but one crime, guilty to a lesser included offense;

d. If the indictment charges two or more crimes, guilty to one of the charges, a lesser included offense or any combination thereof;

e. Not responsible due to mental disease or defect.

The defendant may as a matter of right enter a plea of not guilty to the entire indictment. It constitutes a denial of every allegation in the indictment (200.40). He may likewise enter a plea of guilty to the entire indictment; however, a defendant may not plead guilty to the crime of murder 1st degree since the state constitution prohibits the waiver of a jury trial in a capital offense (N.Y.S. Const., art.1 sec. 2).

Plea Bargaining

Other guilty pleas, meaning to less than the entire indictment, the subject of plea bargaining, require the permission of the court and consent of the people and are not a matter of right. In requiring the court's and prosecutor's joint consent to any plea to an offense less than that charged, the legislature sought to prevent collusive and corrupt arrangements (*People v. Selikoff*, 35 N.Y.2d 227 (1974)). Most cases are resolved through plea bargaining; but, the statute sets ground rules and limitations on the practice in order to assure that defendants charged with serious felony offenses are not permitted to avoid prison sentences or, when it is necessary, to establish a record for purposes of sentencing the defendant as a 2d felony offender. Such limitations do not apply to juvenile offenders; but, if the juvenile offender is charged with murder or a serious, violent felony offense a plea bargain must be to an offense for which he is criminally responsible. Otherwise, with the consent of the court and prosecutor, the plea may be to a reduced charge so as to permit referral to the family court, in the interest of justice.

Although plea bargaining is an essential part of the administration of criminal justice, an accused does not have a fundamental constitutional right to negotiate or plead to anything less than the entire indictment against him (*People v. Gardner*, 359 N.Y.S.2d 196 (1974)). A plea is a bargain struck between a defendant and a prosecutor and where the court has no reason to believe it is unfair or inappropriate the bargain becomes final (*People v. McCasland*, 391 N.Y.S.2d 31 (1977)). A plea conditioned upon the defendant's waiver of his right to appeal denial of a suppression motion is permissible as long as it is voluntarily entered into with full comprehension on the defendant's part both as to the plea and the conditions associated with the plea (*People v. Jasper*, 436 N.Y.S.2d 185 (1981)). Reasonable conditions may be attached to permission to enter a guilty plea, although such conditions must not amount to overreaching or a denial of the defendant's entitlement to fundamental fairness, particularly when the court brings its naturally intimidating power into play during plea negotiations (*People v. Miller*, 434 N.Y.S.2d 36 (1980)). The people will be strictly held to the terms of a plea bargain and a defendant, fully aware of the consequences, will similarly be bound, absent constitutional, statutory or other public policy violations (*People v. Cates*, 480 N.Y.S.2d 512 (1984)). To avoid dispute over what promises were in fact made when the defendant plead guilty, the terms of the plea agreement should be explicitly and unambiguously on record (*People v. Rosenberg*, 538 N.Y.S.2d 558 (1989)). A guilty plea may not be coerced either by actual physical compulsion, threats and the like or by the duress of circumstances(*People v. White*, 345 N.Y.S.2d 513 (1973)). A guilty plea should not be accepted if the defendant claims innocence or denies knowledge of the crime (*People v. Leite*, 383 N.Y.S.2d 71 (1976)).

The Meaning of Lesser Included Offense for Plea Purposes (220.20)

A **lesser included offense** is defined in 1.20/37, in essence, as an offense, the definition of which is necessarily included in the definition of another offense. This definition comes into play after trial. It prevents a finding of guilt for a lesser offense which has an element different from those contained in the greater offense for which indicted; and, it precludes a finding of guilt for the lesser included offense based upon the conduct of the defendant in committing the alleged greater offense due to this differing element. However, where the defendant does not contest his guilt and desires to plead guilty, a much broader, more flexible view of lesser included offense, as set forth in this section, is utilized solely for the purpose of facilitating a plea bargained guilty plea. Therefore, when a defendant seeks to plead guilty to an offense of a lesser grade than that charged in the indictment, he may plead to a lesser included offense as set forth in 1.20/37 or pursuant to any of the following:

a. Culpable mental state: the defendant may plead guilty to an offense requiring a lesser state of mental culpability than the offense charged, i.e., intentional to reckless to criminally negligent behavior;

b. Anticipatory offenses: where the allegations of a count consist in whole or in part of solicitation, conspiracy, or facilitation, such anticipatory offenses may be deemed to constitute a lesser included offense;

c. Harassment: where the offense charged is assault or menacing, harassment is a lesser included offense;

d. Felony murder: if the offense charged constitutes felony murder, the underlying felony may be a lesser included offense;

e. Narcotic offenses: for a charge of criminal sale of a controlled substance any lesser offense of sale or possession; or, if the charge is criminal possession, any lesser charge of criminal possession, may be a lesser included offense;

f. Hazardous wastes: where the charge is unlawful possession or disposal of hazardous wastes under the environmental conservation law, some lesser offenses of unlawful possession or disposal may be lesser offenses;

One of the principles behind the doctrine of lesser included offenses is that a defendant should not be convicted and punished more than once for conduct which, though constituting only one prohibited act, may, because of statutory definition, be theorized as constituting separate criminal acts (*People v. Perez*, 45 N.Y.2d 204 (1978)).

Plea of Guilty to Part of an Indictment; or Covering Other Indictments (220.30)

A plea of guilty to part of an indictment disposes of the entire indictment. A plea of guilty may also be conditioned so as to dispose of another indictment pending against the defendant with the consent of the court and the people. If such other indictment is pending in a different court it shall not be so disposed of without the written permission of that court and the appropriate district attorney. The restrictions on plea bargaining set forth in 220.10/5 are carried over to this section relating to pleas conditioned to dispose of other indictments as well.

Hearing on Predicate Felony Conviction (220.35)

One of the restrictions on plea bargaining bars a defendant previously convicted of a violent felony offense from pleading guilty to a misdemeanor in satisfaction of a subsequent felony offense (220.10.5b). If there is any uncertainty relative to the applicability of the previous conviction, the court may hold a hearing to resolve the uncertainty.

Plea of Not Responsible Due to Mental Disease or Defect (220.15)

The plea of not responsible due to mental disease or defect is neither a plea of guilt nor innocence but a special pleading maintaining the defendant should not be punished criminally because at the time he committed the offense, as a result of mental disease or defect, he lacked substantial capacity to know or appreciate the nature of his act or that the act was wrong (40.15 PL). This plea may be allowed with the consent of the court and the people. The statute sets forth detailed requirements of the parties and the court which must be followed in order to assure the rights of the public and defendant as well are protected.

Counsel for the defendant must state the following:

a. In his opinion the defendant has the capacity to understand the proceedings and the consequences of the plea and is able to assist in his defense;

b. Whether there is any viable defense to the charge other than the affirmative defense of mental disease or defect;

c. In detail, the psychiatric evidence of the defendant relative to that affirmative defense.

The defendant instead of using the plea of mental disease or defect may use the affirmative defense of mental disease or defect and go to trial bearing the burden of proof of that defense by a preponderance of the evidence. If he does not prevail, a finding of guilty as charged in the indictment would follow and the defendant would be punished criminally; on the other hand, should he prevail and be found not responsible due to mental disease or defect, he would not be set free but committed to a mental hospital for further proceedings (*see* 40.15 PL and 330.20 CPL). If allowed to utilize this plea, the defendant will spend some time committed to a mental hospital until such time as the doctors determine he is cured of his mental illness or is no longer a threat to others. Generally speaking, the defendant upon adjudication by verdict or plea of mental disease or defect could possibly remain at least under conditional release for the remainder of his life (*see* 330.20).

The district attorney must put on the record his consent to such plea and state:

a. he is satisfied the defendant would prove the affirmative defense of mental disease or defect if they went to trial;

b. in detail, the people's evidence supporting the charge, including all psychiatric evidence known to him and the reasons for consenting to the plea.

The court, before accepting such plea must address the defendant in open court and determine that he understands each of the following:

a. The nature of the charge and the consequences of such plea;

b. His right to plead not guilty, to a jury trial, the assistance of counsel, to confront and cross examine witnesses against him and the right not to be compelled to incriminate himself;

c. If he pleads mental disease or defect he waives his right to a trial, and his right against self-incrimination as to mental disease or defect and that such plea is the equivalent of a verdict of not responsible due to mental disease or defect after trial.

The court shall not accept such a plea without first determining there is a factual basis for it, and addressing the defendant in open court to determine:

a. that the plea is voluntary and knowing and not the result of force, threats or promises; and,

b. satisfactorily, that the defendant understands the proceedings, can assist in his own defense and understands the consequences of such a plea.

The court may hold a hearing or conduct an inquiry as it deems necessary to make such determinations or to determine whether or not to accept such plea.

Before accepting such plea the court must, in detail, put on the record that it is satisfied:

    a. each element of the crime charged in the indictment would be established beyond a reasonable doubt at a trial;

    b. the affirmative offense of mental disease or defect would be proven by the defendant at trial;

    c. the defendant can understand the proceedings and assist in his own defense;

    d. that such plea is knowing and voluntary and has a factual basis; and,

    e. the acceptance of such plea is required in the interest of justice.

When such plea is accepted by the court the provisions of 330.20 shall govern all subsequent proceedings against the defendant. If it subsequently be found such plea was fraudulently induced by the defendant the acceptance of such plea may be set aside, the indictment reinstated and the defendant proceeded against without running afoul of double jeopardy (*Lockett v. Juviler*, 65 N.Y.2d 182 (1985)).

Change of Plea (220.60)

A defendant may withdraw a not guilty plea any time before the verdict; and,

    a. as a matter of right, enter a plea of guilty to the entire indictment; or,

    b. with the consent of the court and prosecutor, enter a plea of guilty to less than the entire indictment or the plea of not responsible due to mental disease or defect.

A defendant may, with the court's discretion, withdraw a plea of guilty or not responsible due to mental disease or defect any time before the imposition of sentence and in such event the entire indictment will be restored. The decision to allow a defendant to withdraw his guilty plea rests within the trial court's discretion (*People v. Kelsch*, 466 N.Y.S.2d 535 (1983)). Where no valid ground for withdrawal of the guilty plea was asserted or found in the record, the trial court was justified in concluding the defendant's motion was a delaying tactic and no substantial basis existed for the withdrawal (*People v. Luke UU*, 472 N.Y.S.2d 782 (1984)). The motion to withdraw the guilty plea or that of mental disease or defect must be supported by a showing the defendant was deprived of some right in conjunction with the entering of the plea.

See Illustrative Cases

People v. Selikoff, 35 N.Y.2d 227 (1974), p. 357
People v. Allen, 86 N.Y.2d 599 (1995), p. 359
People v. Harris, 61 N.Y.2d 9 (1983), p. 361

8.2 Removal of the Action (Article 230)

The defendant and the people have the right to a trial before an unbiased jury and judge. If either party is of the opinion that this is not possible in the court and or county in which the trial is to be held that party may move for a "change of venue" or, in lay terms, a change in the place where the trial should be held. The initial motion by the defendant, if the grounds supporting the motion are believed to be present, must be made as a part of the defendant's omnibus pre-trial motion as set forth in 255.20. If the defendant is able to satisfy the court as to the existence of the grounds, the motion may be granted. It is extremely difficult to prove the existence of the grounds prior to getting to the *voir dire* proceedings and in most cases the motion will be denied. At this point the provisions of 230.20/2 come into play. The problem is usually that publicity or notoriety will make it impossible to seat an unbiased jury.

This section provides that at any time during the period specified in 255.20 (within 45 days of arraignment or securance of counsel, ordinarily), on motion of either party, demonstrating reasonable cause to believe that a fair and impartial trial cannot be had in such county, the appellate division of the department embracing the county in which the superior court is located may order either:

a. the indictment and action be removed to a designated superior court in another county; or,

b. jurors be brought in from another county to expand the pool of jurors in order to cure the taint.

If the defendant is in custody and the venue is changed, arrangements must be included in the order to transfer the defendant to the custody of the sheriff or other authorized custodial official in the county to which the case has been removed. If the order is issued upon motion of the people, the appellate division may impose such conditions as it deems equitable and appropriate to insure that the defendant is not subject to an unreasonable burden in making his defense. The burden of proving the grounds for removal varies depending upon the movant. A defendant in order to obtain a change of venue must submit clear evidence that he cannot obtain a fair trial by reason of bias, passion and prejudice against him in the community. The state carries a heavier burden in attempting to subject a defendant to the onus of trial in a distant court and to defeat his declared right of trial in the county where the indictment was found, and such right is not to be lightly disregarded. Only the most compelling reason will justify trial by jury not drawn from the vicinage (*People v. Grennan*, 134 N.Y.S.2d 676 (1954)). The mere existence of widespread comment or belief in the guilt of the accused does not prevent the accused from obtaining a fair trial, unless there exists, in addition, a real prejudice in the community which may warp the judgment of those surrounded by such prejudice; but, where such real prejudice exists, a change of place of trial will be granted (*People v. Hyde*, 133 N.Y.S. 306 (1912)). To entitle a defendant to removal of a criminal action to another county because of pre-trial publicity, or for any other reason, it must appear that he cannot obtain a fair and impartial trial in the court where the indictment is pending (*People v. DiPiazza*, 24 N.Y.2d 342 (1969)). The difficulty in obtaining pre-voir dire removal is illustrated by *People v. Boudin*, 457 N.Y.S.2d 302 (1982)) in which the court stated that in seeking pre-voir dire change of venue, the defendant must show that her case is extraordinary, and pre-trial publicity, even if pervasive and concentrated, does not necessarily lead to an unfair trial warranting change of venue.

Newspaper comment alone, even though extensive, does not establish an inability to get a fair trial in the county so as to justify a change in venue (*People v. Broady*, 90 N.Y.S.2d 864 (1949)). Publicity attending a murder case did not entitle the defendant to a change of venue since more than half of the potential jurors questioned expressed ability to fairly judge the defendant based upon the evidence in the case despite any prior knowledge they may have had of the case, although a substantial number of potential jurors had been disqualified because they had formed an opinion based upon prior knowledge (*People v. Ryan*, 542 N.Y.S.2d 665 (1989)). On the other hand, where defendants under indictment for crimes committed during a riot at Auburn Prison, Cayuga County, moved for change of venue on reasons of the size of Cayuga County, publicity attendant on the alleged riot and the economic importance of the prison in the community, the motion was granted and the venue was changed (*People v. Lewis*, 322 N.Y.S.2d 833 (1971)). Where defendant seeks transfer of a trial to another county because of local prejudice, he must show that the hostility and prejudice are so deep that there is an unconscious bias in the minds of potential jurors rather than widespread unfavorable opinion (*People v. Sollazzo*, 106 N.Y.S.2d 600 (1951)).

The moving party may also, for good cause, ask for a stay in the trial pending determination of the motion. Such stay is not to exceed 30 days; and, application for the stay may only be made once. If denied the party may not make it to another justice (230.30).

Upon removal of the indictment to another court, previous rulings and determinations by the original court are not rendered invalid and all subsequent rulings are to be made by the court to which the action was removed (230.40). If the grounds are judicial bias and the movant seeks to have a different judge for the action, the motion should be directed to the trial judge, and if there is a showing of judicial bias, a different judge can be assigned administratively (*People v. Blake*, 520 N.Y.S.2d 92 (1987)).

8.3 Discovery (Article 245)

Discovery is a procedural device designed to take the element of surprise out of criminal actions. Surprise witnesses and the introduction of unexpected evidence at trial makes for entertaining drama in works of fiction depicting criminal trials. In reality, however, courts of law actually try to avoid the element of surprise. Therefore, pre-trial discovery not only helps prevent surprises at trial, it also helps achieve the ever-present objective of judicial economy and the prepotent goals in matters of equity. Discovery helps provide a sense of equity by leveling the playing field, so to speak, between a defendant of limited means, and the people, with seemingly limitless resources. Pre-trial discovery also helps improve efficiency, something that is beneficial for all parties to a criminal action. The fiscal benefits of judicial economy achieved through automatic pre-trial discovery benefits all, including taxpayers. Most importantly, however, efficiencies achieved through pre-trial discovery helps enable better assessment of the case, competent preparation for trial and informed plea negotiations.

New York's legislature recently enacted a completely new discovery statute (Article 245), which is replete with reforms that enhance protections for defendants while increasing prosecutorial accountability. Statutes are, at times, the result of compromise between competing factions of lawmakers with competing interests and goals. Unfortunately, it sometimes takes somewhat vague statutory language to bring compromise to a legislative body by competing visions of reform. Such statutory compromises leave courts with the challenge of interpreting legislative intent. New York's new discovery article, however, is an example of a uniquely clear and precise piece of legislative reform.

This text provides students with the gravamen of key provisions of New York's Criminal Procedure Law in order to gain comprehensive survey of this fascinating and critically important area of criminal justice. It is recommended that the student read at least one unedited section of an article of New York's Criminal Procedure in its entirety for exposure to the nuances and minutiae of criminal procedure statutes. If one chooses the discovery article (245) for this exercise, they will find a uniquely clear and unambiguous example of a statute that leaves little to the imagination of legislative intent. Being that the new discovery article is merely months old as this edition goes to press, time will tell how the courts interpret its legislative intent. Regardless of the outcome of future case law, it is clear that the New York legislature intended to make significant strides in balancing individual liberties and the interests of the state in criminal prosecutions with significant burden shifting reforms.

Article 245 replaced Article 240, which was repealed in its entirety. This legislative reform struck down the defendant's *right to elect* "discovery upon demand," and replaced that mere elective right with an "automatic" privilege to receive (Article 245.20) "initial" pre-trial discovery from the prosecution (Article 245.20(1)). Moreover, prosecutors must also expeditiously produce "initial discovery" material within 15 days of the initiation of a criminal action (245.10(1)(a)). The statute intends near immediate discovery disclosure, and provides a fifteen day outer limit for the production of initial discovery, which tolls from commencement of an action, which, depending upon the type of criminal action, is the defendant's arraignment, information or complaint (Article 245.10(1)(a)). The prosecution may elect to exercise an extension, but they may only do so in limited circumstances discussed in Timing of Discovery, *infra*.

As noted, it is too soon for courts to weigh-in on the new reforms that usher in a new era of discovery with a "presumption of openness" (Article 245.20(7)). Notwithstanding new privileges and provisions of Article 245, it should, like its predecessor (Article 240), be strictly construed and applied in the light of the factual complexities involved in each particular case, with a view to affording a defendant the fair trial mandated by both the state and federal constitutions (*People v. McLoughlin*, 429 N.Y.S.2d 149 (1980)). In like manner, the newly revised article goes even further in reducing the element of surprise frowned upon in *People v. Copicotto* (50 N.Y.2d 222 (1980)), which stated that the legislature determined that a criminal matter should not be a sporting event where each side remains ignorant of facts in the hands of an adversary until events unfold at trial. The court in *Copicotto* further explained that discovery enables a defendant to make a more informed plea decision, minimizes the tactical and often unfair advantage to one side, and increases, to some degree, a more accurate determination of guilt or innocence. In short, pre-trial discovery by and between the defense and prosecution contributes substantially to the fair and effective administration of justice.

Timing of Discovery (245.10)

The prosecutor has a near immediate obligation to meet initial automatic discovery obligations after commencement of an action. The legislature mandates compliance as soon as practicable but no later than 15 days after defendant's arraignment, indictment or information, depending on the venue (Article 245.10(1)(a)). Consistent with the spirit of reform, the prosecution must notify the defendant in writing if any material believed to be non-discoverable is being withheld. The prosecution, however, may elect to grant itself a good faith stay of thirty days, if despite diligent efforts, more time is needed to produce "exceptionally" voluminous materials or obtain materials not their possession (Article 245.10(1)(a)). The defendant must likewise comply with pre-trial discovery obligations within 30 days of being served with the prosecution's certificate of compliance (Article 245.10(2)).

Automatic Discovery (245.20)

The process of discovery begins with the prosecution's automatic production of "initial" discovery material.

1. The Process of Discovery

The prosecution shall disclose to the defendant, and permit the defendant to discover, inspect, copy, photograph and test, all items and information that relate to the subject matter of the case and are in the possession, custody or control of the prosecution or persons under the prosecution's direction or control, including but not limited to:

   a.   All written or recorded statements, and the substance of all oral statements, made by the defendant or a co-defendant to law enforcement personnel or those engaged as their agents;

b. All transcripts of testimony before a grand jury, including but not limited to the defendant or a co-defendant;

c. The names and contact information (*excluding physical addresses unless directed by the court upon good cause shown*) for all persons other than law enforcement personnel known to have evidence or information relevant to any offense charged or to any potential defense thereto, including a designation by the prosecutor as to those persons who may be called as witnesses;

d. The name and work affiliation of all law enforcement personnel (*excluding undercover agents*) whom the prosecutor knows to have evidence or information relevant to any offense charged or to any potential defense thereto, including a designation by the prosecutor as to which of those persons may be called as witnesses;

e. All statements, written or recorded or summarized by persons who have evidence or information relevant to any offense charged or to any potential defense thereto, including all police reports, notes of police and other investigators and law enforcement agency reports (*including witnesses at pre-trial hearings*);

f. Expert opinion evidence, including the name, business address, current curriculum vitae, a list of publications, and all proficiency tests and results administered or taken within the past ten years of each expert witness whom the prosecutor intends to call as a witness at trial or a pre-trial hearing, and all reports prepared by the expert that pertain to the case, or if no report is prepared, all reports prepared by the expert pertaining to the case, or (*if no reports are prepared*) a written statement of the facts and opinions to which the expert is expected to testify and a summary of the grounds for each opinion;

g. All tapes or other electronic recordings, including all electronic recordings of 911 telephone calls made or received in connection with the alleged criminal incident, and a designation by the prosecutor as to which of the recordings the prosecution intends to introduce at trial or a pre-trial hearing;

h. All photographs and drawings made or completed by a public servant engaged in law enforcement activity, or which were made by a person whom the prosecutor intends to call as a witness at trial or a pre-trial hearing, or which relate to the subject matter of the case;

i. All photographs, photocopies and reproductions made by or at the direction of law enforcement personnel of any property prior to its release pursuant to Section 450.10 of the penal law;

j. All reports, documents, records, data, calculations or writings, including but not limited to preliminary tests and screening results and bench notes and analyses performed or stored electronically, concerning physical or mental examinations, or scientific tests or experiments or comparisons, relating to the criminal action or proceeding. Information under this paragraph also includes laboratory information management system records relating to such materials, any findings of nonconformance with accreditation, industry or governmental standards or laboratory protocols, and any conflicting analyses or results by laboratory;

k. All evidence and information, including that which is known to police or other law enforcement agencies acting on the government's behalf in the case, that tends to: (i) negate the defendant's guilt; (ii) reduce the degree of or mitigate culpability; (iii) support a potential defense; (iv) impeach the credibility of a testifying prosecution witness; (v) undermine evidence of the defendant's identity as a perpetrator of a charged offense; (vi) provide a basis for a motion to suppress evidence; or (vii) mitigate punishment. Information under this subdivision shall be disclosed whether or not such information is recorded in tangible form and irrespective of whether the prosecutor credits the information. **The prosecutor shall disclose the information expeditiously upon its receipt and shall not delay disclosure if it is obtained earlier than the time period for disclosure in subdivision one of Section 245.10 of this article;**

l. A summary of all promises, rewards and inducements made to, or in favor of, persons who may be called as witnesses, as well as requests for consideration by persons who may be called as witnesses and copies of all documents relevant to a promise, reward or inducement;

m. A list of all objects obtained from, or allegedly possessed by, the defendant or a co-defendant including those objects allegedly possessed by the defendant and recovered during a search or seizure, or after allegedly being abandoned by the defendant;

n. Supporting documents related for search warrants, transcripts of testimony and oral communications in support of the warrant application, and an inventory of property seized from the warrant;

o. All tangible property that relates to the subject matter of the case, along with a designation of which items the prosecution intends to introduce in its case-in-chief at trial or a pre-trial hearing (along with a continuing duty to provide written updates);

p. A complete record of judgments of conviction for all defendants and all persons designated as potential prosecution witnesses pursuant to paragraph (c) of this subdivision, other than those witnesses who are experts;

q. When it is known to the prosecution, the existence of any pending criminal action against all persons designated as potential prosecution witnesses pursuant to paragraph (c) of this subdivision;

r. The approximate date, time and place of the offense or offenses charged and of the defendant's seizure and arrest;

s. In alleged violations of the vehicle and traffic law subject to this article, all records of calibration, certification, inspection, repair or maintenance of machines and instruments utilized to perform any scientific tests and experiments, including but not limited to any test of a person's breath, blood, urine or saliva, for the period of six months prior and six months after such test was conducted, all reference standards and the certification certificate, if any, held by the operator of the machine or instrument;

t. (*et seq.* for crimes involving computers).

Brady v. Maryland, 373 U.S. 83 (1963), identified the constitutional right of defendants to be apprised of exculpatory evidence known to the prosecutor, i.e., evidence which is favorable to the defendant. All states must recognize the minimum rights afforded by the U.S. Constitution. However, the states may see fit to grant rights above and beyond the minimum rights guaranteed by the U.S. Constitution. There is much litigation in this area, and recent reforms in New York promises to usher in a new chapter of litigation to settle challenges that will arise as result of these reforms.

Before the discovery reforms in Article 245, New York case law recognized that the People have a duty to disclose exculpatory material under their control, including evidence material to the defense, which would have in all likelihood affected the judgment of the jury (*People v. McMullen*, 461 N.Y.S.2d 565 (1983)). In like manner, the Rosario rule (*People v. Rosario*, 9 N.Y.2d 286 (1961)), which is codified in § 245 is to ensure that the defense is given the benefit of any information that can legitimately tend to overthrow the case made for the prosecution or to show that it is unworthy of belief (*People v. Johnson*, 608 N.Y.S. 2d 995 (1994)). Moreover, it was not for the district attorney's office to unilaterally speculate as to what evidence would be useful to the defendant as potentially exculpatory material (*People v. Davis*, 432 N.Y.S.2d 350 (1980)). Historically, courts recognized that there should be some deference to the prosecutor's discretion in determining which evidence must be turned over to the defense, which may be challenged before the trial court (*People v. Jones*, 448 N.Y.S.2d 543 (1982)). The question begged is, to what degree, if any, will courts follow these cases in light of the discovery reforms.

For instance, it is clear that Article 245 disturbs the holding (*Metts v. Miller*, 995 F. Sup. 283 (1997)) (Article 245) which recognized that the prosecutor has no duty to disclose a prospective witness's name or address prior to trial absent a court order. Prior to the reforms, there was neither constitutional nor statutory obligation mandating pre-trial disclosure of the identity of prosecution witnesses; to be entitled to such disclosure, the defendant must first demonstrate material need for such information and the reasonableness of such request (*People v. Miller*, 484 N.Y.S.2d 183 (1984)). The plain language of legislative reforms contained in the "initial," "automatic discovery" provisions found in Article 245.20(1)(c) takes the process in a new, more transparent, direction. Now the prosecution must disclose, "the names and adequate contact information," of prospective witnesses, excluding those from law enforcement.

Certain aspects of prior case law pertaining to disclosure of witness information from (*Vergari v. Kendall*, 352 N.Y.S.2d 383 (1974)) and (*Metts, supra*) are now in conflict with the intent and plain language of (Article 245) reforms. Consistent with *Vergari* and *Metts*, the legislature continues to limit the release of physical addresses for prospective witnesses, by limiting such disclosure "for good cause shown" (Article

245.20(1)(c)). Although legislative reforms in (Article 245), however, clearly abandon the former presumption of secrecy over witness identity by mandating automatic disclosure of basic or "adequate" contact information (Article 245.20(1)(c)). If challenged, the courts may have to settle questions over the meaning of "adequate" contact information in order to determine whether it includes e-mail addresses and cell phone numbers.

Another reform appears to reverse course on discovery of **internal** police notes. Prior to Article 245 there was no requirement to make internal notes or memoranda made by police available for pre-trial discovery, unless exculpatory matter is contained therein or the prosecutor intends to introduce same at trial (*People v. Finkle*, 427 N.Y.S.2d 374 (1980)). Automatic discovery, however, now includes "all police reports, notes of police and other investigators, and law enforcement agency reports," (Article 245.20(1)(e)).

2. Duties of the Prosecution

Discovery reforms now place an affirmative duty on the prosecution to "make a diligent, good faith effort to ascertain," material and information subject to discovery (Article 245.20(2)). The prosecution is not, however, responsible for doing work on behalf of the defense that the defense could otherwise do. "[T]he the prosecutor shall not be required to obtain by subpoena duces tecum material or information which the defendant may thereby obtain," although all that is "in the possession of any New York state or local police or law enforcement agency shall be deemed to be in the possession of the prosecution" (Article 245.20(2)).

3. Supplemental Discovery for Defendant

The prosecution now, must also disclose a list of prior bad acts not charged in the instant case, intended for impeachment of defendant at trial, in the event defendant testifies.

4. Reciprocal Discovery for the Prosecution

The defense also bears the burden of the reciprocal automatic discovery reforms. They include:

(a) All that is in defendant's possession deemed discoverable under paragraphs (f), (g), (h), (j), (l) and (o) of subdivision one of this subsection, which defendant intends to introduce at trial or a pretrial hearing. In addition, The defendant must also provide detailed contact information, along with all written or recorded statements of those whom the defendant intends to call as witnesses at trial or a pre-trial hearing;

(b) Disclosure of the name, address, birth date, and all statements, written or recorded or summarized in any writing or recording, of a person whom the defendant intends to call as a witness for the sole purpose of impeaching a prosecution witness is not required until after the prosecution witness has testified at trial;

(c) The defendant must also exercise due diligence with regard to discovery obligations, and may likewise exercise a stay in good faith without need for a motion. Although, consistent with the prosecutor's duty, disclosure shall be made as soon as practicable and defendant remains subject to the continuing duty to disclose in Section 245.60 of this article.

Disclosure Prior to Certain Guilty Pleas (245.25)

Discovery privileges are not waived or exchanged in lieu of a pre-indictment plea offer from the prosecution. The legislature made sure to limit the likelihood of any gaming of the rules for in the event of pre-indictment plea offers with possible consequences for non-compliance. Therefore, the prosecutor must disclose items and information that would be discoverable prior to trial under subdivision one of Section 245.20 at least 3 days prior to the expiration date of any guilty plea offer by the prosecution or any deadline imposed by the court for acceptance of the guilty plea offer.

See Illustrative Cases

People v. Rosario, 9 N.Y.2d 286 (1961), p. 362
See also, In the Matter of David M. v. Dwyer, 107 A.D.2d 884 (3rd Dept. 1985), p. 364
See also, People v. Wesley, 140 Misc. 2d 306 (Albany Cty Ct. 1988), p. 366

8.4 Pre-Trial Notices of Defenses (Article 250)

There are 4 notices of defenses in Article 250:

1. Notice of intent to use psychiatric evidence (250.10)

2. Notice of alibi (250.20)

3. Notices of defenses involving computer crimes (250.30)

4. Notice of intent to seek the death penalty (250.40)

The purpose of these notice provisions is to prevent surprise to the prosecutor of defense witnesses and evidence. They also reciprocally require the prosecution to timely notify the defense of rebuttal witnesses and evidence the prosecutor intends to utilize.

Notice of Intent to Use Psychiatric Evidence (250.10)

As used in this section psychiatric evidence means:

a. Evidence of mental disease or defect offered in furtherance of defendant's **affirmative defense** claiming lack of criminal responsibility by reason of mental disease or defect;

    b.   Evidence of mental disease or defect in furtherance of the **affirmative defense** of extreme emotional disturbance as defined in (PL 125.25(a) & 125.27);

    c.   Evidence of mental disease or defect in furtherance of any other defense.

Defense Examination. Psychiatric evidence is not admissible at trial unless the defendant serves upon the people and files with the court a written notice of her intention to present psychiatric evidence, before trial and not more than thirty days after entry of the plea of not guilty. However, an exception that may be granted by the court for good cause shown, at any later time prior to the close of the evidence.

State's Examination. The district attorney may apply for an order directing that the defendant submit to an examination by a psychiatrist or licensed psychologist designated by the district attorney. Defense counsel and the district attorney may be present; however, the role of each counsel at such examination is that of an observer, and neither counsel shall be permitted to take an active role at the examination.

After the conclusion of the examination, the psychiatrist or psychologist must promptly prepare a written report of his findings and evaluation. A copy of such report must be made available to the district attorney and to the counsel for the defendant. No transcript or recording of the examination is required, but if one is made, it shall be made available to both parties prior to the trial.

If the defendant willfully refused to cooperate fully with the **state's examination**, the court may preclude testimony and evidence pursuant to the **defense examination** at trail. However, other evidence in furtherance of defendant's affirmative defense shall be permissible, if otherwise competent. In such case, the court must instruct the jury that the defendant did not submit to or cooperate fully in the **state's pre-trial psychiatric examination** ordered by the state and that such failure may be considered in determining the merits of the affirmative defense.

This notice requirement applies to any defense which the defendant intends to prove through the testimony of a psychiatrist or licensed psychologist (*People v. Berk*, 88 N.Y.2d 257 (1996)). Examples include the "fight or flight syndrome" (*People v. Berk*, ibid), "battered woman's syndrome" (*People v. Herrera*, 631 N.Y.S.2d 660 (1995)), or "torture syndrome" (*People v. Tumerman*, 519 N.Y.S.2d 880 (1987)). The statute requiring the defendant to give notice of his intent to introduce psychiatric evidence was designed to allow the prosecution the opportunity to acquire relevant information from any source to counter the defense of mental infirmity, to promote fairness and to avoid delay at trial. Whether to allow the filing of a late notice of intent to file psychiatric evidence is within the discretion of the trial judge, but his discretion is not absolute. The exclusion of relevant and probative testimony as sanction for the defendant's failure to comply with the statutory notice requirement implicates the defendant's constitutional right to present witnesses in his own defense. The trial court must weigh this right against the resultant prejudice to the people's case caused by a belated notice (*People v. Berk*, *supra*).

Notice of Alibi (250.20)

An **alibi** is a defense that at the time of the commission of the offense charged the defendant was at some place other than the scene of the crime and therefore could not have committed it. The purpose of the notice of alibi provision is to afford the prosecutor an opportunity to fairly investigate the merits of the alibi, for an alibi is one defense which is easy to manufacture (*People v. Ruiz*, 419 N.Y.S.2d 864 (1979)).

Within 20 days after the arraignment, the people may serve a demand upon the defendant, that if the defendant intends to use an alibi defense, he must, within 8 days of receipt of such demand, serve upon the people a "notice of alibi" stating:

a. the place or places the defendant claims to have been at the time of the commission of the crime; and,

b. the names and addresses and places of employment and addresses thereof of every witness he intends to call to testify to the alibi defense.

At least 10 days before trial the people must give the defendant a list of the witnesses, including their names, addresses, places of employment and addresses thereof, the people intend to call to rebut the testimony of the defendants alibi witnesses. A witness who will testify that the defendant was at the scene of the crime is not considered to be a rebuttal alibi witness. The rebuttal witness must be someone who will testify the defendant was not at the place he claims to have been in his alibi notice. Where a defendant offers an alibi defense, the people may not in rebuttal offer evidence which only indirectly contradicts the alibi by placing the defendant at the scene of the crime, but the people may directly contradict the alibi with the rebuttal testimony that the defendant was not where he claims to have been (*People v. Baylis*, 347 N.Y.S.2d 892 (1973)). Any evidence which places the defendant at the scene of the crime should be presented as part of the people's direct case and not held for rebuttal of expected alibi testimony (*People v. Guthman*, 348 N.Y.S.2d 109 (1973)).

The court, for good cause shown, may extend the time periods specified in the above sections. If at trial, the defendant attempts to call an alibi witness or the prosecutor a rebuttal witness, without having complied with the notice provisions, the court may exclude any testimony of such witness relating to the alibi defense; but, the court may in its discretion receive such testimony after granting an adjournment of up to three days to the adverse party to allow time to investigate the alibi or rebuttal. Both the defendant and prosecutor are under a continuing duty to disclose additional alibi or rebuttal witnesses which come to their attention subsequent to their submission of their original list of such witnesses.

Notice of Computer Defenses (250.30)

Article 156 P.L. makes the unauthorized use of a computer, or the duplication of or tampering with computer data or programs, a criminal offense. It also contains defenses to each of the above acts if authorization had been given the defendant to use, alter or otherwise do something to or with computer data or programs.

In a prosecution for Article 156 computer offenses, if the defendant seeks to invoke any of the defenses specified in Article 156.50, the defendant must, within 45 days of arraignment and at least 20 days before trial serve written notice upon the people of the intention to use such a defense or defenses.

The notice must specify:

a.   the subdivision or subdivisions upon which the defendant relies on, and,

b.   state the reasonable grounds that led the defendant to believe that he had the authorization required by the statute, or the right required thereby, to engage in such conduct.

The court may exclude any testimony or evidence in regard to such defense if defendant failed to provide required notice. However, the court may, in its discretion, for good cause shown, allow such defense but before doing so, upon application of the people, grant an adjournment.

Notice of Intent to Seek the Death Penalty [Life Sentence] (250.40)

New York's highest court held that the death penalty statute, as written, fails to satisfy protections afforded by the state's constitution (*People v. LaValle*, 3 N.Y.3d 88 (2004); *People v Taylor*, 9 N.Y.3d 129 (2007)). Therefore, the death penalty is struck down for the time being, and there does not appear to be any appetite to revise the statute in an attempt to restore the death penalty. The statute, however, remains relevant to the extent that it is the statutory source for a lifetime sentence, which remains a lawful sentencing option.

8.5 Pre-Trial Motions (Article 255)

A "pre-trial motion" as used in this article means any motion by a defendant which seeks an order of the court:

a.   dismissing or reducing an indictment pursuant to Article 210 or removing an action to the family court pursuant to Article 722;

b.   dismissing an information, prosecutor's information, simplified information or misdemeanor complaint pursuant to Article 170;

c.   granting discovery pursuant to Article 245;

d.   granting a bill of particulars pursuant to Sections 100.45 or 200.90;

e.   removing the action pursuant to Sections 170.15, 230.20 or 230.30;

f.   suppressing evidence pursuant to Article 710;

g.   granting separate trials pursuant to Article 100 or 200.

Section 255.20 sets forth the following procedures for pre-trial motions:

Except as otherwise provided, all pre-trial motions shall be made before commencement of trial, within 45 days of arraignment, or within such additional time as the court may fix upon application of the defendant made prior to entry of judgment. In an action in which either (a) material or information has been disclosed pursuant to paragraph (m) or (n) of subdivision one of Section 245.20 of this title, (b) an eavesdropping warrant and application have been furnished pursuant to Section 700.70 of this chapter, or (c) a notice of intention to introduce evidence has been served pursuant to Section 710.30 of this chapter, such period shall be extended until forty-five days after the last date of such service. If the defendant is not represented by counsel and has requested an adjournment to obtain counsel, or to have counsel assigned, such forty-five day period shall commence on the date counsel initially appears on defendant's behalf.

All pre-trial motions, including supporting materials, shall be included within the same set of motion papers and made returnable on the same date, unless:

a.   the defendant shows it would be prejudicial to the defense for a single judge to decide all the pre-trial motions; or,

b.   one motion seeks to provide the basis for another motion, it shall be deemed impracticable to include both in the same set of motion papers.

Notwithstanding the aforementioned, the court must entertain any pre-trial motions before the end of trial, defendant could not have been aware with due diligence, or for other good cause shown, could not have been raised within the aforementioned period. Any other pre-trial motion made after the requisite 45 day period may be summarily denied, but the court, in the interest of justice, and for good cause shown, may, in its discretion, at any time before sentence, entertain and dispose of the motion on its merits.

The court may refer any pre-trial motion to a judicial hearing officer. In the discharge of this responsibility, the judicial hearing officer shall have the same powers as a judge of the court making the assignment, except that the judicial hearing officer shall not determine the motion but shall file a report with the court setting forth findings of fact and conclusions of law. The rules of evidence shall be applicable at any hearing conducted hereunder by a judicial hearing officer. A transcript of any testimony taken, together with the exhibits or copies thereof, shall be filed with the report. The court shall determine the motion on the motion papers, affidavits and other documents submitted by the parties thereto, the record of the hearing before the judicial hearing officer, and the judicial hearing officer's report.

The pre-trial motion rulings become the rule of the case and it must proceed in accordance therewith (*People v. Brensic*, 460 N.Y.S.2d 979 (1983)). It must be remembered that not all motions made before the trial commences are "pre-trial motions" under Article 255. For instance, Sandoval motions (use of prior convictions for impeachment purposes) are not "pre-trial motions" under 255 (*People v. Innis*, 470 N.Y.S.2d 26 (1983)). Moreover, in exercising its discretion to decide an untimely motion the court should rarely allow and decide the motion with respect to matters which go neither to fairness or the accuracy of the truth finding process or the jurisdiction of the court (*People v. Frigenti*, 397 N.Y.S.2d 313 (1977)).

Good cause for delay has been found by the courts to exist, for example, in light of confusion surrounding defendant's obtaining counsel and the fact that problems with the evidence did not become widely known until more than a year after arraignment (*People v. Colon*, 580 N.Y.S.2d 95 (1992)) and the delay occasioned by voluminous discovery material provided by the people and the long period of time taken to dispose of other preliminary motions (*People v. Melillo*, 448 N.Y.S.2d 108 (1982)). The bottom line is, despite the failure of the defendant to make timely motion, the defendant may be entitled to relief when the consequences affect the accuracy and fairness of the truth finding process of the trial (*People v. Coleman*, 452 N.Y.S.2d 503 (1982)).

See Illustrative Cases

People v. Coleman, 452 N.Y.S.2d 503 (1982), p. 368

Chapter 9

Prosecution of Indictments in Superior Court: From Trial to Sentence

Sec. **9.1** Article 260; Jury Trial—Generally
Sec. **9.2** Article 270; Jury Trial—Formation and Conduct of Jury
Sec. **9.3** Article 280; Jury Trial—Motion for a Mistrial
Sec. **9.4** Article 290; Jury Trial—Trial Order of Dismissal
Sec. **9.5** Article 300; Jury Trial—Court's Charge and Instructions to Jury
Sec. **9.6** Article 310; Jury Trial—Deliberation and Verdict of Jury
Sec. **9.7** Article 320; Waiver of Jury Trial and Conduct of Non-Jury Trial
Sec. **9.8** Article 330; Proceedings from Verdict to Sentence

9.1 The Jury Trial—Generally (Article 260)

Generally (260.10)

A defendant is entitled to a jury trial of an indictment unless said defendant validly waives the right to a jury trial (260.10). This codifies the N.Y.S. constitutional requirement that crimes prosecuted by indictment must be tried by a jury of 12 persons unless a jury trial is waived (N.Y.S. Const., art. VI, sec. 18a). The defendant may at any time before trial, waive the right to a jury trial in the superior court in which the action is pending (320.10/1).

The jury trial commences with the selection and swearing in of the jury and ends with the verdict (1.20/11). The role of the judge at a jury trial is to decide questions of law that arise while the jury's role is to answer questions of fact on the basis of evidence presented at the trial. The judge's duties also include matters such as keeping the proceedings within the reasonable confines of the issues (*People v. Moulton*, 43 N.Y.2d 944 (1978)); controlling the proceedings to insure a fair trial (*People v. Lozado*, 394 N.Y.S.2d 460 (1977)); and enforcing propriety, orderliness, decorum and expedition of the trial (*People v. DeJesus*, 399 N.Y.S.2d 196 (1977)). Although it is the trial judge's prerogative to take an active role in the proceedings in the interest of the effective and orderly administration of justice, an excessive intrusion on the part of a trial judge into the conduct of the trial may constitute grounds for reversal of the decision in the case (*People v. Melero*, 433 N.Y.S.2d 859 (1980)).

Presence of Defendant at Trial (260.20)

A defendant must be personally present during the trial of an indictment, unless:

a. the defendant conducts himself in so disorderly and disruptive a manner that the trial cannot be carried out with him in the courtroom; and,

b. after the court has warned him that he will be removed from the courtroom, if he continues such conduct; and,

c. he continues to engage in such conduct;

d. he may be removed from the courtroom (260.20).

The defendant's right to be present at her trial is encompassed within the confrontation clauses of the N.Y.S. (art.1, sec. 6) and U.S. (amend. 6) Constitutions (*People v. Trendell*, 61 N.Y.2d 728 (1984)). Due process also requires the defendant to be personally present at his trial to the extent that a fair and just trial would be thwarted by his absence (*People v. Mullen*, 44 N.Y.2d 1 (1978)). The statute's purposes (260.20) are twofold: to prevent the ancient evil of secret trials and to guarantee the defendant's right to be present at all important stages of her trial (*People v. Huggler*, 378 N.Y.S.2d 493 (1976)). The statute also insures that the defendant's right to be present at trial includes all proceedings in impaneling the jury, receiving evidence, the summations of counsel, the court's charge and admonitions to the jury and the verdict (*People v. Ciaccio*, 47 N.Y.2d 431 (1979)).

Trial includes not only the core proceedings such as the taking of testimony, but also a myriad of ancillary proceedings (*People v. Sprowal*, 84 N.Y.2d 113 (1994)), such as pre-trial hearings on motions to suppress evidence (*People v. Huggler*, 378 N.Y.S.2d 493 (1979)); pre-trial conferences, e.g., Sandoval hearing in judge's chambers re: admissibility of previous convictions for impeachment purposes by the prosecutor (*People v. Dokes*, 79 N.Y.2d 656 (1992)); and, sidebar questioning, e.g., of prospective jurors on matters of bias or prejudice (*People v. Vargas*, 88 N.Y.2d 363 (1996)).

Waiver of the Right to Be Present at Trial

The defendant may waive her right to be present at her trial by direct words or by her absence under specified circumstances. The defendant's right to be present at her trial may be waived, but the waiver must be voluntary, intelligent and knowing and the court must assure itself of the validity of the waiver before proceeding in the defendant's absence (*People v. Manzi*, 558 N.Y.S.2d 337 (1990)). For example, a defendant voluntarily and knowingly waives his right to be present at trial where, being fully advised of his rights and the fact that the trial could proceed without him, he informs his assigned counsel and the court that he does not wish to remain in the courtroom and that the trial should proceed in his absence (*People v. Johnson*, 357 N.Y.S.2d 892 (1974)). A defendant who was informed of his right to be present at his trial and of the consequences of failing to appear for trial forfeited his right to be present at trial by voluntarily absconding following assignment of the case for trial (*People v. Marcano*, 511 N.Y.S.2d 684 (1987)).

However, even assuming a valid waiver of the defendant's right to be present at trial, a trial in absentia is not automatically authorized, but requires a careful balancing of pertinent factors including the possibility that the defendant could be located within a reasonable period of time, the difficulty of rescheduling the trial and the chance that evidence will be lost or witnesses will disappear (*People v. Thompson*, 463 N.Y.S.2d 650 (1983)). Where there was no indication that the defendant was advised that, in his absence, the trial would proceed without him, no indication of any implied waiver of his right to be present at his trial, and no indication that the defendant was ever informed of the consequences of his failure to appear at trial, it was improper to try the defendant in absentia (*People v. Gilbert*, 466 N.Y.S.2d 750 (1983)). The determination whether a defendant has voluntarily absented himself, and thus knowingly and intelligently waived his right to be personally present at trial. is within the discretion of the trial judge; and, the burden of proving that a voluntary absence constitutes a waiver of the defendant's right to be present at trial is on the prosecution (*Whitley v. Cioffi*, 427 N.Y.S.2d 23 (1980)).

Disruptive Conduct

The statute provides for the removal of the defendant from the courtroom based upon disruptive conduct. The defendant's right to be present at every stage of his trial is deemed waived when he engages in misconduct so disruptive that the trial cannot properly proceed with him present (*People v. Byrnes*, 33 N.Y.2d 343 (1974)). A trial court may properly exclude a defendant from the courtroom during his trial, where he is disruptive, engages in outbursts and is admonished by the court that further outbursts would be cause for removal (ibid). If it is necessary to remove the defendant from the courtroom, provision should be made for a communication hookup (closed circuit television where possible) for the defendant to remain in contact with counsel (ibid). A disruptive defendant may also be restrained by handcuffs or shackles (ibid) or gagged (*People v. Palermo*, 32 N.Y.2d 222 (1973)). The Court of Appeals in Palermo held that the trial court did not abuse its discretion in restoring order to the courtroom by gagging the defendant, where the defendant was warned he would be gagged if he continued his outbursts, the gag was used for no more than a few minutes and the gag was removed upon the defendant's concession to observe reasonable and responsible court procedures. While it is within the discretion of the court to exercise control over the defendant in the courtroom, the power is not absolute. There should be a rational, justifiable reason for taking the extreme measures of removal or otherwise restraining the defendant.

The Steps in a Jury Trial (260.30)

The order of a jury trial, in general, is as follows:

1. The jury must be selected and sworn.
2. The court must deliver preliminary instructions to the jury.
3. The people must deliver an opening address to the jury.

4. The defendant may deliver an opening address to the jury.

5. The people must offer evidence in support of the indictment.

6. The defendant may offer evidence in her defense.

7. The people and then the defendant may offer rebuttal and surrebuttal evidence.

8. At the conclusion of the evidence, the defendant may deliver a summation to the jury.

9. The people may then deliver a summation to the jury.

10. The court must then deliver a charge to the jury.

11. The jury must then retire to deliberate and, if possible, render a verdict.

It is well established that the order of trial prescribed should be followed unless a compelling reason exists for a variation (*People v. Theriault*, 428 N.Y.S.2d 365 (1980)). Those parts of the trial preceded by the word "must" are mandatory and must be carried out in the trial. Those that are proceeded by "may" are not. Notice the defendant is not mandatorily required to do anything at her trial. The court has the power, however, in its discretion, to alter the order of proof in the furtherance of justice (*People v. Olsen*, 34 N.Y.2d 349 (1974)).

The prosecutor's opening statement generally should set forth the nature of the charge against the defendant, the facts he intends to prove and the evidence he intends to introduce in support of the facts and charge (*People v. Kurtz*, 51 N.Y.2d 380 (1980)). During summation it is the right of counsel to comment upon every pertinent fact bearing upon the issues the jury must decide; however, the summation is not an unabridged rhetorical debate, and the final arguments to the jury of both sides must stay within the confines of the evidence in the case (*People v. Brewer*, 463, N.Y.S.2d 297 (1983)). At the close of the case the court must, in its charge to the jury, instruct the jurors on all the law applicable to the case and it should not assume the jury recalls and remembers all the instructions given them in the court's preliminary instructions (*People v. Cardinale*, 316 N.Y.S.2d 369 (1970)).

See Illustrative Cases

People v. Morales, 80 N.Y.2d 450 (1992), p. 371
People v. Antommarchi, 80 N.Y.2d 247 (1992), p. 373
People v. Byrnes, 33 N.Y.2d 343 (1974), p. 374

9.2 The Formation and Conduct of the Jury (Article 270)

Selection of the Jury (270.05 to 270.30)

For a trial of an indictment a trial jury consists of 12 jurors and in addition from 1 to 6 alternate jurors may be chosen depending upon the perceived length of the trial. If the defendant is charged with murder 1st degree (P.L.125.27, for which a life sentence might be imposed), the judge may in his discretion direct as many alternates to be chosen as he deems fit. In such cases if the defendant is found guilty there may be a second phase of the proceeding in order to determine if the death penalty shall be invoked. A second *voir dire* will be held to determine if any juror cannot render an impartial decision as to the death penalty and if so that juror will be replaced by an alternate. If no alternate was available a new jury would be required to be selected for the penalty phase and much of the evidence in the case represented to them so they could determine the appropriate penalty, death or life imprisonment. This would be costly and time consuming, at the least (400.27).

Challenge to the Panel

The jurors are selected from a panel of jurors chosen from the roll of registered voters of the county or from motor vehicle registration records in order to secure a cross section of the population in the formation of the jury. The selection of the panel and of individual jurors is governed by the provisions of the Judiciary Law (sec. 500 et seq.). Before the selection of the jury commences the defendant may challenge the panel, that is, make an objection to the appropriateness of the panel, on the grounds of a significant departure from the provisions of the Judiciary Law in the drawing of the panel so as to result in substantial prejudice to the defendant. The court may hold a hearing in order to determine the issue. The defendant's burden is to show a substantial and identifiable segment of the community was excluded from the panel and that this was the result of a systematic process (*People v. Guzman*, 60 N.Y.2d 403 (1983)). The grounds may be, for example, the systematic exclusion from the panel or underrepresentation of age, economic, gender, race or ethnic groups.

Voir dire

The process of selection of individual jurors from the panel for the makeup of the required 12 person jury and alternates is called "*voir dire*" (to speak the truth). The prospective jurors may be required by the court to fill out a questionnaire relative to their qualifications to serve. Twelve members of the panel are then selected and seated in the jury box and sworn to answer truthfully the questions asked of them relative to their qualifications to serve. The court shall initiate the examination of the jurors by identifying the parties and their counsel and briefly outlining the nature of the case. The court shall then, in turn, examine each individual juror sitting in the jury box as to her qualifications to serve. Each party will then be given a fair opportunity to question the prospective jurors on any unexplored matters; but, the court shall not permit questioning that is repetitious or irrelevant or which relates to the prospective jurors knowledge of the law. The court may then further question the prospective jurors as it deems proper regarding the qualifications of each prospective juror. Upon completion of this examination the parties may challenge (object) to a prospective juror, or jurors, for cause or peremptorily. The jurors excused on the basis of the challenges must leave the jury box and the remainder are sworn as jurors and either remain in the jury box while the process of selection of the additional jurors continues, or, in the discretion of the court, may be removed to another part of the court. The voir dire process will continue as set forth above until all 12 and any alternate jurors deemed appropriate by the court are selected and sworn. The juror first selected must be designated by the court as the foreman.

Challenge for Cause

A challenge for cause is an objection to a prospective juror that may be made only on the ground that:

a.   He does not have the qualifications required by the judiciary law; or,

b.   His state of mind is that he is unlikely to render an impartial verdict based upon the evidence adduced at trial; or,

c.   He is related within the sixth degree of consanguinity or affinity to the defendant, victim, witness or counsel of either party; or was an adverse party in a civil action, or complained against or was accused in a criminal action by any such person; or that he bears some other relationship to any such person that is likely to preclude him from rendering an impartial verdict; or,

d.   He served on the grand jury which found the indictment, or was a witness before it, or at the preliminary hearing, or is to be a witness at the trial, or served as a juror in a previous civil or criminal action involving the same incident as charged in the indictment; or,

e.   There is the possibility of the death penalty in the case and the prospective juror has such conscientious opinions either for or against it that he would not be able to render an impartial verdict.

The court shall decide the challenge and if the challenge is allowed the prospective juror will be excused from service on that jury. Subjective areas of challenge are those related to bias as set forth in b. above. Unless the challenged juror is willing to state unequivocally that her prior knowledge or opinion will not affect her verdict and that she will be able to decide the case solely on the evidence she must be excused from serving. This is known as an expurgatory oath (*People v. Culhane*, 33 N.Y.2d 90 (1973)).

Peremptory Challenges

After the challenges for cause are decided the court will then entertain peremptory challenges. A peremptory challenge is a challenge for which no reason need be given. Upon a peremptory challenge the court must exclude a prospective juror from serving on the jury. The number of peremptory challenges available to a party are limited depending upon the offense with which the defendant is charged:

When two or more defendants are tried jointly, such defendants are treated as a single party and no increase in the number of peremptory challenges is allowed. The people must exercise their peremptory challenges first and then the defendant. The

Number of Peremptory Challenges Allowed Each Party

Highest Crime Charged	For the Regular Jurors	For Alternate Jurors
Class A felony	20	2 for each to be chosen
Class B or C felony	15	2 for each to be chosen
Other felonies	10	2 for each to be chosen

jurors remaining in the jury box after the exercise of the challenges for cause and peremptory challenges are then sworn by the judge and thereafter may only be challenged for cause, based upon new material or actions of the juror which may raise questions as to the jurors qualifications to serve. Although peremptory challenges are those for which no reason need be given, the state and federal constitutions prohibit the exclusion of a prospective juror solely on the factor of race (*People v. Thompson*, 435 N.Y.S.2d 739 (1981) and (*Batson v. Kentucky*, 476 U.S. 79 (1986)). Since the Batson decision there has been much controversy over the appropriateness of peremptory challenges in their entirety, and there appears to be a growing sentiment they should be eliminated. The prohibition against the use of peremptory challenges has been extended to gender discrimination (*J.E.B. v. Alabama*, 511 U.S. 127 (1994)).

Discharge of Juror and Replacement with Alternate (270.35)

After the jury has been sworn and before the verdict is rendered the court must discharge any juror who is unable to continue serving by reason of:

a. illness or other incapacity; or,

b. for any other reason is unavailable for continued service; or,

c. the court finds the juror is grossly unqualified or has engaged in substantial misconduct.

The discharged juror will be replaced by the first chosen alternate juror available or, if none is available, the court must declare a mistrial. If however the jury has entered deliberations, the defendant must consent to such replacement in person, in writing and before the court. This constitutes a waiver of the defendant's constitutional right to be tried by the particular jury, chosen by law and in which the defendant participated (N.Y. Const. art. I, sec. 2). The decision to discharge the juror in question due to any of the above circumstances is within the discretion of the judge; however, the judge must make a thorough inquiry as to the reasons for the illness or other incapacity and as to when such juror will be available to serve. The parties will be afforded an opportunity to be heard. If the court finds the juror will not be able to appear within two hours of the time the trial is due to resume, the court may presume the juror is unavailable and may discharge such juror. Some of the circumstances leading to discharge of a juror have been found to be illness of a juror, death in the juror's family, economic hardship, conversations with others regarding the case, falling asleep and bias or partiality. To remove a juror from trial due to misconduct, the misconduct must be found to be substantial (*People v. Phillips*, 384 N.Y.S.2d 906 (1975)).

Preliminary Instructions by the Court (270.40)

After the jury has been sworn and before the people's opening address the court must instruct the jury on its basic duties, functions and conduct including:

   a. not to converse amongst themselves or anyone else about the trial;

   b. not to read or listen to any news media accounts of the case;

   c. not to visit or view any premises or place connected with the case on their own;

   d. that prior to discharge they may not accept anything for or give any information about the case to anyone; and,

   e. that they must promptly report to the court any incident involving an attempt to improperly influence any member of the jury.

Failure of the court to include these statutory instructions in its preliminary instructions to the jury constitutes grounds for a mistrial (*People v. Wright*, 627 N.Y.S.2d 13 (1995)). The court's preliminary instructions should not go into the substance of the case and should not include an outline of the elements of the crime charged since such instructions could cause jurors to conclude the defendant was guilty before the defense could present its evidence (*People v. Harper*, 818 N.Y.S.2d 113 (2006)) and deprive the defendant of his right to a fair trial (*People v. Townsend*, 67 N.Y.2d 815 (1986)).

When Separation of the Jurors Is Permitted (270.45)

From the time the jurors are sworn to the time they retire to deliberate, the court, in its discretion, may permit them to separate during recesses or adjournments or keep them together under the supervision of a public servant. The public servant shall not communicate with them about the trial or permit anyone else to do so and must then return the jurors to the courtroom at the next session. Sequestration of the jury during deliberations is governed by 310.10. When the jury finds the defendant guilty of murder 1st degree (P.L. 125.27, for which death may be the sentence), the court in its discretion as above may keep the jury separate or sequester it until it retires to deliberate on the sentence to be imposed (270.55).

Viewing of Premises (270.50)

When the court is of the opinion that a viewing of the place of the crime or any other premises or place involved in the case will be helpful to the jury in determining any material factual issue, it may in its discretion, at any time before the summations commence, order such a viewing under the supervision of a public servant. The jury must be kept together and the court itself must be present. The prosecutor, defendant and counsel may, as a matter of right, also be present but may waive such right. The purpose of the viewing is solely to permit visual observation and no one is permitted to discuss the significance or implications of anything observed or concerning any issue in the case. The court in its discretion may refuse to allow viewing of a premises or place if it has changed (*People v. Berger*, 653 N.Y.S.2d 461 (1996)). Unauthorized visits by jurors are not permitted and may be cause for reversal of conviction or a mistrial (*People v. Crimmins*, 26 N.Y.2d 319 (1970)).

See Illustrative Cases

People v. Bolling, 79 N.Y.2d 317 (1992), p. 375
People v. Payne, 88 N.Y.2d 172 (1996), p. 377
People v. Crimmins, 26 N.Y.2d 319 ((1970), p. 378

9.3 The Jury Trial — Motion for a Mistrial (Article 280.10)

A motion for a mistrial may be made by either the defendant or the people. At any time during the trial, the court must declare a mistrial and order a new trial of the indictment:

1. upon motion of the defendant, when there occurs during the trial

    a. an error or legal defect in the proceedings, or

    b. conduct inside or outside the courtroom, which is prejudicial to the defendant and deprives him of a fair trial.

At a trial of more than one defendant, if the mistrial motion is not made by all the defendants but granted nonetheless, the trial of the other defendant(s) must continue.

2. upon motion of the people, when there occurs during the trial

    a. inside or outside of the courtroom, gross misconduct by the defendant, or one acting on his behalf or by a juror, resulting in substantial and irreparable prejudice to the defendant's case.

At a trial of more than one defendant, if the court concludes the occurrence was not caused by one or more of the defendants and it did not result in substantial prejudice to the people's case against such defendant, the trial must continue as to such defendant(s).

3. upon motion of either party or the court on its own motion

    a. when it becomes physically impossible to proceed with the trial in conformity with the law.

A motion for a mistrial should only be granted as a last resort. The trial court's power to declare a mistrial must be exercised with the greatest caution, under urgent circumstances, and for very plain and obvious causes. The authority to discharge the jury is limited to those situations where, taking all circumstances into consideration, there is a manifest necessity for the act (*People v. Baptiste*, 72 N.Y.2d 356 (1988)). The defendant has a constitutional right under the federal and state constitutions (U.S. Const. amend. V; N.Y. Const. art. I, sec. 6) to be tried by the first jury selected and absent manifest necessity a mistrial will result in a 2d trial being barred by double jeopardy. If the court can eliminate any prejudice to either the defendant or the people by curative instructions to the jury it must do so or run the risk of double jeopardy precluding a retrial. The trial court's discretion to decide a mistrial is not abused when the judge provides curative instructions that are sufficient to alleviate any possible prejudice to the defendant (*People v. Owens*, 625 N.Y.S.2d 524 (1995)). Both conduct and prejudice which would justify a mistrial on behalf of the people's case must be more exaggerated than as to the defendant's case (*People v. Mallette*, 399 N.Y.S.2d 63 (1977)). The judge's discretion is not without limits. The reasons underlying a grant of mistrial must be necessitous, actual and substantial. If the judge acts abruptly so as not to consider alternatives or otherwise acts irrationally or irresponsibly, or solely for the convenience of the court or jury, a retrial will be barred (*Enright v. Siedlecki*, 59 N.Y.2d 195 (1983)). The behavior of the prosecutor, defense counsel, defendants, witnesses and jurors, among others, can give rise to the motion for mistrial. Upon a new trial after an order of dismissal, the indictment is deemed to contain all the counts it contained at the time the previous trial was commenced including any count dismissed by the court prior to the mistrial order (280.20), except counts dismissed under circumstances that would equate to an acquittal, such as a dismissal based upon insufficient evidence (*People v. Anderson*, 489 N.Y.S.2d 721 (1985)).

See Illustrative Cases

In the Matter of Enright v. Siedlecki, 59 N.Y.2d 195 (1993), p. 380

9.4 Trial Order of Dismissal (Article 290.10)

Upon motion of the defendant, at the conclusion of the people's case or at the conclusion of all the evidence, the court may:

1. (a) issue a trial order of dismissal upon any count in the indictment on the ground the trial evidence was not legally sufficient to establish the offense charged or any lesser included offense; or,

    (b) reserve decision on the motion until after the verdict has been rendered and accepted by the court.

If the court renders a guilty verdict and the court determines the motion should have been

granted, it shall issue an order setting aside the verdict and dismissing the count in the indictment.

2. Issuance of a trial order of dismissal is not authorized and constitutes error when the trial evidence would have been legally sufficient had the court not erroneously excluded admissible evidence offered by the people.

3. When the court excludes trial evidence offered by the people not in the record, the people may, in anticipation of a dismissal emanating from the allegedly improper exclusion, may place upon the record, out of the presence of the jury, an "offer of proof" summarizing the excluded evidence. In the absence of such an order and an appeal therefrom, such offer of proof is not deemed a part of the record and does not constitute such for purposes of an ensuing appeal by the defendant from a judgment of conviction.

4. If the court's trial order of dismissal dismisses the entire indictment, the defendant shall be immediately released from custody and any bail exonerated.

Where the judge enters the trial order of dismissal before submitting the case to the jury, the principles of double jeopardy bar the prosecutor from taking an appeal from the dismissal order and reprosecuting the defendant upon the charge (*People v. Marin*, 478 N.Y.S.2d 650 (1984)). If the court reserved decision on the motion and the jury finds the defendant guilty, and the court then determines the motion in favor of the defendant, thus overturning the jury's verdict, the people may then appeal the judge's trial order of dismissal. This does not involve the defendant's double jeopardy right not to be twice prosecuted for the same offense since there is no necessity for a reprosecution. The jury verdict may simply be reinstated (*People ex rel. Pendleton v. Smith*, 388 N.Y.S.2d 426 (1976)).

See Illustrative Cases

People v. Marin, 478 N.Y.S.2d 650 (1984), p. 382

9.5 The Court's Charge and Instructions to the Jury (Article 300)

Generally (300.10)

At the conclusion of the summations the court must deliver a charge (instructions) to the jury.

1. The court must state the fundamental legal principles applicable to criminal cases in general, including:

    a. the presumption of innocence;

    b. guilt must be proved beyond a reasonable doubt;

    c. in determining guilt or innocence, not to speculate on the sentence or punishment for the offense;

    d. on request of a defendant who did not testify on his own behalf, that no unfavorable inference may be drawn from that fact;

e. the material legal principles applicable to the case;

f. an explanation of the application of the law to the facts.

2. Where the defendant has raised the affirmative defense of not responsible due
    to mental disease or defect, the court must specifically instruct the jury:

    a. not to speculate on the consequences of its verdict; and,

    b. if they decide to find the defendant not responsible due to mental disease
        or defect there will be hearings as to the defendant's present mental con-
        dition and where appropriate involuntary commitment proceedings.

3. The court must submit the counts in the indictment to be considered, define
    each offense, and instruct the jurors to render a separate verdict on each count
    as either guilty, not guilty or where appropriate, not responsible due to mental
    disease or defect.

In addition to these required general instructions, particular circumstances may
give rise to instructions relative to such circumstances in any given case. The parties
may submit requests to the court to include specific matters in the charge. The court
must rule promptly on such requests; but, a failure to rule upon a request is deemed
to be a denial. For a charge of enterprise corruption (P.L. 460) special instructions
must include the requirement they separately and unanimously agree the defendant
has committed at least three of the criminal acts alleged as part of the pattern of criminal activity, including any lesser included offenses, as required by the penal law
statute. The court may submit to the jury only those counts of the indictment remaining at the time of its charge, which are supported by legally sufficient trial evidence. Any count not so supported should be dismissed (300.40). In submitting a
count to the jury the court in its discretion may submit in the alternative any lesser
included offense when there is reasonable evidence the defendant committed such
offense but did not commit the greater offense. If the defendant was under sixteen
at the time the offense was committed and the lesser offense is one for which he
would not be criminally responsible by reason of infancy, the lesser offense may still
be submitted but a verdict of guilty thereon would not be considered a criminal conviction (300.50).

9.6 Deliberation and Verdict of the Jury (Article 310)

Deliberation

Following the court's charge the jury must retire to the jury room to deliberate
upon its verdict. It must be continuously kept together under the supervision of court
personnel unless the defendant consents to their being separated; or, the court in its
discretion permits them to be separated in cases where the charge is other than a
class A felony or a class B or C violent felony offense. Upon permission to separate,

the court must admonish the jurors regarding communicating with anyone relative to the case or receiving media accounts thereof. No communication is permitted between the supervisory personnel and the jurors except that which is administratively necessary or directed by the court and the jurors are not permitted to communicate with anyone else (310.10). The court may permit the jurors to take with them into the jury room any exhibits of evidence received at the trial after giving all the parties an opportunity to be heard as to whether or not it is proper and in addition a written list of the charges to be considered and the possible verdicts thereon (310.20). At any time during its deliberations the jury may request further instructions from the court on the law, the evidence in the case or any other matter pertinent to their consideration of the case. The court must notify the parties of such request and give them an opportunity to return to the courtroom. The court then will direct the jury to be returned to the courtroom and in the presence of the parties render such information or instruction as the court deems proper. If the request of the jury is for further instructions regarding a statute, the court with the consent of the parties may also give the jury copies of the text of any statute it deems proper (310.30). The request should ordinarily be in writing and the mode of proceeding is in the discretion of the judge depending upon the circumstances of each situation (*People v. O'Rama*, 78 N.Y.2d 270 (1991)).

The Verdict

When the jury has reached a verdict it will so notify the court through the court officer supervising the jury. The judge shall notify the parties. When the jury is brought into the courtroom the judge will ask the foreman if the jury has reached a verdict and the foreman will answer in the affirmative. The verdict must then be announced by the foreman in the presence of the parties. The defendant may knowingly and willingly waive his right to be present, however, even though he has a fundamental right to be present (310.40). The form of the verdict must be in accordance with the instructions of the court. If it is not or if it is legally defective, the court must explain the error and direct the jury to resume its deliberations. If the jury persists in rendering an improper verdict the court in its discretion, depending upon its perception, may order an acquittal or discharge the jury and direct the prosecutor to retry the indictment or a count thereof (310.50). The verdict is not final until it is properly recorded and accepted by the court (*People v. Salemmo*, 38 N.Y.2d 357 (1976)).

A deliberating jury may be discharged by the court without having reached a verdict only when:

a. The jury is deadlocked after having deliberated for an extensive period of time; or,

b. The court and the parties consent to such discharge; or,

c. A mistrial is declared pursuant to 280.10 (on motion due to error or defect in the proceeding).

When the jury is so discharged, the defendant may be retried on the indictment except for counts which were dismissed or deemed to have resulted in an acquittal

(310.60). The court may accept a partial verdict on one or more but not all the counts in the indictment if the court is reasonably satisfied that a complete verdict cannot be reached (310.70).

After rendition of the verdict the judge will ask the jurors as a whole if that is their verdict. Even though no negative answer is received either party may ask the individual jurors to be polled. In such case the individual jurors must be asked if that is their verdict. In either case if a negative response is made by one or more of the jurors the verdict will not be accepted and the jurors will be ordered back to the jury room to resume its deliberations. If no disagreement is expressed, the jury must be discharged unless the charge against the defendant was murder 1st degree in which case the jury may be required to determine the sentence of either death or life imprisonment (310.80). If the defendant is a juvenile offender convicted of only an offense for which he is not criminally responsible the matter shall be referred to the family court for disposition; but, if he is convicted also of a crime for which he is criminally responsible, the conviction for the charge for which he is not criminally responsible will be declared a nullity and set aside (310.85).

See Illustrative Cases

People v. O'Rama, 78 N.Y.2d 270 (1991), p. 384
People v. Baptiste, 72 N.Y.2d 356 (1988), p. 386

9.7 Waiver of Jury Trial and Conduct of Non-Jury Trial (Article 320)

Under the state constitution the defendant has the right to waive a jury trial of an indictment except upon a charge of 1st degree murder (N.Y. Const., art. 1, sec. 2); however, if the prosecutor elects not to seek the death penalty, the defendant may waive the right to be tried by a jury (*People v. Elliott*, 662 N.Y.S.2d 701 (1997)). The defendant may waive the right to a jury trial at any time before trial in the superior court in which the indictment is pending. The waiver must be in writing, signed by the defendant, in open court, in the presence of and with the consent of the court. The court must accept the waiver, unless it finds it is merely a stratagem designed to get an impermissible procedural advantage or the defendant is not fully aware of the consequences of the waiver. If the court disapproves the waiver the reasons must be entered on the record (320.10). The defendant's motion for a bench trial was denied where the reasons advanced were that a codefendant had committed perjury and that there had been extensive pre-trial publicity which indicated the lack of a knowing, intelligent and voluntary waiver, and it appeared to be merely a stratagem to cause delay of the trial and to obtain a severance (*People v. Ahalt*, 529 N.Y.S.2d 250 (1988)). The right of a defendant to a trial by jury of an indictment is a fundamental constitutional right; therefore, any waiver must be voluntary, intelligent and knowing (*People v. Cannady*, 487 N.Y.S.2d 294 (1985)).

Conduct of Non-Jury Trial

The procedures to be followed for a bench trial are the same as those for a jury trial (260.30) with the exception of those matters pertaining to juries. For example, there is no charge to the jury delivered by the court. After the summations the court must then consider the case and render the verdict. The court determines all issues of law and fact, and in multiple count indictments, it must indicate to the parties upon which counts it will render a verdict and against which defendants if more than one (320.20).

9.8 Proceedings from Verdict to Sentence (Article 330)

Verdict of Acquittal or Not Responsible Due to Mental Disease or Defect (330.10)

Upon a verdict of complete acquittal, the court must immediately discharge the defendant if she is in custody, or if at liberty on bail, the court must exonerate the bail. On a verdict of not responsible due to mental disease or defect a detailed procedure in 330.20 governs all subsequent proceedings against the defendant.

Procedure on Verdict or Plea of Not Responsible Due to Mental Disease or Defect (330.20)

The verdict or plea of not responsible due to mental disease or defect means the defendant committed a criminal act but due to a mental defect or illness at the time of its commission she cannot be held criminally liable for such act but the state may require the defendant to be committed to custody and undergo mental evaluation in order to determine her present mental condition.

Examination Orders

Upon acceptance of the plea or the finding of the verdict of not responsible due to mental disease or defect the court will issue an examination order which directs the State Commissioner of Mental Health or Mental Retardation to designate two qualified psychiatrists or psychologists to examine the defendant and commits the defendant to a secure facility designated by the Commissioner, for up to thirty days, to undergo the requisite examination. If the defendant is on bail the court may direct the examination be done on an outpatient basis unless the Commissioner informs the court confinement is necessary for an effective examination. The period of commitment may be extended an additional thirty days. At the conclusion of the examinations the Commissioner shall submit the reports of the psychiatric examiners to the court which must furnish copies to the district attorney, counsel for the defendant and the mental hygiene legal service.

Hearing and Commitment Order

Within ten days of receipt of such reports the court must hold a hearing to determine the defendant's mental condition. At this initial hearing the district attorney bears the burden of proving the defendant:

a. has a dangerous mental disorder; or,

b. is otherwise mentally ill but poses no danger.

In the absence of such a finding the court must:

c. determine the defendant is not mentally ill and direct her release with or without conditions.

If the court finds the defendant to be mentally ill but poses no danger (b above) the court must issue an order of commitment, with conditions, under the Mental Hygiene Law, to the Commissioner for treatment in accordance with the provisions of said law. From that point on the matter will be governed by the provisions of the Mental Hygiene Law. The court may condition the commitment or release set forth in b or c above with the requirement the defendant undergo a treatment plan for five years (extendable another five years) and if at any time during this period, if the defendant is found to be suffering from a dangerous mental disorder, she will be confined to a secure mental facility and proceeded against as if the original finding was that she had a dangerous mental disorder.

Initial and Subsequent Retention Orders

If the court finds the defendant has a dangerous mental disorder it will commit the defendant to the custody of the Commissioner for necessary treatment. The status of the condition of the defendant in such commitment is reviewed periodically, initially after six months, then after a year and subsequently every two years to determine what to do with the defendant. The Commissioner may recommend:

a. if found to still have a dangerous mental condition, continued retention in a secure facility; or,

b. if found mentally ill but not dangerous, retention of custody in a non-secure facility, with conditions as set forth above for cases originally so found; or,

c. if found no longer mentally ill, release from custody, with conditions.

The court may hold a hearing upon the Commissioner's recommendation. If it is for continued retention in a secure facility the burden of proof is upon the commissioner. If it is for release or transfer to a non-secure facility the district attorney may oppose such recommendation on the ground the defendant has a dangerous mental condition. In any case the burden of proof is by a preponderance of the evidence. The Commissioner may also apply to the court for a furlough order, which also may be opposed by the district attorney.

Ancillary Matters

Within thirty days of any retention order the defendant may apply for a rehearing. The defendant also has all the rights granted mentally ill persons under the Mental Hygiene Law. No defendant shall be released by the Commissioner without at least four days' notice to the district attorney, the police department having jurisdiction of the place to which the defendant is to be released or any other person the court may designate. If the defendant should escape from custody, the facility from which the escape has been made must notify the district attorney, the police and any person believed to be endangered by such escape. The defendant may be apprehended and returned to the facility by any peace officer and it is the duty of any peace officer, upon request, to assist a representative of the Commissioner to take the defendant into custody. Any party to these proceedings may appeal the decisions of the court.

Removal of Juvenile Offender to Family Court after Verdict (330.25)

Where a defendant is a juvenile offender and has not been convicted of murder 2d degree, upon motion and with consent of the court, the conviction may be set aside and the action removed to the family court in the interest of justice. If the district attorney consents to the motion she must file a signed memorandum with the court recommending removal in the interests of justice and if the conviction is for rape or sodomy 1st degree or an armed felony, specific factors which support the recommendation, showing:

a. mitigating circumstances relative to the manner of commission of the crime; or,

b. if the defendant was not the sole participant, that his role was relatively minor; or,

c. no previous record of delinquent criminal acts and this act is not likely to be repeated.

If the court is of the opinion, based upon the factors in the district attorney's memorandum, that the interests of justice would best be served by removal of the action to family court, the verdict shall be set aside and a plea of guilty accepted for an act which is not a crime for which the defendant may be held criminally responsible. The court must put on the record the reasons relied upon for such determination from the district attorney's memorandum. The plea shall be deemed a juvenile delinquency fact determination and the action removed to the family court.

Motion to Set Aside a Verdict (330.30, 40, 50)

After a verdict of guilty but before sentence the court may, upon motion of the defendant, set aside or modify the verdict upon the following grounds;

1. Any ground in the record that would result in an appellate court reversal or modification, as a matter of law; or,

2. That during the trial, out of the presence of the court, there occurred jury misconduct or jury tampering, which may have affected a substantial right of the defendant and this was not known by the defendant until now; or,

3. new evidence is discovered which creates the probability the verdict would have been more favorable to the defendant.

Except if the motion to set aside is based upon the ground specified in subdivision 1 (above), the motion must be in writing with notice to the people. The defendant bears the burden of proving the grounds by a preponderance of the evidence. If the essential facts in the motion are not contested the motion may be decided without a hearing. If the motion to set aside the verdict is granted on the grounds specified in subdivision one above, the court will take such action as the appellate court would take, depending upon the circumstances (i.e., order a new trial, dismiss the indictment, change to a lesser included offense, etc.). If granted on the grounds in subdivision 2 above, a new trial must be ordered; and, if on the grounds in paragraph 3, the court will order a new trial or modify the verdict according to the effect the court believes the new evidence would have had on the verdict (e.g., reduce the conviction to that of a lesser included offense).

See Illustrative Cases

In re Francis S., 87 N.Y.2d 554 (1995), p. 388
People v. Suarez, 469 N.Y.S.2d 752 (1983), p. 390

Chapter 10

Prosecution of Informations in Local Criminal Court: From Plea to Sentence

Sec. 10.1 Article 340; Pre-Trial Proceedings
Sec. 10.2 Article 350; Non-Jury Trials
Sec. 10.3 Article 360; Jury Trial
Sec. 10.4 Article 370; Proceedings from Verdict to Sentence

10.1 Pre-Trial Proceedings (Article 340)

Except as otherwise provided, the procedures governing the trial of indictments in superior courts also govern the trial of informations, and other local criminal court accusatory instruments, in local criminal courts. A plea to an information by a defendant must be made orally and in person before the court unless the defendant in writing waives her right to plead in person and authorizes entry of the plea by counsel. A plea to an information against a corporation must be entered by counsel. When a plea bargained sentence is agreed to the agreed upon sentence must be entered in the record by the prosecutor or the court (340.20). The provisions of Articles 245, governing discovery, and 250, governing pre-trial notice of defenses to the people in the trial of indictments, are applicable to the trial of an information (340.30).

Modes of Trial

A trial of an information in a local criminal court must be a single judge trial unless:

1. outside the City of New York, the information charges a misdemeanor; or,

2. in the City of New York, the information charges a misdemeanor punishable by more than six months imprisonment.

In such cases the defendant has the right to a jury trial of the information.

The defendant at any time before trial may waive, in writing, her right to a jury trial and consent to a single judge trial. Youthful offenders who have not been previously convicted of a crime or adjudicated a youthful offender have no right to a jury trial and must proceed with a single judge trial (340.40). The differences in the right to a jury trial outside of and within New York City are attributable to the provisions of the New York State and United States Constitutions and the workload of the courts in New York City. The New York State Constitution only provides for a jury trial for the trial of indictments in superior court (art. 1, sec. 2) while the U.S. Constitution has been interpreted to require a jury trial for serious offenses, meaning offenses punishable by statute by more than six months in prison (*Baldwin v. New York*, 399 U.S. 66 (1970) and *Blanton v. City of North Las Vegas*, 789 U.S. 538 (1989)). Thus, statutorily, due to the differences in case workload, in New York City the defendant to be tried on an information in the New York City Criminal Court is only entitled to a jury trial as required by the federal constitution. A defendant may waive her right to be personally present during the trial of an information in the local criminal court in writing, without objection by the people, and authorizing her attorney to conduct her defense. In addition, a defendant who conducts herself in a disorderly and disruptive manner, to the extent the trial cannot continue, after warning of the court that she will be removed from the court and the trial held in her absence if she does not desist, will be removed from the court if she continues the disorderly and disruptive conduct (340.50). A defendant who deliberately absents herself from court may be tried in absentia, if the trial court conducts an inquiry into the circumstances of the absence and finds the absence is deliberate. Such a defendant forfeits her right to be present at her trial (*People v. Charles*, 575 N.Y.S.2d 886 (1991)).

See Illustrative Cases

People v. Foy, 88 N.Y.2d 742 (1966), p. 391

10.2 Non-Jury Trials (Article 350)

A single judge trial of an information in a local criminal court generally follows the procedures for bench trials in the superior courts. In a single judge trial of an information the judge, in addition to deciding all legal questions, is also the exclusive trier of the facts and must render the verdict at the close of the case. The court in its discretion may allow the parties to deliver opening addresses and summations. If the court grants such permission to one party it must do the same for the other party. The people deliver the first opening address and the defendant the first summation. Except where the trial is of an information charging a class A misdemeanor, the judge, with the consent of the parties, may assign the case for trial by a judicial hearing officer. The judicial hearing officer will hold the trial in the same manner as the judge and must render the verdict as well. Judicial hearing officers are retired judges appointed under the authority of Article 22, Judiciary Law, to perform certain civil and criminal court functions such as provided here.

See Illustrative Cases

People v. O'Brien, 381 N.Y.S.2d 972 (1976), p. 393

10.3 The Jury Trial (Article 360)

A jury trial of an information in the local criminal court follows the procedures set forth for the jury trial of indictments in a superior court as set forth in 260.30. The order in which the trial is to proceed is not inflexible and every deviation from it will not constitute reversible error (*People v. Humphreys*, 308 N.Y.S.2d 81 (1970)). Mandatory requirements of the statute, such as the opening address by the people, may not be waived or dispensed with by consent (*People v. Klein*, 7 N.Y.2d 264 (1959)). The trial jury for the trial of informations consists of six persons and, in the discretion of the court, one or two alternates. As for the trial of indictments (*see* 270.10) challenges to the panel may be made upon the ground of a serious departure from the requirements of the Judiciary Law so as to result in systemic substantial prejudice to the defendant (360.10,15). *Voir dire* follows the procedures for jury selection for the trial of indictments in 270.15; however, for the trial of informations, since six jurors are to be selected, six will be seated and sworn to commence the process (360.20). Challenges for cause and peremptory challenges are permitted and the procedures for entering and deciding them parallel those set forth for the trial of indictments in 270.20 and 270.25. The main difference in procedures is in the number of peremptory challenges allowed each party which, for the trial of the information, numbers three.

Conduct of the Jury Trial of Informations — In General (360.40 to 360.55)

The jury trial must generally be conducted in the same manner and in accord with the procedures set forth for the jury trial of indictments governing preliminary instructions to the jury, supervision of the jury, motion practice, the court's charge to the jury, the submission of the counts and offenses to be submitted and the deliberation and verdict of the jury (*see* 300.10 to 300.30).

See Illustrative Cases

People v. Warren, 536 N.Y.S.2d 337 (1988), p. 395

10.4 Proceedings from Verdict to Sentence (Article 370)

The provisions of Article 330, governing the procedures from verdict to sentence for the trial of indictments in superior court, are applicable to the trial of informations in a local criminal court. If the trial has been held by a judicial hearing officer, all references to the court or judge shall be references to the judicial hearing officer.

Chapter 11

The Sentence

Sec. 11.1 Article 380; Sentencing in General
Sec. 11.2 Article 390; Pre-Sentence Reports
Sec. 11.3 Article 400; Pre-Sentence Proceedings
Sec. 11.4 Article 410; Sentences of Probation and Conditional Discharge
Sec. 11.5 Article 420; Fines, Restitution and Reparation
Sec. 11.6 Article 430; Sentences of Imprisonment

11.1 Sentencing in General (Article 380)

In every case in which a conviction is had after a trial verdict of guilty or a guilty plea, the court must pronounce sentence on each count of the accusatory instrument for which the conviction was had (380.20). Failure of the court to pronounce sentence on each count of a multiple count indictment requires the defendant to be resentenced (*People v. Mohammed*, 511, N.Y.S.2d 99 (1987)).

The court may impose concurrent or in some cases consecutive sentences for each count of a multiple count indictment for which a conviction has been had on more than one count. Sentencing is largely a matter of discretion of the trial judge. In determining an appropriate sentence the judge may consider many factors relating to considerations such as deterrence, rehabilitation, retribution and isolation of the defendant (*People v. Patterson*, 483 N.Y.S.2d 55 (1984)). Sentences are to be formulated so as to deal with the particular needs and circumstances of a specific defendant before the court (*People v. McAdams*, 472 N.Y.S.2d 769 (1984)). The defendant's background, plea bargain agreements, pre-sentence reports, prior criminal record, recommendations of the prosecutor and defense counsel and the nature of the specific offense are among the factors the court may consider. However, a defendant may not be punished for doing what the law allows him to do and if the defendant refuses to plead guilty and goes to trial, retaliation or vindictiveness may play no role in sentencing following a conviction (*People v. Patterson, supra*).

Time for Pronouncing Sentence (380.30)

The sentence must be pronounced without unreasonable delay. Following an adjudication of guilt, sentence must be imposed, and it may not be deferred or postponed indefinitely (*Hogan v. Bohan*, 305 N.Y. 110 (1953)). The court must fix a date for

pronouncing sentence, or for pre-sentence proceedings that will lead to the determination of an appropriate sentence, or pronounce sentence on the date of conviction.
The court may sentence the defendant on the date of conviction if:

a. a pre-sentence or fingerprint report is not required; or,

b. if required, such report has been received; but,

c. the court may not pronounce sentence at this time without first asking the de-
    fendant if he desires an adjournment. If requested, the defendant must state
    the purpose of the requested adjournment, and the court in its discretion may
    allow a reasonable time.

The defendant must be present at the sentencing except in a misdemeanor or petty
offense case. In such instance the defendant may in writing waive her right to be
present and acknowledge the maximum sentence the court may impose. In any case
the defendant may be sentenced in absentia for either voluntary absence or if disorderly and disruptive and, after warning of the court, the defendant persists in such
conduct and the court orders her removed. Corporations appear by counsel but in
the absence of counsel's presence, after reasonable notice, the court may pronounce
sentence in the absence of counsel (380.40). The defendant has a right to be present
at sentencing and to be represented by counsel.

Statements at Time of Sentence (380.50)

At the time of sentencing, the court must afford the prosecutor, the defense counsel,
the victim (if the conviction has been had on a felony charge) and the defendant an
opportunity to speak relative to the sentence to be imposed. Before pronouncing
sentence the court must ask the victim if she wishes to make such a statement. The
victim may make the statement personally but if a minor or mentally incapacitated,
or if for any other reason the victim prefers another person to speak for her, the court
must allow such other person to address the court. Whether or not the victim makes
a statement regarding sentencing, if the defendant is sentenced to prison as a violent
felony offender, the prosecutor must give to the victim a form upon which the victim
may request notification upon the release of such defendant from prison under any
circumstances. The victim may fill out the form and return it to the prosecutor who
in turn will cause it to be delivered to the correctional institution so that the requisite
notification may be made upon defendant's release from custody. A certificate of
conviction is also sent to the correctional facility which authorizes the execution of
sentence (380.60) and, in the case of an indeterminate sentence, a copy of the stenographic minutes of the sentencing proceeding in order to inform the prison personnel
of the details of the sentence and as an aid in developing programs for the prisoner
while incarcerated (380.70). The court must also deliver a copy of the certificate of
conviction to the commissioner of social services (380.80).

See Illustrative Cases

People v. Rodney E., 77 N.Y.2d 672 (1991), p. 395

11.2 Pre-Sentence Reports
(Article 390)

Prior to sentencing, fingerprint reports and pre-sentence reports may be required.

Fingerprint Reports (390.10)

When the defendant is convicted for any offense for which fingerprints were required to be taken (160.10) the court may not pronounce sentence until it has received a fingerprint report from either the division of criminal justice services or a police department with respect to the defendant's prior arrest record. The court may use the original fingerprint report gotten upon the arrest of the person or direct the preparation and receipt of a new report.

Pre-Sentence Investigation and Report (390.15, 60)

Pre-sentence investigations and reports must be ordered by the court and no sentence may be pronounced without receipt of such report, where the defendant has been convicted of:

a. felony; or,

b. misdemeanor for which

  i) a sentence of over ninety days imprisonment is to be imposed; or,

  ii) a sentence of probation which has been agreed to by the parties is to be imposed.

Pre-sentence reports are not required otherwise; however, the court in its discretion may order a pre-sentence report in any case. Notwithstanding these provisions, the pre-sentence investigation and report may be waived upon mutual consent of the parties and the judge, in writing and on the record, whenever:

a. a sentence of imprisonment has been agreed upon for time served; or,

b. a sentence of probation has been agreed upon by the parties and will be imposed; or, a sentence of probation has been revoked and a prison sentence is to be imposed; or,

c. a report has been prepared in the last twelve months.

Whenever the pre-sentence report has been waived, if the court determines it would be relevant to the sentence, the victim impact statement, ordinarily a part of such report, will be required. If the defendant is to be sentenced to an indeterminate sentence, the pre-sentence report cannot be waived (390.20). The pre-sentence report requirement is designed not merely to make the sentence more meaningful for the offender, but also to bring before the court factors that may call for treatment in the community (*People v. Bentley*, 359 N.Y.S.2d 391 (1974)). The sentence must reflect facts known to the sentencing judge at the time of sentence, not merely those known at the time of plea or as agreed to by the prosecutor and defendant (*People v. Valdes*, 467 N.Y.S.2d 550 (1983)). Any sentence "promise" at the time of the plea is, as a matter of law and strong public policy, conditioned upon its being lawful and appropriate in light of the subsequent pre-sentence report or other information obtained from other reliable sources (*People v. Selikoff*, 35 N.Y.2d 227 (1974)).

The pre-sentence investigation is carried out by the probation department of the court. It consists of gathering information with respect to the circumstances of the offense, the defendant's background, a victim impact statement, any matter the court directs to be included and any matter relating to sentencing that the investigating agency deems relevant (390.30). The pre-sentence investigation report must contain an analysis of as much of the information gathered in the investigation as the investigative agency deems relevant to the question of sentence including any other information the court directs to be included and a victim impact statement. The victim impact statement, which must be in the report in all cases unless deemed to be irrelevant to the issue of sentencing, advises the court on the victim's views on her personal and economic losses, and the amount of reparation and restitution sought by the victim. The victim cannot be required to supply the information required for the preparation of the report, however. Where the conviction is of a misdemeanor, a short form pre-sentence investigation report may be made; but, in no case may it exclude a victim's impact statement or any matter relevant to the sentence that the court directs to be included (390.30). The fullest possible information on a defendant's background should be brought before the court before imposing a sentence for a serious crime (*People v. Halaby*, 430 N.Y.S.2d 717 (1980)). It is important in all criminal cases for the court to know that there are victims and to appreciate their concerns about plea bargaining and sentencing (*People v. Michael M.*, 475 N.Y.S.2d 774 (1984)).

The defendant and prosecutor may submit to the court a written memorandum setting forth any information deemed important to the question of sentence. The prosecutor's memo should be served upon the defendant's attorney at least ten days before the date set for sentencing and the defendant may annex written statements of others in support of his memorandum (390.40). The key to proper sentencing procedures is whether the defendant has been afforded an opportunity to refute those aggravating factors which may negatively influence the court (*People v. Gregorio*, 443 N.Y.S.2d 589 (1981)). As a matter of law and fairness the pre-sentence memorandum of the defense counsel must be made available to the prosecutor and probation department conducting the pre-sentence investigation except for those matters which in the discretion of the court are required to be kept confidential (*People v. Washington*, 402 N.Y.S.2d 542 (1978)).

The pre-sentence reports and memoranda are confidential and may not be disclosed to anyone except the defense counsel and prosecutor. Even in these cases the court, in its discretion, may exclude information it deems not relevant to sentencing or would be detrimental to the rehabilitation of the defendant. The victim impact statement prepared as part of the pre-sentence investigation report must be made available by the prosecutor to the victim or the victim's family; and, in addition, the prosecutor must notify the victim or the victim's family of the right to address the court personally at the sentencing and the requirement that the court be notified if the defendant intends to avail herself of such opportunity. The probation department may make the pre-sentence report available to any other court or its probation department that subsequently acquires jurisdiction over the defendant, and to similar agencies outside the state. All are bound by the requirements of confidentiality (390.50). Whenever the defendant is sentenced to prison a copy of the pre-sentence report and memoranda must be submitted to the head of the correctional facility to which the defendant has been committed (390.60).

Requirement of HIV Related Testing in Certain Cases (390.15)

A defendant convicted of an offense under Article 130 P.L. (rape, sodomy or sexual abuse). at the request of the victim of said offense, must be ordered by the court to undergo HIV related testing, by a government public health officer designated by the court. The test results shall not be communicated to the court but shall only be disclosed to the victim and the defendant. If the victim is an infant or an incompetent person the request may be made by a representative. The court shall conduct a hearing only if necessary to determine the applicant is the victim of the offense. The results of the test may not be used as evidence against the defendant in any criminal or civil proceeding related to the offense for which the defendant was convicted; however, this does not prevent a witness in a hearing held in relation to this procedure from being prosecuted for perjury.

See Illustrative Cases

See also, Donald P. v. Palmieri, 246 A.D. 2d. 597 (2nd Dept. 1998), 396
People v. Michael M., 475 N.Y.S.2d 774 (1984), p. 398

11.3 Pre-Sentence Proceedings (Article 400)

Before pronouncing sentence, the court, in its discretion, may hold one or more *pre-*sentence conferences, in open court or chambers, in order to resolve any discrepancies in information it has from the pre-sentence report and the parties pre-sentence memoranda, or other information the court has received, or to assist the court in its consideration of any other matter relevant to the sentence to be imposed (400.10). The pre-sentence conference is not mandatory. If there is no question regarding the information the court has relative to sentence, it may be imposed without such conference. The parties may be present at the conference as well as any other person the court decides has information which may be relevant to the sentence. The court may hold a summary hearing at the conference, take testimony under oath, record it as part of the record and include it as part of the pre-sentence report.

In order to determine if the defendant would respond favorably to a drug or alcohol treatment program prior to imposing sentence the court may also adjourn sentencing to a subsequent date. When imposing sentence thereafter, the court shall take into consideration the defendant's compliance with the pre-sentence conditions ordered by the court. The court may impose any of the conditions set forth in P.L. 65.10/2a–f,l (conditions of probation and conditional discharge) such as refrain from bad habits or violent behavior, undergo medical or psychiatric treatment or participate in drug or alcohol treatment programs (400.10/4).

Procedures for Determining If Defendant Is a Felony Recidivist (400.15, 16, 20, 21)

Persons convicted of certain felonies on two or more subsequent occasions may be given increased penalties due to their record of recidivism and the threat they pose to society. These defendants are classified in P.L. Article 70 as either a:

a. second violent felony offender,

b. persistent violent felony offender,

c. second felony offender, or

d. persistent felony offender.

These procedures must be followed in order to determine if any previous convictions of the defendant qualify as predicate felony convictions for the purpose of applying the mandatory enhanced penalties prescribed by the penal law provisions regarding recidivist felons. The procedures for such determinations are the same for each classification as listed above other than that of the persistent felony offender, for which the enhanced punishment is not mandatory:

a. The prosecutor must file a statement with the court alleging the prior conviction and a copy given to the defendant. Only convictions within the past ten years are applicable and the ten year period is tolled for any periods of incarceration of the defendant during that ten year period. Convictions in any United States jurisdiction are applicable.

b. The court must ask the defendant if he wishes to controvert any of the prior convictions alleged and if he does, the court must hold a hearing to determine if the alleged prior conviction qualifies as a predicate felony conviction for enhanced sentencing purposes. Any uncontroverted allegations shall be deemed to be admitted.

c. The burden of proving the existence of a controverted conviction rests upon the prosecutor by proof beyond a reasonable doubt.

d. Any previous conviction found to have been had as a result of a violation of the defendant's constitutional rights shall not be applicable.

e. At the conclusion of the hearing, the court must determine if the defendant has been subjected to a predicate felony conviction.

f. Any admitted allegation, or finding after a hearing, of a predicate felony conviction is binding upon the defendant for all future proceedings in which the issue may arise.

Any question as to the issue of double jeopardy due to the use of a previous conviction to increase the punishment of a defendant upon an instant conviction has been laid to rest by the Supreme Court, which has ruled the double jeopardy clause is inapplicable to noncapital recidivist sentencing proceedings (*Monge v. California*, 118 S. Ct. 2246 (1998)).

The procedure for determining the existence of predicate felony convictions for persistent felony offenders (400.20) is different in some respects from that described above for the other classifications of recidivist felons.

a. The increased punishment is not mandated by the penal law provision (70.10) but is in the discretion of the court. The court therefore initiates the hearing. If the court does not believe the increased penalty is appropriate it may choose not to initiate the proceeding or it may end it at any time.

b. The judge must consider, in addition to predicate felony convictions, the background and character of the defendant in order to determine if the enhanced penalty should be provided.

c. At the hearing the prosecutor is also required to prove allegations of the defendant's bad character but only by a preponderance of the evidence.

d. The defendant must also have been imprisoned as a result of the conviction (70.10).

The imprisonment of the defendant for enhanced sentencing under 400.20 or to prove the tolling period may be proved by a certificate of the person in charge of the prison to which the defendant had been confined (400.22).

When necessary to prove previous convictions of recidivist misdemeanants, the court must follow a procedure similar to that described above for felony recidivists. The defendant must be given a statement setting forth the previous conviction and, if he denies or remains mute, a hearing must be held at which the prosecutor bears the burden of proof of said conviction beyond a reasonable doubt (400.40).

Procedure for Determining a Fine Based on Defendant's Gain from the Offense (400.30)

In certain instances the court may impose a fine as part of the sentence and if the defendant has realized a monetary gain from the commission of the offense, the fine may be based upon the amount of such gain (*see* P.L. Article 80). In order to determine the amount of gain the court may hold a hearing. The defendant and counsel and the district attorney shall be notified of said hearing. If the defendant states the amount of such gain and the court accepts it as accurate no hearing need be held. If the defendant remains mute, or the court does not accept the defendant's statement as to the amount of the gain, a hearing will be held to determine the amount of defendant's gain. Any relevant evidence not legally privileged is admissible to prove the amount of defendant's gain and the burden of proof is upon the people by a preponderance of the evidence.

Procedure for Determining Sentence for Conviction of Murder 1st Degree (400.27)

In 1972 the Supreme Court held unconstitutional a Georgia statute that provided a jury with complete discretion to impose the death penalty (*Furman v. Georgia*, 92 S. Ct. 2726). In 1974 the New York State legislature amended its death penalty statute (which provided for the jury to decide if the death sentence should be imposed such as Georgia's had) to provide a mandatory death sentence for its capital crimes. However, in 1976 the Supreme Court, in *Gregg v. Georgia* (96 S. Ct. 2909), declared mandatory death penalty statutes to be unconstitutional and that a sentencing system that authorized the jury to exercise discretion within structured, statutory guidelines, taking into account both aggravating and mitigating factors, was constitutional. The Court of Appeals declared New York's mandatory death penalty statute unconstitutional in 1977 (*People v. Davis*, 43 N.Y.2d 17). New York was without a death penalty statute until September 1, 1995, when the legislature redefined murder 1st degree (P.L. 125.27) and provided a structured procedure within which a jury, considering aggravating and mitigating factors, could determine if the death penalty should be the sentence for a person convicted of such crime. As noted in Chapter 8, New York's highest court held that the death penalty statute, as written, fails to satisfy protections afforded by the state's constitution (*People v. LaValle*, 3 N.Y.3d 88 (2004); *People v Taylor*, (9 N.Y.3d 129 (2007)). Therefore, the death penalty was struck down, and there does not appear to be any appetite to revise the statute in an attempt to restore the death penalty. The statute, however, remains relevant to the extent that it is the statutory source for a lifetime sentence, which remains a lawful sentencing option.

See Illustrative Cases

See also, People v. McIntosh, 178 Misc. 2d. 433 (Dutchess Cty. Ct. 1998), p. 400
See also, People v. Arroyo, 683 N.Y.S.2d 788 (1998), p. 401

11.4 Sentences of Probation and Conditional Discharge (Article 410)

Conditions of the Sentence (410.10, 20, 30, 40)

A defendant upon conviction may be sentenced to probation or conditional discharge. In these instances the defendant does not go to jail but is released and must comply with conditions specified by the court during the period of release under the sentence. Where the sentence is one of probation the defendant must be given a written copy of such conditions at the time of sentencing (410.10). The conditions must be set by the court and may not be delegated to others such as the probation department (*People ex rel. Perry v. Cassidy*, 250 N.Y. S.2d 743 (1964)). The purpose of probation is the rehabilitation of the defendant (*People v. Mauro*, 246 N. Y.S.2d 687 (1964)) and the conditions should be sufficiently clear and explicit so that the defendant and probation officer will have notice of them (*People v. Turner*, 276 N.Y.S.2d 409 (1967)). The court's failure to give the defendant a written copy of the conditions will not invalidate the sentence where it is clear the defendant was aware of the precise conditions imposed (*People v. Nazarian*, 541 N.Y.S.2d 262 (1989)). The commission of an offense other than a traffic infraction during the period of probation or conditional release is a ground for revocation of the sentence regardless of whether such fact is specified as a condition of the sentence. The court may change the conditions during the period of probation or conditional release. If the conditions are to be enlarged the defendant must be present (410.20).

If the court has reasonable cause to believe the defendant has violated the conditions of his release it may file a written "Declaration of Delinquency," and promptly take steps to bring the defendant before the court in order to make a final determination as to the alleged delinquency. Such declaration and prompt action will toll the period of probation or conditional release and thus prevent the defendant's sentence to end while there is reasonable cause to believe he is not complying with the conditions laid down at sentencing (410.30). The court may at any time order the person on probation or conditional discharge, in writing, to appear before it. Failure to appear without reasonable cause constitutes a violation of the conditions of release regardless of whether such requirement is specified as a condition. Likewise the court may issue a warrant for the arrest of such person upon reasonable grounds to believe he has violated the conditions specified. The warrant may be issued to a police officer or probation officer (410.40).

Custody and Supervision of Probationers (410.50)

While on probation the probationer is in the legal custody of the court that imposed the sentence and that court's probation department has the duty of supervising the defendant during the period of probation. The probationer is subject to reasonable search and seizure while on probation. His Fourth Amendment right to be free from unreasonable search and seizure is not abrogated but the circumstances of the right depend upon what might be considered reasonable in searching or arresting a parolee under the supervision of the court (*People v. Jackson*, 46 N.Y.2d 171 (1978)). The probationer is still in legal custody during probation which by its very nature and purpose entails a degree of supervision (*People v. Adams*, 336 N.Y.S.2d 533 (1972)).

If the court has reasonable cause to believe the probationer has violated the conditions of his release it may issue a search order. No search warrant is required. If his probation officer has reasonable cause to believe the probationer has violated the conditions of release such officer may, without a warrant, take such probationer into custody and search his person. Note the requirement of reasonable cause to believe which circumscribes the authority of the court and probation officer in search and arrest situations. In executing the search order or in taking the probationer into custody, a probation officer may call upon the assistance of a police officer.

A probationer taken into custody must forthwith be brought before the court that imposed the probation sentence unless such court is not in session. In that case the probationer may at his request be brought before another court to determine if a securing order should be issued or release of the probationer should be made in order to facilitate an appearance before the court that imposed the sentence (*see* 120.90). When the probationer appears before the court that imposed the sentence, if such court finds reasonable cause to believe the probationer violated the conditions of probation, it shall either commit him to the custody of the sheriff or release him on his own recognizance for future appearance at a hearing as to whether or not the violation has occurred. If the court does not find reasonable cause to believe such violation has occurred it must direct that the probationer be released (410.60).

The Hearing on the Violation (410.70)

The court may not revoke probation without a hearing at which the probationer has an opportunity to be heard and the court finds the probationer has violated a condition of probation. There must be filed with the court a statement setting forth the condition(s) of the probation sentence violated and a reasonable description of the date, time, place and manner of such violation. The defendant must appear before the court (unless voluntarily absent) and the court must furnish him with a copy of the statement. The court must advise the defendant of his right to make a statement, the right to counsel at all stages of the proceeding, and an adjournment in order to secure counsel and/or prepare for the hearing.

The hearing must be a summary one, conducted by the court without a jury. The court may hear any relevant evidence not legally privileged. The defendant may cross examine witnesses and present evidence on his own behalf A finding that the defendant has violated a condition of his sentence of probation must be based upon a preponderance of the evidence presented at the hearing. At the conclusion of the hearing the court may revoke, continue or modify the sentence of probation.

The courts have ruled upon a number of issues arising from 410.50. For example, the use of the preponderance of evidence standard is constitutionally permissible since the probation hearing is not a criminal proceeding (*People v. Neuroth*, 568 N.Y.S.2d 837 (1991)). The summary nature of the proceeding is permissible since probation is a matter of grace and its revocation also depends upon the sound discretion of the court (*People v. Oskroba*, 305 N.Y. 113 (1953)). No formal procedure or strict adherence to the rules of evidence is required relative to an alleged violation of parole, save that the defendant be arraigned and given an opportunity to be heard. Once these conditions have been met the court retains jurisdiction to revoke probation and impose a new sentence (*Whitree v. State*, N.Y.S.2d 319 (1966), and *People v. Tyrrell*, 475 N.Y.S.2d 937 (1984)).

Transfer of Supervision and Termination of Sentence (410.80, 90)

If the defendant resides in, at the time of sentence, or desires to reside in after probation has been sentenced, a place outside the jurisdiction of the sentencing court, such court may transfer the supervision of the probationer to the probation department of the court having jurisdiction over such place. The court may also transfer its powers and duties as the sentencing court to the court supervising said probation department (410.80). The court may at any time during the probation period terminate the period of probation, other than a period of lifetime probation. The court may terminate a period of lifetime probation for a probationer who has been on unrevoked probation for a period of at least five years. The court shall grant a request for termination when it is of the opinion that:

a. the probationer no longer is need of the supervision, guidance and training available through probation supervision;

b. the probationer has diligently complied with the conditions of probation; and,

c. the termination of probation would not be adverse to the protection of the public.

No termination shall be granted where a financially able probationer has failed to make a good faith effort to comply with an order of the court for financial restitution or reparation.

A procedure for supervising 2d felony offenders under the drug laws who had received a life sentence and were released on lifetime parole for having cooperated with the police investigating the drug crimes was added to Article 410 in 1995 and is scheduled to expire in 2005 (410.91). The procedure is similar to that set forth for probationers.

11.5 Fines, Restitution and Reparation (Article 420)

As part of a sentence the court may impose monetary payments against convicted defendants in the form of fines, restitution or reparation payments, mandatory surcharges and crime victim assistance fees. If a defendant fails or refuses to make such payments when able to do so, the court may resentence the defendant and impose additional imprisonment time.

Collection of Fines, Restitution or Reparation (420.10)

When the court imposes a fine or restitution or reparation payment it may direct the entire amount be paid at the time of sentencing or at some later date or that it be paid in scheduled installments. It shall also designate an official or organization, other than the district attorney, to whom such payment shall be made. If the payments are in the form of restitution or reparation a surcharge may be imposed which covers the administrative costs of such collections. The payment of fines, restitution or reparation may be made conditions of probation. In the event the person to whom restitution or reparation payments are to be made dies, the remaining payments shall be made to the estate of the deceased. An order directing said payments is also entered as a civil judgment against the defendant and is collectable as any other civil judgment.

If a defendant fails to make the payments as ordered when he has the ability to pay, the defendant must be imprisoned. If the defendant is at liberty, the court may issue a warrant directed to a peace officer or police officer to take him into custody and bring him before the court. The official or organization designated by the court to collect the payments is required to notify the court if such payments are not made. Any money earned by the defendant for work performed while imprisoned may be utilized to make the required payments. There are limits to the period of imprisonment the court may impose for failure to make payments as directed:

a. For a felony conviction, not more than one year;

b. For a misdemeanor conviction, not more than one third the maximum authorized term of imprisonment;

c. For a petty offense conviction, not more than fifteen days.

In no case shall the aggregate period of imprisonment exceed the maximum term of authorized imprisonment. In any case where the defendant is unable to make the ordered payments, he may apply to the court for resentence. If the court is satisfied the defendant is unable to pay, it may adjust the terms of payment, revoke the portion of the sentence imposing the payments or revoke the original sentence and resentence the defendant.

The statute permitting the incarceration of a defendant who is unable to pay is constitutional, as it permits the court to consider all sentencing alternatives and does not mandate imprisonment (*People v. Montero*, 480 N.Y.S. 2d 70 (1984)). A defendant who asserts inability to pay must show such inability to the court. A defendant who receives public assistance will be required to pay ordered payments if she fails to prove her inability to pay (*People v. Jenkins*, 316 N.Y.S.2d 475 (1970)). Payments may be ordered against co-defendant but a defendant could be ordered to pay the entire monetary amount assessed for restitution or reparation (*People v. Turco*, 515 N.Y.S.2d 853 (1987)). Fines imposed for Vehicle and Traffic Law violations may be paid by credit card and an administrative fee may be assessed in connection with this method of payment (410.05). When a corporation is assessed a payment it must be paid at the time sentence is imposed. If not so paid it may be collected in the form of a civil action against the defendant corporation (420.20).

Remission of Fines, Restitution or Reparation (420.30)

Monies paid by the defendant in satisfaction of fines, restitution or reparation may be returned to the defendant by the superior court that imposed the sentence upon application of the defendant. Mandatory surcharge or crime victim assistance fees may not be remitted. If the fine, restitution or reparation was imposed by a local criminal court such court may not remit. Application for remittance in such a case must be made to a superior court in the county where the local criminal court sits. Before the superior court remits it must give five days' notice to all interested parties and afford each an opportunity to be heard.

Mandatory Surcharge and Crime Victim Assistance Fee Procedures (420.35, 40)

Under no circumstances shall the mandatory surcharge or crime victim assistance fee be waived by the court at the time of sentence. If there is an issue raised as to defendant's indigence and whether the requirement to pay would create an unreasonable hardship upon the defendant and /or his family, a separate post sentencing proceeding will be held, giving the defendant an opportunity to be heard on the matter. Based upon the unreasonable hardship hearings, the court may defer the payment in whole or in part. If the court defers payment it must enter a written order to that effect and direct a civil judgment for the owing amount to be filed against the defendant. On the other hand, if the court finds payment would not create an unreasonable hardship, it shall direct payment of the fees and may imprison the defendant for up to fifteen days for non-payment, if otherwise not sentenced to imprisonment.

11.6 Sentences of Imprisonment (Article 430)

The substantive terms of imprisonment for various criminal offenses are set forth in the Penal Law sections dealing with sentencing (e.g., Article 70). The CPL provisions are procedural in nature. Once a lawful sentence of imprisonment has been imposed by the court it may not be changed, suspended or interrupted once the term or period of sentence has commenced (430.10). The sentence commences when the defendant is given over to the custody of the department of correction (*People v. Ladone*, 556 N.Y.S.2d 215 (1990)). There are lawful exceptions to this rule. The court may correct mistakes or errors that had an effect on the substance of the sentence (*People v. Minaya*, 54 N.Y.2d 353 (1981)); or, for example, it may set aside a sentence on grounds it was legally invalid, on motion of either party or upon appeal (*People v. Baraka*, 439 N.Y.S.2d 827 (1981)).

The judgment or sentence of the court may also be contested upon a motion to set aside the judgment or sentence (Article 440) or an appeal (Article 450) in appropriate circumstances as indicated in Chapter 12, *infra*.

Chapter 12

Proceedings after Judgment

Sec. 12.1 Article 440; Post-Judgment Motions
Sec. 12.2 Article 450; Appeals — In What Cases Authorized and to What
     Courts Taken
Sec. 12.3 Article 460; Appeals — Taking and Perfecting; and, Stays during
     Pendency
Sec. 12.4 Article 470: Appeals — Determination

12.1 Post-Judgment Motions
(Article 440)

After the judgment is entered in a case, the judgment may be contended by a post-judgment motion or an appeal. There are two basic post-judgment motions contained in Article 440; a motion to vacate judgment and a motion to set aside sentence. Article 440 is a codification of the relief historically available to defendants under the ancient writ of error coram nobis and court decisions that expanded its coverage. The statute embraces all non-appellate post-judgment remedies and motions to challenge the validity of a judgment of conviction unless the basis for the contention is not covered by the provisions of the statute. This article which codifies the common law writ of error coram nobis, is designed to inform the court of facts not reflected in the record and not known at the time of judgment that would, as a matter of law, undermine the judgment (*People v. Harris*, 491 N.Y.S.2d 678 (1985)).

Motion to Vacate Judgment (440.10)

1. At any time after the entry of judgment, the court in which the judgment was entered may, upon motion of the defendant, vacate such judgment on the ground that:

    a. the court lacked jurisdiction; or,

    b. the judgment was secured through fraud, misrepresentation or duress; or,

    c. false material evidence was used at trial and was known to be false by the prosecutor before the entry of judgment; or,

    d. the judgment was based upon unconstitutionally procured evidence; or,

    e. by reason of mental disease or defect, the defendant was incapable of understanding or participating in the proceedings; or,

    f.   improper or prejudicial conduct, not appearing in the trial record occurred, which if it had appeared in the record, would on appeal, have resulted in a reversal of the conviction; or,

    g.   new evidence has been discovered since the entry of the judgment, and such evidence could not have been discovered earlier by due diligence of the defendant, and it is of such a character that if it had been received at trial the verdict probably would have been more favorable to the defendant; or,

    h.   the judgment was obtained in violation of a constitutional right of the defendant.

If the defendant's ground does not fall within the statute, the defendant may still utilize the writ of error coram nobis, e.g., a claim of ineffective assistance of appellate counsel (*People v. Bachert*, 69 N.Y.2d 593 (1987)). Though the motion may be made at any time after the judgment, the length of time between the judgment and the filing of the motion may be relevant to its outcome, e.g., a defendant having pleaded guilty to a charge, should not, years later, at a time when the prosecution is unable to prove its case, be allowed to assert his constitutional right to appeal has been obstructed (*People v. Lynn*, 28 N.Y.2d 196 (1971)).

  2. The court however must deny the motion to vacate based upon any of the above grounds, if:

    a.   the ground was previously determined on the merits on an appeal; or,

    b.   the judgment is, at the time of the motion, appealable or on appeal; or,

    c.   the defendant unjustifiably failed to appeal during the prescribed period of time; or,

    d.   the ground raised has solely to do with the validity of the sentence and not the validity of the conviction.

  3. The court *may* deny the motion to vacate in the event the ground was previously the subject of a motion and denied and not determined upon an appeal; but, it may in the interest of justice and for good cause shown, in its discretion, grant the motion if it is otherwise meritorious, and vacate the judgment.

If the court grants the motion to vacate, it must vacate the judgment and dismiss the accusatory instrument, or order a new trial, or take such other action as is warranted under the circumstances (e.g., modify the judgment by reducing it to a conviction for a lesser offense) (440.10).

Motion to Set Aside Sentence — by Defendant; by People (440.20, 40)

The post-judgment motion to set aside sentence may be made either by the defendant or by the people.

Any time after the entry of the judgment, the court in which the judgment was entered may, upon motion of the defendant, set aside the sentence on the ground that it was unauthorized, illegally imposed or otherwise invalid as a matter of law. The court, however, must deny the motion when the grounds raised were previously adjudicated on the merits upon an appeal. The court may deny the motion if the grounds raised were previously determined on a motion. In this instance however, as in the motion to set aside judgment, the court in its discretion, in the interest of justice and for good cause shown, may grant the motion if it is otherwise meritorious. The order setting aside a sentence doesn't affect the validity of the underlying conviction, merely the sentence, and the court must then resentence the defendant in accordance with the law (440.20). Claims of harsh or excessive sentences are not allowable as a post-judgment remedy but must be brought by appeal. Examples of sentencing errors which may be attacked by post-judgment motion are the erroneous imposition of consecutive sentences or sentencing as a second or third offender or lack of counsel at sentencing. Not more than one year after the entry of judgment, the court in which it was entered may, upon motion of the people, set aside the sentence upon the ground that it was invalid as a matter of law. The court must deny the motion when the ground was previously determined on appeal and it may deny the motion if it was previously determined on a motion. In the latter case the court may grant the motion, in its discretion, for good cause shown if it is otherwise meritorious. The motion by the people must be made upon reasonable notice to the defendant and the defendant's attorney. The defendant has the right to appear at any hearing on the motion and must be given adequate opportunity to appear in opposition to the motion (440.40). The defendant has no right to a sentence based on an inadvertent mistake (*People v. White*, 450 N.Y.S.2d 866 (1982)). Where the prosecutor did not file appropriate information on defendant's prior felony conviction as required for sentencing as a second felony offender, the initial sentence was invalid as a matter of law and subject to vacatur upon motion of the people (*People v. Brown*, 387 N.Y.S.2d 470 (1976)).

Procedure on Defendant's Motions (440.30)

A specific procedure is set forth to be utilized in bringing, answering and determining motions of a defendant to vacate a judgment and to set aside a sentence. The basic provisions are quite similar to those set forth in Article 210 (*supra*) for determining other motions of the defendant. By and large the procedure requires the defendant to make the motion in writing with notice to the people. Every ground for the motion must be set forth along with sworn allegations of fact and supported by other documentary evidence where available. The people have the right to answer the allegations of the defendant and may support the answer by documentary evidence as well. When all the papers have been submitted, the court must consider them and determine whether a hearing is necessary to resolve questions of fact. If a hearing is not deemed necessary the motion will be decided without one. If the court determines there are questions of fact that require determination, a hearing will be held. The defendant has a right to be present at the hearing and he may waive such right in writing. If the defendant does not waive the right to be present, the court must cause him to be present at the hearing. At the hearing the defendant bears the burden of proof by a preponderance of evidence of every fact essential to support the motion. When the court decides the motion, either with or without a hearing, it must set forth on the record its findings of fact, conclusions of law and the reasons for its determination.

Miscellaneous Provisions

In addition to post-judgment motions, Article 440 contains a number of notification procedures.

1. Upon the request of a crime victim, the district attorney must notify the victim by letter of the final disposition of the case against the defendant. If the defendant is imprisoned, the notice to the victim will also inform him of the right to submit a written victim's impact statement to the parole authorities or to meet personally with them in order to make his (the victim's) views known, on each occasion upon which the defendant is to appear before the board for parole consideration (440.50).

2. The district attorney shall give written notice to the department of education upon the conviction of a felony of any person holding a license under title eight of the Education Law (teachers and other professionals). In addition such notice will be given upon the vacatur or reversal of any felony conviction of such person (440.55).

3. The appropriate director of the probation department must notify the district attorney of the county in which the conviction of a defendant was had of any sentence to probation which is invalid according to law, in order for the people to move to set such sentence aside (440.60).

See Illustrative Cases

People v. Machado, 90 N.Y.2d 187 (1997), p. 403
People v. Reyes, 680 N.Y.S.2d 493 (1998), p. 405
People v. Harris, 682 N.Y.S.2d 808 (1998), p. 406
People v. Tookes, 639 N.Y.S.2d 913 (1996), p. 408

12.2 Appeals — In What Cases Authorized and to What Courts Taken (Article 450)

In addition to the non-appellate post-judgment remedies discussed above there are appellate remedies available to the defendant and, in a constitutionally limited fashion, to the people. This article deals with the right to appeal and the courts to which appeals are to be taken. The procedure for taking appeals (art. 460) and rules the courts must follow in deciding appeals (art. 470) follow. The appellate courts of New York State are classified as the intermediate appellate courts and the Court of Appeals, the highest court in New York State. In most instances appeals may be taken to the intermediate appellate courts as a matter of right but there are instances when permission from a court is required before such an appeal may be taken. On the other hand, appeals to the Court of Appeals, other than those involving the death penalty, require permission.

Appeals by Defendant

An appeal to an intermediate appellate court may be taken by the defendant as a matter of right from a judgment or sentence, other than one involving death, or an order setting aside a sentence, other than one of death (450.10). Appeals involving the death penalty are taken directly to the Court of Appeals as a matter of right (450.70). Certain judgments and sentences arising from plea bargains are also excluded from these defendant's intermediate appeal rights (450.10).

If an appeal by the defendant is not authorized as a matter of right, he may appeal, with the permission of a judge, an order denying a post-judgment motion to vacate a judgment (440.10) or to set aside a sentence (440.20). You will recall that these motions by the defendant may be made at any time after the judgment is entered and appeals regarding these decisions are permissive as opposed to as a matter of right in order to eliminate unwarranted work for the appellate courts (450.15). An order denying a motion to vacate judgment in a criminal case is not final but intermediate in nature and, as such, the legislature may constitutionally impose conditional limitations on the right of appeal (*Rivera v. Justices of N.Y.S. Supreme Court*, 606 N.Y.S.2d 667 (1994)).

The right to appeal in a criminal action is purely statutory (*People v. Taylor*, 472 N.Y.S.2d 155 (1984)). The concept of appeal to a higher court was unknown at common law and is not a natural or inherent right (*People v. Kearse*, 295 N.Y.S.2d 192 (1968)). Upon a guilty plea, the defendant waives statutory grounds for appeal; but, a guilty plea does not amount to a waiver of appeal of constitutional guarantees. However, issues stemming from a guilty plea which involves the legality of the sentence or the voluntariness of the plea itself are always appealable (*People v. Francabandera*, 33 N.Y.2d 429 (1974)).

Appeals by the People

The appellate rights of the people are limited by the defendant's constitutional and statutory protections against being twice put in jeopardy for the same offense, "double jeopardy" (U.S. Const. amend. V; N.Y. Const. art. I, sec. 6; N.Y. CPL art. 40). The people may not appeal a verdict of acquittal, but they may appeal certain orders of the court made during the course of the criminal action. For example, the people may take an appeal to an intermediate court as a matter of right from an order of a criminal court dismissing an accusatory instrument or count thereof; or, setting aside a verdict; or, one involving a sentence other than death; or, suppressing evidence; or, a finding that the defendant is mentally retarded in a death penalty case (450.20). When appealing a pre-trial order of the criminal court suppressing evidence, the people must file a statement with the appellate court asserting the inability to use the

Trial Court	Intermediate Appellate Court
Superior Court	
Supreme County	Appellate division of the department in which the trial court is located
Local Criminal Courts	
One outside of New York City	County Court of the county in which the trial court is located
The New York City Criminal Court	
New York or Bronx County	Appellate Division, 1st Department
Kings, Queens or Richmond County	Appellate Division, 2nd Department

evidence suppressed makes the criminal charge unable to be proven as a matter of law or due to the weakening of the people's overall case. The taking of this appeal by the people acts as a bar to future prosecution unless and until the suppression order is reversed (450.50). This and the right to appeal an order dismissing an indictment and the ordering of the filing of a prosecutor's information (450.20/1a) are the only two instances where interlocutory appeals may be had in a criminal case (450.55). The people may take an appeal directly to the Court of Appeals from an order of a superior court vacating or setting aside a sentence of death (450.80).

The defendant and the people both have the right to appeal a sentence other than death to an intermediate appellate court. The defendant upon the ground that the sentence is invalid as a matter of law or that it is harsh or excessive. The people may appeal only on the ground that the sentence is invalid as a matter of law (450.30).

To What Court Should Intermediate Appeals Be Taken?

New York State is divided into four appellate departments with an Appellate Division of the Supreme Court presiding over each department. You will recall the criminal trial courts of the state are divided into the superior courts (the supreme and county courts) in which trials of indictments are held, and the local criminal courts (the district courts, New York City Criminal Court and the various city, town and village courts) in which trials of misdemeanors and lesser criminal offenses are usually held (CPL, art. 10). Each of the trial courts is located in a specific appellate department. The proper court to which an intermediate appeal should be taken depends upon the court whose determination is being appealed.

In the case of the local criminal courts, if the appellate division of the department in which the trial court is located has established an appellate term of the supreme court, and directed that appeals from the local criminal courts be taken to the appellate term, appeals from the local criminal court must be taken to that appellate term (450.60).

Appeals from Decisions of Intermediate Appellate Courts

The defendant or the people may appeal from an adverse order of an intermediate appellate court. There is no right to an appeal to the Court of Appeals except for appeals involving a judgment of death. In order to take a permissive appeal from the intermediate appellate court the prospective appellant must obtain permission from a judge of the Court of Appeals or from a justice of the appellate division department that decided the intermediate appeal; and, the appeal must involve a question of law in whole or in part (450.90). The Court of Appeals is restricted to review of questions of law by the New York State Constitution (art. VI, sec. 3a).

See Illustrative Cases

People v. Calvi, 664 N.Y.S.2d 313 (1997), p. 410

12.3 Appeals — Taking and Perfecting, and Stays during Pendency (Article 460)

The procedure for taking appeals is set forth in this article. The procedures differ slightly for appeals as a matter of right and permissive appeals; and, the court to which the appeal is to be made.

Appeals as a Matter of Right

For an appeal as a matter of right, to an intermediate appellate court or the Court of Appeals, the party seeking to appeal must file a written notice of appeal, in duplicate, within thirty days, with the clerk of the court that imposed the judgment, sentence or order, stating that such party appeals therefrom, to a designated appellate court:

a. If the defendant is the appellant, he must, within such thirty day period, forward a copy of the notice of appeal to the district attorney of the county in which the court that rendered the decision to be appealed is located. If the appeal is directly to the Court of Appeals, the district attorney must immediately give written notice to the public servant having custody of the defendant.

b. If the people are the appellant, they must within such thirty day period, serve a copy of such notice upon the defendant or upon his attorney.

When these steps have been completed the appeal is deemed to have been taken. The clerk of the court must enter the filing date upon the notices served upon him and forward the duplicate to the clerk of the court to which the appeal is to be taken.

Appeals, as a matter of right to the county court or the appellate term of the supreme court, in which the underlying proceedings were recorded by a court stenographer are taken in the same manner as those taken to the intermediate appellate court or the Court of Appeals. However, if the court does not have a clerk, the filing must be to the judge of said court and the appellant must also file a copy of the notice of appeal with the clerk of the court to which the appeal is taken. If the proceedings to be appealed were not recorded by a court stenographer, the appellant must also file within the prescribed time an affidavit of errors, setting forth the alleged errors or defects in the proceedings being appealed. The appellant must file a copy of the affidavit of errors upon the respondent within 3 days (the district attorney or defendant or defendant's counsel). When these steps have been taken the appeal is deemed to have been taken. Within ten days after the filing of the affidavit of errors, the court must forward, to the appellate court, a copy of the affidavit and a court return setting forth the evidence and facts and circumstances which constitute the factual foundation for the contentions alleged in the appeal (460.10).

Permissive Appeals

For a permissive appeal by a defendant to an intermediate appellate court, the defendant must within thirty days make application for a certificate granting leave to appeal, to a single judge of the court to which the appeal is to be taken. If the judge grants the application and issues the certificate (which states the case involves questions of law and/or fact which should be reviewed by the court, 460.15) the defendant must, within fifteen days of the issuance of such certificate, file with the court from whose order the appeal is being taken, the certificate and a written notice of appeal or, in an appropriate case, an affidavit of errors. Not more than one application may be made for such certificate (460.15). Thereafter the defendant follows the steps set forth for an appeal as a matter of right, *supra*.

All appeals to the Court of Appeals, except in death penalty cases which may be appealed as a matter of right, are permissive requiring the application for and the granting of a certificate by either a judge of an appellate division or the Court of Appeals itself. The appellant must, within thirty days, apply for a certificate granting leave to appeal. If the certificate is granted, its granting constitutes the taking of the appeal:

   a.   Where the appeal sought is from an order of the appellate division, the certificate may be issued by a judge of the Court of Appeals or the appellate division of the appellate department within which the order was issued.

   b.   Where the appeal is sought from an order of an intermediate appellate court other than the appellate division (county court or appellate term) the certificate may only be issued by a judge of the Court of Appeals.

   c.   The judge issuing or denying such certificate shall forward a copy of the certificate to the clerk of the Court of Appeals (460.20).

Where a notice of appeal, affidavit of errors or application for leave to appeal is filed prematurely or contains an inaccurate description of the matter being appealed, it is within the discretion of the court, in the interest of justice, to treat such instrument as valid. When the appellant files a notice of appeal within the designated time but through mistake or inadvertence fails to serve a copy on the respondent within the designated time, the appellate court may, in its discretion, in the interests of justice, for good cause shown, permit such service to be made within a designated period of time and upon such service the appeal is deemed to be taken (460.10).

The time for taking an appeal may be extended by the appropriate intermediate appellate court or the Court of Appeals on the ground the failure to timely file resulted from:

a. improper conduct of a public servant or the improper conduct, death or disability of the defendant's attorney; or,

b. inability of an incarcerated defendant and his attorney to communicate concerning the appeal (460.30).

In certain cases the taking of an appeal may allow a stay of the judgment or sentence being appealed (460.40,50,60).

Perfecting the Appeal

After an appeal has been taken to the appropriate court there are steps that must be taken to complete the appeal process. These steps are called **perfecting** the appeal. Appeals taken to the appellate division are perfected by following the rules of the appellate department in which the appellate court is located. The Court of Appeals has its own set of rules for perfection of appeals to that court. The county courts and the appellate terms have their own rules to be followed and are also governed by the Uniform Rules of the New York State Trial Courts. Among the matters to be determined by these court rules are the times when the appeal must be noticed for and brought to argument, the time for, and the content and form of the records and briefs to be served and filed. Transcripts of the record of proceedings in the trial court are needed for the appeal. Therefore when an appeal has been taken, the court reporter of the trial court will prepare the transcript and file it in the trial court. The expense for such transcript and any required copies shall be paid for by the defendant. If the defendant is declared a "poor person" by the appellate court the expense shall be borne by the state and payed from funds of the office of court administration (460.70).

12.4 Appeals — Determination Thereof (Article 470)

An appellate court must determine an appeal without regard to technical errors which do not affect the substantial rights of the parties, which means that "harmless errors" are not appealable or to be considered by the appellate court once determined to be harmless. The rule that a judgment of conviction need not be reversed on appeal for a trial error which was harmless was originally enacted to relieve courts and the public of the needless expense of retrying cases in which the result would be the same after the error was corrected (*People v. Grant*, 45 N.Y.2d 366 (1978)). For purposes of appeal, a question of law is preserved for appeal when:

a. the appealing party protested at the time the court ruling was made or any subsequent time when the court had a chance to change its ruling. Such protest need not be in the form of an "exception" but is sufficient if the party made his position known to the court or, if in response to a protest by a party, the court expressly decided the question raised upon appeal; or,

b. a party without success sought a particular ruling or instruction (470.05).

Matters on appeal may be subject to "reversal," "modification" or "corrective action."

These terms are defined as:

a. "**Reversal**" means vacating a judgment, sentence or order.

b. "**Modification**" means vacating a part of an order and affirmance of the rest.

c. "**Corrective action**" means affirmative action taken or directed, upon reversing or modifying the action of the lower court, consistent with the appellate court's decision, e.g., remanding the matter to the lower court for future action not inconsistent with the appellate court's decision or a reversal of a conviction in the lower court (470.10).

Determination of Appeals by Intermediate Appellate Courts

1. Scope of Review

Upon appeal the intermediate appellate court may consider and determine questions of law or issues of fact involving error or defect which may have adversely affected the appellant. Upon appeal the court must affirm, reverse or modify the criminal court judgment, sentence or order. For instance, the court may modify a judgment in the following ways:

a. If the trial evidence is found not legally sufficient to establish the defendant's guilt of the offense for which he was convicted but is legally sufficient to establish his guilt of a lesser included offense, the court may modify the judgment by changing it to one of conviction for the lesser included offense; or,

b. If the sentence imposed upon a valid conviction is found to be illegal or unduly harsh, the court may modify the judgment by reversing it with respect to the sentence and by otherwise affirming it.

A reversal or modification must be based upon the law, or the facts, or as a matter of discretion in the interest of justice, or upon any combination of these reasons. Determinations deemed to be on the law are, for example:

a. a ruling or instruction of the court deprived the defendant of a fair trial; or,

b. the evidence at trial was not legally sufficient to establish the defendant's guilt; or,

c. a sentence was unauthorized, illegally imposed or otherwise invalid as a matter of law.

Determinations deemed to be on the facts are, for example:

a. a verdict of conviction was in whole or in part against the weight of evidence.

Determinations deemed to be as a matter of discretion in the interest of justice are, for example:

a. an error or defect at trial was not duly protested so as to present a question of law, but such error or defect deprived the defendant of a fair trial; or,

b. a sentence, though legal, was unduly harsh or severe (470.15).

The appellate powers of the intermediate appellate courts are very broad compared to those of the Court of Appeals and the trial courts. The latter courts may only take action based upon questions of law.

2. Corrective Action upon Reversal or Modification

Upon reversing or modifying a judgment, sentence or order of a criminal court, the intermediate appellate court must take or direct such corrective action as is necessary and appropriate both to rectify any injustice to the appellant and to protect the rights of the respondent. For example:

a. Upon reversal for a defect that resulted in prejudice to the defendant or deprived him of a fair trial, the court must order a new trial and remit the case to the criminal court.

b. Upon reversal for legal insufficiency of evidence, the court must dismiss the accusatory instrument.

c. Upon modification for legal insufficiency of evidence with respect to one or more but not all of the counts of the accusatory instrument, the court must dismiss the counts found to be unsupported and affirm the others. The court may then reduce the sentence to that imposed by the criminal court for the counts not dismissed or remit the case to the criminal court for resentencing. The court might also, as it may do in any appropriate case, in its discretion, in the interest of justice, on the ground the sentence is unduly harsh, impose some legally authorized lesser sentence.

d. Upon modification to conviction for a lesser offense the court must remit the case for resentencing (470.20).

Determination of Appeals by the Court of Appeals

1. Appeals Taken Directly from Criminal Courts

The scope of review and corrective action to be taken by the Court of Appeals follows that set forth above for the intermediate appellate courts. In addition there are special provisions and a mandatory review of death sentence cases to determine:

a. if the penalty of death is excessive, arbitrary, legally impermissible or against the weight of evidence;

    b.   if the penalty is disproportionate or excessive compared to the penalty imposed in similar cases, by virtue of the race of the defendant or victim of the crime for which the defendant was committed.

The court shall include in its decision:

    a.   the aggravating and mitigating factors in the record on appeal; and,

    b.   those similar cases it took into consideration.

In addition to any other corrective action it is authorized to take, the court may affirm the sentence of death or remit the case to the criminal court to determine if the sentence should be:

    a.   Death, life imprisonment without parole or life other than without parole; or,

    b.   Life imprisonment without parole or life other than without parole (470.30).

2. Appeals from Intermediate Appellate Courts

Scope of Review

    a.   Upon appeals to the Court of Appeals from an order of an intermediate appellate Court:

        1)   affirming a judgment, sentence or order of a criminal court, the Court of Appeals may consider any question of law the intermediate appellate court could have considered. It is not restricted to considering only those that the appellate court ruled upon.

        2)   reversing or modifying a judgment, sentence or order, the Court of Appeals may consider and determine:

            i.   any question of law determined by the appellate court; or,

            ii.   any question of law not considered by the appellate court but which was connected to a different question of law the court decided, which is now being contested; or,

           iii.   any question concerning the legality of the corrective action taken by the appellate court.

    b.   Upon any such appeal the Court of Appeals must affirm, reverse or modify the decision of the appellate court (470.35).

Corrective Action upon Reversal or Modification

    a.   Upon reversing or modifying an order of the intermediate appellate court *affirming* a criminal court judgment, the Court of Appeals must take or direct such corrective action as the intermediate appellate court would have been required to take or direct had it reversed the criminal court judgment on the same grounds.

    b.   Upon reversing an order of the intermediate appellate court reversing or modifying a criminal court judgment, on the ground that questions of law were erroneously determined by the appellate court in favor of the appellant therein, the court of appeals must take or direct corrective action. If the facts underlying the original criminal court judgment were considered by the appellate court, the Court of Appeals must reinstate and affirm the criminal court judgment and remit the case to the criminal court for whatever action should be taken. If however, the appellate court did not consider the facts, the case shall be remitted to the appellate court for further determination of the facts.

c. Upon modifying an intermediate appellate court order reversing or modifying a criminal court judgment, upon the ground that the corrective action was illegal, the Court of Appeals itself must either, take the appropriate corrective action or remit to the appellate court to take the appropriate action (470.40).

Remission of Case by Appellate Court to the Criminal Court

Upon reversing or modifying a judgment and directing corrective action, the appellate court must remit the case to the trial court which must execute the direction of the appellate court and, depending upon the nature of the direction, either discharge the defendant, exonerate his bail or issue a securing order (470.45).

Reargument of an Appeal

After the determination of an appeal, the court may in its own discretion or on motion of a party adversely affected by the appellate court's decision, in the interest of justice and for good cause shown, order reargument or reconsideration of the appeal. If it does so, the court must again determine the appeal. All appellate courts may establish rules limiting the time within the motion must be made. If a court has no such rule the motion may be made at any time (470.50).

Dismissal of the Appeal

Any time after the appeal has been taken and before its determination, the court upon its own motion or that of the respondent may dismiss the appeal. The grounds are mootness, jurisdiction, untimeliness or other substantial defect, irregularity or failure of the appellant. Such motion must be made with reasonable notice to the appellant with an opportunity to be heard. The notice must be served by ordinary mail to the appellant at his place of residence or if he is incarcerated, at the jail and to his attorney. If the court dismissing the appeal is an intermediate appellate court the defendant, if granted a certificate of permission to appeal, may appeal the decision to the Court of Appeals. Upon such an appeal, the Court of Appeals must affirm or reverse the order of the appellate court (470.60).

See Illustrative Cases

People v. Crimmins, 36 N.Y.2d 230 (1975), p. 411
People v. Schaeffer, 56 N.Y.2d 448 (1982), p. 413
People v. Robinson, 36 N.Y.2d 224 (1975), p. 414
People v. Bleakley, 69 N.Y.2d 490 (1987), p. 415

Part Three

Special Proceedings and Miscellaneous Procedures

Chapter 13

Securing Attendance at Court of Defendants and Witnesses under Control of the Court— Recognizance, Bail and Commitment

Sec. 13.1 Article 500; Recognizance, Bail and Commitment—Definitions
Sec. 13.2 Article 510; Recognizance, Bail and Commitment—Application for; Securing Orders and Related Matters
Sec. 13.3 Article 520; Bail and Bail Bonds
Sec. 13.4 Article 530; Recognizance or Bail Re: Defendants; When and by What Courts Authorized
Sec. 13.5 Article 540; Forfeiture of Bail and Remission Thereof

13.1 Recognizance, Bail and Commitment— Definitions (Article 500.10)

There are 23 definitions set forth in Article 500.10 relating to bail, recognizance and commitment. It is necessary to understand them in order to understand the provisions of the CPL which contain them. These terms appear not only in the articles in this chapter, specifically on bail and recognizance, but throughout the CPL where bail and recognizance are addressed. The following are definitions or summaries of key words and terms necessary to the understanding of substantive materials on bail and recognizance.

Bail means cash bail or a bail bond or money paid with a credit card. **Cash bail** is money posted upon the condition it will be forfeited if the defendant does not comply with the court's instructions regarding appearance in court and other conditions of their release. A **bail bond** is a written undertaking by one or more obligors that they will pay to the state a sum of money in the event the principal does not comply with the court's instructions regarding appearance in court and other conditions of his release. A **principal** is a defendant, material witness or any other person who might be compelled to appear before the court. An **obligor** is the person who executes the undertaking in a bail bond. The principal himself may be an obligor. A **surety** is an obligor who is not a principal. In making an **application for recognizance or bail**, a principal asks the court to release him on his own recognizance (ROR) or bail, permitting the principal to be at liberty during the pendency of the criminal action, rather than commit (jail) him. The court at arraignment or other stages of the proceeding may issue a **securing order**, committing the principal or fixing bail or releasing him on his own recognizance or release under non-monetary conditions (NMC). Such conditions may include that the principal be in contact with a pretrial services agency serving principals in that county; that the principal abide by reasonable, specified restrictions on travel that are reasonably related to an actual risk of flight from the jurisdiction; and that the principal refrain from possessing a firearm, destructive device or other dangerous weapon. Electronic monitoring may also be used when certain crimes are charged, at no cost to the principal, if no other monetary or non-monetary option would reasonably assure principal's return to court. If the court orders **commitment to the custody of the sheriff** the principal will be confined to the custody of the sheriff or in a city, its department of correction. To **fix bail** means the court will designate a sum of money and stipulate, when it is posted, the principal will be permitted to be at liberty during the pendency of the criminal action or proceeding; or, in the alternative, the court may **release on own recognizance** the principal upon his promise to appear when required and comply with other orders of the court. To **post bail** means to deposit it in the form and amount fixed by the court, with the court or other authorized public servant or agency.

There are different kinds of bail bonds:

a. **Appearance bond** — the principal is the only obligor

b. **Surety bond** — the obligor is the surety or a surety and the principal

c. **Insurance company bail bond** — a surety bond in which the surety obligor is a licensed bail bond corporation

d. **Secured bail bond** — a bail bond secured by personal or real property

e "Partially secured bail bond" means a bail bond secured only by a deposit of a sum of money not exceeding ten percent of the total amount of the undertaking.

f. **Unsecured bail bond** — a bond other than an insurance company bail bond, not secured by a deposit of or lien upon property.

These terms when found in the CPL are to be given the meaning indicated above (500.10).

13.2 Recognizance, Bail and Commitment— Application for; Securing Orders and Related Matters (Article 510)

New York enacted bail reform on January 1, 2020, to ensure a defendant's return to court. It mandates that the court must impose the "least restrictive" securing order that will reasonably assure a defendant's return to court. CPL 510.10(1), and individualized non-monetary conditions of release (510.40(3). The law's guiding principle is no jail, no bail. The reforms immediately proved controversial and were amended in April 3, 2020, with a rollback providing more circumstances eligible for the imposition of cash bail.

The following are the four available types of securing orders:

1. Release on the defendant's own recognizance (ROR). These are low flight risks.

2. Release on non-monetary conditions (NMCs). These are significant flight risks on non-bailable offenses and moderate flight risks on bailable offenses.

3. Monetary bail (also referred to as a monetary condition) for significant flight risks.

4. Commitment to the custody of the sheriff (i.e., remand) for overwhelming flight risks.

There is a presumption is that a defendant should be released on their own recognizance ("ROR"). Only upon a court's determination that a defendant poses a risk of flight to avoid prosecution may a court impose one of the three more restrictive securing orders listed above. When imposing one of these more restrictive securing orders, the court must always impose the least restrictive means of ensuring the defendant's return to court and give its rationale either on the record or in writing.

Determining the "Least Restrictive" Means

The Court "must" take into account the following "relevant" criteria when determining the least restrictive means of reasonably assuring the defendant's return to court:

a. The principal's activities and history (510.30(1)(a);

b. The charges that have been alleged (CPL 510.30(1)(b));

c. Prior criminal conviction(s) (CPL 510.30(1)(c));

d. Prior adjudications as a juvenile delinquent or a youthful offender (CPL 510.30(1)(d);

e. History of flight to avoid prosecution (CPL 510.30(1)(e)); and

f. History of family or household crimes (CPL 510.30(1)(g)).

Where the defendant is charged with a crime against a member of their family or household, the court must also consider any previous violation of an order of protection for a member of the defendant's family or household and any history of use or possession of a firearm (CPL 510.30(1)(g)(i)–(ii)); Additionally, the court must also take into account the defendant's individual financial circumstances, ability to post bail without undue hardship, and ability to obtain a secured, unsecured, or partially secured bond if it is considering imposing monetary. CPL 510.30(1) (f).

Qualifying Offenses

The following are the qualifying offenses where the Court can impose bail.

a. Any crime that is alleged to have caused the death of another person (CPL 510.10[4][j]).

b. Any felony committed while serving a sentence of probation or while released to post release supervision (CPL 510.10[4][r]).

c. Any felony where the defendant qualifies for sentencing on such charge as a persistent felony offender under Penal Law § 70.10 (CPL 510.10[4][s]).

d. Any felony or class A misdemeanor involving harm to an identifiable person or property, where such charge arose from conduct occurring while the defendant was released on his own recognizance or released under conditions for a separate felony or class A misdemeanor involving harm to an identifiable person or property, provided that the prosecutor must show reasonable cause to believe that the defendant committed the instant crime and any underlying crime. The underlying crime need not be a qualifying offense (CPL 510.10[4][t]).

e. Failure to register as a sex offender (Correction Law § 168-t) when the defendant is required to maintain Level 3 sex offender registration (CPL 510.10[4][p]).

Under CPL 530.60(2)(b)(i) & CPL 530.60(2)(b)(iv) if an individual who has committed an offense had been released on their own recognizance and is accused of a felony, or persistently and willfully fails to appear in court, the Court may revoke the order and impose bail.

510.10(4) et seq. Offenses Qualifying for Sheriff's Custody

Where the defendant is charged with a qualifying felony, the court may commit the principal to the custody of the sheriff. Various crimes are specified pertaining to burglary, robbery, witness intimidation, witness tampering, sex offences such as incest, homicide, terrorism, criminal contempt, and crimes that exploit or abuse children. The reforms were rolled back, however, within 3 months of the major reform on April 3, 2020, with the expansion of qualifying criteria. Offenses also include promoting sexual performance of a child, crime causing death, strangulation, unlawful imprisonment, vehicular assault, hate crime assault, aggravated assault of a child, weapons possession on school grounds, grand larceny, money laundering, failure to register as a sex offender, endangerment of a child by a registered sex offender, bail jumping, escaping from custody, commission of a felony while on probation, persistent felony offender, and commission of a class A misdemeanor harming an identifiable person or property when released on one's own recognizance.

510.15 Commitment of Principal under Seventeen or Eighteen

When a principal who is under the age of sixteen is committed to the custody of the sheriff the court must direct that the principal be taken to and lodged in a place certified by the office of children and family services as a juvenile detention facility for the reception of children.

As of October 1, 2019, when a principal who is sixteen or seventeen years of age is committed to the custody of the sheriff, the court must direct that the principal be taken to and lodged in a place certified by the office of children and family services in conjunction with the state commission of correction as a specialized secure juvenile detention facility for older youth. No principal designated in this section shall be detained in any prison, jail, lockup or other place used for adults convicted of a crime or under arrest and charged with the commission of a crime without the approval of the office of children and family services which shall consult with the commission of correction if the principal is sixteen years of age or older in the case of each principal and the statement of its reasons therefore.

13.3 Bail and Bail Bonds (Article 520)

Forms of Bail

The authorized forms of bail are cash bail or one of seven various types of bail bonds listed below:

a. Cash bail.

b. An insurance company bail bond.

c. A secured surety bond.

d. A secured appearance bond.

e. A partially secured surety bond.

f. A partially secured appearance bond.

g. An unsecured surety bond.

h. An unsecured appearance bond.

i. Credit card or similar device, provided, however, that notwithstanding any other provision of law, any person posting bail by credit card or similar device also may be required to pay a reasonable administrative fee.

Under the new bail law, if a court specifies the forms in which monetary bail may be posted, **the court must specify at least three of the available forms of bail** (i.e., cash; an insurance company bail bond; a secured, partially secured, or unsecured surety bond; and a secured, partially secured, or unsecured appearance bond), **one**

of which must be either an unsecured or partially secured surety bond. CPL 520.10(1), (2) (b).

Cash Bail

Where a court has fixed bail in any of its authorized forms, at any time after the principal has been committed to the custody of the sheriff pending its posting, cash bail may be deposited in the amount designated in the order fixing bail, even though cash bail was not specified in the order. The person posting the cash bail must complete and sign a form which sets forth:

a.   information about the depositor, the criminal action involved, the principal, and the amount of cash bail deposited; and,

b.   an undertaking that the principal will appear in court whenever required; and,

c.   an acknowledgement that the cash bail will be forfeited if the principal does not appear in court as required.

Money posted as cash bail is and shall remain the property of the person posting it unless forfeited to the court (520.15).

At common law, cash could not be accepted as or in lieu of bail (*People v. Molinari*, 174 N.Y.S.2d 512 (1919)). Absent statutory authority there is no right to deposit cash as bail. Cash bail deposited with the court, is held by the court as a trustee of such money. The terms of the trust are that, if the defendant appears, the money shall be returned to the depositor, but if the defendant fails to appear it shall be given to the appropriate authorities. In bail bonds the law looks to the surety to guarantee the defendant's appearance. In cash bail the law looks to the money already in the hands of the state to insure the defendant's appearance (*People v. Castro*, 464 N.Y.S.2d 650 (1983)).

Bail Bonds

When a bail bond is to be posted in satisfaction of bail, the obligor(s) must submit a bond in the amount and form required, and a justifying affidavit containing information as to the security set forth for the bond. The bond must be subscribed to by the obligors and contain information as required from the depositor of cash bail as set forth in 520.15, *supra*. The bail bond posted is effective and binding upon the obligors until the termination of the action unless prior to such termination:

a.   the bail is judicially revoked or vacated; or,

b.   the principal is surrendered to custody; or,

c.   the effectiveness of the bond is expressly limited by time in the terms of the bond (520.20).

The obligor is responsible for the principal's appearance, not only on the first but upon all subsequent appearances (*People v. Parisi*, 217 N.Y.24 (1916)).

The court may conduct an inquiry as to the sufficiency of the bail. In the inquiry the court will look at the background, character and reputation of any obligor for a bail bond or depositor of cash bail; the source of any money or property deposited as security or bail and whether it constitutes the fruits of criminal behavior or unlawful conduct; and, whether any feature of the undertaking contravenes public policy. The inquiry is usually precipitated by application of the district attorney. The court may examine, under oath, any person having material information. The district attorney has the right to call witnesses and to examine any witness in the proceeding. At the conclusion of the inquiry, the court must issue an order either approving or disapproving the bail (520.30). If cash bail is deposited with a local criminal court and the case is subsequently transferred to a superior court, the accused may request the transfer of the cash bail to the superior court. The depositor will be notified of such request and the superior court shall order the cash bail transferred to, and for the use of, the superior court (520.40).

13.4 Recognizance or Bail Re: Defendants; When and by What Courts Authorized; Orders of Protection (Article 530)

The procedures governing recognizance and bail determinations by various courts and protective procedures for victims of potential violence, such as orders of protection, are addressed in this article. During a criminal action or an appeal, a defendant may apply to a court for release on recognizance or bail. Whether a court may issue an order for such release is dependent upon the factors enumerated above. (530.10).

Orders of Bail or Recognizance by Local Criminal Courts

Upon application of a defendant charged with an offense below the grade of felony, the local criminal court in which the charge is pending, must order release of the defendant on recognizance or bail. If the defendant is charged with a felony, the recognizance or bail decision is within the discretion of the court, however:

a. A city, town, or village court may not order recognizance or bail when the defendant is charged with a class A felony or if it appears the defendant has two previous felony convictions.

b. No local criminal court may order recognizance or bail for a defendant charged with a felony, unless and until;

    i. the district attorney has been notified and given an opportunity to be heard, and, the court has received a copy of the defendants previous criminal record report.

A copy of the report must be given to the defendant. If the report is not available, the court may dispense with the report with the consent of the district attorney. In an emergency which impairs the ability of the authorities to furnish such report (e.g., an electrical blackout) the court may proceed without the consent (530.20). Despite the provision precluding release of a defendant set forth in "a," above, a failure to timely dispose of a felony complaint in violation of Section 180.80 requires the court to release such defendant on his own recognizance (*People v. Davis*, 460 N.Y.S.2d 260 (1983)).

Orders of Recognizance or Bail by Superior Courts

1. When the Criminal Action Is Pending in a Local Criminal Court

When an action is pending in a local criminal court, upon application of the defendant to a judge of a superior court in the same county, such judge may order recognizance or bail when the local criminal court:

a.   Lacks authority to order bail or recognizance; or,

b.   Has denied the defendant's application; or,

c.   Has fixed bail in an amount deemed to be excessive.

Before the superior court judge may order bail or recognizance, such judge must notify the district attorney and provide an opportunity to be heard on the matter, and such judge must be furnished a copy of the defendant's previous criminal record. Not more than one such application may be made by the defendant (530.30).

2. When the Action Is Pending in the Superior Court

Upon application of a defendant charged with an offense less than a felony only, the court must order recognizance or bail. If the defendant is charged with a felony, the court in its discretion may order recognizance or bail. If the defendant is on release upon an order of the local criminal court in the same action, the superior court may continue the effectiveness of the previous order. As in all felony cases, before the judge can order recognizance or bail he must give notice to the district attorney and an opportunity to be heard, and be furnished with a copy of the defendant's prior criminal record. However, after a defendant has been convicted of a class A felony, the superior court may not order or continue his release on recognizance or bail (530.40).

Although the state may afford an opportunity for bail, traditionally and acceptably, there are offenses of a nature as to which the state may properly refuse to make provisions for the right to bail (*Gold v. Shapiro*, 45 N.Y.2d 849 (1978)). One charged with a felony has no absolute right to bail and whether bail will be fixed and in what amount is for the state to decide (*People ex rel. Devore v. Warden of N.Y.C. Prison*, 244 N.Y.S.2d 505 (1963)). The discretionary power to deny bail in felony cases cannot be exercised arbitrarily. The decision needs to be buttressed by a real showing of the reasons therefore (*People ex rel. Singer v. Corbett*, 271 N.Y.S.2d 921 (1966)).

Order of Recognizance or Bail after Conviction and before Sentence

When a defendant in a criminal action for other than a class A felony at liberty on recognizance or bail is convicted, and the trial court judge revokes his bail and remands him to the custody of the sheriff while awaiting sentence, the defendant may make application for release on recognizance or bail:

a. If the criminal action was in a superior court, the application will be made to, and the order for release on recognizance or bail issued by, a justice of the appellate division of the department in which the trial court was located; or,

b. If the criminal action was pending in a local criminal court, the application is made to, and release issued by, a superior court judge of the county in which the local court is located.

The application must be made with reasonable notice to the people and an opportunity to be heard. Only one such application may be made by the defendant. The defendant must allege in his application that he intends to appeal the conviction immediately after sentence is pronounced. If the defendant is released as a result of this application but does not take the appeal within thirty days or perfect it within one hundred twenty days, he must surrender himself to the trial court in order that execution of the sentence upon the judgment of conviction may be commenced. If he fails to do so, a bench warrant for his arrest may be issued by the trial court (530.45).

Order of Recognizance or Bail during Pendency of an Appeal

A judge of the appropriate court (*see* 460.50, 60) may issue an order of recognizance or bail for a defendant pending the determination of his appeal, unless the defendant received a class A felony sentence (530.50). There is no constitutional right to bail, including after conviction. There was a rational basis for the legislature's determination not to extend the entitlement to post conviction bail to persons receiving a class A III felony sentence relating to drug offenses. The statute is constitutional (*Gold v. Shapiro*, 503 N.Y.S.2d 906 (1978)). It is not a conviction for a class A felony that bars bail during pendency of an appeal, but a class A felony sentence (*People v. Vasquez*, 450 N.Y.S.2d 606 (1982)).

Revocation of Order of Recognizance or Bail

1. General Provision

When a defendant is at liberty during a criminal action on a recognizance or bail order, and the court believes it necessary to review such order, it may, and by a bench warrant if necessary, require the defendant to appear before the court. The court may revoke the release order for good cause. If the defendant is entitled to recognizance or bail as a matter of right (less than a felony charge) the court must issue another such order. Otherwise, the court may issue another order or commit the defendant to the custody of the sheriff.

2. Revocation of Release

Revocation of release may be made during course of a course of a criminal proceeding of a defendant who has been released pursuant to a securing order for "good cause shown." Such may be done by the court *sua sponte*, or upon motion by the People. When reviewing an existing securing order, the court may order the defendant to appear, by a bench warrant if necessary. CPL 530.60(1). If the People seek to increase the non-monetary or the monetary conditions, a hearing is required. CPL 510.40(3), 530.60(2)(c).

Upon a finding of good cause shown to revoke the existing securing order, the court may either issue a new order releasing the defendant on his own recognizance, releasing the defendant on non-monetary conditions, fixing bail, or remanding the defendant to custody. Under the new law, the court may order bail or remand even if the defendant is not charged with one of the qualifying offenses listed above. CPL 530.60

Further, there are specific scenarios which are grounds for revocation of a securing order. They are where:

a. The defendant "persistently and willfully" failed to appear after notice of scheduled appearances in the case before the court (CPL 530.60(2)(b)(i));

b. The defendant violated an order of protection while at liberty pursuant to subdivision (b), (c), or (d) of Section 215.51 of the penal law (criminal contempt in the first degree) (CPL 530.60(2)(b)(ii));

c. The defendant intimidated a victim or witness (pursuant to PL Section 215.15, 215.16, or, 215.17) or tampered with a witness (pursuant to PL Section 215.11, 215.12, or 215.13) (CPL 530.60(2)(b)(iii));

d. The defendant is charged with a felony and committed another felony while at liberty (CPL 530.60(2)(b)(iv)).

See Illustrative Cases

People v. Torres, 446 N.Y.S.2d. 969, p. 417

The Bench Warrant

The function of a bench warrant is to achieve the court appearance of a defendant in a pending criminal action for a purpose other than initial arraignment (1.20/30). Those issued by a superior court, a district court, the N.Y.C. Criminal Court or a superior court judge sitting as a local criminal court may be executed anywhere in the state. One issued by a city, town or village court may only be executed in the county of issuance or an adjoining county; and, it may be executed anywhere else in the state upon the written endorsement of a local criminal court judge of the county in which it is to be executed. A bench warrant may be addressed to and executed by:

a. a police officer whose geographical area of employment is the place where the offense was committed or where the issuing court is located; or,

b. a uniformed court officer of a court in New York City, the county of Nassau or Suffolk for execution in the court building in which the officer is employed or its vicinity; or,

c. a parole or probation officer when the person named in the warrant is on parole or probation and the officer is authorized to execute the warrant by his director.

The warrant must be executed in the same manner as a warrant of arrest (120.80) and the arrested person must be brought to the issuing court without unnecessary delay (530.70).

Surrender of a Defendant

Under the new law, in most cases a court will be required to provide at least forty-eight hours' notice to the defendant or the defendant's attorney that the defendant is required to appear in court before the court may issue a bench warrant for a defendant for failure to appear for a scheduled court appearance. CPL 510.50(2). The exceptions to this rule are where there is "relevant," credible evidence that the defendant's failure to appear was willful or the defendant has been charged with a new crime.

At any time before the forfeiture of bail the obligor of a bail bond or the depositor of cash bail may surrender the defendant. The surrender should be made to the court in which the case is pending or the sheriff in whose custody he had been committed at the time bail was given. The defendant may also surrender himself. For purposes of surrender the defendant may be taken into custody any place in the state by the obligor or depositor or any person over age twenty empowered by either to do so. Upon five days' notice to the district attorney the court must order the bail exonerated. Upon filing such order the bail is exonerated (530.80). The people have the right to insist on a forfeiture of bail when the defendant has violated the terms of his freedom (*People v. Alvarez*, 404 N.Y.S.2d 509 (1978)).

Procedures for Family Offense Matters

The family court and the criminal courts have concurrent jurisdiction over the following offenses, when they involve the persons indicated. They are deemed family offenses:

a. disorderly conduct (other than in a public place),

b. harassment 1st and 2d degree,

c. aggravated harassment 2d degree,

d. stalking 1st, 2nd, 3rd and 4th degree,

   e. criminal mischief,

   f. menacing 2d and 3d degree,

   g. reckless endangerment, or

   h. assault 2d or 3d degree or attempted assault;

between:

   a. spouses or former spouses,

   b. parent and child; or,

   c. members of the same family or household, meaning persons:

      i. related by consanguinity or affinity;

      ii. legally married to one another;

      iii. formerly married to one another;

      iv. who have a child in common, whether they have been married or have lived together at any time; or

      v. persons in an intimate relationship, regardless of whether or not the parties lived together. The court will consider the nature or type of relationship, regardless of whether the relationship is sexual in nature; the frequency of interaction between the persons; and the duration of the relationship. Neither a casual acquaintance nor ordinary fraternization between two individuals in business or social contexts shall be deemed to constitute an "intimate relationship."

If the respondent is a juvenile under P.L. 30.00, the family court will have exclusive jurisdiction over such proceeding.

The petitioner or complainant bringing a family offense proceeding shall be informed, by an official designated by the court, of the procedures available, including, but not limited to:

   a. the concurrent jurisdiction of the family and criminal courts;

   b. a family court proceeding is a civil proceeding whose purpose is to stop the violence, end family disruption and obtain protection. Those referrals for counseling are available for this purpose;

   c. the purpose of a criminal court proceeding is the prosecution of the offender and can result in a criminal conviction;

   d. the proceeding starts with the filing of the accusatory instrument or family court petition, not with arrest or request for arrest;

   e. an arrest may precede the commencement of a criminal court or family court proceeding but is not a requirement for commencing either proceeding.

No official shall discourage or prevent any person who wishes to file a complaint or petition from having access to any court for that purpose.

When a person is arrested for a family offense, violation of an order of protection or arrested on a warrant for a family offense, and the applicable court is not in session, such person shall be brought before the local criminal court of the county of arrest or the county in which the warrant is returnable. In addition to the usual arraignment responsibilities, the local criminal court may issue any order authorized under Section 530.12/11 (revoke a release order and commit the defendant to custody, restore the case to the calendar when there has been an adjournment in contemplation of dismissal, revoke probation or a conditional discharge) (530.11).

Protection for Victims of Family Offenses

The protection provided for victims of family offenses comes in the form of an order of protection. The order of protection may be a "temporary order of protection" which is issued by a court prior to conviction of an offense and after conviction, the court may issue an "order of protection," which has a different life span.

1. The Temporary Order of Protection

The court may issue a temporary order of protection in family offense cases as a condition of any order of recognizance or bail or an adjournment in contemplation of dismissal. In addition to any other conditions, such an order may require the defendant:

a. to stay away from the home, school, business or place of employment of the family or a household member;

b. to permit a person entitled to visitation to visit a child at stated periods;

c. to refrain from committing a family offense or any criminal offense against the child, family or household member or any person to whom custody of the child is awarded, or from harassing, intimidating or threatening such persons;

d. to refrain from acts or omissions that creates an unreasonable risk to the health, safety and welfare of a child, family or household member's life or health;

e. to permit a designated party to enter a residence during a specified time to remove personal belongings not in issue in any proceeding.

A temporary order of protection ex parte, may be issued under the following circumstances:

a. The court may issue a temporary order of protection ex parte upon the filing of an accusatory instrument and for good cause shown. The court at this time may also modify one issued by the family court.

b. When the family court is not in session, upon request of the petitioner, a local criminal court may issue a temporary order of protection ex parte pending a hearing in the family court. The matter is then adjourned to the next session of the family court, but in no event in excess of four days later, where additional proceedings will take place.

c. The court may issue or extend a temporary order of protection ex parte simultaneously with the issuance of an arrest warrant. It may continue in effect until the day the defendant appears in court pursuant to such warrant.

2. The Order of Protection

Upon conviction of any family offense in addition to any other disposition the court may enter an order of protection, not a temporary order of protection. The duration of this order of protection shall be fixed by the court, and in the case of:

    a. a felony conviction, shall not exceed the greater of

        i. five years from the date of such conviction; or,

        ii. three years from the expiration of a prison sentence imposed.

    b. a misdemeanor conviction, shall not exceed three years from the expiration of a prison sentence imposed.

    c. a conviction for any other offense shall not exceed one year from the expiration of a prison sentence imposed.

In addition to any other condition imposed, such order may require the defendant to comply with the same conditions which may be imposed for a temporary order of protection, as listed above, e.g., stay away from the home, or abstain from offensive conduct.

A copy of the order of protection or temporary order of protection shall be filed with the sheriff or police department having jurisdiction over any of the places set forth in the order as well as any modifications or its revocation. A copy of the order will also be given to the complainant, defendant and counsel and any other person affected by the order. The presentation of this copy to a police officer or a peace officer acting pursuant to his special duties shall constitute authority for him to arrest the person who has violated the terms of the order, bring him before the court and aid in securing the protection such order was intended to afford. Violation of an order may result in punishment for contempt of court. If a defendant is brought before the court for violation of an order of protection of any type and the court is satisfied after a hearing that the defendant willfully failed to obey such order, the court may:

    a. revoke an order of recognizance or bail and commit the defendant; or,

    b. restore the case to the calendar if there had been an adjournment in contemplation of dismissal and commit the defendant to custody; or,

    c. revokes a conditional discharge or probation and takes additional appropriate steps under the law.

When applicable, an order of protection or temporary order of protection may be entered against a former spouse and persons who have a child in common whether they have been married or have lived together at any time (530.12).

3. Modification

Either a Temporary Order of Protection or Order of Protection may be modified by the Court at the request of either the People or the Defendant in three significant ways:

Subject to incidental contact: This is reserved for instances where the Defendant and the protected person may live in the same building, or may occasionally see each other in common areas such as the hallway or lobby, or may work together. In such circumstances the Defendant may be allowed to be in the same area as the protected person, but must immediately leave the area when they see them and may not make any contact with the protected person.

Limited: In such circumstances a defendant may contact, communicate, and be in the same location as a protected person without a violation of the order of protection so long as the defendant refrains from committing any new crimes against the protected person. This order of protection is usually issued in family, co-worker, or roommate situations where the crime committed is minimal and the threat of future incidents is slight.

Subject to family court modification: in certain cases where Family Court has concurrent jurisdiction, the Family Court may modify the Order of protection as they see fit at a subsequent hearing. This is usually applicable in domestic violence cases where the individuals have a child in common.

Protection of Victims of Crimes Other Than Family Offenses

Prior to 1981 an order of protection was only available in family offense cases. Legislation in that year added the protections afforded by temporary orders of protection, temporary orders of protection ex parte and orders of protection for victims of crimes other than family offenses. The procedures for the issuance, modification, disposition and content of these protective orders are essentially the same as those set forth for protective orders in family offense cases. The specific language of the statute is adjusted to take into account the application of the protective order to criminal cases in general, as opposed to the specialized situations found in family offense cases. Therefore you are referenced to the above Section (530.12) for details; e.g., the three types of protective orders are available, requirements of the defendants set forth on the order are similar, copies of the order are given to police and persons affected by the order and expiration dates for the various orders are basically the same. There are no substantive differences between the two (530.13).

Suspension, Revocation and Ineligibility for Firearms Licenses; Order to Surrender Firearms

Whenever the court issues a temporary order of protection, temporary order of protection ex parte or order of protection:

    a. the court shall suspend any firearm license possessed by the defendant, order the defendant ineligible for any such license and order the immediate surrender of any firearms possessed by him; where the court

b. receives information that gives the court good cause to believe that:

   i. the defendant has a prior conviction for a violent felony offense; or,

   ii. the defendant previously violated an order of protection and such violation involved the infliction of serious injury, or use of a deadly weapon or instrument, or behaved in such a manner as to constitute a violent felony offense; and,

c. where the court finds a substantial risk the defendant may use or threaten to use a firearm unlawfully against the person the protective order was designed to protect, it may take such action.

Upon conviction of a family offense (530.12) or a violent offense against a person affected by the protective order (530.13) the court shall revoke any such license, and/or, order the other alternatives listed in the above paragraph.

Any suspension order issued shall remain in effect for the duration of the protective order, unless modified or vacated by the court. Where any order of revocation, suspension or ineligibility is ordered, it shall be noted on the protective order; and, the appropriate police authorities will be notified of such order, as well as a surrender order. The defendant is entitled to a hearing either before or within fourteen days of any such order relating to the licensing or surrender of firearms affecting him (530.14).

See Illustrative Cases

People v. Davis, 460 N.Y.S.2d. 260 (1983), p. 419
People v. Boop, 397 N.Y.S.2d (1977), p. 421

13.5 Forfeiture of Bail and Remission Thereof (Article 540)

Forfeiture of Bail; Generally

A bail bond or cash bail is forfeited when, without sufficient cause, a principal does not appear or render himself amenable to the orders of the court wherein the bail is posted, and the court enters such facts on its record. The court may direct the forfeiture to be discharged if the principal appears at any time before the final adjournment of the court and satisfactorily excuses his neglect. If the forfeiture is not discharged the district attorney must proceed against the obligor or the depositor. The bond or the cash bail and a copy of the forfeiture order must be filed by the district attorney with the county clerk.

a. If the forfeiture consisted of a bail bond, when docketed by the county clerk, it becomes a lien against the obligor and may be collected as any other judgment.

b. If the forfeiture is not discharged and the bail consisted of cash bail, the county treasurer with whom the cash bail was deposited must give written notice of the forfeiture to the depositor and after final adjournment or forty five days, whichever is longer, apply the money to the use of the county (540.10).

When an individual is out on bail, it is the duty of the obligor to provide for his presence at trial and all other proceedings. If he fails in that responsibility the bail may be forfeited (*People v. Dizdar*, 397 N.Y.S.2d 340 (1977)). A depositor of cash bail is presumed to know at the time he posted bail the exact circumstances in which the deposit may be forfeited and the depositor is assumed to have consented to all provisions of the bail forfeiture statutes (*People v. Castro*, 464 N.Y.S.2d 650 (1983)).

If the bail is posted in a city, town or village court in connection with a local criminal court accusatory instrument other than a felony complaint and thereafter is forfeited the procedures described above are not applicable. The following procedures take effect:

a. If the bail consisted of a bail bond, the financial officer of the city, town or village must promptly file an action to recover the money specified in such bond. Any money recovered becomes the property of the city, town or village in which the offense is alleged to have been committed.

b. If the bail consisted of cash bail, the court must:

    i.   if it is a city court, pay the forfeited bail to the treasurer of the city; or,

    ii. if it is a town or village court, pay the forfeited bail to the state comptroller, but it becomes the property of the town or village (540.20).

Remission of Forfeiture

After the forfeiture of bail, an application for remission of such forfeiture may be made to a court:

a. If the forfeiture was by a superior court, application is made in such court.

b. If the forfeiture was by a local criminal court, other than a district court, the application is made to a superior court in the county.

c. If the forfeiture was by a district court, the application may be made to a superior court in the county or to that district court.

The application must be made within one year after the forfeiture of bail is declared and with five days' notice to the district attorney accompanied by service of copies of the affidavits and papers upon which the application is founded. The court in its discretion may grant the application and remit the forfeiture or any just part thereof, and only upon payment of the costs of forfeiture (540.30).

The right to remission of bail is not a vested right but an act of grace by the legislature (*People v. Castro, supra*). Statutes relating to remission of forfeited bail must be strictly construed. A surety seeking remission of bail has the burden of proving exceptional circumstances and that there is no loss of rights by or prejudice to the people (*People v. Public Service Mut. Ins. Co.*, 352 N.Y.S.2d 209 (1974)). The remission of forfeiture of bail should generally be denied regardless of the excuse for defendant's nonappearance if the defendant has contributed by a careless, reckless or willful act to the event offered as an excuse. That the bailed defendant was ultimately acquitted or convicted does not of itself establish that there was no prejudice to the people by the failure of the defendant to appear as required, for the purpose of determining whether to remit the forfeiture of bail (*People v. Peerless Ins. Co.*, 253 N.Y.S.2d 91 (1964)).

Chapter 14

Securing Attendance at Court of Defendants Not Securable by Conventional Means and Related Matters

Sec. 14.1 Article 550; In General

Sec. 14.2 Article 560; Confined in Institutions within the State

Sec. 14.3 Article 570; Outside the State but within the United States; Rendition to Other Jurisdictions of Defendants within the State — The Uniform Criminal Extradition Act

Sec. 14.4 Article 580; Confined as Prisoners in Other U.S. Jurisdictions and Rendition to Other Jurisdictions of Prisoners in N.Y.S. — Agreement on Detainers

Sec. 14.5 Article 590; Outside the United States

Sec. 14.6 Article 600; Corporate Defendants and Related Matters

Defendants are usually gotten before the court through an arrest or court process such as a summons. There are situations where these conventional means are not possible due to the fact the defendant is outside the jurisdiction of the state or is confined upon court order in an institution. In this chapter we deal primarily with the processes and procedures involved in extradition. Extradition involves the surrender by one state to another of a person accused or convicted of crime. It is provided for in the United States Constitution (art. 4, sec. 2) and detailed procedures of implementation are set forth in the Uniform Criminal Extradition Act (18 USCA sec. 3182). The purpose of extradition is to prevent the escape of persons accused or convicted of crime over state lines and to secure their return to the state from which they fled for trial and punishment.

14.1 In General (Article 550)

If a defendant has never been arraigned in a criminal action and he is at liberty within the state his attendance at court may be secured by an arrest warrant or superior court warrant of arrest, or a court summons. If the defendant has been arraigned:

    a. but is in custody as a result of a securing order, the court may direct the sheriff to produce him; or,

    b. and is at liberty on recognizance or bail, the court may secure his attendance by notification or by the issuance of a bench warrant.

If the defendant's attendance cannot be secured by one of the above methods, either because he is out of the state or confined in an institution as a result of an order issued in some other action or proceeding, his attendance may be secured by one of the methods set forth below (550.10).

14.2 Defendants Confined in Institutions within the State (Article 560)

When a criminal action is pending against a defendant who is confined in an institution under court order, his attendance at court may be secured by the court for purposes of arraignment or prosecution.

    a. If the action is pending in a superior court, a district court, the N.Y.C. criminal court or a local criminal court with a superior court judge sitting as a local criminal court, upon application of the district attorney, such court may order the production of the defendant.

    b. If the action is pending in a city, town or village court, upon application of the district attorney, the court may order the production of a defendant confined in the county jail of such county. If the defendant is confined in any other institution of the state, the application of the district attorney must be made to a superior court judge in the county where the action is pending and such judge may issue the order of production.

The application of the district attorney must be made with notice to (and opportunity to be heard) the district attorney of another county if one is involved and the defendant's attorney. If the order of production is issued, upon application of such district attorney or the defendant's attorney, a judge of the appellate division may vacate such order for good cause shown (560.10).

14.3 Defendants Outside the State but within the U.S., Rendition to Other Jurisdictions of Defendants within the State; the Uniform Criminal Extradition Act (Article 570)

This article is New York's uniform criminal extradition act (570.02). As mentioned at the beginning of this chapter, extradition is governed by the federal constitution and federal law. States may pass their own legislation implementing these provisions within their own state and adding provisions that are not covered by the primary federal law. The terms governor and executive authority are synonymous, and state means a state or territory of the United States (570.04). In some cases extradition is mandatory and governed by the provisions of federal law. In others it is discretionary and depends upon comity between the states. The article also deals with procedures for the extradition of fugitives from New York State.

Mandatory Extradition — Fugitives from Justice

It is the duty of the governor of New York State to have arrested and delivered to the executive authority of another state, any person charged in such state with crime and who has fled from justice and is found in this state (570.06). The demand of the governor of the demanding state must be in writing and allege the accused was present in the demanding state at the time of the commission of the crime and that thereafter he fled from the state, or that he escaped from confinement or jumped bail, probation or parole. The demand must be accompanied by a copy of the indictment; or, an affidavit; or, judgment of conviction or sentence in order to allow review of the legality of the demand (570.08). A **"fugitive from justice"** is a person who commits a crime within a state and leaves the state without waiting to abide the consequences of such act. No one can be held to be a fugitive from justice unless he was in the demanding state when the crime was committed (*People ex rel. Higley v. Millspaw*, 281 N.Y. 441 (1939)). The test on extradition is not whether the acts charged constituted a crime in the asylum state but whether they are criminal in the demanding state (*People ex rel. Shurburt v. Noble* 169 N.Y.S.2d 181 (1957)). Where one whose extradition is sought was not corporally present in the demanding state at the time of the commission of the offense, such state cannot demand his return under this provision of law (*People v. Chief of Police, City of Rochester*, 162 N.Y.S. 845 (1916)). When a demand is made upon the governor he may call upon the attorney general or any district attorney to investigate the demand and to report to him the situation and circumstances of the person so demanded and whether he ought to be surrendered (570.10). When a person is imprisoned or held under pending criminal charges in another state, the governor of this state may agree with the governor of the other state for the extradition of such person and to his return to the other state as soon as the prosecution in this state is terminated (570.12).

Discretionary Extradition — Those Who Left under Compulsion; or, Were Not in Demanding State at the Time of Commission of the Crime

The governor of this state may also surrender a person in this state on demand of the governor of another state:

a. even though such person left the demanding state involuntarily (570.14); or,

b. a person who committed an act in this or another state, other than the demanding state, intentionally resulting in a crime in the demanding state, and the results of said act, if committed in this state, would be a crime in this state. In his discretion the governor may condition the surrender upon an agreement by the demanding state that the defendant will not be prosecuted for any other crime after acquittal, or release from prison after a conviction, until given a reasonable opportunity to return to this state (570.16).

Technically the persons described by the above acts would not be fugitives. The procedure for processing these demands is the same as that for extradition of a fugitive. These extradition procedures do not violate the federal constitution nor the federal statutes enacted thereunder, but are a valid exercise of the police power of the state (*People ex rel. Faulds v. Herberich*, 93 N.Y.S.2d 272 (1949)). Substantial rights of citizens must be protected, but constitutional and statutory provisions relating to extradition must be liberally construed. Courts must avoid a view of their duties so narrow as to avoid permanent asylum to offenders against laws of another state (*People ex rel. Robert v. Warden of New York City Prison*, 114 N.Y.S.2d 13 (1952)). In considering the validity of an extradition warrant where the person was not present in the demanding state at the time of the crime, the court is not restricted to the four corners of the indictment. It may consider evidence in determining whether the acts committed would constitute crime under New York law. The draftsman of this section contemplated investigation to determine factually whether the accused had done such acts as would be punished under New York law (*In re Taylor*, 323 N.Y.S.2d 128 (1971)).

If the governor decides the demand should be complied with, he will sign a warrant of arrest, which will be sealed by the state seal and direct it be served by a police officer or other person he deems fit. The substantial facts needed to validate the warrant must be recited in the warrant (570.18). The governor has a duty upon an appropriate showing to grant a warrant of extradition, but if he refuses there is no means of compulsion (*People ex rel. Higley v. Millspaw*, 281 N.Y.S.2d 44 (1939)). The officer or person to whom the warrant was issued may arrest the accused at any time or place within the state and may command the aid of other police or any other person to assist in the arrest (570.20). Anyone who would refuse to assist is subject to punishment under the law (*see* PL sec. 195) (570.22).

Rights of the Accused; Application for Writ of Habeas Corpus

The person arrested under the governor's warrant shall not be turned over to the agent of the demanding state until he is first taken before a judge of a court of record. The court shall inform him of the demand for his surrender, the crime involved, his right to counsel and to contest the legality of the proceeding. If the prisoner or his counsel wish to contest the proceeding, the court shall fix a reasonable time within which the person may apply for a writ of habeas corpus. When such writ is applied for notice must be given to the district attorney of the county and the agent of the demanding state as to its time and place (570.24). **Habeas corpus**, from the Latin, literally translated means, you have the body. A writ of habeas corpus is a procedure for obtaining a judicial determination of the legality of a person's custody. It is a felony if an officer delivers the prisoner to the agent of the demanding state without first taking him before a judge of a court of record (570.26). The one executing the governor's warrant or the agent of the demanding state to whom the prisoner has been delivered, may when necessary confine the person in a county or city jail. The expenses involved are chargeable to the officer delivering the prisoner for safekeeping (570.28). An agent of a demanding state transporting prisoners following extradition proceedings through this state must show the jailer satisfactory written evidence that he is transporting such prisoner to the demanding state after extradition proceedings or the waiver thereof (570.30).

Arrest of Accused before Requisition or without a Warrant

Before Requisition

Whenever a credible person makes a complaint or charge before a local criminal court, that a person in this state is extraditable to another state due to the commission of crime in, or escape from prison or jumped bail, or probation from such other state, the court shall issue a warrant of arrest to a police officer. The court will direct the police officer to arrest the person and bring him before a local criminal court to answer the charge against him. A certified copy of the complaint or charge will be attached to the warrant (570.32). The federal constitution and statutes on extradition do not bar New York from arresting a person within its borders for a crime committed in another state in advance of a requisition from the demanding state. The power of a state to arrest a person within its borders for a crime committed elsewhere and the manner of such arrest is left to the individual states (*Burton and Heeren v. N.Y.C. Co.*, 132 N.Y.S. 628 (1911)).

Arrest without a Warrant

An arrest of a person in this state may also be made by a police officer or any other person upon reasonable grounds to believe the person to be arrested is extraditable to another state for the commission of a felony. When arrested the accused must be taken to a local criminal court, and a sworn complaint made against him setting forth the grounds for the arrest (570.34). If upon examination it appears to the local criminal court that the defendant is the person as charged, the court must commit him to custody for up to thirty days to enable the arrest of the accused on a governor's warrant, unless the accused is released on bail (570.36). A justice of a superior court may release the accused on bail unless the charge against him is punishable by death or life imprisonment in the demanding state. Bail may be conditioned upon his appearance before the superior court not later than thirty days after the examination in the local criminal court as specified above (570.38). If the accused is not arrested on the governor's warrant within the thirty day period the accused may be discharged or recommitted by the local criminal court for a further period or periods of up to sixty days. A superior court may also release him on bail as indicated above, during this period (570.40). The maximum period the accused may be held to await the governor's warrant is then, ninety days. The accused may demand his release if not arrested on the governor's warrant within ninety days; but, this time limit does not immunize him from extradition and upon receipt of a governor's warrant it loses all effect and cannot interfere with the court's obligation to comply with the requisition (*People ex rel. Brandolino v. Hastings*, 421 N.Y.S.2d 893 (1979)). If the prisoner is released on bail and doesn't appear as required, the superior court judge shall forfeit the bail and order his arrest without a warrant (570.42). If a criminal prosecution is pending against such person in this state, the governor, in his discretion, may either surrender him or hold him until he has been tried and discharged or convicted and punished in this state (570.44). The guilt or innocence of the accused as to the crime charged in the demanding state may not be inquired into by the governor or in any subsequent proceeding regarding extradition in this state. Inquiry may be made however, as to the identity of the accused as the person charged in the demanding state (570.46). The governor may recall his warrant of arrest or issue another whenever he deems it proper (570.48).

Written Waiver of Extradition Proceedings

A person arrested for purposes of extradition to another state may waive the extradition procedures. He must sign a written waiver, stating his consent to return to the demanding state, before a superior court judge who must first advise him of his rights to extradition procedures and a writ of habeas corpus. When the waiver is executed the prisoner shall be turned over to an agent of the demanding state, with a copy of the waiver, for return to the demanding state (570.50).

Fugitives from New York State

When a person charged with crime, escape from prison or jumping bail, probation or parole in this state, flees to another state, the governor shall demand of the executive authority of such other state or a justice of the supreme court of the District of Columbia, the return of such fugitive to New York State. The governor shall issue a governor's warrant to an agent of this state and direct he take the person so charged, if delivered to him, to the proper officer in the county in which the crime was committed (570.52).

a. In order to request the governor to seek return of a fugitive who has been charged with a crime in this state, the district attorney of the county in which the offense was committed or in a proper case the attorney general, shall make written application for the return of the person to the governor. If the person required to be returned has escaped from jail, or jumped bail, probation or parole, the application may be made by the district attorney of the county in which the offense was committed, the warden of the institution escaped from or the sheriff of the escape county or the state correctional services commissioner.

b. In each case the application will contain the identity of the fugitive, the details of the crime or escape, the state he is believed to be in and the specific location therein, and in the case of the person charged with crime, a statement of the district attorney that the ends of justice require the arrest and return of the fugitive to this state for trial. The application shall be accompanied by an affidavit of verification, a copy of the indictment or judgment of conviction and any other documents deemed necessary. All papers must be in duplicate.

c. The governor shall indicate his action by endorsement on the application. One copy of the papers shall be filed in the office of the secretary of state for purposes of record. The other copy of the papers shall be forwarded with the governor's requisition through his agent, to the executive authority of the asylum state (570.54).

The expenses of the extradition will be paid for by a county, the state division of correction or the state division of parole depending upon the reason for the application and who made it (570.56). A person brought back into this state on extradition or after a waiver of extradition shall not be subject to a civil action arising from the same facts as the crime until he has been convicted or if acquitted, until he has reasonable opportunity to return to the asylum state (570.58). He may be tried, however, for other criminal offenses (570.60).

See Illustrative Cases

People v. Culwell, 621 N.Y.S.2d 490 (1995), p. 422
People v. LaFontaine, 682 N.Y.S.2d (1998), p. 424

14.4 Securing Attendance of Prisoners from Other U.S. Jurisdictions and Rendition to Other Jurisdictions of Prisoners in N.Y.S. Prisons; Agreement on Detainers (Article 580)

A defendant in a criminal action in New York who is confined as a prisoner in another state or a federal prison may be secured for attendance at the criminal action in one of three ways (580.10):

   a. under the uniform criminal extradition act (570.12, *supra*); or,

   b. by the agreement on detainers (580.20); or,

   c. if a federal prisoner, in accord with 580.30.

Under the uniform extradition act, return is accomplished by executive agreement of the governors of the two states concerned.

The Agreement on Detainers

The Agreement on Detainers is an interstate compact, which was adopted in 1957. The states that join it do so in order to simplify interstate rendition of prisoners for trial from one state to another. The text of the compact has been incorporated into 580.20 CPL and is the statutory procedure for New York State; but as indicated above it is not the only method which may be utilized to secure the attendance of prisoners between jurisdictions. If a person is charged with a criminal offense in one state and is serving a prison term in another, the state that seeks to bring him to trial may file a detainer with the state in which he is imprisoned. The detainer is a written request to detain the prisoner after his sentence is completed so that the requesting state may take him into custody and bring him to trial. One of the purposes of the agreement on detainers is to protect the prisoners right to a speedy trial. When the detainer is filed in the receiving state the prisoner and appropriate state officials must be notified of the filing. Under the agreement, the prisoner or the prosecutor in the sending state may initiate the process in order to cause the prisoner to be temporarily placed in the custody of the sending state, so that trial of the accusatory instrument may be had in the sending state.

The prisoner may deliver a written notice and request for final disposition on the pending charge in the sending state to the official having custody of him. This official shall send it, and a certificate detailing the status of the prisoner, to the prosecutor and court in the sending state. The prisoner must then be brought to trial in the sending state within 180 days of the receipt of such notice by the prosecutor and court. The court may in its discretion grant any reasonable or necessary continuances.

If the prosecutor of the sending state initiates the process by forwarding a request for temporary custody of the prisoner for purposes of trial, the trial must be commenced within one hundred twenty days of the prisoner's arrival in the sending state. Continuances may be granted by the court in this instance as well.

In either of the above instances, if the trial is not had prior to the prisoner being returned to prison, the accusatory instrument underlying the charge shall not be of any further force or effect and the court shall enter an order dismissing it without prejudice.

This agreement does not apply to any person who is adjudged to be mentally ill (580.20).

The agreement on detainers is designed to standardize interstate rendition procedures in order to protect an inmates right to a speedy trial and reduce any uncertainties which might obstruct programs of prisoner treatment and rehabilitation (*People ex rel. Capalongo v. Howard*, 453 N.Y.S.2d 45 (1982)). Since the terms of the agreement on detainers place a more stringent burden on the prosecutor than does the federal constitutional guarantee of a speedy trial, the prisoner must comply with all the statutory provisions before judicial relief may be had (*Baker v. Schubin*, 339 N.Y.S.2d 360 (1972)). The provisions of the agreement do not become applicable until the defendant commences service of a term of imprisonment (*People ex rel. Albuquerque v. Ward*, 455 N.Y.S.2d 1002 (1982)). If a state lodging a detainer warrant is not a signatory to the agreement on detainers, the detainer warrant is of no force or effect except as the detaining state is inclined as a matter of comity to honor it (*Baker v. Schubin*, 339 N.Y.S.2d 360 (1972)). The defendant must be ready for trial before he can invoke the limitation on the time in which he can be brought to trial after his arrival in the state, as provided by the agreement on detainers (*People v. Cook*, 406 N.Y.S.2d 643 (1978)).

Securing the Attendance of Defendants Who Are Federal Prisoners

The agreement on detainers constitutes an interstate compact and does not apply to the securance of federal prisoners. In order to secure a defendant for trial who is a federal prisoner, a superior court, upon application of the district attorney, issues a certificate known as a writ of *habeas corpus ad prosequendum*, addressed to the attorney general of the United States. The certificate includes the particulars of the prisoner and charge against him and a request the prisoner be produced in court under the custody of a federal public servant in order to stand trial. The certificate and a copy of the accusatory instrument are delivered to the attorney general or his authorized representative (580.30). The decision on the request is strictly within the discretion of the attorney general.

See Illustrative Cases

New York v. Hill, 528 U.S. 110 (2000), p. 427

14.5 Securing Attendance of Defendants Who Are outside the United States (Article 590)

When a defendant is in a foreign country with which the United States has an extradition treaty and the offense with which he is charged is an extraditable one under such treaty, the district attorney of the county in which such offense was allegedly committed, may make application to the Governor, asking him to apply to the President of the United States to institute extradition proceedings. If the Governor is satisfied the defendant is in the foreign country in question and the offense is an extraditable one, he may, in his discretion, make the requested application to the secretary of state of the United States, requesting the President to institute extradition proceedings. If the Governor's application is granted, all expenses incurred must be borne by the county. This section applies equally to the extradition of fugitives after a conviction in a criminal court (590.10).

14.6 Securing Attendance of Corporate Defendants (Article 600)

The attendance of a corporation as a defendant may be secured by the service of a summons or an appearance ticket if the action is in a lower criminal court, or a corporate summons if the case is in a superior court. The service may be made upon any agent of the corporation authorized to accept such service. The corporate defendant must appear by counsel. Upon failure to appear at the time the corporate defendant is required to enter a plea, the court may enter a plea of guilty and impose sentence.

Chapter 15

Securing Attendance of Witnesses

Sec. 15.1 Article 610; By Subpoena
Sec. 15.2 Article 620; By Material Witness Order
Sec. 15.3 Article 630; Persons Confined in Institutions within New York State
Sec. 15.4 Article 640; The Uniform Witness Act: Persons at Liberty outside
       N.Y.S. and Rendition to Other Jurisdictions of Witnesses at
       Liberty within N.Y.S.
Sec. 15.5 Article 650; Prisoners of Other U.S. Jurisdictions and Rendition to
       Other Jurisdictions of Prisoners in N.Y.S.

The processes for securing the attendance of witnesses are similar to those for the securance of defendants. There are rules for securing witnesses from within the state by subpoena, material witness order or court order for those not at liberty; and, within the framework of the Uniform Witness Act, for securing witnesses from outside the state either at liberty or confined in institutions; and, for rendition of witnesses to other states from New York.

15.1 Securing Attendance of Witnesses by Subpoena (Article 610)

A person at liberty within the state may be required to be a witness in a criminal action by the issuance and service upon him of a subpoena. A **subpoena** is a court process directing the person named to appear as a witness in a designated court at a specific time and any recessed or adjourned date as well. The term subpoena also includes a **subpoena duces tecum** which requires the witness to bring specific physical evidence to court (610.10).

Any criminal court may issue a subpoena for an action in such court. The district attorney may issue a subpoena for a witness he intends to call in a criminal action or before the grand jury. Defense counsel may similarly issue a subpoena for a witness the defense intends to call. An attorney for the defendant may not issue a subpoena duces tecum for a state agency or one of its political subdivisions; but, upon application to the court for same, the court may issue such subpoena (610.20).

Court	Where Service May Be Made
Superior	Anywhere in the state
District Ct. or NYCCCt.	Anywhere in state; but, if outside the county of issuance or an adjoining county it must have the endorsement of a judge of the county of issuance
City, Town or Village	Same as for District or NYCCCt., but with the endorsement of a superior court judge.

Where a subpoena duces tecum is issued, the court or grand jury shall have the right to possession of the subpoenaed evidence. Possession shall be for a reasonable period of time and terms. In determining reasonableness the court shall consider, among other things:

a. good cause by the party issuing the subpoena;

b. the rights and reasonable needs of the subpoenaed person; and,

c. the feasibility of making copies of the evidence.

The costs of reproduction and transportation shall be borne by the party issuing the subpoena unless the court deems otherwise, in the interest of justice (610.25). The limited retention of subpoenaed documents upon good cause shown, does not violate the U.S.C.A. Const. amend. 4 proscription against unreasonable searches and seizures (*Hynes v. Moscowitz*, 44 N.Y.2d 383 (1978)).

Where a subpoena may be served depends upon the court that issued it. The general rule is that a subpoena of any criminal court may be served in the county of issuance or an adjoining county. Then there are special rules for the various criminal courts:

The subpoena may be served by any person over eighteen years of age and in the same manner as for the service of subpoenas in civil actions (CPLR 2303) (610.30,40).

See Illustrative Cases

People v. Jovanovic, 676 N.Y.S.2d 392 (1997), p. 431
People v. Riggins, 678 N.Y.S.2d 469 (1998), p. 433
People v. Woodson, 630 N.Y.S.2d 670 (1995), p. 434

15.2 Securing Attendance of Witnesses by Material Witness Order (Article 620)

A **material witness order** is a court order;

a. adjudging a person a material witness in a pending criminal action; and,

b. fixing bail to secure his future attendance (620.10).

The order may be issued on the ground the witness possesses material information and will not be responsive or amenable to a subpoena at the time needed in court. It may be issued by the appropriate court only after an indictment or felony complaint has been filed or a grand jury proceeding is commenced or pending. Unless vacated sooner (*see* 620.60) the order remains in effect during the pendency of the action in the superior court (620.20).

The proceeding to adjudge a person a material witness is commenced by either party making application to the appropriate court. The application must contain the grounds required. If the court is satisfied as to the facts, it may issue an order directing such person to appear before the court to determine if the person should be declared a material witness. If the facts are that the person would in all likelihood not respond to such an order, the court may issue a warrant to a police officer to bring such person before the court for such determination (620.30). When the person appears before the court, the court must inform him of the nature of the proceeding and his rights, such as the right to counsel and others as available to defendants arraigned on a felony complaint (*see* 180.10). If the proceeding is adjourned to permit the person to obtain counsel the court may fix bail and in default of same, commit him to the custody of the sheriff (620.40).

At the hearing the applicant has the burden of proof by a preponderance of the evidence of all the essential facts based upon testimony given under oath. The prospective witness may testify under oath or give an unsworn statement and call witnesses in his behalf. If the court is satisfied there is reasonable cause to believe the person possesses material information and will not be amenable or respond to a subpoena when needed, it may issue a material witness order declaring such person a material witness and fix bail to assure his attendance. If bail is not met, he must be committed to the custody of the sheriff (620.50). Since these procedures interfere with the personal liberty of a person, they should be strictly construed (*People ex rel. Fusco v. Ryan*, 124 N.Y.S.2d 690 (1953)). The seriousness of the crime under investigation, the character of the material witness, his relationship to those he will be called to testify against, the possibility of flight to avoid testifying and the difficulty of procuring his return should he flee should be considered in fixing bail of a material witness. However, bail should not be used simply to keep a material witness confined (*People ex rel. Richards v. Warden of City Prison*, 98 N.Y.S.2d 173 (1950)). The duty to disclose knowledge of crime rests upon all citizens and is so vital that one known to be innocent may be detained, in the absence of bail, as a material witness (*People ex rel. Van Der Beek v. McCloskey*, 238 N.Y.S.2d 676 (1963)).

The material witness status and the amount of bail may be reviewed on application of the material witness, alleging new evidence. The party upon whose application the order was issued may similarly make such application. Notice of the parties is required in either case and upon a hearing the judge will determine if the order should be vacated, modified or otherwise amended (620.60). If a material witness on bail cannot be found at the time his appearance is required the court shall issue a warrant, addressed to a police officer directing his arrest (620.70). A material witness held in custody of the sheriff must be paid $3.00 for each day he is held in custody (620.80).

15.3 Securing Attendance of Witnesses Confined in Institutions within the State (Article 630)

If a party to a criminal action seeks as a witness a person confined by court order to an institution within this state, he may make application to the court. If the party demonstrates reasonable cause to believe such confined person possesses material information, the court will issue an order compelling the attendance of the witness (630.10). If the witness is confined in a state institution, the order must be issued by a superior court; but, if confined in a local institution, such as a county or city jail, the order will be issued by a local criminal court. In any case, if the witness is a prisoner who has been sentenced to death the order may only be issued by a justice of the appellate division and only upon a showing that the prisoner's attendance is clearly necessary in the interests of justice (630.20).

15.4 The Uniform Witness Act; Securing as Witnesses Persons at Liberty outside the State and Rendition to Other States of Witnesses at Liberty within New York State (Article 640)

The procedures for securing witnesses from outside a state are governed by the Uniform Witness Act (Uniform Act to Secure Witnesses From Without a State in Criminal Proceedings) and they are similar in concept to those for securing defendants under the Uniform Extradition Act. The Uniform Witness Act also governs the procedures for securing as witnesses, prisoners from other states (see art. 650).

Rendition of Witnesses from New York to Another State

If a judge of a court of record of another state, that subscribes to the Uniform Witness Act, certifies:

a. that there is a criminal prosecution pending or a grand jury investigation has commenced in such state; and,

b. a person in New York State is a material witness in such proceeding; and,

c. his presence will be required for a specified number of days;

upon presentation of such certificate to a New York superior court judge, a hearing will be ordered and an order issued directing the witness to appear at the hearing. If at such hearing the judge determines:

a. that the witness is material and necessary,

b. that no undue hardship will accrue to the witness if compelled to attend, and,

c. he will be protected against arrest or service of process while in such state,

he shall issue a subpoena with the certificate attached and direct the witness to attend and testify in the proceeding as requested. If the certificate recommended the witness be taken into immediate custody and delivered to an officer of the requesting state to assure his attendance, the judge may direct the witness to be brought immediately before him for said hearing. The witness who is subpoenaed must be paid a fee of ten cents a mile and five dollars for each day of attendance and after such payment, if he fails to appear and testify, he will be punished for disobeying the subpoena (640.10).

Securing Witnesses from Another State to Testify in New York State

The procedures for New York State to follow in order to secure a witness from another state, mirror those set forth above for the rendition of a witness from New York to another state, under the Uniform Witness Act. New York has a statute exempting persons either passing through or appearing as witnesses from arrest or process while in New York State, as required by the Act (640.10).

The subpoenaing of an out of state material witness intrudes on individual liberty and is in derogation of the common or customary law; thus, there must be strict compliance with the requirements of the statute (*Broughton v. City of New York*, 398 N.Y.S.2d 397 (1977)). While the U.S.C.A. Const. amend. 6 mandates that an accused has the right to present his own witnesses to establish a defense, including the right to compel their attendance if necessary, such right is subject to the limitation that no state, without being party to a compact, has the power to compel attendance of witnesses who are beyond the limits of the state (*People v. Carter*, 37 N.Y.2d 234 (1975)). This section could not be used to allow a prosecutor to obtain a person's photograph and fingerprints when the "witness" was an obvious target of the grand jury investigation and a potential defendant. It should not be used against any person unless that person is slated strictly as a statutory witness. (*State v. Motte*, 437 N.Y.S.2d 48 (1981)). This section comprehends subpoenas duces tecum as well as subpoenas ad testificandum (*Superior Court v. Farber*, 405 N.Y.S.2d 989 (1978)). The burden of proof to establish the witness is material and necessary rests upon the party seeking the witness's testimony and the order denying the application to compel witnesses to testify in a sister state is appealable (*State of N.J. v. Bardoff*, 459 N.Y.S.2d 878 (1980)).

See Illustrative Cases

People v. McCartney, 38 N.Y.2d 618 (1976), p. 436
State of New Jersey v. Bardoff, 459 N.Y.S.2d 878 (1983), p. 438

15.5 Securing Attendance as Witnesses, and Rendition as Witnesses, of Prisoners (Article 650)

There are three provisions relating to the securance of prisoners as witnesses:

a. prisoners in New York State to be witnesses outside the state,

b. prisoners outside the state to be witnesses in New York State, and

c. federal prisoners to be witnesses in New York State.

Prisoners in New York State — Rendition to Other States

In order for another state to secure as a witness in that state, a person confined as a prisoner in New York State, a judge of a court of record of such state must:

a. certify that there is a criminal prosecution or grand jury investigation in such court; and,

b. a prisoner in New York is a material witness in such proceeding; and,

c. his presence is required for a specific number of days.

A person confined as criminally mentally ill, or as a defective delinquent, or confined in the death house awaiting execution cannot be the subject of this procedure. Upon presentment of this certificate to a judge of a superior court in the county of confinement of the prisoner, and upon notice to the attorney general, the judge shall order a hearing and direct the person having custody of the prisoner to produce him for the hearing. If at the hearing the judge determines the prisoner is a material and necessary witness, he shall order the prisoner to attend as requested by the other state. He will also set terms and conditions, such as measures for the return of the prisoner to custody, proper safeguards during the custody and provisions for proper payment for the expenses incurred in the production and return of the prisoner to custody in New York (650.10).

Prisoners outside of New York State to Be Witnesses in New York

The procedure for New York to follow in seeking a prisoner from another state to be a witness in a New York criminal proceeding mirrors that set forth above for other states seeking the appearance of a prisoner in New York to appear in their state as a witness. Either party in the New York proceeding may make the application (650.20).

Federal Prisoners to Be Witnesses in New York State

When a federal prisoner is sought as a witness the procedures also mirror those set forth above, with a few differences in nomenclature. The certificate required is known as a writ of habeas corpus ad testificandum and it is addressed to the attorney general of the United States.

Chapter 16

Securing Testimony for Future Use and Using Testimony from a Prior Proceeding

Sec. 16.1 Article 660; Securing Testimony for Future Use — Examination of Witnesses Conditionally
Sec. 16.2 Article 670; Use of Testimony Previously Given
Sec. 16.3 Article 680; Securing Testimony outside the State for Use in the State — Examination of Witnesses on Commission

This chapter deals with securing testimony from witnesses who may not be available as such at the time of trial. Specific procedures are established which must be followed in order to insure the reliability of such testimony and that the constitutional rights of the parties are not abused.

16.1 Securing Testimony for Future Use — Examination of Witnesses Conditionally (Article 660)

The Application Procedure and Its Grounds

Any time between the arraignment and termination of a criminal action, a criminal court may, upon written application of either party, order that a witness be examined, conditionally under oath, so that such testimony may be received at subsequent proceedings related to the action, in the event the witness is unavailable at such time (660.10). The grounds for such order must be based upon reasonable cause to believe that such witness:

a. possesses material information; and,

b. will not be available as a witness when needed because he is;

    i. about to leave the state for a substantial period of time; or,

    ii. is physically ill or incapacitated (660.20).

If the action is pending in a local criminal court, the application must be made in such court. If the defendant has been held by a local criminal court on a felony complaint for the action of the grand jury or if held on an indictment, the application must be made in the superior court (660.30). The application must contain particulars as to the offense charged, the grounds, and a request the examination be recorded by videotape. A copy of the application, with reasonable notice and opportunity to be heard, must be served upon the adverse party (660.40). The court may make any inquiry it deems appropriate and if satisfied grounds for the application exist, it must order an examination of the witness conditionally at a specific time and place. The party securing the order must serve a copy on the adverse party and issue a subpoena for the attendance of the witness (660.50).

The Examination Proceeding

The examination must be conducted in the same manner as if the witness was testifying at trial and must be recorded. The witness must testify under oath. The applicant party will first examine the witness and then the respondent party may cross-examine. Each party is entitled to register objections and have them ruled upon by the court. Upon conclusion of the examination, a transcript and any videotape must be certified and filed with the court (660.60).

See Illustrative Cases

People v. Cotton, 92 N.Y.2d 68 (1998), p. 439

16.2 Use of Testimony Previously Given (Article 670)

Testimony given by a witness at:

a. a trial of an accusatory instrument; or,

b. a felony complaint hearing (180.60 CPL); or,

c. an examination of such witness conditionally (art. 660 CPL),

may be received into evidence at a subsequent proceeding relating to the same action (including post judgment challenges to a conviction) when the witness is unable to attend due to:

a. death, illness, or incapacity; or,

b. the inability to locate the witness with due diligence; or,

c. his being outside the state or in federal custody and cannot with due diligence be brought before the court.

When received into evidence the testimony may be read and any videotape played (670.10).

Grand jury testimony given by a witness who was not available at trial did not qualify within any of the prescribed prior proceedings for admission of a transcript of prior testimony given by an unavailable witness (*People v. Johnson*, 380 N.Y.S.2d 187 (1976)).

Prior testimony at a police disciplinary hearing by a witness, since deceased, was not admissible at the trial of criminal charges against a police lieutenant (*People v. Harding*, 37 N.Y.2d 130 (1975)).

The party who desires to offer previous testimony as evidence must make a motion to the court showing the legal facts and justification for its reception. In determining the motion the court must make an inquiry and hold a hearing. If the court grants the motion the party may read into evidence the transcript and play any videotape. The adverse party may enter objections and the court must rule thereon. Without obtaining any court order the district attorney may enter such previously given testimony in a grand jury proceeding under the same circumstances as specified in 670.10 (670.20).

See Illustrative Cases

People v. Arroyo, 54 N.Y.2d 567 (1982), p. 440
People v. Robinson, 89 N.Y.2d 648 (1997), p. 442

16.3 Securing Testimony outside the State; Examination of Witnesses on Commission (Article 680)

Testimony material to a trial of a crime may be taken by, "examination on a commission," outside the state, and received in evidence at such trial. A "**commission**" is a process of a superior court, designating one or more persons as commissioners and authorizing them to conduct a recorded examination of a witness under oath, primarily by way of questions attached to the commission, and to remit to the court a transcript of the examination (680.10).

Only a defendant may initiate this commission process. If the court is satisfied the witness has material information, which in the interest of justice should be disclosed at trial, and lives outside the state, the court may issue a commission for examination of such witness at a designated time and place outside the state. The moving papers must be served on the prosecutor with reasonable notice and opportunity to be heard. The papers must contain the details of the offense, the witness and the grounds for the motion (680.20). The determination as to whether a commission shall issue is within the discretion of the court. Courts should exercise great restraint and grant such an application only in exceptional circumstances (*People v. Carter*, 37 N.Y.2d 234 (1975)).

If the court grants the defendant's application, the district attorney may apply to the court for the same commission to examine a person designated by the people.

The same justification is required as for the defendant's motion (680.30). The people at this time may also move for another commission to examine witnesses in the same or another jurisdiction. If the court grants the application, the defendant may piggy back upon this commission, a request for it to interview also, a person designated by the defendant. Each request must be justified as is required in the first instance. Note that without the initial request of the defendant and its granting by the court, the people have no authority to initiate this commission process (680.40).

When the court grants the application, each party must submit questions to be asked of the witness by the commission. The court will examine them with opportunity for counsel to be heard and may exclude any question it considers irrelevant, incompetent or otherwise inadmissible at trial (680.50). If the examination is to be conducted in the United States or one of its territories, the court may designate any attorney authorized to practice in that jurisdiction or a person designated to administer an oath therein, as a commissioner. If the examination is to take place in a foreign country, a diplomatic representative of the United States employed as such in that country or a commissioned officer of the armed forces may be designated (680.60).

For the examination each witness must testify under oath. The examination must be recorded and transcribed. The witness will first be asked the questions submitted by the party requesting the examination and then the adverse party's cross questions. Each party may be present and after the questions of the commission, may ask further questions of the witness. Documentary and physical evidence may be produced by the witness, which shall be annexed to the transcript prepared for the court (680.70). The transcript and a record of the examination must be filed with the trial court. Upon the trial either party may read into evidence the transcript or that portion containing the testimony of the witness examined on commission. Prior to the introduction of the evidence at trial, the court may review the transcript, hear any objections by the parties and exclude any evidence that would not be admissible at trial. At the trial the court must entertain and rule on any objections of the parties as the transcript is read (680.80).

Chapter 17

Securing Evidence by Court Order and Suppressing Evidence Unlawfully or Improperly Obtained

Sec. 17.1 Article 690; Search Warrants
Sec. 17.2 Article 700; Eavesdropping and Video Surveillance Warrants
Sec. 17.3 Article 705; Pen Registers and Trap and Trace Devices
Sec. 17.4 Article 710; Motion to Suppress Evidence
Sec. 17.5 Article 715; Destruction of Dangerous Drugs

The Fourth Amendment to the United States Constitution and Article 1, Section 12 of the New York State Constitution prohibit unreasonable searches. They do not prohibit all searches, only those which are unreasonable. They have two clauses, the reasonableness clause and the warrant clause:

"No person shall be subject to an unreasonable search or seizure of his person, houses papers or effects" (the reasonableness clause); and,

"no warrants shall but upon probable cause, particularly describing the place to be searched and the person or things to be seized" (the warrant clause).

In order for a search to be reasonable it must be based upon probable cause. In New York, probable cause is called, "reasonable cause to believe." The articles in this chapter constitute New York's statutory procedures governing search and seizure. They attempt to codify the principles and intent of the language of the constitutional provisions and have been subject to an enormous number of court decisions, both at the federal and state level.

17.1 Search Warrants (Article 690)

A **search warrant** is a court order, directing a police officer to search a designated premises, vehicle or person, in order to seize designated property and to deliver it to the court that issued the warrant. It is the process of a local criminal court and may be issued upon the application of a police officer, district attorney or other public servant acting in the course of his official duties (690.10). Search warrants are in derogation of common law rights and statutes governing their issuance should be strictly construed (*People v. Prisco*, 232 N.Y.S.2d 837 (1962)). U.S.C.A. Const. Amend. 4 protects not against all searches and seizures but only against unreasonable ones (*People v. Vasquez*, 275 N.Y.S.2d 14 (1966), rev'd on other grounds, 57 Misc. 138 (2nd Dept. 1968)). Searches conducted outside the judicial process, without prior approval by a judge are per se unreasonable under U.S.C.A. Const. Amend. 4, subject only to a few specifically established and well delineated exceptions (*People v. Avasino*, 338 N.Y.S.2d 73 (1972)). Preference is to be accorded searches under a warrant, and in doubtful or marginal cases, a search under a warrant may be sustainable, where without one it would fail (*People v. DiBernardo*, 392 N.Y.S.2d 1001 (1977)). The statutory provisions governing the issuance of search warrants are designed to protect a person's privacy in his home, office, and automobile, and even a public telephone booth, where he has a reasonable expectation of privacy (*People v. Perel*, 34 N.Y.2d 462 (1974)). The mere fact that it would be burdensome to obtain a warrant, standing alone, is never justification for not obtaining the search warrant (*People v. Spinelli*, 35 N.Y.2d 77 (1975)).

Property Subject to Seizure

Personal property is subject to seizure under a search warrant if there is reasonable cause to believe it to be:

1. stolen,

2. unlawfully possessed,

3. related to crime, or,

4. evidence of crime or that a particular person committed a crime (690.10).

A search warrant may be issued on probable cause, and it is not required that the officer possess enough evidence to convict the person whom he arrests or searches (*People v. Rooks*, 229 N.Y.S.2d 923 (1962)). When a search warrant directs a search of a designated place, premises or vehicle it may also direct a search of any person present thereat or therein (690.15). The application for a warrant authorizing the search of "any other person present" should state whether any person apparently unconnected with the illegal activity has been seen at the premises; and, the warrant itself must limit the locus of the search to the area in which the criminal activity is believed to be confined and, according to the circumstances, may also specify the time for the search (*People v. Nieves*, 36 N.Y. 2d 396 (1975); *see also People v. Covlin*, 58 Misc. 3d 996 (Sup. Ct., N.Y. Co (2018)).

Where and When It May Be Executed

A search warrant issued by a district court, the New York City criminal court or a superior court judge sitting as a local criminal court may be executed anywhere in the state. One issued by a city, town or village court may only be executed in the county of issuance or an adjoining county (690.20). The warrant must be addressed to a police officer whose geographical area of employment embraces or is embraced by the county of issuance. It need not be addressed to a specific police officer but may be addressed to a class of police officers. The police officer to whom the warrant is issued may execute it anywhere in the county of issuance or an adjoining county (690.25).

The warrant must be executed within ten days of its issuance. It may be executed on any day of the week between the hours of 6:00 A.M. and 9:00 P.M., unless the warrant expressly authorizes execution at any time of the day or night (690.30). Such authorization may be granted upon the ground it cannot be executed between 6:00 A.M. and 9:00 P.M., or, the property sought will be removed or destroyed if not seized immediately (690.35). After its execution it must be returned to the court without unnecessary delay (690.30). The intent of the legislature in requiring a specific direction in the search warrant for its execution at night was to protect persons and premises, except in special cases, from being searched during full hours of darkness and rest (*People v. Watson*, 241 N.Y.S.2d 934 (1963)).

The Application

The application for a search warrant is usually made in writing but it may be made orally by telephone or similar electronic device. It is usually made orally from the scene of an event when time is of the essence. It must be signed and sworn to by the applicant. In either case it must contain:

a. The name of the court and name and title of the applicant;

b. A statement that there is reasonable cause to believe authorized property may be found in the place to be searched; and, allegations of fact known by the applicant's personal knowledge or information and belief, the sources of such information and belief and any depositions in support thereof;

c. A request that the court issue the search warrant.

d. If appropriate, a request;

   i.   the warrant be authorized for night service on the grounds mentioned above; or,

   ii. the warrant authorize the entry of premises to be searched without giving notice of the officer's authority and purpose. The grounds for such authorization are;

     a) reasonable cause to believe the property may be easily and quickly disposed of, or may endanger the life or safety of the officer or another person; or,

     b) if the warrant is for a search for a person who is the subject of an arrest warrant for a felony, the person sought is likely to commit another felony, or may endanger the life or safety of the officer or another (690.35).

In the case of an oral application the conversation between the judge and the applicant must be recorded or verbatim stenographic notes taken. If the only record are the long hand notes of the judge, he must sign them and file them with the court within 24 hours of the issuance of the warrant (690.36).

The application for a search warrant is criminal, rather than civil, in nature and its purpose is to aid in the detection and punishment of crime (*B.T. Productions Inc. v. Barr*, 388 N.Y.S.2d 483 (1976)). The warrant application must set forth how the information was acquired so the magistrate may judge for himself the persuasiveness of the facts relied upon to establish probable cause (*People v. Simon*, 460 N.Y.S.2d 998 (1983)). The details of the defendant's drug selling operation were sufficient to establish "reasonable suspicion" the drugs were easily disposable, as was required to support a "no knock" provision of the search warrant (*People v. Skeete*, 684 N.Y.S.2d 198 (1999)). Under the Fourth Amendment, all that is required is "reasonable suspicion" that knocking and announcing would be dangerous or futile or would inhibit effective investigation (*People v. Richards*, 520 U.S. 385 (1997)).

In determining the application for the search warrant the court may examine under oath any person whom it believes may have pertinent information. If the court is satisfied there is reasonable cause to believe the property is seizable and in the place to be searched it may issue the search warrant. If the court is also satisfied there are grounds for a night time search or a no knock authorization it may enter such authorization on the warrant. If it is an oral application, the applicant must prepare the application and read it verbatim to the judge (690.40).

Affidavits in support of applications for search warrants must be tested by magistrates and courts in a common sense and realistic fashion (*see generally People v. Wirchansky*, 367 N.Y.S.2d 94 (1975)). They should not be read in a hypertechnical manner but considered in the light of everyday expectations and accorded all reasonable inferences (*Matter of Marcario*, 462 N.Y.S.2d 1000 (1983)). The purpose of the search warrant procedure is to subject the facts claimed to show probable cause to the informed and deliberate scrutiny of a neutral and detached magistrate (*People v. Loewel*, 378 N.Y.S.2d 521 (1976)). The validity of the search warrant depends upon whether probable cause existed to support its issuance (*People v. Pagano*, 244 N.Y.S.2d 214 (1963)). The court must exercise its discretion only in light of the evidence the magistrate has before him (*People v. Hendricks*, 25 N.Y.2d 129 (1969)). In considering whether probable cause exists for the issuance of a search warrant, the court considers probabilities as perceived by a cautious, reasonable, prudent police officer and evaluated by an independent magistrate. Of particular relevance is the evaluation of the sources of the information, the manner in which it was acquired, the experience and expertise of the officers involved and the extent to which the information has been verified (*People v. Hanlon*, 36 N.Y.2d 549 (1975)). Affidavits upon which a search warrant is issued must contain something more than mere conclusions in order to justify the issuance of a search warrant (*People v. Rodgers*, 15 N.Y.2d 422 (1965)). It may be issued on a showing of probable cause and it is not required that the officer possess sufficient admissible evidence to convict the person he arrests or searches (*People v. Rooks*, 229 N.Y.S.2d 923 (1962)). The search warrant may be based on hearsay evidence provided there is a substantial basis for crediting it (*People v. Brown*, 40 N.Y.2d 183 (1976)). The probable cause may be based on unsworn hearsay only when the two prong Aguilar-Spinelli test is satisfied, i.e., if there is a reasonable showing that the informant is reliable and had a basis of knowledge for the statement (*People v. Burke*, 690 N.Y.S.2d 897 (1999)). This test applies only to information given by an undisclosed informant. A sworn statement of an identified member of the community, attesting to facts directly and personally observed by him, is in and of itself sufficient to support the issuance of the warrant (*People v. Bourdon*, 686 N.Y.S.2d 162 (1999)).

The Search Warrant

A search warrant must contain:

a. The name of the issuing court, judge and police officer or department to whom issued and the signature of the judge unless an oral warrant.

   i.   If an oral warrant, the time and date of its issuance.

b. A description of the property to be searched for and the place to be searched.

c. Where authorized, a direction for night service or no knock entry.

d. A direction that the warrant and any property seized be returned to the court without unnecessary delay (690.45).

Search warrants which are couched in vague language and which are not sufficiently specific to identify places to be searched and items to be sought for and seized are void (*People v. Sohmers*, 286 N.Y.S.2d 714 (1968)). Once probable cause is present, only warrants which particularly describe the place to be searched and the things to be seized may lawfully be issued (*People v. Hay*, 245 N.Y.S.2d 705 (1963)).

The Execution of the Search Warrant

In executing a search warrant:

a. the officer must give notice of his authority and purpose to an occupant of a premises or vehicle before entry and show the warrant upon request, unless the warrant authorizes a no knock entry or it is unoccupied or the officer reasonably believes it to be unoccupied.

b. The officer may use necessary physical force to effect the entry against any person resisting the entry.

c. Deadly physical force may only be used if the officer reasonably believes it to be necessary to defend himself or another from what he reasonably believes to be the use or imminent use of deadly physical force.

d. Upon seizing the property, the officer must prepare an itemized receipt containing the name of the court, and leave it with the person from whom taken or at the place searched, if no one is present. He must then, without unnecessary delay, return the property, the warrant and a written inventory of the property seized to the court.

e.   Upon arresting a person during a search for him pursuant to a search warrant, the officer must comply with the terms of the arrest warrant and report the arrest and disposition of the prisoner to the court that issued the search warrant (690.50).

f.   Upon receiving the property seized, the court either retains it or directs it to be held by the police pending further disposition (690.55).

The basic purpose of the knock and announce rule is to protect the individual's right to privacy and to reduce the possibility of harm to the police inherent in an unannounced entry. A strict interpretation of a police officer's conduct under the knock and announce rule is applied where actual entry is effected through force, use of a pass key supplied by a third person or unannounced entry is made through an unlocked door (*People v. DiBernardo*, 392 N.Y.S.2d 1001 (1977)). The nighttime search provisions of this article are statutory requirements that are not of constitutional stature (*People v. Arnow*, 436 N.Y.S.2d 950 (1981)). When a valid "no knock" warrant is executed in a premises used to sell drugs, the officers are entitled to protect themselves from harm, by patting down a tenant of the premises for weapons (*People v. Soler*, 460 N.Y.S.2d 537 (1983)). A search warrant which authorized the search of the defendant's apartment and his person did not authorize the search of the defendant 19 blocks from his home (*People v. Green*, 33 N.Y.2d 496 (1974)). The scope, intensity and duration of a search pursuant to a warrant may depend on many factors, such as the size of the area to be searched, type of items to be examined, conditions prevailing at the time of the search, and whether or when the purposes of the search are completed. The "plain view" doctrine permits, during the execution of a search warrant, the seizure of items other than those enumerated in the warrant itself, providing the initial intrusion, which enables the officer to view the items in question is lawful, that the discovery is inadvertent and the incriminating nature of the evidence seized is immediately apparent (*People v. Martinelli*, 458 N.Y.S.2d 785 (1982)).

See Illustrative Cases

People v. Nieves, 36 N.Y. 2d 396 (1975), p. 444
People v. Betts, 90 A.D.2d 641 (1982), p. 447
People v. Burke, 690 N.Y.S.2d 897 (1999), p. 448

17.2 Eavesdropping and Video Surveillance Warrants (Article 700)

Traditionally the Fourth Amendment of the federal constitution was interpreted so as to protect a person's papers, houses, person and effects against unreasonable search and seizure. These are all tangible, physical objects and property. However, in 1967, the United States Supreme Court, in deciding *Katz v. U.S.* (388 U.S. 41), determined the Fourth Amendment protects people not places and decided eavesdropping or wiretapping involves the privacy interests protected by the Fourth Amendment. As a result of *Katz*, wiretapping and bugging (the seizing of a person's words) by government agents must not be unreasonable; otherwise, the seizure violates the Fourth Amendment and the words seized and any evidence derived therefrom are subject to the protections of the Fourth Amendment, i.e., the exclusionary rule. In 1968 Congress passed federal legislation regulating wiretapping under the Fourth Amendment (18 U.S.C. sec. 2516). This statute establishes the national law for wiretapping. Any state regulation of wiretapping must conform to the provisions of this federal statute. In 1970 New York enacted the provisions of Article 700, in order to conform New York's law on eavesdropping with the federal law. Section 250.05, P.L, makes unlawful eavesdropping a felony and art.1, sec.12, N.Y. Const., in addition to containing the same provision as does the U.S. Const. Fourth Amendment, also goes on to provide protection against unreasonable interception of communications. A person who engages in unlawful wiretapping (including a police officer) can be prosecuted for the federal or state offenses of illegal eavesdropping.

Article 700 begins by setting forth definitions of technical terms:

1. **Eavesdropping** means "wiretapping" or "mechanically overhearing of conversation," as these terms are defined in 250 P.L.

   a. **Wiretapping** is the intentional overhearing or recording of a telephonic or telegraphic communication, by a person other than the sender or receiver, without the consent of either.

   b. **Mechanical overhearing of a conversation** is the intentional overhearing or recording of a conversation, without the consent of at least one of the parties, by a person not present, by means of any instrument or device (this is commonly called "bugging").

2. **Eavesdropping warrant** is an order of a judge authorizing eavesdropping.

3. **Intercepted communication** is one intercepted by wiretapping or bugging.

4. **Justice** means an appellate division judge or judge of the supreme or county court in whose jurisdiction the eavesdropping warrant is to be executed.

5. **Applicant** means a district attorney, the attorney general or the deputy attorney general in charge of the organized crime task force, if authorized by the attorney general to be an applicant.

6. **Exigent circumstances** are conditions requiring secrecy and where a continuing investigation would likely be thwarted by alerting a person subject to surveillance that it had occurred.

7. **Designated offense.** The statute lists numerous specific crimes, the investigation of which may allow an eavesdropping warrant to be issued. In addition to the specific crimes specified, a conspiracy, or an attempt to commit one of them, if a felony, is also a designated offense. The list is too lengthy to be set forth

here, however, each crime listed is a felony and has been found to be dangerous to life, limb or property by legislative enactment. The list is exclusive (700.05).

The Eavesdropping Warrant

Eavesdropping warrants may be issued upon an *ex parte* application and for a period only as necessary to achieve the objective of the authorization, but in no case longer than thirty days. Extensions may be granted (700.10). It is public policy that eavesdropping is a dangerous intrusion into the right of privacy and should only be countenanced when done within constitutional limitations (*People v. Szymanski*, 310 N.Y.S.2d 587 (1970)). The requirements of this article providing for eavesdropping warrants, which are reflective of controlling federal law, must be strictly complied with (*People v. Sher*, 38 N.Y.2d 600 (1976)). Under preemption principles, any state law drawn more broadly than the *Federal Omnibus Crime Control and Safe Streets Act of 1968,* 18 U.S.C.A. sec. 2510, which imposes on the states the minimum constitutional criteria for electronic surveillance legislation, runs afoul of the supremacy clause, U.S.C.A. Const., art. 6, cl. 2 *(People v. Shapiro*, 50 N.Y.2d 747 (1980)). The purpose of the eavesdropping law was to provide a comprehensive scheme for the issuance of eavesdropping warrants, based upon strict standards of probable cause and necessity, and demanding scrupulous particularity in the description of both the person and place upon which eavesdropping is to be conducted and the nature of the evidence sought thereby (*People v. Sciandra*, 319 N.Y.S.2d 516 (1971)). It is not unlawful to eavesdrop on telephone conversations with the consent of one of the parties (*People v. Lasher*, 58 N.Y.2d 962 (1983)).

An eavesdropping warrant may be issued only:

a. upon an appropriate application; and,

b. upon probable cause a particularly described person is committing, about to commit, or has committed a particular designated offense; and,

c. upon probable cause that particular communications about such offense will be obtained through eavesdropping; and,

d. upon a showing that normal investigative procedures have been tried and failed, or reasonably appear to be unlikely, or to be too dangerous to employ; and,

e. upon probable cause the place where the communications are to be intercepted are being used in the commission of the offense, or are in the name of the designated person (700.15). (Note: All five subdivisions must be satisfied before a warrant may be issued.)

In striking a balance between society's interest in privacy and in ferreting out crime, Congress and the legislature sought to insure that electronic surveillance be resorted to only when it was absolutely necessary and that it was not routinely used as the initial step in criminal investigation (*People v. Gallina*, 466 N.Y.S.2d 414 (1983)). Neither the New York nor the federal statute requires that any particular investigative procedures be exhausted before a wiretap may be authorized (*U.S. v. Lilla*, 699 F.2d

99 (1983)). The standard of probable cause for a wiretap is the same as the standard for a regular search warrant (*U.S. v. Fury*, 554 F. 2d 522 (1977)). An eavesdropping warrant, like any other warrant, is subject to the command of the U.S. Const. Amend. 4 that it be supported by probable cause and particularly describe the place to be searched and the persons or things to be seized (*People v. Frank*, 447 N.Y.S.2d 558 (1982)).

The warrant must contain:

a. the name of the applicant, the judge, the person whose communication is to be intercepted and the law enforcement agency authorized to do the eavesdropping;

b. the place where the tap is to be installed, the time period of the authorization, the type of communication sought to be intercepted and the designated offense to which it relates;

c. a provision the intercept will be executed as soon as practicable, in such a way as to minimize the interception of other communications, terminate upon attainment of the authorized objective and in any event, in thirty days; and,

d. an express authorization to make secret entry upon the place to install the eavesdropping device if necessary (700.30).

The minimization provisions of this section are mandatory (*People v. Sturgis*, 352 N.Y.S.2d 942 (1973)). The requirement that authorization to intercept be conducted so as to minimize the interception of communications not subject to eavesdropping is designed to insure that communications intercepted conform, as nearly as possible, to those subject to interception under the eavesdropping authorization. **Minimization** may be defined as a good faith and reasonable effort to keep the number of nonpertinent calls intercepted to the smallest number practicable (*People v. Floyd*, 41 N.Y.2d 245 (1976)). An eavesdropping warrant was null and void where it failed to include the requirements of minimization and of particularity of the description of the types of conversations to be overheard and the identity of the person whose conversations were to be overheard (*People v. Sturgis* (*supra*)). In other cases the courts have decided the absence of a minimization directive in the original wiretap order did not violate this section, where the officers conducting the wiretap were aware of minimization requirements and abided by them (*U.S. v. Austin*, 399 F. Supp. 698 (1975)); and, the law does not require that persons whose conversations are to be recorded pursuant to an eavesdropping warrant be named but simply that they be named if they are known (*People v. Sher*, 329 N.Y.S.2d 2 (1972)).

The Application

The *ex parte* application for an eavesdropping warrant is made in writing except in emergency situations when it may be made orally. It must be signed and sworn to by the applicant. It must contain a full and complete statement of the facts establishing:

a. probable cause as to the designated offense and the particularity of the place, the type of communication and the person subject to the request for the warrant; and,

b. that normal investigative procedures have been tried or not and why; and,

c. all previous applications involving the same person or place; and,

d. the period of time requested for the warrant and that such communications are not legally privileged.

The facts may be based on the applicant's personal knowledge or information and belief. If based on someone else's statements, the reliability of such person and the basis for such person's belief must be established. Affidavits of such persons may be submitted with the application if they tend to support any fact or conclusion in the application (700.20). An affidavit in support of an eavesdropping warrant, though based entirely on hearsay, is permissible provided that there is a substantial basis for crediting the hearsay. The disclosure of the identity of the informant upon whose information affidavit the application was based was not necessary where there was sufficient evidence apart from the arresting officer's testimony as to informer's communication to establish probable cause (*People v. Sturgis (supra)*). A magistrate cannot find probable cause for issuance of an eavesdropping warrant upon mere conclusions of the affiant. The affidavit must have details of underlying circumstances upon which the affiant bases his conclusions (*People v. Holder*, 331 N.Y.S.2d 557 (1972)). Independent observation and investigation by the police after receiving a tip concerning crime confirmed the tip and established both the reliability and credibility of his information, for purpose of the issuance of a wiretap order (*People v. Fusco*, 348 N.Y.S.2d 858 (1973)).

In an emergency situation where imminent danger of death or serious physical injury exists, and where it is impractical for a written application to be prepared without risk of the death or injury occurring, the application need not be made in writing but may be made by telephone, radio or other means of electronic communication. The procedure then follows essentially that for the written application. A record must be made of the conversations between the judge and applicant. When the judge finds the emergency situation exists and the other requirements for the issuance of the warrant (700.15) have been met, he may issue a temporary eavesdropping warrant for a period not to exceed 24 hours (700.21). The judge determines each application (in writing or telephonic) on the basis of the facts and whether the grounds exist for the issuance of the warrant. If he is not so satisfied the application must be denied (700.25). A judge issuing a wiretap warrant has considerable discretion in determining the sufficiency of the application. The sufficiency may not be judged by the results obtained in executing the warrant. In reviewing the validity of the wiretap warrant, the court should determine whether a minimal showing was lacking so that the judge abused his discretion in issuing the warrant (*People v. Romney*, 433 N.Y.S.2d 941 (1980); abrogated by *People v. Guerra*, 77 AD2d 482 (1980)). Eavesdropping warrants are based on substantially the same principles applicable to search warrants for physical evidence (*People v. DiStefano*, 382 N.Y.S.2d 5 (1976)). Given the dangers and susceptibility to abuse inherent in unrestrained electronic surveillance, only the most exacting and meticulous standards should be required before permitting an intrusion into an individual's right of privacy (*People v. Brenes*, 385 N.Y.S.2d 530 (1976)). Where an informant of unknown reliability appeared personally before the magistrate and gave direct evidence in support of the application, the two-prong Spinelli-Aguilar test need not be met (*People v. Meranto*, 448 N.Y.S. 2d 59 (1982)).

At any time prior to the expiration of the warrant, the applicant may apply for an order of extension. The form and process for the extension is the same as that for the original application. In addition it must set forth the results thus far obtained (700.40). It was to avoid the necessity of removing and then reinstalling eavesdropping devices that the legislature directed that extension of eavesdropping orders be applied for prior to the expiration of the original warrants (*People v. Glasser*, 396 N.Y.S.2d 422 (1977)).

Executing the Warrant

The eavesdropping warrant must be executed by an officer of the law enforcement agency authorized to execute it. Any communication intercepted must be recorded by tape or similar device, if possible, and done in such a way as will protect the recording from editing or other alteration. Upon termination of the warrant, the eavesdropping must cease, and any device installed must be removed or permanently disabled. The warrant is authorization to enter a private place for such removal or disablement (700.35). In executing the warrant there must be a good faith and reasonable effort to keep the number of non-pertinent calls intercepted to the smallest practicable number (*People v. Frank*, 447 N.Y.S.2d 558 (1982)). Factors to be considered are: the nature and scope of the investigation; the character and sophistication of the targets and their associates; the extent of the official supervision devoted to each step of the surveillance; and, the possibility and practicality, contemporaneously with the interception, whether particular conversations are in fact pertinent to the objectives of the investigation. Ultimately, the primary question is whether there was a good faith attempt to avoid the interception of conversations unrelated to the crimes authorized to be investigated by the terms of the court order authorizing the eavesdropping (*People v. Brenes*, 42 N.Y.2d 41 (1977)). The intercepting authorities may monitor the initial portion of any telephone conversation, to determine its pertinency, and if not pertinent cease its monitoring. The authorities may, indeed must, tape record anything which they monitor, since to hold otherwise, would permit a far greater intrusion of permitting police agents to monitor without recording, and, thereby not preserving that which they listen to for review by the courts (*People v. Estrada*, 410 N.Y.S.2d 757 (1978)).

Progress Reports and Notices

The justice issuing the warrant may require reports as to the progress of the investigation toward achievement of its objectives. Immediately upon the expiration of the warrant or its extension, the recordings of the communications intercepted must be made available to the justice and sealed under his direction (700.50). The sealing requirement must be strictly construed and, absent a satisfactory explanation for failure to comply with such requirement, the tapes must be suppressed as evidence (*People v. Pecoraro*, 397 N.Y.S.2d 60 (1977)). A delay in sealing was not excused by the fact that the judge had gone home. The judge was available at home and in any event, the prosecutor could have used the services of the judge on call to handle special situations (*People v. Fonville*, 681 N.Y.S.2d 420 (1998)). The policies underlying the sealing provisions are to prevent tampering, alteration or editing, to establish the chain of custody and to protect the confidentiality of the tapes secured by eavesdropping (*People v. Scaccia*, 390 N.Y.S.2d 743 (1977)).

Notice must be given to the person named in the warrant as to the facts of the eavesdropping warrant within a reasonable time after its termination, but in no case more than ninety days thereafter; unless, on a showing of exigent circumstances, the issuing judge postpones such notice for a reasonable period of time. Thereafter, the justice, upon motion of the person served, may in his discretion make available such portions of the intercepted communications, applications and warrants, as he deems to be in the interest of justice (700.50). Failure of the people to give notice of the facts of the wiretapping rendered the recordings inadmissible as evidence (*People v. Tartt*, 336 N.Y.S.2d 919 (1972)). Delay in service of the notice of the eavesdropping warrant, where the circumstances of the investigation warranted postponement of such notice and defendant did not demonstrate any prejudice and, as a result, was reasonable (*U.S. v. Lilla*, 534 F. Supp. 1247 (1982)).

Notice must also be given a defendant before the use of any evidence at his trial, of intercepted communications or any evidence derived therefrom, within fifteen days of arraignment and before the commencement of the trial. The people must furnish the defendant with a copy of the warrant and the application under which the interception was authorized. The court may extend the time for good cause shown if it finds the defendant will not be prejudiced by the delay in receiving such notice and papers (700.70). The purpose of this provision is to promote timely pre-trial motions while at the same time protecting the defendant's right to seek suppression of the evidence (*People v. Merced*, 462 N.Y.S.2d 555 (1983)). If appropriate the trial judge in his discretion, may order a hearing during trial on a defendant's claim of undisclosed electronic surveillance. To use without notice to the defendant, any evidence derived from electronic surveillance is impermissible, even if the surveillance itself is legal (*People v. Cruz*, 34 N.Y.2d 362 (1974)).

Custody, Reports and Disclosure

Applications and warrants, after sealing by the justice, shall be delivered to the applicant and a copy kept by the justice. Even after denial of the application, the papers may not be shown to anyone without a showing of good cause before the court and must be kept for ten years by the justice. Custody of the recordings made may be wherever the justice determines and they must also be kept for ten years.

Duplicate copies may be made in the event disclosure is ordered by the court (700.55). Care and keeping of the recordings obtained pursuant to an eavesdropping warrant prior to their delivery to the justice who issued the warrant fall within the ambit of rules of evidence governing the "chain of custody" (*People v. Blanda*, 362 N.Y.S.2d 735 (1974)).

Within thirty days after termination of the warrant the issuing justice must forward a report of the eavesdropping warrant to the administrative office of the United States courts with a duplicate forwarded to the state office of court administration. In January of each year the attorney general and each district attorney must forward a report of eavesdropping warrants to the same offices (700.60).

Any law enforcement officer who, by any means authorized, has obtained knowledge of the contents of any intercepted communication or evidence derived therefrom, may:

a.   disclose such contents to another law enforcement officer in connection with his official duties; and,

b.   use such contents in the proper performance of his duties.

When a law enforcement officer engaged in intercepting communications under the eavesdropping warrant intercepts a communication which was not otherwise sought, containing evidence of crime, he may also disclose it and use it in the performance of his official duties. If such evidence is to be used as testimony in a criminal proceeding under oath it must first be added to the eavesdropping warrant by the issuing justice upon application by the applicant, as soon as practicable. Any person who receives information or evidence may give testimony as to it in a criminal proceeding, under oath, as long as the seal required on the recordings is present or its absence is satisfactorily explained (700.65).

The section providing that a law enforcement officer who, while engaged in the authorized interception of communications, intercepts evidence of another crime may, use such evidence before a grand jury or in a criminal proceeding when the justice amends the eavesdropping warrant, is constitutional. The question as to whether the application to amend was made as soon as practicable must depend in each case upon the circumstances then existing (*People v. Sher*, 329 N.Y.S.2d 2 (1972)). The failure to comply with the sealing requirements makes any evidence derived from the tapes inadmissible at trial (*People v. Sher*, 38 N.Y.2d 600 (1976)). The purpose of the requirement that the eavesdropping warrant be amended when new criminal matters come to light over a wiretap is to legalize the continuance on the wiretap to discover further evidence of newly disclosed crimes (*People v. Ruffino*, 309 N.Y.S.2d 805 (1970)). By enacting this section the legislature intended to engraft a "plain view" exception upon the general constitutional requirement that seized evidence must be particularly described in the application for the warrant (*People v. DiStefano*, 38 N.Y.2d 640 (1976)).

See Illustrative Cases

People v. Floyd, 26 N.Y.2d 558 (1970), p. 452

17.3 Pen Registers and Trap and Trace Devices (Article 705)

A "**pen register**" is a device which records electronic impulses, which identify numbers dialed or transmitted over a telephone line to which the device is attached. It does not include a device used by the telephone provider for billing purposes. A "**trap and trace device**" captures incoming impulses from which the identity of the transmitting telephone number can be ascertained (705.00).

Before law enforcement may use these devices, authorization must be gotten from a justice authorized to issue eavesdropping warrants under 700.05 (an appellate court judge or judge of the supreme or county court with jurisdiction over the location where the device is to be installed) (705.05). The procedures for authorization to utilize a pen register or trace device, are similar to those established for the securance of an eavesdropping warrant. Upon application of the district attorney or attorney general the justice may authorize a law enforcement agency to use these devices in the investigation of "designated crimes" as set forth in the eavesdropping section, 700.05/8 (705.00). The big difference between the eavesdropping statute and this statute is in the amount of evidence needed to secure the pen register authorization. To secure the pen register or trace device authorization, the facts and circumstances required are those which amount to reasonable suspicion that the designated crime is being committed. In order to get an eavesdropping warrant, the requisite amount of evidence required is probable cause (705.10).

The application must contain the facts establishing reasonable suspicion and who, when and where the device is to be installed. It must be in writing and is made *ex parte* (705.15). If the justice is satisfied as to reasonable suspicion and the other requisite information in the application, he shall issue the authorization to install the device. The authorization is in the form of an order and is not called a warrant. The order will contain the particulars as to where and when the device is to be installed (705.20). The order may be issued for up to sixty days and extensions for up to sixty days may be granted upon the filing of another application containing the information as required for the original authorization (705.25). The order must be sealed and not disclosed unless authorized by the court (705.30). Upon request of the applicant permission may be granted to a provider of the electronic service or the subscriber or owner of a premises to assist in the installation of the device. All are required to comply with the non-disclosure provision listed above. Such company or person must be reasonably compensated for their services and they are clothed with immunity for assisting in furtherance of the order (705.35).

17.4 Motion to Suppress Evidence (Article 710)

In 1961, the United States Supreme Court, in *Mapp v. Ohio* (367 U.S. 643) applied the federal **exclusionary rule** to the states, "… all evidence obtained by search and seizure in violation of the constitution is, by that same authority, inadmissible in a state court." The function of the exclusionary rule is to act as a deterrent to unlawful police conduct (*People v. Anthony*, 461 N.Y.S.2d 399 (1983)). There is no one specific method designed to be followed to enforce the rule. The purpose of this article pertaining to motions to suppress evidence is to provide for an orderly hearing, to prevent interruption of trial and to afford defense counsel the opportunity to prepare a defense (*People v. Slater*, 386 N.Y.S.2d 134 (1976)). Through the years many decisions have modified the application of the exclusionary rule but New York has chosen, in some instances, not to follow the federal rule but to choose a different rule under the state constitution giving the defendant more protection than that provided by the federal constitution. For example, the Court of Appeals rejected the "good faith exception" to the exclusionary rule of *U.S. v. Leon* (468 U.S. 897), in *People v. Bigelow* (66 N.Y.2d 417 (1985)), on state constitutional grounds, finding that to embrace the exception would put a premium on unlawful police activity and give others the incentive to commit lawless acts in the future. In order to effectuate the exclusionary rule, in this state, the defendant must use the procedures set forth in this article, Motion to Suppress Evidence. The motion to suppress is also one of the pre-trial motions required to be made in accordance with Section 255.10 (*supra*). **Evidence** means any tangible property or potential testimony in the possession of, or available to, the prosecutor, which may be offered in evidence at a criminal action (710.10).

Grounds for the Motion

Upon motion of a defendant who:

1. is aggrieved by unlawful or improper acquisition of evidence and has reasonable cause to believe it may be used against him; or,

2. claims that improper identification testimony may be offered against him, a court may order such evidence to be suppressed or excluded upon the ground that it:

    a. is tangible property obtained by an unlawful search and seizure; or

    b. consists of a record of, or testimony, gotten by unlawful eavesdropping or video surveillance; or a statement of the defendant involuntarily made, as per 60.45, *supra* (confession or admission generally); or,

    c. consists of evidence derived from one of the above; or,

    d. is the result of a chemical test of the defendant's blood to determine intoxication while driving a vehicle, boat or snowmobile in violation of the law; or,

    e. consists of inadmissible eyewitness identification testimony; or,

    f. consists of information gotten through the unlawful use of a pen register or trap and trace device (710.20).

A claim of a legitimate expectation of privacy is necessary to have standing to contest a search and seizure as unlawful (*People v. Ycasa*, 531 N.Y.S.2d 183 (1988)). A legitimate expectation of privacy, sufficient to confer standing to seek suppression of evidence, exists where the defendant has manifested an expectation of privacy that society recognizes as reasonable. The test is both whether the defendant exhibited an expectation of privacy in the place or items searched or seized, and whether society generally recognizes the defendant's expectation of privacy as reasonable *(People v. Ramirez-Potoreal*, 88 N.Y.2d 99 (1996)). With regard to standing, where evidence was seized from his person, defendant's expectation of privacy is beyond question (*People v. Hibbler*, 494 N.Y.S.2d 191 (1985)). A defendant who is a casual visitor to an apartment does not have any reasonable expectation of privacy in it and therefore no standing to contest a warrantless entry of it (*People v. Ortiz*, 83 N.Y.2d 840 (1994)). The fact that the defendant was showering and had left his clothing in another room, was entirely consistent with transient presence without a reasonable expectation of privacy, and did not, in and of itself, establish that he was a houseguest with such an expectation and concomitant standing to challenge the search and seizure of the house (*People v. Garrett,* 576 N.Y.S.2d 604 (1991)). In another case, the defendant was at least an overnight guest at the apartment and as such had standing to challenge the search warrant for the apartment. He told the officer he lived in the apartment and the officer could come back at any time. Police reports reflected the defendant's residence as the apartment and at the time of the arrest, at 6:30 AM, he was found in bed (*People v. Chandler,* 581 N.Y.S.2d 530 (1991)). A defendant, for example, does not have a reasonable expectation of privacy in, the hallway of a public housing building (*People v. Grier,* 552 N.Y.S.2d 383 (1990)); a vacant apartment (*People v. Alicia*, 493 N.Y.S.2d 841 (1985)); a trash pile on a city sidewalk or a paper bag secreted in the trash pile (*People v. Ramirez-Portoreal*, (supra)); an illegal search and seizure of another person (*People v. Rodriguez*, 395 N.Y.S.2d 222 (1977)); an automobile when he is merely a passenger in the back seat (*People v. Hernandez*, 679 N.Y.S.2d 790 (1997)); a car he has stolen (*People v. Gittens*, 488 N.Y.S.2d 457 (1985)) or in which he is a passenger (*People v. Cacioppo*, 479 N.Y.S.2d 264 (1984)). These are examples of the myriad of cases, in one area only, decided by the courts involving the motion to suppress. Many times if the defendant can prevail on the motion, the charge against him will be required to be dismissed due to lack of evidence to establish guilt beyond a reasonable doubt at trial.

When Notice to Defendant Is Required

When the people intend to offer at trial:

a. evidence of a statement by the defendant to a public servant, which if involuntarily made would make it inadmissible; or,

b. eye witness identification testimony,

they must serve a notice of such intention on the defendant, within fifteen days of arraignment and before trial, in order to give the defendant a reasonable opportunity to move for its suppression. For good cause shown the court may allow the notice to be made thereafter but it must give the defendant a reasonable opportunity to move to suppress. Such evidence will not be admissible at trial if the people fail to give this notice, unless the defendant moves to suppress such evidence without having received such notice and the motion to suppress it is denied (710.30).

The purpose of this section is to promote timely pre-trial motions and to protect the defendant's rights to prepare a challenge to and seek suppression of evidence (*People v. Merced*, 462 N.Y.S.2d 555 (1983)). The notice is not required for the prosecutor to use such evidence for impeachment purposes only, and not as evidence in chief (*People v. Sanzotta*, 595 N.Y.S.2d 152 (1993)). An involuntary statement under 60.45 includes one that is physically or psychologically coerced, obtained by a promise or statement that creates a risk of falsely incriminating oneself or is obtained by the failure to give Miranda warnings (*People v. Chase*, 85 N.Y.2d 493 (1995)). Good cause for late notice cannot be established by the prosecutor by office failure, mere neglect or absence of prejudice to the defendant (*People v. Moore*, 682 N.Y.S.2d 798 (1998)).

Motion Procedures

The pre-trial motion to suppress must be made in accordance with the procedures set out for pre-trial motions in Article 255. The motion must be made within forty five days of arraignment or securance of counsel, unless for good cause, the court may permit it to be made at a later time, even during trial. When the pre-trial motion is made the trial may not commence until the motion has been determined by the court (710.40). The purpose of this provision is to allow the defendant a fair opportunity to contest admissibility while avoiding unfair surprise, to preserve judicial economy by preventing interruption of trials to resolve suppression issues that would otherwise arise mid-trial, and to afford the people the option to appeal an adverse ruling without risk of jeopardy having attached (*People v. Sorbo*, 649 N.Y.S.2d 318 (1996)). If the accusatory instrument is a felony complaint or indictment, the motion must be made in the superior court having jurisdiction. On an information or a misdemeanor complaint, the motion must be made in the local criminal court with jurisdiction (710.50).

The pre-trial motion must be in writing with notice to the people and an opportunity to be heard. It must state the grounds and contain sworn allegations of fact based upon personal knowledge or information and belief, with the sources indicated.

The people may file an answer, denying or admitting any or all of the allegations in the moving papers. The court may summarily grant or deny the motion on the papers submitted. If the motion cannot be decided on the papers the court must hold a hearing to determine findings of fact necessary to the determination. All persons giving information must testify under oath and hearsay evidence is admissible to establish any material fact. A motion permitted to be made at trial may be in writing or made orally. If the court can't decide it without a hearing, the hearing must be held out of the presence of the jury, if any. Upon determining the motion, the court must set forth on the record its findings of fact, conclusions of law and the reasons for its determination (710.60). Where the defendant contends he was the victim of an unconstitutional search and seizure, the prosecution has the burden of production, requiring that it come forward with evidence of the legality of the police action in the first instance; but, the burden of proof remains with the defendant to show his constitutional rights were violated (*People v. Sanders*, 433 N.Y.S.2d 854 (1980)).

Upon granting the motion, the court must order the evidence be excluded, and upon request of the defendant, order restored to him, any tangible property lawfully possessed by the defendant that was seized and the subject of the motion. If the court denies the motion, the defendant may appeal the denial after a judgment of conviction, including one based upon a plea of guilty. If a defendant does not make the motion to suppress he waives his right to raise it upon appeal of a judgment of conviction (710.70).

See Illustrative Cases:

People v. Ramirez-Portoreal, 230 A.D.2d 943 (1996), p. 455
People v. Spencer, 84 N.Y.2d 749 (1995), p. 459
People v. Hill, 110 A.D.3d 410 (2013), p. 460

17.5 Destruction of Dangerous Drugs (Article 715)

A **dangerous drug** means any substance listed in Schedules I through V, Section 3306, of the Public Health Law (715.05). This section includes all the controlled substances listed in Article 220 and marijuana, which is not included in the Penal Law definition of controlled substances. This article establishes a procedure for the destruction of dangerous drugs seized by the government in connection with an arrest for their sale or possession before trial. If the procedures are followed, Section 60.70 permits evidence relating to the drugs to be admitted into trial despite their unavailability. There is also a procedure for their destruction if seized not in conjunction with an arrest.

The district attorney may make a written motion in a superior court for an order for the destruction of dangerous drugs, with a copy of the report of their quantitative and qualitative analysis attached. The motion will be made *ex parte*, where no arrest has been made in connection with their seizure, with a showing that the likelihood of an arrest in connection with them is nonexistent. The court may then order the destruction of all or part of the subject drugs (715.10).

The motion upon notice to a defendant must be made after the defendant has been arraigned in the superior court on a felony charge for the possession or sale of the dangerous drugs and they are material to the prosecution of the indictment (715.10). In every felony case involving the possession or sale of a dangerous drug, the head of the agency charged with custody of the drugs shall have a quantitative and qualitative analysis made of the drugs, within forty five days of their receipt. Within ten days after receipt of the analysis report, a copy shall be forwarded to the district attorney, with the location where the drugs are being held (715.50). When the motion on notice is received, the court must order a hearing to be held on the motion, within thirty days. If the court finds neither the people nor the defendant will be prejudiced, it may order all or part of the drugs destroyed. The defendant may waive the hearing and consent to their destruction (715.20). The order of destruction, issued either on motion with notice or *ex parte*, shall state the time within which the order is to be carried out and direct the destruction to be witnessed by at least two witnesses, one of whom must be a police officer (715.30). An affidavit of destruction, with a copy of the order attached, must then be filed with the court by the person who destroyed the drugs and each of the witnesses to the destruction (715.40).

Chapter 18

Special Proceedings Which Replace, Suspend or Abate Criminal Actions

Sec. 18.1 Article 720; Youthful Offender Procedure
Sec. 18.2 Article 722; Establishment of Youth Part
Sec. 18.3 Article 722.23; Removal of Adolescent Offender to Family Court
Sec. 18.4 Article 725; Removal of Proceeding against a Juvenile Offender to Family Court
Sec. 18.5 Article 730; Mental Disease or Defect Excluding Fitness to Proceed

18.1 Youthful Offender Procedure (Article 720)

Generally speaking, a **youthful offender** is a person 13 to 19 years old, who is convicted of a certain designated crime and the circumstances are such that the court, in its discretion, may set aside the conviction and replace it with an adjudication of youthful offender. The purpose of the adjudication is to spare young persons who have violated criminal laws from the stigma and adverse consequences necessarily flowing from a criminal conviction (*Drayton v. N.Y.*, 556 F.2d 644 (1977)).

Specifically, a "**youth**" means:

a. a person charged with a crime allegedly committed when he was sixteen and not yet nineteen years of age; or,

b. a person charged with being a juvenile offender as per 1.20/42 (a person thirteen but not yet sixteen years of age, charged with one of a number of class A felonies and who may be tried either as an adult criminal or proceeded against as a juvenile delinquent).

Either of these persons is eligible to be adjudicated a youthful offender upon conviction of the crime charged, unless:

a. previously convicted and sentenced for a felony; or,

b. previously adjudicated a youthful offender following a conviction for a felony; or, a juvenile delinquent and the underlying crime therefore was a designated felony under the Family Court Act, sec. 301.2; or,

279

c. the conviction to be replaced by a youthful offender adjudication in the instant case is for a class A-I or II or an armed felony; or rape or sodomy in the first degree or aggravated sexual abuse; however, for the armed felony and sex case convictions, if, in the opinion of the court there were mitigating circumstances, or if the defendant was not the sole participant and his role was minor, the court may adjudge the youth a youthful offender (720.10).

When the accusatory instrument against an apparently eligible youth is filed, the court, with the defendant's consent, shall order it sealed with respect to the public, unless the youth has previously been adjudicated a youthful offender or convicted of a felony; and, all proceedings in the action conducted in private, unless, the charge is a felony (720.15). The purpose of the confidentiality provisions is to remove the stigma of alleged criminal activity and its adverse effect on the accused, thereby affording protection to the accused in pursuit of employment, education, professional licensing and insurance opportunities (*People v. Gallina*, 488 N.Y.S.2d 249 (1985)).

The Process

In order to determine if an eligible youth is a youthful offender, upon conviction the court must order a pre-sentence report. At sentencing, the court must make such determination based upon the following criteria:

a. In the opinion of the court, would the interest of justice be served by relieving the eligible youth from the onus of a criminal record and by not imposing an indeterminate term of imprisonment of more than four years.

b. If the court so finds, it may, in its discretion, find the youth is a youthful offender.

c. If the court is a local criminal court and the youth has no previous conviction of a crime or adjudication as a youthful offender, it must find the youth a youthful offender.

If the conviction is for two or more crimes, to be adjudicated a youthful offender, he must be found a youthful offender for all such crimes. If the youth is found a youthful offender, the conviction is deemed vacated and replaced by the youthful offender finding and the youth sentenced as per Section 60.02 P.L. (generally, not more than that for an "E" felony conviction in a felony case; and, in a misdemeanor case, not more than six months). Upon determining the youth is not a youthful offender, the accusatory instrument is unsealed and the action continues pursuant to the ordinary rules of a criminal action (720.20). There is no constitutional right to youthful offender treatment. Such treatment is afforded only on a favorable exercise of discretion by the sentencing court and such court is under no statutory compulsion to afford such relief (*People v. Williams*, 418 N.Y.S.2d 737 (1979)). The sound discretion of the sentencing court will not be disturbed on appeal where there is no clear abuse of such discretion (*People v. Allen*, 686 N.Y.S. 2d 216 (1999)). The factors to be considered for a youthful offender determination include gravity of the crime and the manner in which it was committed, mitigating circumstances, prior criminal record and acts of violence, recommendations and pre-sentence reports, reputation and cooperation with authorities, attitude towards society and respect for the law and prospects for rehabilitation and hope for a future constructive life (*People v. Shrubsall*, 562 N.Y.S.2d 290 (1990)).

The person adjudged a youthful offender has the same right to post judgment motions and remedies and appeals as in criminal cases, wherever such provisions may be reasonably applied (720.30). A trial court's exercise of discretion in affording youthful offender treatment is reviewable on appeal (*People v. Nudelman*, 419 N.Y.S.2d 674 (1979)). The granting of youthful offender status is within the sound discretion of the sentencing court and will not be disturbed on appeal where there is no clear abuse of such discretion (*People v. Allen*, 686 N.Y.S.2d 216 (1999)). Although the county court did not necessarily abuse its discretion in denying youthful offender treatment to a seventeen year old defendant convicted of 1st degree manslaughter in regard to the shooting death of her father, the Appellate Division exercised its discretion by vacating the conviction and adjudicating the defendant a youthful offender, where the defendant had no previous criminal record or other past violent or anti-social conduct, was remorseful about the shooting and cooperated fully with authorities, the probation department recommended she be treated as a youthful offender, she was sexually abused as a child and the crime arose out of that fact, and the jury found that defendant acted under the influence of severe emotional disturbance for which there was a reasonable explanation or excuse (*People v. Cruickshank*, 484 N.Y.S.2d 328 (1985)).

The youthful offender adjudication is not a criminal conviction and does not operate as a disqualification to hold public office or public employment, or to receive any license granted by a public authority. Except as permitted by statute or the court, all official records on file with the court, police or division of criminal justice services relating to the case and youthful offender determination are confidential and may not be disclosed to any person or agency except an institution to which the youth has been committed or the division of probation or parole for the purpose of carrying out their duties (720.35). The submission of the youthful offender record of an applicant for the position of patrolman to the civil service commission defeated the purpose of the statute and was in direct violation of the spirit and letter thereof (*Cuccio v. Department of Personnel*, 243 N.Y.S.2d 220 (1963)). While a civil service applicant cannot be disqualified from holding a license or public employment based on a youthful offender adjudication, this does not mean that in appropriate circumstances facts underlying the youthful offender adjudication cannot be probed in order to aid in determining the moral fitness of an applicant for a position sought (*Bell v. Codd*, 395 N.Y.S.2d 116 (1977)). The use of a youthful offender adjudication for the purpose of impeachment is prohibited; however, the cross examiner may bring out the facts underlying the adjudication so long as he does not elicit the adjudication itself (*U.S. v. Canniff*, 521 F.2d 565 (1975)).

See Illustrative Cases

Cacchioli v. Hoberman, 313 NY.2d 287 (1992), p. 462
Bell v. Codd, 395 N.Y.S.2d 16 (1977), p. 464

18.2 Establishment of Youth Part
(Article 722)

A new law went into effect on October 1, 2018, which created a new class of defendants called "Adolescent Offenders" (AOs), charged with certain felonies committed on or after October 1, 2018, when the defendant was 16 years old, or effective October 1, 2019, when the defendant was 17 years old (CPL 1.20 (44)). The statute mandates creation of a youth part in the superior court of every county with exclusive jurisdiction over AO and Juvenile Offender defendants (*see* CPL 1.20 (42)), to be presided over by specially trained family court judges (CPL 722.10 (1)); *see also* CPL 410.90-a).

18.3 Removal of Adolescent Offender to
Family Court (Article 722.23)

The case is commenced by the filing of a youth felony complaint directly in the youth part rather than in the local criminal court. If, however, the accusatory instrument alleges a non-drug class A felony or a violent felony defined by PL § 70.02, the court must review the accusatory instrument within six calendar days from the arraignment (CPL 722.23 (2)(a)).

If the district attorney proves by a preponderance of the evidence that any one of three aggravating factors exist, the case remains in the youth part for adjudication under the criminal law (CPL 722.23 (2)(c)). If the parties agree or the court determines that none of the aggravating factors apply to the case, the case is transferred to the family court unless the district attorney files a motion within 30 days to prevent removal alleging that extraordinary circumstances exist to retain the case in the youth part (CPL 722.23 (1) (a)).

The court is required to deny the motion to prevent removal unless it finds that "extraordinary circumstances exist that should prevent the transfer of the action to family court" (Penal Law § 722.23 (1) (d)). The term extraordinary circumstances is not defined in the statute. When a case is removed to the Family Court, further criminal proceedings are prohibited regarding the offenses subject to the removal (Penal Law § 722.21 (6)(e); *see People v. D.L.*, 62 Misc. 3d 900 (2018).

18.4 Removal of Proceeding against a
Juvenile Offender to Family Court
(Article 725)

The classification of juvenile offender was added to the law by the legislature in 1978. It lowered the age of criminal responsibility from sixteen to thirteen years of age for certain serious felonies (*see* 1.20/42). A person thirteen but less than sixteen years of age who commits or allegedly commits one of the designated offenses listed under 1.20/42 may be charged and tried as an adult in the criminal court or may be proceeded against as a juvenile delinquent in the family court. As in the case of the youthful offender, the juvenile offender then receives less harsh treatment under the law due to the factors of immaturity and in the hopes of rehabilitation due to factors present in the circumstances of the youth and the criminal act committed.

The criminal court may direct the action or charge be removed to the family court by an order of removal. The court may direct this at various stages of the proceedings:

a. upon the establishment of reasonable cause to believe the offender committed or allegedly committed the offense or a lesser offense, at the direction of the grand jury or after a hearing on a felony complaint in the local criminal court;

b. after a plea or verdict of guilty;

c. upon a motion to dismiss on the grounds of insufficient evidence for the juvenile offender charge; or,

d. in the interest of justice with the district attorney's consent.

The order must direct the defendant appear before the family court within ten days of the removal order and, if in custody, at the next session of the family court. All papers regarding the action in the criminal court including the grand jury minutes, if any, must be transferred to and filed with the clerk of the family court (725.05). In order to balance society's interests against the interests of the individual child, the criminal court is vested with the discretion to refer the errant child to family court or to compel the minor to face the consequences of his wrongdoing as an adult. The discretion entrusted to the criminal court must be exercised in a sober and meticulous fashion, on the basis of as much information about the juvenile and the crime as can be obtained, including records of the department of social services bearing on the recent social and psychological history of the juvenile (*Matter of Roman*, 412 N.Y.S.2d 325 (1979)).

Upon filing of the order of removal in the family court a juvenile delinquency proceeding must be initiated and the criminal action is terminated. All proceedings then follow the provisions of the family law (725.10). The legislature intended that absent removal, juvenile offender cases should be heard only in the court where upon a finding of guilt, criminal responsibility can attach. By criminalizing certain conduct committed by persons thirteen, fourteen and fifteen years of age, and by creation of a detailed and specific set of procedures that govern the removal of actions to the family court, the legislature has divested the family court of initial jurisdiction over acts that are juvenile offenses. The family court did not have jurisdiction over a petition charging a fourteen year old juvenile with robbery, where the district attorney had exercised his discretion not to proceed with a criminal action against said juvenile, and the criminal court had not issued a removal order (*Matter of Nick C.*, 659 N.Y.S.2d 969 (1997)).

All official records and papers in the matter are confidential and are not to be divulged to any person or agency except as provided by the family law (725.15). The clerk of the family court shall maintain a separate file for copies of such papers. He must delete all portions that would identify the defendant. He will keep two separate files, one confidential and the other, after making such deletions, available for public inspection (725.20).

18.5 Mental Disease or Defect Excluding Fitness to Proceed (Article 730)

This article has to do with a defendant's mental competency to stand trial and must be differentiated from the issue of defendant's mental capacity at the time of the commission of the crime. Due process prohibits criminal prosecution of a defendant who is not mentally competent to stand trial. Such a person is deemed an **"incapacitated person,"** who is defined as a defendant who as a result of mental disease or defect lacks capacity to:

a. understand the proceedings against him; or,

b. assist in his own defense (730.10).

In defining incapacitated person the legislature had in mind the situation where the defendant, because of a current inability to comprehend, or at least a severe impairment to that existing mental state, could not with a modicum of intelligence assist counsel (*People v. Francabandera*, 33 N.Y.2d 429 (1974)). To be excused from being a party to criminal proceedings as a result of a mental condition, there must be a showing that the condition from which the defendant suffers is of such nature that his reasoning power is impaired to the extent that he cannot understand the nature of the charges against him and make a defense thereto. A mental disturbance which does not affect one's reasoning powers cannot act as a shield to the defendant (*People v. Pugach*, 225 N.Y.S.2d 822 (1962)). The test for competency to stand trial is whether defendant has sufficient present ability to consult with his attorney with a reasonable degree of rational understanding and whether he has a rational as well as a factual understanding of pending proceedings (*Mead v. Walker*, 839 F.Supp.1030 (1993)). A defendant need not be competent independent of medication before he can be put on trial. Synthetic or pharmacologically induced competency is sufficient (*People v. Parsons*, 371 N.Y.S.2d 840 (1975)).

The Process

After a defendant is arraigned and before the imposition of sentence, if the court becomes of the opinion that the defendant may be incapacitated, it must issue an order of examination in order to assist the court in determining the mental competence of the defendant (730.30). The order of examination is transmitted to the Commissioner of Mental Health who then forwards it to the director of a state or local government mental facility who must direct an examination of the defendant by at least two qualified psychiatric examiners (licensed psychiatrists or psychologists). After the examination, each examiner must prepare a report of the results of his examination and submit it to the director. If the examiners are not unanimous as to their opinion of the defendant's mental capacity, the director must designate another examiner to examine the defendant and submit a report as well. The reports are sent to the court that issued the examination order. The defendant may be examined as an outpatient or, at the direction of the director, confined to a hospital for a reasonable period of time for such purpose, depending upon the circumstances. Any statement by the defendant for the purpose of the examination shall be inadmissible in evidence against him on any issue other than his mental condition (730.20). The determination of competence to proceed at trial is a judicial rather than medical one, and the court is not required to adopt the opinion of the mental health examiners (*People v. Villanueva*, 528 N.Y.S.2d 506 (1988)). The receipt in evidence of the psychiatrist's report containing defendant's admissions required reversal of his conviction for murder (*People v. Roth*, 11 N.Y.2d 80 (1962)).

When the examination reports are received by the court, the court on its own motion may conduct a hearing to determine the mental capacity of the defendant. Upon motion of the defendant or the district attorney, or if the reports of the examiners are not unanimous, it must conduct a hearing. If no motion is made or if after the hearing the court is of the opinion the defendant is not mentally incapacitated, the criminal action must proceed (730.30). The test for determining the fitness of a defendant to stand trial is whether he is able to understand the nature of the charges against him, and capable of assisting in his own defense. In making this determination, the court must take into consideration expert medical proof, coupled with all other evidence, and the court's own observations of the defendant (*People v. Tortorici*, 671 N.Y.S.2d 162 (1998)). The determination of whether to order a hearing to determine defendant's competence to stand trial lies within the sound discretion of the court (*People v. Tortorici*, 92 N.Y.2d 757 (1999)). The defendant is presumed competent and is not entitled, as a matter of law, to a competency hearing unless the court has reasonable grounds to believe that, because of mental disease or defect, the defendant is incapable of assisting in his own defense or of understanding the proceedings against him (*People v. Medina*, 671 N.Y.S.2d 550 (1998)). The people have the burden of proving defendant's competence by a fair preponderance of the evidence (*People v. Wright*, 482 N.Y.S.2d 591 (1984)). Factors which the court should consider on the issue of competency to stand trial are whether defendant is oriented as to time and place; is able to perceive, recall and relate; has an understanding of the process of trial and the roles of judge, jury, prosecutor and defense attorney; can establish a working relationship with his attorney; has sufficient intelligence and judgment to listen to the advice of counsel and, based on that advice, appreciate without necessarily adopting the fact that one course of conduct may be more beneficial than another; and is sufficiently stable to withstand the stresses of trial without suffering prolonged or permanent breakdown (*People v. Picozzi*, 482 N.Y.S.2d 335 (1984)).

Defendants Found Incapacitated

If no motion is made or if after a hearing the court is of the opinion the defendant is mentally incapacitated, the court must order a final order of observation (less than a felony case) or an order of commitment (in a felony case). In the case of a final order of observation for the less than felony situation, the court may commit defendant to the custody of a mental health facility for not more than ninety days and dismiss the accusatory instrument against him. In a felony case the court must order the defendant to a mental health facility, for care and treatment for not more than one year. If the defendant is still deemed to be incapacitated after the year, the commitment is renewed and continues to be renewed thereafter at two year intervals. At the end of each of the intervals reports are sent to the court and the parties as to the mental capacity of the defendant. The court will hold hearings on motions to determine the mental capacity of the defendant. If the court finds the defendant no longer incapacitated, the criminal action will then be continued. If the court finds the defendant still mentally incapacitated it issues an order of retention and the defendant remains in the mental health facility for additional care and treatment. The sum total of all the commitment periods may not exceed two-thirds of the maximum sentence the defendant could receive. When that time limit is reached, with the defendant still confined to the mental facility, its superintendent must reexamine the defendant and if still mentally incapacitated, take the steps necessary to have him civilly committed to a mental institution (*see* 730.70) and the court must dismiss the accusatory instrument against the defendant (730.40,50). Fixing the maximum period during which one, charged with a criminal offense and committed on account of incapacity to proceed to trial, may be retained, solely on the basis of the maximum sentence for the crime with which he is charged, does not meet the constitutional standard. The defendant may be committed for a reasonable period for determination of whether there is a substantial probability that he will attain the capacity to proceed to trial in the foreseeable future (*People v. Anonymous*, 351 N.Y.S.2d 869 (1974)). The due process right of a defendant to be released after a reasonable period of time, necessary to determine whether there is substantial probability that he will attain the capacity to proceed to trial in the foreseeable future, does not automatically entitle an incapacitated defendant to a dismissal of the charges. Although entitled to release, such defendant does not have the corollary right to dismissal of charges given the public's countervailing interest in the court's continuing jurisdiction over defendant to monitor his condition and location (*People v. Schaffer*, 86 N.Y.2d 460 (1995)).

Dismissal of Indictment and Leaves

When the defendant is in the custody of the commissioner in a mental facility under the order of the criminal court, the criminal action is suspended until the defendant is found to be no longer incapacitated. In such case, the court is notified of such determination and must take steps to determine if the defendant is no longer incapacitated (*see* 730.30 re: hearings). If the defendant is found by the court to remain incapacitated the order of confinement will be continued, and the defendant will remain in the mental facility. Upon motion of the defendant, with the consent of the district attorney, the court may dismiss the indictment against the defendant, if it is satisfied:

a. the defendant is a resident or citizen of another state or country, and he will be removed thereto upon dismissal of the indictment; or,

b. the defendant has been continuously confined in the custody of the commissioner for more than two years; and,

    i. the dismissal is consistent with the ends of justice; and,

    ii. custody is not necessary for the protection of the public; and,

    iii. care and treatment can be effectively provided without the criminal order of commitment.

While in the custody of the commissioner the defendant may not be released, discharged, or placed on any less restrictive status such as vacation, furlough or temporary leave, without delivery of written notice by the commissioner of at least four days, excluding Saturdays, Sundays and holidays, to the district attorney, state and local police, sheriff, any person who may be reasonably expected to be the victim of violence from the defendant and any other person the court may designate. The district attorney, upon receipt of such notice, may apply to the court for a hearing to determine whether such person is a danger to himself or others. Upon a finding the defendant is a danger to himself or others the court shall issue an order of retention for a specified period, not to exceed six months (730.60). When petitioner had been held in a mental hospital as an indicted defendant, incompetent to stand trial, long enough to determine whether he was likely to attain the capacity to stand trial and when there is no likelihood that the petitioner would attain such capacity nor make any progress to that goal, civil commitment or outright release is constitutionally compelled (*People ex rel. Anonymous v. Waugh*, 351 N.Y.S.2d 594 (1974)). In a hearing to convert to civil status a person, who was held in commitment to a state hospital, as being competent to stand criminal trial, the people had the burden of proof, once the petitioner raised the initial question of his status. The standard of evidence is proof by a preponderance of evidence (*People v. Arendes*, 400 N.Y.S.2d 273 (1977)).

Part Four

Illustrative Cases for Analysis

Illustrative Cases for Analysis

Chapter 1; Introduction

Sec. 1.3; Basic Constitutional Law Summary

People v. Gokey
60 N.Y.2d 309 (1983)

OPINION OF THE COURT: (Re: Search of containers, incident to arrest)

A duffel bag that is within the immediate control or "grabbable area" of a suspect at the time of his arrest may not be subjected to a warrantless search incident to the arrest, unless the circumstances leading to the arrest support a reasonable belief that the suspect may gain possession of a weapon or be able to destroy evidence located in the bag. There being no such exigency present at the time police searched defendant's bag here, the motion to suppress should have been granted.

On the afternoon of March 12, 1981, the Watertown City Police Department received a tip from an informant that defendant was traveling on a bus from New Jersey to Watertown with marihuana and hashish in his possession. With an arrest warrant for an unrelated larceny charge in hand, three Watertown police officers and two officers from the Jefferson County Sheriff's Department waited at the bus terminal. With them was a dog specially trained to detect marihuana. Defendant was observed to be carrying a duffel bag when he disembarked from the bus.

One of the officers approached defendant and informed him that he was under arrest. Defendant was then ordered to place his hands against the wall and to spread his feet so that he could be frisked. When led to the duffel bag, which lay on the ground between defendant's feet, the dog's reaction indicated the presence of marihuana. Defendant was then handcuffed. An officer searched the duffel bag and found approximately 11 ounces of marihuana.

After being indicted, defendant moved to suppress the seized marihuana as the fruit of an unlawful warrantless search. County Court, relying on *New York v. Belton* (453 U.S. 454), denied the motion. Defendant pleaded guilty to criminal possession of marihuana in the third degree and the Appellate Division affirmed the conviction, without opinion. This court now reverses.

In *New York v. Belton* (453 U.S. 454, 461, supra), the Supreme Court set forth a general rule under the Fourth Amendment of the United States Constitution that a custodial arrest will always provide sufficient justification for police to search any container within the "immediate control" of the arrestee. Under this standard, it is clear that defendant's Federal constitutional rights were not violated.

This court has declined to interpret the State constitutional protection against unreasonable searches and seizures so narrowly (see *People v. Smith*, 59 NY2d 454; NY Const, art I, § 12; see, also, *People v. Langen*, 60 NY2d 170, 181). Under the State Constitution, an individual's right of privacy in his or her effects dictates that a warrantless search incident to arrest be deemed unreasonable unless justified by the presence of exigent circumstances. When an individual subjected to arrest has a privacy interest in property within his or her immediate control or "grabbable area," this court has identified two interests that may justify the warrantless search of that property incident to a lawful arrest: the safety of the public and the arresting officer; and the protection of evidence from destruction or concealment (see *People v. Smith*, 59 NY2d 454, 458, supra; *People v. Belton*, 55 NY2d 49, 52–53).

The reasonableness of a police officer's assertion of the presence of either or both of these predicates to justify a warrantless search is measured at the time of the arrest. Moreover, the search must have been conducted contemporaneously with the arrest. In *People v. Smith* (supra), for example, this court upheld a search by police of an arrestee's briefcase that was within the arrestee's possession at the time of arrest as a reasonable search incident to arrest. Determinative of the search's validity were the facts that police reasonably believed that defendant was in possession of a weapon as was evidenced by his wearing a bulletproof vest, that the briefcase was large enough to contain a weapon, and that it was not so securely fastened that defendant would have been unable to gain access to it. The officers' reasonable fear for their safety was found not to have dissipated merely because defendant was moved off a subway platform into a porter's room less than 10 feet away before the search was initiated. The search of the briefcase was conducted virtually contemporaneously with the arrest and immobilization, by handcuffing, of defendant.

Similarly, in *People v. Johnson* (59 NY2d 1014), a warrantless search of a handbag located approximately two feet from defendant at the time of his arrest, was upheld because police reasonably believed at the time of the search that defendant might gain access to a weapon. In that case, police had received a radio call about a "man with a gun" and were instructed to investigate the premises. When police arrived, the building superintendent warned them that a man had just struck him over the head with an automatic pistol and had attempted to shoot him. Police entered the apartment and, contemporaneously with the defendant's arrest, dumped out the contents of the bag, which was in easy reach of the defendant, who had not yet been handcuffed.

In the present appeal, the People have not asserted the presence of any exigency to justify the warrantless search of defendant's duffel bag. The police sought defendant's arrest for two nonviolent crimes and the People concede that "in all frankness there was no immediate suspicion by the police officers that the defendant was in fact armed." Indeed, the officers' conduct leading up to the search of the bag confirms the absence of exigency. The police did not seize the bag from defendant upon his arrest but permitted him to keep the bag between his legs while he was frisked. The police officers' interest in the bag focused solely on the possibility that it contained marihuana. A search was undertaken only after the dog's conduct had corroborated the information that the bag contained marihuana.

Furthermore, the police have not asserted nor, on the facts of this case, could they reasonably rely on a belief that the search was justified by the need to preserve evidence located in the bag. Again, the presence of any exigency is belied by the police officers' failure to seize the bag immediately upon encountering defendant. By the time the search was undertaken, defendant's hands were handcuffed behind his back and he was surrounded by five police officers and their dog. Therefore, because the police concededly did not fear for their safety, and because they could not have reasonably believed that the search of the bag was necessary to preserve any evidence that might have been located in it, the warrantless search of the bag was invalid.

Accordingly, the order of the Appellate Division should be reversed and the indictment dismissed.

Order reversed.

People v. Settles
46 N.Y.2d 154 (1978)

OPINION OF THE COURT: (Re: Waiver of right to counsel at post indictment line-up)

Following a joint trial with codefendant Osborne (Sonny) Boalds, defendant appeals from his judgment of conviction upon a jury verdict for robbery in the first degree.

The threshold issue we address is whether the identifications made by witnesses at a postindictment, prearraignment corporeal viewing of the then unrepresented defendant should have been excluded where defendant, in the absence of counsel, orally waived his right to have an attorney present at the lineup.

The order of the Appellate Division affirming the conviction should be reversed. The filing of an indictment constitutes the commencement of a formal judicial action against the defendant and is equated with the entry of an attorney into the proceeding. This being the case, a defendant in a postindictment, prearraignment custodial setting, even though not then represented by an attorney, may not in the absence of counsel waive his right to have counsel appear at a corporeal identification. Hence, any actions taken by the police with respect to an indicted but unarraigned defendant which impinge upon his right to counsel may not be used against him at trial.

The facts are uncomplicated and undisputed. On the night of March 9, 1974, two men robbed a bar, its manager and one of its patrons in Queens County. Responding to a radio call, two police officers arrived at the location just as one of the perpetrators was leaving the scene. In an exchange of gunfire one of the officers was fatally wounded, and his partner, after giving chase, soon lost sight of the suspect. Fortunately, later that night the police were directed to proceed to the apartment of Boalds' common-law wife. After receiving permission to enter and search the premises, they discovered fruits of the earlier robbery, clothes apparently worn by the perpetrators and a gun which later proved to be the weapon which fired the fatal shots. Also in the apartment were Boalds and the defendant. While Boalds was immediately placed under arrest, defendant was merely brought to a police station for further investigation and was released the following morning.

On May 1, 1974, the Queens County Grand Jury returned an indictment charging defendant and Boalds with two counts of murder, two counts of robbery and another of possession of a dangerous weapon arising out of the events of the night of March 9. At that time, however, defendant could not be found and a warrant was issued for his arrest. He was later apprehended and placed in custody in Atlanta, Georgia, and was returned to New York on August 14, 1974. Immediately upon his arrival, defendant was transported to the 113th Precinct in order that he be placed in a lineup. Although not advised that he was under indictment, defendant was given his four-fold Miranda warnings, whereupon he agreed to appear in the lineup without an attorney present. Of the five individuals who were present in the bar on the night of the crimes and who viewed the lineup, two were able to identify defendant as one of the perpetrators.

In this State, the right of a criminal defendant to interpose an attorney between himself and the sometimes awesome power of the sovereign has long been a cherished principle. This need, moreover, has been recognized as all the more vital with respect to the unsophisticated, who are often uneducated in the ways of the criminal justice system and unaware of the role counsel can play in protecting their interests. When a person charged with a crime has been unable to engage counsel because of financial circumstances, it has long been the duty of the court before whom he is brought to assign counsel. In short, we recognize that the assistance of counsel is essential not only to insure the rights of the individual defendant but for the protection and well-being of society as well. The right of any defendant, however serious or trivial his crime, to stand before a court with counsel at his side to safeguard both his substantive and procedural rights is inviolable and fundamental to our form of justice.

So valued is the right to counsel in this State (NY Const, art I, § 6), it has developed independent of its Federal counterpart (US Const, 6th Amdt). Thus, we have extended the protections afforded by our State Constitution beyond those of the Federal — well before certain Federal rights were recognized. A criminal defendant under indictment and in custody may not waive his right to counsel unless he does so in the presence of an attorney.

Once an indictment is returned against a particular defendant, the character of the police function shifts from investigatory to accusatory. For this reason, the warnings which are sufficient to comply with the strictures against testimonial compulsion do not satisfy the higher standard with respect to a waiver of the right of counsel.

Prior to indictment, there may be valid reasons why an uncounseled suspect might wish to deal with the police. He may nourish the hope, however vain, that he can avoid any legal entanglement by simply clearing up a few loose ends. Alternatively, he may feel that by getting into the good graces of the police as an informer he might be able to avoid indictment and trial. No such opportunity is afforded him once the Grand Jury has spoken.

Any delay in arraigning an indicted defendant can have no rationale unless done for the purpose of buttressing what at that point is a prima facie case. For example, here, rather than arraigning defendant immediately, the police subjected him to uncounseled corporeal viewing. They were not merely trying to ascertain whether there was probable cause to believe a crime had been committed or even whether the defendant had committed the crime. They already knew that a crime had occurred and that defendant was to stand trial therefor. This is precisely the juncture at which legal advice is crucial. Once a matter is the subject of a legal controversy any discussions relating thereto should be between counsel. The fact that defendant did not have an attorney appointed at the time the police sought their waiver is a distinction without a difference as far as the right to counsel is concerned.

Of course, a postindictment defendant may knowingly and intelligently waive his right to counsel at any stage of the judicial proceedings. But no knowing and intelligent waiver of counsel may be said to have occurred without the essential presence of counsel, the likelihood of a defendant incriminating himself is diminished when custodial interrogation takes place in the presence of an attorney. That is not the point. At the time when legal advice is most critically needed, our Constitution strikes the balance in favor of the defendant by placing a buffer, in the form of an attorney, between himself and the coercive power of the State. This court has long jealously guarded an indicted defendant's right to counsel, and we refuse to predicate a waiver of so valued a right on the recitation of a formula printed on a card. Should the police desire to have any dealings with an indicted defendant, except of course in connection with such ministerial matters as pedigree declarations and his processing as an arrestee, they must do so in the presence of an attorney.

We reject the contention of the People that the purpose of the rule against an indicted defendant waiving his right to counsel in the absence of an attorney loses its force at a corporeal viewing. While we have noted that "the need for and right to a lawyer at an identification lineup is insignificant compared to the need in an ensuing interrogation," this in no way signifies that the assistance of counsel at a postindictment lineup may be ignored.

A defendant is entitled to the assistance of an attorney at any critical stage of the prosecution. Generally, the critical stage commences upon the filing of an accusatory instrument but certain other procedures, such as a court order of removal, are "'sufficiently "judicial" in nature'" to permit invocation of that right. In any of these situations, if an attorney has entered the proceedings, the right to counsel may be waived only in his presence and with his acquiescence. Similarly, where the investigatory stage of a prosecution has concluded and formal judicial proceedings have commenced, whether by indictment or arraignment, the right to counsel may be waived only in the presence of counsel. Thus, where an indictment has been returned, we equate the indictment with the entry of a lawyer into the proceedings and invoke the requirement of counsel's presence to effectuate a valid waiver.

Order reversed.

People v. Griminger
71 N.Y.2d 635 (1988)

OPINION OF THE COURT: (Re: Aguilar-Spinelli, two prong test, required in New York)

The primary issue presented is whether the Aguilar-Spinelli two-prong test, or the Gates totality-of-the-circumstances test, should be employed in determining the sufficiency of an affidavit submitted in support of a search warrant application (see, *Illinois v. Gates*, 462 U.S. 213; *Spinelli v. United States*, 393 U.S. 410; *Aguilar v. Texas*, 378 U.S. 108). We conclude that, as a matter of State law, our courts should apply the Aguilar-Spinelli test.

Special agents of the United States Secret Service arrested a counterfeiting suspect, and, in the course of interrogation, he signed a detailed statement accusing defendant of keeping large quantities of marihuana and cocaine in his bedroom and adjacent attic. Consequently, one of the agents prepared an affidavit for a warrant to search defendant's home. According to the affidavit, a confidential informant known as source "A" observed substantial quantities of marihuana and quantities of cocaine in defendant's bedroom and attic on numerous occasions, saw defendant sell drugs on numerous occasions, and, as recently as seven days ago, "A" observed 150 to 200 pounds of marihuana in defendant's bedroom and adjacent attic. The affidavit further stated that, pursuant to a consent search, approximately four pounds of marihuana were found in a garbage can at defendant's residence.

Although the agent did not personally know the counterfeiting suspect, his affidavit said that the undisclosed informant was "a person known to your deponent." The agent also omitted the fact that the informant was under arrest when he provided this information. Based solely upon this affidavit, a Federal Magistrate issued the search warrant. On August 26, 1983, the warrant was executed by 2 Federal agents and 6 or 7 Nassau County policemen. The search produced 10 ounces of marihuana, over $ 6,000 in cash and drug-related paraphernalia. Additionally, the Federal agents turned over the marihuana discovered during the consent search referred to in the warrant to Nassau County law enforcement officials.

Defendant was charged with two counts of criminal possession of marihuana, as well as with criminal sale of marihuana arising out of an unrelated May 1984 incident. Defendant sought to suppress the evidence obtained as a result of the August 26 search, but County Court denied the motion. Although the court found that the agent's affidavit failed to satisfy the "reliability" prong of the Aguilar-Spinelli test, it concluded that the Gates test should be applied in assessing the sufficiency of a search warrant. Under that test, the court determined that there was probable cause to issue the warrant.

Defendant then pleaded guilty to all charges with the understanding that he would receive concurrent sentences in return for his pleas. The Appellate Division, however, reversed and remanded for further proceedings, holding that as a matter of State constitutional law, County Court should have applied *Aguilar-Spinelli*. The Appellate Division, agreeing with County Court that the reliability of the informant was lacking, found that the warrant had, therefore, been improperly issued, and that the fruits of that illegal search must be suppressed.

A Judge of this court granted the People leave to appeal. We now affirm.

Prior to *Illinois v. Gates*, Federal courts applied the two-pronged Aguilar-Spinelli test in probable cause determinations when evaluating hearsay information from an undisclosed informant. Under this test, the application for a search warrant must demonstrate to the issuing Magistrate (i) the veracity or reliability of the source of the information, and (ii) the basis of the informant's knowledge. We adopted this standard as a matter of State constitutional law. In *Illinois v. Gates* (supra), the United States Supreme Court altered its position and adopted the seemingly more relaxed "totality-of-the-circumstances approach."

In *People v. Johnson* (supra), this court expressly rejected the *Gates* approach for evaluating warrantless arrests. In *People v. Bigelow* (66 NY2d 417, although the People urged us to adopt the Gates test in the search warrant context, we found it unnecessary to decide the question, since "the People's evidence [did] not meet minimum standards of probable cause even if *Gates* was applied." This appeal squarely presents the issue left undecided in Bigelow. We are not persuaded, however, that the *Gates* approach provides a sufficient measure of protection, and we now hold that, as a matter of State constitutional law, the Aguilar-Spinelli two-prong test should be applied in determining whether there is a sufficient factual predicate upon which to issue a search warrant.

We reaffirm today that in evaluating hearsay information the Magistrate must find some minimum, reasonable showing that the informant was reliable and had a basis of knowledge. Our courts should not "blithely accept as true the accusations of an informant unless some good reason for doing so has been established." The *Aguilar-Spinelli* two-pronged inquiry has proven a satisfactory method of providing reasonable assurance that probable cause determinations are based on information derived from a credible source with firsthand information, and we are not convinced that the *Gates* test offers a satisfactory alternative.

The reasons advanced by the People in support of the Gates test are similar to those enunciated by the Supreme Court itself in *Illinois v. Gates*. They contend that the less stringent Gates test will encourage the use of warrants, a highly desirable goal. They assert that the Aguilar-Spinelli test has been applied in a rigid, inflexible manner to the detriment of law enforcement. The commonsense approach of *Gates*, posit the People, is a more reasonable rule of law, since the hypertechnical two-prong test places an unnecessary burden on law enforcement officers who are not lawyers, but rather public officials "acting under stress and often within the context of a volatile situation."

Although we agree with the People that the use of warrants should be encouraged there is no reason to believe that police will refrain from obtaining a warrant merely because this State continues to apply the Aguilar-Spinelli test. With limited exceptions, carefully circumscribed by our courts, it is always incumbent upon the police to obtain a warrant before conducting a search. Furthermore, whether there was probable cause will generally be raised by the defendant at a suppression hearing. If a Magistrate has already determined that probable cause existed, great deference will be accorded that finding, resulting in far fewer suppression problems. This, in turn, results in a more efficient use of police resources; it is indeed wasteful to make an arrest or conduct a search without a warrant only to have those efforts invalidated by a suppression court.

Nor is the Aguilar-Spinelli test a hypertechnical approach to evaluating hearsay information. In the real world, we are confronted with search warrant applications which are generally not composed by lawyers in the quiet of a law library but rather by law enforcement officers who are acting under stress and often within the context of a volatile situation. Consequently such search warrant applications should not be read in a hypertechnical manner as if they were entries in an essay contest. On the contrary, they must be considered in the clear light of everyday experience and accorded all reasonable inferences

Accordingly, the order of the Appellate Division should be affirmed and the defendant's cross appeal dismissed.

Chapter 3; Exemption from Prosecution
Sec. 3.1; Article 20; Geographical Jurisdiction
People v. Fea
47 N.Y.2d 70 (1979)

OPINION OF THE COURT: (Re: Particular effect of an offense, 20.10)

The question presented upon this appeal is whether, pursuant to CPL 20.40 (subd. 2, par [c]), Bronx County had territorial jurisdiction to indict and convict defendant of assault in the second degree and assault in the third degree arising out of vicious beatings he inflicted in Rockland County.

The events leading up to this prosecution had their inception in April, 1974. At that time, Harold Mazza, a person who had previously been involved in a number of illicit enterprises, joined two others in organizing a partnership known as the McLean Painting Company in the City of Yonkers, Westchester County. Soon after formation, the firm was engaged as a subcontractor at a construction site in Westchester. Mazza soon encountered difficulty meeting his rather substantial weekly payroll.

His unsavory past precluded the use of traditional banking channels to secure interim financing.

An acquaintance, Paul Zerbo, sympathized with Mazza's plight and informed him that defendant would be able to provide him with a short-term loan enabling him to meet his payroll. At a meeting in The Bronx, defendant offered Mazza a $ 15,000 loan, which Mazza was to repay at a rate of $ 750 per week until $ 18,000 was returned to Fea. Four payments were made when Mazza again found himself in need of more funds to meet the company payroll. A new $ 10,000 loan was arranged in The Bronx under the condition that Mazza would pay $ 200 per week interest on the additional sum until the entire principal was repaid. Defendant again informed Mazza that he would collect the weekly payments at his Yonkers office but if no one arrived by the close of business Friday, Mazza was to bring the installment to defendant at the Rosedale bar in Bronx County.

In the months that followed, 9 or 10 weekly installments were made, approximately half of them in The Bronx. Two or three of these payments were made by checks drawn on insufficient funds. By November, 1974, McLean Painting was in economic extremis and unable to meet any of its obligations, including those to defendant. Apparently fearful of the consequences of default, Mazza absented himself from his Yonkers office for the next three months. During that period, defendant asked Zerbo to relay a message to Mazza that defendant was looking for him. Defendant finally located Mazza on February 3, 1975.

That morning, as Mazza and Zerbo arrived at a construction site in Westchester County, they noticed defendant and an associate waiting for them. The pair were intercepted and ordered to follow defendant's car over the Tappan Zee Bridge into Rockland County, where Mazza and Zerbo were forced at gunpoint to enter a deserted bar. Once inside, the two were savagely beaten by defendant and his associate. At various intervals, Mazza was informed in most forceful terms that the consequences would be even greater should he continue to fail to meet his obligations in the future.

An ongoing investigation by the Bronx County District Attorney's office into defendant's activities soon revealed his role in the Rockland County assaults. Both Mazza and Zerbo agreed to cooperate and this prosecution resulted. The defendant was subsequently indicted for the assaults against Mazza and Zerbo occurring in Rockland County as well as a separate assault against a different victim in Bronx County

During the course of trial, defendant moved that those counts relating to the Rockland County assaults be dismissed on the ground that Bronx County had no territorial jurisdiction over the transactions. Although expressing grave doubt over the power of Bronx County to prosecute defendant for assaults allegedly committed outside that county's borders, the court reluctantly agreed to charge the jury that, to convict defendant, "they must find the fact that [the assaults were] likely to have a particular effect in Bronx County" beyond a reasonable doubt. Although territorial jurisdiction need not be proved beyond a reasonable doubt (*People v. Moore*, 46 NY2d 1, 6), under no view of the evidence may Bronx County be deemed a proper forum within the meaning of CPL 20.20 (subd. 2, par [c]). Therefore, we are constrained to reverse so much of the order of the Appellate Division which affirmed the judgment of conviction relating to the Rockland County assaults and to dismiss the counts of the indictment pertaining to those assaults.

At common law, the power of the sovereign to enact laws proscribing conduct and attaching criminal liability to the commission of the prohibited acts extended only within the confines of its territory. The theory underlying the common-law rule stems from the concept that the accused had a right to be tried by a jury drawn from the neighborhood where the acts giving rise to criminal liability took place. Of necessity, certain exceptions to the early common-law territorial theory of jurisdiction emerged. Thus, in instances where conduct perpetrated outside the jurisdiction was done with the intent to obstruct the governmental affairs of the sovereign and such extraterritorial conduct actually produced that effect, it could prosecute the acts as if actually committed within its borders. This common-law exception to the strict territorial theory of jurisdiction was the precursor of the injured forum and protective jurisdiction sections of the Criminal Procedure Law (see CPL 20.20, subd. 2; 20.40, subd. 2).

Absent statutory exception, in this State the territorial unit for criminal prosecutions is the county. The Legislature has, however, created a number of statutory exceptions to strict territorial principles of geographic jurisdiction (e.g., CPL 20.20, subd. 2, pars [a], [d]; 20.40, subd. 2, pars [a], [b] [adopting the objective territorial or injured forum theory of jurisdiction. Relevant to this case is the adoption of the protective theory of jurisdiction, which is premised on the postulate that the jurisdiction of the State, or one of its counties, may be exercised over conduct outside its geographical borders where such conduct was intended to have a deleterious effect within its territory.

As presently drafted, the statute adopting the protective theory of county jurisdiction over criminal offenses (CPL 20.40, subd. 2, par [c]), is rather limited in scope. The statute provides that a county may prosecute an offense occurring outside its borders when: "Even though none of the conduct constituting such offense may have occurred within such county: "(c) Such conduct was likely to have, a particular effect upon such county or a political subdivision or part thereof, and was performed with intent that it would, or with knowledge that it was likely to, have such particular effect therein."

The definition of "particular effect" within a county is provided by CPL 20.10 (subd. 4): "When conduct constituting an offense produces consequences which, though not necessarily amounting to a result or element of such offense, have a materially harmful impact upon the governmental processes or community welfare of a particular jurisdiction, or result in the defrauding of persons in such jurisdiction, such conduct and offense have a 'particular effect' upon such jurisdiction."

The People maintain that the Rockland County assaults were committed with the intent to produce a materially harmful impact upon the community welfare of Bronx County by compelling Mazza to resume usurious loan payments in The Bronx. However, even assuming that the attacks could be deemed to have been intended to compel payment in Bronx County alone, that conduct would not have the "materially harmful impact" presently contemplated by the statute. Extraterritorial jurisdiction is to be applied only in those limited circumstances where the out-of-jurisdiction conduct is violative of a statute intended to protect the integrity of the governmental processes or is harmful to the community as a whole.

For example, an attempt in county B to bribe an executive officer of county A to effectuate a decision favorable to the offeror's interests in county B, if accomplished, would have a perceptible detrimental impact upon the governmental integrity of county A and would support that county's exercise of territorial jurisdiction over the bribe offeror. Such conduct would clearly be intended to have a dramatic effect upon the governmental processes of county A. A variation of Professor Denzer's example (Denzer, Practice Commentary, McKinney's Cons Law of NY, Book 11A, CPL 20.40, p. 55) aptly illustrates a situation in which a county could assert its protective jurisdiction on the ground that the intended conduct, if brought to its logical conclusion, would have a materially harmful impact upon the community welfare of the county: if a person were to attempt to blow up a dam in Putnam County near the Westchester County line, knowing or intending that his act would cause substantial flooding in Westchester County, either Westchester or Putnam could prosecute the conduct. If the dam were destroyed, Westchester County's jurisdiction would lie as it would be an injured forum. However, if for some reason the charge did not ignite, Westchester could assert its protective jurisdiction over the transaction, for that theory looks to the intent of the actor rather than the consequences of his act

In both of these examples, the particular effect intended by the criminal conduct is to cause a materially harmful impact, not to any particular individual, but rather to the well being of the community as a whole. Moreover, the conduct was intended to impact upon one particular jurisdiction. Thus, the county in which the criminal conduct is intended to result may properly prosecute the actor if only to protect the integrity of its governmental processes or the welfare of the citizens. Here, in contrast, any impact upon Bronx County arising out of the assaults committed in Rockland County is amorphous at best. The result intended to be effected by the assaults was not intended to cause harmful impact upon the community [*78] as a whole, but rather only upon the recalcitrant debtor. Indeed, defendant's sole motivation in beating Mazza was the simple desire to compel repayment of the debt. Whether he was repaid in Bronx County, Westchester County or elsewhere was at most incidental, the place of payment not being a constituent element of the motive. The interest of Bronx County in prosecuting these assaults was nonexistent.

Accordingly, the order of the Appellate Division dismissing those counts of the indictment is affirmed.

People v. Alvaro Carvajal

812 N.Y.S.2d 395 (2005)

OPINION OF THE COURT: (Re: Geographic jurisdiction, 20.30)

In this prosecution for first degree criminal possession of a controlled substance and conspiracy, we are called upon to determine whether New York rightly exercised territorial jurisdiction over the possession offenses, when the defendant resided, and the cocaine was seized, in California. We conclude that, pursuant to the authority granted by CPL 20.20 (1) (c), New York was vested with jurisdiction to prosecute.

Based on a series of calls intercepted between May 13 and May 19, 1994, the New York State Drug Enforcement Task Force learned of plans to use three cars to transport cocaine from San Francisco to New York. Defendant was in New York City for four days, from May 13 to May 16, meeting with his cohorts. During his stay, he made telephone calls to his California subordinates. He gave detailed instructions to them on preparing the cocaine for shipment to New York City via automobile, and planned to pay the travel expenses of a driver.

After returning to California, defendant continued his preparations. On May 17, he told Freddy Lasso that he would put 21 kilograms of cocaine in the white car for Hans Vargas (a Chicanero employee) to pick up. Defendant later reassured Freddy Lasso that he would "dress up the girls" (prepare the cocaine) for delivery to New York. Freddy Lasso told him to "fill up the space" in the blue and green cars.

On May 19, task force members stopped Vargas just outside the San Francisco airport; after a brief search of his white Mazda, no drugs were located and Vargas was sent on his way. Vargas parked in the airport garage and entered the terminal, and upon his return to the car, the task force team intervened, finding 21 kilograms of cocaine in hidden compartments in the panels of the car's rear doors. Later that evening, task force members stopped a blue Volvo which had been left at a suburban San Francisco shopping center by defendant's employee Victor Hugo. At the time of the stop, Chicanero employee Hector Rivas was driving the Volvo. Thirty kilograms of cocaine were found in a hidden trap behind the dashboard. Following these setbacks, defendant and Freddy Lasso spoke by telephone and made plans to move their drug inventory to a new location.

The task force learned that the cohorts stored a large amount of cocaine in a "stash house" in Daly City, outside San Francisco. On the night of June 15, 1994, police recovered 23 kilograms of cocaine and more than $433,000 from the stash house. Apparently, defendant and an underling entered the garage at the stash house while task force agents were inside; defendant later told Freddy Lasso that he saw some strange people in the house and left. Defendant said that he doubted whether the people he had seen in the house were police. Grueso angrily told defendant that he had 48 hours to get him "that material." Freddy Lasso told defendant to "load up" a car with drugs bound for New York as soon as possible.

Defendant was arrested in California in September 1994; Freddy Lasso and other conspirators were also arrested. On October 15, 1994, defendant, Freddy Lasso, Grueso, Lasso's brothers Raul and Nelson Lasso, and others were charged in a special narcotics indictment with second degree conspiracy. Defendant, Freddy Lasso and Grueso were also charged, acting in concert, with three counts of first degree criminal possession of a controlled substance (Penal Law § 220.21 [1]) for the separate quantities of drugs seized in California.

The court instructed that to convict on drug possession, the jury had to find that the defendants committed the elements of that crime in the County of Queens, in New York City, and in the State of California. The court further advised the jury, without objection by defense counsel, that

> "[y]ou should be aware that I have referred to many of the alleged overt acts as telephone conversations. The law in this regard says under Article 20.60 of the Criminal Procedure Law, '[a]n oral or written statement made by a person in one jurisdiction to a person in … another jurisdiction by means of telecommunications is deemed to be made in each such jurisdiction.'"

Defendant was convicted of three counts of first degree criminal possession of a controlled substance, as well as one count of conspiracy in the second degree, and was sentenced as a second felony offender to an aggregate term of 35 years to life. The Appellate Division affirmed defendant's convictions, concluding that territorial jurisdiction over the possessory offenses had been established under CPL 20.20 (1) (a) in that defendant's telephone conversations with his New York-based accomplices were deemed New York conduct sufficient to establish an element of the offense. Defendant's cohorts in the conspiracy were also convicted as charged.

Discussion

We conclude that territorial jurisdiction over the possessory offenses in this case was established under CPL 20.20 (1) (c), which provides that

> a person may be convicted in the criminal courts of this state of an offense defined by the laws of this state, committed either by his own conduct or by the conduct of another for which he is legally accountable pursuant to section 20.00 of the penal law, when:

> 1. Conduct occurred within this state sufficient to establish: …

> (c) A conspiracy or criminal solicitation to commit such offense, or otherwise to establish the complicity of at least one of the persons liable therefor; provided that the jurisdiction accorded by this paragraph extends only to conviction of those persons whose conspiratorial or other conduct of complicity occurred within this state" (CPL 20.20 [1] [c]).

Plainly, jurisdiction over an offense exists based on a conspiracy occurring in New York to commit that offense. Further, jurisdiction exists only for those defendants whose criminal acts in furtherance of the conspiracy occurred in New York. Here, the question is whether there was evidence of defendant's conduct in New York sufficient to establish his conspiracy to commit first degree criminal possession of a controlled substance. We conclude that there was.

Defendant contends that his telephone calls from California to New York counterparts amount merely to conduct having some "nexus" to this state, not conduct occurring within this state. However, under CPL 20.60 (1), defendant's telephonic statements to his accomplices here are deemed to be New York conduct "the Criminal Procedure Law provides that oral statements made over the telephone are deemed to be statements made in both the sending and receiving" jurisdictions pursuant to CPL 20.60 (1). In those calls, he spoke with Freddy Lasso and others concerning their joint efforts to move drugs from California to New York.

Dissent

In summary, the controlled substances at issue were seized from persons and a house located in California, not recovered from an area or person located in New York. These drugs were never possessed in New York by defendant. Nor were they possessed within an area or by a person under defendant's dominion and control. Accordingly, the crime of criminal possession of a controlled substance never occurred within the territorial borders of New York. Thus, the trial court could not acquire jurisdiction over the crime.

By affirming the Appellate Division's holding that Supreme Court acquired territorial jurisdiction over the three criminal possession counts, the majority: (1) incorrectly credits the People's theory that defendant, under a constructive possession theory, committed the crime of criminal possession of a controlled substance in the first degree; and (2) incorrectly concludes that a New York criminal trial court can acquire jurisdiction over a criminal offense that was not actually committed in New York. The majority holds that "jurisdiction over an offense exists based on a conspiracy occurring in New York to commit that offense." This holding can only be correct if the possession offense which is the object of the conspiracy has been committed in New York and the defendant possessed drugs in New York. The majority's holding sets a dangerous precedent because it will allow a trial court to try a defendant for a completed crime where only an attempted crime or no crime has been committed.

Based on the foregoing, defendant's conviction on the drug possession counts should be vacated and the indictment on those counts dismissed.

Order affirmed.

People v. Moore
46 N.Y.2d 1 (1978)

OPINION OF THE COURT: (Re: Offenses on bridges, tunnels, in cars, etc., 20.40)

The defendant was indicted and convicted in Kings County for rape and sexual abuse in the first degree. The offenses allegedly occurred in the defendant's car while parked in Queens County near the Kings County border. The trial court held, as a matter of law, that Kings County had jurisdiction to prosecute the offenses pursuant to CPL 20.40 (subd. 4, pars [c], [g]). The Appellate Division reversed and ordered a new trial on the ground that a question of fact was presented as to whether the crimes were committed within 500 yards of the boundary between the two counties (see CPL 20.40, subd. 4, par [c]). On this appeal the prosecutor urges that Kings County had jurisdiction pursuant to CPL 20.40 (subd. 4, par [g]) which states: "An offense committed in a private vehicle during a trip thereof extending through more than one county may be prosecuted in any county through which such vehicle passed in the course of such trip."

At the trial the complainant testified that she resided in Brooklyn and had been acquainted with the defendant for approximately three years prior to the incident. On May 12, 1974, she went with the defendant to a Brooklyn social club where he was employed. They went in the defendant's car. Later, while driving the complainant home the defendant entered Highland Park, stopped in a parking lot and told her that he wanted to have intercourse with her. When she refused, he assaulted and raped her. Afterwards, as they were leaving the park, the defendant stopped for a traffic light and the complainant jumped from the car and escaped. A police officer testified that Highland Park is on the border between Kings and Queens County and that the parking lot is located in Queens County.

During the trial the defendant argued that the jurisdictional issue should be submitted to the jury as a question of fact. However, before formally charging the jury, the court advised the parties that it had decided to deny the defendant's motion and that it would not permit the jury to pass on the question of jurisdiction. The court expressly relied on CPL 20.40 (subd. 4, par [g]) and noted that "There isn't any question from the evidence so far adduced in this case that this vehicle started the trip in the Borough of Brooklyn, went through the Borough of Queens and went back into the Borough of Brooklyn."

At common law and under the State Constitution the defendant has the right to be tried in the county where the crime was committed unless the Legislature has provided otherwise. The burden is on the People to prove that the county where the crime is prosecuted is the proper venue because either the crime was committed there or one of the statutory exceptions is applicable. Venue, however, need not be proven beyond a reasonable doubt; a preponderance of the evidence will satisfy the People's burden Any question with respect to where a boundary lies should usually be decided by the court (but generally it is for the jury to decide, as a matter of fact, the place where the crime was committed or any other fact relevant to venue.

In any event in this case even if the complainant's testimony were credited, Kings County could not establish jurisdiction by relying solely on the private vehicle trip statute (CPL 20.40, subd. 4, par [g]) in view of the complainant's ability to otherwise identify the place where the crime was allegedly committed. Statutory exceptions to the rule that the prosecution should be held at the place where the crime was committed were created out of necessity. Strict adherence to the common-law rule often created insurmountable obstacles to prosecution. For instance, if part of the crime had been committed in one county and part in another the defendant could not be tried in either. In this and similar cases where the law would otherwise be frustrated, the general rule was altered by statute to insure that there would always be some forum where the crime could be prosecuted

The private vehicle trip statute (CPL 20.40, subd. 4, par [g]) went into effect in 1971. The drafters noted that CPL 20.40 (subd. 4) — of which the private vehicle statute is a part — was designed to apply "in certain narrow situations, such as those involving offenses committed on bridges, trains, and ships, or on designated bodies of water." The purpose of the statute is readily apparent. When a crime is committed in an automobile during the course of a trip it may be impossible to determine in what county the offense occurred. In those cases the statute insures a forum by authorizing prosecution of the offense in any county through which the vehicle passed in the course of the trip. The problem, however, was never encountered in this case since here the complainant was able to identify the place where the crime was committed despite the use of the automobile. Thus the statute is inapplicable.

Accordingly the order of the Appellate Division should be affirmed.

Sec. 3.2; Article 30; Speedy Trial

People v. Taranovich
37 N.Y.2d 442 (1975)

OPINION OF THE COURT: (Re: Speedy trial, 30.20)

The question presented for our determination may be phrased as follows: under the particular circumstances attending this criminal prosecution, was the 12-month delay between the appellant's arraignment and his subsequent indictment violative of his constitutional and statutory rights to a speedy trial? The County Court of Nassau County granted defendant's motion to dismiss the indictment filed against him on the ground that he had not been afforded a speedy trial. The Appellate Division unanimously reversed this order, denied the motion to dismiss and reinstated the indictment.

We affirm.

In the early morning hours of January 13, 1972, an officer of the Nassau County Police Department stopped a vehicle which was being operated in an erratic manner on a highway in Mineola. The defendant placed his automobile in reverse gear and ran over the officer with the vehicle. Although he immediately sped away from the scene, defendant was apprehended a short distance away by other officers. The injured officer was hospitalized for lacerations, contusions and a cerebral concussion.

He was arraigned the same day on District Court informations charging attempted murder, possession of a dangerous drug, and resisting arrest, leaving the scene of an accident, operating a motor vehicle while impaired and operating a motor vehicle without a license.

Eight days following his arrest and arraignment on these charges, defendant was admitted to bail and he has since remained free on bail.

When the defendant waived a felony examination, he was held for the action of the Grand Jury, which, on February 10, 1972 voted a true bill charging him with assault in the first degree and leaving the scene of an accident. The District Attorney has candidly admitted that the papers on defendant's case were inadvertently misplaced due to clerical error, and, as a result thereof, the defendant was not indicted until January 19, 1973.

A defendant's right to a speedy trial is guaranteed both by the Constitution (US Const, 6th and 14th Amdts) and by statute (CPL 30.20; Civil Rights Law, § 12). However, before examining the various factors which must be weighed in ascertaining whether or not the defendant has been denied his constitutionally protected right to a speedy trial, we note, of course that if there has been a determination of an infringement of defendant's speedy trial right by the State, a dismissal of the indictment is required. For example, unlike the invocation of the exclusionary rule which permits a second trial of the defendant so long as "tainted" evidence is not utilized by the prosecution, the only available remedy in a speedy trial situation is necessarily more drastic since it completely precludes the defendant's prosecution (*Barker v. Wingo*, 407 U.S. 514, 522).

As our prior decisions indicate, there is no specific temporal duration after which a defendant automatically becomes entitled to release for denial of a speedy trial. Instead, the assertion by the accused of his right to a speedy trial requires the court to examine the claim in light of the particular factors attending the specific case under scrutiny. As this case illustrates, there are no clear cut answers in such an inquiry, and the trial court must engage in a sensitive weighing process of the diversified factors present in the particular case. Moreover, the various factors must be evaluated on an ad hoc basis since no rigid precepts may be formulated which apply to each and every instance in which it is averred that there has been a deprivation of the speedy trial right (*Barker v. Wingo*, supra, at p.530). Additionally, we hasten to add that no one factor or combination of the factors set forth below is necessarily decisive or determinative of the speedy trial claim, but rather the particular case must be considered in light of all the factors as they apply to it.

The following factors should be examined in balancing the merits of an assertion that there has been a denial of defendant's right to a speedy trial: (1) the extent of the delay; (2) the reason for the delay; (3) the nature of the underlying charge; (4) whether or not there has been an extended period of pretrial incarceration; and (5) whether or not there is any indication that the defense has been impaired by reason of the delay.

The first factor, the extent or duration of the delay, is, of course, important inasmuch as it is likely that, all other factors being equal, the greater the delay the more probable it is that the accused will be harmed thereby. However, as crucial as the length of the delay may be, this court has steadfastly refused to set forth a per se period beyond which a criminal prosecution may not be pursued.

The second factor, the reason for the delay, may be in the appellant's favor since the District Attorney's failure to indict is attributable to clerical error within his own office. While such inadvertence may seem inexcusable, it will not, in and of itself, be sufficient to warrant the drastic measure of dismissal of the indictment. As far as this factor is concerned, we note also that the delay in handing up the indictment does not appear to have been a deliberate attempt by the prosecution to hamper the appellant in the preparation of his defense and, indeed, no such claim is here made.

The third factor, the nature of the underlying charge, would appear to be in the People's favor. Appellant was arrested for attempted murder, a class B felony, and indicted for assault in the first degree, a class C felony. Upon such a serious charge, the District Attorney may be expected to proceed with far more caution and deliberation than he would expend on a relatively minor offense. Of course, this is not to say that one's right to a speedy trial is dependent upon what one is charged with, but rather that the prosecutor may understandably be more thorough and precise in his preparation for the trial of a class C felony than he would be in prosecuting a misdemeanor.

The fourth factor, whether or not there has been an extended period of pretrial incarceration, is not, in this case, a motivation for dismissal of the indictment on defendant's application since appellant was incarcerated for but eight days before he was released on bail. Historically, this factor has been considered significant because the speedy trial guarantee affords the accused a safeguard against prolonged imprisonment prior to the commencement of his trial. Moreover, a defendant confined to jail prior to trial is at an obvious and distinct disadvantage in the sense that he can only assist in the preparation of his defense to a limited degree because he is unable to gather evidence or to contact prospective witnesses.

The fifth factor, whether or not there is any indication that the defense has been impaired by reason of the delay, is most critical in view of the facts of this particular case. While, of course, it is not incumbent upon a defendant to show that he has been prejudiced by the delay in the commencement of his trial, a questionable period of delay may or may not be unreasonable depending upon whether or not the likelihood of the defendant's acquittal has been effected thereby. For instance, if the delay precipitated by the prosecution resulted in the defendant's being unable to call certain witnesses, or if the duration of the delay was such that it might be expected that the witnesses would be less able to articulate exactly what had transpired, then the defendant would have a strong argument for dismissal of the indictment. To be sure, we do not depart from the now traditional view in this court that where in the circumstances delay is great enough there need be neither proof nor fact of prejudice to the defendant. In this case, we are primarily concerned with the testimony of only two witnesses, the appellant and the police officer he allegedly ran over; and it seems highly improbable that the officer is likely to fail to recall what transpired on the morning of January 13, 1972.

Balancing all of these factors, we hold that this defendant was not deprived of his constitutional right to a speedy trial. A one-year delay between the alleged occurrence of a crime and an indictment for a class C felony, even when it results from prosecutorial inattention, in and of itself does not entitle a defendant to a dismissal of the indictment where there is no lengthy pretrial incarceration and no apparent impairment of his defense caused by the delay.

Accordingly, the order of the Appellate Division should be affirmed.

People v. Anthony Romeo
849 N.Y.S.2d 666 (2008)

OPINION OF THE COURT: (Re: Right to Speedy Trial, 30.20)

In November 1985 the defendant killed John Starkey in Suffolk County (hereinafter the Starkey homicide). During the course of the People's investigation of this homicide, the County Court issued an order that the defendant provide blood and hair samples. The defendant's attorney arranged that the defendant would surrender on March 5, 1987. Instead of surrendering, the defendant fled to Canada, where, on March 8, 1987, he killed a New Brunswick constable. The defendant recrossed the border into the United States and was arrested in Boston for that crime. On March 9, 1987, he appeared before a federal magistrate, who ordered that he be held without bail pending extradition to Canada. Suffolk County law enforcement officials, who were made aware of the defendant's presence in the United States, obtained blood and hair samples from him while he was incarcerated in Boston. Within a week, testing of those samples linked the defendant to the Starkey homicide. In that same month, March 1987, a grand jury in Suffolk County returned an indictment charging the defendant with two counts of murder in the second degree in connection with the Starkey homicide, and an arrest warrant and a detainer were issued.

In March and April 1987, while the defendant remained in federal custody, hearings were held on the Canadian extradition request, and the People agreed to permit the Canadian case to be tried first. The defendant, through counsel, objected, and asserted the defendant's constitutional right to a speedy trial. In May 1987, the defendant, who was then in federal custody in Springfield, Missouri, moved for an order directing the People to obtain the defendant's presence in Suffolk County for arraignment. At the oral argument on the motion, the People, in opposing the motion, argued in part that they believed the Canadian trial would not affect or delay the timing of the ultimate trial date under the Suffolk County indictment for the Starkey homicide.

By order dated June 17, 1987, more than three months after the defendant had been taken into federal custody, the County Court denied his motion. The court noted that the People's decision to defer its prosecution of the Starkey homicide might implicate the defendant's speedy trial rights: "[i]n the event that this procedure results in the violation of the defendant's right to a speedy trial he may seek the ultimate remedy of dismissal at the appropriate time and in the appropriate manner." At oral argument on the motion on June 15, 1987, the County Court had characterized the People's strategy as "one that they will have to live with." The defendant was extradited to Canada in 1987, convicted of the constable's murder, and sentenced to an indeterminate term of 25 years to life imprisonment. The People did not seek to extradite the defendant from Canada after his conviction and sentencing in 1987.

In July 1999, while incarcerated in Canada, the defendant moved in the County Court, Suffolk County, to dismiss the Starkey indictment on constitutional and statutory speedy trial grounds. The People argued in opposition, as they do now, that under the extradition treaty between the United States and Canada, it would have been futile to seek extradition because it would have required the Canadian authorities to commute the defendant's sentence on his conviction for the murder of the constable. The motion was denied in December 1999.

On April 30, 2003, an amendment to the extradition treaty became effective and, on June 3, 2003, the People sought extradition of the defendant. In November 2005, upon the defendant's return to the United States, he was finally arraigned on the Suffolk County indictment. In February 2006, the defendant pleaded guilty to manslaughter in the first degree pursuant to the Suffolk County indictment and was sentenced to an indeterminate term of 7 to 21 years imprisonment with respect to the Starkey homicide, to run concurrently with the term imposed upon his Canadian conviction. During the 2005 and 2006 proceedings in the County Court, Suffolk County, the defendant did not renew or reassert his constitutional speedy trial claim. As part of his allocution to the guilty plea to manslaughter in the first degree, he expressly waived his right to appeal his "plea and sentence as well as any prior rulings that remain in the case."

After the defendant was sentenced in Suffolk County, he was returned to Canada to continue serving the sentence imposed in connection with the constable's murder and the concurrent sentence on the Starkey homicide.

The defendant now appeals his conviction for the Starkey homicide, arguing that his constitutional right to a speedy trial has been violated.

The People's claim that the defendant's "failure to file a motion to dismiss the indictment in 2005 or 2006 constitutes nonpreservation" of his constitutional speedy trial claim is without merit. Here, however, the defendant's 1999 constitutional speedy trial motion was, in fact, decided by the County Court in 1999. The defendant was, thus, not required to reassert this claim when he pleaded guilty in 2006. Nor could the defendant's waiver of the right to appeal encompass the claim.

On the merits, in evaluating a speedy trial claim under the United States Constitutions, we must consider the extent of the delay, the reason for it, the nature of the underlying charge, whether there has been an extended period of pretrial incarceration, and whether there is any indication that the defense has been prejudiced by the delay.

The defendant's constitutional speedy trial claim must be evaluated in light of the delay as of the time the defendant made his speedy trial motion in 1999. We agree with the defendant that he was denied his constitutional right to a speedy trial.

Here, the delay we consider is the 12 years from 1987 to 1999. That lengthy period is extraordinary. Two of the Taranovich factors militate in favor of the People's position. The seriousness of the charges in connection with the Starkey homicide is self-evident, and the defendant was not incarcerated before trial on those charges at all. Nevertheless, under the circumstances of this case, we find that the length of the delay, the prejudice to the defendant, and the People's responsibility for the delay — despite having been aware before the defendant was extradited to Canada that he was asserting his constitutional right to a speedy trial — outweigh the other factors. The defendant was denied his constitutional right to a speedy trial.

Sec. 3.3; Article 40; Double Jeopardy

People v. Rivera

60 N.Y.2d 110 (1983)

OPINION OF THE COURT : (Re: Subsequent prosecution permitted, 40.20)

Defendant was tried previously on charges of attempted intentional murder, intentional assault, reckless endangerment and criminal possession of a weapon. He was convicted of reckless endangerment and criminal possession of a weapon. After the trial, the victim died and defendant was indicted for depraved mind murder. He has moved to dismiss the murder indictment claiming that this subsequent prosecution is barred. The People rely upon CPL 40.20 (subd. 2, par [d]). It permits a second prosecution as an exception to the prohibition against separate prosecutions for two offenses based on the same act or criminal transaction, in cases of delayed death where the victim subsequently dies from the physical injuries resulting from the "assault or * * * other offense" for which the assailant was previously prosecuted.

In July, 1976, defendant Rivera and his codefendant, Suarez, were indicted in Bronx County. The attempted intentional murder count was dismissed by the court at the close of the People's case because the People's proof was insufficient to establish an intent to kill Fonseca, the victim. The remaining counts were submitted to the jury and it returned a verdict acquitting both defendants of the intentional assault count but convicting them of reckless endangerment and criminal possession of a weapon in the fourth degree.

Nearly four years later, in November, 1980, Felix Fonseca died. Defendant and Suarez were again indicted in Bronx County, but this time they were indicted for the crime of murder in the second degree arising from the alleged reckless killing of Fonseca under circumstances evincing a depraved indifference to human life. Defendant moved to dismiss the indictment on double jeopardy and statutory grounds.

The trial court dismissed the indictment holding that reckless endangerment in the first degree requires proof of the same elements as depraved mind murder and that the two crimes were substantially the "same offense." The Appellate Division unanimously reversed the order of dismissal and reinstated the indictment.

On this appeal defendant maintains that a subsequent prosecution for murder is permissible in cases of delayed death only when an earlier prosecution results in a conviction of assault (not when it results in an acquittal).

It is a fundamental principle of our constitutional system that a defendant may not be placed twice in jeopardy for the same offense (US Const, 5th Amdt; NY Const, art I, §6). The Legislature, however, has extended the constitutional protections further by enactment of CPL 40.20 (subd. 1) which prohibits a second prosecution arising from the same transaction as an earlier one. This statutory prohibition against separately prosecuting a person for the same offense was enacted primarily to supersede the "dual sovereignties" doctrine which permitted successive State and Federal prosecutions based on the same transaction or conduct and it extended protection for second prosecutions beyond that required by the constitutional double jeopardy clause. Recognizing that the general rule barring subsequent prosecutions was too broad, however, the Legislature added to the statute six exceptions in which a second prosecution is expressly permitted (CPL 40.20, subd. 2, pars [a]–[f]; Relevant here is the fourth of these which deals with cases of delayed death and is found in paragraph (d). It authorizes a second prosecution when: "One of the offenses is assault or some other offense resulting in physical injury to a person, and the other offense is one of homicide based upon the death of such person from the same physical injury, and such death occurs after a prosecution for the assault or other nonhomicide offense."

The need for the exception is obvious. It is impossible to prosecute anyone for homicide until the victim is dead and death which occurs subsequent to trial of one of the offenses within the reach of the statute is a supervening fact which creates a new offense which was not chargeable originally. Thus, charging defendant with murder for a death occurring after the first conviction arising out of the injury does not place him in jeopardy twice (see *Diaz v. United States*, 223 U.S. 442).

Moreover, there are sound policy reasons why this should be so. The defendant should be tried as soon as possible for offenses already consummated — the death did not occur until almost four years later in this case — while the evidence is available and witnesses' recollections fresh. If he is guilty he should be punished promptly. Conversely, if he is innocent he should not be held for lengthy periods until the full consequences of his conduct are known.

Turning to the language of the exception, it permits a subsequent prosecution for death occurring after a prosecution for assault or some other offense resulting in physical injury. The offenses involved in the initial prosecution of defendant were assault and reckless endangerment. Both are consistent with physical injury, and although physical injury is not an element of reckless endangerment, the evidence established that in this instance physical injury resulted from the prior reckless endangerment and that is sufficient. Accordingly, both the assault and reckless endangerment offenses are encompassed within the statutory language. The statutory requirements having been met, it is irrelevant that the crime charged in the prior prosecution is based on the same act or transaction, contains similar elements to that crime subsequently charged or whether it resulted in conviction or acquittal. This follows logically because the rationale underlying the exception is that the two prosecutions are for different crimes. The point is illustrated in *Diaz v. United States* (223 U.S. 442, supra), in which the defendant was tried and convicted of assault and subsequently prosecuted for murder when his victim died. In holding the subsequent murder prosecution permissible, the Supreme Court noted that while assault and homicide shared many common elements, the principal element of death distinguished them. Indeed, the homicide offense was not consummated and subject to prosecution until the moment of death.

In sum, the prosecution is permitted by the language of the exception set forth in section 40.20 (subd. 2, par [d]) and there is no violation of the second prosecution provision. The new offense is one of homicide, arising from the death of the victim from the same injury which resulted from the offense prosecuted. Thus, the only factor distinguishing the depraved mind murder prosecution from the prior charge of reckless endangerment, was the delayed death. The statutory exception was designed to encompass that event, and it applies here.

Accordingly, the order of the Appellate Division should be affirmed.

People v. Kurtz
434 N.Y.S.2d 200 (1980)

OPINION OF THE COURT: (Re: Double Jeopardy, 40.30)

This appeal presents the issue whether constitutional or statutory double jeopardy provisions prohibit retrial after the trial court dismisses the accusatory instrument on the defendant's own motion for the reason that the prosecutor failed to make an adequate opening statement as required by CPL 260.30.

On March 2, 1979, the defendant was arrested and charged in a simplified traffic information with speeding and driving while intoxicated. On June 20, 1979, trial was held in City Court, City of Watertown. After the jury was selected and sworn, the prosecutor delivered his opening statement. Immediately thereafter, defense counsel moved to dismiss the information on the ground that the People's opening statement was inadequate as a matter of law. After arguments were heard in chambers, the trial court reserved decision on the motion. Over the objection of the prosecutor, who offered to amplify any inadequacies in his opening, the trial continued at the behest of defense counsel. After one witness had testified, the trial was recessed for the afternoon. The following day, the prosecutor moved for permission to supplement his opening statement to the jury. Defense counsel objected to this motion on procedural grounds. Shortly thereafter, the trial court denied the prosecutor's motion to supplement his opening and then dismissed the information on the ground that the prosecutor's opening statement to the jury was insufficient as a matter of law.

On appeal, County Court, Jefferson County, reversed and remanded the case to City Court for a new trial. While County Court agreed with the trial court that the prosecutor's opening statement was inadequate in that it failed to state any of the facts constituting the offenses which the prosecutor intended to prove, County Court disapproved of the procedure utilized by the trial court subsequent to the defendant's motion to dismiss. The court stated that the trial court should have determined the motion before allowing the trial to continue and, upon deciding the prosecutor's opening statement was inadequate, it should have permitted the prosecutor to supplement his opening to the jury. Finally, County Court rejected defendant's contention that a reversal and new trial was barred by the doctrine of double jeopardy. The court held that retrial was not precluded as "it was the defendant's motion that concluded the trial proceedings prior to an evidentiary determination on the merits." There should be an affirmance.

At the outset, we note our agreement with the determination reached by the courts below that the prosecutor's opening statement was inadequate. CPL 260.30, which sets forth the order of events in a criminal jury trial, provides that the "people must deliver an opening address to the jury." This opening statement should be a capsulized version "of the evidence that [the prosecutor] expects to present, and the claim that he will make with reference thereto, to the end that the jury, upon listening to the evidence, may better understand and appreciate its connection and bearing upon the case."

Although the Criminal Procedure Law does not specify the requisite contents of the prosecutor's opening statement, at a minimum the prosecutor generally should set forth the nature of the charge against the accused and state briefly the facts he expects to prove, along with the evidence he plans to introduce in support of the same. In this case, the opening statement merely consisted of a brief summary of the evidence to be introduced and a listing of the names of the witnesses who were to testify. The prosecutor failed in all respects to delineate the particular offenses with which the defendant was charged and how these charges were to be proven. Such an incomplete recitation simply fails to satisfy the statutory requirement that the prosecutor make an opening statement to the jury.

Under no circumstances should the court allow the trial to proceed without first ruling on the motion. As mentioned earlier, it was the belated disposition of the motion which has created the difficulty in this case, a problem which should be avoided in all other cases. However, our analysis does not end here for now we must determine whether defendant's retrial is prohibited by the doctrine of double jeopardy.

In this State, a defendant's right not to be twice put in jeopardy for the same crime is protected by the double jeopardy clauses of the Federal and State Constitutions as well as by statutory double jeopardy provisions. Specifically, as the doctrine of double jeopardy has developed in New York in relation to midtrial dismissals, "reprosecution is permitted whenever a dismissal has been granted on motion by defendant, so long as the dismissal does not constitute an adjudication on the facts going to guilt or innocence [even where] dismissal occurs after jeopardy has attached." Indeed, in its most recent excursion into the double jeopardy area, the Supreme Court has implicitly approved of this approach. As presently constituted under this recent line of cases, the doctrine distinguishes between trial orders terminating the trial in the defendant's favor prior to any determination of guilt or innocence and those orders which terminate the trial based on evidentiary insufficiency. Because a dismissal based on insufficient evidence is tantamount to an acquittal, reprosecution is precluded in the latter category of cases. Retrial of cases falling within the former category of dismissals, however, is permissible because "the defendant, by deliberately choosing to seek termination of the proceeding against him on a basis unrelated to factual guilt or innocence of the offense of which he is accused, suffers no injury cognizable under the Double Jeopardy Clause."

In the case before us, the trial court dismissed the action on defendant's motion solely because of the insufficiency of the prosecutor's opening statement. As mentioned earlier, this dismissal was not premised on any evidentiary determination that the People were not entitled to a conviction or that the prosecutor had acted in bad faith by deliberately delivering an incomplete opening in order to terminate the trial over defendant's objection. Rather, dismissal here was the result of the trial court's misconception of the requirements of CPL 260.30 (subd 3) and occurred without any evaluation on the trial court's part as to the factual elements of the offenses with which defendant was charged. Inasmuch as this dismissal, erroneous as it was, in no sense resembles an acquittal of the defendant and indeed appears functionally indistinguishable from the declaration of a mistrial, retrial of defendant is prohibited neither by the double jeopardy clauses of the State and Federal Constitutions nor by the statutory double jeopardy provisions.

Accordingly, the order of the County Court, Jefferson County, should be affirmed.

DISSENT

Defendant moved to dismiss on the People's opening, after jeopardy had attached (CPL 40.30, subd 1, par [b]). The motion was granted on the ground that "the prosecutor's statement was insufficient in that it failed to state any facts constituting the crime of driving while intoxicated which the prosecutor intended to prove," i.e., specifically, that there was no statement with respect to proof of intoxication. Conceptually this must be likened to the granting of a motion, on the defendant's application made at the close of the People's case, for a trial order of dismissal on the ground that the trial evidence is not legally sufficient to establish the offense charged (CPL 290.10, subd 1). The dismissal, terminating the trial proceedings in defendant's favor, was "an adjudication on the facts going to guilt or innocence." It was expressly predicated on a determination with respect to the sufficiency of the People's proof; it was not a termination of the trial on grounds unrelated to factual guilt or innocence. While the majority ascribes to CPL 260.30 the effect of requiring the prosecution to "adequately amplify the charges against defendant and the facts to be proven in support thereof," it refuses to regard the trial court's dismissal on the ground that the prosecution's statement was defective as to facts to be proved as an evaluation by the trial court "as to the factual elements of the offenses with which defendant was charged" — which appears to me to be a patent inconsistency.

That the dismissal was thought by the trial court to be on the factual merit of the People's case is apparent. In granting defendant's motion to dismiss the trial court also considered the possibility of reprosecution of the charge and concluded, "I therefore find that this is a final determination, outside of any rights of appeal, that the People have, and that a resubmission is precluded by Section 210.20(4)." Thus, to the extent that the characterization of the dismissal by the trial court may be relevant, it is clear in this instance that the dismissal was not "in contemplation of" a second prosecution.

Sec. 3.4; Article 50; Immunity

In the Matter of Brockway v. Monroe

59 N.Y.2d 179 (1983)

OPINION OF THE COURT: (Re: The immunity process)

Where the court, the prosecutor, the defense attorney and counsel for the witness have chosen to depart from the normal question-by-question conferral of transactional immunity on a prosecution witness as contemplated by CPL 50.20 and 50.30, and have charted their own course, agreeing that the witness shall receive immunity for all testimony given by him subject only to rulings by the court on objections by the prosecutor, whether the witness received transactional immunity must be determined by reference to the procedure which the principals chose to follow. In such a case, in the absence of timely objection by the prosecutor to the question, if the testimony given in answer is responsive to the question asked, the witness receives immunity for the transaction to which he testified.

Petitioner, Daniel Brockway, was indicted by a Chemung County Grand Jury on January 9, 1981 for criminal sale of a controlled substance in the third degree and conspiracy in the second degree. The indictment alleged that Brockway had sold cocaine to one Camille Comfort on November 1, 1980. Subsequently, Brockway was subpoenaed by the Steuben County District Attorney's office to testify for the prosecution's case against Joseph and Larry Comfort, who were standing trial in Steuben County Court on charges of murder and attempted murder of State Police officers investigating cocaine sales in Steuben County.

On January 20, 1982, Brockway appeared with counsel at the Steuben County trial. Before he was called to the witness stand, his attorney informed the prosecutor that Brockway, on being called to testify, would invoke his Fifth Amendment privilege and refuse to answer any questions on the ground that the answers might tend to incriminate him. In a chambers conference, the Steuben County Judge was advised of Brockway's position, and the prosecutor asked the court to confer immunity on him pursuant to CPL 50.20. The prosecuting attorney indicated that it would not be necessary to proceed by way of a question-by-question grant of immunity on direct examination and that such a procedure would also not be necessary on cross-examination so long as the questions concerned the transactions in issue. The prosecutor agreed to be guided by the court's direction as to the scope of answers to questions on collateral matters but took the position that he would recommend against immunity on collateral issues, so as to leave it up to the witness and his attorney to decide whether to invoke his Fifth Amendment rights regarding such questions.

Brockway's attorney informed the court that to the extent that the prosecutor was suggesting something less than full transactional immunity he would counsel his client not to answer any questions. He contended that the court only had authority to grant full transactional immunity subject to any evidentiary rulings. The court then indicated that any immunity granted would be full transactional immunity and that the witness would be clothed with immunity as to anything to which he testified. As to collateral matters, the court informed the attorneys that it would determine whether answers to the questions would be allowed and that if in its discretion the court directed the witness to answer and allowed the question even if it were collateral then immunity would attach. The court noted that the prosecutor would have the opportunity to object to collateral or immaterial matters and that rulings would be made as they went along.

The court instructed Brockway's attorney to counsel his client that if there were an objection to a collateral matter the witness was not to answer until the court had an opportunity to rule on the objection. If the witness were to answer in violation of this direction, the court indicated that it would strike the answer so that it could never be used against him. Brockway's counsel stated that he would so advise his client and that he had already informed him that all answers must be responsive to the questions.

After being sworn in as a witness and answering several preliminary questions, Brockway asserted his Fifth Amendment right not to answer a question as to whether he knew Larry Comfort, one of the defendants in the Steuben County trial. The court then conferred transactional immunity on the witness in accordance with the prior discussion and ordered him to answer.

After direct examination by the prosecutor, the witness was cross-examined by defense counsel. During this cross-examination, the following testimony was elicited:

"Q. And did you subsequently undertake to sell that cocaine?

"A. Yes, I guess.

"Q. Did you or didn't you?

"A. I don't really remember. Yes.

"Q. You did?

"A. Yes.

"Q. To whom?

"A. I don't know.

"Q. You don't know?

"A. I'm sorry. I didn't sell this cocaine. I sold cocaine earlier.

"Q. To whom?

"A. Camille Comfort.

"Q. When was that?

"A. Around the first of November."

At this point, the prosecutor broke in and asked to approach the Bench. He contended that the witness' response — that he had sold cocaine earlier — to the question whether he sold this particular cocaine was volunteered and nonresponsive. The court agreed that it was nonresponsive and directed the jury to disregard the witness' answer as well as the questions and answers that followed. Defense counsel's exception to the court's ruling was noted.

By notice of motion dated March 15, 1982, Brockway moved to dismiss his Chemung County indictment for criminal sale of a controlled substance in the third degree and conspiracy in the second degree. He asserted that he had received transactional immunity by testifying at the Steuben County trial about the November 1 sale of cocaine to Camille Comfort which was the subject of the Chemung County indictment. The motion was denied by Chemung County Court in a decision dated April 27, 1982. The court found that the immunity given was limited to the transaction in Steuben County and that petitioner's answer to the question was not responsive but was volunteered so that it could not form the basis for transactional immunity.

Brockway then commenced this article 78 proceeding in the Appellate Division, third Department, by an order to show cause signed on June 2, 1982. He sought a judgment directing the Chemung County Judge to dismiss the indictment on the ground that he had obtained immunity on the charges and restraining the Judge from proceeding to trial of the indictment until further direction from the Appellate Division.

By order entered August 9, 1982, the Appellate Division granted the petition and ordered the indictment dismissed. The court found that Brockway's statements were reasonably responsive to the questions asked and that a review of the record failed to disclose that the responses were made in bad faith or could not have been anticipated. According to the court, the Steuben County Judge had ruled that if questioning were allowed and Brockway answered in a responsive fashion he would be clothed with immunity, and this is exactly what had happened here.

We now affirm the judgment of the Appellate Division from which respondents have appealed.

The Legislature by enacting CPL 50.20 and 50.30 n2 has created a multistep procedural scheme by which a court at the express request of the prosecutor in any criminal proceeding other than a Grand Jury proceeding may confer transactional immunity on a witness. Under these provisions, immunity is granted in the following fashion: the witness invokes his right not to give evidence on the ground that it may incriminate him; the prosecutor requests the court to grant immunity to the witness; the court orders the witness to give the requested evidence notwithstanding his assertion of his privilege against self incrimination and advises him that he will receive immunity on doing so; and the witness complies with the order by giving the requested evidence. This procedure contemplates that the witness will be given immunity on a question-by-question basis under which the witness claims his privilege not to answer a specific question, the prosecutor seeks immunity as to the answer to that question, and the court orders the witness to respond to the question conferring immunity for the particular response. Although use of this procedure may prove cumbersome and overly mechanical when applied to extended questioning, it has the salutary effect of permitting the court, the prosecutor, and the witness to know whether immunity is being granted and the prosecutor to decide whether the anticipated response to a particular question will be of sufficient assistance to the prosecution's case to justify requesting immunity for the response. In fact, this orderly, multistep process was designed by the Legislature to avoid conferring overly broad and unnecessary grants of immunity.

Although nothing in the statute expressly precludes the prosecutor and counsel for the witness with the approval of the court from adopting a different procedure in an individual instance or prevents the court from granting immunity to a witness' entire testimony subject to specific rulings on collateral questions and other evidentiary objections, the immunity at issue here is of legislative creation which ordinarily should be conferred in accordance with the statutory mandate.

Here, the answer given by the witness, Brockway, was unquestionably responsive to the question put to him — as to whom he had earlier sold cocaine — and was not gratuitously volunteered. It has been observed that it is very difficult to deprive a witness of immunity based on a nonresponsive or volunteered answer and that a high burden is placed on the prosecutor to establish nonresponsiveness. In this instance a reading of the transcript leaves no room for doubt. The witness' memory had faltered, and he was having difficulty remembering whether and to whom he had sold cocaine. When asked for a second time whether he knew to whom he had sold cocaine, already having indicated that he did not know, he apologized for his prior answers and corrected himself by saying "I didn't sell this cocaine. I sold cocaine earlier." Then came the critical question by defense counsel to which the prosecutor failed to object — "To whom?" The witness responded, "Camille Comfort," and was then further questioned — "When was that?" — to which he responded, "Around the first of November." It was only after both questions had been asked and answered that the prosecutor came to life, at a point too late to deny the witness immunity with respect to the responsive answers he had already given. In these circumstances we agree with the majority at the Appellate Division that the witness received transactional immunity with respect to the sale of cocaine to Camille Comfort on or about November 1, 1980.

This case, in which Brockway was granted an immunity apparently unnecessary for the prosecution of the Steuben County trial and presumably unintended by the prosecutor, illustrates the compelling desirability of strict adherence to the procedures prescribed by sections 50.20 and 50.30.

For the reasons stated, the judgment of the Appellate Division should be affirmed, without costs.

Chapter 4; Rules of Evidence, Standards of Proof and Related Matters

Sec. 4.1; Article 60; Rules of Evidence

People v. Felder

485 N.Y.S.2d 576 (1985)

OPINION OF THE COURT: (Re: Bolstering of eye witness identification, 60.25, 30)

Appeal by defendant from a judgment of the County Court, Nassau County rendered January 18, 1983, convicting him of two counts of robbery in the second degree, upon a jury verdict, and imposing sentence. Judgment reversed, on the law, and new trial ordered.

On the same night as the robbery involved herein, police officers arrested defendant and one other individual after the complainant pointed out these people to the officers. Complainant testified as to this identification at trial. When the prosecutor started to elicit testimony from one of the arresting officers concerning this out-of-court identification, the trial court sustained defense counsel's objections, told the prosecutor at a sidebar that this constituted an attempt to bolster the complaining witness's identification and warned him not to pursue this line of questioning. Following this, the prosecutor nonetheless persisted in pursuing this line of questioning and thereby compounded the prejudice. After stating that the complainant had pointed out the two men as being his assailants, the officer testified that he "asked him if he was positive * * * these were the two people who had robbed him earlier in the evening." He then testified that the complainant made a response following which "we patted down both subjects, placed them in handcuffs, and removed them from the bar."

The testimony served to highlight the significance of complainant's identification. Even though his response was not admitted into evidence, the testimony left the jurors with the clear impression that he was particularly sure and that the arrests were made as a result of this response. The "inevitable effect" of the testimony was "to impress in the minds of the jurors that the identification evidence was of such high reliability as to justifiably warrant prompt official police action. These improper questions were addressed to the witnesses for no other purpose than to obtain answers which would endow 'such proof with an undeserved aura of trustworthiness' (*People v. Trowbridge*, 305 NY 471, 477). Moreover, the testimony was elicited in blatant disregard of the trial court's warning.

Evidence of defendant's guilt rested solely upon the identification by the complainant, and the evidence of [the perpetrator's] identity is [not] so strong that there is no serious issue upon the point. This testimony therefore deprived defendant of a fair trial.

Reversed and remanded.

People v. Sandoval

34 N.Y.2d 371 (1974)

OPINION OF THE COURT: (Re: Proof of previous convictions, 60.40)

We affirm the order of the Appellate Division. In doing so we take the occasion to approve and comment on the procedure made available to defendant in this case to obtain a prospective ruling limiting the prosecutor's reference, in cross-examination impeachment of defendant, to prior specific criminal, vicious and immoral acts.

This defendant was indicated for common-law murder. Immediately prior to selection of the jury, counsel for defendant made a motion to the trial court requesting it, in its discretion, to prohibit the use of prior crimes or convictions to impeach the credibility of defendant if he decided to testify. The trial court then considered the various prior charges against defendant and the crimes of which defendant had been convicted to the extent they were then made known to the court. The trial court ruled that the District Attorney could use a 1964 conviction of disorderly conduct and a 1965 conviction of assault in the third degree and could inquire as to the underlying facts with respect to either. At the same time the court ruled that he would not permit use of a 1960 charge of contributing to the delinquency of a minor, 1963 and 1965 convictions of driving while intoxicated, a 1965 arrest for felonious assault resulting in dismissal, a 1965 traffic violation, and a 1967 charge of gambling. We agree with the Appellate Division that there was no abuse of discretion in these rulings.

It is appropriate, however, to consider the procedural and substantive rights of a defendant to obtain a prospective ruling as to the permissible scope of his cross-examination concerning prior commission of specific criminal, vicious and immoral acts, on the basis of which, inter alia, he will decide whether to take the witness stand in his own defense.

Initially we note that CPL 60.40 (subd. 1), while relevant to the subject under consideration, now merely authorizes the introduction, by way of contradiction, of independent proof of a prior conviction in the event of the denial of such conviction by the defendant or any other witness. It is not addressed to questions of when and to what extent a defendant may be cross-examined concerning prior convictions. The nature and extent of cross-examination have always been subject to the sound discretion of the Trial Judge We now hold that in exercise of that discretion a Trial Judge may, as the Trial Judge in this case did, make an advance ruling as to the use by the prosecutor of prior convictions or proof of the prior commission of specific criminal, vicious or immoral acts for the purpose of impeaching a defendant's credibility.

The rules governing the admissibility of evidence of other crimes represent a balance between the probative value of such proof and the danger of prejudice which it presents to an accused. When evidence of other crimes has no purpose other than to show that a defendant is of a criminal bent or character and thus likely to have committed the crime charged, it should be excluded. Thus, a balance must here be struck between the probative worth of evidence of prior specific criminal, vicious or immoral acts on the issue of the defendant's credibility on the one hand, and on the other the risk of unfair prejudice to the defendant, measured both by the impact of such evidence if it is admitted after his testimony and by the effect its probable introduction may have in discouraging him from taking the stand on his own behalf.

The particular limitations of proof must always depend on the individual facts and circumstances of each case. Such determination will best be made by the trial court. The procedural vehicle therefore would be a motion, accompanied in rare instances, in the discretion of the Judge to whom the motion is made, by an appropriate evidentiary hearing.

In most cases, as in this case, but not necessarily in all cases, a pretrial motion will be preferable.

Thereby, the defendant with definitive advance knowledge of the scope of cross-examination as to prior conduct to which he will be subjected, can decide whether to take the witness stand. Revelation of the impeachment testimony and announcement of the trial court's ruling in advance of trial are consistent with the objectives today of broad pretrial discovery and disclosure.

The sensitive, informed reconciliation of the interests of the People and the rights of the defendant must here as in other instances, be committed principally to the reviewable discretion of the trial court, to be exercised in the light of all the facts and relevant circumstances disclosed in the given case.

In the fact-finding process, the function, in cross-examination, of evidence of a defendant's prior criminal, vicious or immoral acts (unless such evidence would be independently admissible to prove an element of the crime charged) is solely to impeach his credibility as a witness. From the standpoint of the prosecution, then, the evidence should be admitted if it will have material probative value on the issue of defendant's credibility, veracity or honesty on the witness stand. From the standpoint of the defendant it should not be admitted unless it will have such probative worth, or, even though it has such worth, if to lay it before the jury or court would otherwise be so highly prejudicial as to call for its exclusion. The standard — whether the prejudicial effect of impeachment testimony far outweighs the probative worth of the evidence on the issue of credibility — is easy of articulation but troublesome in many cases of application.

At the threshold it must be recognized as inevitable, and thus not determinative, that evidence of prior criminal, vicious or immoral conduct will always be detrimental to the defendant. Similarly, it does not advance analysis to note that such evidence will have a propensity to influence the jury or the court; that objective and purpose attend the introduction of all evidence. The issue to be resolved has a double aspect in determining whether the defendant will be deprived of a fair trial. Will the testimony to be elicited in cross-examination have a disproportionate and improper impact on the triers of fact? Will the apprehension of its introduction undesirably deter the defendant from taking the stand and thereby deny the jury or court significant material evidence?

Evidence of prior specific criminal, vicious or immoral conduct should be admitted if the nature of such conduct or the circumstances in which it occurred bear logically and reasonably on the issue of credibility. Lapse of time, however, will affect the materiality if not the relevance of previous conduct. The commission of an act of impulsive violence, particularly if remote in time, will seldom have any logical bearing on the defendant's credibility, veracity or honesty at the time of trial. Further, proof of such a crime may be highly prejudicial and inadmissible when it has no purpose other than to show that a defendant is of a criminal bent or character and thus likely to have committed the crime charged. To the extent, however, that the prior commission of a particular crime of calculated violence or of specified vicious or immoral acts significantly revealed a willingness or disposition on the part of the particular defendant voluntarily to place the advancement of his individual self-interest ahead of principle or of the interests of society, proof thereof may be relevant to suggest his readiness to do so again on the witness stand. A demonstrated determination deliberately to further self-interest at the expense of society or in derogation of the interests of others goes to the heart of honesty and integrity. On the other hand, crimes or conduct occasioned by addiction or uncontrollable habit, as with alcohol or drugs may have lesser probative value as to lack of in-court veracity. Commission of perjury or other crimes or acts of individual dishonesty, or untrustworthiness (e.g., offenses involving theft or fraud, bribery, or acts of deceit, cheating, breach of trust) will usually have a very material relevance, whenever committed. By contrast, questions as to traffic violations should rarely, if ever, be permitted.

From another aspect, cross-examination with respect to crimes or conduct similar to that of which the defendant is presently charged may be highly prejudicial, in view of the risk, despite the most clear and forceful limiting instructions to the contrary, that the evidence will be taken as some proof of the commission of the crime charged rather than be reserved solely to the issue of credibility. Thus, in the prosecution of drug charges, interrogation as to prior narcotics convictions (unless proof thereof is independently admissible) may present a special risk of impermissible prejudice because of the widely accepted belief that persons previously convicted of narcotics offenses are likely to be habitual offenders. On the other hand, proof of prior convictions of perjury or other crimes of individual dishonesty should usually be admitted on trial of another similar charge, notwithstanding the risk of possible prejudice, because the very issue on which the offer is made is that of the veracity of the defendant as a witness in the case.

This case reflects a recognition of the principles underlying broadened discovery in criminal procedure and a growing awareness that there may be undue prejudice to a defendant from unnecessary and immaterial development of previous misconduct. To that extent therefore it sets some boundaries to the scope of cross-examination permitted.

Order affirmed.

People v. Jovanovic

263 A.D.2d 182 (1st Dept 1999)

OPINION OF THE COURT: (Re: Rape Shield Law, 60.42)

On this appeal of his conviction for kidnapping, sexual abuse and assault, defendant Oliver Jovanovic asks us to examine certain issues regarding the application of the Rape Shield Law (CPL 60.42). We conclude that the trial court's evidentiary rulings incorrectly applied the Rape Shield Law and, as a result, improperly hampered defendant's ability to present a defense, requiring reversal of his conviction and remand for a new trial.

The criminal charges arose from a date between Jovanovic and the complainant which took place after weeks of on-line conversations and e-mail correspondence. This appeal focuses on a number of statements made by the complainant in e-mails sent to Jovanovic. In these statements, she indicated an interest in participating in sadomasochism. Defendant's purpose in seeking to offer these statements in evidence was not to undermine complainant's character by demonstrating that she was unchaste. Rather, it was to highlight both the complainant's state of mind on the issue of consent, and his own state of mind regarding his own reasonable beliefs as to the complainant's intentions.

Nevertheless, the trial court concluded that these statements were inadmissible under the Rape Shield Law. Initially, we hold that a careful reading of the statute discloses it to be inapplicable to much of the evidence precluded at trial.

The Evidence at Trial

The People's case against Jovanovic was primarily founded upon the testimony of the complainant. She told a detailed story of becoming acquainted with Jovanovic through communications over the Internet, both by e-mail and by so-called "instant messages," as well as in a number of lengthy telephone conversations.

Subsequent Events: The complainant took the subway to her dormitory at about 10:00 p.m., fell asleep, woke up, showered, and after Luke called her at 1:00 a.m., she went to Luke's apartment, where she reported to him that she had been tied up, sodomized with a stick, hit with a baton, and burned by Jovanovic. The next morning she returned to her dormitory.

On Sunday night, November 24, 1996, she logged on to the computer at her school library and retrieved an e-mail message sent by Jovanovic the night before at 10:35 p.m. In it, he said she had forgotten her gold chain when she left the apartment, and that he could mail it if she gave him her zip code, or he could drop it off. He also said, "I have a feeling the experience may not have done you as much good as I'd hoped, because you weren't acting much smarter at the end than you were at the beginning." He closed with the words, "I hope you managed to get back all right."

The complainant sent Jovanovic a long e-mail the following day, in which her remarks included assertions that she was "purged by emotions, and pain," and that she was "quite bruised mentally and physically, but never been so happy to be alive." She said "Burroughs best sums up my state * * * the taste is so overpoweringly delicious, and at the same time, quite nauseating."

They continued their on-line communications later that day.

The Redacted Statements: With the narrative by the complainant, the People were able to present to the jury a compelling story of a woman being drawn into a cyber-space intimacy that led her into the trap of a scheming man. However, its compelling quality was due in part to its one-sided and unbalanced nature. This imbalance resulted from the trial court's ruling precluding Jovanovic from effectively challenging certain aspects of the complainant's presentation. Where he should have been given free rein to explore the complainant's truthfulness, her accuracy in relating her experiences and her grip on reality, he was instead precluded from inquiring into several highly relevant statements contained in the complainant's e-mails to him.

The following discussion sets forth the portions of the complainant's e-mails to defendant that were subject to the court's preclusion order.

First Redacted E-Mail: On November 17, 1996, in the complainant's e-mail to Jovanovic, she told him of "dragging" a girl to the emergency room after the girl reported that she had been raped. After further additional messages were sent back and forth between the two that same evening, on November 18, 1996, the complainant wrote to explain to Jovanovic how, over the Internet, she had first made contact with Luke, who she described as "attached to one skitzophrenic [sic] stalker x-intrest [sic] d'amour." One sentence was deleted from this e-mail. It read, "So said intrest [sic] plotted my death as well as a means of getting attention, thus the rape."

Second Redacted E-Mail: "the boy calls, tells lots and lots of a life led like burroughs: heroin addicted, bisexual atheist. My kinda comrad. so he seduced me. come to Ufm, I did[,] come to my appartment, I did[,] then he got me."

Third Redacted E-Mail: Jovanovic answered, shortly thereafter on November 19th, "[t]hen he got you? How suspenseful," although the court precluded the first four words, "[t]hen he got you?" The complainant's response on November 20th, contained a further personal confession that the court also deleted from the evidence, in which the complainant had replied, "No duh, there's more, more interesting than sex, yes he did catch me, no sex, but he was a sadomasochist and now I'm his slave and its [sic] painful, but the fun of telling my friends 'hey I'm a sadomasochist' more than outweighs the torment."

Fourth Redacted E-Mail: Jovanovic's responsive e-mail on November 20th said, "You're submissive sometimes? Should have told me earlier." The complainant's next message in reply, also on November 20th included the following critical information, which was also redacted: "and yes, I'm what those happy pain fiends at the Vault call a 'pushy bottom'."*

---

* The defense explains that The Vault is a club catering to sadomasochists, and a "pushy bottom" is a submissive partner who pushes the dominant partner to inflict greater pain.

While the vast majority of the electronic correspondence between Jovanovic and the complainant was introduced into evidence, the preclusion of the foregoing statements, particularly the last three, had an enormous impact on the defense. Basically, it left the jury with a distorted view of the events. Moreover, in the absence of proof that Jovanovic had reason to believe, prior to their meeting, that they both had intended to participate in consensual, nonviolent sadomasochism that night, his ability to testify in a credible manner as to this defense was irreparably impaired. Indeed, the limitation imposed by the court served to insulate the complainant from being fully cross-examined even as to those statements which were admitted into evidence, which evinced or implied some degree of interest in sadomasochism.

These messages were ruled inadmissible on the ground that they were covered by the protection of the Rape Shield Law (CPL 60.42), in that they constituted evidence of the complainant prior sexual conduct, having the effect of demonstrating her "unchastity." In addition to the messages themselves, based upon the trial court's understanding of the Rape Shield Law, Jovanovic was precluded from questioning either the complainant or Luke as to whether the two had mutually engaged in consensual sadomasochism.

The distinction between evidence of prior sexual conduct (to which the statute expressly applies), and evidence of statements concerning prior sexual conduct, is more than merely semantic. Direct evidence of the complainant's conduct with others would generally be introduced (if admissible) as a basis to infer that she had voluntarily behaved in such a way on prior occasions with others. In contrast, the use of a statement is not so straightforward. It is frequently relevant not to prove the truth of the matter stated, but rather, for the fact that the speaker made the statement. That is, a statement may be relevant as proof of the speaker's, or the listener's, state of mind.

For instance, here, the complainant's statement to Jovanovic regarding sadomasochism were not necessarily offered to prove the truth of what she said, i.e. that she actually was a sadomasochist. Rather, much of their importance lay in the fact that she chose to say these things to Jovanovic in the context of her electronic, online conversation with him, so as to convey to him another message, namely, her interest in exploring the subject of such activities with him.

In addition, redaction of the long narrative in the second e-mail, in which the complainant told Luke's story of a sadistic sexual encounter, was not justifiable under the Rape Shield Law, as it did not report past conduct on the part of the complainant. In any case, it was highly relevant to the attempted defense that the claim of attack was concocted, particularly in view of the similarity between that narrative and Jovanovic's complained-of conduct on the night in question.

We conclude that the trial court's rulings erroneously withheld from the jury a substantial amount of highly relevant, admissible evidence. Furthermore, these errors were of constitutional dimension.

Sec. 4.3; Article 70; Standards of Proof

People v. Graham

211 A.D. 2d 55 (1995)

OPINION OF THE COURT: (Re: Probable cause (reasonable cause to believe), 70.10)

This appeal presents the issue of whether the observation by an experienced police officer, in a "drug-prone" location, of five separate transactions in each of which defendant exchanged money for a small object he removed from a brown paper bag and thereafter placed the bag on the ground next to a fence about 10 feet away, gives rise to probable cause.

On April 23, 1992, shortly before 2:00 p.m., Police Officers Smith and McDonald, uniformed and on foot patrol in the Lincoln Projects, stationed themselves in the lobby of a building directly across the street from 2101 Madison Avenue, a playground and a drug-infested area. Smith, a police officer for over five and one-half years and assigned to patrolling the Lincoln Projects for over four years, had personally made 50 narcotics-related arrests involving crack cocaine in the area around 2101 Madison Avenue and had assisted in over 100 more such arrests. On that particular day, bright, sunny and providing Officer Smith with a clear, unobstructed view of the area between the two buildings, the playground was littered with empty crack vials.

At about 1:55 p.m., Smith, using binoculars, observed a man approach defendant, who was sitting on a bench in the playground area in front of 2101 Madison Avenue. Defendant got up and the two men met between the bench and a fence. The man handed money to defendant, who reached into a brown paper bag he was holding, took out a small object and handed it to the man who, at that point, walked off. Defendant then took the brown paper bag, placed it on the ground next to a fence about 10 feet away and sat back down on the bench. A few minutes later, at approximately 1:59 p.m., and 2:01 p.m. Smith observed two other men approach defendant and then two women. The defendant engaged in the same transaction with each of these parties.

Although Smith could, through the binoculars, observe money being exchanged in each of these transactions, he could not see what was being taken out of the brown bag and given in return. Asked to explain why, Smith, who believed that the objects were less than an inch in length, stated: "A vial is very small. It was kind of cupped. It was a fast transaction."

After observing a fifth transaction, Smith and McDonald left their observation post and walked across to where defendant was seated. McDonald approached defendant while Smith walked over to the bag, picked it up and, looking inside, saw six vials of what he knew from experience was crack cocaine. At Smith's direction, McDonald then arrested defendant.

Finding the testifying police officer credible and "an experienced officer trained in narcotics investigation in evaluating his observation," the hearing court found that Officer Smith had good reason to believe, given that the "stash" was kept not on defendant's person but was "secrete[d] ... within reasonably close distance," that what he saw was not an "innocent transaction." Accordingly, the court, citing *People v. McRay* (51 NY2d 594), denied suppression.

The thrust of defendant's argument on appeal is that Officer Smith's observations of defendant as he exchanged unidentified objects for money in a drug-infested area, in the absence of other significant factors, are insufficient to establish probable cause. The standard for probable cause justifying a search or seizure is not the same as that required to establish guilt. Probable cause does not require proof to a mathematical certainty, or proof beyond a reasonable doubt. Probable cause is defined as the body of information available to a police officer which would lead a reasonable person who possesses the same expertise as the officer to conclude, under the circumstances, that a crime is being or was committed. (*People v. McRay*, 51 NY2d, supra, at 602.) Since the Fourth Amendment's commands are "practical and not abstract," they must be interpreted in a commonsense and realistic fashion. Clearly, if Officer Smith had observed vials, glassine envelopes, tinfoil packets or any other type of package commonly associated with a drug transaction, probable cause would have existed. (See, e.g., *People v. McRay*, 51 NY2d, supra, at 606 [glassine envelopes]; *Matter of James P.*, 194 AD2d 467, lv denied 82 NY2d 659 [vial]; *People v. Balas*, 104 AD2d 1039, 1040 [tinfoil packet].) But the observation of a drug package is not a sine qua non for the existence of probable cause in a drug sale. (See, e.g., *People v. Shaw*, 193 AD2d 390, lv denied 82 NY2d 853 ["objects" extracted from a bag and exchanged for money]; *People v. Owens*, 155 AD2d 696, 697 ["object(s)" were passed through a missing windowpane in the front door of an apartment building in exchange for money]; *People v. Bittner*, 97 AD2d 33, 37 [unidentified object exchanged].)

In a probable cause analysis, the emphasis should not be narrowly focused on a recognizable drug package or any other single factor, but on an evaluation of the totality of circumstances, which takes into account the realities of everyday life unfolding before a trained officer who has to confront, on a daily basis, similar incidents

As this Court noted in *People v. Shaw* (193 AD2d, supra, at 391), the jurisprudence in this area "has moved beyond such niceties as distinctions based on the color or degree of opacity of the envelope" to the point where the visual identification of the object exchanged for money is merely one element in the totality of circumstances to be considered in any probable cause assessment. Since street-level drug sales typically involve small, easily concealable packages, utilization of a totality of the circumstances analysis is both reasonable and necessary. Street sellers of narcotics should not enjoy an immunity from arrest or search merely because they are able to conceal their wares during the exchange; concealment is itself a common characteristic of illegal conduct.

In *People v. McRay* (51 NY2d, supra, at 604) the Court of Appeals identified certain factors which, when combined with the passing of a glassine envelope, may give rise to a finding of probable cause. The Court initially pointed to the exchange of money, noting, "To begin with the most obvious, if money is passed in exchange for the envelope, probable cause almost surely would exist [citations omitted]. Exchange of currency negates all but the most implausible explanations for the transaction, and thus conveys more than sufficient indicia of a drug sale to warrant an arrest" (51 NY2d, supra, at 604). The Court also noted that "additional evidence of furtive or evasive behavior on the part of the participants suffices to establish probable cause [citations omitted]. Such evidence, suggesting consciousness of guilt, has traditionally been considered some proof of a crime [citations omitted]." (supra, at 604.) In addition, the Court indicated that among the other factors to be considered were the police officer's experience and whether the area involved is a "drug-prone" location. (Supra, at 601.)

In the instant case, any person observing defendant and his five customers and his method of operation, using good common sense, would have, in the totality of circumstances, concluded that defendant was involved in the sale of narcotics. From a succession of customers, defendant received cash in exchange for an object less than an inch in length, which he removed from a brown paper bag. While defendant had been holding the bag before the first transaction, after the first exchange, he placed the bag on the ground next to a nearby fence before returning to the bench on which he had been sitting some 10 feet away. In each subsequent transaction, Smith observed defendant go over to the fence, retrieve the bag, remove a small object which he gave to the customer in exchange for cash, return the bag to the ground near the fence and then walk back to the bench. By placing his bag near the fence, retrieving it only to remove small objects that he concealed in his cupped palm, exchanging them for cash and then replacing the bag in the same place near the fence, defendant was obviously distancing himself from the contents of the bag and taking caution to conceal whatever he was selling. This is hardly the type of behavior engaged in by legitimate street vendors, who advertise their wares openly. Defendant's behavior is typical of a drug dealer plying his trade in a known drug location. The use of a stash has been held to constitute furtive behavior indicative of drug dealing.

Moreover, of course, any person with Officer Smith's expertise, which included participation in over 150 cocaine-related arrests in the very area where these transactions occurred, an area which, on the day in question, was littered with empty crack vials, would have unhesitatingly so concluded. Considerable deference was due his conclusion that he was observing drug transactions. While the observation of one such transaction under these circumstances might leave room for doubt, the observation of the same exchange repeated five times within a matter of minutes removed any such doubt. In each, while Officer Smith could not observe the object exchanged, he could tell that it was less than an inch in length—consistent with the length of a vial. Moreover, the purposeful concealment of the objects exchanged in the palm of defendant's hand, as Smith observed, was consistent with the conduct of a low-level street seller.

In sum, considering the totality of the circumstances, we are of the view that any experienced police officer, confronted with what Officer Smith, an experienced officer, particularly with respect to narcotics activity in the location in question, witnessed, would reasonably have concluded that what he had observed were five drug sales from a brown bag which defendant used as a stash. The officer's observations and assessment of defendant's actions in the circumstances demonstrated probable cause to search the brown bag for drugs and to arrest defendant.

Judgment, Supreme Court, New York County, rendered on or about April 6, 1993, affirmed.

People v Guarino

56 A.D.2d 638 (2nd Dept 1977)

OPINION OF THE COURT: (Re: Guilt Beyond Reasonable Doubt, 70.20)

Appeal by defendant from a judgment of the County Court, Rockland County, rendered December 3, 1975, convicting him of murder in the second degree and criminal possession of a weapon in the second degree, after a nonjury trial, and imposing sentence. Judgment modified, on the law and the facts, by reducing the conviction of murder in the second degree to one of manslaughter in the second degree, and by reversing the sentence imposed thereon. As so modified, judgment affirmed and case remanded to the County Court for resentence. Defendant was charged in a four-count indictment with the crimes of murder in the second degree, manslaughter in the first degree, manslaughter in the second degree and criminal possession of a weapon in the second degree.

The indictment arose out of the fatal shooting of defendant's wife, Grace Guarino, at approximately 1:30 A.M. on Saturday, January 25, 1975, in the crowded bar of the Boom Boom Room in Nyack, New York.

Defendant was present in the bar and was arrested for the shooting shortly thereafter. After a nonjury trial he was convicted of the crimes of murder in the second degree and criminal possession of a weapon in the second degree. The thrust of the People's case rested on (1) defendant's confession to a police officer, shortly after the shooting, wherein he stated "I shot my wife and I killed my wife" and (2) the testimony of several witnesses who were present in the bar that night and who, cumulatively, testified that they heard several shots, saw a gun in defendant's hand and saw the deceased fall to the floor. However, it must be noted that the language of the confession does not, by itself, prove the element of intent beyond a reasonable doubt, which element is a prerequisite to a conviction for murder in the second degree (see Penal Law, § 125.25, subd 1). Moreover, the testimony of the witnesses was at times unclear, a fact which was understandable in view of the crowding and lighting conditions in the bar. Specifically, none of the witnesses actually saw defendant shoot the deceased. The People's proof also included testimony that defendant first came into the bar at approximately 11:00 P.M. on the evening of January 24, 1975. Although defendant asked his wife to leave the bar and return home to care for her sick child, she refused to do so.

The whole thrust of the defense was that the shooting was a tragic accident. Defendant testified that he had bought the gun two years earlier because he worked in a dangerous area. He stated that he had never fired the gun and never had any intention to kill his wife. Although right-handed, defendant testified that he pulled the gun out of his left pocket with his left hand and hoped that his wife would return home with him when she saw the gun. His wife ran toward him, pulled his arm and put her hand on the gun. As he pulled away from her, the gun went off. Specifically, defendant testified: "Well, I had a gun in my left pocket. I just pulled it out. She saw it. She ran towards me and she was pulling and pulling at me and I was trying to pull away from her and the gun just went off. She was struggling with me for about thirty seconds." The remaining portion of defendant's case was devoted to testimony regarding his excellent reputation for honesty and peaceableness and the nature of the marital relationship between defendant and the deceased. With regard to the murder charge, the trial court based its conclusion on the fact that the defendant had a loaded gun "ready to fire and there is complete absence of any credible evidence or supporting testimony indicating any struggle or, indeed, any action on the part of the deceased." This statement by the trial court reflects an erroneous view of the burden of proof applicable in criminal trials.

At a criminal trial the burden is on the People to prove every material element of the crime charged beyond a reasonable doubt. It was not incumbent on defendant to produce testimony to support his version of the occurrence. Rather, it was incumbent on the People to establish all of the material elements of the murder charge, including intent, beyond a reasonable doubt. In our view, the evidence adduced at the trial did not, as a matter of law, establish an intentional shooting, and thus the People failed to sustain its burden of proof on the issue of intent beyond a reasonable doubt. The evidence presented was as consistent with a lack of intent as with a presence thereof, i.e., it did not exclude to a moral certainty every reasonable hypothesis of innocence. Consequently, defendant could not be convicted of murder in the second degree. Since the evidence established defendant's guilt of manslaughter in the second degree (which was charged in the indictment), i.e., "recklessly causes the death of another person," the judgment of conviction has been modified accordingly and the case remanded for resentencing on that charge.

Chapter 5; Preliminary Proceedings in Local Criminal Court

Sec. 5.5; Article 140; Arrest without a Warrant

People v. De Bour

40 N.Y.2d 210 (1976)

OPINION OF THE COURT: (Re: Interference with a person's liberty, 140.10)

This case raises the fundamental issue of whether or not a police officer, in the absence of any concrete indication of criminality, may approach a private citizen on the street for the purpose of requesting information. We hold that he may. The basis for this inquiry need not rest on any indication of criminal activity on the part of the person of whom the inquiry is made but there must be some articulable reason sufficient to justify the police action which was undertaken.

At 12:15 a.m. on the morning of October 15, 1972, Kenneth Steck, a police officer assigned to the Tactical Patrol Force of the New York Police Department, was working the 6:00 p.m. to 2:00 a.m. tour of duty, assigned to patrol by foot a certain section of Brooklyn. While walking his beat on a street illuminated by ordinary street lamps and devoid of pedestrian traffic, he and his partner noticed someone walking on the same side of the street in their direction. When the solitary figure of the defendant, Louis De Bour, was within 30 or 40 feet of the uniformed officers he crossed the street. The two policemen followed suit and when De Bour reached them Officer Steck inquired as to what he was doing in the neighborhood. De Bour, clearly but nervously, answered that he had just parked his car and was going to a friend's house.

The patrolman then asked De Bour for identification. As he was answering that he had none, Officer Steck noticed a slight waist-high bulge in defendant's jacket. At this point the policeman asked De Bour to unzip his coat. When De Bour complied with this request Officer Steck observed a revolver protruding from his waistband. The loaded weapon was removed from behind his waistband and he was arrested for possession of the gun.

At the suppression hearing Officer Steck testified to the above facts noting that the encounter lasted "a few minutes." On cross-examination, Officer Steck stated that at the time he believed defendant might have been involved with narcotics and crossed the street to avoid apprehension. On the other hand the defendant testified that he never saw the police until they crossed the street in front of him and that he continued walking straight ahead. He stated that the police asked him where he was going and also whether he had any dope in his pockets. He answered that he had been visiting at his mother's home with relatives. De Bour further testified that during this encounter, Steck's partner proceeded to pat his clothing and two or three minutes later Steck found the gun and fired it in order to see whether it was operable. At the conclusion of this hearing the court found Officer Steck's testimony to be credible and denied the motion to suppress. Subsequently De Bour pleaded guilty to felonious attempted possession of a weapon and was sentenced to a conditional discharge. The Appellate Division unanimously affirmed, without opinion.

Whether or not a particular search or seizure is to be considered reasonable requires a weighing of the government's interest against the encroachment involved with respect to an individual's right to privacy and personal security. Thus, we must consider first whether or not the police action was justified in its inception and secondly whether or not that action was reasonably related in scope to the circumstances which rendered its initiation permissible.

Considering the justification at its inception, we first address the People's interpretation of the *Cantor* opinion (36 N.Y.2d 106). Their argument that the patrolmen were authorized to ascertain whether there was any criminal activity is a sheer bootstrap. Before the police may stop a person pursuant to the common-law right to inquire there must exist at that moment a founded suspicion that criminal activity is present (*People v. Cantor*, supra; *People v. Rosemond*, 26 NY2d 101). The police may not justify a stop by a subsequently acquired suspicion resulting from the stop. This reasoning is the same which refuses to validate a search by what it produces (e.g., *People v. Scott D.*, 34 NY2d 483, 490). To validate this stop under the common-law power to inquire, we must examine the knowledge possessed at that moment and any reasonable inferences. Although this analysis involves a less stringent degree of belief than probable cause, it should be approached in the same manner so as to permit the use of familiar signposts as points of reference.

We have frequently rejected the notion that behavior which is susceptible of innocuous behavior alone will not generate a founded or reasonable suspicion that a crime is at hand. Here, we agree with the appellant that this encounter was supported by less than reasonable suspicion and consequently would not justify a stop involving actual or constructive restraint.

We turn now to the appellant's interpretation of *Cantor* (supra). Contrary to the appellant's assertions, *Cantor* should not be read as a blanket prohibition of all police-citizen encounters conducted in the absence of probable cause or reasonable suspicion based on concrete observations. To be sure, police officers may not seize an individual, either physically or constructively, without some articulable justification. However, not every encounter constitutes a seizure.

We have defined a seizure of the person for constitutional purposes to be a significant interruption with an individual's liberty of movement (*Cantor*, supra). Our recent decisions have emphasized the primacy of the right to be free from aggressive governmental interference. In *Cantor* (supra) the actions of three plain-clothes officers in surrounding the defendant with revolvers drawn and blocking his vehicle with their own was considered an unconstitutional seizure. Similarly, in *People v. Ingle* (36 NY2d 413, 418) where a motorist was "accosted" and "restrained" for a "routine traffic check" we held that this constituted a "limited seizure within the meaning of constitutional limitations." The conduct of the policemen in the instant case presents a sharp contrast to these last-mentioned cases. Here De Bour was merely approached and questioned by two uniformed officers whose conduct bespoke no violent or forcible apprehension. Clearly then, De Bour was not seized in the sense that Cantor and Ingle were.

Despite the lack of a forcible seizure here all constitutional considerations do not disappear. The basic purpose of the constitutional protections against unlawful searches and seizures is to safeguard the privacy and security of each and every person against all arbitrary intrusions by government. Therefore, any time an intrusion on the security and privacy of the individual is undertaken with intent to harass or is based upon mere whim, caprice or idle curiosity, the spirit of the Constitution has been violated and the aggrieved party may invoke the exclusionary rule or appropriate forms of civil redress. It is in this vein that the defendant urges that his right as a citizen to walk the streets unimpeded by the State has been trammelled.

While we agree that the patrolmen here had no articulable reason to seize forcibly, or arrest the defendant, we cannot say that the defendant's right to be free from an official interference by way of inquiry is absolute. Were we to carry the defendant's interpretations of Cantor and the Constitution to their logical extreme we would have to conclude that when the police possess a need or desire to initiate an encounter with a private individual they must be prepared to seize him or else do nothing. This approach is hardly reasonable and if adopted would probably lead to an overcompensation in the form of a dilution of the standards embracing reasonable suspicion or probable cause. "The history of the use, and not infrequent abuse, of the power to arrest cautions that a relaxation of the fundamental requirements of probable cause would 'leave law-abiding citizens at the mercy of the officers' whim or caprice'" (*Wong Sun v. United States*, 371 U.S. 471, 479). Common sense and a firm grasp of the practicalities involved compel us to reject an all or nothing approach. The crucial factor is whether or not the police behavior can be characterized as reasonable which, in terms of accepted standards, requires a balancing of the interests involved in the police inquiry.

The role of the police in our society is a multifaceted one. On the one hand the police are mandated to enforce the law; yet the extent to which this authorizes the police to investigate or to prevent crime is ambiguous at best. On the other hand, and more important, we must recognize the multiplicity and complexity of tasks assumed by the police. As public servants, the police perform the lion's share of services expected of local government. Among other functions, the police in a democratic society are charged with the protection of constitutional rights, the maintenance of order, the control of pedestrian and vehicular traffic, the mediation of domestic and other noncriminal conflicts and supplying emergency help and assistance. To consider the actions of the police solely in terms of arrest and criminal process is an unnecessary distortion. We must take cognizance of the fact that well over 50% of police work is spent in pursuits unrelated to crime. Consequently unrealistic restrictions on the authority to approach individuals would hamper the police in the performance of their other vital tasks. This is not to say that constitutional rights to privacy and freedom from unreasonable searches and seizures must be abandoned to accommodate the public service aspect of the police function. The overriding requirement of reasonableness in any event, must prevail.

Generally, in the performance of their public service functions, not related to criminal law enforcement, the police should be given wide latitude to approach individuals and request information. For instance, no one would quarrel with a police officer's right to make inquiry of passers-by to find the parents of a lost child. We have consistently recognized the obligation of policemen to render assistance to those in distress (e.g., *People v. Mitchell*, 39 NY2d 173). However, when police officers are engaged in their criminal law enforcement function their ability to approach people involves other considerations and will be viewed and measured by an entirely different standard of reasonableness. Unfortunately, there is scant appellate authority on this subject, even the majority of the Supreme Court in the Terry trilogy explicitly avoided resolving the constitutional propriety of an investigative confrontation (*Terry v. Ohio*, 392 U.S., at p 19, n 16, supra, but see the separate concurrences of Justices Harlan and White, who maintained that there is no doubt that a policeman can address questions to anyone on the street, at pp. 32, 34). Nevertheless the practical necessities of law enforcement and the obvious fact that any person in our society may approach any other person and attempt to strike up a conversation, make it clear that the police have the authority to approach civilians. While the extent of this power may defy precise definition it would be unrealistic to say it does not exist at all.

Due to the tendency to submit to the badge and our belief that the right to be left alone is too precious to entrust to the discretion of those whose job is the detection of crime, a policeman's right to request information while discharging his law enforcement duties will hinge on the manner and intensity of the interference, the gravity of the crime involved and the circumstances attending the encounter. Thus, while it might be reasonable for the police at the scene of a crime to segregate and interview witnesses, the same procedures would not be justified if done on a whim or caprice. One aspect of law enforcement warrants particular mention and that is the area of crime prevention. Since this function is highly susceptible to subconstitutional abuses it will be subject to the greatest scrutiny; for whereas a policeman's badge may well be a symbol of the community's trust, it should never be considered a license to oppress.

Applying these principles to the instant case, we believe that the police officers legitimately approached De Bour to inquire as to his identity. The encounter here was devoid of harassment or intimidation. It was brief lasting only a few minutes and the questions were circumscribed in scope to the officers' task as foot patrolmen. Significantly, the encounter did not subject De Bour to a loss of dignity, for where the police degrade and humiliate their behavior is to be condemned. In addition, the crime sought to be prevented involved narcotics and the Legislature has declared that to be a serious crime. Moreover, the attendant circumstances were sufficient to arouse the officers' interest. The encounter here occurred after midnight in an area known for its high incidence of drug activity and only after De Bour had conspicuously crossed the street to avoid walking past the uniformed officers. In evaluating the police action in light of the combined effect of these factors we conclude that rather than being whimsical it was reasonable. Hence the police officers were authorized to make the brief limited inquiry that they did.

Our next concern is whether or not the pistol was properly confiscated. The Appellant contends that the undefined bulge at the waistband did not justify Officer Steck's request that he unzip his jacket. We cannot agree. Here, the patrolman testified that when he noticed the bulge at the waistband he "took it to be a gun." The location of the bulge is noteworthy because unlike a pocket bulge which could be caused by any number of innocuous objects, a waistband bulge is telltale of a weapon. Viewed in the context of a late night encounter on a lonely street coupled with the apparently evasive crossing of the street, the officers should have been expected to request clarification as to the source of the waistband bulge which was in fact a .38 caliber Smith & Wesson revolver. The patrolman did not throw the defendant against the wall and thrust his hand into his pockets, nor did he embrace the defendant in a bear hug. In contrast the intrusion here was extremely minimal—Officer Steck simply requested that De Bour open his jacket and the officer never touched him until after he saw the pistol butt protruding from the belt. In our view, the officer's justifiable apprehension that De Bour was armed coupled with the minimal intrusion rendered the police action consonant with the respect and privacy of the individual and as such was reasonable.

Having concluded that the initial encounter was lawful in its inception and that the subsequent intrusion was reasonably limited in scope and intensity we agree that there should have been no suppression and the order of the Appellate Division should be affirmed and the conviction of De Bour sustained.

People v. Carroll
22 Misc. 3d 755 (Rock. Cty Ct. 2008)

OPINION OF THE COURT: (Re: Warrantless Arrests by Private Persons, 140.30)

In separate accusatory instruments, defendant Timothy C. Carroll is charged with the violation of harassment in the second degree and the misdemeanor of resisting arrest. The resisting arrest accusatory instrument accuses defendant of resisting a police officer's attempt to take him into custody following a citizen's arrest of defendant for the noncriminal violation.

As drafted, the resisting arrest charge raises critical issues regarding the complex relationships between the laws governing police arrests, citizens' arrests, and the crime of resisting arrest. Whether the People can prosecute defendant for resisting arrest under the circumstances here depends upon an analysis of these relationships.

On May 19, 2008, defendant was arraigned on the charges of harassment in the second degree and resisting arrest. The harassment accusatory instrument, signed by the putative victim, alleges that defendant struck him in the eye with his closed fist. The resisting arrest accusatory instrument, signed by a police officer, alleged that defendant kicked and pushed the officer when the officer attempted to handcuff defendant after informing him that he was under arrest for harassment in the second degree.

LEGAL DISCUSSION

I. Upon His Arrest By A Citizen for a Noncriminal Violation that Occurred Outside the Police Officer's Presence, Defendant Cannot Lawfully Be Prosecuted For Resisting Arrest under NY Penal Law § 205.30

Under NY Penal Law § 205.30, a defendant can lawfully be prosecuted for resisting arrest only if the underlying arrest was "authorized." Stated differently, that the underlying arrest was authorized is an essential element of the crime of resisting arrest. For that reason, legally sufficient facts demonstrating that the underlying arrest was authorized must be pleaded properly in an accusatory instrument charging a defendant with the misdemeanor of resisting arrest.

Therefore, according to the People, the resisting arrest charge is properly pleaded and defendant's prosecution for resisting arrest can proceed.

Whether the People are correct depends upon the answers to the following legal questions:

(1) Where a defendant has been arrested by a citizen for a noncriminal violation committed outside a police officer's presence, is the officer legally authorized to take physical custody of the defendant without a warrant?

(2) Does a police officer act as a police officer or as an agent of the arresting citizen when he or she takes physical custody of the alleged offender?

(3) Does New York's resisting arrest statute criminalize a defendant's attempts to prevent a police officer, acting in the capacity of an arresting citizen's agent, from taking defendant into custody without a warrant for a noncriminal violation that occurred outside the officer's presence?

No judicial authority in New York directly analyzes these questions. Whether defendant can lawfully be prosecuted for resisting arrest under the circumstances alleged in this case, however, requires that these questions be answered.

A. Where a defendant has been arrested by a citizen for a noncriminal violation committed outside a police officer's presence, is the officer legally authorized to take physical custody of the defendant without a warrant

NY Criminal Procedure Law § 140.10(1) bars a police officer from making a warrantless arrest of a person for a noncriminal violation unless the officer has reasonable cause to believe that the noncriminal violation was committed in the officer's presence. Similarly, under New York's citizen's arrest statute, NY Criminal Procedure Law § 140.30, a private individual is legally authorized to arrest a person for a noncriminal offense only when the offense was actually committed in the arresting individual's presence.

When a private person effects a citizen's arrest, the arresting citizen must comply with the procedures set forth in NY Criminal Procedure Law § 140.40. These procedures require the arresting citizen to: without unnecessary delay deliver or attempt to deliver the person arrested to the custody of an appropriate police officer as defined in subdivision [six]. For such purpose, he may solicit the aid of any police officer and the latter, if he is not himself an appropriate police officer, must assist in delivering the arrested person to an appropriate police officer.

B. Does a Police Officer Act as a Police Officer or as an Agent of the Arresting Citizen When He or She Takes Physical Custody of the Alleged Perpetrator

If, as the People maintain, a police officer is authorized, without a warrant, to take physical custody of an alleged offender arrested by a citizen for a noncriminal offense committed outside the officer's presence, it is essential to determine whether the officer acts as an arresting police officer or as the arresting citizen's agent when doing so. This distinction is legally significant because, as discussed below, the crime of resisting arrest arises only when a defendant resists an authorized arrest made by a police or peace officer, not by a citizen.

Although no court in New York State has yet considered this question, other state courts have. Courts in Idaho, Alaska and California have held that when a police officer assumes custody of a person who has been arrested by a citizen, the police officer is deemed to be assisting the citizen in the course of the citizen's arrest. In other words, when a police officer comes to the aid of citizen who has made a citizen's arrest, he or she acts merely as an agent of the citizen, and the arrest is not converted into a police arrest.

The analyses and conclusions drawn by those courts are equally applicable to New York law. When a private person has made a citizen's arrest of an alleged offender, a police officer who comes to the arresting citizen's aid acts in the capacity of the arresting citizen's agent, not of an arresting police officer. Stated differently, the assistance provided by a police officer to an arresting citizen does not convert the citizen's arrest into a police officer's arrest.

C. Does New York's Resisting Arrest Statute Criminalize a Defendant's Attempts to Prevent a Police Officer, Acting in the Capacity of an Arresting Citizen's Agent, from Taking the Defendant into Custody for a Noncriminal Violation That Occurred Outside the Officer's Presence

NY Penal Law § 205.30 provides that the crime of resisting arrest is committed when a person: intentionally prevents or attempts to prevent a police officer or peace officer from effecting an authorized arrest of himself or another person.

As written, this statute criminalizes only the conduct of a person who resists an authorized arrest made by a "police officer or peace officer." It does not criminalize the conduct of a person who resists an authorized arrest made by a citizen under N.Y. Penal Law § 140.30. Nor does the statute criminalize the conduct of a person who, having been arrested by a citizen, resists being taken into custody by the arresting citizen's agent.

According to the accusatory instrument, the alleged victim, not the police officer, made the authorized arrest of defendant in this case. As such, because the officer was acting in the capacity of the arresting citizen's agent and not in the capacity of an arresting police officer, defendant cannot be prosecuted for the crime of resisting arrest under NY Penal Law § 205.30.

CONCLUSION

Pursuant to NY Criminal Procedure Law § 140.40, the police officer was not legally authorized to take defendant into custody without a warrant following a citizen's arrest of defendant for a noncriminal violation that occurred outside the police officer's presence. Defendant, who was arrested by a citizen for a noncriminal offense that occurred outside the police officer's presence, cannot lawfully be prosecuted for resisting arrest under NY Penal Law § 205.30 in connection with the officer's attempts to take defendant into custody.

Accordingly, the refiled accusatory instrument charging defendant with resisting arrest is dismissed.

So ordered

People v. Floyd

26 N.Y.2d 558 (1970)

OPINION OF THE COURT: (Re: No knock entry, 140.15)

Because the police, otherwise authorized to make a lawful arrest, effected the arrest by unlawful means, the evidence obtained as a result of the arrest may not be used and defendant's conviction must be reversed and the indictment dismissed. This result is required as a consequence of the application of the search and seizure provision of the Federal Constitution to the States under the Fourteenth Amendment (U. S. Const., 4th Amdt.; 14th Amdt.), and the exclusionary rule applied to the States under the holding in *Mapp v. Ohio*, (367 U.S. 643).

Defendant, after a jury trial, was convicted of a felony and two misdemeanors based on his possession of narcotics (heroin) and a hypodermic instrument ("eyedropper" and "spike"). The conviction was affirmed by the Appellate Division, two Justices dissenting. Prior to the trial, defendant's motion to suppress the seized evidence upon which his conviction was subsequently based, was denied, and the present appeal brings that denial up for review.

Defendant's arrest was precipitated by an anonymous telephone call to the New York City police to the effect that he was wanted for forgery on a Federal warrant. After verifying the accuracy of the information three police officers went to the hotel where defendant sojourned, obtained a passkey from the clerk, and entered defendant's room at 7:00 o'clock in the morning, without knocking and without notice to him of their authority or the purpose of their entry. Upon entry the police observed in open display a narcotic "fix," described as an eyedropper, spike, and a bottle cap with a piece of cotton. After arresting and handcuffing defendant, a thorough search of the room yielded the packages of heroin, containing glassine envelopes, secreted in a pillowcase, upon which defendant had been lying before the entry.

In this State, for a long time by statute, and at the common law, police in breaking open and entering premises for the purpose of making an otherwise lawful arrest must give notice to the occupants of who they are and the purpose for which they seek entry. It makes no difference whether the arrest is with or without a warrant, or whether it is an escaped prisoner who is being recaptured. Case law has made exceptions from the statute or common-law rules for exigent circumstances which may allow dispensation with the notice.

In this case there was matter that was both contraband and evidence, but before entry the police did not have the slightest reason to believe that the matter was present in the premises. Defendant was wanted for a crime but there was no reason to believe that he would or could escape. Nor was the crime for which he was wanted a violent one. Nor was there any reason to believe that he was armed or would offer violence or resistance to the officers. That he occupied a second-story room in the hotel did not increase the risk of escape but provided the police, three in number, an excellent and obvious opportunity to post one of their number outside the window of the room if they believed defendant might try to escape. That defendant had once eluded a Federal officer on the street is quite irrelevant to predicting what he might do when cornered in a room. Nor does the circumstance that the arresting officers drew their guns before entering defendant's room prove anything, especially since they were engaging in the extrahazardous act of entering his room by stealth without notice.

Consequently, an arrest effected in this manner is unlawful.

Accordingly, the judgment of conviction should be reversed and the indictment dismissed. Judgment reversed and indictment dismissed.

People ex rel. Maxian v. Brown

164 A.D. 2d 56 (1st Dept. 1990)

OPINION OF THE COURT: (Re: Arraignment without unnecessary delay, 140.20)

Petitioners in these consolidated habeas corpus proceedings are persons arrested without warrants and thereafter detained by the police for varying periods while awaiting arraignment. Petitioners have challenged the legality of their prearraignment detention arguing, in reliance upon certain state statutory and constitutional provisions, that their detention was impermissibly prolonged. It is not disputed that among the petitioners are numerous persons held by the police in prearraignment custody for more than 24 hours and that, of these, some were detained in excess of 72 hours, and a few for more than 90 hours. While all of the petitioners had been either arraigned or released as of the argument of this appeal, the within proceedings raise important issues as to the limitations imposed by state law upon prearraignment detention. As these are novel issues, classically "capable of repetition, yet evading review" (*Gerstein v. Pugh*, 420 U.S. 103, 110 n.11) due to the temporary nature of the challenged detention, appellate consideration is not foreclosed by the mootness doctrine (*Williams v. Ward*, 845 F2d 374, 380).

Section 140.20 of the Criminal Procedure Law provides in relevant part:

1. Upon arresting a person without a warrant, a police officer, after performing without unnecessary delay all recording, fingerprinting and other preliminary police duties required in the particular case, must except as otherwise provided in this section, without unnecessary delay bring the arrested person or cause him to be brought before a local criminal court and file therewith an appropriate accusatory instrument charging him with the offense or offenses in question.

In *People ex rel Roundtree v. Brown*, the first of the two decisions presented for our review, Justice Soloff, in a thorough and well-reasoned opinion, held that in applying the above-quoted provision it would be presumed that an arraignment delayed for more than 24 hours was "unnecessarily delayed" within the meaning of the statute. Justice Soloff was careful to explain that the presumption, would be rebuttable, but only upon a showing by the respondent that there was an acceptable explanation for the delay. Failing such an explanation, the petitioner was entitled to be released. Justice Soloff's holding in *Roundtree* was subsequently followed by Justice McQuillan in *People ex rel Lovells v. Brown*, the second of the decisions here to be reviewed.

Respondents-appellants take issue with Justice Soloff's construction of CPL 140.20(1). Finding no mention of any 24 hour limitation on prearraignment detention within the statute, they claim that Justice Soloff essentially rewrote the statute to impose a rigid limitation where none had been prescribed by the legislature.

While we agree with respondents that the legislature did not mandate in CPL 140.20(1) that arraignments take place within any unvarying interval following a warrantless arrest, we think it clear that Justice Soloff did not do so either. Nothing in *Roundtree* may be fairly read to impose an inflexible time limit on prearraignment detention. All that was done in *Roundtree* was to establish a means for arrestees to vindicate their unarguable right to be arraigned without unnecessary delay. It seems plain then that if CPL 140.20(1) is to confer any enforceable benefit on those held pending arraignment, there must be a point at which the presumption of regularity gives way and the arrestee may, therefore, require his custodian to come forward with an explanation for the delay in arraignment. Indeed, unless we wish to entertain the suggestion that CPL 140.20(1) is nothing more than a hortatory flourish, there does not appear to be any question that there must come a time at which prearraignment delay is presumed to be unnecessary. The more difficult question is when this presumption may be said to arise.

By contrast, as we have noted, the application of CPL 140.20(1) is intimately concerned with the question of necessity. The statute's evident purpose is not to define the "absolute temporal limits" (*Williams*, supra) placed on an arrestee's detention before a probable cause determination, but rather to assure that prearraignment detention is not prolonged beyond the time reasonably necessary to accomplish the administrative prerequisites to arraignment.

In construing the obligation imposed by CPL 140.20(1) so strictly, we recognize that the deprivation entailed by prearraignment detention is very great with the potential to cause serious and lasting personal and economic harm to the detainee. We recognize also that this deprivation is one as to which no predicate is established in advance and, indeed, which may ultimately be found to have been unwarranted. It is, moreover, a deprivation frequently more severe than would be exacted from a defendant whose guilt had been proven.

Extended deprivations of liberty, unilaterally imposed and bearing no conceivably just relation to any crime which might be charged, would be profoundly troubling under any circumstances; they are, however, unconscionable under the circumstances of prearraignment detention which are notoriously harsh. Abruptly severed from all that is familiar and sustaining in the world they are used to travel, detainees are consigned, often in chains, to chronically overcrowded and squalid holding facilities where they will likely be subjected to extraordinary physical and emotional strain. They are, in such degrading, demoralizing and altogether intolerable circumstances, uniquely vulnerable to pressures which may compromise not only their personal integrity but their legal defense. The questionable validity of confessions obtained after prolonged prearraignment detention is, of course, a recurrent subject of judicial concern.

When the State is allowed to retain, past the point of necessity, an advantage as overwhelming and potentially coercive as that which it holds over the individual during prearraignment detention, the most serious and irreversible damage may be done both to the individual and to the capacity of the courts to do justice. Arraignment then, may not be prepared for at leisure. It must be afforded, as the statute commands, "without unnecessary delay." In applying this standard, we must assume that the custodial authority possesses adequate resources and that it is prepared to discharge the administrative tasks incident to arraignment in a reasonably efficient way. Were we to assume otherwise, the state would be deprived of all force and effect since the extent of the delay would then be permitted to vary inversely with the government's commitment of resources. Obviously, the purpose of the statute was not to sanction delay, but to limit it in view of the overriding and urgent importance of a prompt arraignment to the arrestee and to the administration of justice. We conclude then that delay is not necessary within the meaning of the statute unless it is delay which could not have been reasonably foreseen and either reduced or eliminated. Clearly, there is nothing necessary about delays resulting from the longstanding failure of government to take reasonable remedial measures, including, of course, the allocation of resources adequate to the efficient discharge of its prearraignment responsibilities. We do not say what the government must do, only that if it is not to run afoul of CPL 140.20(1) it must do all it is reasonably capable of to expedite the processing of arrestees for arraignment.

At what point then may it be presumed that the considerable obligation imposed by CPL 140.20(1) has not been met?

After an arrest, the custodial authority is, of course, initially entitled to a presumption that it is acting in accordance with CPL 140.20(1) — that it is moving the suspect through the steps leading to arraignment without unnecessary delay. This presumption, however, is not eternal. It fades and it fades rapidly. Indeed, once the suspect is in custody, continued detention in advance of the probable cause determination or, as here, of the arraignment at which the probable cause determination is to be made, is justified only by the custodial authority's need of a "brief period" (id.) to complete the administrative steps incident to arrest or arraignment. Although the length of that "brief period" has been permitted, under the authority of *Williams*, to balloon to 72 hours, CPL 140.20(1) requires that it, nevertheless, be limited to the time necessary to bring a suspect to arraignment. Accordingly, under the law of this state, the presumption in favor of the custodian can last no longer than the period reasonably necessary to produce an arrestee for arraignment.

After carefully reviewing the extensive record before her, Justice Soloff observed: "The 'totality of the processes', at least of those which can be identified and timed, can usually be completed in 24 hours with time to spare...." We do not hesitate to characterize these findings as factual and to affirm them as such. We agree with Justice Soloff that close examination of the numerous petitions and returns in the proceeding, discloses no reason why the prearraignment process cannot be completed within 24 hours. Factually, it appears probable that delay in excess off 24 hours is unnecessary and socially, the desirability of a prompt arraignment is unarguable. In addition, as has already been noted, the utility of the statute depends on the existence of such a presumption.

Accordingly, the judgment of the Supreme Court, New York County (Brenda Soloff, J.), should be affirmed, without costs or disbursements.

People v. Carney
58 N.Y.2d 51 (1982)

OPINION OF THE COURT: (Re: Stop and frisk, 140.50)

A suspect may not be frisked by a police officer who has no knowledge of facts that would provide a basis for suspecting that the individual is armed or dangerous. The absence of such circumstances leads to the conclusion that the search here was unreasonable as a matter of law and, therefore, the order of the Appellate Division should be reversed.

Shortly before midnight on January 4, 1974, two black men armed with a hot gun attempted to rob a liquor store, shooting the owner while doing so. Officer John Morris went to the scene, but found that other officers had already arrived and that the victim had been taken to the hospital. Officer Morris returned to his radio car and began driving back to the precinct house. Two blocks from the robbery scene, he was flagged down by a man who identified himself as a patron of an establishment named "Fat Man's Bar," located approximately one-half block from the liquor store. The man stated that he had heard about the shooting and that two black men who looked "suspicious" had just entered the Fat Man's Bar.

Officer Morris drove back to the bar, called for additional officers, and entered the establishment. The citizen who had stopped Officer Morris also entered and pointed out defendant and his companion. Without ever asking why the man believed defendant and his companion to be suspicious and without himself making any inquiry or observation of the two men, Officer Morris frisked defendant and his friend. The police officer found and removed a loaded .32 caliber revolver from defendant's waistband. The other man had no weapon. The two suspects were taken to the hospital where the liquor store owner was being treated; he stated that the men were not the ones who had attempted to rob him.

Defendant pleaded guilty to attempted felonious possession of a weapon after his motion to suppress was denied.

The seminal case in the area of stop-and-frisk is, of course, *Terry v. Ohio* (392 U.S. 1). There, the Supreme Court upheld the validity of a stop-and-frisk when "the police officer [is] able to point to specific and articulable facts which, taken together with rational inferences from those facts, reasonably warrant that intrusion." (Id., at p. 21.) The court added: "This demand for specificity in the information upon which police action is predicated is the central teaching of this Court's Fourth Amendment jurisprudence." (Id., at p. 21, n. 18.). Manifestly, the basis for determining the propriety of the pat down is the officer's personal knowledge of the circumstances, evaluated "in light of his [or her] experience."

This focus on the officer's personal observation and experience has been recognized in this court's analysis of stop-and-frisk situations. Thus, in *People v. Benjamin* (51 NY2d 267, 270–271), it was noted that a mere anonymous tip of "men with guns" was insufficient to justify a pat down, but that the observations of the experienced officer when he arrived at the scene, in conjunction with the anonymous information, were such as would justify the frisk. In *People v. Klass* (55 NY2d 821), two officers on foot patrol were approached by an unidentified person who described a man with a gun in the hallway of an adjacent building. The officers immediately ran into the building and found Klass, who matched the description just received. Only after Klass refused to give his name or an explanation for his presence did the officers frisk him, thereby discovering a gun. Implicit in this court's affirmance was the recognition that, although initially acting on secondhand information, the officers had articulable knowledge of circumstances tending to support a reasonable suspicion that Klass was dangerous.

In the present case, the police officer had no knowledge of anything to suggest that defendant possessed a firearm or otherwise posed a threat to the officer's safety. The citizen's report that two men were suspicious, without more, does not provide adequate grounds for a frisk. Indeed, whether a person is "suspicious" is the ultimate determination that is to be reached by the officer on the basis of his or her own observations and experience. A frisk would not be justifiable if supported by only the officer's conclusory statement that the subject looked suspicious; so, too, the infirmity rising from the absence of articulable facts is compounded when the officer relies on an inexperienced lay person's conclusion that is not grounded on any objective factual elaboration.

In so holding, the court is cognizant of the holdings in *Adams v. Williams* (407 U.S. 143) and *People v. Moore* (32 NY2d 67, cert den 414 U.S. 1011). Critical to the decisions in both those cases was the relevant content and apparent reliability of the information received by the police. In *Adams*, the officer was approached by an informant personally known to him and from whom he had obtained tips previously. In addition, the information was immediately verifiable at the scene. Notably, the officer's suspicions were further aroused when the defendant rolled down his car's window, rather than opening the door as requested by the officer. Similarly, in *Moore*, the information that the defendant possessed a gun was apparently quite reliable, coming from a man who claimed to be her husband and who was being taken to the police station after brandishing a knife in culmination of a three-day quarrel. These cases require that, before stopping and frisking an individual, the officer must have reliable knowledge of sufficient facts to justify the frisk (see *Adams v. Williams*, supra; cf. *People v. Green*, 35 NY2d 193; *People v. Moore*, supra). The tip here lacked any indicia of reliability and was totally subjective, nonparticularized and conclusory in content. Consequently, the circumstances "[required] further investigation before a forcible stop of a suspect would be authorized" (*Adams v. Williams*, supra, at p. 147).

Accordingly, the order of the Appellate Division should be reversed, the motion to suppress granted, and the indictment dismissed.

Chapter 6; Preliminary Proceedings in Local Criminal Court

Sec. 6.1; Article 170; Proceedings on Complaints Other Than Felony Complaints

People v. Ross

67 N.Y.2d 321(1986)

OPINION OF THE COURT: (Re: Right to counsel, 170.10)

Because Justice Court erroneously denied defendant his statutory right to the assistance of either retained or assigned counsel on the misdemeanor charge (see, CPL 170.10), his conviction of driving with a revoked or suspended license (Vehicle and Traffic Law § 511 [1]) must be reversed.

The case arises from the following facts. Early in the morning of February 16, 1984, Riverhead police officers began an investigation of a Buick automobile parked at a Getty gas station. The defendant approached the gas station. When questioned by the police, defendant responded that he had come to get his car, which he had parked at the gas station after it broke down. Defendant was thereupon arrested for driving an unregistered vehicle, and was taken to police headquarters. He was subsequently charged with a misdemeanor count of driving with a revoked or suspended license and with four traffic infractions. The Legal Aid Society was initially assigned as defendant's counsel but, in a letter to the court it asked to be relieved and that counsel be assigned pursuant to County Law article 18-B. The Town Justice denied the request for assignment of substitute counsel. Defendant pleaded not guilty. When the case was called, defendant told the Town Justice that he was not prepared to proceed because he was still attempting to raise money to retain a lawyer. He indicated that he did not want to plead guilty, but he did not know how to handle his defense. The following exchange then ensued:

"The Court: That's what you were told, that you either defend yourself or plead guilty to them, that's exactly what you were told. I said, I had no intention of sentencing you to jail on these charges and therefore I was not granting you Legal Aid.

"Mr. Ross: This is nonsense, this is crazy. You call this a court of law?

"The Court: What do you mean by that? You were not entitled to a free attorney on Vehicle and Traffic charges, where I have no intention of sending you to jail.

"Mr. Ross: I'm being charged with a misdemeanor even though it's Vehicle and Traffic it's still a misdemeanor, I can't afford an attorney. I'm in a predicament either I plead guilty or I'm going to be found guilty so, either way I lose so, let's see what I can do. I'm ready to go to trial."

Later, after defendant's cross-examination of a police officer concerning the legality of the searches that elicited the VIN number and the certificate of title, defendant asked "Is there any way I can postpone this to get a lawyer[?] I don't think I can represent myself good enough." The Justice denied the request.

Defendant was convicted of all five counts. He was fined $ 100 on the misdemeanor conviction for driving while his license was suspended or revoked. He was also fined for the infractions of driving an uninsured vehicle and for improper plates, and he was given a conditional discharge on the other two counts.

The common law and the statutory law of this State impose upon Trial Judges the duty to scrupulously safeguard the right of all defendants to the effective assistance of counsel at every stage of a criminal proceeding. Where a defendant who is charged with a felony or misdemeanor is financially unable to obtain counsel, the court must assign counsel if the defendant so requests. This statutory right is codified at CPL 170.10, which provides, in pertinent part:

"3. The defendant has the right to the aid of counsel at the arraignment and at every subsequent stage of the action. If he appears upon such arraignment without counsel, he has the following rights:

"(a) To an adjournment for the purpose of obtaining counsel; and

"(b) To communicate, free of charge, by letter or by telephone, for the purposes of obtaining counsel and informing a relative or friend that he has been charged with an offense; and

"(c) To have counsel assigned by the court if he is financially unable to obtain the same; except that this paragraph does not apply where the accusatory instrument charges a traffic infraction or infractions only.

"4. Except as provided in subdivision five, the court must inform the defendant:

"(a) Of his rights as prescribed in subdivision three; and the court must not only accord him opportunity to exercise such rights but must itself take such affirmative action as is necessary to effectuate them."

CPL 170.10 (6) further mandates that the trial court may allow a defendant in a felony or misdemeanor case to proceed pro se only when the statute's prerequisites are met. Thus, it provides: "6. If a defendant charged with a traffic infraction or infractions only desires to proceed without the aid of counsel, the court must permit him to do so. In all other cases, the court must permit the defendant to proceed without the aid of counsel if it is satisfied that he made such decision with knowledge of the significance thereof, but if it is not so satisfied it may not proceed until the defendant is provided with counsel, either of his own choosing or by assignment. Regardless of the kind or nature of the charges, a defendant who proceeds at the arraignment without counsel does not waive his right to counsel, and the court must inform him that he continues to have such right as well as all the rights specified in subdivision three which are necessary to effectuate it, and that he may exercise such rights at any stage of the action."

Although we have had little occasion to construe these provisions of the Criminal Procedure Law an indigent defendant's right to assigned counsel, except in traffic infraction cases, has long been recognized. The statute now requires that a defendant's request for assistance of counsel, or a reasonable adjournment to obtain counsel, must be honored. It should not be met with bullying tactics by the court or obvious expressions of its impatience, resentment or anger. Once this defendant indicated to the Town Justice that he was reluctant to proceed pro se, he was entitled to the court's "affirmative action" to effectuate his right to counsel on the misdemeanor charge (see, CPL 170.10 [4]). At the very least, the court should have granted defendant an adjournment so that his eligibility for assigned counsel pursuant to County Law article 18-B could be determined.

The People raise two arguments to support their contention that, on the facts of this case, defendant was not entitled to assigned counsel, or an adjournment. First, they claim that CPL 170.10 should be read in light of recent Federal constitutional law holding that a court must appoint assigned counsel for indigent defendants only when the Trial Judge determines that a sentence of imprisonment will be imposed (relying on *Argersinger v. Hamlin*, 407 U.S. 25; *Scott v. Illinois*, 440 U.S. 367). Defendant is asserting his statutory right to counsel, however, not a constitutional right and the Criminal Procedure Law clearly provides broad statutory protection to all defendants accused of felonies and misdemeanors without reference to the potential sentence attached to the crime.

The Town Justice's refusal to make an 18-B referral, or to adjourn the proceeding while defendant obtained private counsel clearly violated the prerequisites that the Legislature intended would preserve a defendant's right to counsel at all stages of a criminal proceeding.

Accordingly, the order of the Appellate Term should be modified by reversing defendant's conviction for violation of Vehicle and Traffic Law and ordering a new trial on the misdemeanor charge.

People v. O'Grady

175 Misc. 2d 61 (Crim. Ct. Bx Cty, 1997)

OPINION OF THE COURT: (Re: Dismissal in the interests of justice, 170.40)

During the sixth game of the 1996 baseball World Series more than 56,000 people were assembled at Yankee Stadium and millions were observing the game on television as the defendant allegedly ran shirtless onto the baseball field. On his bare torso were written two messages. On his chest and stomach was written "Howard Stern for President." On his back was written "Guilliani [sic] kiss my....," with an arrow pointing down to the defendant's buttocks.

As a result, the game was disrupted for 1 1/2 minutes and the defendant now stands charged with criminal trespass in the third degree (Penal Law § 140.10 [a]) and disorderly conduct (Penal Law § 240.20 [1]). The defendant moves for dismissal in the interest of justice pursuant to CPL 170.30 (1) (g) and 170.40.

The mass exhilaration at the sixth game of the World Series was phenomenal and one can imagine how this could inspire the urge to run onto the field. The emotion and adrenalin at Yankee Stadium can be ignitable and one can envisage a Yankees fan being enraptured by exhilaration — you crave more adrenalin, you run onto the Bronx diamond, you're in the eye of the most electrifying milieu in the universe! At the ceiling of this excitation, under the scrutiny of over 56,000 pairs of frenzied eyes, among hoots, hollers and cheers, the adrenalin rush comes to a crash as you are seized, arrested, brought to the station house and — here's the most harrowing part — you miss the rest of the game. With the power to interrupt millions of people the world over, from world leaders to little league youngsters with memories of the bygone spring and aspirations of forthcoming renown, the realization arrives that the season has ended and that this enthusiastic fan has missed the last of the competition.

The defense moves for dismissal in the interest of justice. A court may grant a dismissal in the furtherance of justice, even when there is no other legal basis requiring a dismissal, when there exists "some compelling factor, consideration or circumstance clearly demonstrating that conviction or prosecution of the defendant upon such accusatory instrument or count would constitute or result in injustice." (CPL 170.40 [1].) Dismissal lies within the discretion of the Trial Judge but such discretion is neither absolute nor uncontrolled. CPL 170.40 (1) provides 10 criteria that a court must examine and weigh collectively and individually, to the extent appropriate, in deciding whether to exercise its discretionary power to dismiss:

"(a) the seriousness and circumstances of the offense;

"(b) the extent of [****] harm caused by the offense;

"(c) the evidence of guilt, whether admissible or inadmissible at trial;

"(d) the history, character and condition of the defendant;

"(e) any exceptionally serious misconduct of law enforcement personnel in the investigation, arrest and prosecution of the defendant;

"(f) the purpose and effect of imposing upon the defendant a sentence authorized for the offense;

"(g) the impact of a dismissal on the safety or welfare of the community;

"(h) the impact of a dismissal upon the confidence of the public in the criminal justice system;

"(i) where the court deems it appropriate, the attitude of the complainant or victim with respect to the motion;

"(j) any other relevant fact indicating that a judgment of conviction would serve no useful purpose."

When viewing these criteria, the court must look to compelling factors that warrant dismissal. A compelling factor is present if denial of the motion would be such an abuse of discretion so as to shock the conscience.

This court has examined and considered, individually and collectively, all of the criteria enumerated in CPL 170.40 (1) and finds that there are not sufficient compelling factors warranting dismissal. Indeed, the defendant's alleged actions clearly warrant prosecution. To begin with, security guards and police charged with restraining and removing those entering unlawfully onto the ball field risk physical injury. Furthermore, the defendant interrupted more than 56,000 fans attending the game and perhaps millions of people worldwide. Finally, the defendant created a vulgar spectacle that was inappropriate, especially for children. (There were surely many and maybe thousands of children at this game who did not turn their eyes from the field like the television cameras.)

It has been often said that "In the great department store of life, baseball is in the toy department." And baseball is a game for kids of all generations: When at a ball park, we may all go back to a childhood dream. For the children at the sixth game of the [****] 1996 World Series, the message on the defendant's torso may have diminished the innocence of the game and detracted from the purity of the enchantment.

Accordingly, the motion to dismiss in the interest of justice is denied.

Hollender v. Trump Village Cooperative, Inc.
58 N.Y.2d 420 (1983)

OPINION OF THE COURT: (Re: ACD as ground for false arrest and malicious prosecution 170.55)

The issue on this appeal is whether an accused's acceptance of an adjournment in contemplation of dismissal, popularly referred to by the acronym ACD or ACOD, constitutes a bar to a subsequent civil suit for false imprisonment or malicious prosecution. We hold that an ACOD disposition, authorized by CPL 170.55, is neither a conviction nor an acquittal. We further hold that while it, therefore, does not interdict an action for false imprisonment, it does bar one for malicious prosecution.

At about 8:00 p.m. on January 8, 1975, plaintiff Joanne Hollender, then 17 1/2 years of age, and some friends congregated in an outdoor area between two buildings which were part of a group of co-operative housing units in a development known as Trump Village in Brooklyn. Two of the co-operative's security guards approached the young people and ordered them to disperse. When Joanne objected to doing so, they summoned the police who, at the insistence of one of the guards, placed her under arrest for criminal trespass. Ultimately, before her criminal trial was to get underway, she was offered and accepted the ACOD disposition.

Thereafter, Joanne brought this civil action against the co-operative and its prosecuting guard. As pertinent here, her complaint sounded separately in false imprisonment and malicious prosecution. In due course, she recovered separate awards for compensatory and punitive damages on each cause. But the Appellate Division, reversing on the law, dismissed the complaint, essentially on the ground that the acceptance of the adjournment in contemplation of dismissal precluded the suit on both counts. For the reasons which follow, we now modify its order insofar as it affects the false imprisonment cause.

We begin our analysis by recounting that CPL 170.55 is rooted in an informal mechanism first developed in the New York City court system. The interest of justice section applicable to lesser offenses, CPL 170.55 provides a means of disposing of relatively minor charges. Provided that the defendant, the prosecutor and the court agree, this procedural path makes it possible for such charges — often family or neighbor related and usually involving an individual facing his or her initial encounter with the criminal justice system — to be kept in a state of suspense for a period of six months, during which the subject's habitual behavior pattern can be tested by time. The trial court, in its discretion, also is empowered to condition ACOD status on a willingness to participate in a dispute resolution program (CPL 170.55, subd. 4) and, subject to the accused's consent, on performance of community service (CPL 170.55, subd. 5).

Under the statutory scheme, once the six-month period is at an end, absent any untoward event, the case will be dismissed as a matter of course unless, on application of the prosecutor, the court is convinced "that dismissal of the accusatory instrument would not be in furtherance of justice" (CPL 170.55, subd. 2). As per CPL 170.55 (subd. 6), such dismissal is not to connote either a conviction or, as in the case of a plea, an admission of guilt. * So it is that, in the eyes of the criminal law, once the accusatory instrument is dismissed the arrest and the prosecution are rendered a "nullity" (CPL 170.55, subd. 6).

Moreover, to avoid stigmatizing one who has been granted the ACOD dismissal, such a person expressly is included among those entitled to the full benefit of the record sealing and expunging provisions which come into play when a criminal action or proceeding has been terminated in favor of an accused (CPL 160.50, subds. 1, 2). The over-all effect of a consummated ACOD dismissal is then to treat the charge as though it never had been brought. Nevertheless, the fact is that the occasion for determination of the merits of the events underlying the charge will have gone by without their resolution. Thus, in a subsequent civil litigation to which a finding of guilt or innocence of the charge is germain, adjournment in contemplation of dismissal, by reason of its sui generis character, will leave the question unanswered.

This in mind, it must be remembered that in an action for damages for false imprisonment, the burden of establishing that the detention was privileged is on those charged with the commission of that tort. Hence, it was error for the Appellate Division to rule that the adjournment in contemplation of dismissal in this case was legally decisive of the issue.

Contrariwise, in a malicious prosecution action, it is for the one who brings the suit to establish that the criminal proceeding allegedly instigated by the defendant terminated in favor of the accused. Indeed, it is only when the final disposition is such as to indicate innocence, that this burden is met. So viewed, the Appellate Division's dismissal of the malicious prosecution claim was correct. The adjournment in contemplation of dismissal, being as unadjudicative of innocence as it was of guilt, by its very nature operated to bar recovery.

Accordingly, the order of the Appellate Division should be modified and the case remitted to that court for further proceedings in accordance with this opinion.

Sec. 6.2; Article 180; Proceedings on Felony Complaints

People v. Hodge

53 N.Y.2d 313 (1981)

OPINION OF THE COURT: (Re: Right to counsel at hearing, 180.10)

Defendant Gabriel Hodge has been convicted of the felonies of burglary in the third degree and escape in the first degree. On appeal from an Appellate Division order of affirmance, the main issue we confront is whether he is entitled to a reversal of the escape conviction because a preindictment preliminary hearing on that charge, held pursuant to CPL 180.10 (subd. 2), was conducted in the absence of retained counsel. For the reasons which follow, we hold that he is and that the appropriate corrective action is a new trial.

Hodge was arraigned on a charge of escape in the Princetown Town Court. The case was adjourned for a week in order to afford him an opportunity to retain an attorney. On the appointed date, the defendant appeared alone, but informed the court that he had retained counsel, whose name he furnished to the court and for whose absence on this day he was unable to account. When defendant demurred at having the hearing go forward without the presence of his lawyer, the court insisted, "You have had a chance to obtain counsel. Your counsel is not present. So we are going to proceed without your counsel for this matter."

In this case the handicap this represented is not dependent on inference alone. The record reveals, for instance, that during the examination of one of the People's witnesses, when the defendant was offered an opportunity to examine a document before it was received into evidence, he stated, "I am not an attorney. So I have never seen a preliminary hearing conducted without an attorney present. So it would be senseless to show this to me, you know." At another point, offered an opportunity to cross-examine, he responded similarly. To this the court rejoined, "You were informed of your rights to an attorney. You have talked to your attorney in the meantime and your attorney is not present. In the criminal procedure law, if your attorney is not present after adequate time the court can proceed to examine the case."

At the conclusion of the hearing, the court found that there was reasonable ground to believe that the crime charged had been committed. The defendant was then bound over for the Grand Jury, which was to indict him for escape in the first degree, and, after proceeding to trial with counsel, he was convicted.

We begin our analysis with the observation that, since most constitutional rights are not self-executing, the right to counsel may be the most basic of all. Conscious of its role, in criminal cases in particular, we have called for "the highest degree of vigilance in safeguarding the right of an accused to have the assistance of an attorney at every stage of the legal proceedings against him" (*People v. Cunningham*, 49 NY2d 203, 207). And, in so protecting the right to a lawyer's assistance from the time the criminal process is initiated, an explicit and implicit goal is that a system which ideally seeks equal representation for the State and for the defendant should move in that direction in fact as well as in theory.

With these concerns in mind, it is hardly surprising that the Supreme Court has ruled that a preliminary hearing is "a 'critical stage' of the State's criminal process," thus triggering the United States Constitution's guarantee that a defendant be afforded "the guiding hand of counsel." A hearing is no vestigial remnant of an earlier day. It has many functions besides the obvious formal ones, such as reduction of excessive charges, prompt arrangement for release where appropriate and, above all, early screening of unjustifiable and unprovable charges against the innocent. In a very real sense, as scholars and practitioners agree, since the prosecutor must present proof of every element of the crime claimed to have been committed, no matter how skeletally, the preliminary hearing conceptually and pragmatically may serve as a virtual minitrial of the prima facie case. In its presentation, the identity of witnesses, to greater or lesser degree, testimonial details and exhibits, perforce will be disclosed.

Since the hearing provides an occasion for appraising witnesses and others who are likely to participate in the ultimate trial, at least as often as not, attentive and sensitive counsel gain knowledge and insight that will be of invaluable assistance in the preparation and presentation of the client's defense. Most important, early resort to that time-tested tool for testing truth, cross-examination, in the end may make the difference between conviction and exoneration.

In this perspective, we must reject the People's suggestion that, because the Grand Jury subsequently indicted the defendant, any infirmities that occurred at the flawed hearing may be excused. True, the State, by presenting the case to a Grand Jury in the first instance, may bypass the preliminary hearing stage entirely. And, though a preliminary hearing results in dismissal, it may nevertheless succeed in obtaining an indictment at the hands of a Grand Jury. But, though in the former case the People will have obviated the preliminary hearing process and, in the latter, rendered the favorable disposition ineffectual, once it pursues the path of the preliminary hearing, the defendant becomes entitled to have it conducted with full respect for his right to counsel.

Accordingly, the order of the Appellate Division should be modified by reversing the conviction of escape in the first degree, vacating the sentence imposed thereon, and remitting the case to the Schenectady County Court for a new trial in accordance with this opinion.

Chapter 7; Preliminary Proceedings in Superior Court

Sec. 7.1; Article 190; The Grand Jury and Its Proceedings

People v. Di Napoli

27 N.Y.2d 229 1970

OPINION OF THE COURT: (Re: Grand jury secrecy, 190.25)

We are called upon to decide whether the courts below were warranted in authorizing the Public Service Commission to inspect the grand jury minutes in a proceeding long concluded.

We start with the proposition that secrecy of grand jury minutes is not absolute. A copy of the minutes may be furnished to any person upon the written order of the court. Firmly settled is the rule that determination of the question whether disclosure should be permitted is addressed to, and rests in, the trial judge's discretion. In exercising this discretion, the court must balance the competing interests involved, the public interest in disclosure against that in secrecy.

It is our view that Special Term and the Appellate Division properly found that the public interest would best be served by allowing inspection by the Commission. As to the interest in disclosure, we need but note that charges to consumers arising from the decade-long conspiracy, involving millions of dollars, may depend upon the agency's ascertainment of the degree of Consolidated Edison's — and Brooklyn Union's — involvement in the criminal conspiracy. Moreover, only by obtaining a complete record will the Commission be able to take steps to prevent similar victimization of utilities and their customers in the future.

Ranged against these considerations are the reasons for maintaining the secrecy or confidentiality of grand jury minutes. Those most frequently mentioned by courts and commentators are these: (1) prevention of flight by a defendant who is about to be indicted; (2) protection of the grand jurors from interference from those under investigation; (3) prevention of subornation of perjury and tampering with prospective witnesses at the trial to be held as a result of any indictment the grand jury returns; (4) protection of an innocent accused from unfounded accusations if in fact no indictment is returned; and (5) assurance to prospective witnesses that their testimony will be kept secret so that they will be willing to testify freely.

Applying these criteria to the case before us, it is evident that the courts below were justified in exercising their discretion as they did. At this time — more than two years after the conclusion of the grand jury proceedings, the conviction of the appellants by guilty pleas and the payment of fines — there is no danger of any escape of persons who may be indicted, no interference with the grand jury's freedom to deliberate, no danger of subornation of perjury and no need to protect any innocent accused person.

Concerning the last reason listed above — assurance to prospective witnesses that their testimony will be kept secret to encourage their giving of testimony — we believe it may not be said that the disclosure here ordered will have a chilling effect on the ability of future grand juries to obtain witnesses. The Commission, far from being an "outsider," is a governmental investigatory body, with specific authority over the subject matter into which the grand jury was inquiring. Having in mind the nature of the conspiracy under investigation by the grand jury, witnesses before it could reasonably have anticipated that some investigating body, even though it might not be the Public Service Commission, would be set up to consider the impact of such criminal activity upon the public utility, as well as its consumers, and procure a copy of the minutes to assist it in such investigation. Quite obviously, our affirmance will not sanction any general disclosure or widespread publication of the minutes. Authorization to inspect was granted solely to enable the Commission's staff to utilize the minutes to assist it in its investigation and preparation for the public hearings which it will hold.

In short, as we have already noted, the grant of the Commission's motion may not be said to have been an abuse of discretion. Since there was ample basis for the conclusion that the inspection will serve the public interest and that the reasons for the rule of secrecy no longer exist, it follows that the order appealed from should be affirmed.

People v. Straehle

30 A. D. 2d 452 (2nd Dept 1968)

OPINION OF THE COURT: (Re: Immunity before grand jury, perjury, 190.40)

An indictment for perjury in the first degree against a police officer of the City of New Rochelle has been dismissed and the People appeal. The officer executed a waiver of immunity and testified before a Grand Jury concerning a telephone conversation he allegedly had had with a gambler. The gambler and the officer were indicted for perjury. A trial was held in which the gambler was convicted, but the jury could not reach a verdict as to the officer and a mistrial resulted as to him. It was then that the motion to dismiss the indictment was made and granted.

The issue is: may a police officer who has signed a waiver of immunity, under the compulsion of losing his job, be indicted for perjury for willfully testifying falsely before a Grand Jury?

The waiver, signed by the defendant in this case, was obtained under an illegal compulsion and was therefore ineffective. Thus, when officer Straehle appeared before the Grand Jury under an invalid waiver of immunity, he retained all the protection available to a nonwaiving witness. Such immunity is granted to enable a witness to aid the State by his truthful testimony. He is not given the immunity for the purpose of deceiving a Grand Jury and misleading its investigation. Thus, if the witness, having been given the protection of the immunity from prosecution for substantive crimes, willfully gives false testimony, he is subject to indictment, prosecution and conviction for that perjury.

Accordingly, we reverse, on the law, deny defendant's motion and reinstate the indictment.

People v. Feerick

93 N.Y.2d 433 (1999)

OPINION OF THE COURT: (Re: Claim of immunity, fabricated transactions, 190.40)

Defendants are all members of the New York City Police Department convicted of various crimes arising out of their entry into two apartments in a Manhattan building where they restrained and threatened the occupants in an attempt to recover a police radio. All four defendants challenge the legal sufficiency of the evidence supporting their convictions for official misconduct (Penal Law § 195.00). Defendant Rosario individually contends that he received immunity from prosecution by virtue of his testimony before a Grand Jury. The Appellate Division considered these issues and affirmed the convictions. We conclude that these claims either lack merit or are unreviewable, and affirm the convictions in all respects.

On September 26, 1990, in attempting to recover defendant DeVito's police radio — which had been lost during a prior drug-related incident — defendants pushed their way into the apartment of Denise Jackson, with weapons drawn. Theresa Johnson, who was staying with Jackson at the time, was sleeping; Ben Stokes, whom defendants sought to question, rented a room from Jackson, but was not present at the time. When Maribel Delgado, Stokes's girlfriend, knocked on the door, she too was searched and detained. Delgado told them that Stokes might be in another apartment in the building. They proceeded to the second apartment and again forced their way in, with weapons drawn. Finding Stokes in the second apartment, defendants demanded the return of the police radio in exchange for which they would not prosecute Stokes for the 591 vials of crack cocaine they found while searching the second apartment. Defendant DeVito, back at the precinct, vouchered the vials of crack, falsely indicating on various forms that they had been recovered in the alleyway behind the building, where Stokes had dropped them while running away to avoid arrest.

After defendants left, Jackson called 911 to report the incident. Stokes was interviewed but was unwilling to cooperate in any prosecution of defendants. The District Attorney's office declined to prosecute defendants, but urged the Police Department to follow up with appropriate disciplinary action. Pursuant to Patrol Guide section 118–9, which requires a member of the police force to respond to questions under the penalty of dismissal, hearings were held for all four defendants. At his hearing on January 18, defendant Rosario stated that he had arrested Stokes for the drugs vouchered on September 26. Rosario had also testified before the Grand Jury on January 11 regarding that arrest. Advised of these developments, the District Attorney's office reopened the investigation of defendants, leading to the indictment. After the jury trial Defendant Rosario was found guilty of perjury in the first degree for his testimony at the Grand Jury regarding Stokes's drug arrest.

Immunity Based on Grand Jury Testimony

Having been convicted of perjury for his false testimony before the Grand Jury regarding Stokes's drug charge, defendant Rosario claims immunity from prosecution for any charges arising out of the September 26 incidents. Understandably, he does not contest the perjury conviction, which is specifically exempted from the statute (see, CPL 50.10 [1]).

In order for there to be immunity, the connection between the "transaction, matter or thing" about which a witness testifies before the Grand Jury and the criminal charges must be real and of some substantiality, not merely trifling, imaginary or speculative. Rosario, however, did not testify to an actual transaction. He falsely testified that the drugs were obtained when Stokes dropped them in the alley, rather than from the apartment the officers had improperly searched. As a result, there can be no question that the connection between the crimes with which Rosario was charged and the transaction about which he testified was illusory, because that transaction itself was imaginary.

Fabricated transactions do not confer immunity under CPL 190.40. To hold otherwise would allow — indeed encourage — witnesses to invent encounters with real people in the hope that the mention of actual objects and real persons will shield them from prosecution. This Court has refused to burden the immunity inquiry with "chance and gamesmanship" as "inconsistent with the ends of justice, [un]warranted by any legitimate interests of the defendant, and ... [un]intended by the Legislature" (*People v. Sobotker*, 61 NY2d 44, 49). Allowing Rosario the benefit of his "imaginary transaction" testimony would do precisely that.

In sum, we conclude that defendant Rosario was not entitled to immunity from prosecution based on his Grand Jury testimony. Accordingly, the order of the Appellate Division should be affirmed.

People v. Williams
56 N.Y.2d 916 (1982)

OPINION OF THE COURT: (Re: Immunity before grand jury, 190.40)

Appeal, by permission of an Associate Judge of the Court of Appeals, from an order of the Appellate Division of the Supreme Court in the Second Judicial Department, entered July 6, 1981, which affirmed an order of the Supreme Court, entered in Queens County, dismissing the indictment against defendant.

In June, 1978, defendant was called to testify before the Grand Jury which was investigating the homicide of one Delores Taylor; defendant never signed a waiver of immunity nor was informed that he was entitled to counsel or that he might remain silent. Defendant testified that on the night in question he and a friend visited the deceased at her apartment; that deceased and a third man, who had been in deceased's apartment, quarreled; that when defendant returned from an errand, he found his friend and the third man fighting; that he broke up the fight, the third man left and deceased told defendant and his friend that she would lock her door, and that defendant and his friend then left. Ms. Taylor was subsequently found dead; the third man, who had been the apparent target of the Grand Jury investigation, was indicted for murder, but when the defendant later made statements implicating himself in the homicide to the prosecutor, the latter successfully moved to dismiss the indictment against the third man. Defendant was then indicted for manslaughter in the second degree, but that indictment was dismissed by Criminal Term on the ground that defendant's testimony before the Grand Jury had immunized him from prosecution under CPL 50.10 (subd. 3) and CPL 190.40.

The Appellate Division concluded that the language of the statutes, construed as a whole, appeared clear: absent a waiver, a witness before a Grand Jury who responded directly to questioning legally addressed to him, cannot be convicted of an offense for any transaction concerning which he gave testimony; that "[it] is enough, to wake the privilege into life, that there is a reasonable possibility of prosecution, and that the testimony, though falling short of proving the crime in its entirety, will prove some part or feature of it, will tend to a conviction when combined with proof of other circumstances which others may supply" (*Matter of Doyle*, 257 NY 244, 256 [Cardozo, Ch. J.]); that references in other cases to the testimony as reflecting a link in the chain of facts against the witness were but an expressive means of describing Cardozo's test in *Doyle*, and that defendant's testimony, which placed him at the scene of the crime near the time of the homicide and could lead to an inference that the victim might have opened her locked door to him with whom she was friendly, tended to incriminate him of the crime concerning which he testified.

The decision of the Appellate Division is affirmed.

People v. Evans
79 N.Y.2d 407 (1992)

OPINION OF THE COURT: (Re: Defendant's right to appear before grand jury, 190.50)

The issue is whether these three defendants were deprived of their statutory right to appear and testify before a Grand Jury under CPL 190.50 (5) where, despite their written requests served on the People at their arraignments on felony complaints, the prosecutor nevertheless proceeded to present criminal charges to the Grand Jury in order to avoid the automatic and imminent consequences of the People's failure to satisfy CPL 180.80. We also consider whether the statutory right to appear was satisfied when the prosecutor offered these defendants the opportunity to have their say after the Grand Jury had already voted to indict them.

These appeals stem from independent arrests and felony complaints. At their separate arraignments the day after their arrests, the People served defendants with notice under CPL 190.50 (5) (a) that criminal charges would be presented to a Grand Jury. Defendants responded with written notices under that statute that they intended to exercise their right to testify before the Grand Jury.

However, on the dates for their production before the Grand Jury, Evans and Oquendo were not produced until after the indictments were already voted. Defendant

Davis was produced in timely fashion, but he was returned to the detention facility before being given the opportunity to testify "due to the lack of security." According to the prosecutor's affirmations, the Assistant District Attorneys presented the respective cases to the Grand Jury, instructed it on the law, and obtained indictments in order to avoid the consequences of CPL 180.80.

The People, however, did not immediately file the indictments with the court. The Assistant District Attorneys offered to further delay filing the indictments, to reopen the Grand Jury proceedings, and to allow defendants to testify before the same Grand Jury that had already voted to indict them. The attorneys for the defendants rejected this suggestion and the indictments were filed with the court.

Our reading of CPL 190.50 (5) together with its history and purpose warrants the conclusion that the Legislature intended that individuals who give timely notice reasonably prior to the prosecution's presentment of evidence and prior to the Grand Jury vote on an indictment are entitled to testify before the vote. This interpretation properly effectuates the purposes underlying the statute by protecting defendants' valued statutory option to appear at this critical accusatory stage to offer testimony that may affect the Grand Jury's consideration of the otherwise exclusive, ex parte presentment of evidence by the prosecution. Further, the District Attorney's statutory obligation to notify the Grand Jury foreperson when an accused has served notice of intent to appear (CPL 190.50 [5] [b]) surely contemplates that defendant will be afforded a prevote appearance, since the statute fixes the time in such circumstances as within a "reasonable time" (CPL 190.50 [5] [a]). We discern nothing in the statutory language or the legislative history justifying a dilution of an accused's personal right to appear before the Grand Jury before that body has been instructed on the law by the prosecutor and before it has deliberated on the evidence and voted on the criminal charges against the defendant. This view comports with the raison d'etre of indictment by Grand Jury: "to prevent the people of this State from potentially oppressive excesses by the agents of the government in the exercise of the prosecutorial authority vested in the State" (*People v. Iannone*, 45 NY2d 589, 594; NY Const, art 1, § 6).

The failure of the Department of Correction to produce defendants provides no excuse or good cause for the District Attorney's failure to give effect to a properly invoked right under CPL 190.50 (5). Nor should we give legal effect to the practical difficulties the prosecution may encounter in satisfying its obligations under CPL 180.80.

Accordingly, the order of the Appellate Division in each case, affirming the dismissal of the indictments, should be affirmed.

Chapter 8; Prosecution of Indictments in Superior Court; from Plea to Pre-Trial Motions

Sec. 8.1; Article 220; The Plea

People v. Selikoff

35 N.Y.2d 227 (1974)

OPINION OF THE COURT: (Re: Plea bargaining, 220.10)

These three appeals by defendants present issues arising from convictions based on negotiated guilty pleas. They raise the question whether a defendant may show that his guilty plea to a lesser crime was induced by an off-the-record unfulfilled promise, although contradicted by the recorded colloquy on the taking of the plea. Also at issue is whether a defendant is entitled to be sentenced as promised, or, if the court cannot or will not sentence as promised, whether the defendant is entitled to no more than the right to withdraw his guilty plea. In each case the order of the intermediate appellate court affirming the conviction should be affirmed.

Throughout history the punishment to be imposed upon wrongdoers has been subject to negotiation. Plea negotiation, in some form, has existed in this country since at least 1804. Even in England, where there are no public prosecutors, no inflexible sentencing standards, and considerably less pressure on the trial courts, a limited form of plea negotiation seems to be developing. Moreover, convictions upon guilty pleas, pleas probably to lesser crimes, have been high since 1839 both in rural, where there is little trial court congestion, and in urban areas, where there is much congestion. History and perspective suggest, then, that plea negotiation is not caused solely, or even largely, by overcrowded dockets. This is not to say, however, that plea negotiation is not acutely essential to relieve court calendar congestion, as indeed it is. In budget-starved urban criminal courts, the negotiated plea literally staves off collapse of the law enforcement system, not just as to the courts but also to local detention facilities.

Plea negotiations, of course, serve many other needs. They relieve the prosecution and the defense too, for that matter, from the inevitable risks and uncertainties of trial. The negotiation process which results in a guilty plea telescopes the judicial process and the necessarily protracted intervals involved in charge, trial, and sentence, and even appeals, hopefully starting the offender on the road to possible rehabilitation. The process also serves significant goals of law enforcement by permitting an exchange of leniency for information and assistance.

Perhaps most important, plea negotiation serves the ends of justice. It enables the court to impose "individualized" sentences, an accepted ideal in criminology, by avoiding mandatory, harsh sentences adapted to a class of crime or a group of offenders but inappropriate, and even Draconian, if applied to the individual before the court. Obviously no two defendants are quite alike even if they have committed, in legal definition, identical offenses. The negotiation process often brings to light mitigating circumstances unknown when the defendant was charged.

There is the much-maligned, but almost universally used, discretion by prosecutors and courts in accepting lesser pleas. It is sometimes a finer adjustment to the particular crime and offender than the straight application of the rules of law would permit. Plea negotiations serve other laudable purposes. Like procedures to protect the integrity of the fact-finding process at trial, still-developing modern practices are available to assure the integrity of the guilty plea. Where a defendant denies guilt, or if the court believes defendant may be innocent, and the guilty plea is not otherwise justified as knowingly and intelligently made, the guilty plea may be and should be rejected.

In *People v. Selikoff*, the pleading court stated on the record that based on the representations made by the prosecution and defense counsel, as well as on the facts known to him, it was his then opinion that no sentence of imprisonment would be imposed. As the result of his experience in the trial, the Judge concluded that the pleading defendant's role in the fraudulent scheme had not been peripheral, as he had been advised during the plea negotiations, but that defendant had been a principal participant. The presentence report stated that defendant denied both his role in the fraud and his guilt of the obscenity charge.

On sentence, based upon his later information and views, the sentencing Judge stated that he could not and would not perform his conditional promise of no imprisonment. He offered defendant an opportunity to withdraw his guilty pleas. Defendant rejected the opportunity and insisted on performance of the "promise." Consequently, the court sentenced defendant to an indeterminate five-year sentence on the grand larceny charge and a $ 1,000 fine on the obscenity charge. The Appellate Division affirmed the convictions.

Significant factors suggest affirmance in the *Selikoff* case. A Judge may not ignore those provisions of law designed to assure that an appropriate sentence is imposed. Thus, any sentence "promise" at the time of plea is, as a matter of law and strong public policy, conditioned upon its being lawful and appropriate in light of the subsequent presentence report or information obtained from other reliable sources. That the court in the *Selikoff* case did not explicitly condition its "promise" (although the implication could hardly be clearer) upon its later evaluation after reading the presentence report, or the facts it learned from the trial of the codefendants, is therefore of no consequence.

Defendant Selikoff was afforded an opportunity to withdraw his plea of guilty. This opportunity he was entitled to receive since the foundation for the plea, regardless of fault, had proven to be without substance. He could have requested that the trial be presided over by a Judge other than the one who had received the guilty plea.

The views expressed are consonant with the rationale and holding in *Santobello v. New York*. There, the Supreme Court held that the failure of a prosecutor to honor his off-the-record promise to make no sentence recommendation rendered invalid the guilty plea induced by the promise. The court left it to the discretion of the State courts whether either to allow defendant to withdraw his plea, or to fulfill the aborted promise by vacating the sentence and remanding the proceedings for resentence before a different Judge, without a prosecutor's sentence recommendation.

In the *Selikoff* case, the record shows that the court in promising no imprisonment, relied upon what it was led to believe to be the minimal involvement of defendant. Upon subsequently discovering that defendant was a major piece rather than a pawn in the fraudulent scheme, the court acted quite correctly in refusing to impose the promised sentence but allowing defendant to withdraw his guilty plea. The case demonstrates that it is useful for the pleading court to note on the record its reasons or qualifications in proposing to impose any given sentence. A defendant, sophisticated in the criminal process, who has misled, or lied to the court, should not, at least on this record, be heard to contend that his plea was induced by an off-the-record promise.

Accordingly, the orders in each of the appeals should be affirmed.

People v. Allen
86 N.Y.2d 599 (1995)

OPINION OF THE COURT: (Re: Waiver of rights in plea bargain, 220.10)

After a jury was selected and sworn and opening arguments scheduled in defendant's trial, the prosecutor requested and was granted a one-day continuance because his first witness had suffered a heart attack that morning and was hospitalized. The next day, after speaking with the witness' physician, the court informed counsel and the defendant that the heart attack had been massive and the witness would be unavailable for at least seven weeks. The prosecutor requested a second continuance which was denied by the court. The People then moved for a mistrial, which was granted over objection by the defense. In granting the motion for a mistrial, the court found that a mistrial was manifestly necessary owing to the critical nature of the witness' testimony. On the day defendant's second trial was scheduled to begin, defendant entered a plea of guilty to two counts. As a condition of the plea to the lesser charges, defendant waived his right to appeal, and expressly waived any claim of double jeopardy.

After sentencing, defendant appealed the judgment of conviction to the Appellate Division, arguing that his purported waiver of his right to appeal on the constitutional double jeopardy ground was invalid, and that the trial court erred in finding manifest necessity for a mistrial. The Appellate Division affirmed the conviction holding that although the waiver was invalid, the trial court properly granted the motion for a mistrial based on manifest necessity. Leave was granted to defendant by a Judge of this Court and, for a reason different from that stated by the Appellate Division, we affirm.

Defendant asserts that as a matter of State double jeopardy law (NY Const, art I, §6) the double jeopardy defense is among the categories of defenses that are not waivable as part of a plea bargain, and thus, that he may raise his double jeopardy claim on this appeal despite his express waiver of the claim as part of his plea bargain. He contends that because the double jeopardy defense has such strong ties with the concept of, it goes directly to the power of the courts to prosecute the defendant. Thus, he argues, a court has no jurisdiction over a defendant who has objected to a mistrial and, therefore, like other defenses that are fundamental to the integrity of the criminal process, a double jeopardy defense cannot be validly waived. Defendant's claims are unsupported by our precedents and are otherwise unpersuasive. We have expressly recognized that a double jeopardy objection may be waivable in certain unusual cases, as where a defendant explicitly consents to retrial despite a double jeopardy defense. Moreover, when a defendant by the conduct of counsel impliedly consents to a retrial after a mistrial, double jeopardy does not bar a retrial. We can discern no substantive basis to make a distinction between an implied consent to retrial, as in Ferguson, and the express waiver of a double jeopardy defense to retrial presented here.

A defendant's claim of double jeopardy is different from those narrow categories of appellate claims that cannot be waived as part of a plea bargain. Plea bargaining is now established as a vital part of our criminal justice. It enables the parties to avoid the delay and uncertainties of trial and appeal and permits swift and certain punishment of law violators with sentences tailored to the circumstances of the case at hand. The pleading process necessarily includes the surrender of many guaranteed rights but when there is no constitutional or statutory mandate and no public policy prohibiting it, an accused may waive any right which he or she enjoys.

To be sure, we have recognized narrow exceptions to the general rule that an accused may waive any right he or she enjoys as part of a plea bargain; certain categories of appellate claims may not be waived. These include the constitutionally protected right to a speedy, challenges to the legality of court-imposed sentences and questions as to the defendant's competency to stand trial. These appellate claims cannot be waived because of a larger societal interest in their correct resolution.

Society has a recognized interest in speedy trials because trial delay may result in the loss of evidence or an accused's inability to respond to criminal charges, thereby compelling innocent persons to plead guilty out of necessity. Because of this societal interest, a defendant may not waive such claims. Similarly, a defendant may not waive the right to challenge the legality of a sentence or his competency to stand trial. These rights are recognized as a matter of fairness to the accused but they also embrace the reality of fairness in the process itself.

None of the societal interests which formed the basis of our decisions in the cases holding that a certain appellate claim is nonwaivable is presented in the case of double jeopardy. For although double jeopardy has jurisdictional overtones, the purpose of applying the double jeopardy bar to situations in which no final determination of guilt or innocence has been made is to protect the valued right of a defendant to have his trial completed by the particular tribunal summoned to sit in judgment on him. The defendant who expressly waives a double jeopardy defense as part of a plea bargain after a mistrial may forgo the right to be tried by a particular tribunal in exchange for a definite sentence and protection against the possibility of conviction on the highest counts because such waiver does not implicate a larger societal value.

As the foregoing discussion demonstrates, no policy or societal interest requires us to place double jeopardy in a category with other nonwaivable defenses. Thus, the general rule applies and the defendant is bound by his express waiver of his double jeopardy claim.

Accordingly, the order of the Appellate Division should be affirmed.

People v. Harris

61 N.Y.2d 9 (1983)

OPINION OF THE COURT: (Re: Waiver of constitutional rights on guilty plea, 220.50)

The critical issue common to this six appeal is whether a prior felony conviction, based upon a guilty plea which was entered without the defendant having been advised by the court of the specific constitutional rights being waived by that plea, may constitute a predicate felony for the purpose of sentencing the defendant as a second felony offender. In each case, the People have sought an increased sentence of imprisonment under section 70.06 of the Penal Law, which authorizes harsher penalties for second felony offenders. The defendant has challenged the use of his respective prior felony conviction alleging a defective guilty plea.

At the outset, it should be stated that the procedure to be followed for determining whether a defendant is a second felony offender is set forth in CPL 400.21. This section places upon the People the burden of proving beyond a reasonable doubt the existence of the previous felony conviction, but not its constitutionality. Once the fact of the prior conviction has been established, it is then incumbent upon the defendant to allege and prove the facts underlying the claim that the conviction was unconstitutionally obtained. Upon reviewing the records on this appeal, we conclude, for the reasons stated, that the defendant did not sustain his burdens, and the presumptions of the validity and regularity of the previous felony convictions were not overcome by substantial evidence to the contrary.

A conviction obtained in violation of one's constitutional rights may not be used to enhance punishment for another offense. Consistent with that principle, CPL 400.21 provides that a previous conviction which was obtained in violation of the rights of the defendant under the applicable provisions of the constitution of the United States must not be counted in determining whether the defendant has been subjected to a predicate felony conviction. Likewise, this court has on numerous occasions repeated that an alleged second or third felony offender could question the validity of the predicate conviction at the time he was resentenced.

But this court has never held, and we refuse to so hold now, that a predicate conviction upon a guilty plea is invalid solely because the Trial Judge failed to specifically enumerate all the rights to which the defendant was entitled and to elicit from him or her a list of detailed waivers before accepting the guilty plea. There is no requirement for a uniform mandatory catechism of pleading defendants. Though a rigorous and detailed colloquy may be appropriate in certain instances, under most ordinary circumstances such questioning by the Trial Judge would be an unnecessary formalism. The seriousness of the crime, the competency, experience and actual participation by counsel, the rationality of the "plea bargain," and the pace of the proceedings in the particular criminal court are among the many factors which the Trial Judge must consider in exercising discretion. But as we have emphasized on a previous occasion, there is no requirement that the Judge conduct a pro forma inquisition in each case on the off-chance that a defendant who is adequately represented by counsel may nevertheless not know what he is doing. Overall, a sound discretion, exercised in cases on an individual basis is preferable to a ritualistic uniform procedure.

On the other hand, a record that is silent will not overcome the presumption against waiver by a defendant of constitutionally guaranteed protections. To be sure, the record must show an intentional relinquishment or abandonment of a known right or privilege. Presuming waiver from a silent record is impermissible. The record must show, or there must be an allegation and evidence which show, that an accused intelligently and understandingly rejected his constitutional rights. Anything less is not waiver. The key issue is whether the defendant knowingly, voluntarily and intelligently relinquished his rights upon his guilty plea.

Turning to the appeal before us, in People v. Harris, the trial court sentencing defendant as a second felony offender rejected defendant's claim that the predicate felony conviction had been unconstitutionally obtained. The record of the prior proceeding revealed that Harris had offered to plead guilty on the condition that he be immediately paroled and placed under the supervision of a drug rehabilitation program. It further showed that Harris was represented by counsel, that he was advised by the Trial Judge that by pleading guilty he was waiving his rights to a jury trial and to confront witnesses against him, that he stated that he had discussed his plea with his attorney, that he was pleading freely, and that he admitted his guilt and acknowledged the facts underlying his commission of the crime. Upon examining the record, the trial court found that the allocution had been sufficient and that the predicate felony conviction had been constitutionally obtained, and Harris was sentenced as a second felony offender. The Appellate Division likewise rejected Harris' challenge of the earlier guilty plea and we agree that the record affirmatively demonstrates that the plea was entered intelligently and freely.

Accordingly, the order of the Appellate Division should be affirmed.

Sec. 8.3; Article 245; Discovery

People v. Rosario
9 N.Y.2d 286 (1961)

OPINION OF THE COURT: (Re: Previous statements of prosecution witnesses, 245)

The appellant Luis Rosario stands convicted of murder in the first degree stemming from the death of a restaurant proprietor shot during the course of a robbery which the appellant and two accomplices committed and, on the record before us, there can be no possible doubt of his guilt. Indeed, he does not contest the sufficiency of the evidence, but he does raise a question which involves an important problem in the administration of the criminal law and merits our attention and consideration. It is the appellant's contention that the trial judge committed reversible error in refusing to turn over to defense counsel, for cross-examination purposes, statements given some time before the trial by three prosecution witnesses.

After each of these three witnesses had concluded his or her direct testimony, defense counsel requested that the witness' prior statements be turned over to them for possible use on cross-examination. Instead, the statements were submitted to the trial judge for his inspection. After reading each statement, he announced that he found some "variances" between statement and testimony and told defense counsel that they might examine and use only those portions of the statement containing the variances. In other words, he refused the request that the entire statement be given to the defense so that counsel might "determine for themselves" whether any other portions would be helpful upon cross-examination.

When it appears that a witness for the prosecution has made a statement, to police, district attorney or grand jury, the attorney for the defendant, naturally enough, desires to see it in the hope that it may assist him to impeach and discredit that witness. The question then arises whether the statement should forthwith be delivered to the defense or whether it should be handed over only if it is found, on inspection by the court, to contain material at variance with the witness' testimony in court. The United States Supreme Court has held that a defendant "is entitled to inspect" any statement made by the Government's witness which bears on the subject matter of the witness' testimony (see *Jencks v. United States*, 353 U.S. 657) whereas in New York we have allowed the defendant to see and use the statement only if it contains matter which is inconsistent with the testimony given by the witness from the stand.

The procedure to be followed turns largely on policy considerations, and upon further study and reflection this court is persuaded that a right sense of justice entitles the defense to examine a witness' prior statement, whether or not it varies from his testimony on the stand. As long as the statement relates to the subject matter of the witness' testimony and contains nothing that must be kept confidential, defense counsel should be allowed to determine for themselves the use to be made of it on cross-examination.

A pretrial statement of a witness for the prosecution is valuable not just as a source of contradictions with which to confront him and discredit his trial testimony. Even statements seemingly in harmony with such testimony may contain matter which will prove helpful on cross-examination. They may reflect a witness' bias, for instance, or otherwise supply the defendant with knowledge essential to the neutralization of the damaging testimony of the witness which might, perhaps, turn the scales in his favor. Shades of meaning, stress, additions or omissions may be found which will place the witness' answers upon direct examination in an entirely different light. As the United States Supreme Court has so well observed, "Flat contradiction between the witness' testimony and the version of the events given [previously] * * * is not the only test of inconsistency. The omission from the reports of facts related at the trial, or a contrast in emphasis upon the same facts, even a different order of treatment, are also relevant to the cross-examining process of testing the credibility of a witness' trial testimony." (*Jencks v. United States*, 353 U.S. 667, supra.)

Furthermore, omissions, contrasts and even contradictions, vital perhaps, for discrediting a witness, are certainly not as apparent to the impartial presiding judge as to single-minded counsel for the accused; the latter is in a far better position to appraise the value of a witness' pretrial statements for impeachment purposes. Until his attorney has an opportunity to see the statement, it is asked, how can he effectively answer the trial judge's assertion that it contains nothing at variance with the testimony given or, at least, useful to him in his attempt to discredit such witness?

It is our conclusion, therefore, that the trial judge should have turned over to the defendant the requested statements in their entirety. In this instance, though, we deem it not amiss to consider whether the ruling which he made prejudiced the defendant, whether, in other words, there was a rational possibility that the jury would have reached a different verdict if the defense had been allowed the use of the witness' prior statements. We believe not. On the record before us, there can be no possible question of the appellant's guilt, even apart from the testimony of the witnesses whose statements had been requested and refused. Not only was there evidence of admission to friends before and after the fatal robbery, not only was there proof of a confession to the district attorney, not only was there evidence of flight, but there was ballistics testimony indicating that the lethal bullet had issued from the appellant's gun. And, of the utmost significance, examination of the prior statements discloses that the few variances contained in them were of a most inconsequential character.

This court is exceeding slow to disregard error as harmless particularly in a capital case. However, in the one before us, we are as convinced as judges may ever be, in view of the overwhelming proof of guilt and the absence of any real inconsistency between prior statement and trial testimony, that the jury would not have decided the case differently even if defense counsel had had the use of the statements in question. In other words, it may not be said that any substantial right of the appellant was prejudiced by the trial court's erroneous ruling.

The judgment of conviction should be affirmed.

In the Matter of David M. v. Dwyer
107 A.D.2d 884 (3rd Dept. 1985)

OPINION OF THE COURT: (Re: Bodily intrusions, 245)

Proceeding pursuant to CPLR article 78 to prohibit respondents from obtaining blood and hair samples of petitioner. Petitioner is a 17-year-old male who was arrested and charged with murder in the second degree, robbery in the first degree and burglary in the first degree. Following a preliminary examination, the City of Troy Police Court dismissed these charges for lack of probable cause. Petitioner was thereupon discharged from custody as to the felony charges, but remained incarcerated in the

Albany County Jail on pending unrelated matters. To further their investigation of the felony charges, the People thereafter sought an order compelling petitioner to provide blood and hair samples. The County Court of Rensselaer County granted this application in an order dated October 3, 1984; that order has been stayed pending determination of this proceeding.

A CPLR article 78 proceeding in the nature of prohibition is a remedy which may be availed of by a suspect who seeks protection from a court order directing that he furnish bodily samples. To secure such an order, the People must establish the following three elements:

(1) probable cause to believe the suspect has committed the crime,

(2) a 'clear indication' that relevant material evidence will be found, and

(3) the method used to secure it is safe and reliable.

In addition, the issuing court must weigh the seriousness of the crime, the importance of the evidence to the investigation and the unavailability of less intrusive means of obtaining it, on the one hand, against concern for the suspect's constitutional right to be free from bodily intrusion on the other.

Initially, petitioner contends that probable cause to believe that he committed the crimes under investigation was lacking, not only because the People have not yet indicted him but also because the evidence purporting to incriminate him is hearsay. A formal charge, however, is not a precondition for a judicial directive compelling a suspect to make himself available for the drawing of his blood. A finding of "reasonable cause" or "probable cause," which terms are interchangeable here can, by statute, be based on reliable hearsay evidence. Attached to the People's moving papers in support of their application for permission to take petitioner's blood and hair samples are statements from various people containing inculpatory admissions allegedly made by petitioner. The People also have possession of a sweat shirt allegedly worn by petitioner at the time of the crime; the sweat shirt was bloodstained, presumably as a result of petitioner's participation in the crime. In our view, probable cause was established.

There is merit, however, to petitioner's contention that there is no clear indication that the intrusion sought will supply substantial probative evidence. While the scientific validity and reliability of tests used to identify and collate blood samples are not open to question, the only evidence put before County Court by the People consists of an affidavit from an evidence technician with the Troy Police Department who "observed numerous blood stains in and about the area where the deceased was lying," and the bloodstained sweat shirt worn by petitioner. There are no serological tests establishing that blood other than that of the decedent was found at the crime scene or that the blood on the sweatshirt was of the decedent's type. Furthermore, petitioner is not the only suspect; another person already has been indicted. In short, the People have not satisfactorily demonstrated the conclusiveness or probative value of the blood test they seek.

Nor, on the present record, is the taking of hair samples from petitioner warranted. To support this request, the People merely offer the evidence technician's averment that: "at the autopsy, [he] personally removed several hairs from the body of the deceased, which did not appear to be in a natural state. * * * These hairs were found lying upon the body of the deceased, not attached to [it] in any way, and were of such a nature that they did not appear to belong on that portion of the deceased's person." What, if any, scientific importance comparison tests of hair have and whether performing them will narrow the field of suspects to any appreciable degree is not set forth.

Since the conclusiveness or probative value of the proposed tests comparing blood and hair samples has not been satisfactorily established, a hearing should be held and expert testimony received on these). In the interim, determination of this proceeding will be held in abeyance. Decision withheld, and matter remitted to the County Court of Rensselaer County for further proceedings not inconsistent herewith.

People v. Wesley
140 Misc. 2d 306 (Albany Cty Ct. 1988)

OPINION OF THE COURT: (Re: admissibility of DNA evidence, 245)

In each of the cases herein the People move for an order to extract blood from the respective defendant for the purpose of comparing the DNA therein with DNA contained in biological evidence reasonably believed to be relevant in each respective case. In People v. Bailey, the defendant is charged with rape in the first degree; the evidence believed to be relevant is an aborted fetus. In People v. Wesley, the defendant is charged with burglary in the second degree and suspected of murder in the second degree. Bloodstained clothing was retrieved from the defendant; the People proposed to compare the DNA contained in said bloodstains with DNA extracted from the deceased victim and for control purposes with DNA to be extracted from a known blood sample of defendant Wesley.

The process sought to be used by the People is colloquially and most frequently referred to in forensic science as "DNA fingerprinting," by which name the test will in this decision be hereinafter called.

DNA fingerprinting is at the "cutting edge" of forensic science, just as molecular biology and genetic engineering are at the "cutting edge" of revolutionary applications in medicine and control of such genetic or genetic-influenced diseases as diabetes, diverse forms of cancer, muscular dystrophy, Down's Syndrome, and Acquired Immune Deficiency Syndrome (AIDS).

DNA fingerprinting is a genetic and molecular biological process that has its basis in the fact that each individual has an entirely unique genetic "signature," derived in turn from the fact that the over-all configuration of the DNA, found in every cell in the human body (and for that matter, in every living organism) containing a nucleus — over 99% of the cells of the human body is different in every individual except in the case of identical twins. This fact is not only generally accepted by the scientific community to which it is related, but is uniformly accepted therein.

Related to this fact and fully accepted by the scientific community is the further fact that in each individual the configuration of DNA contained in one cell is the same for every cell in the body of that individual. Thus, for the purpose of DNA fingerprinting, DNA for comparative purposes can be obtained from blood, semen, hair roots, skin, and indeed from over 99% of the cells of the human body.

The immediate advantage of DNA fingerprinting, in addition to its ability to utilize a vaster source of obtainable biological evidence than heretofore was the case — practically any portion of the human body — is the claimed certainty of identification. Blood-grouping identification tests often can narrow down the number of suspects to from 30 to 40% of the population. The laboratory the People propose to utilize claims a mean power of certainty of identification for American Whites of 1 in 840,000,000; for American Blacks, 1 in 1.4 billion. There are approximately only five billion people in the entire world.

The overwhelming enormity of these figures, if DNA fingerprinting proves acceptable in criminal courts, will revolutionize the administration of criminal justice. Where applicable, it would reduce to insignificance the standard alibi defense. In the area of eyewitness testimony, which has been claimed to be responsible for more miscarriages of justice than any other type of evidence, again, where applicable, DNA fingerprinting would tend to reduce the importance of eyewitness testimony. And in the area of clogged calendars and the conservation of judicial resources, DNA fingerprinting, if accepted, will revolutionize the disposition of criminal cases. In short, if DNA fingerprinting works and receives evidentiary acceptance, it can constitute the single greatest advance in the "search for truth," and the goal of convicting the guilty and acquitting the innocent, since the advent of cross-examination.

Further, the compilation of a DNA fingerprint data base, such as that in existence for ordinary fingerprints, will enormously enhance the ability of law enforcement to reduce the number of unsolved crimes that currently occur daily.

The matter of the admissibility of DNA fingerprinting as a contested issue in the courts of the State of New York is a matter of first impression. Thus it was necessary herein that a Frye hearing be held to determine the admissibility of this new kind of scientific evidence. Because of the above and other overwhelming implications of DNA fingerprinting, it was necessary that this hearing be both extensive and intensive, so that a record be produced of a quality and thoroughness sufficient for the Court of Appeals ultimately to decide this matter. This resulted in a sharply contested hearing commencing December 11, 1987, and continuing on diverse dates thereafter, entailing the testimony of numerous witnesses prominent in the scientific fields of molecular biology, population genetics, and other diverse areas of genetics and human genetics, producing a transcript of over a thousand pages.

THE LAW

The ultimate standard for the admission of scientific evidence in the State of New York, even though refinements have been added by the appellate courts of the State of New York, is *Frye v. United States* (293 F 1013 [Dec. 3, 1923]). In that case the

Court of Appeals of the District of Columbia stated:" Just when a scientific principle or discovery crosses the line between the experimental and demonstrable stages is difficult to define. Somewhere in this twilight zone the evidential force of the principle must be recognized, and while courts will go a long way in admitting expert testimony deduced from a well-recognized scientific principle or discovery, the thing from which the deduction is made must be sufficiently established to have gained general acceptance in the particular field in which it belongs." (supra, at 1014.)

The New York Court of Appeals refined the Frye standard, stating the test is not whether a particular procedure is unanimously indorsed by the scientific community, but whether it is generally acceptable as reliable.

THE SCIENCE — THEORY, PRINCIPLES AND TECHNOLOGY

A Genetic and Biological Primer

The particular scientific fields that govern DNA fingerprinting are molecular biology, genetics, and a specialized branch of genetics known as population genetics. In order to understand DNA fingerprinting it is helpful to have a basic knowledge of genetics and cellular biology. To this end the court presents the following brief genetic and biological primer: (Omitted here)

The DNA evidence is admissible in the rape and murder prosecutions. DNA fingerprinting is a scientific test that is reliable and has gained acceptance in the scientific community. The evidence indicated the procedures used by the laboratory conducting the DNA fingerprinting were accurate and it is generally accepted in the scientific community that the DNA fingerprinting test is incapable of giving a false match or false positive results.

Sec. 8.5; Article 255; Pre-Trial Motions

People v. Coleman

452 N.Y.S.2d 503 (1982)

OPINION OF THE COURT: (Re: Failure to comply with 45-day rule, 255.20)

Defendants Thomas Coleman, Michael Dukes and Derrick Hoover were, inter alia, indicted for robbery in the first degree and arraigned on February 11, 1982. No pretrial motions were made by any of the defendants within the following 45 days. Thereafter the People moved on April 2, 1982 to preclude the defendants from serving pretrial motions and demand for discovery. CPL 255.20 (subds. 1, 3) in part provides:

"1. Except as otherwise expressly provided by law, whether the defendant is represented by counsel or elects to proceed pro se, all pretrial motions shall be made within forty-five days after arraignment and before commencement of trial, or within such additional time as the court may fix upon application of the defendant made prior to entry of judgment * * *

"3. Notwithstanding the provisions of subdivisions one and two hereof, the court must entertain and decide on its merits, at anytime before the end of the trial, any appropriate pretrial motion based upon grounds of which the defendant could not, with due diligence, have been previously aware, or which, for other good cause, could not reasonably have been raised within the period specified in subdivision one of this section or included within the single set of motion papers as required by subdivision two. Any other pre-trial motion made after the forty-five day period may be summarily denied, but the court, in the interest of justice, and for good cause shown, may, in its discretion, at any time before sentence, entertain and dispose of the motion on the merits."

Contemporaneously with the People's application Coleman's attorney made an "omnibus motion" to which the District Attorney has responded. Hoover has not answered the motion at all while Dukes' attorney responded by first preparing an omnibus motion which was dated April 13, 1982 (making it returnable on April 14, 1982 and presumably serving it on the return day). In a supporting affirmation, Dukes' attorney sought to explain and excuse the failure to make the pretrial motions within the required period. He states that although an attorney from his office appeared at the arraignment on February 11, 1982, he did not receive the case until approximately one week thereafter. Upon reviewing the file he discovered that Dukes was represented by a Victor Kleinfeld on a prior matter pending in Criminal Court. Knowing that said Victor Kleinfeld was representing codefendant Hoover in the instant matter, he initiated an intraoffice procedure to determine the exact circumstances of the legal representation and whether there was a conflict of interest. Dukes' attorney argues that this period of approximately 24 days should toll the statute. He argues further that he was actually engaged on trial in other matters and this time should also be excluded. Finally, he argues that despite the expiration of the 45-day period, the court, in the exercise of its discretion, should allow the pretrial motions since the People have suffered no prejudice by the delay.

The District Attorney, on the other hand, contends that the defendant waives his right to pretrial motions in the absence of good cause once the 45-day period has expired (and that the motion to preclude should not be treated as a notice of demand but rather as a means by which the waiver is confirmed).

The issue therefore presented is whether CPL 255.20 mandates preclusion against the defendants, and if so, to what extent. As to Hoover there can be little doubt that there should be preclusion since, as previously indicated he never made any pretrial motions nor answered the People's motion to preclude. As to Coleman, he should be precluded also as to the remaining pretrial motions which it might have been possible to make. With Dukes, since it is not disputed that more than 45 days have elapsed since arraignment, the question becomes whether there are any circumstances or legal reasons why certain periods should be excluded so as to toll the statute. Stripped to its essentials, Dukes' attorney alleges that during part of the period he was both on trial in other matters and also trying to determine whether he should continue to represent the defendant. It is readily apparent that these reasons, with overtones of law office failure, would hardly excuse a civil default and are just as obviously insufficient to justify a failure to make pretrial motions in a criminal case. To hold otherwise would mean that defense attorneys could, with impunity, take no action on a pending indictment so long as they were involved in any other trial or inquiry.

It must also be noted that there are strong policy reasons supporting strict enforcement of CPL 255.20. The CPL places upon the People the burden of giving the defendant a speedy trial (CPL 30.30). It seems consistent and fair that another provision of the CPL which seeks to speed the administration of criminal justice be accorded the same importance even where the burden of such provision falls on the defendant. CPL 255.20 creates an unambiguous requirement that the defendant show good cause before an untimely omnibus motion may be determined favorably on his behalf. Thus the fact that the People appear not to be prejudiced by the delay cannot inure to the benefit of the defendant.

The affirmation presented to the court is so insufficient in explanation that I must conclude that Dukes has failed to show good cause for failing to make the motion within 45 days following arraignment. Preclusion therefore appears warranted by CPL 255.20. This conclusion may appear harsh especially since the tardiness is of relatively short duration. Nevertheless, for the court to disregard the violation of the 45-day requirement where no good cause has been shown would arbitrarily negative a very clear legislative injunction. Final determination of the matter, however, demands resolution of an issue which pertains to all the defendants herein. That is, would preclusion, regardless of delay, constitute a violation of a defendant's right to due process and a fair trial?

This issue turns on whether the matters precluded adversely affect the truth-determining process and so undermine fundamental constitutional rights. In the absence of such factors a defendant's unexcused failure to move within 45 days of arraignment should be deemed a waiver. In sum, what emerges is the realization that despite a failure to act within the time parameters of CPL 255.20, a defendant may still be entitled to relief when the consequences affect the accuracy and fairness of the truth-finding process of the trial.

Applying the above principles to the motion at bar, it becomes apparent that insofar as Dukes' pretrial motion would seek to suppress an inculpatory statement as well as tangible evidence, the motion should be summarily denied. There are no compelling reasons to abandon the 45-day requirement as to those matters. They do not affect the truth-finding process since a failure to suppress evidence may well enhance such process. Moreover, the issue of voluntariness of the statement can be raised anew at the trial itself.

Similarly, insofar as the motion seeks to dismiss the indictment after inspection of the Grand Jury minutes, it too may be summarily denied since a defect in this regard would be deemed cured. A conviction supported by legally sufficient evidence. The remaining items of Dukes' omnibus motion regarding a bill of particulars and discovery, may not be denied because they relate directly to the accuracy of the truth-finding process. The inability to obtain information to prepare his case would infringe upon the defendant's constitutional right to a fair trial pursuant to the Sixth Amendment.

It should be noted that the Sandoval motion, while included with Dukes' omnibus motion, is not a "pretrial motion" within the purview of CPL 255.10 and hence is not subject to the time strictures of CPL 255.20. A hearing on that issue should accordingly be allowed.

The People's motion to preclude is therefore granted as to defendants Hoover and Coleman (relating to those pretrial motions not heretofore made and not mandated in the interest of a fair trial) and further granted as to defendant Dukes except that it is denied as to items 6 (bill of particulars and discovery) and 7 (Sandoval) of Dukes' omnibus motion. Of course, if any of the defendants can show that the interest of justice warrants the grant of pretrial relief at this late date they may submit such motion as permitted by CPL 255.20 (subd. 3).

Chapter 9; Prosecution of Indictments in Superior Court; from Trial to Sentence

Sec. 9.1; Article 260; Jury Trial — Generally

People v. Morales

80 N.Y.2d 450 (1992)

OPINION OF THE COURT: (Re: Defendant's right to be present, 260.20)

Did defendant have a right to be present when the trial court preliminarily examined a child-witness to determine whether she understood the nature of an oath? We conclude that defendant did not have that right, and accordingly sustain his conviction.

In March 1988, defendant was indicted for rape, sodomy and other crimes against R.H. and E.T., children with whom he lived for several years in the role of stepfather. Both children testified at trial; E.T. was at that time 13 years old and R.H. nine. As R.H. was less than 12, the trial court was required to find that she understood "the nature of an oath" before she could give sworn testimony (CPL 60.20 [2]).

The court conducted a competency inquiry after trial had commenced, but outside the jury's presence. Informing defense counsel that the proceeding was "not something that your client has a right to be present at," the Judge excluded defendant from the hearing so the child would not be "distracted by anyone at all." The court permitted defense counsel and the prosecutor to attend but not directly examine the witness, asking instead for submission of any additional questions the attorneys might wish to have posed.

After several general questions about school, the Judge asked R.H. if she knew why she was in court, to which she answered: "Because Edwin, the father of my brothers, he did fresh things to me." The court then ascertained whether the child knew the difference between telling the truth and a lie, and her understanding of the consequences of lying. The court also assured itself that the child would testify only from personal knowledge, and would respond "I don't know" or "I forgot" as necessary. Finally, at defense counsel's request, the court asked R.H. if she understood the roles of the Judge, prosecutor and defense counsel.

At the conclusion of the inquiry, the court found that R.H. was capable of giving sworn testimony. The jury convicted defendant of rape and sodomy. Defendant appealed, arguing his statutory rights to be present at trial were violated when he was barred from the competency hearing. The Appellate Division unanimously rejected defendant's claims, and we affirm.

As the only purpose of a CPL 60.20 hearing is to determine a witness' testimonial capacity, it is plain that the proceeding is unrelated to the basic issues at trial. No evidentiary testimony is taken — that is the function of trial; rather, the sole issue under consideration is the mental capacity of a prospective witness. Consequently, although the hearing may take place in the midst of trial, it can also be conducted pretrial. Indeed, pretrial inquiry may lead to a finding that a child lacks capacity to testify, and thus to dismissal of all or part of the case. Alternatively, a finding that a child could provide only unsworn testimony would alert the parties to the need for corroboration.

The Criminal Procedure Law mandates that a "defendant must be personally present during the trial of an indictment" (CPL 260.20). This statute serves a dual purpose: "To prevent the ancient evil of secret trials" and to "guarantee the defendant's right to be present at all important stages" of trial. Interpreting the statute, we have held that the word "trial" includes "impaneling the jury, the introduction of evidence, the summing up of counsel, and the charge of the court to the jury, receiving and recording the verdict." To the extent there is a concern about secret trials, defendant's presence serves a symbolic function, and thus the right does not rest exclusively on defendant's potential contribution to the proceedings. Indeed, a defendant's appearance at rendition of the verdict could serve little practical function, yet defendant has a right to be present. Trial in absentia is impermissible except in limited circumstances (see, CPL 260.20 [disorderly and disruptive defendant may be removed from courtroom]).

Apart from the core segments of trial, prosecutions entail myriad ancillary proceedings, some conducted pretrial, others during trial (e.g., Sandoval hearing, voir dire of prospective jurors, hearing on admissibility of alleged threats, hearing on disqualification of seated juror, pretrial motion to suppress).

That is not to say that Our statutory provision is not coextensive with Federal due process — some of our decisions give greater protections than appear to be constitutionally required. Rather, based on our own body of State law, we look to the effect that defendant's absence might have on the opportunity to defend.

Accordingly, we found no abrogation of the defendant's rights when he was absent from a precharge conference, or a colloquy regarding sufficiency of a readback, but have held that where defendant has something valuable to contribute, presence is generally required. The distinction between core segments of trial and ancillary proceedings is important for a State law analysis because a defendant usually has an un-fettered right to attend trial — regardless of his or her potential contribution — but only a qualified right to attend ancillary proceedings. As discussed earlier, a CPL 60.20 hearing is not a core part of the trial and indeed could have been conducted pretrial. Therefore, we must evaluate the extent to which defendant's exclusion affected his ability to defend.

Accordingly, the order of the Appellate Division should be affirmed.

People v. Antommarchi
80 N.Y.2d 247 (1992)

OPINION OF THE COURT: (Re: Right to be present at voir dire, 260.20)

A jury has convicted defendant of criminal possession of a controlled substance in the third degree and the Appellate Division has affirmed. He seeks reversal con-tending that (1) he was denied his statutory right to be present during a material stage of the proceedings (see, US Const. 6th, 14th Amends; NY Const, art I, § 6; CPL 260.20). We agree that defendant was denied the right to be present during a material stage of the trial.

Defendant's claim is based upon his absence during part of the proceedings when the jury was impaneled. He was present in the courtroom when the court began the voir dire by asking prospective jurors to respond orally to questions contained in a questionnaire and to follow-up questions posed by the court and counsel. Thereafter, several prospective jurors, at the court's invitation, went to the bench to speak about matters they did not wish to discuss publicly. The discussions were held on the record and in the presence of counsel, but without defendant. They addressed such matters as whether individual jurors would be able to remain objective despite experiences as crime victims or relationships with people who had been arrested, and whether they thought that defendant was guilty merely because he had been charged with participating in a drug sale. The court also asked at least one juror whether she could objectively assess the testimony of a police officer without being influenced by her friendships with other police officers.

As we have noted before, a defendant has a fundamental right to be present during any material stage of the trial and questioning during the side-bar discussions with prospective jurors in a defendant's absence if the questions relate to juror qualifications such as physical impairments, family obligations and work commitments. The court may not, however, explore prospective jurors' backgrounds and their ability to weigh the evidence objectively unless defendant is present. Defendants are entitled to hear questions intended to search out a prospective juror's bias, hostility or predisposition to believe or discredit the testimony of potential witnesses and the venire person's answers so that they have the opportunity to assess the juror's "facial expressions, demeanor and other subliminal responses."

By questioning the prospective jurors' ability to weigh evidence objectively and to hear testimony impartially, the court violated defendant's right to be present during a material part of the trial. Moreover, because defendant had a fundamental right to be present, his failure to object to being excluded from the side-bar discussions is not fatal to his claim.

Accordingly, the order of the Appellate Division should be reversed and a new trial ordered.

People v. Byrnes
33 N.Y.2d 343 (1974)

OPINION OF THE COURT: (Re: Removal of defendant for disruptive behavior, 260.20)

Following a jury trial in Nassau County Court, the defendant Thomas Byrnes was convicted of rape, sodomy and incest. His conviction was unanimously affirmed by the Appellate Division and leave to appeal was granted by a Judge of this court.

At the trial, the complainant, defendant's daughter, then 11 years of age, testified that on two occasions, in November, 1970 and March, 1971, she and her father went to the home of one Gene Abrams, where Abrams photographed them in the nude engaging in various sexual acts. A series of photographs, produced from negatives seized at the Abrams home pursuant to a warrant and admitted into evidence over defendant's objection, variously depicted an adult male and a young female engaged in acts of intercourse and sodomy.

The Trial Judge excluded the defendant from the courtroom during the testimony of the complaining witness because of what he characterized as deliberate disruptive behavior by the defendant calculated to intimidate the witness. The defendant contends that the exclusion was an accommodation to the witness and an impermissible punishment for his prior disruptive behavior, all in violation of his right to confront the witnesses against him.

While the right of an accused to be present at every stage of a trial is guaranteed by constitution and statute, the right may be lost where the defendant engages in misconduct so disruptive that the trial cannot properly proceed with him in the courtroom.

On the record before us, we find that the Trial Judge acted well within his discretion in excluding the defendant from the courtroom during the testimony of the complaining witness. Four outbursts punctuated by profane and abusive language preceded defendant's removal. Each related in some way to the prospect of the complainant testifying in court. On one of these occasions, it was necessary for the defendant to be restrained by Sheriff's Deputies. The court was careful to admonish the defendant that further outbursts would be cause for removal. At one point the defendant promised that he would comport himself properly, only again to become disruptive. The last of the four outbursts occurred when the complainant was called as a witness. As she entered the courtroom and took her seat, the defendant "leaped on the counsel table and lunged in the direction of the witness chair in an assaultive manner." He was again restrained by Sheriff's Deputies and this time was shackled. The witness was excused, as was the jury. The court again admonished the defendant, who said in substance that he did not intend to listen. The trial was then recessed for the day. The following day, when trial resumed, the court announced its decision to exclude the defendant during the complainant's testimony. Careful provision was made to insure communication between the defendant and his attorney during this period. Under these circumstances, we conclude that the defendant lost his right to be present.

For the reasons stated, the order of the Appellate Division is affirmed.

Sec. 9.2; Article 270; Jury Trial — Formation and Conduct of Jury

People v. Bolling
79 N.Y.2d 317 (1992)

OPINION OF THE COURT: (Re: Discriminatory peremptory challenges, 270.25)

These appeals, involving application of the rules developed in *Batson v. Kentucky* (476 US 79), raise two questions: (1) whether a prima facie showing of discrimination may be established before completion of the jury selection process and (2) whether defense counsel established a prima facie case that the prosecution had violated the Equal Protection Clauses of the Federal and State Constitutions by exercising peremptory challenges for discriminatory purposes. In *People v. Bolling*, we hold that defense counsel established a prima facie case and, inasmuch as the prosecutor failed to provide racially neutral reasons for his challenges, the judgment must be modified. In *People v. Steele*, we hold that a prima facie case was not established and consequently affirm the order of the Appellate Division.

In *Batson v. Kentucky* the prosecutor used peremptory challenges to strike four African-Americans from the jury so that defendant, an African-American, was tried by an all-Caucasian jury. The Supreme Court held that the Equal Protection Clause of the Fourteenth Amendment forbids the use of peremptory challenges solely for discriminatory purposes. Finding that a prima facie case of discrimination had been established, the Court remanded the case to enable the prosecutor to provide racially neutral reasons for the strikes or, in the absence thereof, for a new trial. The Court set forth three steps for establishing prima facie that the prosecutor used peremptory challenges to discriminate in selecting the petit jury. The defendant must show (1) that he or she is a member of a cognizable racial group, (2) that the prosecutor's use of peremptory challenges resulted in the exclusion of members of defendant's race from the jury, and (3) facts and other relevant circumstances sufficient to raise an inference that the prosecutor used the challenges for discriminatory purposes. Once the defendant makes a prima facie showing of discrimination, the burden shifts to the prosecution to present racially neutral explanations for the challenges. It cannot rebut defendant's prima facie case, however, by merely alleging its good faith or by claiming that the stricken jurors would be biased because they shared defendant's race. In the matters before us, defendants satisfied the first two requirements by showing that they are African-Americans and that the prosecution struck several African-American jurors. To satisfy the third, and raise an inference of discrimination, defendants allege a "pattern" of strikes used by the prosecution against African-Americans during the jury selection process. We conclude that a defendant may assert a claim that peremptory challenges are being used for discriminatory purposes when those challenges are exercised, regardless of whether jury selection has been completed.

There are no fixed rules for determining what evidence will give rise to an inference sufficient to establish a prima facie case of discrimination. In *Batson* the Supreme Court listed, as examples, a pattern of strikes or questions and statements made by the prosecutor during voir dire suggesting discriminatory motives. The defendant may also raise an inference of discrimination by making a record comparing Caucasians accepted with similarly situated African-Americans challenged, or by establishing objective facts indicating that the prosecutor has challenged members of a particular racial group who might be expected to favor the prosecution because of their backgrounds. The mere inclusion of some members of defendant's ethnic group will not defeat an otherwise meritorious motion. Although the racial distribution of those on the jury, as compared to the population generally, is not relevant to establish a prima facie case, a disproportionate number of strikes challenging members of a particular racial group within a venire may be sufficient to create an inference establishing a prima facie claim. Generally, however, percentages will not be conclusive of the issue. Finally, when a *Batson* objection has been made, defendant is entitled to the benefit of the proposition that peremptory challenges permit those inclined to discriminate to do so.

Because we have no record of the questions posed during voir dire in these cases, our determination must rest upon the claimed discriminatory pattern of strikes as they relate to the prospective jurors examined and the few facts developed during colloquy.

In *Bolling*, the prosecution exercised five peremptory challenges, four to exclude African-American members of the venire. African-Americans comprised 42% of the 12 prospective jurors, and 80% of them were excluded by the prosecution. This disproportionate number of challenges to African-American prospective jurors coupled with defendant's uncontested assertion that two of the four jurors excused by the Assistant District Attorney had pro-prosecution backgrounds was sufficient to raise an inference that the Assistant District Attorney had used his peremptories to discriminate. Accordingly, the court should have required the prosecutor to give reasons establishing that the strikes were for racially neutral reasons. If he was unable to do so, the court should have sustained the objection, and seated the juror notwithstanding the prosecutor's challenge. The reasons given for denying the motion, that the prosecution had subsequently accepted two African-American jurors, was legally irrelevant.

Defendant Steele also relies on a pattern of strikes. In her case, the prosecution struck three of the six African-Americans available. While the prosecutor exercised three of her four challenges against African-Americans, that alone is not sufficient to establish a pattern of exclusion of African-Americans. In the absence of a record demonstrating other facts or circumstances supporting a prima facie case, the defendant failed to establish a pattern of purposeful exclusion sufficient to raise an inference of discrimination.

Accordingly, in *People v. Bolling* the order of the Appellate Division should be modified by remitting to Supreme Court, New York County, for a hearing to afford the People an opportunity to provide racially neutral reasons for the exercise of their peremptory strikes. In the absence of such explanation, the judgment of conviction should be vacated and a new trial ordered. Should satisfactory explanation be provided by the People, the judgment of conviction should be amended to show that result. In *People v. Steele* the order should be affirmed.

People v. Payne

88 N.Y.2d 172 (1996)

OPINION OF THE COURT: (Re: Discriminatory peremptory challenges; application of procedures to determine allegations of discrimination, 270.25)

This Court recently refined the three-step procedure that trial courts are required to follow in determining allegedly discriminatory use of peremptory challenges against prospective jurors. These appeals in three unrelated cases require the Court to review the application of these procedures when the People assert discriminatory use of peremptory challenges by the defense. In all three cases, the trial courts upheld several objections from the People that defense peremptory strikes discriminated on the basis of race.

When one side in a criminal case claims that the other side's exercise of peremptory strikes is infected by purposeful discrimination, the trial court must engage in a three-step process. Initially, the party contesting the peremptory challenges — the prosecution in these three cases — must satisfy the court with a prima facie showing that the peremptory strikes related to the race of the jurors sought to be removed. If that threshold showing is met, the lawyer seeking the excusals — the defense in these three cases — has the burden of coming forward to overcome the inference of purposeful discrimination. To do so, that party must voice a "race-neutral explanation for striking the jurors in question. When the proffered explanations appear facially race-neutral, the trial court must then determine whether the opponent of the strike [here, the People] has proved purposeful racial discrimination. The focus at this third step is whether the "race-neutral" explanation is a mere pretext for racial discrimination. The ultimate burden of persuasion at the third stage rests unalterably on the party objecting to the peremptory strikes — in these three cases, the People.

A. In *People v. Payne*, the trial court required defense counsel to "[g]ive me race-neutral reasons." Defense counsel's explanation for his challenge to juror Number Eight was as follows:

"I just note for him, he's lived in the same neighborhood in Brooklyn for 50 years and that his criteria for judging a witness' credibility was limited. He seemed to believe that one would judge the credibility of a witness just by observing their body language and I think the Court Officers are going to be more calm witnesses than Mr. Payne will. So, I had a problem with that."

As to Number Nine, counsel stated: "[A]ll I could say was that I had trouble getting any information out of him. He sat there quietly for the most part. All his answers were yes or no and I'm insecure with that because I have no idea who this person is and that makes both me and Mr. Payne uncomfortable. We'd like to elicit dialogue from jurors and, so, we couldn't be confident that he could be fair and impartial."

Notably, counsel did not challenge other similarly situated jurors who had either lived in one place for a long time or gave laconic answers to counsel's questions.

After hearing defense counsel's proffered reasons, the trial court ruled that the peremptory challenge to juror Number Eight could not stand because the race-neutral explanation was "totally disingenuous." As to Number Nine, the trial court stated, "the fact that he answered yes or no, other jurors answered yes or no. You didn't challenge them. I find that to be a racially motivated challenge and I will disallow that challenge." The court allowed the defense peremptory challenges to Numbers Two and Six.

The Appellate Division affirmed, and on the pertinent issue ruled: "[T]he Supreme Court properly determined that the explanations proffered by defense counsel for the exercise of his peremptory challenges against the two subject panelists were mere pretext offered in an attempt to conceal a racially discriminatory intent. This determination is entitled to great deference on appeal and will not be disturbed where, as here, it is supported by the record"

B. In *People v. Jones*, as to juror Number Two, defense counsel stated: "[He] was challenged based on a consultation with my client. He, based on his own feelings regarding the types of individuals that he wanted to sit on the jury that would judge him, felt that juror number two did not respond in a way that he felt that that individual would be fair to him." Counsel articulated his challenge to juror Number Six as follows: "[H]is wife is a legal secretary and has experience in that area and, again, number six was one of the jurors that on consultation with my client, he again felt that one of the peremptory challenges that we have that he felt was to be used because of the way he felt about this particular person." The court found, however, that "the reasons given for [Numbers Two and Six] are pretextual and those jurors will be seated."

C. In *People v. Lowery*, defense counsel gave the following explanation for his challenge to juror Number Three, the only juror at issue on this appeal: "[B]asically, I looked at her, she's from Bay Ridge. I'm looking at — I would like to increase, have more the type of people who come from the neighborhood he comes from. She's from Bay Ridge. She's a high school teacher. "She didn't appeal to me, she didn't appeal — it's a peremptory challenge. She did not appeal to me." The court ordered Number Three to be seated over defendant's objection, but upheld the defense peremptory strikes for the other five. The court stated, "That one is overruled on the basis of the objection made. It's not race neutral, in my view."

People v. Crimmins
26 N.Y.2d 319 (1970)

OPINION OF THE COURT: (Re: Unauthorized juror visits to scene, 270.50)

Defendant was indicted for, and convicted of, killing her daughter. Two of the People's witnesses, Sophie Earomirski and Joseph Rorech, presented substantially all of the evidence which connected defendant to the crime. The former testified that at about 2:00 a.m., on July 14, 1965, she saw defendant carrying a bundle and holding the hand of a little boy; she was accompanied by a man. Defendant's companion took the bundle and threw it into an automobile, and Mrs. Earomirski, from her third floor window across the street, heard defendant say, "My God, don't do that to her." Mr. Rorech testified that at a subsequent time defendant admitted to him, "Joseph, please forgive me, I killed her."

Although defendant raised several alleged errors in the Appellate Division, reversal was predicated on only one — an unauthorized visit by three jurors to the neighborhood which was the subject of Mrs. Earomirski's testimony. Leave to appeal to this court was granted on the People's application. They argue that reversal is mandated only when prejudice to the defendant is shown and that, as found by the Trial Justice, such prejudice is absent herein. They also argue that the evidence is legally sufficient to establish defendant's guilt beyond a reasonable doubt.

After the trial but before the imposition of sentence, defendant moved, on the basis of a juror's affidavit, to set aside the verdict because members of the jury had made an unauthorized visit to the street on which Sophie Earomirski lived. A hearing was held, and the juror, Samuel Ehrlich, testified that, after Mrs. Earomirski had testified, he wanted to see that area. He went there between 1:00 and 2:00 a.m. Ehrlich further testified that his visit did not influence his opinion. Another visit was made by Ehrlich and two other jurors, Harry Tunis and Irving Furst, at about 5:30 p.m.

During the jury's deliberations the lighting in the area was discussed in "small talk" and, according to Ehrlich, someone mentioned that the area was well-lit. Another juror, Philip Seidman, testified that the subject was discussed. During the length of the trial, the jurors were never admonished not to visit any place which had been the subject of testimony. Ironically, after Mrs. Earomirski had testified, defense counsel requested that the court arrange a controlled visit to the area. The court denied the visit as unnecessary.

In this type of case, proof of the fact of the unauthorized visit is sufficient to warrant a new trial without proof of how such visit may have influenced individual jurors in their jury room deliberations. Such a visit, in and of itself, constitutes inherent prejudice to the defendants.

The attempt to distinguish the view made herein from one of the scene of a crime is without merit. Mrs. Earomirski's ability to see and hear the events to which she testified depended very much on the lighting in the area and the distances involved. And the credibility of her testimony is essential to the prosecution's case. The Legislature perceived the evil in such a view and directed court supervision of views of the place where the crime is alleged to have been committed or where "any material fact occurred." The statutory inclusion is sound, and we ought not to make a tenuous distinction.

Finally, appellant argues that the error is harmless. The question is moot. Although, as the People argue, the evidence is legally sufficient to sustain the verdict of guilt, it was not so overwhelming that we can say, as a matter of law, that the error could not have influenced the verdict. Only two witnesses gave evidence which connected defendant directly with the crime. Rorech, of course, testified that defendant confessed to the slaying, and that testimony, together with that of the coroner, is sufficient to establish a prima facie case. But that testimony was seriously challenged, and the witness was subjected to searching cross-examination. Mrs. Earomirski was the other witness who implicated defendant, and it is the value of her testimony which may have been affected by the impropriety. Given such limited evidence, we cannot find the error harmless beyond a reasonable doubt.

Accordingly the order of the Appellate Division should be affirmed.

Sec. 9.3; Article 280; Jury Trial — Motion for a Mistrial

In the Matter of Enright v. Siedlecki

59 N.Y.2d 195 (1983)

OPINION OF THE COURT: (Re: Factors court considers, 280.10)

Manifest necessity for the declaration of a mistrial in a criminal case exists when after opening statements referring to a confession have been made, the prosecutor discovers a Miranda warnings statement indicating that defendant had requested counsel and the confession is, after a hearing, suppressed. Therefore, the judgment of the Appellate Division should be reversed.

Petitioner Enright was indicted for robbery in the second degree. Following a lengthy Huntley hearing the suppression court denied his motion to suppress a confession given to the police. At the ensuing trial the confession was referred to in the opening statements of both the prosecutor and defense counsel. The next day, however, the trial prosecutor discovered a Miranda rights warning statement indicating that Enright had requested counsel before his statement was taken. The hearing was then reopened and, at its conclusion the statement was suppressed.

During discussion concerning the necessity for a mistrial, petitioner's counsel agreed with the prosecutor that reference to the confession during opening statements constituted a major problem and expressed doubt that the jury could be "sanitized" with respect to defendant's inculpatory statement, but refused to consent to a mistrial. The prosecutor, stating that he felt "penalized in the sense that I now have to fly a flag with different colors and I don't know that anything the court says can dispel the doubt," moved for a mistrial. The Trial Judge, noting that he had admonished the jury to listen carefully to the opening statements and concluding that "there is no way we can proceed to a trial with this panel at this time and be sure that this defendant has a fair trial" granted the mistrial, stating that he was doing so on the prosecutor's motion and on the court's own motion.

Petitioner then commenced the present proceeding to prohibit the scheduled retrial The Appellate Division held any prejudice to the People arising from the unavailability of the confession to be of their own making and no basis for mistrial, and that, no inquiry having been made by the Trial Judge into the jury's ability to render a fair verdict or curative instruction given, the Trial Judge had abused his discretion in granting a mistrial without defendant's consent.

The rules governing the effect of declaring a mistrial in a criminal case without the consent or over the objection of the defendant are well settled. When such a mistrial is declared the prohibition against double jeopardy contained in the Fifth Amendment to the United States Constitution and in section 6 of article I of the New York Constitution precludes retrial for the same offense unless there is a manifest necessity for [the mistrial], or the ends of public justice would otherwise be defeated. This principle is at the root of CPL 280.10, which requires the declaration of a mistrial upon motion of the People when there has been "gross misconduct by the defendant or some person acting on his behalf" (subd. 2) or on motion of either party or on the court's own motion "when it is physically impossible to proceed with the trial in conformity with law" (subd. 3). Under either the constitutional or statutory provisions a defendant's valued right to have his trial completed by a particular tribunal must in some circumstances be subordinated to the public's interest in fair trials, but the Trial Judge must exercise sound discretion to assure that, taking all relevant circumstances into account, there was manifest necessity for the declaration of a mistrial without defendant's consent.

A corollary of the discretion granted Trial Judges is the principle that a reviewing court will be hesitant to interfere with the discretion exercised out of deference to the fact that the Trial Judge is in the best position to determine whether a mistrial is in fact necessary in a particular case. The Trial Judge's discretion is not without limits, however. The reasons underlying the grant of a mistrial may not be illusory; rather, in order fully to protect the defendant's right to trial by a particular tribunal they must be necessitous, actual and substantial. Thus, if the Judge acts so abruptly as not to permit consideration of the alternatives or otherwise acts irrationally or irresponsibly or solely for convenience of the court and jury or other similar abuse of discretion, retrial will be barred.

The Trial Judge's grant of a mistrial will be subjected to strict scrutiny when the basis for doing so is the unavailability of critical prosecution evidence, for the People are not entitled to a mistrial merely to gain a more favorable opportunity to convict. On the other hand, the trial judge's evaluation of the likelihood that the impartiality of one or more jurors may have been affected by improper comment, will be accorded the highest degree of respect. The decision whether a mistrial is necessary because of juror bias [is] often based on subtle indications of discontent, not always apparent on the cold face of the record presented to an appellate court. Hence a Trial Judge is entrusted with considerable discretion in making such determinations, for it is the Trial Judge, better than any other, who can detect the ambience of partiality.

In finding an abuse of discretion in *Matter of Enright*, the Appellate Division placed undue emphasis on the prosecution's error and the Trial Judge's failure to question the jurors concerning their ability to act impartially. Defendant does not suggest that the oversight which resulted in the confession reaching the jury was other than inadvertent. But the question for decision is not whether it would have been an abuse of discretion to continue the trial, but whether it was an abuse of discretion not to allow it to continue. The jury's awareness that defendant had confessed prejudiced both sides. In determining whether a trial should be permitted to continue, a Trial Judge need not necessarily explore every ramification by juror questioning before declaring a mistrial. Enright's attorney, asked for his feeling as to a mistrial, responded "I don't see how the jury could be sanitized" and, the prosecutor having stated that the inability to mention during trial the statement the jurors had been told about on voir dire "is a big problem right now," expressed his agreement. He nevertheless declined, as was his right, to consent to the prosecutor's motion for a mistrial. The Trial Judge's ruling on the motion, made as its language shows to protect the defendant's right to a fair trial and then joined in by the court of its own motion because "I don't see how he could get a fair trial with all this," was not predicated on prejudice to the People. Moreover, defendant's attorney's concession that the jury could not be "sanitized" and the difficulty inherent in jurors disregarding a confession of which they have been told, made unnecessary the questioning of the jurors by the Trial Judge. Nor in view of the public interest in fair trials designed to end in just, inherent in the due process provisions of the Federal and State Constitutions, did the fact that the provisions of CPL 280.10 did not exactly fit the situation limit the Trial Judge's authority to declare a mistrial on the basis of prejudice to the defendant. The Trial Judge was justified in concluding that there was no acceptable alternative to a mistrial.

Sec. 9.4; Article 290; Jury Trial — Trial Order of Dismissal

People v. Marin

102 A.D. 2d 14 (2nd Dept. 1984)

OPINION OF THE COURT: (Re: Right to dismiss v. double jeopardy, 290.10)

On December 4, 1980, a conflagration at the Stouffer's Inn of Westchester claimed the lives of 26 people. Defendant, Luis Marin, was subsequently indicted, tried and found guilty by a jury of murder in the second degree and arson in the fourth degree in connection with the tragedy. That verdict was set aside by the trial judge and the indictment was dismissed. The issue on this appeal is whether the evidence presented at trial was legally sufficient to prove that the defendant had intentionally caused the fatal fire.

At the outset, the procedural posture in which the case reaches this court should be noted. At the close of the prosecution's case, and again at the close of the evidence, the defendant moved for a trial order of dismissal (see CPL 290.10, subd. 1, par [a]). In effect, he argued that, because the evidence in its entirety was so weak and lacking in probative value, the trial judge should dismiss the case outright rather than submit it for consideration by the jury. Although the judge expressed full agreement with the defense's position on the deficiency of the evidence, he reserved decision on the motion and permitted the jury to consider the charges. In doing so, the Judge was seeking to preserve the prosecution's right to appellate review. Where, after the taking of evidence, a Trial Judge dismisses a case without submitting it to the jury, principles of double jeopardy bar the prosecutor from pursuing an appeal from the dismissal. In such circumstances, the case, whether rightly or wrongly, is resolved in the defendant's favor for all time. Where, on the other hand, a Trial Judge dismisses a case after the jury has returned a guilty verdict, as the Judge did here, the prosecutor's right to appeal is preserved. If he is successful, the verdict is simply reinstated with no double jeopardy implications. Thus, the practice of reserving decision on a motion to dismiss until such time as the jury returns a guilty verdict is entirely appropriate.

Mindful of these considerations, the Trial Judge in this case, after assessing the evidence, submitted the charges to the jurors "fully [expecting] that the jury would dismiss the case." Nevertheless, after some five days of deliberations, the jury returned a guilty verdict and the Judge was then called upon to decide the motion to dismiss. He ultimately granted the motion, finding the evidence legally insufficient to sustain the verdict. In doing so, he expressed the belief that the jury had been led to its determination by the trial prosecutor's summation which, although "brilliant," had persuaded the jurors "to go beyond the proven facts." Indeed, the Judge stated that, were he not dismissing the case for evidentiary insufficiency, he would have declared a mistrial based upon the prosecutor's summation.

We need not speculate as to the reasons for the jury's verdict, or pass upon the propriety of the prosecutor's summation, for, after a painstaking review of this lengthy record, we are in agreement with the Trial Judge's assessment that the evidence was insufficient to prove the defendant's guilt beyond a reasonable doubt.

At trial, the prosecution called many witnesses including hotel employees, persons who were attending conferences at the hotel on the day of the fire, arson investigators, scientific experts and firemen who responded to the scene. Notwithstanding all this testimony, however, the People never directly connected the defendant, Luis Marin, with the fire itself or with the means to start it and never firmly established how the Stouffer's fire had actually begun.

In sum, careful analysis of the record discloses too much speculation and too many gaps in the People's proof to establish the defendant's guilt beyond a reasonable doubt. The jurors in this case did precisely that which the rules governing circumstantial evidence are designed to guard against, viz.: they [leaped] logical gaps in the proof offered and [drew] unwarranted conclusions based on probabilities of low degree.

Accordingly, the order granting the defendant's motions for a trial order of dismissal must be affirmed.

Sec. 9.6; Article 310; Jury Trial — Deliberation and Verdict of Jury

People v. O'Rama
78 N.Y.2d 270 (1991)

OPINION OF THE COURT: (Re: Jury deliberations; request for information, 310.30)

Following a jury trial, defendant was convicted of driving while under the influence of alcohol as a felony (see, Vehicle and Traffic Law § 1192 [3]; § 1193 [1] [c]). His appeal requires us to decide the extent to which the specific contents of jurors' notes must be disclosed to the defendant and defense counsel before a response is given. We hold that the trial court committed reversible error when it failed to disclose the note's contents.

One of the jurors asked permission to speak to the Judge but was told to put his query in the form of a note. After receiving this juror's note, the Judge brought the jury and counsel back into the courtroom and had the note marked as a court exhibit. The Judge declined to read the note aloud, however, because, in his view, reading it "would [not] serve any particular purpose at this point." Instead, the Judge summarized the "substance" of the note's contents, stating that it "indicates that there are continued disagreements among the jurors." After questioning five of the jurors and eliciting from four of them that a unanimous verdict was still possible, the Judge "implor[ed]" the jurors to try again. When the jury was ushered out of the courtroom, the Judge elaborated upon his reasons for withholding the precise contents of the individual juror's note, stating that he did not read it because "it indicate[d w]hat the present posture is as far as votes." Defense counsel then unsuccessfully sought disclosure of the note's contents.

The jury deliberated for the remainder of the afternoon, returning to the courtroom for one more testimonial readback. At 5:08 p.m., the jury brought in its guilty verdict. The primary issue he raises on this appeal is whether the trial court's actions in relation to the individual juror's note constitute reversible error.

We begin our analysis of this issue with CPL 310.30, which provides that a deliberating jury may request additional information or instruction "with respect to any matter pertinent to [its] consideration of the case." The statute further provides that "[u]pon such a request, the court must direct that the jury be returned to the courtroom and, after notice to both the people and counsel for the defendant, must give such requested information or instruction as the court deems proper" (emphasis supplied). CPL 310.30 thus imposes two separate duties on the court following a substantive juror inquiry: the duty to notify counsel and the duty to respond. The latter duty requires the court to give a response that is "meaningful." We have not, however, previously addressed the separate, albeit related, question raised in this appeal — i.e., the scope of the court's CPL 310.30 duty to provide counsel with "notice."

The requirement that "notice" be given to counsel is not a mere formality or a procedural device designed only to ensure counsel's presence in the courtroom when the court gives its response to the jurors' request for information or instruction. While that is undoubtedly one of the statute's purposes, an equally important purpose is to ensure that counsel has the opportunity to be heard before the response is given. Such an opportunity is essential to counsel's ability to represent the client's best interests and, further, to ensure the protection of the client's constitutional and statutory rights at these critical postsubmission proceedings. Supplemental instructions, which are given in direct response to the jurors' own questions, may well be determinative of the outcome. Thus, just as CPL 310.30's requirement that juror inquiries be answered mandates a "meaningful" response, so too does that statute's "notice" requirement mandate notice that is meaningful.

We conclude that "meaningful" notice in this context means notice of the actual specific content of the jurors' request. Manifestly, counsel cannot participate effectively or adequately protect the defendant's rights if this specific information is not given. Indeed, the precise language and tone of the juror note may be critical to counsel's analysis of the situation in the jury room and ability to frame intelligent suggestions for the fairest and least prejudicial response. Concomitantly, the Trial Judge's summary of the "substance" of an inquiry cannot serve as a fair substitute for defense counsel's own perusal of the communication, since it is defense counsel who is best equipped and most motivated to evaluate the inquiry and the proper responses in light of the defendant's interests.

We further hold that, in most cases, this requirement of meaningful notice is best served by following the procedure that was outlined in *United States v. Ronder* (639 F2d 931, 934, supra; accord, *People v. Miller*, 163 AD2d 491). Under this procedure, jurors' inquiries must generally be submitted in writing, since, as the trial court in this case recognized, written communications are the surest method for affording the court and counsel an adequate opportunity to confer. Further, whenever a substantive written jury communication is received by the Judge, it should be marked as a court exhibit and, before the jury is recalled to the courtroom, read into the record in the presence of counsel. Such a step would ensure a clear and complete record, thereby facilitating adequate and fair appellate review. After the contents of the inquiry are placed on the record, counsel should be afforded a full opportunity to suggest appropriate responses. As the court noted in *Ronder* (supra, at 934), the trial court should ordinarily apprise counsel of the substance of the responsive instruction it intends to give so that counsel can seek whatever modifications are deemed appropriate before the jury is exposed to the potentially harmful information. Finally, when the jury is returned to the courtroom, the communication should be read in open court so that the individual jurors can correct any inaccuracies in the transcription of the inquiry and, in cases where the communication was sent by an individual juror, the rest of the jury panel can appreciate the purpose of the court's response and the context in which it is being made.

Viewed in light of these principles, the trial court's actions in this case were clearly inadequate. Accordingly, for the reasons stated above, the order of the Appellate Division should be reversed and a new trial ordered.

People v. Baptiste

72 N.Y.2d 356 (1988)

OPINION OF THE COURT: (Re: Discharge of jury before verdict and effect thereof, 310.60)

Defendant appeals from an order of the Appellate Term which affirmed a judgment entered on a guilty plea convicting him of the misdemeanor of sexual abuse in the third degree. The guilty plea was entered after an earlier trial had been terminated without his consent because the jury was unable to reach a verdict. Defendant contends that the trial was unnecessarily aborted and thus his reprosecution violated the Double Jeopardy Clauses of the United States and New York Constitutions (US Const. 5th Amend; NY Const; art I, § 6). We agree and reverse the order of Appellate Term and dismiss the information.

Defendant and a codefendant were charged with assault, third degree, sexual misconduct and sexual abuse, third degree. The jury was charged on the morning of April 4 and, at the conclusion of the instructions, retired to deliberate. Shortly after retiring, the jury requested a readback of the testimony of the complainant, the codefendant and the arresting officer. After the readback, the jury continued deliberating for about an hour and then requested the exhibits and a readback of a doctor's testimony. They recessed for dinner and at 9:15 p.m. the jury requested that the testimony of the complainant, codefendant and arresting officers be read back again. The court asked the jurors to specify which portions of the testimony they were interested in and when they had not responded by 10:00 p.m., the Judge summoned them to the courtroom and clarified his earlier instructions. After the jury left the courtroom, the Judge advised counsel, "If they have not reached a verdict by eleven-thirty we'll have to declare a mistrial, so if they can't reach a verdict it has to be a mistrial." The jury was in the courtroom again from 11:40 p.m. to midnight as selected testimony was read back in response to the jury's earlier request. At the conclusion, the court directed the jurors to return to the jury room and decide whether the court had complied sufficiently with their request and "whether or not you feel that further deliberations will be fruitful in arriving at a verdict." After the jury left, the court asked defendant's counsel to consent to a mistrial. He refused. At 12:25 a.m., the court, sua sponte and over defendant's objection, returned the jury to the courtroom and declared a mistrial.

Both the State and Federal Constitutions provide that the State may not put a defendant in jeopardy twice for the same offense. Because jeopardy attaches as soon as a jury has been sworn our constitutional provisions also embrace the defendant's right to be free from reprosecution if the first trial has not continued to conclusion. As a general rule, the prosecutor is entitled to one, and only one, opportunity to require the accused to stand trial for a defendant possesses a "valued right" to have his trial completed by a particular tribunal on the first presentation of the evidence. If the merits of the charges against the defendant have not been resolved, the "valued right" to have the trial concluded by a particular tribunal may be subordinate to the public interest "in seeing that a criminal prosecution proceed to verdict. The "classic example" of charges which may be retried when the first trial has been aborted without defendant's consent, arises when the jurors reach an impasse and are unable to arrive at a verdict. Retrial is not prohibited in such cases.

The determination of a Trial Judge that deadlock has occurred and that a mistrial is necessary involves the exercise of discretion. The trial court's judgment is entitled to great deference by reviewing courts for it is best situated to take all the circumstances of the particular proceeding into account and determine whether a mistrial is in fact required. Nevertheless, Trial Judges are not free to act without restraint. The defendant's right to obtain a verdict from the first jury selected should not be foreclosed. The court's power to declare a mistrial must be exercised with the greatest caution, under urgent circumstances, and for very plain and obvious causes; the authority to discharge the jury is limited to those situations where, taking all the circumstances into consideration, there is a manifest necessity for the act.

The record in this case does not demonstrate a manifest necessity for terminating defendant's trial. The Trial Judge himself first raised the issue when he mentioned the possibility of a mistrial to counsel around 10:00 p.m. and announced to counsel that if the jury had not reached a verdict by 11:30 p.m. a mistrial would be declared. This was after he had satisfied the jury's request for a readback but before they had even had an opportunity to consider the testimony just read to them. The jury had not given any indication that it was unable to reach a verdict and the court's statement was apparently made without consulting counsel. When the court did discuss the possibility of deadlock with the jury, it was because the Judge had decided to summon them to the courtroom to discuss the possibility of an impasse, not because the jury had notified him they were in any difficulty.

The impetus for the declaration of mistrial having come solely from the Judge, he was under a particular obligation to demonstrate on the record that the jury believed it was unable to decide the case. His colloquy with the foreperson fell far short of establishing that to be so. Indeed, the foreperson indicated that there had been recent "movement" among the jurors and the logical inference arising from the foreperson's equivocal statement, repeated twice, that the jury was not able to resolve the matter "at this time" is that the jury was exhausted, not deadlocked. But further than that, because the court acted sua sponte, the jury did not know why it was being returned to the courtroom. Thus, the foreperson's answers to the court's questions may well have been his answers alone. All the jurors were present in the courtroom during this colloquy and prudence dictated that under the circumstances the court should have obtained confirmation of the foreperson's answers from other jurors before deciding the question.

There is, of course, no mechanical formula for determining the necessity for a new trial and no minimum time a jury must deliberate before a mistrial is considered. These jurors, however, had little opportunity to decide this case. Although the trial had been relatively short, nine witnesses had been sworn and there were serious discrepancies in their versions of the underlying incident. In an effort to resolve these discrepancies, the jury had requested the court to read back testimony several times and was in the process of considering some of this testimony when the mistrial occurred. There is no support in the record for the court's determination that the jury had found the problem insoluble or believed itself hopelessly deadlocked and in the absence of such evidence, the trial court abused its discretion in declaring a mistrial, as a matter of law.

Accordingly, the order should be reversed and the information dismissed.

Sec. 9.8; Article 330; Proceedings from Verdict to Sentence

In Re Francis S.

87 N.Y.2d 554 (1995)

OPINION OF THE COURT: (Re: After verdict of mental disease or defect, finding dangerous mental condition, 330.20)

In 1987, with the permission of the court and the consent of the People, defendant Francis S. entered a plea of not responsible by reason of mental disease or defect to charges of attempted assault in the first degree and possession of a weapon in the third degree. Following a psychiatric examination and initial hearing to assess his present mental condition, he was determined to be a "track 2" insanity acquittee, that is, mentally ill but not suffering from a dangerous mental disorder, and was remanded to the custody of the Commissioner of Mental Health to be civilly committed for a four-month period. The hearing court also issued a five-year order of conditions, which required defendant, inter alia, to comply with the terms of the treatment plan prescribed for him by the Office of Mental Health (OMH).

Pursuant to that plan, defendant was treated on both an inpatient basis in a non-secure facility and on an outpatient basis at various State psychiatric clinics over the next several years. However, in early 1991, he unilaterally changed his treatment center in violation of his order of conditions. That order of conditions was due to expire August 7, 1992. On August 4, 1992, the Commissioner applied for a recommitment order seeking to have S. placed in a secure facility on the ground that because of his mental condition he currently presented a danger to himself or others. OMH reached this conclusion based on S.'s persistent noncompliance with the order of conditions, his psychiatric history, and the circumstances underlying his arrests on several occasions during 1991 and 1992.

S. moved to dismiss the application on both constitutional and statutory jurisdictional grounds. The court denied the motion in all respects and held a hearing to determine whether S. currently suffered from a dangerous mental disorder — the requisite statutory basis for recommitment under CPL 330.20.

The hearing evidence consisted primarily of expert psychiatric evaluations and evidence of S.'s treatment history and his numerous arrests in the more than five years since he was permitted to plead not responsible. Six psychiatrists testified, three on behalf of the State petitioners and three on behalf of defendant. All six agreed that S. was suffering from a mental disorder; the primary source of disagreement was over whether S. currently suffered from a dangerous mental disorder requiring in-patient care.

At the conclusion of the hearing, Supreme Court found that S. was mentally ill. The court nevertheless felt constrained to order recommitment because, as a result of his present hospitalization and enforced medication, S.'s dangerous behavior had diminished.

The Commissioner of Mental Health and the District Attorney appealed. Upon its review of the hearing evidence, the Appellate Division found that S. was suffering from a dangerous mental disorder, reversed and granted the recommitment appli-cation. That Court granted defendant leave to appeal, and we now affirm.

Initially, we reject defendant's contention that the Appellate Division's finding that he was suffering from a dangerous mental disorder is erroneous. Both Supreme Court and the Appellate Division found that defendant suffered from a mental illness, the first element of a dangerous mental disorder, and because that finding is supported by evidence in the record it is beyond our further review. Moreover, Supreme Court applied an erroneous legal standard in finding that the second element of a dangerous mental disorder — his current dangerousness as a result of his mental illness — had not been established solely because S.'s condition was stabilized during hospitalization. On the other hand, the Appellate Division majority quite properly based its deter-mination that S. had a dangerous mental disorder on his history of prior relapses into violent behavior and of recurrent substance abuse and noncompliance with treatment programs upon release. Thus, in our view, the Appellate Division's finding of S.'s present dangerousness more nearly comports with the evidence in the record.

As we have repeatedly recognized, the provisions of CPL 330.20 reflect a legislative judgment that, having concededly once engaged in criminal conduct as a result of mental illness, the insanity acquittee continues to present a serious risk of a recurrence of dangerous behavior derived from mental illness.

We recognize the inability of modern psychiatry to guarantee the safety of the public through effective treatment permanently removing the potentiality of recurrent violent acts by persons found not responsible by reason of mental illness, thereby justifying extended continuous supervision over the acquittee by the criminal court through an order of conditions. And we rely upon one legal commentator who had demonstrated that the legislative judgment of the continued latent risk of recurrence of an insanity acquittee's dangerous mental disorder has a sound basis in clinical studies of recidivism among insanity acquittees. The very imprecision of the field of psychiatry militates in favor of judicial deference to such legislative judgments. The lesson we have drawn from the uncertainty of diagnoses in the field of the psychiatry of violent behavior is not that government may not act in the face of this uncertainty, but rather that courts should pay particular deference to reasonable legislative judgments.

Accordingly, the order of the Appellate Division should be affirmed.

People v. Suarez

98 A.D. 2d. 678 (1st Dept. 1983)

OPINION OF THE COURT: (Re: Motion to set aside verdict; newly discovered evidence, 330.30)

Order of Supreme Court, New York County granting defendant's motion to set aside a jury verdict of guilty of burglary in the second degree on the basis of newly discovered evidence, unanimously reversed, on the law, the motion to set aside the verdict denied, and the verdict reinstated. The case is remitted to Criminal Term for imposition of sentence.

Defendant and his companion, Vizcoriando, were alleged to have invaded the victim's apartment early one morning and ransacked the premises, tying the victims up and robbing them at knifepoint. The victims were able to identify the perpetrators; the female victim was Vizcoriando's stepniece. Inasmuch as Vizcoriando remained at large after defendant's arrest, the two were indicted separately. When ultimately arrested and indicted, Vizcoriando pleaded guilty to attempted robbery in the second degree. After defendant's trial, Vizcoriando was brought in to testify in support of defendant's motion to set aside the verdict. Basically, Vizcoriando stated that he had committed the crime alone. Although the Trial Judge found this testimony "somewhat incredible" and "quite incredible," inasmuch as the victims had testified that two perpetrators had tied them up and ransacked the apartment, the Judge set aside the verdict, ruling that such "material" evidence could not have been discovered with due diligence prior to trial, and "could possibly change the verdict."

This was error. The power to set aside a verdict on the ground of evidence newly discovered since trial is purely statutory. It must be shown that the evidence could not with due diligence have been produced by the defendant at the trial, and is of such character as to create a probability that such evidence would have resulted in a verdict more favorable to the defendant (CPL 330.30, subd. 3). To conform to the requirements of the statute, the criteria for granting such an application are sixfold. The "newly discovered evidence" (a) must be such as will probably (not merely possibly) change the result if a new trial is granted; (b) must have been discovered since trial; (c) could not have been discovered before trial by the exercise of due diligence; (d) must be material to the issue; (e) must not be cumulative to the former issue; and (f) must not be merely impeaching or contradictory to former evidence.

There is no probability that this evidence would have altered the jury's verdict. The evidence merely goes to contradict the victims' testimony that there had been two perpetrators. In this respect the Trial Judge appropriately termed such evidence "quite incredible," and her consideration of the application should have terminated at that point. In fact, the Trial Judge herself recognized only a possibility that such evidence might change the verdict, which was clearly insufficient to set it aside. Upon the hearing "the defendant has the burden of proving by a preponderance of the evidence every fact essential to support the motion." (CPL 330.40, subd. 2, par [g].)

The Trial Judge's expressed doubts demonstrate the insufficiency of the evidence to meet the statutory requirement. Vizcoriando was arrested just as defendant's trial was beginning, before presentation of any evidence. The jury did not return its verdict for another three days. Thus, it is questionable whether this "new evidence" could not have been discovered with due diligence prior to conclusion of trial.

If Vizcoriando's testimony was withheld from defendant's trial as a deliberate tactic, defendant would not be entitled to a new trial based on the later availability of this testimony. The Court of Appeals has noted that, especially suspect is the belated exculpation of defendant by an individual after he has nothing to lose i.e., where the individual does not come forward with this information until his own fate has been sealed by criminal conviction. Vizcoriando's testimony did not warrant the setting aside of this verdict and the granting of a new trial.

Chapter 10; Prosecution of Informations in Local Criminal Courts; Plea to Sentence

Sec. 10.1; Article 340; Pre-Trial Proceedings

People v. Foy

88 N.Y.2d 742 (1996)

OPINION OF THE COURT: (Re: Right to jury trial, 340.40)

Defendant-appellant was charged with multiple petty offenses. None carries a maximum term of incarceration greater than six months upon conviction when prosecuted individually. The issue framed for our consideration is whether defendant is constitutionally entitled to a jury trial because the maximum aggregate sentences for the charged offenses, as consolidated, may exceed six months. The Appellate Term affirmed a judgment of New York City Criminal Court convicting defendant of harassment, after a bench trial, and sentencing him to a conditional discharge. A Judge of this Court granted leave to appeal and we now affirm.

Criminal Court rejected defendant's demand for a jury trial. It concluded that a jury trial is not constitutionally mandated when the maximum statutory sentence for a petty charge does not exceed six months. Furthermore, the court noted that CPL 340.40 (2) requires a trial before a Judge where no one charge carries an authorized sentence of more than six months. The court reasoned that because the two informations here involved entirely separate incidents which occurred on different dates, there was no constitutional authority or precedent requiring a jury trial.

The Appellate Term held that each count was a "petty" offense within the meaning of the Sixth Amendment and, thus, not triable by jury if prosecuted individually. The court found unavailing defendant's argument that a jury trial was required because he could have been sentenced to an aggregate jail term in excess of six months had he been convicted of more than one of the petty offenses joined under the consolidation. The court reasoned that the central point of inquiry in determining whether a jury trial is required is the seriousness of the offense with which the defendant is charged, and not the sheer number of accumulated offenses tried on a given day or on a given accusatory instrument. Furthermore, the court noted that the administrative convenience of litigating these multiple charges in one trial did not serve to enhance the ultimate risk faced by the defendant or to somehow transform the 'petty' offenses alleged to the level of a 'serious' crime. Finally, the court stated that the widespread application of an aggregate sentence rule in our already overburdened criminal justice system would only serve to 'overwhelm the courts and prosecutors by consuming large amounts of time for selecting juries and would cause unmanageable delay.

Defendant argues that, when a defendant is charged with multiple petty offenses in a joined prosecution, carrying a potential aggregate sentence greater than six months' imprisonment, both the New York and United States Constitutions mandate that the defendant be afforded a jury trial. Defendant urges this Court to adopt the "aggregate-sentence approach" for determining the constitutional right to a jury trial. We reject defendant's arguments and agree with the Appellate Term that the determination as to whether a defendant is constitutionally entitled to a jury trial hinges on the seriousness of the offense, not the potential aggregate sentence for a series of petty offenses that may be consolidated for trial.

It is well settled that offenses carrying a maximum statutory term of imprisonment of greater than six months are "serious" offenses for which the New York and United States Constitutions unquestionably afford defendants the right to a jury trial. Equally settled is the proposition that offenses carrying sentences of less than six months are "petty" offenses, to which no right to a jury trial attaches. Courts are required to examine each offense in a prosecution individually and separately, to determine whether the Legislature has ascribed a serious level classification fixed by the measurement of whether any of the individual offenses carry a potential maximum sentence of greater than six months. When a court determines that none does, the defendant is not constitutionally entitled to a jury trial.

We are satisfied that the inescapably interrelated history and development of this Court's and the United States Supreme Court's rulings on the right to a jury trial for prosecution of petty offenses dictates an affirmance of the rulings of the courts below. No persuasive justification is presented for us to adopt defendant's contention that prosecution of consolidated petty offenses, with a potential aggregate sentence in excess of six months, adds up to a constitutionally compelled right to a jury trial. Multiple petty crimes remain "petty" by legislative classification and their nature, and are not transformed by their sheer number alone into matters of a serious level and nature.

In sum, even in aggregate sentence circumstances for petty offenses, the unalterable fact remains that the defendant is not charged with any offense that qualifies as serious, thus invoking the guarantee of a jury trial. Since it is the discrete petty offense itself in these circumstances, and not the accumulation of them, which determines the constitutional entitlement to a jury trial, defendant-appellant's arguments cannot prevail.

Accordingly, the order of the Appellate Term should be affirmed.

Sec. 10.2; Article 350; Non-Jury Trial

People v. O'Brien
381 N.Y.S.2d 972 (1976)

OPINION OF THE COURT: (Re: Time of verdict, 350.10)

The defendant was charged with disorderly conduct in violation of subdivisions 5 and 6 of section 240.20 of the Penal Law, for acts which allegedly occurred in the Village of Newark, New York, on or about October 31, 1975. The defendant was arraigned in Newark Village Court on November 5, 1975, before the Newark Village Justice. The matter was adjourned to November 12, 1975, for trial. However, the District Attorney informed the court that he was not prepared for trial and moved for an adjournment, which was opposed by defendant's attorney but granted by the court, and the matter was adjourned.

Trial was held on November 19, 1975, starting at about 3:00 p.m. At the end of the trial (at about 5:00 p.m.), over the specific objection of defendant's attorney, the procedure was "very irregular," and that it was being done "because not only is this case before the Court but there are at least four, and perhaps five, that arise out of this same time and place." The trial court also stated "I am reserving decision until I hear the other cases because the other cases have been set down for trial on December 10th at 1:30." In his objection, defendant's attorney indicated his concern "that the court may get entangled with testimony from other cases unrelated to this defendant." It was not until December 24, 1975, that the Village Justice found the defendant guilty and sentenced the defendant to a conditional discharge for a period of one year.

An appeal has been taken to this court by defendant. His attorney contends that the Village Justice erred in not rendering his decision at the conclusion of the trial, and in reserving his decision to a later date so that he might read the transcript of the trial.

CPL 350.10 (subd. 3, par [d]) provides that in a single-judge trial of an information in a local criminal court, after summations, "The court must then consider the case and render a verdict." Identical language is found in CPL 320.20 (subd. 3, par [d]) with respect to a nonjury trial of an indictment by one Judge of a superior court.

The words "then" and "verdict" demand further consideration. Had the word "immediately" or the words "within thirty days" or other similar words been used in place of the word "then," there would be no problem. The word "then" can be construed in different ways, and it is evident that the Justice in the local criminal court construed it to mean merely "in due course as the next step in the trial procedure."

As will appear more fully below, this court construes the word "then" in a different manner.

The word "verdict" points up the fact that in a situation where the single Justice is determining all questions of fact, he is in effect serving as a one-man jury. He is not required to write a decision or to make findings and conclusions, but is merely required to render a verdict of "guilty" or "not guilty." The possibility of a "hung" jury situation does not exist, since the verdict is being rendered by a single individual.

Article 310 contemplates that a jury will render a verdict at the close of the case, unless it is "hung" or there is a mistrial, in which latter event a retrial is provided for. Obviously, a jury is entitled to a reasonable length of time in which to deliberate, but unless it is "hung" or there is a mistrial, it must render a verdict and cannot reserve its verdict to some later date.

As noted above, a jury is entitled to a reasonable length of time in which to deliberate, and it seems to this court that a Judge in either a superior court or a local criminal court is entitled to a like amount of time. He should have time to consider his notes, the exhibits, and the testimony of the witnesses, and to have the latter read back to him if necessary, and time to go over the evidence as he remembers it, but within a relatively short time he should render a verdict of "guilty" or "not guilty," just as a jury would have been required to do. As noted above he is not required to make a written decision or findings and conclusions, but only to render a verdict. In criminal matters it seems to this court that a reasonable time for rendition of a verdict would be, in the absence of a specific statute to the contrary or of the acquiesence of counsel, a matter of no more than a few hours. Certainly it would be far less than the 35 days which the local court took in this case. An additional factor exists in the present case, to wit: It appears that it is possible that the defendant could have been prejudiced by the consideration of other cases in the interim period, and defendant's counsel expressed on the record his concern in the latter regard at the time he objected to the reservation.

The policy of the law is and must be to afford a defendant a prompt trial, which must include a prompt verdict at the conclusion of the evidence and summations and also of the charge if there is a jury. It is clearly improper to keep a defendant dangling for days or weeks or even longer. It is logical that a verdict should be required to be rendered when the facts are the freshest in the mind or minds of the person or persons who is or are rendering the verdict, and certainly before there is an opportunity to consider, either consciously or unconsciously, extraneous matters not in evidence in the case before the court particularly when they involve other persons accused of committing the same or closely related acts.

This court determines that the requirements of CPL 350.10 (subd. 3, par [d]) were not complied with in this case and that the conviction and sentence herein were not valid.

The conviction of the defendant is reversed and the sentence imposed is set aside.

Sec. 10.3; Article 360; Jury Trial

People v. Warren

536 N.Y.S.2d 337 (1988)

OPINION OF THE COURT: (Re: Number of jurors, 360.10)

Judgment unanimously reversed on the law and new trial granted, in accordance with the following memorandum: Defendant moved, pursuant to CPL 170.25, for an order directing the District Attorney to prosecute the charges against him by indictment. Thereafter, defendant was indicted on misdemeanor charges of obstructing governmental administration and resisting arrest arising out of an incident on January 11, 1983. Defendant, over his objection, was subsequently tried and convicted of both misdemeanor counts before a six-person jury. Defendant now contends that he was denied his constitutional right to be tried before a jury of 12 persons. We agree.

Article VI (§ 18 [a]) of the NY Constitution authorizes the State Legislature to provide for both six-person and 12-person juries, but specifically provides that "crimes prosecuted by indictment shall be tried by a jury composed of twelve persons." This language is mandatory in nature and it is without limitation or qualification. Therefore, a defendant when prosecuted on an indictment is entitled to be tried by a jury composed of 12 persons even if the indictment, as here, does not charge a felony.

Chapter 11; The Sentence

Sec. 11.1; Article 380; Sentencing in General

People v. Rodney E.

77 N.Y.2d 672 (1991)

OPINION OF THE COURT: (Re: Interim probation not permitted, 380.20)

The question on this appeal is whether a court can place a defendant on "interim probation" after conviction but before sentence.

Courts have power to sentence persons convicted of specified crimes to serve a period of probation but as the Appellate Division recognized and the prosecutor concedes, there is no express statutory authority for "interim probation" pending the sentence. Nor can such authority be inferred from the court's power to prescribe the contents of a presentence probation report. The court, of course, may consider the defendant's activities after conviction in determining the appropriate sentence, and may direct the Probation Department to include such information in the presentence report (CPL 390.30 [1]). But probation involves more than reporting; it also requires the Probation Department to supervise the defendant's activities to insure compliance with the conditions of probation imposed by the court, as indeed the court ordered the agency to do in this case. The Probation Department's supervisory powers, however, are conferred by the Legislature and under the existing statutes the Department only assumes this supervisory role with respect to persons convicted of a crime, after the defendant has been sentenced to a term of probation and not before (CPL 410.50 [2]; Penal Law § 65.10 [3]). Thus in this State, probation is only available as a sentencing option; there is no statute which, expressly or by implication, permits a court to place a person convicted of a crime on probation before sentence is imposed.

In sum, the court erred in placing the defendant on probation prior to sentence and in basing the sentence in part on allegations that the defendant had violated the conditions of the interim probation. Thus the sentence should be set aside and the defendant should be resentenced. We note that if the court finds that it is unable to impose the sentence which was agreed upon when the defendant pleaded guilty, the defendant should be permitted to withdraw the plea.

Order reversed and case remitted to Onondaga County Court for further proceedings in accordance with the opinion herein.

Sec. 11.2; Article 390; Pre-Sentence Reports

Donald P. v. Palmieri

246 A.D. 2d. 597 (2nd Dept. 1998)

OPINION OF THE COURT: (Re: HIV testing, 390.15)

Ordered that the motion is granted, and, upon reargument, it is

Ordered that the decision and judgment of this Court, dated July 29, 1996, is recalled and vacated, and the following decision and order is substituted therefor:

Proceeding pursuant to CPLR article 78 in the nature of prohibition to enjoin the Honorable Daniel R. Palmieri, a Judge of the County Court, Nassau County, from enforcing an order of that court, dated March 29, 1996, made in a criminal action entitled People v Donald P., under Indictment No. 93056, directing the petitioner to submit to an HIV test pursuant to CPL 390.15 (1) (a), upon his conviction of attempted sexual abuse in the first degree.

Upon the petition, the papers filed in support of the proceeding, and the papers filed in opposition thereto, it is

Adjudged the petition is granted, without costs or disbursements, and the respondent is prohibited from enforcing the order dated March 29, 1996.

The petitioner was indicted on charges of rape in the first degree, sodomy in the first degree, and sexual abuse in the first degree (see, Penal Law § 130.35 [1]; § 130.50 [1]; § 130.65). He testified before the Grand Jury that he had sexual intercourse with the complainant but claimed that the acts were consensual. The charges in the indictment were reduced (see, CPL 210.20), and the petitioner was permitted to plead guilty to attempted sexual abuse in the first degree based on his admission that he attempted forcible sexual contact with the complainant. Before sentence was imposed, the complainant applied to the court for an order pursuant to CPL 390.15 requiring the petitioner to submit to Human Immunodeficiency Virus (hereinafter HIV) testing.

The court granted the application (see, People v Doe, 169 Misc 2d 29) and thereafter imposed sentence. The petitioner commenced this proceeding pursuant to CPLR article 78 in which he contends that the County Court lacked authority under the statute to order him to submit to HIV testing.

We conclude that a proceeding in the nature of prohibition is the appropriate vehicle to address the petitioner's claim. "Prohibition may be maintained solely to prevent or control a body or officer acting in a judicial or quasi-judicial capacity from proceeding or threatening to proceed without or in excess of its jurisdiction ... and then only when the clear legal right to relief appears and, in the court's discretion, the remedy is warranted." The writ will not lie if another adequate legal remedy is available.

The HIV test in the instant case was not sought for use in the prosecution of a pending criminal proceeding (see, CPL 240.40 [2] [b] [v]). Thus, the court had no statutory authority to order the petitioner to submit to an HIV test except that conferred by CPL 390.15. The petitioner may not obtain review of the order issued pursuant to CPL 390.15 on a direct appeal from the judgment, as the order is not part of the conviction or sentence (see, CPL 450.10, 450.30). The statute specifically provides that the test results shall not be disclosed to the court and that the failure to comply with its provisions shall not affect the validity of any sentence imposed by the court (see, CPL 390.15 [1], [7]). Furthermore, CPL 390.15 does not grant a right to appeal to any of the parties to the application. Therefore, a proceeding pursuant to CPLR article 78 is the only avenue available to the petitioner to obtain appellate review of his claim that the court exceeded its authority when it granted the complainant's application under CPL 390.15.

CPL 390.15 (1) (a) provides that "(i)n any case where the defendant is convicted of a felony offense enumerated in any section of article one hundred thirty of the penal law, or any subdivision of section 130.20 of such law, where an act of 'sexual intercourse' or 'deviate sexual intercourse'... is required as an essential element for the commission thereof, the court must, upon a request of the victim, order that the defendant submit to ... (HIV) related testing." A victim is defined as "the person with whom the defendant engaged in an act of sexual intercourse or deviate sexual intercourse, ... where such conduct with such victim was the basis for the defendant's conviction of an offense specified in paragraph (a) of this subdivision" (CPL 390.15 [1] [b]).

We agree with the petitioner that the phrase "where an act of 'sexual intercourse' or 'deviate sexual intercourse' is required as an essential element for the commission thereof" applies to a felony conviction under Penal Law article 130, as well as to a misdemeanor conviction under Penal Law § 130.20. Common sense dictates that the Legislature did not intend to mandate HIV testing based on the conviction of any felony in Penal Law article 130, as that would encompass defendants convicted of acts of sexual contact which carry no risk of HIV transmission. Moreover, the definition of a "victim" in the statute includes a requirement that sexual intercourse or deviate sexual intercourse form the basis for the defendant's conviction, rather than the basis for the charges in the indictment. The statute does not make any provision for circumstances such as these, where the charges are reduced pursuant to a plea. Accordingly, since the court did not have the statutory authority to order the petitioner to be tested, he established a clear legal right to relief, and the petition is granted.

Coppertino, J. P., Thompson, Krausman and Florio, JJ., concur.

People v. Michael M.

124 Misc. Cty. 1984)

OPINION OF THE COURT: (Re: Victims' statements, 390.40)

The Courtroom is the focal point of the entire criminal justice system, particularly for the victim, the judge is the personification of justice. Certainly the Trial Judge should ideally be perceived as "the personification of justice" by everyone involved in the system, including the defendant. More particularly, however, victims' rights in the criminal justice system are now being asserted more forcefully than ever before. Certainly these rights have long languished, overwhelmed by other considerations.

Victims' rights should be recognized, asserted and protected by the judiciary without doing harm to fundamental rights of defendants. The court, ever mindful of balancing those rights, is asked to disqualify itself from presiding over this matter because prior to a resolution of this case, the victim's family and friends have written to this Trial Judge demanding "justice." Is a defendant's right to a fair trial compromised by the Trial Judge being aware of the outrage of the alleged victim's friends and family? Are communications by the victim's family to the Trial Judge prior to verdict or plea an appropriate manner for the victim to exercise his right to participate in plea and sentence negotiations? Should these communications be encouraged or discouraged?

In this case the defendant, 16 years old, is indicted for the crime of sodomy in the first degree. It is alleged that he anally sodomized a 22-month-old infant. By the nature of these charges, it is understandable that those closest to this incident have responded with intense feelings. The parents and grandparents of the alleged infant victim have reacted with anger, outrage, and a cry for just retribution. The friends of the defendant have reverted to bewilderment, mystified that their "student," "parishioner" or "friend" as the case may be, might be responsible for these charges. Nevertheless, they remain supportive of the defendant.

Having said this by way of introduction, the issue before this court is defendant's application that the court recuse itself in the instant matter. The grounds for this particular request are: (1) that the court has become prejudiced against the defendant by virtue of a "deluge" of letters to the court by the victim's family and friends.

In the first instance, what the defendant has characterized as a "deluge" of letters is not fittingly so described. The defendant has certainly "won the battle" on any quantifiable basis.

On the other hand, this court perceives little or no distinction between the manner in which this case has proceeded, including the submission of letters, and a myriad of other cases that have come before this Trial Judge. Indeed, many more notorious cases before this and other courts have resulted in larger and more vociferous outcries from the victims and, indeed, the entire community.

On the most personal level, this court, having examined its conscience, states categorically and without reservation that it harbors no prejudice against this defendant by reason of the letters, plea discussions or any other facts now known to this Trial Judge. Accordingly, the application then turns on whether the court must, as a matter of law, recuse itself because of some apparent prejudice to the defendant or an appearance of impropriety created by virtue of the letters.

Recently the National Conference of the Judiciary on the Rights of Victims of Crime issued a Statement of Recommended Judicial Practices. This manifesto was the product of a conference of Judges of courts of general jurisdiction of all our States. Those recommendations state, in part, that "victims shall be allowed to participate and, where appropriate, to give input through the prosecutor 'concerning' plea and sentence negotiations." Furthermore, "victim impact statements prior to sentencing should be encouraged and considered." On the other hand, the Canons of Judicial Conduct require that "A judge should except as authorized by law, neither initiate nor consider ex parte or other communications concerning a pending proceeding." The ethical standards of the prosecutor and defense counsel also prohibit ex parte communications with the court.

A Judge should not consider ex parte communications; but, written documents provided to the court, whether supplied by either side or unsolicited, can be considered by the court where they are openly disclosed to the parties. This court concludes, therefore, that all of these letters are not ex parte communications under these circumstances. The court is satisfied that they can be considered in plea and sentence negotiations.

Moreover, this court believes that a victim's communications to the court, when done in the foregoing manner, at any stage of a criminal proceeding should be encouraged and considered by the judiciary. It is important in all criminal cases for the court to know that there are "victims," and to appreciate their concerns about plea bargaining and sentencing. In most instances, victims can and should communicate to the court through the prosecutor, but they should not be limited to that form of communication and participation in the system. Indeed if the crime victim cannot vent his frustrations to the Trial Judge, that "personification" of justice, it undermines all of our efforts to ensure that justice is done under law. This is particularly so in the most heinous of crimes, where the system tries to channel the victim's desire for revenge into a civilized form. By all means, this the judiciary must encourage.

Again, having examined its own conscience, this court states categorically and without reservation that it harbors no prejudice against this defendant and sees no reason in law or in conscience why it cannot preside over a fair trial for this defendant. The motion is therefore denied.

Sec. 11.3; Article 400; Pre-Sentence Proceedings

People v. McIntosh

178 Misc. 2d. 433 (Dutchess Cty. Ct. 1998)

OPINION OF THE COURT: (Re: Constitutionality of standard for jury to follow in determining if death penalty should be applied, 400.27 [11])

Defendant, Dalkeith McIntosh, stands indicted for five counts of murder in the first degree, Penal Law § 125.27. The District Attorney has filed notice pursuant to CPL 250.40 of his intention to seek the death penalty. Defendant has moved for an order invalidating and striking down CPL 400.27 (11) to the extent that the second clause of this provision provides for a vague and standardless determination by a capital sentencing jury whether to impose a sentence of death or a sentence of life in prison without parole on a defendant.

CPL 400.27 (11) (a) provides in relevant part: "The jury may not direct imposition of a sentence of death unless it unanimously finds beyond a reasonable doubt that the aggravating factor or factors substantially outweigh the mitigating factor or factors established, if any, and unanimously determines that the penalty of death should be imposed."

Defendant contends that this provision is inconsistent with the exacting standards and heightened protections associated with the death penalty law, and violates State and Federal law. For the reasons that follow, this court rejects the defendant's contentions and denies the defendant's motion to invalidate CPL 400.27 (11).

The Supreme Court has set forth clear constitutional mandates that must be satisfied for CPL 400.27 (11) to stand. It is uncontested that the death penalty may not be imposed under sentencing procedures that create a substantial risk that it [will] be inflicted in an arbitrary and capricious manner. Accordingly, a State must establish rational criteria that narrow the decisionmaker's judgment as to whether the circumstances of a particular defendant's case meet the threshold.

A State may narrow the category of death-eligible defendants at the guilt phase by narrowing the definition of capital offenses so that the jury finding of guilt responds to this concern. Once the jury finds that the defendant falls within the legislatively defined category of persons eligible for the death penalty, the jury then is free to consider a myriad of factors to determine whether death is the appropriate punishment. Further, states cannot limit the sentencer's consideration of any relevant circumstance that could cause it to decline to impose a penalty. In this respect, the State cannot channel the sentencer's discretion, but must allow it to consider any relevant information offered by the defendant.

In accordance with the mandates above, CPL 400.27 (11) is constitutionally sound. First, the New York Legislature has sufficiently narrowed its category of capital crimes by classifying homicides into six categories and providing that only defendants charged under Penal Law § 125.27 face the possibility of the death penalty. Accordingly, those defendants who are death-eligible must satisfy certain explicitly delineated circumstances and, therefore, stand apart from those who are convicted of other killings.

After a defendant is considered death-eligible, a sentence of death can only be imposed if the jury finds, unanimously and beyond a reasonable doubt, that there exist aggravating factors which "substantially outweigh" any mitigating factors. (CPL 400.27 [11] [a].) Further, the court will instruct the sentencing jury on the proper manner in which to weigh the aggravating factors and any mitigating factors found.

Finally, the New York death penalty statute includes a catch-all mitigating provision and permits the defendant to raise, subject to the rules of evidence, "any evidence relevant to any mitigating factor" contained in CPL 400.27 (9). Moreover, CPL 400.27 (6) allows a defendant to introduce "reliable hearsay evidence" in support of mitigation. Therefore, CPL 400.27 (11) satisfies the constitutional mandates set out by the United States Supreme Court.

CPL 400.27 (11) (a) further safeguards a defendant's constitutional rights. The New York statute permits a jury to decide that the aggravating circumstances, substantially and beyond a reasonable doubt, outweigh the mitigating circumstances, but, nevertheless decline to impose the death penalty. (See, CPL 400.27 [11].) This court sees nothing wrong with permitting—for a defendant's benefit—a narrow window through which human mercy can fit.

Moreover, defendant's complaint that, since the statute is "vague," the jury's sentencing determination is unreviewable by an appellate court, is also without merit. CPL 400.27 (11) (b) specifically provides, "If the jury directs imposition of either a sentence of death or life imprisonment without parole, it shall specify on the record those mitigating and aggravating factors considered and those mitigating factors established by the defendant, if any." Therefore, any sentencing decision rendered by the jury will not be vague, and will be reviewable. Finally, statutes are presumed constitutional.

Therefore, for the foregoing reasons, this court finds New York's death penalty statute to be constitutionally sound. Accordingly, defendant's motion, challenging this portion of the statute, is denied.

People v. Arroyo

683 N.Y.S.2d 788 (1998)

OPINION OF THE COURT: Re: Constitutionality of notice of intent to seek death penalty, 400.27)

On May 28, 1997, the Schoharie County Grand Jury, in a single indictment charged defendants Donna Arroyo, Cary Wayne McKinley and Daniel Edwards with murder in the first and second degrees in the shooting death of Frank Arroyo on May 12, 1997. Defendant Arroyo was also charged with criminal solicitation in the second degree. Notice of intent to seek the death penalty was filed by the District Attorney against all three defendants, and was withdrawn in the case of Cary McKinley.

The defendants move to strike the notice of intent to seek the death penalty on the grounds that Penal Law § 125.27 and CPL 400.27, as enacted and as applied, constitute cruel and unusual punishment, violate the defendants' fundamental right to life, and invite the arbitrary and discriminatory, including racially discriminatory, imposition of the death penalty.

It is well established that State statutes have a strong presumption of constitutionality. The United States Supreme Court has held that the death penalty is not unconstitutional per se. Furthermore, the Supreme Court upheld a bifurcated procedure which called for the sentencing jury to consider the circumstances of the offense together with the character of the defendant. New York's death penalty scheme includes the safeguards approved.

As set forth in this court's decision on motion, the evidence presented to the Grand Jury supports the indictments for the crimes as charged. This court's decision on motion determined that the aggravating circumstance included in Penal Law § 125.27 (1) (a) (vi), murder "for hire," satisfies the constitutional requirement that a capital punishment scheme narrows the class of people eligible for the death penalty and reasonably justifies the imposition of a more severe penalty on the defendant as opposed to others convicted of murder. Prosecutors are given wide discretion in deciding when to seek the death penalty. The defendants have made no showing of prosecutorial conduct indicating arbitrary prosecution or that the prosecutor's decision to seek the death penalty was improperly or illegally made. Furthermore, this court's decision has determined that CPL 400.27 ensures that a jury will not make an arbitrary or discriminatory decision to impose the death penalty.

Defendant Edwards argues that the death penalty has been sought in his case because he is white and the prosecutor needs white conviction statistics to balance the number of black convictions. Defendant Arroyo argues that the death penalty is sought against her because she is a woman and conviction statistics for women are needed to balance those for men; and also, that the death penalty is sought most frequently in cases in which a white person, in this case a white Hispanic, is the victim. The defendants' statistical analysis of death cases to date is unpersuasive on the issue of discriminatory enforcement of the death penalty statutes; the appropriateness of the penalty must be determined in each case on its own merits. Considering that the conduct underlying the crimes charged satisfy the statutory criteria of Penal Law § 125.27 (1) (a) (vi), and the lack of specific abuse on the part of the prosecutor in electing to seek the death penalty, the court finds no discriminatory enforcement in this prosecution on the basis of race, gender or any other impermissible basis of the defendants or of the victim.

However, it should be noted that New York's capital punishment scheme ensures a standard and uniform application by including an extra protection for the defendant: review of the defendant's case in the context of all other similar cases. Whenever a sentence of death is imposed, the Court of Appeals is mandated to review the judgment and sentence; the scope of review includes determining whether a death sentence was imposed under the influence of passion, prejudice, or any other arbitrary or legally impermissible factor including the race of the defendant or a victim of the crime; and whether the death sentence is excessive or disproportionate to the penalty imposed in similar cases, considering both the circumstances of the crime and of the defendant (CPL 470.30 [3].)

The court has considered the defendants' argument that the death penalty runs counter to prevailing societal standards of decency and finds this argument erroneous in light of the United States Supreme Court acceptance of capital punishment and in light of this State's significant and persistent history of death penalty legislation.

All other arguments posed by defendant are lacking in merit.

Chapter 12; Proceedings after Judgment

Sec. 12.1; Article 440: Post-Judgment Motions

People v. Machado

90 N.Y.2d 187 (1997)

OPINION OF THE COURT: (Re: Motion to vacate judgment, Rosario claim, 440.10)

On direct appeal from a judgment of conviction, reversal is required when the prosecution has failed to turn over Rosario material. On CPL 440.10 motions made after direct appeal has been concluded, however, for vacatur of a conviction a defendant must demonstrate prejudice — meaning a reasonable possibility that the prosecution's failure to make Rosario disclosure materially contributed to the verdict. This appeal raises yet another novel question in our Rosario jurisprudence: which of the two standards applies when a CPL 440.10 motion is made before a defendant's direct appeal has been exhausted — the "per se" rule, or a requirement of prejudice? We conclude that a uniform standard governs CPL 440.10 motions, and remit to the Appellate Division to determine whether defendant has been prejudiced by the Rosario violation.

Motivated by the "right sense of justice," this Court 36 years ago in *People v. Rosario* (9 NY2d 286,) established a new rule regarding the disclosure of statements by prosecution witnesses. Before *Rosario*, a trial court determined which documents were relevant to the defense and ordered production accordingly; where discovery was erroneously denied the appellate court applied a harmless error test. *Rosario* changed the practice by requiring the People to turn over pretrial statements of prosecution witnesses, leaving it for the single-minded counsel for the accused rather than trial courts to determine the value of those statements to the defense.

With harmless error still the standard, this equilibrium continued for 15 years, until *People v. Consolazio* (40 NY2d 446). *Consolazio* articulated a rule of per se reversal, in order to assure the People's scrupulous adherence to their obligation to turn over Rosario material. The price for the People's failure to disclose prior statements of their own witnesses thus became automatic reversal of the conviction, a standard this Court has continued during the past two decades to apply to Rosario claims raised on direct appeal.

In formulating these principles, which balanced the various societal and individual interests involved, the Court was guided solely by its own precedents, as a matter of common law. Although the Legislature codified the Rosario rule (CPL 240.45 [1] [a]), it prescribed no other standard of review.

People v. Jackson (78 NY2d 638), however, presented a different calculus. In *Jackson*, the Court was asked to decide whether the automatic reversal rule also should apply to Rosario claims raised in a CPL 440.10 motion, after defendant's direct appeal had been concluded — in that case a full three years after defendant's direct appeal had been exhausted. There, for the first time the Court was faced with the task of harmonizing the common-law Rosario rule with a statute, the enactment of a coequal branch of government. Noting that *Rosario* was not based on State or Federal constitutional principles, but rather on our own balancing of interests, we acknowledged in Jackson that CPL 440.10 involved new policy considerations.

As determined in *Jackson*, the controlling statute is CPL 440.10 (1) (f), which provides that a judgment may be vacated on the ground that the conduct at issue is "improper and prejudicial." Thus, the Court observed, the statute explicitly affords a remedy only if the defendant can demonstrate prejudice. Moreover, just as the Rosario rule reflected the Court's balancing of interests, CPL 440.10 represented the Legislature's own weighing, and reflected the Legislature's overriding concern about society's interest in the finality of judgments. Agreeing with the Legislature that this finality interest was "formidable," and concluding that fairness to defendants would not be unduly compromised by an inquiry into prejudice, we refused to "eviscerate the language of CPL 440.10 (1) (f)" and held that a prejudice standard — not a per se rule — was applicable to Rosario violations raised by postappeal CPL 440.10 motions.

The issue before us concededly presents yet another balance of factors, and neither party offers a wholly satisfactory answer as to where the line should be drawn. We are persuaded, however, that the better course is to apply Jackson: Rosario claims raised by way of CPL 440.10 motions made before direct appeal is exhausted should be rejected unless the violation prejudiced defendant.

Additionally, we are satisfied that the test of prejudice in the Rosario context — a "reasonable possibility" that the nondisclosure materially contributed to the verdict — safeguards both the interest in fairness to defendants and the interest in assuring the People's careful discharge of their disclosure obligation. The "reasonable possibility" test is, after all, "perhaps the most demanding test yet formulated" for harmless error analysis (see, *People v. Crimmins*, 36 NY2d 230). And we have recognized that the "reasonable possibility" test "properly encourages compliance" with the People's Brady obligations *People v. Vilardi*, 76 NY2d 67. That should be no less true with respect to the People's Rosario obligations.

People v. Reyes

255 A.D.2d. 261 (1st Dept. 1998)

OPINION OF THE COURT: (Re: Motion to vacate judgment, new evidence claim, 440.10)

Order, Supreme Court, New York County entered May 21, 1997, which granted defendant's motion pursuant to CPL 440.10 (1) (g) to vacate a judgment rendered March 25, 1988, convicting him, after a jury trial, of criminal possession of a controlled substance and criminal possession of a weapon, on the ground of newly discovered evidence, unanimously reversed, on the law, the motion denied and the judgment reinstated.

Defendant was indicted in May 1987 for illegal possession of narcotics and a weapon after the police found more than 4 ounces of cocaine and a loaded gun in a car in which defendant was a passenger. A Mapp/Huntley hearing was held on February 22, 1988, after which the court denied defendant's motion to suppress in all respects. The court found the prosecution's only witness at the hearing, Police Officer Parson (Parson), to be credible, and rejected defendant's arguments that the stop of the car was unlawful and that his statement to the police that the cocaine belonged to him had been coerced. We affirmed defendant's conviction in November 1990, and leave to appeal to the Court of Appeals was denied in January 1991.

In 1996, Parson was convicted of the crimes of tampering with public records, falsifying business records and filing a false instrument in connection with a 1991 incident where he allegedly stole money from a suspected drug dealer and falsified police reports. He was sentenced to five years probation and 500 hours of community service.

In 1997, defendant filed a pro se motion to vacate his conviction pursuant to CPL 440.10 (1) (g) and (h) on the grounds of newly discovered evidence. The newly discovered evidence claim was based on Parson's 1996 criminal conviction. In his motion, defendant argued that the outcome of the suppression hearing and trial would likely have been different had the evidence of Parson's conviction been available, since Parson was the only witness at the suppression hearing and his crucial testimony at trial regarding his observation of the gun in plain view was not corroborated by his partner. In opposition, the People argued that Parson's conviction was not the type of newly discovered evidence warranting vacatur of a conviction since it was not material to the issue of defendant's possession of the drugs order entered on or about May 21, 1997, the trial court granted defendant's motion, finding that the result of the suppression hearing and trial might have been different had Parson's conviction for falsifying evidence been available.

The order should be reversed and the judgment of conviction reinstated. A court may vacate a criminal conviction rendered after trial on the grounds of newly discovered evidence where such evidence (1) will probably change the result if a new trial is granted; (2) is discovered since the previous trial; (3) was not discoverable before the trial by the exercise of due diligence; (4) is material to an issue at defendant's trial; (5) is not cumulative; and (6) is not merely impeachment testimony (*People v. Salemi*, 309 NY 208).

The evidence of Parson's 1996 conviction is not newly discovered evidence warranting vacatur of defendant's conviction since it fails to meet the fourth and sixth criteria mentioned above, namely, that the evidence is material and not merely impeachment evidence. The evidence is not material because it has nothing to do with defendant's case. The illegal acts committed by Parson occurred three years after defendant was convicted, and therefore have no logical bearing on whether the defendant possessed drugs and a gun three years before. The irrelevance of these acts to defendant's case is underscored by defendant's own trial testimony, during which he admitted that the drugs and gun were in the car, but disclaimed ownership of them. Since defendant admitted the prosecution's version of the facts, but merely offered an innocent explanation for them, Parson's misconduct would not have materially aided his defense.

The sixth criterion was also not met since Parson's conviction constituted only general impeachment material. Parson's illegal conduct in an unrelated incident, three years after defendant's trial, had no bearing on defendant's guilt or innocence in this case.

People v. Harris

178 Misc. 2d. 858 (Qns. Cty. Ct. 1998)

OPINION OF THE COURT: (Re: Motion to set aside sentence, Sex Offender Registration Act issue, 440.20)

The People move to have this court reconsider its April 24, 1998 classification of the defendant for purposes of the Sex Offender Registration Act (Correction Law, art 6-C, § 168 et seq.; hereinafter SORA). After reviewing the People's motion, the applicable case law and the court files, the court rules as follows.

Defendant Harris pleaded guilty before this court on March 25, 1998 to violating Penal Law § 130.60, sexual abuse in the second degree. The case was adjourned to April 24, 1998 for a sex offender risk determination pursuant to the Sex Offender Registration Act (commonly known as Megan's Law). On April 24, 1998, the District Attorney advised this court that a stipulation had been entered into with the defendant's attorney providing for the offender to be classified as a "level two" sex offender, despite the defendant's prior record, which included a previous felony conviction for a sex offense. Albeit erroneously, the court agreed to honor the stipulation of the parties, and thereby made a risk level determination that the defendant be classified a level two (moderate risk

The defendant was released from custody on April 1, 1998. The court was not provided with a recommendation from the Board of Examiners until August 16, 1998, just prior to the People's application herein. The court was not, therefore, given the opportunity, prior to the defendant's discharge into the community, to review the Board's recommendations that the defendant be deemed a level three sexually violent predator.

New York's Sex Offender Registration Act was intended by the Legislature to protect the public from the recidivist tendencies of sex offenders, to assist the criminal justice system in identifying, investigating, apprehending and prosecuting sex offenders, and to comply with the Federal Crime Control Act.

In furtherance of same, a "quasi-regulatory" registration and notification scheme was devised with respect to individuals convicted of sex offenses, whereby these individuals would be classified based on a three-tier system. An offender is assigned a presumptive level one (low risk), level two (moderate risk), or level three (high risk) classification. The Board or court may not depart from the presumptive risk level unless it concludes that there exists an aggravating or mitigating factor of a kind, or to a degree, not otherwise adequately taken into account by the Guidelines. The Board is also mandated to submit its sentencing recommendation to the sentencing court within 60 days from the defendant's release from custody "'providing for one of three levels of notification'," based upon the perceived risk of reoffense. Individuals designated as "level three" are deemed to be "sexually violent predators." These individuals are subject to the widest notification and dissemination parameters.

May a court that adopted a sex offender risk level determination stipulated to by the People and the defendant's counsel for purposes of the SORA vacate the stipulation to correct an error in the risk level classification? For the reasons stated below, the court concludes that the aforementioned stipulation should not have been adopted by the court in its classification of the defendant as a "level two" sex offender, and the defendant must now be deemed, nunc pro tunc, a "level three" sex offender.

But for the stipulation by the People, the defendant would have received a presumptive risk assessment level three designation, based upon his prior felony conviction for a sex crime, and the absence of any mitigation warranting a departure from the override. In seeking to give legal force and effect to the parties' stipulation, the court has inadvertently abrogated to the parties a function that is exclusively within the province of the court.

Given the above, and the policy mandates of the statute, the court is mindful of the need to ameliorate the situation as it now stands. Since the risk level classifications are not properly incorporated within a sentence or judgment, they are not properly reviewable pursuant to CPL article 440. Moreover, even assuming that the SORA determination was considered as a part of a plea or sentence, the court would not have inherent power to vacate a plea and sentence for other than to correct a ministerial or clerical error.

However, within the context of SORA, at least one other court has invoked its inherent power to correct its own records in order to remedy an inadvertent omission in failing to certify a sex offender as mandated by statute.

By taking this measure, the court is acting in compliance with the stated objectives of the statute in protecting the community from the risk of sexual victimization and in properly balancing the rights of the individual against the overriding interests of the many in public safety.

Accordingly, in the interest of completeness, public safety, and compliance with Correction Law § 168-d (1), the court certifies the defendant as a level three sex offender nunc pro tunc, to March 25, 1998, the date of his plea, and directs the amendment of the commitment order to include such certification nunc pro tunc to the date of his sentencing, also on March 25, 1998.

People v. Tookes

167 Misc. 2d. 601 (N.Y. Cty. S. Ct. 1996)

OPINION OF THE COURT: (Re: Motion procedure, motion to test DNA, 440.30)

In 1986, defendant-petitioner was convicted after jury trial of first degree rape and related crimes. Nine years later he moves for an order directing DNA testing of genetic material contained in evidence which was recovered in connection with his trial. He rests his application upon a recent statutory amendment authorizing the court to order such testing after judgment has been entered. (CPL 440.30 [1-a].)

The statute upon which defendant relies was enacted as part of legislation designed to establish standards for State and local government forensic laboratories and to establish a DNA data bank for criminal identification purposes. In cases of convictions obtained before January 1996 a defendant may obtain a court order directing DNA testing of evidence obtained in connection with the case.

The enactment of subdivision (1-a) reflects legislative recognition of the need for a procedural mechanism whereby convicted defendants can seek exoneration through DNA testing which may not have been available at the time of trial.

The incorporation of subdivision (1-a) within CPL article 440 confirms the characterization of DNA test results as potential "newly discovered evidence" which may form the basis for a motion to vacate judgment. Although the Legislature has thus endowed courts with the authority to order DNA testing in a postconviction context, the inartfully drawn statute is confusing regarding the circumstances in which such relief should or must be granted. Since the statute requires testing only where the court has determined that the test results probably would have exonerated the defendant, the statute, if read literally, would require the court to know the result of the test before ordering it. A more reasonable interpretation is that the Legislature intended that DNA testing be ordered only upon a court's threshold determination, in the context of the trial evidence, that testing results carry a reasonable potential for exculpation. In the prestatute cases, where applications for postjudgment testing were granted, the exculpatory potential was clear. The evidence adduced in this case, however, presents a very different picture, in which the exculpatory potential of DNA testing is far from apparent.

It was undisputed at trial that defendant and complainant were known to one another before the crime; they lived in the same apartment complex and had been acquainted for several years. The defense was not one of mistaken identification. Rather, the defendant claimed that the complainant had "made the whole thing up" (i.e., had fabricated a claim of sexual assault and had falsely accused him). The complainant, on the other hand, testified to a brutal assault in her apartment during which defendant threatened her with a knife, forced her to undress and sodomized and raped her; that he then tied her arms to the bedpost, bound her legs, gagged and blindfolded her and tried to suffocate her with a pillow. She further related that before leaving he ransacked the apartment and stole jewelry, money and her keys, threatening to return and kill her mother if she reported the crime.

Other witnesses, including the police, corroborated complainant's bruised and hysterical condition just after the attack and the ransacked condition of the apartment, including the cords hanging from the bedpost which, she testified, the assailant had used to bind her. A physician who examined her the same day also testified to her stricken demeanor, her bruises and to lacerations in her vaginal wall which were consistent with forcible penetration. She identified defendant as her attacker that same day.

Defendant testified on his own behalf and a portion of his criminal history was thus made known to the jury. As noted, he claimed that complainant had fabricated the whole story and had falsely implicated him in revenge for his alleged complicity in the murder of her friend four years earlier; he further called witnesses in support of an alibi defense, maintaining he was elsewhere at the time of the crime.

The physician who testified to laceration in the complainant's vagina also prepared a standard Vitullo rape kit of nail, vaginal, oral and hair specimens. The chemist, who tested the kit and other evidence the day after the crime, testified that there was sperm on the vaginal swab, on the victim's panties and on her bed sheet. The chemist also testified that the precise age of the sperm on the vaginal swab could not be determined; that it could have been a week or two old and hence not a product of the attack.

Under these circumstances, the jury's verdict clearly represented an evaluation of the relative credibility of complainant, on the one hand, and defendant and his witnesses on the other. In view of the crime's corroborated violence adduced by the police and the examining physician, including the complainant's bruised and hysterical condition, the damage to her vagina, and the ransacked apartment, the jury reasonably rejected defendant's assertion that the complainant had fabricated the entire event. Further, if the complainant indeed had been as viciously attacked as the evidence indicated, it is entirely unreasonable to infer that she would falsely accuse the defendant, thereby allowing the true assailant to remain at liberty with the keys to her apartment. Nor is mistaken identity a possibility, inasmuch as defendant acknowledged that he and the complainant had been acquainted for years.

In this evidentiary context it is unlikely that there would have been a verdict more favorable to the defendant even if DNA tests excluded him as the source of the recovered sperm, in view of the sperm's indeterminate age. This conclusion is underscored by the equivocal results of the blood and saliva tests, including defendant's decision not to pursue a then-available enzyme analysis. (As noted, while such an analysis would not have been dispositive of guilt or innocence because of the sperm's uncertain age, it at least might have excluded defendant as its source.)

In light of this assessment of the trial evidence, I conclude that if a DNA test had been conducted and if the results had been admitted in the trial resulting in the judgment, there [does not] exist a reasonable probability that the verdict would have been more favorable to the defendant. (CPL 440.30 [1-a].) Accordingly, defendant's motion for an order directing DNA testing is denied.

Sec. 12.2; Article 450; Appeals — In What Cases Authorized and to What Courts Taken

People v. Calvi
244 A.D.2d 349 (2nd Dept. 1997)

OPINION OF THE COURT: (Re: Waiver of right to appeal, 450.10)

The defendant, a former Commissioner of Planning and Development for the City of Yonkers, after being convicted of charges arising from, inter alia, his acceptance of bribes in connection with the awarding of municipal contracts, entered into a co-operation agreement with the New York State Organized Crime Task Force. The agreement contained a provision wherein the defendant agreed to waive his right to appeal from the judgment of conviction.

To be enforceable, a waiver must be knowing, voluntary and intelligent. When accepting a waiver, a trial court must consider the reasonableness of the bargain, its appropriateness under the circumstances, and the effect on the integrity of the judicial process.

The defendant's contention that he felt he was coerced into entering into the co-operation agreement because he had no choice does not make the waiver of his right to appeal involuntary. Such "situational coercion" does not make the agreement unenforceable where, as here, the record reflects that the agreement was voluntarily entered into with full comprehension on the part of the defendant, who has reaped the benefit of the bargain.

Here, the defendant chose to cooperate, thereby admitting his guilt and waiving his right to appeal, rather than risk being incarcerated for several years in a State penitentiary. In view of the defendant's cooperation, the trial court agreed that the defendant's sentence would run concurrently to a sentence he was then serving in a Federal penitentiary on an unrelated Federal conviction. Accordingly, the waiver was a reasonable and appropriate concession under the circumstances.

Ordered that the judgment is affirmed.

Sec. 12.4; Article 470; Appeals — Determination Thereof

People v. Crimmins

36 N.Y.2d 230 (1975)

OPINION OF THE COURT: (Re: Nonconstitutional harmless error, 470.05)

On this appeal we are called on principally to consider the doctrine of harmless error. The definition and elaboration of the doctrine of harmless error as applied to nonconstitutional error involve peculiarly questions of the law of the State of New York to be determined by our State courts. The doctrine has received expression in our court over the last 20 years in various forms, accompanied usually explicitly, always at least implicitly, by a recognition that errors are almost inevitable in any trial, improprieties almost unavoidable, and that the presence of one or the other furnishes no automatic signal for reversal and retrial.

Examination of the language chosen to describe the doctrine and its application in individual cases, as well as analysis of the authorities selected for citation, discloses that we have not always been either consistent in our classification or uniform in our expression. Forms of our verbalization of the doctrine cannot be nicely harmonized.

The presently applicable legislative statement of our State's rule, like its predecessor, has not been helpful. An appellate court must determine an appeal without regard to technical errors or defects which do not affect the substantial rights of the parties. The choice of the adjective "technical" in referring to errors may be said to connote those of a formalistic or minor character. On the other hand, to refer to errors which may affect "substantial" rights suggests errors of a somewhat more serious nature. Notably there has never been incorporated in the statutory language any concept of "harmlessness beyond a reasonable doubt." In any event, our decisions have not turned on or even been significantly affected by the legislative diction of present CPL section.

The ultimate objective, grounded in sound policy considerations, is the wise balancing, in the context of the individual case, of the competing interests of the defendant and those of the People. While we are ever intent on safeguarding the rights of a defendant we recognize at the same time that the State has its rights too. Thus, it does not follow that an otherwise guilty defendant is entitled to a reversal whenever error has crept into his trial. On the other hand, we recognize that a finding that an error has not been harmless does not result in fatal consequences to the People; they are put to a new trial, but the defendant does not go free.

Unless the proof of the defendant's guilt, without reference to the error, is overwhelming, there is no occasion for consideration of any doctrine of harmless error. What is meant here, of course, is that the quantum and nature of proof, excising the error, are so logically compelling and therefore forceful in the particular case as to lead the appellate court to the conclusion that "a jury composed of honest, well-intentioned, and reasonable men and women" on consideration of such evidence would almost certainly have convicted the defendant.

If, however, an appellate court has satisfied itself that there was overwhelming proof of the defendant's guilt, its inquiry does not end there. Under our system of justice a jury is not commanded to return a verdict of guilty even in the face of apparently conclusive proof of the defendant's guilt. Similarly it may and often does exercise a positive sense of moderating mercy. Further inquiry must accordingly be made by the appellate court as to whether, notwithstanding the overwhelming proof of the defendant's guilt, the error infected or tainted the verdict. An evaluation must therefore be made as to the potential of the particular error for prejudice to the defendant.

We hold that an error is prejudicial in this context if the appellate court concludes that there is a significant probability, rather than only a rational possibility, in the particular case that the jury would have acquitted the defendant had it not been for the error or errors which occurred.

Turning then to the record now before us, we of the majority conclude that, excising both the evidence erroneously admitted (with respect to Rorech's taking a truth test and as to Colabella's refusal to sign a waiver of immunity) and the prosecutor's interrogation of Colabella (as to the latter's damaging admission to Sullivan), there was overwhelming proof that this defendant was guilty of manslaughter in the death of her daughter. In addition to other compelling circumstantial evidence, there was eyewitness testimony that on the night before the daughter's body was found, defendant, carrying what was described as a "bundle" and accompanied by an unidentified man, was seen leading her son from the Crimmins home; that as the man threw the "bundle" into a parked car defendant cried out, "Please don't do this to her," to which the man responded, "Does she know the difference now? Now you're sorry." Additionally defendant herself later confessed her guilt to her paramour, "Joseph, forgive me, I killed her." On the other hand the description which defendant offered of the events of the evening preceding the children's disappearance was completely discredited and the prosecution conclusively exploded defendant's theory, of an outside kidnapper. We read this record as leading only to a single, inexorable conclusion, as two juries have indeed found: defendant was criminally responsible for the death of her daughter.

Proceeding further, then, as we must, we also conclude that in the circumstances of this case there is no significant probability in the light of the overwhelming proof that, had it not been for the errors which occurred, this jury would have acquitted the defendant or that a third jury might do so. Our ultimate conclusion, therefore, is that under our State rule the nonconstitutional errors which occurred on this defendant's second trial were harmless.

People v. Schaeffer

56 N.Y.2d 448 (1982)

OPINION OF THE COURT: (Re: Constitutional harmless error, 470.05)

The question presented on this appeal is whether the concededly erroneous admission into evidence of a statement given in violation of his right to counsel by defendant, Charles Schaeffer, was harmless error in light of his other statements which properly were received. At a suppression hearing, Detective McTigue testified, while they were all still at the mother's house, the mother called out that there was a lawyer on the telephone and McTigue replied that he would not speak to any lawyer on the telephone and that, if it was defendant's lawyer, she should tell him to meet them at the station house.

The police then returned the defendant to the station house, where he made a third, this time more detailed, oral statement to McTigue, who related it to the hearing court as follows: "I questioned the defendant some more and he stated that he was in the bar, he had about 20 drinks, scotch and soda. Charlie, the bartender, started to count the receipts. Mr. [Schaeffer] took a $ 5 bill out and put it on the counter as a tip for the bartender. He took out the .45 and pointed it at Charlie and Charlie said, 'Look, don't get excited, I will take my gun out and I will put it on the bar so you can see that everything is all right.' He said with that the gun went off and it kept on going off and Charlie fell down. He then said, 'I went behind the bar and took the gun. I went home. I put the gun in the basement and I went to bed.'"

It was on this record and no more that the hearing court found that defendant's statements were made, "after he was told of his rights and waived his right to remain silent and he waived his right to counsel when he made the statements." No specific finding was made concerning the point at which defendant invoked his right to counsel. All the statements were ruled admissible.

It is clear that admission of defendant's detailed station house statement, taken by McTigue immediately after the detective had refused to speak to counsel on the telephone, was reversible error. Indeed, the People candidly concede that, from that moment, further questioning should have ceased. Surely, defendant's right to counsel had attached and it could not be waived in counsel's absence and any statements taken in violation of that right would be subject to suppression.

The harmless error rule, as it relates to error of constitutional dimension, is, simply stated, "that there is no reasonable possibility that the error might have contributed to defendant's conviction and that it was thus harmless beyond a reasonable doubt."

And, because consideration of whether an error is harmless requires an evaluation not only of the tainted matter, but of the strength of the case absent the taint, the court must focus on the reliability and persuasiveness of the untainted matter and its source. So, for instance, written statements may be "looked at as more reliable than their more evanescent oral counterparts." In short, neither side of the evidentiary equation may be ignored; in the end, the picture must be seen as a whole. The ultimate question, of course, must be whether the People, as the beneficiary of the error, have fully borne the burden of establishing harmlessness by the strict, though not unrealistic standard; fair trial requires no less.

Turning then to the statements in the case before us now, we note at once that the one statement taken in defiance of the fact that the right to counsel had attached not only was by far the longest, but also the most detailed. The tainted statement, independently and noncumulatively, told a tale by which, although the defendant attempted to portray the events of the fatal night as ones culminating in an accident, it readily could have led the jury to believe his motive was robbery, since it included, for the first time, a recounting of how Angelos had started to count his day's receipts immediately before he was killed. Moreover, this dovetailed particularly in its timing, with what might otherwise have been the less significant fact that, when Angelos' body was found, he was clutching money in his hand.

Furthermore, other condemnatory evidentiary interaction between the tainted statement's factual recital and the People's properly admitted proof at trial came to depend on the defendant's assertion therein that the gun went off, presumably by accident, after defendant had placed it on the bar behind which Angelos was standing. This became the very vulnerable target of the People's forensic evidence, which was offered to establish not only that Angelos had been shot after he had already fallen, or been pushed, to the floor, but, as a not inconsequential byproduct, to undermine the credibility of defendant's story as a whole.

In all, on the record here, we conclude as a matter of law that it cannot be said beyond a reasonable doubt that the erroneously admitted statement did not contribute to the defendant's conviction. Accordingly, the order of the Appellate Division should be reversed, the tainted statement suppressed.

People v. Robinson

36 N.Y.2d 224 (1975)

OPINION OF THE COURT: (Re: Timely protest and claim of error, 470.05)

The issue in this case is whether an alleged error in the trial court's charge to the jury, to which no exception was taken, is reviewable in this court on the theory that defendant was deprived of a fair trial.

Defendant was convicted, following a jury trial, of the crimes of murder, attempted robbery and attempted grand larceny. The facts would warrant a jury finding that defendant, acting with the requisite culpable mental state, intentionally aided George and Gargo in the commission of the crime of attempted robbery during which one of the participants, known to him to be armed, caused the death of a victim.

The charge to the jury left something to be desired. In at least two places it misstated a fact by informing the jury that defendant had interposed an affirmative defense. There was no basis in fact for that statement since defendant had denied all knowledge of and participation in the underlying crimes. At other times, the statement of the applicable law was confusing and misleading. Illustrative of the latter defect is the court's statement: "The People have the burden of proving the defendant guilty beyond a reasonable doubt except in certain instances."

However, the charge, read as a whole, though ineptly phrased, correctly informed the jury that the burden of proof of guilt beyond a reasonable doubt was upon the People and that, if defendant was found guilty of attempted robbery, the burden of proof of the affirmative defense to felony murder was upon him to establish by a fair preponderance of the evidence. No request to charge made by defense counsel was rejected by the court and, at the conclusion of the corrective statements requested by counsel, in response to a question by the Trial Judge, said counsel declared "I have no exceptions."

Except in the instance of an appeal taken directly to the Court of Appeals in capital cases, the jurisdiction of the Court of Appeals in criminal cases is limited to considering law. With respect to a ruling or instruction of a criminal court during a trial or proceeding, a question of law is presented "when a protest thereto was registered, by the party claiming error, at the time of such ruling or instruction or at any subsequent time when the court had an opportunity of effectively changing the same." (CPL 470.05, subd. 2.). The failure to object to the charge in this case or to request further clarifications at a time when the error complained of could readily have been corrected preserved no questions of law reviewable in this court. We note in this regard that counsel for both sides are not without responsibility in protecting the substantial rights of the parties and that that responsibility extends to calling the attention of the court to errors of law which adversely affect a client at a time when such errors are correctible.

Although this court cannot review the alleged errors in the charge for the reasons indicated, appellant has not been deprived of a forum in which his arguments can be heard. We recognize that the Appellate Division is statutorily empowered to "consider and determine any question of law or issue of fact involving error or defect in the criminal court proceedings which may have adversely affected the appellant" (CPL 470.15, subd. 1), even though no protest was registered at the trial (CPL 470.15, subds. 3, 6, par. [a]). It was within the sole discretion of the Appellate Division to consider appellant's claim of errors in the charge. That court, however, unanimously affirmed the judgment.

We are constrained here to affirm the order of the Appellate Division since the alleged errors are not reviewable in this court in the absence of a proper exception or request (CPL 470.05, subd. 2).

People v. Bleakley
69 N.Y.2d 490 (1987)

OPINION OF THE COURT: (Re: Weight of evidence, authority of intermediate appellate court to review, 470.15)

We hold that it is reversible error when the Appellate Division manifestly avoids its exclusive statutory authority to review the weight of the evidence in criminal cases.

Each defendant, Timothy Bleakley and Jeffrey J. Anesi, has been found guilty by a jury at a joint trial of two counts of rape in the first degree, one count of sodomy in the first degree and sexual abuse in the first degree. By a divided court, the Appellate Division affirmed the judgments of conviction. The principal issue is whether defendants have been deprived of one of their available statutory standards of intermediate appellate court review, a review based on the weight of the evidence (CPL 470.15 [5]). We discern that in this case they have been so deprived.

The very serious crimes for which both defendants stand convicted started out with some drinking in taverns late in the evening, then some social and amicable bar encounters in the early morning hours which evolved to an automobile setting where the victim and the two defendants planned to "do some coke" together. They did so. The versions of what happened thereafter differ sharply. The victim testified to a horrible and forcible double rape and sodomy. The defendants testified to one consensual sexual incident. There is other evidence of a circumstantial nature dealing with sexual conduct and possible forcible circumstances. There are also serious credibility and discrepancy assertions with respect to all the key witnesses.

Unquestionably, these features all relate principally to the jury's properly exercised function and its resolution in this respect eliminates any further relevant concern with respect to the evidentiary standard of sufficiency or reasonable doubt. But, based on what is before us on this record, the Appellate Division did not do the factual analysis of whether the jury determination was against the weight of the evidence, a review which may take place only in an intermediate appellate court.

Unlike this court which, with few exceptions, passes on only questions of law, intermediate appellate courts are empowered to review questions of law and questions of fact. Indeed, this unique factual review power is the linchpin of our constitutional and statutory design intended to afford each litigant at least one appellate review of the facts.

Although the two standards of intermediate appellate review — legal sufficiency and weight of evidence — are related, each requires a discrete analysis. For a court to conclude, as the Appellate Division did in this case, that a jury verdict is supported by sufficient evidence, the court must determine whether there is any valid line of reasoning and permissible inferences which could lead a rational person to the conclusion reached by the jury on the basis of the evidence at trial and as a matter of law satisfy the proof and burden requirements for every element of the crime charged. If that is satisfied, then the verdict will be upheld by the intermediate appellate court on that review basis.

To determine whether a verdict is supported by the weight of the evidence, however, the appellate court's dispositive analysis is not limited to that legal test. Even if all the elements and necessary findings are supported by some credible evidence, the court must examine the evidence further. If based on all the credible evidence a different finding would not have been unreasonable, then the appellate court must, like the trier of fact below, weigh the relative probative force of conflicting testimony and the relative strength of conflicting inferences that may be drawn from the testimony. If it appears that the trier of fact has failed to give the evidence the weight it should be accorded, then the appellate court may set aside the verdict (CPL 470.20 [2]).

Empowered with this unique factual review, intermediate appellate courts have been careful not to substitute themselves for the jury. Great deference is accorded to the fact-finder's opportunity to view the witnesses, hear the testimony and observe demeanor. Without question the differences between what the jury does and what the appellate court does in weighing evidence are delicately nuanced, but differences there are.

Here the Appellate Division, on a plain reading of the majority and dissenting opinions, failed to provide its exclusive review authority which is expressly withheld from the trial court and even from this court. We must, therefore, remit for that court to complete its consideration of the case, including application of its weight of evidence review.

In directing the corrective action in this case, we do not imply that the Appellate Division must manifest its weight of evidence review power by writing in all criminal cases. But where the order and writings of the intermediate appellate court manifest a lack of application of that review power which appellants are entitled to, then we reverse and remit.

Accordingly, the order of the Appellate Division should be reversed and the case remitted for further proceedings in accordance with this opinion.

Chapter 13; Securing Attendance at Court of Defendants; Recognizance, Bail and Commitment

Sec. 13.2; Article 510; Rules of Law and Criteria Controlling Determinations

People v. Torres

112 Misc.2d. 145 (NY Cty. Crm. Ct. 1981)

OPINION OF THE COURT: (Re: Right to bail, threat to public safety, 510.30)

On this motion by the People to revoke bail, the court ordered a hearing to determine the facts. On September 2, 1981 and on two later occasions, the defendant, through the father of another witness to the first crime, one Anibal Castro, threatened harm to Anibal if the misdemeanor case was not dropped. Subsequently, on September 9, 1981, the defendant, possibly carrying out his threat, stabbed Anibal Castro. Re-arrested for this assault, bail was fixed in the amount of $10,000. Bail was posted and the defendant was released. An indictment was filed on October 7, 1981 for the felony of attempted murder, but no change in bail conditions was made upon arraignment in the Supreme Court. Neither at the time of the bail hearing nor at the arraignment upon the indictment was the court apprised of the underlying misdemeanor charge, nor of the relationship between that charge and the felony. A threat made by a defendant to a witness, after the fixation of bail, is sufficient to warrant a decision revoking bail.

Although there is no constitutional right to bail, and a court is not obligated to release a defendant on bail, when a court does set bail it cannot be set in an unreasonably high amount, and must not be set as a punitive measure. Bail has historically been considered as a security device, the purpose of which is to guarantee the presence of the defendant at trial. Before determining the appropriate amount of bail, a court must first determine whether or not bail should be fixed, i.e., whether the defendant should be permitted to remain at liberty under any circumstances. Both of these decisions are within the sound discretion of the Judge before whom the bail application is made.

Since bail is a security device, it must be fixed only in an amount that is both sufficient and necessary to guarantee the defendant's appearance. Other factors, such as the defendant's potential danger to the community, are not relevant to this issue and cannot be properly considered in fixing the amount of bail. Such factors may, however, be relevant to the court's threshold determination, whether or not any bail should be set at all. If a defendant would present a clear and present danger if free in the community then it would not matter whether he had posted $100,000 bail or was released on his own recognizance. Danger to the community has no relationship to the ability of a defendant to post a bond. Therefore, if a court determines that a defendant would be a threat if released prior to trial its duty is to remand him rather than set an extremely high bail. Courts have remanded defendants without bail finding good cause based on "extraordinary" evidence of danger to the community including involvement in multiple bombings and in cases of witness tampering. Therefore, where, as here, substantial evidence that the defendant, if allowed to remain at liberty, presents a substantial danger to the administration of justice, bail previously set can and should be revoked.

The statutory criteria which the court must consider in determining bail status include (CPL 510.30, subd. 2):

1. Character, reputation, habits and mental condition.
2. Employment status and financial resources.
3. Family ties and length of residence, if any, in the community.
4. Criminal record, if any, including record of previous adjudication as a juvenile delinquent.
5. Previous record, if any, in responding to court appearances when required or with respect to flight to avoid criminal prosecution.
6. The weight of the evidence against him in the pending criminal action and any other factor indicating probability or improbability of conviction.
7. The sentence which may be imposed upon conviction.

These factors are not a catechism or checklist which make the Judge's role ministerial. On the contrary, they are objective indicia of responsibility which, if favorable, generally correlate with a likelihood that the defendant will reappear in court. Upon analysis, it is no surprise that the seriousness of a crime and the weight of the evidence were always considered significant in determining whether or not bail should be granted. The same logic applies with even greater force where a defendant is yet again arrested. A new arrest may, in many, if not most cases, indicate irresponsibility. The underlying evidence may show that the court's initial appraisal of his character, reputation or habits was erroneous. It may be an indication of unstable mental condition. It may, by casting him in a different light, cause a reassessment of the weight of evidence against him in the pending case, and thus may ultimately make a greater sentence more likely. In short, in most cases, rearrest for a serious crime, supported by reasonable cause to believe that he committed that crime, amounts to evidence of both dangerousness to the community and a greater likelihood of flight. It would thus be a sufficient basis for reconsideration of the initial decision to grant bail, and depending on the circumstances, it may well constitute good cause for revocation. A subsequent arrest by itself, however, without evidence of the underlying crime, has never per se constituted good cause for revocation of bail.

The court concludes that the People have met their burden of showing good cause for revocation. The threats, express and oblique, were calculated to frustrate the ability of the court to do justice. Had they been known initially, the defendant should not have been permitted to remain at liberty. The action responsible for the rearrest — the stabbing of complainant in the underlying case — was part of a pattern intended to prevent prosecution. However, it is also evidence of consciousness of guilt and thus substantially increases both the likelihood of conviction on the original charge, and the total potential and likely punishment. At best, it displays a rash, uncontrolled emotionality; at worst, it evinces a depraved act. It therefore shows the kind of irresponsibility which must be considered negatively under the "character, reputation and mental condition" category of the bail statute. In sum, the defendant's conduct not only frustrates the interest of justice but indicates as well a heightened risk that he may flee.

The defendant is accordingly ordered remanded pending trial.

Sec. 13.4; Article 530; Recognizance or Bail; When and by What Courts Authorized

People v. Davis

118 Misc.2d 122 (Westchester Cty. Ct. 1983)

OPINION OF THE COURT: (Re: Mandatory release by local court under 180.80, 530.20)

On August 17, 1982, defendant was arrested by Greenburgh police pursuant to a warrant issued upon a felony complaint charging him with burglary in the second degree. He was promptly fingerprinted and photographed by the police. On the same day, he was directed to be held by the then presiding Town Justice on $10,000 insured bond or cash bail. The securing order provided for the return of the defendant on the next available court date which was then August 24, 1982. He was not arraigned. Other Judges were available to arraign at all times between August 17 and August 24, 1982. On August 24, 1982, assigned counsel for defendant moved for the release of the defendant on his own recognizance pursuant to CPL 180.80 on the grounds that defendant had been confined for 72 hours without being afforded a felony hearing (effective Aug. 21, 1982, the time period was extended to 144 hours). In view of the public interest expressed in this particular matter and the general public interest, a written decision setting forth the reasons for the defendant's release is required.

It is a truism that the lifeblood of individual rights is found in the procedure available to effectuate these rights. Substantial compliance with procedural rights is necessary to prevent a society from sliding into the darkness of totalitarianism. Police power rightfully exercised protects the public. Police power wrongfully used is the dictator's weapon. The Criminal Procedure Law of New York requires prompt arraignment pursuant to a warrant of arrest or arrest without a warrant (CPL 120.90, 140.20). Upon arresting a person with a warrant, the police must record his fingerprints, perform other preliminary police duties, bring the arrested person before a local criminal court, and file an appropriate accusatory instrument charging the defendant with the offense in question, all without unnecessary delay (CPL 120.90.).

Arraignment is not a mere technical formality. It is a means by which essential fairness is introduced into the criminal justice system balancing the rights of the public to be free from criminal activity with the right of the defendant to be clothed with a meaningful presumption of innocence, to allow him to prepare his defense against the power of the State. Prompt arraignment insures that defendant is advised of the charges against him, and of his right to counsel, to seek bail, to communicate with counsel, family and friends and to advise as to whereabouts, to undertake prompt investigation of the charges, and to do all that can be done to meet the challenge of the arrest. The arraignment is a crucial stage in the proceedings and from the defendant's point of view it is the first time that he is brought into neutral territory after being arrested, fingerprinted, photographed and held incommunicado for a reasonable period pending police processing. It would have been at arraignment that the defendant could have made his demand for a felony hearing under the then existing CPL 180.80. The statutory scheme also insists on prompt arraignment to permit the police to remain free of suspicion of threats and brutality in the extortion of confession. Unnecessary delay in arraignment is a violation of the statute; a delay in arraignment from arrest where the defendant could have been arraigned, renders the police guilty of unnecessary delay as a matter of law. Failure to cause a defendant to be arraigned without unreasonable delay may constitute a crime. Police may also be liable for civil damages for violating the defendant's rights. Even where the defendant has been convicted of two previous felonies and the lower criminal court ordinarily would not have jurisdiction to fix bail under CPL 530.20 (subd. 2), the local court must release the defendant on his own recognizance where there has been a violation of CPL 180.80.

Following defendant's arrest, the police properly discharged their duties under CPL 120.90 by promptly fingerprinting and processing the defendant and notifying the then presiding Town Justice of his arrest for the purpose of having him brought before the court. After communicating with the then presiding Town Justice on August 17, 1982, the date of the arrest, the police acted in compliance with his directions (as they were required to do). It was the commitment signed by the then presiding Town Justice which ordered defendant held in lieu of $10,000 secured bond or cash bail until August 24, 1982, one week later. He never ordered the defendant to be arraigned before himself or any other court or Judge in the interim and did not notify any other court or Judge of defendant's arrest and incarceration and did not assign counsel to defendant nor was defendant represented by private counsel. Counsel was assigned on August 24, 1982 when the defendant was brought before the court for the first time.

Holding a prisoner incommunicado for seven days is something that simply should not happen in a democratic society. The defendant is accordingly released on his own recognizance.

People v. Boop
397 N.Y.S.2d 573 (1977)

OPINION OF THE COURT: (Re: Requirement of fingerprint record before release, 530.40)

The defendant was arrested on May 14, 1977, on a charge of driving while intoxicated. He was taken that evening to the county jail. The following day he was fingerprinted and released. The prints were sent to the Division of Criminal Justice Services on May 20, and a report of the defendant's prior criminal record was returned to the Sheriff's office on May 31. Because of defendant's prior conviction of driving while intoxicated in July, 1976, the case was presented to a Grand Jury and this indictment was one of many included in a report to this court on July 27, 1977. The District Attorney scheduled the case for arraignment on the felony indictment for August 10, 1977, and the defendant voluntarily appeared with counsel on that date. Immediately after the arraignment, the defendant entered a plea of not guilty and asked for release under bail. This court then advised that it had not been furnished with a report of the defendant's prior criminal record as required by CPL 530.40.

CPL 160.10 establishes the duty of the police with regard to fingerprinting of arrested persons. CPL 160.20 directs that the prints must be sent to the Division of Criminal Justice Services without unnecessary delay. That division, in turn, must search its records and promptly transmit a report to the forwarding officer or agency. (CPL 160.30.) Finally, the local agency is mandated to transmit promptly a copy of the report to the District Attorney of the county. (CPL 160.40.)

With respect to admission on bail, CPL 530.40 (subd. 4) provides: "a superior court may not order recognizance or bail when the defendant is charged with a felony unless and until the district attorney has had an opportunity to be heard in the matter and such court has been furnished with a report as described in subparagraph (ii) of paragraph (b) of subdivision two of section 530.20." The report referred to is the report of the fingerprint check by the Division of Criminal Justice Services or a local police department report as to the defendant's prior criminal record.

While there is no constitutional guarantee of the right to be admitted to bail in New York, nonetheless the constitutional prohibition of deprivation of liberty without due process is applicable to bail procedures. Due process relates to procedures as well as substance. A law or a procedure may be unconstitutional from the way it operates and the effect it has. Likewise, a law or procedure may be unconstitutional because of the way it is administered. A law which is constitutional as to one matter may violate the Constitution when applied to another. In the present case, the court finds in all, 26 days elapsed and the report has not been transmitted to the District Attorney. To refuse to admit the defendant to bail because of the lack of a report on the facts in this case would be to deprive him of his liberty without due process of law. Accordingly, the defendant must be released although the report has not been furnished to the court.

Chapter 14; Securing Attendance at Court of Defendants Not Securable by Conventional Means and Related Matters

Sec. 14.3; Article 570; Securing Attendance of Defendants from outside the State but within the U.S.; Rendition to Other States; Uniform Criminal Extradition Act

People v. Culwell
621 N.Y.S.2d 490 (1995)

OPINION OF THE COURT: (Re: Fugitive's presence in demanding state, 570.06)

In this habeas corpus proceeding brought by defendant/alleged fugitive William K. Culwell to test the legality of his arrest under the Governor's extradition warrant, this court holds and determines that the writ of habeas corpus is sustained and the alleged fugitive discharged from custody without prejudice to such further proceedings as the sovereign State of Alabama shall deem advisable.

William Culwell left his wife and two minor children in the State of Alabama in August 1989 and has resided in New York State ever since. The alleged fugitive's wife obtained a default judgment of divorce on October 2, 1989 in the Circuit Court of Cullman County, Alabama, which judgment ordered the alleged fugitive to pay $400 per month child support.

The defendant/alleged fugitive since September 7, 1989 has possessed a valid New York State driver's license, and has worked at various jobs in New York State, and has filed Federal and New York State resident income tax returns for the years 1990, 1991, 1992 and 1993. In late 1990 or early 1991, the alleged fugitive flew to Alabama to visit his critically ill father in a hospital. The testimony and documentary evidence adduced by defendant/alleged fugitive conclusively establishes that he has resided in New York State continuously since August 1989.

The request for interstate rendition signed by Alabama Governor Jim Folsom recites that William Kent Culwell stands charged with the crime of failure or refusal to support family "committed in the COUNTY OF CULLMAN while personally present in the State of Alabama." The extradition warrant signed by Governor Mario Cuomo recites "that the accused was present in said State at the time of the commission of the crime, and thereafter fled therefrom and [has] taken refuge in the State of New York."

Extradition contemplates the prompt return of a fugitive once the officials in the State where the charges are pending appropriately demand his or her return. Thus, a court reviewing a petition for a writ of habeas corpus seeking a release from a grant of extradition is extremely limited in its scope of inquiry. The only issues which should concern a reviewing court are: (1) whether the extradition documents are facially sufficient, (2) whether the petitioner has been charged with a crime in the demanding State, (3) whether the petitioner is the person named in the extradition request, and (4) whether the person arrested in the asylum State was a fugitive.

Clearly, Governor Cuomo's extradition warrant was issued under the mandatory provisions of CPL 570.06 and 570.08 reflecting the mandate of US Constitution, article IV, § 2, cl (2) which provides in relevant part: "A Person charged in any State with Treason, Felony, or other Crime, who shall flee from Justice, and be found in another State, shall on Demand of the executive Authority of the State from which he fled, be delivered up, to be removed to the State having Jurisdiction of the Crime." To be a fugitive from justice within the meaning of these sections, the alleged fugitive must have been physically present in the demanding State at the time of the commission of the crime.

In this case, the defendant/alleged fugitive has presented clear and convincing testimony and documentary evidence that between October 2, 1989 and January 1992 he resided continuously in the State of New York and was not physically present in the State of Alabama — except for a period of four days when he visited his critically ill father in a hospital in Alabama. Hence, the defendant/alleged fugitive is not a "fugitive from justice" with respect to the crime of failure or refusal to support family because he was not physically present in the State of Alabama at the time of the commission of the crime; therefore, this court holds and determines that the writ of habeas corpus is sustained and defendant/alleged fugitive is discharged from custody, without prejudice to such future proceedings as the sovereign State of Alabama shall deem advisable.

The extradition warrant should have been requested and issued in compliance with the discretionary provisions of CPL 570.16 which reflect the policy of this State with respect to discretionary extradition and must be complied with.

CPL 570.16 includes requirements that: (1) the Alabama accusatory instrument and supporting affidavits must establish that defendant committed an act which would be a crime in New York and (2) the Alabama accusatory instrument must contain the allegation that defendant committed an act in the State of New York which intentionally resulted in the commission of a crime in the State of Alabama.

This court holds and determines that the writ of habeas corpus is hereby sustained and that the defendant/alleged fugitive is hereby discharged from custody, without prejudice to such further proceedings as the sovereign State of Alabama shall deem advisable.

Former President Ronald Reagan on August 16, 1984 stated: "The failure of some parents to support their children is a blemish on America." This court has no sympathy for the alleged fugitive, who arguably should be criminally prosecuted based upon the substantive allegations against him.

However, this court clearly has a duty and responsibility to enforce compliance with New York statutes and decisional law, and in this case, mandatory extradition under CPL 570.06 and 570.08 is not properly obtainable because the defendant/alleged fugitive was not physically present in Alabama at the time of the commission of the crime, and the provisions of CPL 570.16 with regard to discretionary extradition warrants have not been complied with.

People v. LaFontaine

682 N.Y.S.2d 671 (1998)

OPINION OF THE COURT: (Re: Arrest of accused without a warrant, 570.34)

This is a defendant's appeal to this Court from an order sustaining a trial court denial of suppression of evidence and affirming an ensuing conviction on a guilty plea. We agree with the Appellate Division majority and dissent only to the extent that they unanimously reject the authority of the New Jersey police officers to execute New Jersey or Federal arrest warrants in New York State, under the circumstances presented by this case. Because that resolution removes the only reviewable predicate for a lawful arrest, a reversal is mandated.

The People, as respondent in this Court and at the Appellate Division, offer alternative grounds for the lawfulness of the arrest, and for an affirmance result. We are constrained, however, to reverse the Appellate Division order affirming defendant's conviction, and to remit the matter to Supreme Court for further proceedings. In the unusual procedural posture of this case, the alternative grounds proffered here, and utilized at the Appellate Division, are beyond the statutory review powers of each tribunal.

Defendant was arrested on the fire escape outside his New York City apartment by four police officers of the City of Paterson, New Jersey. They possessed New Jersey and Federal arrest warrants for crimes committed in New Jersey at some prior time.

Two of the officers knocked on the apartment door and identified themselves as police. This announcement apparently precipitated defendant's flight to the fire escape, where he was ultimately apprehended by a third officer stationed outside and one floor below. Immediately after the arrest, the officers entered defendant's apartment, where they observed and seized plastic bags of cocaine and drug paraphernalia. Defendant and the contraband were turned over to the New York City Police Department.

The District Attorney of New York County indicted defendant on two counts of criminal possession of a controlled substance in the third degree (Penal Law § 220.16 [1], [12]) and one count of criminally using drug paraphernalia in the second degree (Penal Law § 220.50). Defendant moved to suppress the evidence seized from his apartment as the fruit of an unlawful arrest.

Following a suppression hearing, Supreme Court denied the motion (159 Misc 2d 751). The trial court determined that, although the New Jersey officers lacked authority to execute their State's arrest warrant in New York, they licitly executed the Federal warrant here. Because the arrest was found lawful, the evidence was also deemed justifiably seized under the plain view exception. Defendant then pleaded guilty to criminal possession of a controlled substance in the third degree.

The Appellate Division, with two Justices dissenting, affirmed the conviction and upheld the denial of suppression, but on a different basis (235 AD2d 93). The majority rejected the trial court's conclusion that the officers were authorized to execute the Federal arrest warrant in New York. Instead, in a thorough opinion, it sustained the denial of suppression on an alternative ground — that the New Jersey police effected an authorized citizen's arrest pursuant to CPL 570.34, a ground explicitly rejected by Supreme Court. One of the dissenting Justices at the Appellate Division granted defendant leave to appeal to this Court. The correspondingly thorough dissenting opinion would have reversed, rejected all arguments in favor of the arrest, and suppressed the evidence (235 AD2d 93, 100–109, supra).

The People try to rebut the thrust of defendant's appeal in this Court by again tendering a kaleidoscope of arguments supporting denial of suppression and affirmance of the conviction. They contend either that the arrest was valid pursuant to the Federal arrest warrant; or that the officers were acting as agents of the New York City Police Department at the time of the arrest; or that the arrest was a valid citizen's arrest pursuant to CPL 570.34, and that, even if the arrest was unauthorized, the exclusionary rule should not apply in these circumstances.

This Court's review is limited by statute to the Federal warrant issue in these procedural circumstances — as is the Appellate Division's (CPL 470.35 [1]; 470.15 [1].

The alternative issues, albeit potentially relevant, and even independently dispositive, were not properly prescribed for review on defendant's appeal to the Appellate Division. CPL 470.15 (1) provides that the Appellate Division can review only errors or defects that "may have adversely affected the appellant" in the criminal court (CPL 470.15 [1]). This Court has construed CPL 470.15 (1) as a legislative restriction on the Appellate Division's power to review issues either decided in an appellant's favor, or not ruled upon, by the trial court. That constraint concomitantly narrows this Court's powers when considered within our own statutorily prescribed regimen.

Upon an appeal to this Court from an intermediate court order affirming a judgment, sentence or order of a criminal court, this Court may consider and determine only questions of law which were raised or considered upon the appeal to the intermediate appellate court, or involve alleged error or defect in the criminal court proceeding resulting in the original criminal court judgment, sentence or order (see, CPL 470.35 [1]). This limitation is not a standard preservation permutation. Rather, a threshold prescription of the legislative devolution of powers to the respective appellate courts is the precise, core problem here. Curiously, the range of available relief is not only different but also more flexible when an appeal arrives on this Court's docket in a reversal procedural mode (CPL 470.35 [2]).

These limitations allow only the Federal warrant issue to be before this Court under these circumstances. Any other facet of the case cannot be said to have led to suppression or to the ultimate judgment of conviction, as those other issues were either decided in defendant's favor or not ruled on by the suppression court (CPL 470.35 [1]).

Moreover, the alternative grounds for affirmance advanced by the People were not properly "raised or considered" at the Appellate Division (CPL 470.35 [1]) because the Federal arrest warrant issue was the only issue decided adversely to defendant at the trial court (CPL 470.15 [1]). It alone constituted the ratio decidendi for upholding the legality of the arrest and denying the suppression of evidence. The Appellate Division's review, therefore, is confined to that issue alone, as is ours.

Once the Appellate Division rejected — unanimously in that respect — the nisi prius court's Federal warrant basis for the arrest, that intermediate appellate court was left with little alternative but to reverse the denial of suppression and remit the case to Supreme Court for further proceedings. In these unusual circumstances, the People might be able to seek reexamination of the alternative suppression justifications that have been part of this case since its onset, either before the nisi prius court on the remittal or, depending on the nature and configuration of eventual new rulings there, on an ensuing appeal.

We are concerned that the fragmented movement up and down for resolution concerning a core issue is less than holistic. In these circumstances, the procedural circuity also contradicts the nostrum that a court should be able to preserve a result from a lower court by sometimes applying an independent alternative rationale where, as here, the issue was properly raised before the nisi prius court. While that tool can still be an available tool for comprehensive handling of cases and fair administration of justice, the exceptional procedural twist exposed again by the instant case blocks that sensible management of this case. Since the anomaly rests on unavoidable statutory language, any modification would be for the Legislature to change, if it so wishes.

Turning then to the only issue before us and the only ground for or against suppression that may be reviewed, we agree with the unanimous analysis of the Appellate Division. Supreme Court erred in determining that the New Jersey officers were authorized to execute the Federal arrest warrant in New York, under the record circumstances presented in this case. Federal Rules of Criminal Procedure, rule 4 (d) (1) provides that a Federal warrant can be executed by a Federal Marshal or "by some other officer authorized by law." The New Jersey officers were not Federal Marshals, nor were they, de jure or de facto, authorized as Federal equivalent officers in these circumstances.

Looking to New York law to determine whether the New Jersey officers were authorized to arrest defendants through the Federal process they possessed, we discover no State common-law predicate for a Federal tie-in authority. Indeed, the sparse case law available indicates that only an officer specially authorized to make arrests in New York can execute a Federal warrant in New York for New York prosecution purposes. Out-of-State police officers may be authorized to make arrests in New York, but generally only when they are in hot pursuit, concededly not the case here (see, CPL 140.55).

Next, we note that the New Jersey officers were not authorized by any New York statute to execute the Federal warrant in New York. CPL 120.60 provides that warrants can be executed only by a police or peace officer and the New Jersey officers do not so qualify (see, CPL 1.20 [33], [34]; 2.10, 120.60).

Having concluded that the only issue decided adversely to defendant at Supreme Court was decided incorrectly at that level, we reverse and remit to Supreme Court for such further proceedings, as may be appropriate.

Accordingly, the order of the Appellate Division should be reversed, and the matter remitted to Supreme Court for further proceedings in accordance with this opinion.

Order reversed

Sec. 14.4; Article 580; Securing Attendance of Prisoners from Other United States Jurisdictions; Agreement on Detainers

New York v. Hill

Supreme Court of the United States
528 U.S. 110 (2000)

OPINION OF THE COURT: (Re: Waiver of 180 day period, speedy trial violation, 580.20)

JUSTICE SCALIA delivered the opinion of the Court.

This case presents the question whether defense counsel's agreement to a trial date outside the time period required by Article III of the Interstate Agreement on Detainers bars the defendant from seeking dismissal because trial did not occur within that period.

I

The Interstate Agreement on Detainers (IAD) is a compact entered into by 48 States, the United States, and the District of Columbia to establish procedures for resolution of one State's outstanding charges against a prisoner of another State. See N. Y. Crim. Proc. Law § 580.20. As "a congressionally sanctioned interstate compact" within the Compact Clause of the United States Constitution, Art. I, § 10, cl. 3, the IAD is a federal law subject to federal construction.

A State seeking to bring charges against a prisoner in another State's custody begins the process by filing a detainer, which is a request by the State's criminal justice agency that the institution in which the prisoner is housed hold the prisoner for the agency or notify the agency when release is imminent. After a detainer has been lodged against him, a prisoner may file a "request for a final disposition to be made of the indictment, information, or complaint." Art. III(a). Upon such a request, the prisoner "shall be brought to trial within one hundred eighty days," "provided that for good cause shown in open court, the prisoner or his counsel being present, the court having jurisdiction of the matter may grant any necessary or reasonable continuance." Ibid. Resolution of the charges can also be triggered by the charging jurisdiction, which may request temporary custody of the prisoner for that purpose. Art. IV(a). In such a case, "trial shall be commenced within one hundred twenty days of the arrival of the prisoner in the receiving state," subject again to continuances for good cause shown in open court. Art. IV(c). If a defendant is not brought to trial within the applicable statutory period, the IAD requires that the indictment be dismissed with prejudice. Art. V(c).

In this case, New York lodged a detainer against respondent, who was a prisoner in Ohio. Respondent signed a request for disposition of the detainer pursuant to Article III of the IAD, and was returned to New York to face murder and robbery charges. Defense counsel filed several motions, which, it is uncontested, tolled the time limits during their pendency.

On January 9, 1995, the prosecutor and defense counsel appeared in court to set a trial date. The following colloquy ensued:

> "[Prosecutor]: Your Honor, [the regular attorney] from our office is engaged in a trial today. He told me that the Court was to set a trial date today. I believe the Court may have preliminarily discussed a May 1st date, and [the regular attorney] says that would fit in his calendar.
>
> "The Court: How is that with the defense counsel?
>
> "[Defense Counsel]: That will be fine, Your Honor."

The court scheduled trial to begin on May 1.

On April 17, 1995, respondent moved to dismiss the indictment, arguing that the IAD's time limit had expired. The trial court found that as of January 9, 1995, when the trial date was set, 167 nonexcludable days had elapsed, so that if the subsequent time period was chargeable to the State, the 180 day time period had indeed expired. However, the trial court concluded that "defense counsel's explicit agreement to the trial date set beyond the 180 day statutory period constituted a waiver or abandonment of defendant's rights under the IAD." Accordingly, the court denied respondent's motion to dismiss.

Respondent was subsequently convicted, following a jury trial, of murder in the second degree and robbery in the first degree. On appeal, respondent argued that the trial court erred in declining to dismiss the indictment for lack of a timely trial under the IAD. The New York Supreme Court, Appellate Division, affirmed the decision of the trial court. The New York Court of Appeals, however, reversed and ordered that the indictment against respondent be dismissed; defense counsel's agreement to a later trial date, it held, did not waive respondent's speedy trial rights under the. We granted certiorari. 526 U.S. 1111 (1999).

II

No provision of the IAD prescribes the effect of a defendant's assent to delay on the applicable time limits. We have, however, "in the context of a broad array of constitutional and statutory provisions," articulated a general rule that presumes the availability of waiver, and we have recognized that "the most basic rights of criminal defendants are ... subject to waiver." In accordance with these principles, courts have agreed that a defendant may, at least under some circumstances, waive his right to object to a given delay under the IAD, although they have disagreed on what is necessary to effect a waiver.

What suffices for waiver depends on the nature of the right at issue. "Whether the defendant must participate personally in the waiver; whether certain procedures are required for waiver; and whether the defendant's choice must be particularly informed or voluntary, all depend on the right at stake." For certain fundamental rights, the defendant must personally make an informed waiver. For other rights, however, waiver may be effected by action of counsel. "Although there are basic rights that the attorney cannot waive without the fully informed and publicly acknowledged consent of the client, the lawyer has — and must have — full authority to manage the conduct of the trial." As to many decisions pertaining to the conduct of the trial, the defendant is "deemed bound by the acts of his lawyer-agent and is considered to have 'notice of all facts, notice of which can be charged upon the attorney.'" Thus, decisions by counsel are generally given effect as to what arguments to pursue, what evidentiary objections to raise, and what agreements to conclude regarding the admission of evidence. Absent a demonstration of ineffectiveness, counsel's word on such matters is the last.

Scheduling matters are plainly among those for which agreement by counsel generally controls. This case does not involve a purported prospective waiver of all protection of the IAD's time limits or of the IAD generally, but merely agreement to a specified delay in trial. When that subject is under consideration, only counsel is in a position to assess the benefit or detriment of the delay to the defendant's case. Likewise, only counsel is in a position to assess whether the defense would even be prepared to proceed any earlier. Requiring express assent from the defendant himself for such routine and often repetitive scheduling determinations would consume time to no apparent purpose. The text of the IAD, moreover, confirms what the reason of the matter suggests: in allowing the court to grant "good-cause continuances" when either "prisoner or his counsel" is present, it contemplates that scheduling questions may be left to counsel. Art. III(a) (emphasis added).

Respondent offers two arguments for affirmance, both of which go primarily to the propriety of allowing waiver of any sort, not to the specifics of the waiver here. First, he argues that by explicitly providing for the grant of "good-cause continuances," the IAD seeks to limit the situations in which delay is permitted, and that permitting other extensions of the time period would override those limitations. It is of course true that waiver is not appropriate when it is inconsistent with the provision creating the right sought to be secured. That is not, however, the situation here. To be sure, the "necessary or reasonable continuance" provision is, by clear implication, the sole means by which the prosecution can obtain an extension of the time limits over the defendant's objection. But the specification in that provision that the "prisoner or his counsel" must be present suggests that it is directed primarily, if not indeed exclusively, to prosecution requests that have not explicitly been agreed to by the defense. As applied to agreed-upon extensions, we think its negative implication is dubious — and certainly not clear enough to constitute the "affirmative indication" required to overcome the ordinary presumption that waiver is available.

Second, respondent argues that the IAD benefits not only the defendant but society generally, and that the defendant may not waive society's rights. It is true that a "right conferred on a private party, but affecting the public interest, may not be waived or released if such waiver or release contravenes the statutory policy." The conditional clause is essential, however: It is not true that any private right that also benefits society cannot be waived. In general, "in an adversary system of criminal justice, the public interest in the administration of justice is protected by the participants in the litigation." We allow waiver of numerous constitutional protections for criminal defendants that also serve broader social interests.

Society may well enjoy some benefit from the IAD's time limits: Delay can lead to a less accurate outcome as witnesses become unavailable and memories fade. On the other hand, some social interests served by prompt trial are less relevant here than elsewhere. For example, because the would-be defendant is already incarcerated in another jurisdiction, society's interests in assuring the defendant's presence at trial and in preventing further criminal activity (or avoiding the costs of pretrial detention) are simply not at issue. In any case, it cannot be argued that society's interest in the prompt resolution of outstanding charges is so central to the IAD that it is part of the unalterable "statutory policy." In fact, the time limits do not apply at all unless either the prisoner or the receiving State files a request. Thus, the IAD "contemplates a degree of party control that is consonant with the background presumption of waivability."

Finally, respondent argues that even if waiver of the IAD's time limits is possible, it can be effected only by affirmative conduct not present here. The New York Court of Appeals adopted a similar view, stating that the speedy trial rights guaranteed by the IAD may be waived either "explicitly or by an affirmative request for treatment that is contrary to or inconsistent with those speedy trial rights." The court concluded that defense counsel's agreement to the trial date here was not an "affirmative request" and therefore did not constitute a waiver. We agree with the State that this makes dismissal of the indictment turn on a hypertechnical distinction that should play no part. As illustrated by this case, such an approach would enable defendants to escape justice by willingly accepting treatment inconsistent with the IAD's time limits, and then recanting later on. Nothing in the IAD requires or even suggests a distinction between waiver proposed and waiver agreed to. In light of its potential for abuse — and given the harsh remedy of dismissal with prejudice — we decline to adopt it.

The judgment of the New York Court of Appeals is reversed.

It is so ordered

Chapter 15; Securing Attendance of Witnesses

Sec. 15.1; Article 610; by Subpoena

People v. Jovanovic

176 Misc. 2d. 729 (N.Y.S. Ct. 1997)

OPINION OF THE COURT: (Re: Purpose of subpoena, subpoena duces tecum, 610.10, 25)

The defendant has been indicted for the crimes of kidnapping, aggravated sexual abuse, sodomy and related crimes. In connection therewith, the defendant subpoenaed from Columbia University copies of all e-mail communications sent to, and received by, the complainant, using her Columbia University e-mail account. Columbia University complied with the defendant's subpoena duces tecum by producing directly to the court several computer disks, which when downloaded and printed consisted of some 2,400 written pages of communications between the complainant and the defendant and the complainant and various third parties. This court determined that it was appropriate for it to review the e-mails, in camera, in order to make a determination as to whether any or all of the materials produced should be disclosed to the defendant.

The court finds that the production by the court to the defendant of these third-party e-mails is not warranted, since the defendant has ultimately failed to establish (i) that the material sought pursuant to the subpoena duces tecum contains "evidence," and (ii) that he cannot obtain the information contained in the e-mails from other sources, i.e., speaking directly with the persons who communicated with the complainant in these e-mails.

A subpoena duces tecum is a judicial subpoena returnable to the court. CPL 610.25 requires only the production to a court of materials subpoenaed, but it does not require the disclosure of such materials to the defense (or otherwise). It is a proper function for a court to conduct an in camera inspection of subpoenaed materials produced in order for the court to make a determination as to whether any of such material should be disclosed.

The court's in camera examination of the third-party e-mails produced by Columbia University pursuant to the defendant's subpoena found nothing in those materials to be directly relevant and material to the defendant's case or which must or should be disclosed to the defendant. Notwithstanding such, as a result of the court's in camera inspection, the defendant was provided with copies of all e-mail communications directly between himself and the complainant.

Although the complainant is not a party to the criminal action against the defendant, any party affected by process of a court has standing to apply to the court for modification, vacatur or reconsideration of a decision or order issued by a court. The right of a defendant to compel a witness pursuant to a subpoena to give testimony or produce documentary or other physical evidence has a constitutional basis predicated upon a defendant's need to compel the production of evidence in order to prepare and present a defense to the charges brought against him or her. That right, however, rather than being an unlimited and unrestricted right to compel by compulsory process any documents sought by a defendant, is a restricted right, whose exercise must satisfy certain relevancy and evidentiary standards and which is further subject to the availability of other means for obtaining the documents sought. The right to compel material pursuant to a subpoena is limited to the compulsion of 'evidence' and is not a right to compel the production of documents that refer to evidence or that provide leads that will assist in the identification of evidence or to ascertain the existence of witnesses or evidence."

New York courts have frequently held that a subpoena "may not be used for the purpose of discovery or to ascertain the existence of evidence." A subpoena may also not be utilized to "fish for impeaching material." In order to benefit from the use of compulsory process a defendant must make a "clear and specific showing that the subpoenaed information is highly material and relevant, is necessary or critical to the maintenance of his defense, and is not obtainable from other available sources." In connection therewith, a defendant's offer of proof may not be predicated upon mere speculation, nor may such be based upon a "potential" for unearthing relevant evidence, it being required that the defendant put forth a factual predicate that would make it "reasonably likely" that the document or documents sought will produce directly relevant and exculpatory evidence. A party cannot utilize compulsory process to search for relevant material, even within a specific set of files, nor should a defendant be allowed to conduct an "'unrestrained "tour of investigation seeking generally useful information."'" Similarly, where the information sought does not bear directly on the issue of a defendant's guilt or innocence, but rather goes towards the issue of a complainant's credibility and the impeachment thereof, such information is not properly disclosable.

In the case at bar, the defendant has failed to establish that the e-mails contain evidence directly relevant to the defendant's guilt or innocence. Moreover, even if the defendant had successfully demonstrated that the e-mails in question constituted evidence, he has failed to demonstrate that there are no other means available to him through investigatory due diligence or otherwise, to obtain the information sought from other sources prior to trial.

Accordingly, I find that the defendant has failed to make a clear and specific demonstration that the third-party e-mails subpoenaed from Columbia University are highly material and relevant, are necessary or critical to his defense and that the information contained therein is not obtainable from other sources. Therefore, such documents will not be disclosed to the defendant. Furthermore, I additionally find that the materials in question are not required to be disclosed to the defendant pursuant to his due process right to a fair trial or pursuant to any other constitutional, statutory or common-law right.

People v. Riggins
178 Misc. 2d 12 (S.Ct. Monroe Cty. 1998)

OPINION OF THE COURT: (Re: Powers of the district attorney, 610.20)

A sealed indictment was returned, in this case, charging the defendant with murder in the second degree. This charge is based upon claims that under circumstances evincing a depraved indifference to human life, she recklessly engaged in conduct which created a grave risk of serious physical injury or death to her daughter, Tysheka Wright, who was less than 11 years old, including leaving the child unclothed in conditions which resulted in death by hypothermia.

The defendant requests that the court fashion an appropriate remedy concerning records of the Catholic Family Center, which were obtained by the Monroe County District Attorney's Office pursuant to a subpoena duces tecum issued following completion of the Grand Jury proceeding and after return of the indictment.

A District Attorney, as an officer of a criminal court, may issue a subpoena of such court, subscribed by himself, for the attendance of a witness in such court or Grand Jury proceedings. (CPL 610.20.) The term "subpoena" includes a "subpoena duces tecum," which may require the witness to produce specified physical evidence. (CPL 610.10.) The physical evidence, subject of a subpoena duces tecum, must be retained by the court, or if subpoenaed for purposes of a Grand Jury proceeding, the evidence must be retained by the Grand Jury or the District Attorney on behalf of the Grand Jury (CPL 610.25.). The Court of Appeals emphatically declared that the power of a District Attorney to compel witnesses to produce physical evidence is limited to a Grand Jury proceeding or a court where a proceeding is pending, and in the latter event, should be made returnable before the court. Thus, the court held that it was improper for the District Attorney to subpoena production of evidence, following completion of a Grand Jury proceeding, and made returnable prior to trial in the District Attorney's Office.

Courts have struggled with the appropriate remedy to be imposed regarding evidence obtained by a District Attorney's Office pursuant to an improperly issued subpoena duces tecum. Such records not infrequently contain material which would be otherwise protected as a confidential communication, such as the physician-patient privilege. In other instances, convictions have been affirmed based upon a determination that the prosecutor did not utilize the information obtained by means of the subpoena duces tecum, but later, obtained the same material as the result of the defendant placing such records in issue at trial.

Indeed, the Court of Appeals, in effect, has held that the improperly issued subpoena duces tecum was harmless error, while at the same time condemning such practice by District Attorneys' Offices. Remedial options available to a court include permitting additional discovery, granting a continuance, issuing protective orders, and prohibiting introduction of evidence. Admittedly, suppression is a drastic remedy, especially in a case of this nature, involving the death of a child.

In this court's opinion, an order precluding the introduction of the improperly subpoenaed records, or other evidence derived therefrom, on the People's direct case would achieve the desired result of being an effective remedy. Arguably, the District Attorney would not be prejudiced because presumably sufficient evidence had already been collected and presented to the Grand Jury in order to obtain an indictment for murder in the second degree.

Based upon the foregoing reasons, it is ordered that the Monroe County District Attorney is precluded from offering records of the Catholic Family Center as evidence on their direct case.

People v. Woodson

165 Misc. 2d 784 (NY Cty. 1995)

OPINION OF THE COURT: (Re: When authority of court required, subpoena duces tecum, 610.20)

On May 8, 1993, the police were summoned to a specific apartment in the Queensbridge Housing Development in response to repeated cries for help. Upon arrival, the officers found a scene of violence at this residence. A young woman, Stephanie Pagan, 26 years of age, and Karisa Ruffin, an infant, were dead as a result of stab wounds. A second child, Melissa Joy Rodriguez, and an adult, Ronicia Rodriguez, were seriously injured but still alive. Later, the wounded child died of her injuries. As they investigated, the police noticed a trail of blood and discovered bloody clothing. They followed this trail and located the defendant on the building roof. Once defendant observed their presence, he jumped from the roof and landed in a nearby grassy courtyard. As a result of his actions, the defendant was seriously injured and required immediate medical attention. He was taken, unconscious, to Elmhurst General Hospital and admitted at 6:45 a.m. on May 8, 1993. The following day, May 9, he was formally arrested based on the homicidal acts. He was still comatose at this time.

The next day, May 10, the District Attorney's office issued a Grand Jury subpoena duces tecum commanding Elmhurst General Hospital to appear with their records before the Grand Jury on that date as a witness in a criminal action against defendant. This subpoena was served on the hospital authorities on May 12 and a detective received a vial of blood (taken on May 8) and a urine specimen (taken on May 11). These items were vouchered and delivered to the Medical Examiner's office. On May 13, the hospital authorities also turned over the defendant's medical records from May 8 through May 13.

Defendant now contends that the blood and urine samples as well as his medical records were illegally obtained and must be suppressed. He also requests suppression of any results of any toxicological examinations performed on his blood and urine based on the fact that these items were the fruit of the poisonous tree.

Was the issuance of a Grand Jury subpoena duces tecum valid under the circumstances of this case? The facts indicate that the defendant was hospitalized on Saturday, May 8; arrested on Sunday, May 9; and a Grand Jury subpoena issued on Monday, May 10. The record further indicates that no court proceedings had been initiated due possibly both to the speed of the investigation and the comatose state of the defendant. Certainly no Grand Jury proceeding had been started when the subpoena was issued so the notation for the hospital to appear on May 10 was an impossibility. In effect, the subpoena was an office subpoena, that is a mandate requiring the party summoned to appear at the District Attorney's office for the sole purpose of furthering an investigation. Neither case nor statutory law grant such authority to the District Attorney. The People have no right to issue a subpoena for the sole purpose of securing evidence in a pending case. Subpoenas, of course, are process of the courts, not the parties.

It has long been recognized that District Attorneys may not issue subpoenas except through the process of the court, and they exercise the power to compel witnesses to produce physical evidence only before a Grand Jury or a court where a proceeding is pending. Where the District Attorney seeks trial evidence the subpoena should be made returnable to the court, which has 'the right to possession of the subpoenaed evidence. It is for the court, not the prosecutor, to determine where subpoenaed materials should be deposited, as well as any disputes regarding production.

By circumventing the court, the District Attorney avoided all the protections provided against abuse of the subpoena process, and succeeded in transforming a court process into a function of his own office. Such conduct is all the more disturbing in light of apparent prior admonitions by Trial Judges to the District Attorney concerning similar misuse in other cases.

Nor can the People be excused by virtue of "exigent circumstances." The facts show that the items sought would not have been disposed of or destroyed or even tampered with since they were simply hospital records and would have been available for future use. Also, there was enough time to have secured a proper court order. Even if the tests and records were intended for the Grand Jury, the court could have granted such an order since the Supreme Court has the authority to issue an order in furtherance of a Grand Jury investigation even though no arrest or indictment has yet occurred. Based on the above, the subpoena must be regarded as a nullity for Grand Jury purposes and this court concludes that the two vials and the hospital records were obtained in violation of defendant's Fourth Amendment rights.

This court finds that the vial of blood and the specimen of urine and the hospital records from May 8 to May 10 were obtained by virtue of an improper subpoena and thus a violation of defendant's Fourth Amendment rights. Consequently, these items must be suppressed as evidence and are inadmissible at trial. Further, any tests based on the vials must also be suppressed. As for the hospital records, since they were also improperly seized, these items must be suppressed as well as any findings that flow directly from these records.

Sec. 15.4; Article 640: Persons at Liberty outside N.Y.S. and Rendition to Other Jurisdictions of Persons at Liberty within the State; the Uniform Witness Act

People v. McCartney

38 N.Y.2d 618 (1976)

OPINION OF THE COURT: (Re: Burden of proof of materiality of testimony, 640.10/3)

This case concerns the construction and application of CPL 640.10 (subd. 3), the "Uniform Act To Secure Attendance Of Witnesses From Without The State In Criminal Cases." We have not previously had occasion to construe and apply this statute which has now been enacted by some 47 States and the District of Columbia. The "Uniform Act" enables a State to secure the attendance of witnesses who are not located within its borders and are, hence, immune to its normal subpoena power. Defendant contends that he was denied the right to secure compulsory attendance of witnesses on his behalf, given to him by the Sixth Amendment of the United States Constitution and held applicable to the States through the due process clause of the Fourteenth Amendment; and he asserts that this right has been violated because the Judge at his pretrial confession suppression hearing refused to utilize the procedures set forth in the "Uniform Act" to compel a Maryland State trooper to testify at the hearing.

The defendant pleaded guilty to the charge of robbery in the second degree (Penal Law, § 160.10) after the court determined, following a hearing, that statements made to New York State Police investigators at the Washington County Jail in Hagerstown, Maryland, were voluntarily made. The Appellate Division unanimously affirmed the conviction. At the suppression hearing, the prosecution produced Investigator Anderson of the New York State Police, who had conducted the interrogation of defendant. Defendant's counsel then sought to compel the attendance of a Maryland State trooper, Officer Miles, who was alleged to have been present during the defendant's questioning in the Maryland jail. The Judge found that Trooper Miles' testimony would not be "of any determinative value to this proceeding," since he did not participate in the questioning of defendant but was merely "in and out" of the room in which defendant was being held, and denied the application for a certificate pursuant to CPL 640.10 (subd. 3).

It should be noted, prefatorily, that a State is not constitutionally required by the Sixth Amendment guarantee of compulsory process to compel the attendance of witnesses beyond its jurisdiction over whom it has no subpoena power. Hence, we must determine whether the defendant was entitled under the "Act" to have the Trial Judge issue a certificate calling for the attendance of Trooper Miles at his Huntley hearing.

It has consistently been held that, in order to be entitled to the issuance of compulsory process under the "Act," the court of the "requesting" State must determine whether the witness sought is "material." Unsupported statements that the witness is material or necessary are not sufficient to require the Trial Judge to grant an application under CPL 640.10 (subd. 3). The party who seeks to secure the presence of an out-of-State witness should present evidence in the form of an affidavit of the witness or otherwise show that the testimony of the desired witness is material and necessary. Indeed, it is established that the burden of showing materiality is upon the party seeking to compel the attendance of an out-of-State witness and in respect of materiality, we think it must be demonstrated by the defendant that the testimony of the witness sought to be subpoenaed is relevant, admissible and of significance to his case. We do not think it unfair to impose upon a defendant such a burden because his right to secure witnesses must be balanced against the rights of the witness whose presence would be compelled. The process for securing the presence of an out-of-State witness has been termed "drastic" because it represents an incursion upon the liberty of a prospective witness, who, although accused of no crime or wrongdoing, is required to attend a criminal proceeding in another State. Two Judges of the United States Supreme Court thought this incursion so serious that they concluded the "Uniform Act" was unconstitutional. While we do not subscribe to this view, we do hold that the burden of proof of materiality should rest upon the party seeking to obtain the benefit of compulsory process for an out-of-State witness under the "Uniform Act."

Turning to the facts of the instant case, we cannot conclude that defendant has met this burden. He has made only an unsupported statement that there were discrepancies in the testimony. Moreover, the Judge found that Officer Miles was not present during the questioning but was "in and out" of the room in which the questioning took place and did not observe any significant portion of the questioning.

A request that the Trial Judge issue a certificate pursuant to CPL 640.10 (subd. 3) seeking the compulsory attendance of a witness in another State is addressed to the discretion of the Trial Judge. In light of the circumstances of this case, it cannot be said that the Trial Judge acted arbitrarily and capriciously in denying defendant's request, and in the absence of an abuse of discretion we may not overturn his determination of nonmateriality. Accordingly, the order of the Appellate Division should be affirmed.

State of New Jersey v. Bardoff

92 A.D. 2d 890 (2nd Dept. 1983)

OPINION OF THE COURT: (Re: Burden of proof of materiality of witnesses, 640.10/10)

Appeal from two orders of the Supreme Court, Richmond County which denied the application of appellant Robert Bardoff for orders pursuant to CPL 640.10 directing Ken Williamson and Charles Picciocco to appear as witnesses at appellant's trial in the Superior Court of New Jersey. Orders reversed and respondents Williamson and Picciocco are directed to appear as witnesses when called to do so in the matter pending in the Superior Court of New Jersey.

Appellant Robert Bardoff is charged in Middlesex County, New Jersey, with the crimes of possession of marihuana and possession of marihuana with intent to distribute. Utilizing the Uniform Act to Secure the attendance of Witnesses from Without a State in Criminal Proceedings, he seeks to secure the testimony of two New York residents, the respondents Williamson and Picciocco. In certificates issued September 28, 1982, Honorable Theodore Appleby, Judge of the Superior Court of New Jersey, certified that each respondent was a "necessary and material" witness. Petitioner presented the certificates in the Supreme Court, Richmond County, which secured the attendance of Williamson and Picciocco for a hearing. After hearing the witnesses and reviewing the papers, Special Term denied petitioner's applications, thus refusing to order the respondents to testify in the New Jersey trial. We reverse.

Initially, we note that an order denying an application to compel witnesses to testify in a sister State is appealable. The Uniform Act mandates a two-step process (1) the Trial Judge may, at his discretion, issue a certificate of materiality and, if he does, then (2) the court of the State where the witness resides is obliged to determine for itself whether the witness is material and necessary.

The burden of proof to establish that a witness is material and necessary rests upon the party seeking the witness' testimony. At the hearing in the State of residence, the out-of-State certificate is entitled to prima facie evidentiary acceptance. In the matter at issue here, appellant submitted his out-of-State certificates of materiality to Special Term. In addition, he explained that his defense at trial would be that he did not know that there was marihuana in the truck that he was driving; that he had simply picked up an order of goods for someone else and unbeknownst to him, marihuana was included; that while a large quantity of marihuana has a strong and particular odor, he could not smell it and neither could the witnesses Williamson and Picciocco who spent time repairing appellant's van shortly before he was arrested.

Contrary to the conclusion reached by Special Term, we find that this evidence is sufficient for appellant to establish that Williamson and Picciocco are necessary and material witnesses. Accordingly, the orders under review are reversed and the applications to require respondents Williamson and Picciocco to appear as witnesses when called to do so in the matter pending in the Superior Court of New Jersey, Law Division (Criminal), Middlesex County, entitled State of New Jersey v. Bardoff are granted.

Chapter 16; Securing Testimony for Future Use and Use of Testimony Previously Given

Sec. 16.1; Article 660; Securing Testimony for Future Use — Examination of Witness Conditionally

People v. Cotton
92 N.Y.2d 68 (1998)

OPINION OF THE COURT: (Re: Exception when witness is unavailable due to defendant's wrongful conduct, 660.60)

Whenever the People allege specific facts which demonstrate a "distinct possibility" that a criminal defendant has engaged in witness tampering, the court must grant a Sirois hearing to test the validity of that claim. Defendant challenges his conviction for second degree murder and related crimes primarily on the ground that the trial court's ruling after a Sirois hearing was flawed in several respects. Perceiving no error warranting a new trial, we affirm the Appellate Division order upholding the conviction.

At defendant's March 1996 trial for the shooting death of Steven Davilla in New York City, the prosecution planned to call eyewitness Anthony echeverria, a 22-year-old neighborhood resident who knew both defendant and the victim. The People indicated in pretrial disclosure to defense counsel and in their March 15 opening statement that echeverria would testify that he was present at the time Davilla was shot and that defendant was the shooter. echeverria had met with prosecutors and the police on March 13 and 14, at which time he had identified defendant as the shooter.

On March 17, the day before he was to testify, echeverria, then incarcerated at Rikers Island on an unrelated charge, telephoned the lead prosecutor and left a voice-mail message that he would no longer testify as to the shooter's identity. He said that his family was "in jeopardy" and "everything is off, I'm not doing nothing. You put me on the stand, do whatever you got to do but I don't know nothing. I didn't see nothing ... Forget everything."

The People at that point noted that echeverria had told a prosecutor that some men had approached members of his family and gave them reason to believe that there was a "contract" out on him, and they moved to introduce the prior statements echeverria had made to law enforcement officials implicating defendant. The court ordered a Sirois hearing to test the People's assertion that defendant had intimidated echeverria.

In *People v. Geraci* (85 NY2d 359), we held that at a Sirois hearing, the People must demonstrate by clear and convincing evidence that the defendant, by violence, threats or chicanery, caused a witness's unavailability. If the People meet that burden, the defendant is precluded from asserting either "the constitutional right of confrontation or the evidentiary rules against the admission of hearsay in order to prevent the admission of the witness's out-of-court declarations." Contrary to defendant's argument, we conclude that the People satisfied their heavy burden, so that Echevarria's out-of-court declarations could be evaluated by the jury.

First, there was sufficient evidence to establish that threats were made against echeverria. Second, the evidence is sufficient to link these threats to defendant. Because of "the inherently surreptitious nature of witness tampering" circumstantial evidence may be used to "establish, in whole or in part, that a witness's unavailability was procured by the defendant." Additionally, as the trial court noted, defendant had previously successfully threatened echeverria when, at the time of the shooting, he looked him in the eye and pointed a gun at him which prompted echeverria to give the police a false name and deny being able to identify the shooter. All of these affirmed facts, together, clearly and convincingly link defendant to the threats.

Initially, we are unpersuaded by defendant's contention that *Geraci* is limited to admitting prior Grand Jury testimony of an intimidated witness. Although *Geraci* itself involved Grand Jury testimony, the Court did not limit its reach to those particular out-of-court statements and indeed made clear that it applied to "hearsay evidence such as the Grand Jury testimony." Nor would the policy objectives underlying *Geraci* be served by foreclosing admissibility of other reliable evidence.

While surely statements admitted pursuant to Geraci cannot be so devoid of reliability as to offend due process, no such danger is presented here. Echevarria's statements were repeated only days after they had first been made, were (according to the affirmed findings) lucid and credible, and described in detail defendant's actions both before and after the shooting. Those same statements were made on two separate occasions, and recounted in the testimony of two witnesses subject to cross-examination, thus making it unlikely that echeverria was misunderstood. Additionally, the testimony indicated that echeverria received no special treatment from the police and had no motive to change his original story and put himself or his family at risk. The statements were thus certainly sufficiently reliable for evaluation by the jurors.

Accordingly, the order of the Appellate Division should be affirmed.

Sec. 16.2; Article 670; Use of Testimony Previously Given

People v. Arroyo
54 N.Y.2d 567 (1982)

OPINION OF THE COURT: (Re: Necessity and reliability, 670.10)

In the main, we are asked to say whether the admission at trial of an unavailable witness' preliminary hearing testimony constituted an unconstitutional application of CPL 670.10 in violation of the right of confrontation. We find it did not.

Defendant was convicted, after a jury trial, of assault in the second degree. The charge stemmed from an incident in which he was alleged to have inflicted multiple stab wounds on his estranged "common-law wife." When the case came on for trial, the People asserted that the victim, who was the sole identifying witness, had disappeared and that diligent attempts to discover her whereabouts had failed. After hearings to determine the question, Trial Term ruled testimony she had given at a preliminary hearing could be read into evidence at trial.

Fundamental to the issues thus raised is the right of a defendant in a criminal case to confront an adverse witness, as guaranteed by both Federal and State Constitutions. This fair trial requirement not only exposes the witness to a face-to-face encounter, but opens the door to that most effective trial tool for testing truth, cross-examination. So vital is the latter that, with narrow and cautious exceptions, the general rule is that testimonial statements which cannot be subjected to this test must be excluded. The corollary is that, for an exception to fall outside the constitutional constriction, it must carry an alternative, though different and perhaps somewhat lesser, assurance of reliability. Even then, it must first have met a threshold criterion of necessity, for, without it, it is difficult to constitutionally justify resort to evidence whose reliability is not necessarily assured by confrontation tests.

In the case here now, that the missing witness was both the individual upon whom the crime was perpetrated, as well as the only one to admit firsthand knowledge of its commission, went far to establish necessity. But this, standing alone, was not enough. Her unavailability also had to be established to satisfy the court that the prosecutor's failure to produce her was not due to indifference or a strategic preference for presenting her testimony in the more sheltered form of hearing minutes rather than in the confrontational setting of a personal appearance on the stand. So, the statute, reflecting the spirit of the underlying constitutional prescriptions, demands a showing that the witness "cannot with due diligence be found." Putting these rules to the test, the trial court, after reviewing the circumstances and motives for her disappearance and the People's efforts to locate her, found as a matter of fact that due diligence indeed had been employed.

The witness' unavailability established, we now turn to the question of the reliability of her former testimony. In this regard, we first note that the solemnity of the occasion on which the preliminary hearing testimony was adduced in the case before us now was emphasized by the defendant's presence as a matter of right, his representation by counsel, the witness' testifying under oath, the furnishing of an opportunity for her cross-examination and, subject to exceptions not material to this case, adherence to the rule against hearsay (CPL 180.60). Furthermore, the hearing, "a virtual minitrial of the prima facie case," delved into substantially the same subject matter as did the trial on which it later was to be used. This identity was calculated to induce, as it did, cross-examination relevant to the purposes to which the examination ultimately was put.

Here, the preliminary hearing at which the witness testified, though guilt or innocence did not hang in the balance, was to determine whether there was enough evidence to hold the defendant on the very crime for which he was convicted. Accordingly, the subject and the scope of the inquiry, even if it never could be foursquare with what might have been developed if essayed anew at trial, was sufficiently close to satisfy the identity factor.

Consequently, though reliability is ordinarily to be judged on the circumstances which present themselves at the time nisi prius passes on admissibility, even in retrospect it could not be said, as a matter of law, that in this case the determination of reliability implicit in the findings by both courts below was not warranted.

All this does not mean, however, that every time a prima facie case is dependent on the introduction of a prior statement the fact that it has overcome the confrontation hurdle automatically will insulate the case against dismissal. There may be instances in which, though the circumstances surrounding prior testimony have rendered it admissible, in the context of the entire case as it develops, the prior testimony, by itself, will be found insufficient to support a guilty verdict beyond a reasonable doubt. But here, the People not only met the test of trustworthiness posed by the confrontation issue, but, on the record already detailed, the prior testimony could serve as a basis on which to uphold the conviction.

For all these reasons, the order of the Appellate Division should be affirmed.

People v. Robinson
89 N.Y.2d 648 (1997)

OPINION OF THE COURT: (Re: Admission of grand jury testimony on motion of defendant, 670.10)

The primary issue in this case is whether a defendant's constitutional right to due process requires the admission of hearsay evidence consisting of Grand Jury testimony when the declarant has become unavailable to testify at trial. Under the circumstances of this case, where the hearsay testimony is material, exculpatory and has sufficient indicia of reliability, we hold that the trial court's failure to admit such evidence was reversible error.

Defendant's conviction stems from an incident which occurred on December 12, 1992 in an apartment in Rochester, New York. Defendant's fiance, in her testimony before the Grand Jury, corroborated defendant's version of the evening's events. She testified that all three were together in the same room, after a night of drinking and dancing, in varying states of undress, while her fiance attempted to have sex with the complainant. She also testified that the complainant made no objection, "[Complainant] didn't say no or stop." After hearing testimony from all three parties, the Grand Jury indicted defendant for sexual abuse in the first degree and sexual misconduct.

Defendant waived his right to a jury trial and was tried before the Bench. Prior to trial, defendant and his fiance were married and defendant specified that his new wife would be a witness for him at trial. However, she left the jurisdiction before trial and refused to return to New York in defiance of an order that defendant secured pursuant to CPL 640.10. Thereafter, defendant made a motion for the admission of his estranged wife's Grand Jury testimony on the grounds that the testimony was material and that she was an unavailable witness despite his due diligence in attempting to return her to New York to testify.

On this appeal, the People argue that the Grand Jury testimony must be excluded because it is not authorized by CPL 670.10, because it does not bear sufficient indicia of reliability or fall within any of the hearsay exceptions and because there has been no violation of due process. Defendant argues that he has a due process right to the introduction of the Grand Jury testimony and that it has been shown to be sufficiently reliable for admission. CPL 670.10 lists only three proceedings for which former testimony may be admissible at trial. We have previously held that Grand Jury proceedings are not encompassed within the statute.

Nevertheless, we have held that certain considerations may support the admission of former testimony that falls beyond the reach of the statute. For example, this Court has sanctioned the admissibility of Grand Jury testimony at a later trial upon proof that the defendant, through violence, threats or chicanery, had caused the disappearance of the witness who gave the prior testimony.

Defendant seeks to admit the Grand Jury testimony of another based upon his constitutional right to due process. "Few rights are more fundamental than that of an accused to present witnesses in his own defense." This constitutional right is limited in the Grand Jury context. In fact, because Grand Jury proceedings are conducted by the prosecutor alone, this function confers upon the prosecutor broad powers and duties, as well as wide discretion in presenting the People's case.

Where the defendant seeks to admit Grand Jury testimony against the People, the party who conducted the original Grand Jury examination, considerations of constitutional dimension are raised notwithstanding the narrow confines of CPL 670.10. We conclude that, under the facts presented here, Grand Jury testimony adduced by the prosecution may be admitted at trial as an exception to the general prohibition against hearsay because the testimony meets certain standards for admissibility.

There is little dispute that the evidence at issue is material. The remaining question concerns the reliability of the proffered hearsay testimony. We have noted that the absence of cross-examination tends to impair the reliability of Grand Jury testimony. However, our discussion of the "especially troubling" issue of the admissibility of Grand Jury testimony in *People v. Geraci* (85 NY2d 359) was precipitated by the fact that the subject hearsay evidence was proffered by the prosecution against the defendant who had no right of cross-examination before the Grand Jury. We are not persuaded that our inquiry into the "indicia of reliability" of former testimony must hinge upon the mere fact that the subject testimony was originally adduced upon direct examination. This single factor does not indicate that Grand Jury testimony is inherently unreliable when proffered against the prosecution.

In this case, the prosecution exercised its full and fair opportunity to examine the witness it chose to call. The fact that some of the testimony could be viewed as unfavorable to the defendant is further indication of its reliability. Moreover, the specific,

leading and probing questioning was sufficient to reveal any relevant, credibility in-
fluencing biases. Here, the prosecutor's direct examination accomplished the general
goal of cross-examination, testing the accuracy of the declarant's testimony. Thus,
the Grand Jury testimony here contains sufficient indicia of reliability such that it
was admissible upon defendant's submission.

Chapter 17; Securing Evidence by Court Order and Suppressing Evidence Unlawfully or Improperly Obtained

Sec. 17.1; Article 690; Search Warrants

People v. Nieves

36 N.Y.2d 396 (1975)

OPINION OF THE COURT: (Re: Search of any persons present on premises provision, 690.15)

Defendant was convicted, on his guilty plea, of attempted possession of gambling
records. He was charged and convicted on the basis of evidence seized from his
person pursuant to a search warrant authorizing the search of certain premises, a
named individual not the defendant, and "any other persons occupying said premises."
Defendant was one of two such "other persons" on the premises. Prior to his plea,
he had moved to suppress the evidence so seized on the ground that the search
warrant did not meet the particularity requirements of the Fourth Amendment and
was in fact an impermissible general warrant. The motion was denied. The Appellate
Term affirmed the conviction and defendant appeals. For reasons which follow, we
conclude that defendant's conviction must be set aside.

The essential facts are not in dispute. Detective Smith, of the Suffolk County Police
Department, obtained a search warrant commanding "any peace officer in the County
of Suffolk" to make a daytime search of the "El Parador Restaurant occupied by Elizar
Vidal and of the person of Elizar Vidal and any other persons occupying said premises,
for the following property: what are commonly known as policy slips and certain writing representing and being runners records, collectors records and tally sheets and
money connected thereto in violation of gambling, of the New York State Penal Law."

The warrant was issued and, at about 6:30 p.m. that same day, it was executed.
Detective Smith proceeded inside the El Parador, which was open, and saw Elizar
Vidal seated at the bar next to one Florencio Riverra. Defendant was seated alone at
a table in the restaurant. According to the detective's testimony at the suppression
hearing, these three were the only people present in the premises. There is no indication that defendant made any attempt to flee or resist, any threatening move, or
that the officer saw any policy slips or other evidence linking defendant in any manner
to the commission of a crime. The officer said he stated that he had a search warrant,

showed it only to Vidal and told all three to empty their pockets. When defendant complied, policy contraband was recovered from his possession. All three persons were placed under arrest.

The challenged language of the warrant in this case — "and any other persons occupying said premises" — would appear to be authorized by CPL 690.15, which provides: "A search warrant which directs a search of a designated or described place, premises or vehicle, may also direct a search of any person present thereat or therein." Defendant contends that the particular search of his person was unreasonable.

The issue is whether mere presence at a specified place may be a sufficiently particular description of a person in a search warrant to meet the standards of the Fourth Amendment. We agree with defendant's contention and have concluded that the warrant in this case, insofar as it commanded the search of the defendant, was too general and that the things seized from him should have been suppressed.

The Fourth Amendment of the United States Constitution and section 12 of article I of the New York Constitution provide: "The right of the people to be secure in their persons, houses, papers and effects, against unreasonable searches and seizures, shall not be violated, and no warrants shall issue, but upon probable cause, supported by oath or affirmation, and particularly describing the place to be searched, and the persons or things to be seized."

The amendment was enacted in reaction to the evils associated with the use of general warrants in England and the detested writs of assistance in the Colonies. By requiring particularity of description of the persons or places to be searched and the things to be seized, it precludes the use of such general warrants. Particularity is required in order that the executing officer can reasonably ascertain and identify the persons or places authorized to be searched and the things authorized to be seized. To protect the right of privacy from arbitrary police intrusion, the "core" of the Fourth Amendment, nothing should be left to the discretion of the searcher in executing the warrant.

This does not mean that hypertechnical accuracy and completeness of description must be attained but rather, from the standpoint of common sense, that the descriptions in the warrant and its supporting affidavits be sufficiently definite to enable the searcher to identify the persons, places or things that the Magistrate has previously determined should be searched or seized.

In addition to particularity of description, the Federal and State Constitutions, of course, also require probable cause. The instant case points up the correlation between these two requirements, for it requires us to probe not only the specificity of the defendant's description in this warrant ("persons occupying said premises"), but also whether there was probable cause to believe that the property described in the warrant would be found on the persons so described at the specified premises. The sufficiency of the description in this case will hinge in part on whether there was probable cause to believe that each and every occupant of the El Parador at any time of day possessed the policy slips and gambling records sought under the warrant.

What will amount to forbidden generality, or, to put it another way, insufficient particularity in a warrant necessarily depends upon the facts and circumstances of each case. Thus, to say that general warrants are outlawed by the Federal and State Constitutions merely initiates the inquiry. The same may be said of their expressed requirement of probable cause and their ultimate mandate of reasonableness. Like "particularity," these depend upon the facts and circumstances.

In reviewing the validity of a search warrant to determine whether it was supported by probable cause or whether it contained a sufficiently particular description of its target, the critical facts and circumstances for the reviewing court are those which were made known to the issuing Magistrate at the time the warrant application was determined.

The circumstances as revealed in the information before the issuing Judge, indicated, at best, that there was probable cause to believe that Vidal, the person named in the warrant, might be engaged in a policy operation from the El Parador. While reasonable inferences may be drawn directly from the circumstances shown in a warrant application, there was no support here for the inference that every occupant of the restaurant might be similarly engaged and hence in possession of the policy records sought in the warrant. In short, there was not probable cause to believe that any person occupying the premises might be in possession of illegal gambling records at the time of the search. As a consequence, the description of defendant merely by reference to his presence at the premises was too general.

The circumstances under which a warrant may issue for the search of all occupants of a particular place are severely limited: the facts before the issuing Judge at the time of the warrant application, and reasonable inferences from those facts, must establish probable cause to believe that the premises are confined to ongoing illegal activity and that every person within the orbit of the search possesses the articles sought.

In sum, if, on the particular facts articulated to the issuing Judge, the locus of the search is carefully confined by description and reasonably appears limited to criminal activity, then the challenged statute authorizing searches of "any person present thereat or therein" may be constitutionally applied. The facts made known to the Magistrate and the reasonable inferences to which they give rise, must create a substantial probability that the authorized invasions of privacy will be justified by discovery of the items sought from all persons present when the warrant is executed. If this probability is not present, then each person subject to search must be identified in the warrant and supporting papers by name or sufficient personal description.

The warrant in this case falls far short of meeting these requirements, since it authorized a search of the entire premises at an apparently public place without any showing of probable cause that the premises were confined to illegal activity and that there was a substantial probability that all persons present at the time of execution would possess the items sought.

In this case, the record contains no indication that defendant's behavior by itself furnished independent probable cause for an arrest and incidental search. The warrant, because too general as to him, afforded no justification for his search. The offending items seized from his person should, therefore, have been suppressed. These being the predicate for the charges against him, his conviction must, in turn, be set aside.

Order reversed, judgment of conviction vacated and information dismissed.

People v. Betts

90 A.D. 2d. 641 (3rd. Dept. 1982)

OPINION OF THE COURT: (Re: Search of any persons present provision, 690.15)

Appeal from a judgment of the County Court of Albany County upon a verdict convicting defendant of two counts of the crime of criminal possession of a controlled substance. On May 16, 1980, Detective Sutton of the Albany Police Department applied for, and secured, a "no-knock" search warrant to search three named persons, "the basement apartment located at 12 Ash Grove Place, Albany," and "any other person or persons therein or thereat." The named persons were believed to be engaged in selling heroin there.

When the search occurred, defendant Janine Betts, who had not been named in the warrant, was found seated on a bed in one of the apartment's bedrooms. After the detective ushered her into the kitchen, he and a fellow officer inspected the bedroom. They found two purses and a cigarette pack lying on the bed. One of the purses belonged to Betts and contained a small quantity of marihuana and a memo pad filled with what Sutton believed were notations of drug transactions. The cigarette pack contained six foil packets of cocaine. Also seized, from the top of the bedroom's television set, were several glassine bags, a brown pharmacist's vial, a playing card, and aluminum foil, materials customarily used to package cocaine and heroin in individual packets. A marihuana cigarette was found on the bedroom floor. Betts was then subjected to a body search, conducted by a police matron, during which a folded $20 bill containing cocaine was discovered. The search of the rest of the apartment uncovered, among other things, several glassine bags of heroin, a foil packet of marihuana and a loaded pistol. Hazel, one of the codefendants, had in his possession $665 in cash and a tinfoil packet of cocaine and heroin. Betts' motion to suppress the evidence seized from her purse and her person was denied and her conviction followed.

The principal issue raised is the validity of the search warrant which neither named nor described defendant, but authorized the search of any unnamed persons encountered in the apartment. Defendant maintains that the presence of language authorizing the search of "any other person therein or thereat" creates an impermissible "open-ended" warrant which violates the Fourth Amendment requirement of particularity of description. We find the warrant unobjectionable.

Warrants issued pursuant to CPL 690.15 (subd. 2), as this one was, sanctioning examination of a particular place and directing "a search of any person present thereat or therein," are not unconstitutional per se (*People v. Nieves*, 36 NY2d 396). Unlike *Nieves*, this is an instance where the facts and circumstances justified an "any other person" search. Significantly, the premises involved, a basement apartment, were private and, therefore, less likely to contain innocent bystanders. Police surveillance, carried out over several days, corroborated in every detail information supplied by a reliable informant that the occupants were vigorously trafficking in drugs. From these facts, the magistrate who issued the warrant could reasonably infer that the apartment was the scene of ongoing illegal activity and that there was a substantial likelihood that anyone present was a participant. Furthermore, the difficulty of specifying each of the individuals who might be in the apartment at any one time rendered this type of search necessary. With respect to the contention that the warrant was improper because Detective Sutton knew Betts had been seen at the apartment, but failed to describe her by name in the warrant, we find no proof in the record that the informant told Sutton of defendant's presence there prior to the application for the warrant.

Judgment affirmed.

People v. Burke

180 Misc. 2d. 715 (kings Cty. S.Ct. 1999)

OPINION OF THE COURT: (Re: Seizure of property not mentioned in the warrant, 690.50)

It is alleged that the defendant, Dennis Burke (hereinafter, defendant), repeatedly sexually assaulted a child over a period of years. In addition, it is alleged that the defendant possessed numerous lewd photographs of children, some of which depicted children engaging in sex acts, as well as videotaped depictions of defendant engaging in sex acts with young children.

Defendant moves to suppress evidence obtained from a search of defendant's home made pursuant to a search warrant signed by a Judge of the Criminal Court. The court held an evidentiary hearing on defendant's motion, at which Detective Kathleen Heavey testified for the People. After reviewing the warrant and the affidavit in support thereof, as well as the papers submitted by both parties on the motion, the court finds that the warrant was supported by probable cause, and was in all other respects legally sufficient. Therefore, the motion to suppress the evidence obtained thereby must be denied, except as to certain items seized which were beyond the scope of the warrant.

On July 21, 1998, at approximately 5:30 P.M., the police were summoned to Fast Photo, in response to a 911 call from an employee at the lab. The employee informed the police that defendant had provided the lab with a roll of undeveloped film to be processed. After the film was developed, the employee saw that one of the resulting photographs depicted a young child posed with her face, mouth agape, in close proximity to the clothed crotch of an adult male; the male depicted in the photographs appeared to be sexually aroused. Police officers waited at the photo lab for defendant to arrive. When defendant presented himself at the photo lab and requested the photographs, he was placed under arrest.

Detective Kathleen Heavey of the New York City Police Department Sexual Exploitation of Children Squad was assigned to investigate the case. On the morning of July 22, 1998, Detective Heavey conferred with the District Attorney's Office about whether to undertake a search of defendant's home. At approximately 8:25 P.M. on July 22, 1998, Detective Heavey submitted an application for a search warrant to a Judge of the Criminal Court. In accordance with Detective Heavey's request, the search warrant authorized the search of "2862 W. 17th Street, First Floor and Garage, Brooklyn, New York," for evidence of "photographs of the complaining witnesses and other children; diaries, journals, computer disks, NAMBLA literature, child-related paraphernalia, photographic equipment, receipts from photo developing stores, and photo albums."

At approximately 9:40 P.M. on July 22, 1998, Detective Heavey and other detectives went to the subject premises to execute the warrant. Detective Heavey brought the warrant to the premises and showed it to the other detectives before commencing the search. As the detectives were walking through the home, John Burke entered the premises. Detective Heavey accompanied defendant's son to the attached garage, where, he said, a green cash box was located. Inside a cabinet in the garage, Detective Heavey found a green metal box. She opened it to find not currency, but numerous photographs of males and females — most of whom clearly appeared to be under the age of 16 — portrayed in sexually explicit poses. In addition, the box contained two videotape cassettes: one inscribed with the name "Eric," and one inscribed with an "X." The box also contained a note which read, "I want to have sex with you" — in Detective Heavey's opinion, the note was written in a child-like scrawl.

Suspecting that the videotape cassettes might contain additional evidence, Detective Heavey gave the tapes to another detective, who played the tape marked "Eric" on a videocassette player located in the living room. This tape contained images of defendant engaging in oral and anal sodomy with a male child who appeared to be under 16 years old. The detectives seized 84 additional unmarked videotape cassettes from the living room and garage. These tapes, along with the tape marked "X" that had been discovered in the green box, were not played while the detectives were inside the subject premises, but were viewed at the police station house in the course of the following week. The "X" tape contained more images of defendant's sexual encounters with minors, but, apart from testimony concerning one tape found under a television set located in the living room, there was no evidence adduced at the hearing that the other tapes contained illicit material.

After viewing the "Eric" videotape, Detective Heavey continued the search. Also found inside the green box was a photograph album marked "VIR" and one inscribed "TRAY — Upstate New York kids." Several photographic albums — described by Detective Heavey as "mini-albums," were also found in the green box. These albums contained photographs of apparent children in states of undress; in some of the photographs, the children are depicted engaging in sex acts. The green box also contained a condom.

Near a television set in the living room, the detectives found more photographs depicting one of the children who had been present when the photographs obtained from the photo lab were taken. From a dresser found in the living room, Detective Heavey seized defendant's passport, Social Security card stub, and some letters. Several pieces of video and still camera equipment were seized from a closet in the living room area. Also, a cardboard box containing numerous pornographic magazines and nine additional "mini-albums" — none of which contained child pornography — was seized from the garage. Various items of clothing were also seized, including a knit pink shirt, four pairs of ladies' underpants, and a lavender nightgown; these articles of clothing were similar in appearance to the items of clothing worn by the child seen in the "Eric" videotape. Also seized from the bedroom were a pair of "camouflage" shorts similar to those worn by defendant in the "Eric" videotape, as well as a tube of surgical lubricant. Defendant was seen to use the lubricant in the course of engaging in a sex act with the male child.

CONCLUSIONS OF LAW

Scope of the Search

Defendant claims that the search of his home was beyond the scope authorized by the warrant because the police seized a number of items that were not specified in the warrant, including videotapes, clothing, and personal papers. With regard to the videotapes marked "Eric" and "X," the court concludes that they were properly seized after it was determined that they constituted evidence of the type authorized by the warrant. As to the remainder of the videotapes and the personal papers, the court finds that there was an insufficient basis to seize these items, and they must be suppressed. The clothing and the tube of surgical lubricant were properly seized as evidence of criminality discovered in plain view during the course of the lawful search.

A. The search and seizure of the "Eric" and "X" Videotapes

The search warrant in this case authorized the police to search for "additional photographs of the complaining witnesses as well as other children, as well as diaries, journals, computer disks, NAMBLA literature, child-related paraphernalia, photographic equipment, receipts from photo developing stores, and photo albums." Clearly, all of the still photographs depicting children in states of undress or engaging in sexual activity were properly seized pursuant to the warrant. However, in the course of searching for photographs and other items specified in the warrant, Detective Heavey also discovered two videotape cassettes, one marked "Eric" and the other marked "X." The tapes were found in a green metal box the detective retrieved from a cabinet in defendant's garage. Also in the box were numerous sexually explicit photographs depicting young children. Defendant argues that because videotape cassettes were not specified in the affidavit or warrant, the tapes were illegally seized. In addition, he claims that the police were not authorized to "search" the contents of the videotapes by playing them on a videocassette recorder.

The police may seize items not specified in the warrant if the warrant authorized the seizure of that type of property. Once the police saw that the videotape cassettes were surrounded by a plethora of sexually explicit still pictures of children, commingled in a closed metal container, they had reason to believe that the videotapes contained recordings of visual images depicting child pornography. Their suspicions were heightened by defendant's son's repeatedly expressed intense desire to obtain the box following his father's arrest, and by the fact that one of the tapes bore a person's name, and the other was inscribed with an "X," perhaps alluding to the illicit subject matter contained therein. Also, Detective Heavey's expert opinion that pedophiles keep "mementos" of their illicit activities lent credence to the belief that the videotapes contained images of the type for which seizure was authorized.

Just as the search of the green box was authorized because there was reason to believe that it could contain the specified, illicit photographs, there was reason to believe that the videotape cassettes found in the green box may have served as "containers" — i.e., a storage medium — for illicit moving images similar in type to the photographs specified in the warrant. Under the circumstances, the police were justified in figuratively "opening" the videocassette by playing the "Eric" tape to determine if, in fact, it contained visual images of the type specified in the warrant. Once the detectives determined that the "Eric" tape contained such images, they were justified in seizing the "X" tape and subsequently reviewing its contents to determine that it, too, contained child pornography.

B. The search and seizure of various items not specified in the warrant

Dozens of additional videotape cassettes, as well as clothing, a condom, and certain of defendant's personal papers were seized from the home's living room and bedroom. Because the unusual circumstances attending the discovery of the "Eric" and "X" videotapes did not apply to the seizure of the remaining cassettes, the court finds that they were not properly seized. The strong indicia that the tapes were of an illicit nature, which supported the search of the "Eric" and "X" tapes, is absent here. The remaining tapes were strewn about the apartment, apparently unmarked, and there was no particular reason to believe that a search of their contents would reveal evidence of the type specified in the warrant. Therefore, all of these tapes must be suppressed.

So, too, must the defendant's personal papers and the condom be suppressed. These items were not specified in the warrant, nor were they the type of evidence sought in the warrant. Moreover, they do not constitute contraband or clear evidence of criminality. (Compare, *People v. Shepard*, 169 Misc 2d 517, 520 [Sup Ct, NY County 1996], citing *People v. Diaz*, 81 NY2d 106 [police may seize item in plain view when incriminating nature is readily apparent].)

The nine "mini-albums" containing innocuous photographs, along with the pornographic magazines, none of which depicted children, must also be suppressed as beyond the scope of the search.

The items of clothing and the tube of surgical lubricant were properly seized under the plain view doctrine. (*People v. Shepard*, supra.) These items were discovered in the course of the detectives' lawful search for items specified in the warrant. Furthermore, the incriminating nature of the clothing and the lubricant were immediately apparent; in the "Eric" tape — viewed by the detectives prior to the seizure of the clothing — items of the clothing resembling the articles that were seized were seen to be worn by defendant or his victim in the course of the videotaped illicit sexual activity and the defendant was seen to use the lubricant in the course of a sexual act. Therefore, the clothing and tube of lubricant were properly seized.

Conclusion

In a long-term, proactive investigation, the police may have the luxury of time and the opportunity for careful reflection as they consider their next investigative move. However, the search in this case was not the culmination of a planned, preexisting operation. Rather, it was the result of a fast-evolving chain of events to which the police had to react, beginning with the 911 call from the photo lab, leading to defendant's arrest, the interview of the young complainant depicted in the photographs taken from the photo lab, and finally, the application for and execution of the warrant.

Therefore, and for the foregoing reasons, the court denies the motion to suppress the fruits of the search of 2862 West 17th Street and the attached garage, except for the videotapes other than the "Eric" and "X" cassettes; the condom; the nine "mini-albums" containing innocuous photographs; the pornographic magazines that do not depict children; and defendant's personal papers. Because these items were beyond the scope of the warrant, they must be suppressed.

Sec. 17.2; Article 700; Eavesdropping and Video Surveillance Warrants

People v. Floyd
41 N.Y.2d 245 (1976)

OPINION OF THE COURT: (Re: Minimization requirement, 700.30)

Defendant claims, on his appeal to this court, that the wire interception of his telephone was not conducted in accordance with the minimization requirement of CPL 700.30 (subd. 7) and, therefore, the approximately 40 intercepted communications admitted at trial concerning defendant's involvement in the distribution of narcotics should have been suppressed.

On defendant's motion to suppress eavesdropping evidence a hearing was held to determine whether the police officers involved in the electronic surveillance had complied with the minimization directive contained in the eavesdropping warrant as mandated by CPL 700.30 (subd. 7). Sgt. McNicholas, the supervising officer, testified that while surveillance had been authorized for 2,880 hours, the eavesdropping was actually conducted for only 1,210 hours. He also testified that he received instructions from two Assistant District Attorneys that only communications of the defendant, Baxter Floyd, were to be intercepted and not those of any other person using the telephone, such as one Patricia Mitchell who was believed to reside at the address at which the subject telephone was located. He was also instructed to intercept only those communications involving the defendant which were pertinent to the crimes under investigation and that privileged communications, such as calls between the defendant and his attorney, priest or doctor were not to be intercepted. These instructions were relayed by the supervising officer to the police officers manning the eavesdropping apparatus. The general aim of the investigation was to determine the extent of the defendant's role in the distribution and sale of narcotics and any narcotics-related crimes, the participation of any other persons such as dealers and buyers in such activity and the involvement of any government agencies.

The procedures utilized during the period of surveillance were described in considerable detail. For most calls, the monitoring officers would intercept the calls for a brief 30- to 40-second interval in order to determine the pertinency of the call to the investigation. If the call was deemed nonpertinent because the defendant was not a party or because the call was innocent in nature, monitoring would cease and the recording device was turned off. If the duration of the call exceeded two to three minutes, the officers would once again monitor the call for a 30- to 40-second period to ascertain whether the parties to the conversation had changed and to redetermine the pertinency of the call. There was never any indiscriminate, automatic overhearing or recording of conversations and police officers were always present operating the monitoring and recording devices. Several calls not involving the defendant were recorded in their entirety but these were of very short duration. The supervising officer also testified that at the inception of the investigation, for the first two or three weeks, when it was necessary to determine a pattern of usage, there was a greater degree of monitoring. Defendant presented no evidence at the minimization hearing. The court then denied appellant's motion to suppress the wiretap evidence, having concluded that the statutory directive to minimize interception of nonpertinent calls had been satisfied. The court specifically held that there was a good faith effort to minimize interception, and that the procedures established by the investigating authorities resulted in a minimization of interception of nonpertinent calls. The defendant proceeded to trial at which approximately 40 tape recordings evidencing defendant's involvement in narcotics trade were admitted into evidence and he was convicted of the crimes of criminal possession and sale of dangerous drugs in the first, second and third degrees.

CPL 700.30 (subd. 7) mandates that an eavesdropping warrant contain a "provision that the authorization to intercept * * * shall be conducted in such a way as to minimize the interception of communications not otherwise subject to eavesdropping under this article."

This case does not involve a claim that the eavesdropping warrant failed to include the talismanic language of CPL 700.30 that the interception of nonpertinent calls be minimized. Rather, the issue presented on this appeal is whether minimization was actually achieved and whether the surveillance procedures utilized by the monitoring police officers were adequate to insure that the smallest practicable number of calls not pertinent to the criminal enterprise under investigation were intercepted. Since previously we have had occasion to comment only briefly on this requirement this case affords an opportunity to discuss in depth the scope of the minimization directive.

The minimization requirement is founded upon the deep-rooted concern expressed by the Supreme Court in *Berger v. New York* (388 U.S. 41, 57) that, in investigations utilizing eavesdropping techniques, "no greater invasion of privacy * * * than was necessary under the circumstances" should be permitted. The requirement also has its underpinnings in the Fourth Amendment interdiction of unreasonable search and seizures and its mandate that search warrants contain provisions "particularly describing the place to be searched, and the persons or things to be seized." The court in Berger sought to prevent the expansion of eavesdropping warrants into full blown "general" warrants prohibited by the Fourth Amendment. The minimization requirement is designed to insure that the communications intercepted conform, as nearly as possible, to those subject to interception by the terms of the eavesdropping warrant.

Minimization does not necessarily require that all nonpertinent communications be free from interception in their entirety, for such a standard would be unrealistic and virtually impossible to satisfy. This is especially true in narcotics conspiracies where crime-related conversations may be prefaced by innocent "chatter" and, thus, in such cases, some minor degree of intrusion must take place before a determination of pertinency can be made. Courts examining interceptions in retrospect cannot fairly expect government agents to be possessed of clairvoyant powers in foreseeing in advance the relevance of particular communications to the crimes under investigation.

Minimization may be defined as a good faith and reasonable effort to keep the number of nonpertinent calls intercepted to the smallest practicable number. The government agents conducting the surveillance must have shown a high regard for the right of privacy and have done all they reasonably could to avoid unnecessary intrusion. This burden may be satisfied by demonstrating that procedures were established to minimize interception of nonpertinent communications and that a conscientious effort was made to follow such procedures.

We hold that in the instant case the People have met their burden and the defendant has failed to rebut the prima facie showing that minimization procedures were established and complied with. Initially, we note that there was no constant, indiscriminate overhearing or recording of all conversations emanating from the subject telephone. Furthermore the monitoring officers were given specific instructions to intercept only calls involving the defendant and only those calls which were pertinent to the investigation and not privileged. The procedures followed by the officers demonstrate compliance with these instructions. If a call was made by an individual other than the defendant the officers monitored the conversation for a brief interval lasting only 30 to 40 seconds to assure that the defendant did not become involved and, if the call was prolonged, they would once again ascertain whether the original parties were "on the line" by monitoring the conversation for the same brief interval. It appears that the same procedure was followed for seemingly innocent calls involving the defendant. This procedure, known as the intrinsic method of minimization, was adequately tailored to protect the expectation of privacy of other persons using the subject telephone as well as the defendant.

We note that the initial monitoring at the outset of the investigation of a greater number of calls was permissible to ascertain the pattern of usage for the telephone.

In light of these procedures, some general guidelines with respect to minimization may be articulated. First, when the government is aware that only a single individual is, or a known group of individuals are, involved in a possible crime, then only communications involving those individuals should be monitored. Where the investigation, however, is directed toward discovery of the participants of what appears to be a broad conspiracy, then the surveillance may be larger in scope in order to accomplish this objective, although steps should be taken to assure, to the extent possible, minimization of "innocent" conversations. Conversations of persons who are not targets of the investigation may be monitored for brief intervals to assure that their use of the phone is not a ruse to mask a suspect's use of the phone or to convey information regarding the crimes being investigated.

Where a conversation occurs between a known suspect and an individual who is not involved in the conspiracy, or whose possible involvement is unknown, great care must be taken to avoid interception of innocent conversation but monitoring officers should be permitted to make an on-the-spot determination of pertinency through a brief period of interception.

Accordingly, the order of the Appellate Division should be affirmed.

Sec. 17.4; Article 710; Motion to Suppress Evidence

People v. Ramirez-Portoreal

88 N.Y.2d 99 (1996)

OPINION OF THE COURT: (Re: Standing, 710.20)

Defendants in these three unrelated appeals have been arrested and prosecuted for various counts of criminal possession of drugs. Prior to their arrests, each had deposited or hidden drugs in a public place and they challenged the legality of the police actions in seizing them. The questions raised are whether, in such circumstances, a defendant has standing to challenge the legality of the police conduct and whether the alleged "abandonment" of the property affects the right to do so. For the reasons which follow we reverse all three orders.

I. People v. Ramirez-Portoreal

On June 10, 1992, three law enforcement officers were on a drug interdiction assignment at the bus terminals in the City of Albany. Defendant Ramirez-Portoreal and two companions arrived on a bus from New York City. When they alighted, defendant was carrying a single piece of luggage; his companions carried none. The three travelers immediately boarded a westbound bus and took seats in different parts of it. Before sitting, defendant placed the bag he carried in an overhead luggage compartment located one row behind his seat and across the aisle from it. The three officers boarded the bus, identified themselves and announced that they were conducting drug interdiction. Defendant produced a ticket but no identification. When Burke asked him whether he had any luggage aboard the bus, he replied that he did not. When asked whether the bag that the officers had seen him place in the luggage rack was his, defendant denied ownership of it. Inspector Burke then asked the bus passengers as a group whether the bag belonged to anyone, and whether anyone objected to his opening it to learn its ownership. None of the passengers responded. Upon opening the bag, the officer discovered a glassine bag containing dime bags of heroin. Defendant and his companions were removed from the bus and arrested. A further search of the bag revealed a quantity of marihuana.

People v. Sanchez

Testimony at the suppression hearing established that on March 1, 1993, an undercover officer in a drug-prone location in Manhattan observed defendant Sanchez surreptitiously place a light brown "package," which bore the characteristics of narcotics packaged for street sale, into the exhaust pipe of a parked van. After placing the drugs there, the defendant walked several feet away but did not leave the immediate area. Two other officers, acting on the undercover's radio transmission, approached defendant and identified themselves. They told him not to move and immediately conducted a safety "pat-down." The undercover officer directed one of the backup officers to remove the package from the exhaust pipe. When the officer did so, he recovered 10 small, pink baggies containing cocaine and held together by masking tape.

People v. Mims

Police Officer Brian Fleming testified at the suppression hearing that on September 27, 1991, he and Officer Edward Lott were stationed on the roof of a building in northern Manhattan. Fleming saw two people approach and give defendant currency in exchange for green-topped vials. Moments later, another pair approached defendant. After a brief conversation, defendant crossed to the south side of 154th Street and reached into a cardboard box that was among a pile of boxes and garbage. He pulled a paper bag from the box, withdrew unidentified items from the bag, replaced the bag in the box, and returned to the other side of the street. Again, Fleming saw defendant conduct what appeared to be a drug sale. Officers Fleming and Lott left the roof, got into their patrol car and drove around the block onto 154th Street to Mims' location. When they got out of the car, Lott detained defendant while Fleming went to retrieve the paper bag from the box in the trash pile. Fleming looked inside the bag and found 18 green-capped vials of crack cocaine. He then recrossed the street, searched defendant and recovered $ 130 from defendant's pocket. Lott found another green-capped vial on the ground near defendant.

II.

A defendant seeking suppression of evidence has the burden of establishing standing by demonstrating a legitimate expectation of privacy in the premises or object searched. Once defendant has established standing, it becomes the People's burden to demonstrate that defendant's action in discarding the property searched, if that is the fact, was a voluntary and intentional act constituting a waiver of the legitimate expectation of privacy. A legitimate expectation of privacy exists where defendant has manifested an expectation of privacy that society recognizes as reasonable. Thus, the test has two components. The first is a subjective component — did defendant exhibit an expectation of privacy in the place or item searched, that is, did he seek to preserve something as private. The second component is objective — does society generally recognize defendant's expectation of privacy as reasonable, that is, is his expectation of privacy justifiable under the circumstances.

Standing to challenge a search is not established by asserting a possessory interest in the goods seized — defendant must assert a privacy interest in the place or item searched. However, constitutional protections against unreasonable searches and seizures are not limited to private premises. Accordingly, and particularly in cases where the search occurred in public, the suppression court must identify the place in which defendant asserts his or her expectation of privacy. For example, the object of defendant Ramirez-Portoreal's claimed expectation of privacy was the piece of luggage he carried. Defendant Sanchez, whose "package" was not in a container and was obviously contraband, could claim an expectation of privacy only in the tailpipe of the van. The object of defendant Mims' asserted expectation of privacy was the paper bag in which Officer Fleming discovered crack vials.

Whether defendant has a legitimate expectation of privacy in the place searched is a substantively different and broader question than whether he or she has a possessory interest in it. While defendant's exercise of dominion and control over premises searched or an item seized may establish constructive possession of it, a legitimate expectation of privacy turns on consideration of all of the surrounding circumstances, including but not limited to defendant's possessory interest.

In sum, standing to seek suppression of evidence requires the defendant to establish, by defendant's own evidence or by relying on the People's evidence that he or she had a legitimate expectation of privacy in the place or item that was searched. The suppression court must identify the object of defendant's expectation of privacy, determine whether defendant exhibited an expectation of privacy in it, and evaluate whether the circumstances would lead society to regard defendant's expectation as reasonable. If the court determines that defendant had a legitimate expectation of privacy in the item searched, standing to challenge the legality of the police conduct is established.

In the context of a challenge to the legality of a police search, the People may argue that the evidence need not be suppressed because defendant has abandoned it. Property is deemed abandoned when the expectation of privacy in the object or place searched has been given up by voluntarily and knowingly discarding the property. The result is a waiver of the constitutional protection. The burden rests upon the People to establish the waiver.

Defendant's intention to relinquish an expectation of privacy will be found if the circumstances reveal a purposeful divestment of possession of the item searched. Standing alone, the surrender of control or disclaimer of ownership does not always establish a waiver. Even where abandoned, moreover, if the abandonment is coerced or precipitated by unlawful police activity, then the seized property may be suppressed because it constitutes "fruit" of the poisonous tree. The inquiry in such cases is whether the contraband itself was revealed as a direct consequence of the illegal nature of the stop or whether defendant's decision to relinquish possession was a calculated decision which attenuated the discovery of the evidence from the illegal police conduct.

In *People v. Ramirez-Portoreal*, the People contend that defendant abandoned the bag. The suppression court correctly determined that defendant had a legitimate expectation of privacy in the bag and the question is whether he gave up that expectation of privacy. If he did, but did so as a result of unlawful police activity, the inquiry then is whether his abandonment was intentional and voluntary as the product of a considered judgment, or a direct and spontaneous consequence of the illegality.

The question of abandonment may also arise in cases such as *People v. Mims* in which a vial of crack cocaine was recovered from the ground near defendant. That obvious contraband was allegedly discarded by defendant in response to a police encounter. Because it was plainly revealed by defendant's action and not discovered as the result of a search, whether such evidence should be suppressed is to be analyzed only under the poisonous fruits analysis, not as a question of waiver of an expectation of privacy.

It should be noted that the legal question of abandonment — i.e., waiver of a legitimate expectation of privacy — is not implicated by the seizure of the 18 crack vials from the trash pile in *Mims* or the contraband discovered in the tailpipe in *Sanchez*. Inasmuch as neither defendant established a legitimate expectation of privacy in the place searched, no question of waiver arises. Applying these rules to the appeals before us requires a reversal in each appeal.

In *People v. Ramirez-Portoreal*, County Court suppressed the evidence because it determined that defendant had standing to contest the search of the bag and that the police conduct in boarding the bus and questioning him was not lawful. The Appellate Division reversed. From the time defendant Ramirez-Portoreal left the first bus until he boarded the second bus and placed the bag in the luggage rack, he was in actual and sole possession of it. The bag was closed, evincing an effort to maintain the privacy it afforded. The fact that defendant seated himself at a distance from the bag does not necessarily indicate that he lacked the right to exclude others from access to it; indeed, it is unlikely that a stranger would have attempted to open the bag or would have been permitted to do so. And even though a prudent traveler might exercise greater care with respect to personal luggage, it cannot be said that society would deem an expectation of privacy in a closed piece of luggage unreasonable merely because it was not stowed in the luggage rack immediately above the traveler. In short, the evidence established defendant's standing to contest the search. Thus, the Appellate Division order denying the motion to suppress should be reversed.

In *People v. Sanchez*, the suppression court and the Appellate Term concluded that defendant had standing to challenge the admissibility of the drugs seized from the tailpipe of the van. An expectation of privacy in the tailpipe of a vehicle not owned by defendant and parked on a busy urban street is not objectively reasonable as a matter of law. Accordingly, we conclude that defendant lacked a legitimate expectation of privacy in the area searched, and his motion to suppress the physical evidence should be denied because he lacked standing to challenge the police conduct.

Similarly, in *People v. Mims* the motion to suppress the 18 vials of crack discovered in the paper bag that defendant had secreted in a trash pile should be denied for lack of standing. Supreme Court and the Appellate Division determined that defendant had not abandoned the property because he remained relatively close to it and returned to it repeatedly, thereby exercising dominion and control over it. While those facts are relevant to defendant's subjective expectation of privacy, the courts did not evaluate the objective component of the expectation of privacy. To the extent Mims' expectation of privacy is asserted in a trash pile on a city sidewalk, society would not accept that expectation as objectively reasonable: defendant claimed no possessory interest in the trash pile and it was readily accessible to animals, children, scavengers, snoops, and other members of the public.

Nor is there an objectively reasonable expectation of privacy in a paper bag secreted in a trash pile. Manifestly, any person or animal having access to the trash pile would have the same access to the container stowed in it, and it is not reasonable to expect that the contents of a paper bag found in a trash pile would remain undisturbed or undiscovered out of respect for the privacy of the person who put it there. Accordingly, we conclude that defendant lacked standing to challenge the police conduct leading to the discovery of the 18 crack vials and the motion to suppress that evidence should be denied.

People v. Spencer

272 A.D.2d. 682 (3rd Dept. 2000)

OPINION OF THE COURT: (Re: Property designated in warrant; plain view, 710.20)

Appeal from a judgment of the County Court of Delaware County, rendered March 22, 1999, upon a verdict convicting defendant of the crimes of burglary, petit larceny and criminal mischief. The charges against defendant arose from a series of incidents in the early morning hours of February 10, 1998 when, based on the evidence adduced at trial, defendant and two minor accomplices committed criminal mischief at a video arcade and burglarized two hardware stores, a restaurant and a laundromat in the Village of Sidney, Delaware County. On appeal, defendant challenges County Court's suppression ruling. We find defendant's claim lacking in merit and affirm the judgment and order.

First, we reject defendant's contention that stolen property discovered in his apartment in plain view during the execution of a valid search warrant was unlawfully "seized" when the police photographed the property, which items were subsequently removed pursuant to a second search warrant. The testimony at the suppression hearing reveals that after both accomplices implicated defendant in the crimes, police obtained a warrant to search defendant's residence for burglar's tools, a dog leash and cash believed to have been stolen from a hardware store. While executing the warrant, police noticed other items in the apartment that they suspected had been stolen during the burglaries so they took photographs of the articles without moving them. The officers then contacted the burglary victims by telephone to ascertain the specific items missing and, after the victims confirmed that items missing from their establishments matched the objects photographed, the police obtained another search warrant which specifically authorized seizure of the items.

Contrary to defendant's argument, we find it was not improper for the police to photograph the suspicious items during the first search. Photographing the articles did not constitute an additional invasion of defendant's privacy beyond that incident to the proper execution of the search warrant. Moreover, it was not inappropriate for the police to use the photographs in an attempt to confirm whether the items were stolen property, as this is analogous to a police officer relying on his or her written description of an item, a practice that is clearly acceptable (see, Arizona v. Hicks, 480 U.S. 321, [officer recorded serial number and make of stereo equipment observed in plain view and used that description to confirm that equipment was contraband]).

Nor, as defendant suggests, can the police conduct be viewed as an improper application of the plain view doctrine. The police may seize contraband or other evidence under the plain view doctrine if three conditions are met: (1) the police are lawfully in the position from which the object is viewed; (2) the police have lawful access to the object; and (3) the object's incriminating nature is immediately apparent" (People v. Diaz, 81 N.Y.2d 106). Upon the facts of this case, although the first two conditions were met through the execution of the first search warrant, the police did not attempt to seize the property during the initial search as "immediately apparent" incriminating evidence. Taking a more prudent approach, the police suspended their search, conducted a further inquiry concerning the suspicious items and then obtained a second search warrant specifically authorizing seizure of the goods. Because the items were seized pursuant to a lawful search warrant, the evidence was properly admitted at trial.

ORDERED that the judgment and order are affirmed.

People v. Hill
262 A.D.2d. 870 (3rd Dept. 1999)

OPINION OF THE COURT: (Re: Stop and frisk, reasonable suspicion, 710.20)

Upon observing two people at approximately 3:00 A.M. walking from the vicinity of a parking lot in the Village of Massena, St. Lawrence County, where several vehicles had been broken into in the recent past, a village police officer began to follow them in his police vehicle. When they walked in different directions at an intersection, the police officer turned at the intersection but was unable to locate the person who had gone in that direction. The police officer radioed for back-up and returned to the intersection where he observed the other person, defendant, and stopped to inquire. Defendant provided straightforward answers to the police officer's questions about where he was going, where he had been and the identity of his companion. In the meantime, a second officer had arrived and discovered defendant's companion hiding nearby.

While talking with defendant, the police officer observed a bulge in the front pocket of the jacket defendant was wearing and conducted a pat-down of the front of the jacket. He discovered several cassette tapes in the front pocket and continued the pat-down until he felt something hard near the small of defendant's back, which turned out to be a gun. After being advised of the Miranda rights, defendant made some statements about the gun. Following a hearing, County Court granted defendant's motion to suppress the gun and his statements, from which order the People appeal.

We affirm. The information possessed by the police officer may have provided, at most, a founded suspicion that criminal activity was afoot, thereby activating the common-law right to inquire; however, the police officer's authority to pat-down or frisk defendant is a corollary to the right to stop and detain, which right is only activated by a reasonable suspicion that defendant had committed, was committing or was about to commit a felony or misdemeanor (see, *People v. De Bour*, 40 NY2d 210). The record supports County Court's conclusion that the police officer had no basis upon which to stop and detain defendant and, therefore, he was not justified in conducting the pat-down.

In any event, no pat-down or frisk was authorized unless the police officer had knowledge of some fact or circumstance to support a reasonable suspicion that defendant was armed or posed a threat to safety. Defendant was generally cooperative and he made no threatening statements or gestures. There is no evidence that the prior criminal activity in the area involved a weapon or that the police officer had any other reason to suspect that defendant was armed or dangerous. The police officer's observation of the bulge in the front pocket of defendant's jacket was insufficient to justify the frisk. In contrast to a waistline bulge, which "is telltale of a weapon," a pocket bulge "could be caused by any number of innocuous objects" (*People v. De Bour*, supra, at 221). There was nothing in the character or location of the bulge to suggest that defendant was carrying a weapon. Defendant did not put his hand in or near the pocket or make any other furtive movements to arouse suspicion that the bulge represented a weapon. On cross-examination, the police officer conceded that his observation of the pocket bulge "had me thinking that maybe he was hiding something possibly from a vehicle." The circumstances of the confrontation with defendant, whether viewed independently or cumulatively, did not supply the necessary reasonable suspicion that defendant was armed or dangerous. In addition, even if the police officer suspected that the pocket bulge was a concealed weapon, any suspicion abated when he determined that the pocket did not contain a weapon, at which time the frisk should have ended. Inasmuch as the gun was unlawfully seized, County Court properly suppressed it and defendant's statements pertaining to the gun, which were the fruit of the unlawful seizure.

The order is affirmed.

Chapter 18; Special Proceedings That Replace, Suspend or Abate Criminal Actions

Sec. 18.1; Article 720; Youthful Offender Procedure

Cacchioli v. Hoberman

31 N.Y.2d 287 (1972)

OPINION OF THE COURT: (Re: Disclosure of adjudication as bar to employment, 720.35)

The court is unanimous in holding—as set forth in the concurring opinion de-nominated part I—that the New York City Transit Authority Police Department would not have been justified in discharging the petitioner on the ground that his failure to divulge his youthful offender adjudication on his job application question-naire did constitute a willful misrepresentation. The court likewise unanimously agrees that the proceeding should be remanded to the court at Special Term to decide whether or not the petitioner's resignation was obtained by duress. The court does not, however, reach or pass upon the further questions—discussed in part II of the concurring opinion—whether the appellant department may, in determining the fitness of the petitioner herein or of any other job applicant, consider an illegal act or arrest which culminates in a youthful offender adjudication. The order appealed from should be modified, without costs, and the proceeding remanded to the Supreme Court, Queens County, for a trial to determine whether the resignation executed by the petitioner was voluntary.

CONCURRENCE:

I.

In June, 1968, petitioner, then 17 years old, passed a competitive civil service ex-amination for the position of Police Trainee with the New York City Transit Authority Police Department. As a candidate for Police Trainee, he was advised that any mis-representation in his application was ground for disqualification or dismissal, and that the "employment of a police trainee may be terminated at any time, if his conduct, capacity or fitness is not satisfactory." Prior to his appointment, petitioner was required to and did execute an "Investigation of Applicant-Questionnaire," which required him to "[list] all arrests and any police investigations not resulting in arrests (Include Juvenile Delinquency, Youthful Offender, Wayward Minor and Family Ct. Proceed-ings)." At the time of his probationary appointment, petitioner was advised that he would be "investigated thoroughly as to character and fitness" before becoming a permanent member of the Transit Authority Police Department.

Subsequent investigation by the Authority indicated that petitioner made several false responses to the questionnaire. Specifically, the investigation revealed that in January, 1967, petitioner had been arrested in Queens County and charged with criminally receiving stolen property (10 stolen automobile tires). This charge was dismissed, apparently so that he could be surrendered on a Dutchess County arrest warrant, which charged him with burglary third degree. Both charges arose out of a single transaction involving a burglary resulting in the theft of 10 tires from a gasoline station in Dutchess County. With respect to the burglary, petitioner pleaded guilty to a reduced charge of malicious mischief and was adjudged a youthful offender.

Since petitioner did not disclose these prior incidents in his questionnaire, he was called to account before a superior officer on September 18, 1969, on which occasion, confronted with the afore-mentioned misrepresentations, he submitted his resignation from the department.

In sum, the proceeding should be remanded to the court at Special Term to decide the factual issue of whether or not the petitioner's resignation was obtained by duress.
II.

This does not mean, however, that the Authority is required to retain the petitioner in the position of Police Trainee, in the event Special Term orders his reinstatement after the hearing upon remand of this proceeding, if the Authority thereafter determines that his integrity, judgment or general fitness falls short of the standards set by it for the position.

At Special Term, the court expressed the view that a public employer, such as the Authority, cannot consider an applicant's youthful offender adjudications, or the illegal and immoral acts which support such adjudications, in evaluating his fitness for public employment. In support of this view, the court relied on former section 913-n of the Code of Criminal Procedure. Former section 913-n, in effect at the time of petitioner's resignation, was carried over into the Criminal Procedure Law, without substantial change as CPL 720.35.

Section 913-n, referring to youthful offenders, provided that: "No determination made under the provisions of this title shall operate as a disqualification of any youth subsequently to hold public office, public employment, or as a forfeiture of any right or privilege or to receive any license granted by public authority."

The language of the statute is quite specific. It states that one is not, ipso facto, disqualified from public employment by reason of his youthful offender adjudication. However, the language of the statute does not expunge one's misconduct so as to prevent the employer from considering the illegal and immoral acts which underlie the youthful offender adjudication. Nor does it permit the youth to conceal mere mention of his youthful offender adjudications or arrests on employment applications. Public policy, in our opinion, rules out such a construction. It would be unreasonable to interpret section 913-n as foreclosing a governmental agency, such as the Authority, from inquiring into an applicant's prior misconduct in evaluating his fitness for employment as a police officer. The public interest requires that law enforcement officers be of impeccable character and integrity, and in order to properly determine an applicant's character and integrity, the department should know of any prior misconduct. This rule should apply not only to law enforcement officers, but, likewise, to other sensitive public positions. For example, a sexual deviate receiving youthful offender status for sexually molesting children would hardly be the one to hire as an attendant at a State school for children. Yet, there is no way to prevent the hiring of one so unfit for such a sensitive position if the employer is barred from all inquiry into the illegal and immoral acts underlying a youthful offender adjudication. Certainly, the Legislature, had it so intended to bar all such inquiry, would have changed the language of section 913-n so as to explicitly state that a youthful offender adjudicature barred employers from making any inquiry into the misconduct which resulted in the adjudication, and that the applicant could conceal his adjudication on employment applications.

We recently held in *People v. Vidal* (26 N Y 2d 249) that notwithstanding section 913-n, it was proper and relevant to cross-examine a witness in a criminal trial as to the underlying and immoral acts which support a prior youthful offender adjudication of the witness.

The reasoning of the court in *Matter of Tucker v. Adams* (141 N. Y. S. 2d 235, 236) is valid: "Here, moreover, petitioner was found guilty of a wrongful act, the elements of which as they bore on the question of his fitness to be a patrolman were within the cognizable discretion of the Commissioner, despite the statutory mandate that it could not be urged as a conclusive bar to his appointment."

While it is true that section 720.35 of the Criminal Procedure Law provides that the official records of a youthful offender adjudication are confidential and may not be made available to a public or private employer unless specifically permitted by statute or upon specific authorization of the court, the statute, by its express terms, is restricted to the public records of the adjudication. Section 720.35 does not prevent the employer from requiring disclosure of youthful offender adjudication on employment applications, or of commencing its own independent investigation into the applicant's fitness and qualifications, which investigation could include misconduct and arrests underlying the applicant's youthful offender adjudication.

Bell v. Codd

57 A.D.2d. 814 (1st Dept. 1977)

OPINION OF THE COURT: (Re: Failure to disclose adjudication, basis for termination, 720.35)

Order, Supreme Court, New York County, annulling the determination of the commissioner and remanding the proceeding to the commissioner for further consideration reversed on the law; the petition dismissed; and the commissioner's determination terminating the petitioner's employment reinstated, without costs or disbursements.

Petitioner, after having taken a competitive civil service examination, was appointed as a probationary police officer with the New York City Transit Authority on December 17, 1973. Prior to his appointment, the petitioner was required to fill out a questionnaire in which he had to list "all arrests and any police investigations not resulting in arrest (Include Juvenile Delinquency, Youthful Offender, Wayward Minor and Family Ct. Proceedings)." The questionnaire also contained the caveat that: "Section 50, Civil Service Law states that a candidate may be rejected 'Who has intentionally made a false statement of a material fact or practiced, or attempted to practice, any deception or fraud in his application, in his examination, or in securing his eligibility for appointment.'" Petitioner omitted to include all matters involving him in which police investigations were conducted, including a youthful offender adjudication. In addition thereto, petitioner while a probationer had one command discipline and five infractions noted against him. On July 3, 1974, petitioner received notice that his services as a probationary police officer were terminated; no reason was assigned therefor. Petitioner then commenced this article 78 proceeding. Special Term annulled the determination of the commissioner and remanded the matter for further consideration. We would reverse and reinstate the commissioner's determination. At the outset, we note that employment of a probationer may be terminated, as occurred in the case at bar, without assigning a specific reason therefor.

In the case at bar, the record reveals that petitioner's lack of candor in regard to answering his questionnaire, and his less than sterling performance as a probationer, afforded more than ample basis for the commissioner's determination. We therefore see no useful purpose in remanding for further consideration of the matter. It is true that an applicant cannot be disqualified from holding a license or public employment based on a youthful offender adjudication (CPL 720.35, subd. 1). This does not mean, however, that in appropriate circumstances the facts underlying a youthful offender adjudication cannot be probed in order to aid in determining the moral fitness of an applicant for a position sought. Public policy would demand that an applicant for the position of police officer, who, by the nature of his duties, is involved in the public welfare in a significant manner, be held to meet a high standard in order to achieve that position (Matter of *Cacchioli v. Hoberman*, 31 NY2d 287, 289 [concurring opn. per Jasen, J.]). We have accordingly reinstated the determination of the commissioner terminating petitioner's employment.

Index

Accusatory Instruments, 8–9, 28–29, 34–35, 46–48, 50, 53–54, 73–75, 79, 82, 85, 90, 95, 98–101, 104, 119, 136, 145, 147, 185, 189, 204, 207, 213, 230–231, 235, 244–245, 256, 275, 280, 282, 286, 294–295, 313, 336–338, 340, 346, 348, 350, 358, 394, 422, 426

ACD, 50, 92–93, 100–101, 349

Adjournment in Contemplation of Dismissal, 50, 100, 109, 143–144, 231–232, 349–350

Appeals, 11–13, 15, 17, 22, 24, 30, 32, 45, 48, 51, 65, 81, 86, 92, 124–126, 144, 169, 177, 183, 196, 202–215, 225, 227, 273, 275–276, 281

Appearance Ticket, 35, 38, 50, 73, 75, 81–85, 89–90, 96, 246

Arraignment, 9, 35–37, 40, 73–75, 78–79, 85, 89–90, 92, 95–98, 100–103, 106, 117, 134, 136–137, 139, 144, 153, 155–156, 163–166, 220, 228, 231, 238, 255, 270, 275, 282, 293, 296, 306, 309, 340–343, 346, 357, 370–372, 419–420, 422–423

Arrest Without a Warrant, 35, 73, 79, 90, 92, 241–242, 331, 422

Bail and Bail Bonds, 5, 8–9, 13, 48–50, 75, 77–78, 82, 89–90, 97, 103, 107, 123, 136–138, 140, 181, 215, 219–228, 231–236, 238–239, 242–243, 248–249, 306, 308–309, 368, 419–424

Commencement of Action, 28, 31, 46–47, 49, 54, 73, 156, 165, 230, 293

Compulsion of Evidence, 41, 55–56, 116, 434

Conduct of Non-Jury Trial, 36, 167, 180–181, 185–186, 395

Criminal Courts, 9, 39–40, 42, 82, 185, 208, 213, 225, 229–230, 248, 303, 359, 369, 393

Criminal Identification Records and Statistics, 8, 30–32, 59–61, 64, 70, 92–93

Destruction of Dangerous Drugs, 22, 64, 259, 276–277

Discovery, 10, 47, 50, 66, 134, 136, 147, 154–156, 159–161, 164, 166, 185, 264, 322–323, 364, 370, 372–373, 405, 434, 436, 448, 454–456, 460–461

Eavesdropping Warrants, 165, 259, 264–266, 268–273, 456

Evidence, 6–11, 14–16, 18–26, 28, 31, 36, 41, 44–46, 49–50, 52–56, 59–70, 77, 79, 81, 87, 92– 93, 99, 101–102, 104–105, 107, 110–114, 116–123, 125, 127, 129, 132–136, 138–142, 151, 153–154, 157–159, 161–172, 174, 176–179, 182, 184, 193, 195–196, 198, 203–208, 210, 212–213, 229, 240–241, 247–249, 256–277, 282–283, 285, 287, 291–293, 296–297, 299, 303, 305, 307–308,

312, 314–315, 318, 320–326, 329,
331, 339, 348, 351, 355, 358, 362–
370, 372, 374–376, 378, 381–385,
388, 390–393, 396, 403, 404, 407–
408, 410–411, 414–421, 425–428,
431, 433–446, 449–455, 457–463
Exemption from Prosecution, 41, 51–57,
60, 298–301

Fines, Restitution and Reparation, 1, 90,
144, 189, 192, 195, 199–201, 354, 360
Fingerprinting and Photographing of
Defendant after Arrest, 8, 191, 251,
340, 368–370, 422–424, 450–454,
462
Forfeiture of Bail, 89, 136, 219, 224, 229,
234–236, 242

Geographical jurisdiction, 37, 39, 41, 43,
45, 75–76, 80, 82–84, 86, 137, 229,
261, 298, 300
Grand Jury, 5, 8–9, 13, 34–35, 50, 53, 56,
65, 68, 97–99, 102–129, 132–134,
136–137, 139–142, 144, 157, 172,
247–252, 256–257, 271, 283, 294–
295, 307, 309, 316, 318, 351–358,
365, 372, 398, 403, 423, 435–437,
442, 444–446

Immunity, 41, 55–57, 60, 98, 111, 116–
118, 139, 272, 316–319, 328, 354–
356, 414
Indictment and Related Instruments, 34,
48, 54, 73–75, 79, 82, 95, 98, 109,
128–129, 185, 336

Jury Trial, 6, 10–11, 36, 120, 148, 151,
167–180, 185–187, 314, 339, 355,
364, 373, 376– 377, 382, 384, 386,
393–395, 397, 407, 410, 416, 431,
443–444

Local Criminal Court Accusatory Instruments, 73–74, 82, 95, 98, 185

Local Criminal Court, 34–35, 40, 73–108,
113, 117, 119–122, 127–129, 136–
137, 140, 144, 185–187, 201, 208,
225–229, 231, 235, 238, 241–242,
250, 256, 259–260, 275, 280, 282–
283, 331, 340, 345, 395–396, 422

Mental Disease or Defect, 25, 60, 63–64,
148, 150–152, 161–162, 178, 181–
183, 203, 279, 284–287, 390
Motion to Suppress Evidence, 10, 158,
168, 259, 273, 450, 457

Non-jury Trials, 36, 167, 180–181, 185–
186, 395

Offer of Immunity, 41, 55–57
Orders of Recognizance, 8, 11, 35. 48–
49, 75, 77–78, 97–98, 100, 103, 108,
124, 128, 136, 138, 144, 198, 219–
223, 225–228, 231–232, 238, 419–
423

Peace officers, 3, 37–38, 74, 79, 83–86,
88, 93, 183, 200, 337–338, 429
Plea, 9, 35–37, 48–50, 53–54, 57, 95–98,
101–102, 104, 109, 118, 134, 136,
143–144, 147–152, 155–156, 161–
162, 181, 183, 185, 189, 192, 207,
246, 276, 283, 310, 345, 350, 359–
364, 388, 390, 393, 398, 400–401,
409–410, 423, 426, 446
Post-judgment Motions, 203–207, 405–
406
Pre-sentence Proceedings, 189–190, 193–
195, 402–405
Pre-sentence Reports, 11, 189, 191–193,
280–281, 398
Pre-trial Motions, 10, 47–49, 54, 57, 66,
98, 110, 135, 147, 153, 164–165, 270,
273, 275, 359, 370–371
Pre-trial Notices of Defenses, 147, 161–
166
Pre-trial Proceedings, 185, 393

Proceedings from Verdict to Sentence, 167, 181, 185, 187, 390

Proceedings in Superior Court, 109–145, 353

Proceedings upon Felony Complaint, 34, 73, 79, 82, 95, 102–108, 248–249, 255, 275, 282, 351, 357, 421

Proceedings upon Information, 34, 48, 74, 79, 82, 98, 101–102, 127, 164, 185–187, 275, 395,

Recognizance, Bail and Commitment, 219–229, 419

Removal of Action, 103–108, 121, 143, 147, 153–154, 183, 279, 282–283

Removal of Proceeding Against Juvenile Offender to Family Court, 73, 106–107, 120–121

Requiring Defendant's Appearance, 13, 35, 50, 136–137, 228–229, 238

Rules of Evidence, 10, 59–70, 112–118, 165, 198, 271, 320, 403

Search Warrants, 14–15, 17–20, 23, 33, 40, 77, 81, 158, 197, 259–272, 274, 296–298, 446–457

Securing Attendance as Witnesses, 247–253

Securing Attendance of Corporate Defendants, 246

Securing Attendance of Defendants, 245–246, 424

Securing Attendance of Witnesses by Material Witness Order, 219, 247–253

Securing Attendance of Witnesses, 247–253, 256, 433

Securing Testimony for Use in a Subsequent Proceeding, 256–258

Securing Testimony Outside the State, 255, 257–258

Sentences of Imprisonment, 148, 189, 191, 201, 232,

Sentences of Probation and of Conditional Discharge, 189, 191, 194, 196–198, 222

Sentencing in General, 189, 397

Simplified Traffic Information, 75, 96–97, 313

Speedy Trial, 41, 46–51, 98, 139, 244–245, 306–311, 362, 372, 429, 433

Standards of Proof, 59–66, 67–70, 320, 327

Summons, 18, 35, 73–75, 79, 89–90, 96, 137, 237–238, 246

Timeliness of Prosecutions, 41, 46–51

Vulnerable Child Witness, 59, 65–67

Waiver of Indictment, 109, 127–128

Waiver of Jury Trial, 36, 147–149, 167, 180, 186, 395

Warrant of Arrest, 7, 17–18, 29, 35, 40, 73–79, 81, 90, 137, 229, 231, 238, 240–242, 264, 291, 309, 422, 426–429

Youthful Offender Procedure, 101, 185, 221, 279–283, 464